Voices of a People's History of the United States

Howard Zinn
Anthony Arnove

SEVEN STORIES PRESS
New York • Toronto • London • Melbourne

Seven Stories Press
140 Watts Street
New York, NY 10013
www.sevenstories.com

IN CANADA
Publishers Group Canada, 559 College Street, Suite 402, Toronto, ON M6G 1A9

IN THE UK
Turnaround Publisher Services, Unit 3, Olympia Trading Estate, Coburg Road, Wood Green, London N22 6TZ

IN AUSTRALIA
Palgrave Macmillan, 627 Chapel Street, South Yarra, VIC3141

LIBRARY OF CONGRESS CATALOGING-IN-PUBLICATION
Zinn, Howard, 1922-
  Voices of a people's history of the United States / Howard Zinn, Anthony Arnove.-- Seven Stories Press 1st ed.
    p. cm.
  Includes bibliographical references and index.
  ISBN-10: 1-58322-647-8 (Hardcover) -- ISBN-10: 1-58322-628-1 (pbk.)
  ISBN-13: 978-1-58322-647-6 (Hardcover) -- ISBN-13: 978-1-58322-628-5 (pbk.)
  1. United States--History--Sources. 2. United States--Biography. I. Arnove, Anthony, 1969- II. Title.
  E173.Z564 2004
  973--dc22   2004018173

College professors may order examination copies of all Seven Stories Press titles for a free six-month trial period. To order, visit www.sevenstories.com/textbook, or fax on school letterhead to 212-226-8760.

For a free copy of the teachers' guide to *Voices of a People's History of the United States* visit www.sevenstories.com/textbook.

Design by Jon Gilbert

Printed in Canada

9 8 7 6

If there is no struggle there is no progress. . . . This struggle may be a moral one, or it may be a physical one, and it may be both moral and physical, but it must be a struggle. Power concedes nothing without a demand. It never did and it never will. Find out just what any people will quietly submit to and you have found out the exact measure of injustice and wrong which will be imposed upon them, and these will continue till they are resisted with either words or blows, or with both.

—FREDERICK DOUGLASS[1]

TO THE REBEL VOICES OF THE COMING GENERATION

Contents

CHAPTER 12: THE EXPANSION OF THE EMPIRE.................... 239

CHAPTER 13: SOCIALISTS AND WOBBLIES 257

CHAPTER 14: PROTESTING THE FIRST WORLD WAR 283

CHAPTER 15: FROM THE JAZZ AGE TO THE UPRISINGS OF THE 1930S

CHAPTER 17: THE BLACK UPSURGE AGAINST RACIAL SEGREGATION

Acknowledgments

We would like to thank, first and foremost, Dan Simon, our editor and friend, who not only envisioned this book and made it possible, but who served as the strongest advocate the readers of this book could ever have.

Two skilled and insightful researchers provided invaluable help and deserve special appreciation: Joey Fox, who helped this project in its daunting initial stages, and Jessie Kindig, who assisted us in the final stages. Without either of them, this book would not now be in your hands.

Brenda Coughlin labored long hours in editorial and research assistance, but more significant, kept us from losing sight of the importance of this project when it seemed it might never be completed.

Thanks to Hugh Van Dusen of Harper Collins, who has so ably published and sustained *A People's History of the United States* for more than twenty years.

Elaine Bernard of the Harvard Trade Union Program generously facilitated the initial meetings and research that began *Voices*.

Ray Raphael, Elizabeth Martínez, and David Williams provided invaluable editorial suggestions, recommendations, and guidance.

George Mürer brilliantly handled the enormous task of securing permissions, for which we are profoundly indebted, and Paul Abruzzo undertook some of the early preliminary research for *Voices* in its first incarnation.

Therese Phillips, Dao X. Tran, Peter Lamphere, Laura Durkay, Monique Jeanne Dols, David Thurston, Chris Peterson, Rosio Gallo, Story Lee Matkin-Rawn, and Meredith Kolodner all contributed importantly to our research efforts, logging long hours with old manuscripts and microfilms, as well as lap tops.

Jon Gilbert deserves special appreciation for his work on the laborious production of this book.

Shea Dean offered her excellent editing skills when the manuscript was completed.

Andrew H. Lee, New York University history librarian, provided critical assistance to our research. For research assistance, we would also like to thank: Ryan Nuckel, Tamiment Library and Robert F. Wagner Labor Archives at New York University; David Kessler and Amelia Hellam, The Bancroft Library, University of California at Berkeley; The University of Washington Harry Bridges Center for Labor Studies in Seattle; Stephen Kiesow, Seattle Public Library; the California Digital Library; the Online Archive of California; Sherri F. Pawson and David G. Horvath, University of Louisville Libraries; Tom Hardin, Louisville Free Public Library; Ann Billesbach, Nebraska State Historical Society; Brian DeShazor, Pacifica Radio Archives; Joseph Ditta, The New York Historical Society; Candace Falk, Emma Goldman Papers Project, University of California at Berkeley; New York Public Library; Ann Bristow, Indiana University, Bloomington, Indiana; William LeFevre, Archives of Labor and Urban Affairs, Wayne State University, Detroit, Michigan; Toni M. Carter, the Virginia Historical Society; Harry Elkins Widener Library and all the Harvard Libraries; the Boston Public Library; the New York Historical Society; the Chicago Historical Society; the Schomburg Center for Research in Black Culture; and all of the other libraries and librarians whose work contributed to our research.

For help with specific readings and permissions, we would like to thank: David Barsamian of Alternative Radio; Joan Miura; Johanna Lawrenson; Julie Diamond; Yolanda Huet-Vaughn; Wini Breines; Alan Maass of *Socialist Worker;* Paul D'Amato of *International Socialist Review;* Bill Roberts of Haymarket Books; Susan Rosenthal; Amy Goodman, *Democracy Now!;* Denis Moynihan, Outreach Director, *Democracy Now!;* Bob Seay, WOMR Radio; Chip Berlet, Political Research Associates; Roberto Barreto; Ismael Guadalupe Ortiz; Marian Wright Edelman; Patti Smith; Robert Bills; Michael Smith, Woody Guthrie Foundation and Archives; Judy Hicks, Librarian, *Peoria Journal Star;* Sheila Lee, Louisiana Newspaper Project; Nadya Cherup, Detroit Public Library; Michael F. Knight, U.S. National Archives and Records Administration, Manuscript Division; Ernest J. Emrich, the Joseph L. Rauh Jr. Papers, Library of Congress, Manuscript Division; Lin Fredericksen, Kansas State Historical Society Reference; and Wade Lee, University of Toledo Libraries; Martha Honey; Martin Duberman; Joe Allen; Winona LaDuke; Orlando and Phyllis Rodriguez; Anita Cameron and Colorado ADAPT; Mike Davis; Paul Robeson, Jr.; and Cindy and Craig Corrie.

We would also like to thank: Ana Bautista, Nita Levison, Carole Sue Blemker, Patty Mitchell, James P. Danky, Woody Holton, Robert Gross, Lawrence Goodwyn, Robert Arnove, Ike Arnove, Suzanne Ceresko, Meredith Blake, John Sayles, Maggie Renzi, Rudy Acuña, Jonathan H. Rees, Peter Nabokov, Hans Koning, Paul Riggs, Marlene Martin, Ahmed Shawki, Sharon Smith, Bill Roberts, Julie Fain, Herbert Aptheker, Philip Foner, Eric Foner, Gerda Lerner, Jeremy Brecher, Manning Marable, Richard Hofstadter, Michael Wallace, Roxanne Dunbar-Ortiz, Bob Wing, Bob Rabin and the Comite Pro Rescate y Desarrollo de Vieques, Frank Abe, Jim Zwick, Lynne Hollander, Jim Crutchfield, the Hudson Mohawk Independent Media Center, Ruth Baldwin of Nation Books,

Maria Herrera-Sobek, Barbara Seaman, Odile Cisneros, Amy Hoffman, Marc Favreau, Andy Coopersmith, Norma Castillo, Maritza Castillo, Lou Plummer, Military Families Speak Out, and Monami Maulik.

Gayle Olson-Raymer wrote the excellent teacher's guide to this book, with Ray Raphael, Ron Perry, Jack Bareilles, Mike Benbow, Tasha Boettcher-Haller, Robin Pickering, Jennifer Rosebrook, Colby Smart, and Eric Vollmers.

Thanks also to Tara Parmiter, for her efforts promoting the book to historians since its early conception.

We are deeply indebted to all of the people who wrote the texts we drew upon, transcribed them, recorded them, published them, and sustained them for all these years—especially those whose names are not recorded.

And, finally, we are especially grateful to Roz and Brenda. Without your love, we'd be nowhere at all.

Introduction

Readers of my book *A People's History of the United States*[1] almost always point to the wealth of quoted material in it—the words of fugitive slaves, Native Americans, farmers and factory workers, dissenters and dissidents of all kinds. These readers are struck, I must reluctantly admit, more by the words of the people I quote than by my own running commentary on the history of the nation.

I can't say I blame them. Any historian would have difficulty matching the eloquence of the Native American leader Powhatan, pleading with the white settler in the year 1607: "Why will you take by force what you may have quietly by love?"

Or the black scientist Benjamin Banneker, writing to Thomas Jefferson: "I apprehend you will readily embrace every opportunity, to eradicate that train of absurd and false ideas and opinions which so generally prevails with respect to us, and that your Sentiments are concurrent with mine, which are that one universal Father hath given being to us all, and that he hath not only made us all of one flesh, but that he hath also without partiality afforded us all the Same Sensations and [endowed] us all with the same faculties."

Or Sarah Grimké, a white Southern woman and abolitionist, writing: "I ask no favors for my sex. . . . All I ask of our brethren, is that they will take their feet from off our necks, and permit us to stand upright on that ground which God designed us to occupy."

Or Henry David Thoreau, protesting the Mexican War, writing on civil disobedience: "A common and natural result of an undue respect for law is, that you may see a file of soldiers, colonel, captain, corporal, privates, powder-monkeys, and all, marching in admirable order over hill and dale to the wars, against their wills, ay, against their common sense and consciences, which makes it very steep marching indeed, and produces a palpitation of the heart."

Or Jermain Wesley Loguen, escaped slave, speaking in Syracuse on the Fugitive Slave Law of 1850: "I received my freedom from Heaven and with it came the command to defend my title to it. . . . I don't respect this law—I don't fear it—I won't obey it! It outlaws me, and I outlaw it."

Or the populist orator Mary Elizabeth Lease of Kansas: "Wall Street owns the country. It is no longer a government of the people, by the people, and for the people, but a government of Wall Street, by Wall Street, and for Wall Street."

Or Emma Goldman, speaking to the jury at her trial for opposing World War I: "Verily poor as we are in democracy, how can we give of it to the world? . . . [A] democracy conceived in the military servitude of the masses, in their economic enslavement, and nurtured in their tears and blood, is not democracy at all."

Or Mississippi sharecropper Fannie Lou Hamer, testifying in 1964 about the dangers to blacks who tried to register to vote: "[T]he plantation owner came, and said, 'Fannie Lou. . . . If you don't go down and withdraw your registration, you will have to leave . . . because we are not ready for that in Mississippi.' And I addressed him and told him and said, 'I didn't try to register for you. I tried to register for myself.'"

Or the young black people in McComb, Mississippi, who, learning of a classmate killed in Vietnam, distributed a leaflet: "No Mississippi Negroes should be fighting in Vietnam for the White Man's freedom, until all the Negro People are free in Mississippi."

Or the poet Adrienne Rich, writing in the 1970s: "I know of no woman—virgin, mother, lesbian, married, celibate—whether she earns her keep as a housewife, a cocktail waitress, or a scanner of brain waves—for whom the body is not a fundamental problem: its clouded meanings, its fertility, its desire, its so-called frigidity, its bloody speech, its silences, its changes and mutilations, its rapes and ripenings."

Or Alex Molnar, whose twenty-one-year-old son was a marine in the Persian Gulf, writing an angry letter to the first President Bush: "Where were you, Mr. President, when Iraq was killing its own people with poison gas? . . . I intend to support my son and his fellow soldiers by doing everything I can to oppose any offensive American military action in the Persian Gulf."

What is common to all these voices is that they have mostly been shut out of the orthodox histories, the major media, the standard textbooks, the controlled culture. The result of having our history dominated by presidents and generals and other "important" people is to create a passive citizenry, not knowing its own powers, always waiting for some savior on high—God or the next president—to bring peace and justice.

History, looked at under the surface, in the streets and on the farms, in GI barracks and trailer camps, in factories and offices, tells a different story. Whenever injustices have been remedied, wars halted, women and blacks and Native Americans given their due, it has been because "unimportant" people spoke up, organized, protested, and brought democracy alive.

• • •

When I decided, in the late 1970s, to write *A People's History of the United States*, I had been teaching history for twenty years. Half of that time I was involved in the civil rights movement in the South, when I was teaching at Spelman College, a black women's college in Atlanta, Georgia. And then there were ten years of activity against the war in Vietnam. Those experiences were not a recipe for neutrality in the teaching and writing of history.

But my partisanship was undoubtedly shaped even earlier, by my upbringing in a family of working-class immigrants in New York, by my three years as a shipyard worker, starting at the age of eighteen, and then by my experience as an air force bombardier in World War II, flying out of England and bombing targets in various parts of Europe, including the Atlantic coast of France.

After the war I went to college under the GI Bill of Rights. That was a piece of wartime legislation that enabled millions of veterans to go to college without paying any tuition, and so allowed the sons of working-class families who ordinarily would never be able to afford it to get a college education.

I received my doctorate in history at Columbia University, but my own experience made me aware that the history I learned in the university omitted crucial elements in the history of the country.

From the start of my teaching and writing, I had no illusions about "objectivity," if that meant avoiding a point of view. I knew that a historian (or a journalist, or anyone telling a story) was forced to choose, from an infinite number of facts, what to present, what to omit. And that decision inevitably would reflect, whether consciously or not, the interests of the historian.

There is an insistence, among certain educators and politicians in the United States, that students must learn *facts*. I am reminded of the character in Charles Dickens's book *Hard Times*, Gradgrind, who admonishes a younger teacher: "Now, what I want is, Facts. Teach these boys and girls nothing but Facts. Facts alone are wanted in life."

But there is no such thing as a pure fact, innocent of interpretation. Behind every fact presented to the world—by a teacher, a writer, anyone—is a judgment. The judgment that has been made is that this fact is important, and that other facts are not important and so they are omitted from the presentation.

There were themes of profound importance to me that I found missing in the orthodox histories that dominated American culture. The consequence of these omissions has been not simply to give a distorted view of the past but, more importantly, to mislead us all about the present.

For instance, there is the issue of class. The dominant culture in the United States—in education, among politicians, in the media—pretends that we live in a classless society, with one common interest. The Preamble to the United States

Constitution, which declares that "we the people" wrote this document, is a great deception. The Constitution was written in 1787 by fifty-five rich white men—slave owners, bondholders, merchants—who established a strong central government that would serve their class interests.

That use of government for class purposes, to serve the needs of the wealthy and powerful, has continued throughout American history, down to the present day. It is disguised by language that suggests all of us, rich and poor and middle class, have a common interest.

Thus, the state of the nation is described in universal terms. When the president declares happily that "our economy is sound," he will not acknowledge that it is not sound for forty or fifty million people who are struggling to survive, although it may be moderately sound for many in the middle class, and extremely sound for the richest 1 percent of the nation who own 40 percent of the nation's wealth.

Class interest has always been obscured behind an all-encompassing veil called "the national interest."

My own war experience, and the history of all those military interventions in which the United States was engaged, made me skeptical when I heard people in high political office invoke "the national interest" or "national security" to justify their policies. It was with such justifications that Harry Truman initiated a "police action" in Korea that killed several million people, that Lyndon Johnson and Richard Nixon carried out a war in Southeast Asia in which perhaps three million people died, that Ronald Reagan invaded Grenada, that the elder Bush attacked Panama and then Iraq, and that Bill Clinton bombed Iraq again and again.

The claim made in spring of 2003 by the new Bush that invading and bombing Iraq was in the national interest was particularly absurd, and could only be accepted by people in the United States because of a blanket of lies spread across the country by the government and the major organs of public information—lies about "weapons of mass destruction," lies about Iraq's connections with Al Qaeda.

When I decided to write *A People's History of the United States*, I decided I wanted to tell the story of the nation's wars not through the eyes of the generals and the political leaders but from the viewpoints of the working-class youngsters who became GIs, or the parents or wives who received the black-bordered telegrams.

I wanted to tell the story of the nation's wars from the viewpoint of the enemy: the viewpoint of the Mexicans who were invaded in the Mexican War, the Cubans whose country was taken over by the United States in 1898, the Filipinos who suffered a devastating aggressive war at the beginning of the twentieth century, with perhaps 600,000 people dead as a result of the determination of the U.S. government to conquer the Philippines.

What struck me as I began to study history, and what I wanted to convey in my own writing of history, was how nationalist fervor—inculcated from childhood by pledges of allegiance, national anthems, waving flags, and militaristic rhetoric—permeated the educational systems of all countries, including our own.

I wondered how the foreign policies of the United States would look if we wiped out the national boundaries of the world, at least in our minds, and thought of children everywhere as our own. Then we could never drop an atomic bomb on Hiroshima, or napalm on Vietnam, or cluster bombs on Afghanistan or Iraq, because wars, especially in our time, are always wars against children.

When I began to write "people's history," I was influenced by my own experience, living in a black community in the South with my family, teaching at a black women's college, and becoming involved in the movement against racial segregation. I became aware of how badly twisted was the teaching and writing of history by its submersion of nonwhite people. Yes, Native Americans were there in the history, but quickly gone. Black people were visible as slaves, then supposedly free, but invisible. It was a white man's history.

From elementary school to graduate school, I was given no suggestion that the landing of Christopher Columbus in the New World initiated a genocide, in which the indigenous population of Hispaniola was annihilated. Or that this was the first stage of what was presented as a benign expansion of the new nation, but which involved the violent expulsion of Native Americans, accompanied by unspeakable atrocities, from every square mile of the continent, until there was nothing to do but herd them into reservations.

Every American schoolchild learns about the Boston Massacre, which preceded the Revolutionary War against England. Five colonists were killed by British troops in 1770.

But how many schoolchildren learned about the massacre of six hundred men, women, and children of the Pequot tribe in New England in 1637? Or the massacre, in the midst of the Civil War, of hundreds of Native American families at Sand Creek, Colorado, by U.S. soldiers?

Nowhere in my history education did I learn about the massacres of black people that took place again and again, amid the silence of a national government pledged by the Constitution to protect equal rights for all.

For instance, in 1917 there occurred in East St. Louis one of the many "race riots" that took place in what our white-oriented history books called the "Progressive Era." White workers, angered by an influx of black workers, killed perhaps two hundred people, provoking an angry article by the African-American writer W. E. B. Du Bois, "The Massacre of East St. Louis," and causing the performing artist Josephine Baker to say: "The very idea of America makes me shake and tremble and gives me nightmares."

I wanted, in writing people's history, to awaken a great consciousness of class conflict, racial injustice, sexual inequality, and national arrogance.

But I also wanted to bring into the light the hidden resistance of the people against the power of the establishment: the refusal of Native Americans to simply die and disappear; the rebellion of black people in the anti-slavery movement and in the more recent movement against racial segregation; the strikes carried out by working people to improve their lives.

When I began work, five years ago, on what would become the present volume, *Voices of a People's History of the United States*, I wanted the voices of struggle, mostly absent in our history books, to be given the place they deserve. I wanted labor history, which has been the battleground, decade after decade, century after century, of an ongoing fight for human dignity, to come to the fore. And I wanted my readers to experience how at key moments in our history some of the bravest and most effective political acts were the sounds of the human voice itself. When John Brown proclaimed at his trial that his insurrection was "not wrong, but right," when Fannie Lou Hamer testified in 1964 about the dangers to blacks who tried to register to vote, when during the first Gulf War, in 1991, Alex Molnar defied the president on behalf of his son and of all of us, their words influenced and inspired so many people. They were not just words but actions.

To omit or to minimize these voices of resistance is to create the idea that power only rests with those who have the guns, who possess the wealth, who own the newspapers and the television stations. I want to point out that people who seem to have no power, whether working people, people of color, or women—once they organize and protest and create movements—have a voice no government can suppress.

Columbus and Las Casas

The *Diario* of Christopher Columbus
(October 11–15, 1492)

Bartolomé de Las Casas, Two Readings on the Legacy
of Columbus (1542 and 1550)
   The Devastation of the Indies: A Brief Account (1542)
   In Defense of the Indians (1550)

Eduardo Galeano, *Memory of Fire* (1982)

There is no more glaring distortion in the history learned by generations of Americans—in textbooks, in schools, in the popular culture—than in the story of Christopher Columbus. He is universally portrayed as a heroic figure, a brave adventurer, a skilled seaman who crossed the ocean not knowing what he would find, and stumbled on an unknown continent.

All that is true. But what is missing from that story is that, when he landed in the Bahamas Islands, Columbus and his men, greeted by peaceful and generous natives, set out on a ruthless quest for gold that led to enslavement, misery, and death for that population.

Profit was the driving force behind Columbus' expedition and behind his actions after he landed. His expedition had been financed by the king and queen of Spain, with the hope that crossing the ocean would bring him to the gold and spices of Asia. There had been overland expeditions to Asia, by Marco Polo and others, but now the Turks, who had conquered the eastern Mediterranean, were a barrier to Asia, and so the Spanish needed a sea route.

Columbus was promised, if he brought back gold and spices, ten percent of the profits and governorship over newfound lands. He never arrived in Asia, because although he knew the world was round, he thought the circumference of the earth was smaller than it really was. But one fourth of the way to Asia he came unexpectedly on land.

Seeing the natives he encountered, the peaceful Taino Arawak Indians, as less than human (though in his diary he described them as gentle and generous), he tortured them to force them to find gold for him. He kidnapped and enslaved hundreds of them, compelling them to work in the mines, under terrible conditions, in the quest for gold. It was the beginning of the annihilation of the Indians on

Hispaniola (the island which is now Haiti and the Dominican Republic). It was the start of the European conquest of the Western Hemisphere.

• • •

We begin the chapter with the diary of Christopher Columbus from his first voyage to the Americas. The only version of the diary of the first voyage that we have is the one transcribed by Bartolomé de Las Casas in the 1530s. "Barring the unlikely discovery of the long-lost original *Diario* or of the single complete copy ordered for Columbus by Queen Isabella, Las Casas's partly summarized, partly quoted version is as close to the original as it is possible to come," note historians Oliver Dunn and James E. Kelley, Jr. The Las Casas manuscript also disappeared, but a single copy was discovered around 1790.

It should be noted that Las Casas is sometimes paraphrasing, rather than quoting, Columbus, and that Columbus often refers to himself in the third person or impersonally as "the Admiral" in his own writing.

The *Diario* of Christopher Columbus
(October 11–15, 1492)[1]

THURSDAY 11 OCTOBER [1492]

He steered west-southwest. They took much water aboard, more than they had taken in the whole voyage. They saw petrels and a green bulrush near the ship. The men of the caravel Pinta saw a cane and a stick, and took on board another small stick that appeared to have been worked with iron, and a piece of cane, and other vegetation originating on land, and a small plank. The men of the caravel Niña also saw other signs of land and a small stick loaded with barnacles. With these signs, everyone breathed more easily and cheered up. On this day, up to sunset, they made 27 leagues.

After sunset, he steered his former course to the west. They made up about 12 miles each hour and, until two hours after midnight, made about 90 miles, which is twenty-two leagues and a half. And because the caravel Pinta was a better sailer and went ahead of the Admiral [Columbus] it found land and made the signals the Admiral had ordered. A sailor named Rodrigo de Triana saw this land first, although the Admiral, at the tenth hour of the night, while he was on the sterncastle, saw a light, although it was something so faint that he did not wish to affirm that it was land. But he called Pero Gutiérrez, the steward of the King's dais, and told him that there seemed to be a light, and for him to look: and thus he did and saw it. He also

told Rodrigo Sánchez de Segovia, whom the king and queen were sending as vee-
dor [accountant or auditor] of the fleet, who saw nothing because he was not in a
place where he could see it. After the Admiral said it, it was seen once or twice; and
it was like a small wax candle that rose and lifted up, which to few seemed to be an
indication of land. But the admiral was certain that they were near land, because of
which when they recited the Salve, which in their own way are accustomed to recite
and sing, all being present, the Admiral entreated and admonished them to keep a
good lookout on the forecastle and to watch carefully for land; and to the man who
first told him that he saw land he would later give a silk jacket in addition to the other
rewards that the sovereigns had promised, which were ten thousand maravedís [cop-
per coins] as an annuity to whoever should see it first. At two hours after midnight
the land appeared, from which they were about two leagues distant. They hauled down
all the sails and kept only the treo, which is the mainsail without bonnets, and jogged
on and off, passing time until daylight Friday, when they reached an islet of the
Lucayos, which was called Guanahani in the language of the Indians. Soon they
saw naked people; and the Admiral went ashore in the armed launch, and Martín
Alonso Pinzón and his brother Vicente Anes, who was captain of the Niña. The
Admiral brought out the royal banner and the captains two flags with the green
cross, which the Admiral carried on all the ships as a standard, with an F and a Y [for
King Ferdinand and Queen Isabella], and over each letter a crown, one on one side
of the + and another on the other. Thus put ashore they saw very green trees and
many ponds and fruits of various kinds. The Admiral called to the two captains and
to the others who had jumped ashore and to Rodrigo Descobedo, the escrivano
[clerk] of the whole fleet, and to Rodrigo Sánchez de Segovia; and he said that they
should be witnesses that, in the presence of all, he would take, as in fact he did take,
possession of the said island for the king and for the queen his lords, making the declarations that were required, and which at more length are contained in the testi-
monials made there in writing. Soon many people of the island gathered there. What
follows are the very words of the Admiral in his book, about his first voyage to, and
discovery of, these Indies. I, he says, in order that they would be friendly to us—
because I recognized that they were people who would be better freed and converted
to our Holy Faith by love than by force—to some of them I gave red caps, and glass
beads which they put on their chests, and many other things of small value, in which
they took so much pleasure and became so much our friends that it was a marvel.
Later they came swimming to the ships' launches where we were and brought us parrots and cotton thread in balls and javelins and many other things, and they traded
them to us for other things which we gave them, such as small glass beads and bells.
In sum, they took everything and gave of what they had willingly. But it seemed to
me that they were a people very poor in everything. All of them go around as naked
as their mother bore them; and the women also, although I did not see more than

one quite young girl. And all those that I saw were young people, for none did I see of more than 30 years of age. They are all very well formed, with handsome bodies and good faces. Their hair coarse—almost like the tail of a horse—and short. They wear their hair down over their eyebrows except for a little in the back which they wear long and never cut. Some of them paint themselves with black, and they are of the color of the Canarians [Canary Islanders], neither black nor white; and some of them paint themselves with white, and some of them with red, and some of them with whatever they find. And some of them paint their faces, and some the whole body, and some of them only the eyes, and some of them only the nose. They do not carry arms nor are they acquainted with them, because I showed them swords and they took them by the edge and through ignorance cut themselves. They have no iron. Their javelins are shafts without iron and some of them have at the end a fish tooth and others of other things. All of them alike are of good-sized stature and carry themselves well. I saw some who had marks of wounds on their bodies and I made signs to them asking them what they were; and they showed me how people from other islands nearby came there and tried to take them, and how they defended themselves; and I believed and believe that they come here from tierra firme to take them by captive. They should be good and intelligent servants, for I see that they say very quickly everything that is said to them; and I believe they would become Christians very easily, for it seemed to me that they had no religion. Our Lord pleasing, at the time of my departure I will take six of them from here to Your Highness in order that they may learn to speak. No animal of any kind did I see on this island except parrots. All are the Admiral's words.

SATURDAY 13 OCTOBER [1492]

As soon as it dawned, many of these people came to the beach—all young, as I have said, and all of good stature—very handsome people, with their hair not curly but straight and coarse, like horsehair; and all of them very wide in the forehead and head, more so than any other race that I have seen so far. And their eyes are very handsome and not small; and none of them are black, but of the color of the Canary Islanders. Nor should anything else be expected since this island is on an east-west line with the island of Hierro in the Canaries. All alike have very straight legs and no belly but are very well formed. They came to the ship with dugouts [canoes] that are made from the trunk of one tree, like a long boat, and all of one piece, and worked marvelously in the fashion of the land, and so big that in some of them 40 and 45 men came. And others smaller, down to some in which one man came alone. They row with a paddle like that of a baker and go marvelously. And if it capsizes on them then they throw themselves in the water, and they right and empty it with calabashes [hollowed out gourds] that they carry. They brought balls of spun cotton and parrots and javelins and other little things that it would be tiresome to write down, and they gave everything for anything that was given to them. I was attentive and labored to find out if there was any gold; and I saw that some of them wore a little piece hung in a hole that they have in their noses. And by signs I was able to understand that, going to the south or rounding the island to the south, there was there a king who had large vessels of it and had very much gold. I strove to get them to go there and later saw that they had no intention of going. I decided to wait until the afternoon of the morrow and then depart for the southwest, for, as many of them showed me, they said there was land to the south and to the southwest and to the northwest and that these people from the northwest came to fight them many times. And so I will go to the southwest to seek gold and precious stones. This island is quite big and very flat and with very green trees and much water and a very large lake in the middle and without any mountains; and all of it so green that it is a pleasure to look at. And these people are very gentle, and because of their desire to have some of our things, and believing that nothing will be given to them without their giving something, and not having anything, they take what they can and then throw themselves into the water to swim. But everything they have they give for anything given to them, for they traded even pieces for pieces of bowls and broken glass cups, and I even saw 16 balls of cotton given for three Portuguese *çeotis* [copper coins], which is a Castilian *blanca* [a copper coin worth half of a maravedí]. And in them there was probably more than an arroba [around 24 pounds] of spun cotton. This I had forbidden and I did not let anyone take any of it, except that I had ordered it all taken for Your Highnesses if it were in quantity. It grows here on this island, but because of the short time I could not declare this for sure. And also the gold that they wear hung in their noses originates here; but in order not to lose time I want to go see if I can find the island of Cipango. Now, since night had come, all the Indians went ashore in their dugouts.

SUNDAY 14 OCTOBER [1492]

As soon as it dawned I ordered the ship's boat and the launches of the caravels made ready and went north-northeast along the island in order to see what there was in the other part, which was the eastern part. And also to see the villages, and I soon saw two or three, as well as people, who all came to the beach calling to us and giving thanks to God. Some of them brought us water; others, other things to eat; others, when they saw that I did not care to go ashore, threw themselves into the sea swimming and came to us, and we understood that they were asking us if we had come from the heavens. And one old man got into the ship's boat, and others in loud voices called to all the men and women: Come see the men who came from the heavens. Bring them something to eat and drink. Many men came, and many women, each one with something, giving thanks to God, throwing themselves on the ground; and they raised their hands to heaven, and afterward they called to us in loud voices to come ashore. But I was afraid, seeing a big stone reef that encircled that island all around. And in between the reef and shore there was depth and harbor for as many ships as there are in the whole of Christendom, and the entrance to it is very narrow. It is true that inside of this belt of stone there are some shallows, but the sea is no more disturbed than inside a well. And I bestirred myself this morning to see all of this, so that I could give an account of everything to Your Highnesses, and also to see where a fort could be made. And I saw a piece of land formed like an island, although it was not one, on which there were six houses. This piece of land might in two days be cut off to make an island, although I do not see this to be necessary since these people are very naive about weapons, as Your Highnesses will see from seven that I caused to be taken in order to carry them away to you and to learn our language and to return them. Except that, whenever Your Highnesses may command, all of them can be taken to Castile or held captive in this same island; because with 50 men all of them could be held in subjection and can be made to do whatever one might wish. And later, near the said islet, groves of trees, the most beautiful that I saw and with their leaves as green as those of Castile in the months of April and May, and lots of water. I looked over the whole of that harbor and afterward returned to the ship and set sail, and I saw so many islands that I did not know how to decide which one I would go to first. And those men whom I had taken told me by signs that they were so very many that they were numberless. And they named by their names more than a hundred. Finally I looked for the largest and to that one I decided to go and so I am doing. It is about five leagues distant from this island of San Salvador, and the others of them some more, some less. All are very flat without mountains and very fertile and all populated and they make war on one another, even though these men are very simple and very handsome in body.

MONDAY 15 OCTOBER [1492]

I had killed time this night for fear of reaching land to anchor before morning, because of not knowing whether the coast was clear of shoals, and as soon as it dawned I spread sail; and as the island was farther than five leagues, rather about seven, and the tide detained me, it was around noon when I reached the said island and I found that the face which is in the direction of San Salvador runs north-south and that there are in it five leagues; and the other, which I followed, runs east-west, and there are in it more than ten leagues. And since from this island I saw another larger one to the west, I spread sail to go forward all that day until night because I would not yet have been able to reach the western cape of the island, to which island I gave the name Santa María de la Concepcíon. And close to sundown I anchored near the said cape in order to find out if there was gold there, because these men that I have had taken on the island of San Salvador kept telling me that they wear very large bracelets of gold on their legs and on their arms. I well believe that all they were saying was a ruse in order to flee. Nevertheless, my intention was not to pass by any island of which I did not take possession, although if it is taken of one, it may be said that it was taken of all.

• • •

In recent years, the idealized, romanticized picture of Columbus has begun to be reconsidered, perhaps because Indians began to assert their importance as the original inhabitants of the American continent. With that reconsideration, Columbus has been seen in a different light, as the first representative of European imperialism in the Western Hemisphere, as a person who, while hypocritically presenting himself as a devout Christian, kidnapped, maimed and killed the indigenous people of Hispaniola in pursuit of gold. The evidence for this revised view comes mainly from Bartolomé de Las Casas, who was a contemporary of Columbus and who himself witnessed the scenes on Hispaniola, which he describes in the following passages.

Bartolomé de Las Casas, Two Readings on the Legacy of Columbus (1542 and 1550)

BARTOLOMÉ DE LAS CASAS, *THE DEVASTATION OF THE INDIES: A BRIEF ACCOUNT* (1542)[2]

The Indies were discovered in the year one thousand four hundred and ninety-two. In the following year a great many Spaniards went there with the intention of settling the land. Thus, forty-nine years have passed since the first settlers penetrated the land, the first so-claimed being the large and most happy isle called Hispaniola, which is six hundred leagues in circumference. Around it in all directions are many other islands, some very big, others very small, and all of them were, as we saw with our own eyes, densely populated with native peoples called Indians. This large island was perhaps the most densely populated place in the world. There must be close to two hundred leagues of land on this island, and the seacoast has been explored for more than ten thousand leagues, and each day more of it is being explored. And all the land so far discovered is a beehive of people; it is as though God had crowded into these lands the great majority of mankind.

And of all the infinite universe of humanity, these people are the most guileless, the most devoid of wickedness and duplicity, the most obedient and faithful to their native masters and to the Spanish Christians whom they serve. They are by nature the most humble, patient, and peaceable, holding no grudges, free from embroilments, neither excitable nor quarrelsome. These people are the most devoid of rancors, hatreds, or desire for vengeance of any people in the world. And because they are so weak and complaisant, they are less able to endure heavy labor and soon die of no matter what malady. The sons of nobles among us, brought up in the enjoyments of life's refinements, are no more delicate than are these Indians, even those among them who are of the lowest rank of laborers. They are also poor people, for they not only possess little but have no desire to possess worldly goods. For this reason they are not arrogant, embittered, or greedy. Their repasts are such that the food of the holy fathers in the desert can scarcely be more parsimonious, scanty, and poor. As to their dress, they are generally naked, with only their pudenda covered somewhat. And when they cover their shoulders it is with a square cloth no more than two varas in size. They have no beds, but sleep on a kind of matting or else in a kind of suspended net called hamacas. They are very clean in their persons, with alert, intelligent minds, docile and open to doctrine, very apt to receive our holy Catholic faith, to be endowed with virtuous customs, and to behave in a godly fashion. And once they begin to hear the tidings of the Faith, they are so insistent on knowing more and on taking the sacraments of the Church and on observing the divine cult that, truly, the missionaries who are here need to be endowed by God with great patience in order to cope with such eagerness. Some of the secular Spaniards who have been here for many years say that the goodness of the Indians is undeniable and that if this gifted people could be brought to know the one true God they would be the most fortunate people in the world.

Yet into this sheepfold, into this land of meek outcasts there came some Spaniards who immediately behaved like ravening wild beasts, wolves, tigers, or lions that had been starved for many days. And Spaniards have behaved in no other way during the past forty years, down to the present time, for they are still acting like ravening beasts, killing, terrorizing, afflicting, torturing, and destroying the native peoples, doing all this with the strangest and most varied new methods of cruelty, never seen or heard of before, and to such a degree that this Island of Hispaniola, once so populous (having a population that I estimated to be more than three millions), has now a population of barely two hundred persons.

The island of Cuba is nearly as long as the distance between Valladolid and Rome; it is now almost completely depopulated. San Juan [Puerto Rico] and

Jamaica are two of the largest, most productive and attractive islands; both are now deserted and devastated. On the northern side of Cuba and Hispaniola lie the neighboring Lucayos comprising more than sixty islands including those called Gigantes, beside numerous other islands, some small some large. The least felicitous of them were more fertile and beautiful than the gardens of the King of Seville. They have the healthiest lands in the world, where lived more than five hundred thousand souls; they are now deserted, inhabited by not a single living creature. All the people were slain or died after being taken into captivity and brought to the Island of Hispaniola to be sold as slaves. When the Spaniards saw that some of these had escaped, they sent a ship to find them, and it voyaged for three years among the islands searching for those who had escaped being slaughtered, for a good Christian had helped them escape, taking pity on them and had won them over to Christ; of these there were eleven persons and these I saw.

More than thirty other islands in the vicinity of San Juan are for the most part and for the same reason depopulated, and the land laid waste. On these islands I estimate there are 2,100 leagues of land that have been ruined and depopulated, empty of people.

As for the vast mainland, which is ten times larger than all Spain, even including Aragon and Portugal, containing more land than the distance between Seville and Jerusalem, or more than two thousand leagues, we are sure that our Spaniards, with their cruel and abominable acts, have devastated the land and exterminated the rational people who fully inhabited it. We can estimate very surely and truthfully that in the forty years that have passed, with the infernal actions of the Christians, there have been unjustly slain more than twelve million men, women, and children. In truth, I believe without trying to deceive myself that the number of the slain is more like fifteen million.

The common ways mainly employed by the Spaniards who call themselves Christian and who have gone there to extirpate those pitiful nations and wipe them off the earth is by unjustly waging cruel and bloody wars. Then, when they have slain all those who fought for their lives or to escape the tortures they would have to endure, that is to say, when they have slain all the native rulers and young men (since the Spaniards usually spare only the women and children, who are subjected to the hardest and bitterest servitude ever suffered by man or beast), they enslave any survivors. With these infernal methods of tyranny they debase and weaken countless numbers of those pitiful Indian nations.

Their reason for killing and destroying such an infinite number of souls is that the Christians have an ultimate aim, which is to acquire gold, and to swell themselves with riches in a very brief time and thus rise to a high estate disproportionate to their merits. It should be kept in mind that their insatiable greed and ambition, the greatest ever seen in the world, is the cause of their villainies. And also, those lands are so rich and felicitous, the native peoples so meek and patient, so easy to subject, that our Spaniards have no more consideration for them than beasts. And I say this from my own knowledge of the acts I witnessed. But I should not say "than beasts" for, thanks be to God, they have treated beasts with some respect; I should say instead like excrement on the public squares. And thus they have deprived the Indians of their lives and souls, for the millions I mentioned have died without the Faith and without the benefit of the sacraments. This is a well-known and proven fact which even the tyrant Governors, themselves killers, know and admit. And never have the Indians in all the Indies committed any act against the Spanish Christians, until those Christians have first and many times committed countless cruel aggressions against them or against neighboring nations. For in the beginning the Indians regarded the Spaniards as angels from Heaven. Only after the Spaniards had used violence against them, killing, robbing, torturing, did the Indians ever rise up against them. On the Island Hispaniola was where the Spaniards first landed, as I have said. Here those Christians perpetrated their first ravages and oppressions against the native peoples. This was the first land in the New World to be destroyed and depopulated by the Christians, and here they began their subjection of the women and children, taking them away from the Indians to use them and ill use them, eating the food they provided with their sweat and toil. The Spaniards did not content themselves with what the Indians gave them of their own free will, according to their ability, which was always too little to satisfy enormous appetites, for a Christian eats and consumes in one day an amount of food that would suffice to feed three houses inhabited by ten Indians for one month. And they committed other acts of force and violence and oppression which made the Indians realize that these men had not come from Heaven. And some of the Indians concealed their foods while others concealed their wives and children and still others fled to the mountains to avoid the terrible transactions of the Christians.

And the Christians attacked them with buffets and beatings, until finally they laid hands on the nobles of the villages. Then they behaved with such temerity and shamelessness that the most powerful ruler of the islands had to see his own wife raped by a Christian officer.

From that time onward the Indians began to seek ways to throw the Christians out of their lands. They took up arms, but their weapons were very weak and of little service in offense and still less in defense. (Because of this, the wars of the Indians against each other are little more than games played by children.) And the Christians, with their horses and swords and pikes began to carry out massacres and strange cruelties against them. They attacked the towns and spared neither the children nor the aged nor pregnant women nor women in childbed, not only stabbing them and dismembering them but cutting them to pieces as if dealing with sheep in the slaughter house. They laid bets as to who, with one stroke of the sword, could split a man in two or could cut off his head or spill out his entrails with a single stroke of the pike. They took infants from their mothers' breasts, snatching them by the legs and pitching them headfirst against the crags or snatched them by the arms and threw them into the rivers, roaring with laughter and saying as the babies fell into the water, "Boil there, you offspring of the devil!" Other infants they put to the sword along with their mothers and anyone else who happened to be nearby. They made some low wide gallows on which the hanged victim's feet almost touched the ground, stringing up their victims in lots of thirteen, in memory of Our Redeemer and His twelve Apostles, then set burning wood at their feet and thus burned them alive. To others they attached straw or wrapped their whole bodies in straw and set them afire. With still others, all those they wanted to capture alive, they cut off their hands and hung them round the victim's neck, saying, "Go now, carry the message," meaning, Take the news to the Indians who have fled to the mountains. They usually dealt with the chieftains and nobles in the following way: they made a grid of rods which they placed on forked sticks, then lashed the victims to the grid and lighted a smoldering fire underneath, so that little by little, as those captives screamed in despair and torment, their souls would leave them. . . .

After the wars and the killings had ended, when usually there survived only some boys, some women, and children, these survivors were distributed among the Christians to be slaves. The repartimiento or distribution was made according to the rank and importance of the Christian to whom the Indians were allocated, one of them being given thirty, another forty, still another, one or two hundred, and besides the rank of the Christian there was also to be considered in what favor he stood with the tyrant they called Governor. The pretext was that these allocated Indians were to be instructed in the articles of the Christian Faith. As if those Christians who were as a rule foolish and cruel and greedy and vicious could be caretakers of souls! And the care they took was to send the men to the mines to dig for gold, which is intolerable labor, and to send the women into the fields of the big ranches to hoe and till the land, work suitable for strong men. Nor to either the men or the women did they give any food except herbs and legumes, things of little substance. The milk in the breasts of the women with infants dried up and thus in a short while the infants perished. And since men and women were separated, there could be no marital relations. And the men died in the mines and the women died on the ranches from the same causes, exhaustion and hunger. And thus was depopulated that island which had been densely populated. . . .

THE ISLANDS OF SAN JUAN AND JAMAICA

The Spaniards passed over to the islands of San Juan and Jamaica (both of them veritable gardens and beehives of activity) in the year one thousand five hundred and nine, with the aim and purpose of making these islands a part of Hispaniola.

And on those islands the Spaniards perpetrated the same acts of aggression against the Indians and the wicked deeds described above, adding to them many outstanding cruelties, massacres and burnings of the people, or executing them by flinging them to the fierce dogs, torturing and oppressing the survivors, condemning them to the hard labor of mines, thus eradicating them from the earth, despoiling the land of those unfortunate and innocent people. Before the arrival of the Spaniards there had lived on these islands more than six hundred thousand souls, it has been stated. I believe there were more than one million inhabitants, and now, in each of the two islands, there are not more than two hundred persons, all the others having perished without the Faith and without the holy sacraments.

THE ISLAND OF CUBA

In the year one thousand five hundred and eleven, the Spaniards passed over the island of Cuba, which I have said is at the same distance from Hispaniola as the distance between Valladolid and Rome, and which was a well-populated province. They began and ended in Cuba as they had done elsewhere, but with much greater acts of cruelty.

Among the noteworthy outrages they committed was the one they perpetrated against a cacique, a very important noble, by the name Hatuey, who had come to Cuba from Hispaniola with many of his people, to flee the calamities and inhuman acts of the Christians. When he was told by certain Indians that the Christians were coming to Cuba, he assembled as many of his followers as he could and said to them: "Now you must know that they are saying the Christians are coming here, and you know by experience how they have put So and So and So and So, and other nobles to an end. And now they are coming from Haiti (which is Hispaniola) to do the same here. Do you know this?" The Indians replied: "We do not know. But it may be that they are by nature wicked and cruel." And he told them: "No, they do not act only because of that, but because they have a God they greatly worship and they want us to worship that God, and that is why they struggle with us and subject us and kill us."

He had a basket full of gold and jewels and he said: "You see their God here, the God of the Christians. If you agree to it, let us dance for this God, who knows, it may please the God of the Christians and then they will do us no harm." And his followers said, all together, "Yes, that is good, that is good!" And they danced round the basket of gold until they fell down exhausted. Then their chief, the cacique Hatuey, said to them: "See there, if we keep this basket of gold they will take it from us and will end up by killing us. So let us cast away the basket into the river." They all agreed to do this, and they flung the basket of gold into the river that was nearby.

This cacique, Hatuey, was constantly fleeing before the Christians from the time they arrived on the island of Cuba, since he knew them and of what they were capable. Now and then they encountered him and he defended himself, but they finally killed him. And they did this for the sole reason that he had fled from those cruel and wicked Christians and had defended himself against them. And when they had captured him and as many of his followers as they could, they burned them all at the stake.

When tied to the stake, the cacique Hatuey was told by a Franciscan friar who was present, an artless rascal, something about the God of the Christians and of the articles of Faith. And he was told what he could do in the brief time that remained to him, in order to be saved and go to heaven. The cacique, who had never heard any of this before, and was told he would go to Inferno where, if he did not adopt the Christian Faith, he would suffer eternal torment, asked the Franciscan friar if Christians all went to Heaven. When told that they did he said he would prefer to go to Hell. Such is the fame and honor that God and our Faith have earned through the Christians who have gone out of the Indies.

On one occasion when we went to claim ten leagues of a big settlement, along with the food and maintenance, we were welcomed with a bounteous quantity of fish and bread and cooked victuals. The Indians generously gave us all they could. Then suddenly, without cause and without warning, and in my presence, the devil inhabited the Christians and spurred them to attack the Indians, men, women, and children, who were sitting there before us. In the massacre that followed, the Spaniards put to the sword more than three thousand souls. I saw such terrible cruelties done there as I had never seen before nor thought to see.

A few days later, knowing that news of this massacre had spread through the land, I sent messengers ahead to the chiefs of the province of Havana, knowing they heard good things about me, telling them we were about to visit the town and telling them they should not hide but should come out to meet us, assuring them that no harm would be done to them. I did this with the full knowledge of the captain. And when we arrived in the province, there came out to welcome us twenty-one chiefs and caciques, and our captain, breaking his pledge to me and the pledge I had made them, took all these chieftains captive, intending to burn them at the stake, telling me this would be a good thing because those chiefs had in the past done him some harm. I had great difficulty in saving those Indians from the fire, but finally succeeded.

Afterward, when all the Indians of this island were subjected to servitude and the same ruin had befallen there as on the island Hispaniola, the survivors began to flee to the mountains or in despair to hang themselves, and there were husbands and wives who hanged themselves together with their children, because the cruelties perpetrated by one very great Spaniard (whom I knew) were so horrifying. More than two hundred Indians hanged themselves. And thus perished a countless number of people on the island of Cuba.

That tyrant Spaniard, representative of the King of Spain, demanded, in the repartimiento, that he be given three hundred Indians. At the end of three months all but thirty of them had died of the hard labor on the mines, which is to say only a tenth of them had survived. He demanded another allocation of Indians, and they also perished in the same way. He demanded still another large allocation, and those Indians also perished. Then he died, and the devil bore him away.

In three or four months, when I was there, more than seventy thousand children, whose fathers and mothers had been sent to the mines, died of hunger.

And I saw other frightful things. The Spaniards finally decided to track down the Indians who had taken refuge in the mountains. There they created amazing havoc and thus finished ravaging the island. Where had been a flourishing population, it is now a shame and pity to see the island laid waste and turned into a desert.

• • •

Bartolomé de Las Casas struggled for many years to persuade the Spanish monarchy to put a stop to the cruelties committed against the Indians. In the year 1550, a debate was arranged between Las Casas and the priest Ginés de Sepúlveda before the Royal Council of Spain in the city of Valladolid, and the central question was: are the Indians human beings and therefore deserving to be treated that way, or are they sub-humans and so deserving of enslavement?

BARTOLOMÉ DE LAS CASAS, *IN DEFENSE OF THE INDIANS* (1550)[3]

Illustrious Prince:

It is right that matters which concern the safety and peace of the great empire placed in your keeping by the divine goodness be reported to you, for you rule Spain and that marvelous New World in the name of the great Charles, your father, and you strive for immortal glory, not just with the imperial power but especially with the generous spirit and with the wisdom implanted in you by Christ. Therefore I have thought it advisable to bring to the attention of Your Highness that there has come into my hands a certain brief synopsis in Spanish of a work that Ginés de Sepúlveda is reported to have written in Latin. In it he gives four reasons, each of which, in his opinion, proves beyond refutation that war against the Indians is justified, provided that it be waged properly and the laws of war be observed, just as, up to the present, the kings of Spain have commanded that it be waged and carried out.

I hear that it is this man's intention to demonstrate the title by which the Kings of Spain possess the empire of the Indies and to bolster his position with arguments and laws, so that from now on no one will be able to slander you even tacitly on this point. I have read and reread this work carefully. And it is said that Sepúlveda drives home various other points at greater length in his Latin work (which I have not yet had the chance to see). What impression it has made on others I do not know. I certainly have detected in it poisons disguised with honey. Under pretext of pleasing his prince, a man who is a theologian offers honey-coated poison. In place of bread, he offers a stone. Great prince, unless this deadly poison is stopped by your wisdom, so that it will not become widespread, it will infect the minds of readers, deceive the unwary, and arm and incite tyrants to injustice. Believe me, that little book will bring ruin to the minds of many.

In the first place, while claiming that he wants to vindicate your jurisdiction over the Indies, he tears to pieces and reduces your rights by presenting arguments that are partly foolish, partly false, partly of the kind that have the least force. Furthermore, if this man's judgment in this matter should be printed [and] sanctioned with the royal license and privilege, there can be no doubt that within a short time the empire of the Indies will be entirely overthrown and destroyed.

Indeed, if so many laws already issued, so many decrees, so many harsh threats, and so many statutes conscientiously enacted by the Emperor Charles and his predecessors have been ineffective in preventing so many thousands of innocent men from perishing by sword, hunger, and all the misfortunes of total war, and extensive areas of their highly civilized kingdoms and most fertile provinces from being savagely devastated; if the fear of God and the dread of hell have not even moderated (I shall not say curbed) the utterly ruthless and cruel spirits of the Spaniards; if the outcries of preachers and holy men that they were barred from the sacraments of the Church and were not forgiven in sacramental confession were of no avail, what will happen when evil men (for whom, according to the old proverb, nothing is wanting except the opportunity) read that a scholar, a doctor of theology, and the royal historian has published books approving those criminal wars and hellish campaigns, and, by supporting arguments, confirms and defends the unheard-of crime whereby Christian men, forgetting Christian virtue, hold in slavery those people, the most unfortunate of all, who appear to have escaped the ferocity of that most cruel race by chance rather than by the mercy of the Spaniards? Furthermore [what will happen when they read] that he teaches that soldiers may lawfully keep everything they take in these wars, even though they undertook the campaign with the evil intention of looting, that is, of pillaging by fire, sword, murder, plunder and violence, upsetting, overturning, and throwing into confusion all laws, divine and human, and that they are not bound to restore such goods because the Spaniards who do these things and shed the blood of the innocent consecrate their hands to God (as I hear Sepúlveda has written) and merit Christ's grace because they prevent the worship of idols?

Whom will they spare? What blood will they not shed? What cruelty will they not commit, these brutal men who are hardened to seeing fields bathed in human blood, who make no distinction of sex or age, who do not spare infants at their mothers' breasts, pregnant women, the great, the lowly, or even men of feeble and gray old age for whom the weight of years usually awakens reverence or mercy? What will they not do if they hear that there is a man teaching that they are consecrating their hands to God when they crush the Indians with massacres, pillaging, and tyranny—that they are doing the same as those who killed the Children of Israel who were adoring the calf? They will give more trust to him, as to someone who tells them what they want to hear, than they would to the son of God himself if he were face to face before us and teaching something different.

If, then, the Indians are being brought to the point of extermination, if as many peoples are being destroyed as widespread kingdoms are being overthrown, what sane man would doubt that the most flourishing empire of the New World, once its native inhabitants have been destroyed, will become a wilderness, and nothing but dominion over tigers, lions, and wild beasts for the Kings of Spain? . . .

Therefore when Sepúlveda, by word or in his published works, teaches that campaigns against the Indians are lawful, what does he do except encourage oppressors and provide an opportunity for as many crimes and lamentable evils as these [men] commit, more than anyone would find it possible to believe? In the meantime, with most certain harm to his own soul, he is the reason why countless human beings, suffering brutal massacres, perish forever, that is, men who, through the inhuman brutality of the Spaniards, breathe their last before they heard the word of God [or] are fed by Christ's gentle doctrine [or] are strengthened by the Christian sacraments. What more horrible or unjust occurrence can be imagined than this?

Therefore, if Sepúlveda's opinion (that campaigns against the Indians are lawful) is approved, the most holy faith of Christ, to the reproach of the name Christian, will be hateful and detestable to all the peoples of the world to whom the word will come of the inhuman crimes that the Spaniards inflict on that unhappy race, so that neither in our lifetime nor in the future will they want to accept our faith under any condition, for they see that its first heralds are not pastors but plunderers, not fathers but tyrants, and that those who profess it are ungodly, cruel and without pity in their merciless savagery.

• • •

Other than Las Casas there are no texts of this period that describe the experiences of the people Columbus "discovered." Eduardo Galeano here re-imagines their plight, drawing on numerous historical sources. Galeano, the Uruguayan people's journalist and radical storyteller, is known around the world for his books *The Open Veins of Latin America* and the trilogy *Memory of Fire*, from which the reading here is selected. In these passages, from the first volume of the trilogy, *Genesis*, Galeano narrates Columbus's voyages, turning some of the many myths about Columbus on their head.

Eduardo Galeano, *Memory of Fire* (1982)[4]

1492: THE OCEAN SEA

THE SUN ROUTE TO THE INDIES

The breezes are sweet and soft, as in spring in Seville, and the sea is like a Guadalquivir river, but the swell no sooner rises than they get seasick and vomit, jammed into their fo'c'sles, the men who in three patched-up little ships cleave the unknown sea, the sea without a frame. Men, little drops in the wind. And if the sea doesn't love them? Night falls on the caravels. Whither will the wind toss them? A dorado, chasing a flying fish, jumps on board and the panic grows. The crew doesn't appreciate the savory aroma of the slightly choppy sea, nor do they listen to the din of the sea gulls and gannets that come from the west. That horizon: does the abyss begin there? Does the sea end?

Feverish eyes of mariners weatherbeaten in a thousand voyages, burning eyes of jailbirds yanked from Andalusian prisons and embarked by force: these eyes see no prophetic reflections of gold and silver in the foam of the waves, nor in the country and river birds that keep flying over the ships, nor in the green rushes and branches thick with shells that drift in the sargassos. The bottom of the abyss— is that where hell starts to burn? Into what kind of jaws will the trade winds hurl these little men? They gaze at the stars, seeking God, but the sky is as inscrutable as this never-navigated sea. They hear its roar, mother sea, the hoarse voice answering the wind with phrases of eternal condemnation, mysterious drums resounding in the depths. They cross themselves and want to pray and stammer: "Tonight we'll fall off the world, tonight we'll fall off the world."

1492: GUANAHANÍ

COLUMBUS

He falls on his knees, weeps, kisses the earth. He steps forward, staggering because for more than a month he has hardly slept, and beheads some shrubs with his sword.

Then he raises the flag. On one knee, eyes lifted toward heaven, he pronounces three times the names of Isabella and Ferdinand. Beside him the scribe Rodrigo de Escobedo, a man slow of pen, draws up the document.

From today, everything belongs to those remote monarchs: the coral sea, the beaches, the rocks all green with moss, the woods, the parrots, and these laurel-skinned people who don't yet know about clothes, sin, or money and gaze dazedly at the scene.

Luis de Torres translates Christopher Columbus's questions into Hebrew: "Do you know the kingdom of the Great Khan? Where does the gold you have in your noses and ears come from?"

The naked men stare at him with open mouths, and the interpreter tries out his small stock of Chaldean: "Gold? Temples? Palaces? King of kings? Gold?"

And then he tries his Arabic, the little he knows of it: "Japan? China? Gold?"

The interpreter apologizes to Columbus in the language of Castile. Columbus curses in Genovese and throws to the ground his credentials, written in Latin and addressed to the Great Khan. The naked men watch the anger of the intruder with red hair and coarse skin, who wears a velvet cape and very shiny clothes.

Soon the word will run through the islands:

"Come and see the men who arrived from the sky! Bring them food and drink!"

1493: BARCELONA

DAY OF GLORY

The heralds announce him with their trumpets. The bells peal and the drums beat out festive rhythms. The admiral, newly returned from the Indies, mounts the stone steps and advances on the crimson carpet amid the silken dazzle of the applauding royal court. The man who has made the saints' and sages' prophecies come true reaches the platform, kneels, and kisses the hands of the queen and the king.

From the rear come the trophies: gleaming on trays, the bits of gold that Columbus had exchanged for little mirrors and red caps in the remote gardens newly burst from the sea. On branches and dead leaves are paraded the skins of lizards and snakes; and behind them, trembling and weeping, enter the beings never before seen. They are the few who have survived the colds, the measles, and the disgust for the Christians' food and bad smell. Not naked, as they were when they approached the three caravels and were captured, they have been covered up with trousers, shirts, and a few parrots that have been put in their hands and on their heads and shoulders. The parrots, robbed of their feathers by the foul winds of the voyage, look as moribund as the men. Of the captured women and children, none has survived.

Hostile murmurs are heard in the salon. The gold is minimal, and there is not a trace of black pepper, or nutmeg, or cloves, or ginger; and Columbus has not brought in any bearded sirens or men with tails, or the ones with only one eye or foot—and that foot big enough when raised to be protection from the fierce sun.

1493: ROME

THE TESTAMENT OF ADAM

In the dim light of the Vatican, fragrant with oriental perfumes, the pope dictates a new bull.

A short time has passed since Rodrigo Borgia, of Xátiva, Valencia, took the name Alexander VI. Not a year ago yet since the day he bought for cash the seven votes he was short in the Sacred College, and could change a cardinal's purple for the ermine cape of the supreme pontiff.

Alexander devotes more time to calculating the price of indulgences than to meditating on the mystery of the Holy Trinity. Everyone knows that he prefers very brief Masses, except for the ones his jester Gabriellino celebrates in a mask in his private chambers, and everyone knows that the new pope is capable of rerouting the Corpus Christi procession to pass beneath a pretty woman's balcony.

He is also capable of cutting up the world as if it were a chicken: he raises a hand and traces a frontier, from head to tail of the planet, across the unknown sea. God's agent concedes in perpetuity all that has been or is being discovered, to the west of that line, to Isabella of Castile and Ferdinand of Aragon and their heirs on the Spanish throne. He entrusts them to send good, God-fearing, erudite, wise, expert men to the islands and mainlands discovered or to be discovered, to instruct the natives in the Catholic faith and teach them good customs. Whatever is discovered to the east will belong to the Portuguese crown.

Anguish and euphoria of sails unfurled: in Andalusia Columbus is already preparing a second voyage to the regions where gold grows in bunches on the vines and precious stones await in the craniums of dragons.

1493: HUEXOTZINGO

WHERE IS THE TRUTH? WHERE ARE THE ROOTS?

This is the city of music, not of war: Huexotzingo, in the valley of Tlaxcala. In a flash the Aztecs attack and damage it, and take prisoners to sacrifice to their gods.

On this evening, Tecayehuatzin, king of Huexotzingo, has assembled the poets from other areas. In the palace gardens, the poets chat about the flowers and songs that come down to earth, a region of the fleeting moment, from within the sky, and that only last up there in the house of the Giver of life. The poets talk and doubt:

Can it be that men are real?
Will our song
Still be read tomorrow?

The voices follow one another. When night falls, the king of Huexotzingo thanks them and says good-bye:

We know something that is real
The hearts of our friends.

1493: PASTO

EVERYBODY PAYS TAXES

Even these remote heights far to the north are reached by the Inca Empire's tax collector.

The Quillacinga people have nothing to give, but in this vast kingdom all communities pay tribute, in kind or in labor time. No one, however far off and however poor, can forget who is in charge.

At the foot of the volcano, the chief of the Quillacingas steps forward and places a bamboo cylinder in the hands of the envoy from Cuzco. The cylinder is full of live lice.

1493: SANTA CRUZ ISLAND

AN EXPERIENCE OF MIQUELE DE CUNEO FROM SAVONA

The shadow of the sails spreads across the sea. Gulfweed and jellyfish, moved by the waves, drift over the surface toward the coast.

From the quarterdeck of one of the caravels, Columbus contemplates the white beaches where he has again planted the cross and gallows. This is his second voyage. How long it will last he doesn't know; but his heart tells him that all will come out well, and why wouldn't the admiral believe it? Doesn't he have the habit of measuring the ship's speed with his hand against his chest, counting the heartbeats?

Below decks in another caravel, in the captain's cabin, a young girl shows her teeth. Miquele de Cuneo reaches for her breasts, and she scratches and kicks him and screams. Miquele received her a while ago. She is a gift from Columbus.

He lashes her with a rope. He beats her hard on the head and stomach and legs. Her screams become moans, the moans become wails. Finally all that can be heard are the comings and goings of sea gulls and the creak of rocked timbers. From time to time waves send a spray through the porthole.

Miquele hurls himself upon the bleeding body and thrusts, gasps, wrestles. The air smells of tar, of saltpeter, of sweat. Then the girl, who seems to have fainted or died, suddenly fastens her nails in Miquele's back, knots herself around his legs, and rolls him over in a fierce embrace.

After some time, when Miquele comes to, he doesn't know where he is or what has happened. Livid, he detaches himself from her and knocks her away with his fist.

He staggers up on deck. Mouth open, he takes a deep breath of sea breeze. In a loud voice, as if announcing an eternal truth, he says, "These Indian women are all whores."

1495: SALAMANCA

THE FIRST WORD FROM AMERICA

Elio Antonion de Nebrija, language scholar, publishes here his "Spanish-Latin Vocabulary." The dictionary includes the first Americanism of the Castilian language:

Canoa: Boat made from a single timber.

The new word comes from the Antilles.

These boats without sails, made of the trunk of a ceiba tree, welcomed Christopher Columbus. Out from the islands, paddling canoes, came the men with long black hair and bodies tattooed with vermilion symbols. They approached the caravels, offered fresh water, and exchanged gold for the kind of little tin bells that sell for a copper in Castile.

1495: LA ISABELA

CAONABÓ

Detached, aloof, the prisoner sits at the entrance of Christopher Columbus's house. He has iron shackles on his ankles, and handcuffs trap his wrists.

Caonabó was the one who burned to ashes the Navidad fort that the admiral had built when he discovered this island of Haiti. He burned the fort and killed its occupants. And not only them: In these two long years he has castigated with arrows any Spaniards he came across in Cibao, his mountain territory, for their hunting of gold and people.

Alonso de Ojeda, veteran of the wars against the Moors, paid him a visit on the pretext of peace. He invited him to mount his horse, and put on him these handcuffs of burnished metal that tie his hands, saying that they were jewels worn by the monarchs of Castile in their balls and festivities.

Now Chief Caonabó spends the days sitting beside the door, his eyes fixed on the tongue of light that invades the earth floor at dawn and slowly retreats in the evening. He doesn't move an eyelash when Columbus comes around. On the other hand, when Ojeda appears, he manages to stand up and salute with a bow the only man who has defeated him.

1496: LA CONCEPCIÓN

SACRILEGE

Bartholomew Columbus, Christopher's brother and lieutenant, attends an incineration of human flesh.

Six men play the leads in the grand opening of Haiti's incinerator. The smoke makes everyone cough. The six are burning as a punishment and as a lesson: They have buried the images of Christ and the Virgin that Fray Ramón Pané left with them for protection and consolation. Fray Ramón taught them to pray on their knees, to say the Ave Maria and Paternoster and to invoke the name of Jesus in the face of temptation, injury, and death.

No one has asked them why they buried the images. They were hoping that the new gods would fertilize their fields of corn, cassava, boniato, and beans.

The fire adds warmth to the humid, sticky heat that foreshadows heavy rain.

CHAPTER TWO

The First Slaves

Three Documents on Slave Revolts (1720 to 1793)
  Anonymous Letter to Mr. Boone in London (June 24, 1720)
  Letter from Petersburg, Virginia (May 17, 1792)
  *Secret Keeper Richmond (Unknown) to Secret Keeper Norfolk
    (Unknown) (1793)*

Four Petitions Against Slavery (1773 to 1777)
  "Felix" (Unknown) Slave Petition for Freedom (January 6, 1773)
  Peter Bestes and Other Slaves Petition for Freedom (April 20, 1773)
  *"Petition of a Grate Number of Blackes" to Thomas Gage
    (May 25, 1774)*
  *"Petition of a Great Number of Negroes" to the Massachusetts House
    of Representatives (January 13, 1777)*

Benjamin Banneker's Letter to Thomas Jefferson (August 19, 1791)

In the year 1619, the first blacks were brought by force to serve the white colonists of Jamestown, Virginia. But the slave trade had begun almost a hundred years before this, when blacks were brought from Africa to the Portuguese and Spanish colonies in the Caribbean and South America.

The Virginians in 1619 were desperate for labor to grow enough food to stay alive. In the winter of 1609–10, the colony had been decimated by starvation, leaving only sixty colonists from an original group of five hundred. They could not force the Indians to work for them, but blacks captured in Africa, brought far from home and helpless, would be useful. And so the importation of slaves began, with the first twenty blacks brought in chains from the West Indies to Jamestown.

• • •

Slaves did not merely accept their lot, as some historians have claimed. Instead, they resisted in many ways, including physical rebellion, as the following three documents reveal. In the first, an anonymous letter, the author describes a slave uprising in the Carolinas, one of many that would happen until slavery was abolished. The second letter describes "a very dangerous Insurrection among the Negroes in the Eastern shore of Virginia." The third document is a rare letter in the archives of the state of South Carolina by a slave who tells of plans for a rebellion involving thousands of slaves. This never came to fruition, but the document, which was found on the street in 1793 in Yorktown, Virginia, reveals the desire of slaves for freedom, despite the great odds against a successful revolt.

Three Documents on Slave Revolts (1720 to 1793)

ANONYMOUS LETTER TO MR. BOONE IN LONDON (JUNE 24, 1720)[1]

I am now to acquaint you that very lately we have had a very wicked and barbarous plott of the designe of the negroes rising with a designe to destroy all the white people in the country and then to take the town [Charles Town] in full body but it pleased God it was discovered and many of them taken prisoners and some burnt some hang'd and some banish'd.

I think it proper for you to tell Mr. Percivall at home that his slaves was the principal rogues and 'tis my opinion his only way will be to sell them out singly or else I am doubtful his interest in slaves will come to little for want of strict management, [since] work does not agree with them. 14 of them are now at the Savanna towne and sent for white and Indians and will be executed as soon as they come down[.] [T]hey thought to gett to [St.] Augustine and would have got a creek fellow to have been their pylott but the Savanna garrison tooke the negroes up half starved and the Creeke Indians would not join them or be their pylott.

LETTER FROM PETERSBURG, VIRGINIA (MAY 17, 1792)[2]

Several alarming accounts have been received in town, of a very dangerous Insurrection among the Negroes in the Eastern shore of Virginia;—Reports state, That about two weeks ago, the Negroes in that part of the State, to the amount of about 900, assembled in different parts, armed with muskets, spears, clubs etc. and committed several outrages upon the inhabitants. A favorite servant of Colonel Savage, who had joined them, met his master on the road, took his horse and some money from him, and treated him in an insolent manner. Celeb, a negro, the property of Mr. Simkins, was to command this banditti; he was also a favorite servant of his master and had long lived with him in the capacity of overseer. A barrel of musket balls, about 300 spears, some guns, powder, provisions, etc. have already been discovered and taken; the spears, it is said, were made by a negro blacksmith on the Eastern shore. A considerable number of the slaves have been taken up, and it is expected will be hanged.

It appears from a letter which has been lately discovered in Norfolk from one of the Negroes on the Eastern shore that they had concerted a plan with the Negroes from Norfolk and Portsmouth to commit some violent outrages in and about those towns. Six hundred of them were to cross the bay, at a certain time in the night, and were to be joined by the Negroes, in that Neighborhood; then they meant to blow up the magazine in Norfolk, and massacre the inhabitants.

SECRET KEEPER RICHMOND (UNKNOWN) TO SECRET KEEPER NORFOLK (UNKNOWN) (1793)[3]

Dear Friend—

The great secret that has been so long in being with our own color has come nearly to a head tho some on our Town has told of it but in such a slight manner it is not believed[.] [W]e have got about five hundred Guns aplenty of lead but not much powder[.] I hope you have made a good collection of powder and ball and will hold yourself in readiness to strike whenever called for and never be out of the way[.] [I]t will not be long before it will take place, and I am fully satisfied we shall be in full possession of the [w]hole country in a few weeks[.] [S]ince I wrote you last I got a letter from our friend in Charleston[:] he tells me has listed near six thousand men, there is a gentlemen that says he will give us as much powder as we want, and when we begin he will help us all he can, the damn's brutes patroles is going all night in Richmond but will soon kill them all, there ain't many, we will appoint a night to begin with fire clubs and shot, we will kill all before us, it will begin in every town in one nite[.] Keep ready to receive orders, when I hear from Charleston again I shall [k]no[w] and will [w]rite to you, be that give you this is a good friend and don't let any body see it, [w]rite me by the same hand he will give it to me out his hand and he will be up next week[.] [D]on't be feared have a good heart, fight brave and we will get free[.] I had like to get each [illegible] but God was for me, and I got away, no more now but remain your friend—Secret Keeper Richmond to secret keeper Norfolk.

• • •

More evidence of resistance to slavery can be found in the various petitions by slaves to state legislatures, seeking release from their bondage. Here are four of them, in part deferential but also impassioned and defiant.

Four Petitions Against Slavery (1773 to 1777)

"FELIX" (UNKNOWN) SLAVE PETITION FOR FREEDOM (JANUARY 6, 1773)[4]

Province of the Massachusetts Bay To His Excellency Thomas Hutchinson, Esq; Governor; To The Honorable His Majesty's Council, and To the Honorable House of Representatives in General Court assembled at Boston, the 6th Day of January, 1773.

The humble PETITION of many Slaves, living in the Town of Boston, and other Towns in the Province is this, namely That your Excellency and Honors, and the Honorable the Representatives would be pleased to take their unhappy State and Condition under your wise and just Consideration.

We desire to bless God, who loves Mankind, who sent his Son to die for their Salvation, and who is no respecter of Persons; that he hath lately put it into the Hearts of Multitudes on both Sides of the Water, to bear our Burthens, some of whom are Men of great Note and Influence; who have pleaded our Cause with Arguments which we hope will have their weight with this Honorable Court.

We presume not to dictate to your Excellency and Honors, being willing to rest our Cause on your Humanity and justice; yet would beg Leave to say a Word or two on the Subject. Although some of the Negroes are vicious, (who doubtless may be punished and restrained by the same Laws which are in Force against other of the King's Subjects) there are many others of a quite different Character, and who, if made free, would soon be able as well as willing to bear a Part in the Public Charges; many of them of good natural Parts, are discreet, sober, honest, and industrious; and may it not be said of many, that they are virtuous and religious, although their Condition is in itself so unfriendly to Religion, and every moral Virtue except Patience. How many of that Number have there been, and now are in this Province, who have had every Day of their Lives embittered with this most intollerable Reflection, That, let their Behaviour be what it will, neither they, nor their Children to all Generations, shall ever be able to do, or to possess and enjoy any Thing, no, not even Life itself, but in a Manner as the Beasts that perish.

We have no Property. We have no Wives. No Children. We have no City. No Country. But we have a Father in Heaven, and we are determined, as far as his Grace shall enable us, and as far as our degraded contemptuous Life will admit, to keep all his Commandments: Especially will we be obedient to our Masters, so long as God in his sovereign Providence shall suffer us to be holden in Bondage.

It would be impudent, if not presumptuous in us, to suggest to your Excellency and Honors any Law or Laws proper to be made, in relation to our unhappy State, which, although our greatest Unhappiness, is not our Fault; and this gives us great

Encouragement to pray and hope for such Relief as is consistent with your Wisdom, justice, and Goodness.

We think Ourselves very happy, that we may thus address the Great and General Court of this Province, which great and good Court is to us, the best judge, under God, of what is wise, just and good.

We humbly beg Leave to add but this one Thing more: We pray for such Relief only, which by no Possibility can ever be productive of the least Wrong or Injury to our Masters; but to us will be as Life from the dead.

Signed,

FELIX

PETER BESTES AND OTHER SLAVES PETITION FOR FREEDOM (APRIL 20, 1773)[5]

Sir,

The efforts made by the legislative of this province in their last sessions to free themselves from slavery, gave us, who are in that deplorable state, a high degree of satisfaction. We expect great things from men who have made such a noble stand against the designs of their fellow-men to enslave them. We cannot but wish and hope Sir, that you will have the same grand object, we mean civil and religious liberty, in view in your next session. The divine spirit of freedom, seems to fire every humane breast on this continent, except such as are bribed to assist in executing the execrable plan.

WE are very sensible that it would be highly detrimental to our present masters, if we were allowed to demand all that of right belongs to us for past services; this we disclaim. Even the Spaniards, who have not those sublime ideas of freedom that English men have, are conscious that they have no right to all the service of their fellow-men, we mean the Africans, whom they have purchased with their money; therefore they allow them one day in a week to work for themselve[s], to enable them to earn money to purchase the residue of their time, which they have a right to demand in such portions as they are able to pay for (a due appraizment of their services being first made, which always stands at the purchase money). We do not pretend to dictate to you Sir, or to the honorable Assembly, of which you are a member: We acknowledge our obligations to you for what you have already done, but as the people of this province seem to be actuated by the principles of equity and justice, we cannot but expect your house will again take our deplorable case into serious consideration, and give us that ample relief which, as men, we have a natural right to.

BUT since the wise and righteous governor of the universe, has permitted our fellow men to make us slaves, we bow in submission to him, and determine to

behave in such a manner, as that we may have reason to expect the divine appro-
bation of, and assistance in, our peaceable and lawful attempts to gain our freedom.

WE are willing to submit to such regulations and laws, as may be made relative
to us, until we leave the province, which we determine to do as soon as we can from
our joynt labours procure money to transport ourselves to some part of the coast
of Africa, where we propose a settlement. We are very desirous that you should have
instructions relative to us, from your town, therefore we pray you to communicate this letter to them, and ask this favor for us.

In behalf of our fellow slaves in this province, And by order of their Committee.

PETER BESTES

SAMBO FREEMAN

FELIX HOLBROOK

CHESTER JOIE

"PETITION OF A GRATE NUMBER OF BLACKES" TO THOMAS GAGE (MAY 25, 1774)[6]

The Petition of a Grate Number of Blackes of this Province who by divine permission are held in a state of Slavery within the bowels of a free and christian
Country

Humbly Shewing

That your Petitioners apprehind we have in common with all other men a
naturel right to our freedoms without Being depriv'd of them by our fellow men
as we are a freeborn Pepel and have never forfeited this Blessing by aney compact
or agreement whatever. But we were unjustly dragged by the cruel hand of power
from our dearest frinds and sum of us stolen from the bosoms of our tender
Parents and from a Populous Pleasant and plentiful country and Brought hither
to be made slaves for Life in a Christian land. Thus are we deprived of every thing
that hath a tendency to make life even tolerable, the endearing ties of husband and
wife we are strangers to for we are no longer man and wife then our masters or
mestreses thinkes proper marred or onmarred. Our children are also taken from
us by force and sent maney miles from us wear we seldom or ever see them again
there to be made slaves of for Life which sumtimes is vere short by Reson of Being
dragged from their mothers Breest[.] Thus our Lives are imbittered to us on these
accounts[.] By our deplorable situation we are rendered incapable of shewing our
obedience to Almighty God[.] [H]ow can a slave perform the duties of a husband
to a wife or parent to his child[?] How can a husband leave master and work and
cleave to his wife[?] How can the wife submit themselves to there husbands in all
things[?] How can the child obey thear parents in all things[?] . . .

How can the master be said to Beare my Borden when he Beares me down whith the Have chanes of slavery and operson [oppression] against my will and how can we fulfill our parte of duty to him whilst in this condition[?] [A]nd as we cannot searve our God as we ought whilst in this situation Nither can we reap an equal benefet from the laws of the Land which doth not justifi but condemns Slavery or if there had bin aney Law to hold us in Bondege we are Humbely of the Opinon ther never was aney to inslave our children for life when Born in a free Countrey. We therefor Bage your Excellency and Honours will give this its deu weight and consideration and that you will accordingly cause an act of the legislative to be pessed that we may obtain our Natural right our freedoms and our children be set at lebety [liberty].

"PETITION OF A GREAT NUMBER OF NEGROES" TO THE MASSACHUSETTS HOUSE OF REPRESENTATIVES (JANUARY 13, 1777)[7]

To the Honorable Council and House of Representatives for the State of Massachusetts-Bay in General Court assembled January 13th[,] 1777.

The Petition of a great number of Negroes who are detained in a state of Slavery in the Bowels of a free and Christian Country Humbly Shewing:

That your Petitioners apprehend that they have, in common with all other Men, a natural and unalienable right to that freedom, which the great Parent of the Universe hath bestowed equally on all Mankind, and which they have never forfeited by any compact or agreement whatever—But they were unjustly dragged, by the cruel hand of Power, from their dearest friends, and some of them even torn from the embraces of their tender Parents, from a populous, pleasant and plentiful Country—and in Violation of the Laws of Nature and of Nation and in defiance of all the tender feelings of humanity, brought hither to be sold like Beasts of Burden, and like them condemned to slavery for Life—Among a People professing the mild Religion of Jesus—A People not insensible of the sweets of rational freedom—Nor without spirit to resent the unjust endeavors of others to reduce them to a State of Bondage and Subjection.

Your Honors need not to be informed that a Life of Slavery, like that of your petitioners, deprived of every social privilege, of every thing requisite to render Life even tolerable, is far worse than Non-Existence—In imitation of the laudable example of the good People of these States, your Petitioners have long and patiently waited the event of Petition after Petition by them presented to the legislative Body of this State, and can not but with grief reflect that their success has been but too similar.

They can not but express their astonishment, that it has never been considered, that every principle from which America has acted in the course of her unhappy difficulties with Great-Britain, pleads stronger than a thousand arguments in favor of your Petitioners.

They therefore humbly beseech your Honors, to give this Petition its due weight and consideration, and cause an Act of the Legislature to be passed, whereby they may be restored to the enjoyment of that freedom which is the natural right of all Men—and their Children (who were born in this Land of Liberty) may not be held as Slaves after they arrive at the age of twenty one years.

So may the Inhabitants of this State (no longer chargeable with the inconsistency of acting, themselves, the part which they condemn and oppose in others) be prospered in their present glorious struggles for Liberty; and have those blessings secured to them by Heaven, of which benevolent minds can not wish to deprive their fellow Men.

And your Petitioners, as in Duty Bound shall ever pray.

• • •

When the Revolutionary army needed more forces, a number of slaves were entreated or forced into the military, often with the promise of freedom as a reward for their service. But these promises were routinely betrayed, and many masters claimed the right to re-enslave blacks who had fought in the Revolution. Numerous petitions, such as the one here—which proved to be successful—testify to the struggle of blacks to claim their rights after their service. Benjamin Banneker, the child of a freed slave, taught himself mathematics and astronomy, predicted accurately a solar eclipse, and was appointed to plan the new city of Washington. Shortly before publishing a scientific almanac in 1792, he wrote to Thomas Jefferson, calling for an end to slavery. The exchange of letters between Banneker and Jefferson was published in pamphlet form by David Lawrence, a printer in Philadelphia.

Benjamin Banneker, Letter to Thomas Jefferson (August 19, 1791)[8]

Sir,

I am fully sensible of the greatness of that freedom, which I take with you on the present occasion; a liberty which Seemed to me scarcely allowable, when I reflected on that distinguished and dignified station in which you Stand; and the almost general prejudice and prepossession which is so prevalent in the world against those of my complexion.

I suppose it is a truth too well attested to you, to need a proof here, that we are a race of Beings who have long labored under the abuse and censure of the world, that we have long been looked upon with an eye of contempt, and that we have long been considered rather as brutish than human, and Scarcely capable of mental endowments.

Sir I hope I may Safely admit, in consequence of that report which hath reached me, that you are a man far less inflexible in Sentiments of this nature, than many others, that you are measurably friendly, and well disposed towards us, and that you are willing and ready to Lend your aid and assistance to our relief from those many distresses and numerous calamities to which we are reduced.

Now Sir if this is founded in truth, I apprehend you will readily embrace every opportunity, to eradicate that train of absurd and false ideas and opinions which so generally prevails with respect to us, and that your Sentiments are concurrent with mine, which are that one universal Father hath given being to us all, and that he hath not only made us all of one flesh, but that he hath also without partiality afforded us all the Same Sensations, and endued [endowed] us all with the same faculties, and that however variable we may be in Society or religion, however diversified in Situation or color, we are all of the Same Family, and Stand in the Same relation to him.

Sir, if these are Sentiments of which you are fully persuaded, I hope you cannot but acknowledge, that it is the indispensable duty of those who maintain for themselves the rights of human nature, and who possess the obligations of Christianity, to extend their power and influence to the relief of every part of the human race, from whatever burden or oppression they may unjustly labor under, and this I apprehend a full conviction of the truth and obligation of these principles should lead all to.

Sir, I have long been convinced, that if your love for your Selves, and for those inestimable laws which preserve to you the rights of human nature, was founded on Sincerity, you could not but be Solicitous, that every Individual of whatsoever rank or distinction, might with you equally enjoy the blessings thereof, neither could you rest Satisfied, short of the most active effusion of your exertions, in order to their promotion from any State of degradation, to which the unjustifiable cruelty and barbarism of men may have reduced them.

Sir, I freely and Cheerfully acknowledge, that I am of the African race, and in that color which is natural to them of the deepest dye (My Father was brought here a S[lav]e from Africa), and it is under a Sense of the most profound gratitude to the Supreme Ruler of the universe, that I now confess to you, that I am not under that State of tyrannical thralldom, and inhuman captivity, to which too many of my brethren are doomed; but that I have abundantly tasted of the fruition of those blessings which proceed from that free and unequalled liberty with which you are favored and which I hope you will willingly allow you have mercifully received from the immediate hand of that Being, from whom proceedeth every good and perfect gift.

Sir, Suffer me to recall to your mind that time in which the Arms and tyranny of the British Crown were exerted with every powerful effort in order to reduce you to a State of Servitude[.] [L]ook back, I entreat you, on the variety of dangers to which you were exposed, reflect on that time in which every human aid appeared unavailable, and in which even hope and fortitude wore the aspect of inability to the Conflict, and you cannot but be led to a Serious and grateful Sense of your miraculous and providential preservation; you cannot but acknowledge, that the present freedom and tranquility which you enjoy you have mercifully received, and that it is the peculiar blessing of Heaven.

This, Sir, was a time when you clearly saw into the injustice of a State of Slavery, and in which you had just apprehensions of the horrors of its condition[.] [I]t was now Sir, that your abhorrence thereof was so excited, that you publicly held forth this true and invaluable doctrine, which is worthy to be recorded and remember'd in all Succeeding ages. "We hold these truths to be Self evident, that all men are created equal, and that they are endowed by their creator with certain unalienable rights, that among these are, life, liberty, and the pursuit of happiness."

Here Sir, was a time in which your tender feelings for your selves had engaged you thus to declare, you were then impressed with proper ideas of the great valuation of liberty, and the free possession of those blessings to which you were entitled by nature; but Sir how pitiable is it to reflect, that altho you were so fully convinced of the benevolence of the Father of mankind, and of his equal and impartial distribution of those rights and privileges which he had conferred upon them, that you should at the Same time counteract his mercies, in detaining by fraud and violence so numerous a part of my brethren under groaning captivity and cruel oppression, that you should at the Same time be found guilty of that most criminal act, which you professedly detested in others, with respect to yourselves.

Sir, I suppose that your knowledge of the situation of my brethren is too extensive to need a recital here; neither shall I presume to prescribe methods by which they may be relieved; otherwise than by recommending to you and all others, to wean yourselves from these narrow prejudices which you have imbibed with respect to them, and as Job proposed to his friends "Put your Souls in their souls stead[.]" [T]hus shall your hearts be enlarged with kindness and benevolence toward them, and thus shall you need neither the direction of myself or others in what manner to proceed herein.

And now, Sir, altho my Sympathy and affection for my brethren hath caused my enlargement thus far, I ardently hope that your candor and generosity will plead with you in my behalf, when I make known to you, that it was not originally my design; but that having taken up my pen in order to direct to you as a present, a copy of an Almanack which I have calculated for the Succeeding year, I was unexpectedly and unavoidably led thereto.

This calculation, Sir, is the production of my arduous Study in this my advanced Stage of life; for having long had unbounded desires to become acquainted with the Secrets of nature, I have had to gratify my curiosity herein thro[ugh] my own assiduous application to Astronomical Study, in which I need not to recount to you the many difficulties and disadvantages which I have had to encounter. . . .

And now Sir, I shall conclude and Subscribe my Self with the most profound respect your most Obedient humble Servant,

BENJAMIN BANNEKER

CHAPTER THREE

Servitude and Rebellion

Richard Frethorne on Indentured Servitude (March 20–April 3, 1623)

A True Narrative of the Rise, Progresse, and Cessation of the Late Rebellion in Virginia, Most Humbly and Impartially Reported by His Majestyes Commissioners Appointed to Enquire into the Affaires of the Said Colony (1677)

Proclamation of the New Hampshire Legislature on the Mast Tree Riot (1734)

Letter Written by William Shirley to the Lords of Trade about the Knowles Riot (December 1, 1747)

Gottlieb Mittelberger, *Gottlieb Mittelberger's Journey to Pennsylvania in the Year 1750 and Return to Germany in the Year 1754* (1754)

Account of the New York Tenant Riots (July 14, 1766)

In England and in other countries of Northern Europe, the desperation of the poor was turned into profit by merchants and ship captains who arranged to transport men and women to the Americas to work as servants. These people, known as indentured servants, had to turn over their pay for five or seven years to cover the cost of passage. They were packed into ships almost as densely as were the black slaves from Africa, in journeys that lasted months. On board they were plagued by sickness and many died, especially the children.

Those who survived and landed in America were bought and sold much like slaves. From that point on, their lives were completely controlled by their masters, the women subject to sexual abuse, the men beaten and whipped for disobeying orders. Indentured servitude continued through the seventeenth and eighteenth centuries, and those who became free after their term of labor came to be a large part of the working classes of the colonies. Some of them became small landowners. Most became tenants or wandering poor, and a good number returned to England, disillusioned with their life in America.

• • •

In early 1623, the indentured servant Richard Frethorne came to the colony of Jamestown. He wrote to his parents soon after about the suffering he observed.

Richard Frethorne on Indentured Servitude
(March 20–April 3, 1623)[1]

Loving and Kind Mother and Father:

My most humble duty remembered to you, hoping in god of your good health, as I myself am at the making hereof. This is to let you understand that I your child am in a most heavy case by reason of the country, is such that it causeth much sickness, as the scurvy and the bloody flux and diverse other diseases, which maketh the body very poor and weak. And when we are sick there is nothing to comfort us; for since I came out of the ship I never ate anything but peas, and loblollie (that is, water gruel). As for deer or venison I never saw any since I came into this land. There is indeed some fowl, but we are not allowed to go and get it, but must work hard both early and late for a mess of water gruel and a mouthful of bread and beef. A mouthful of bread for a penny loaf must serve for four men which is most pitiful. If you did know as much as I, when people cry out day and night—Oh! That they were in England without their limbs—and would not care to lose any limb to be in England again, yea, though they beg from door to door. For we live in fear of the enemy every hour, yet we have had a combat with them . . . and we took two alive and made slaves of them. But it was by policy, for we are in great danger; for our plantation is very weak by reason of the death and sickness of our company. For we came but twenty for the merchants, and they are half dead just; and we look every hour when two more should go. Yet there came some four other men yet to live with us, of which there is but one alive; and our Lieutenant is dead, and [also] his father and his brother. And there was some five or six of the last year's twenty, of which there is but three left, so that we are fain to get other men to plant with us; and yet we are but 32 to fight against 3000 if they should come. And the nighest help that we have is ten mile of us, and when the rogues overcame this place last they slew 80 persons. How then shall we do, for we lie even in their teeth? They may easily take us, but that God is merciful and can save with few as well as with many, as he showed to Gilead. And like Gilead's soldiers, if they lapped water, we drink water which is but weak.

And I have nothing to comfort me, nor is there nothing to be gotten here but sickness and death, except [in the event] that one had money to lay out in some things for profit. But I have nothing at all—no, not a shirt to my back but two rags, nor clothes but one poor suit, nor but one pair of shoes, but one pair of stockings, but one cap, but two bands. My cloak is stolen by one of my fellows, and to his dying hour would not tell me what he did with it; but some of my fellows saw him have butter and beef out of a ship, which my cloak, I doubt, paid for.

So that I have not a penny, nor a penny worth, to help me too either spice or sugar or strong waters, without the which one cannot live here. For as strong beer in England doth fatten and strengthen them, so water here doth wash and weaken these here. . . . But I am not half a quarter so strong as I was in England, and all is for want of victuals; for I do protest unto you that I have eaten more in day at home than I have allowed me here for a week. You have given more than my day's allowance to a beggar at the door; and if Mr. Jackson had not relieved me, I should be in a poor case. But he like a father and she like a loving mother doth still help me.

For when we go to Jamestown (that is 10 miles of us) there lie all the ships that come to land, and there they must deliver their goods. And when we went up to town, as it may be, on Monday at noon, and come there by night, then load the next day by noon, and go home in the afternoon, and unload, and then away again in the night, and [we must] be up about midnight. Then if it rained or blowed never so hard, we must lie in the boat on the water and have nothing but a little bread. . . .

Good father, do not forget me, but have mercy and pity my miserable case. I know if you did but see me, you would weep to see me; for I have but one suit. (But [though] it is a strange one, it is very well guarded.) Wherefore, for God's sake, pity me. I pray you to remember my love to all my friends and kindred. I hope all my brothers and sisters are in good health, and as for my part I have set down my resolution that certainly will be; that is, that the answer of this letter will be life or death to me. Therefore, good father, send as soon as you can; and if you send me any thing let this be the mark.

• • •

A hundred years before the Declaration of Independence, in 1676, a rebellion took place in Virginia led by Nathaniel Bacon and joined by white frontiersmen, slaves, and servants. To quote from *A People's History of the United States:* "[It was] a rebellion so threatening that the governor had to flee the burning capital of Jamestown, and England decided to send a thousand soldiers across the Atlantic, hoping to maintain order among forty thousand colonists." The grievances of this motley group were various: frontiersmen believed they were not getting proper protection from Indian attacks; slaves and servants felt the weight of oppression from their masters and the political leaders of Virginia. The British Crown set up a Commission of Inquiry to report on Bacon's rebellion, which they did as follows.

A True Narrative of the Rise, Progresse, and Cessation of the Late Rebellion in Virginia, Most Humbly and Impartially Reported by His Majestyes Commissioners Appointed to Enquire into the Affaires of the Said Colony (1677)[2]

Bacon in most incens'd manner threatens to be revenged on the Governor and his party, swearing his soldiers to give no quarter and professing to scorne to take any themselves, and so in great fury marches on towards James Towne, onely halting a while about New Kent to gain some fresh forces, and sending to the upper parts of James River for what they could assist him with.

Having increased his number to about 300 in all, he proceeds directly to towne, as he marcheth the people on the high wayes coming forth praying for his happiness and railing ag't [against] the Governour and his party, and seeing the Indian captives which they led along as in a shew of tryumph, gave him many thankes for his care and endeavours for their preservation, bringing him forth fruits and victualls for his soldiers, the women telling him if he wanted assistance they would come themselves after him.

Intelligence coming to Bacon that the Governour had good in towne a 1000 men well arm'd and resolute, "I shall see that," saith he, "for I am now going to try them." . . . .

In the evening Bacon with his small tyr'd body of men comes into Paspahayes old Fields and advancing on horseback himselfe on the Sandy Beech before the towne commands the trumpet to sound, fires his carbyne, dismounts, surveys the ground and orders a French worke to be cast up.

All this night is spent in falling of trees, cutting of bushes and throwing up earth, that by the help of the moone light they had made their French worke before day, although they had but two axes and 2 spades in all to perform this work with.

About day-break next morning six of Bacons soldiers ran up to the pallasadees of the Towne and fired briskly upon the guard, retreating safely without any damage at first (as is reported). [T]he Governor gave comand that not a gun should be fir'd ag't Bacon or his party upon paine of death, pretending to be loath to spill bloode and much more to be beginner of it, supposing the rebells would hardly be so audacious as to fire a gun against him, But that Bacon would rather have sent to him and sought his reconciliation so that some way or other might have bin found out for the preventing of a warr, to which the Governour is said to have shewne some inclination upon the account of the service Bacon had performed (as he heard) against the Indian enemy, and that he had brought severall Indian prisoners along with him, and especially for that there were severall ignorant people which were deluded and drawne into Bacon's party and thought of no other designe than the Indian warr onely, and so knew not what they did.

But Bacon (pretending distrust of the Governor) was so farr from all thought of a Treaty that he animates his men against it, telling them that he knew that party to be as perfidious as cowardly, . . . The better to observe their motion [Bacon] ordered a constant sentinel in the daytime on top of a brick chimney (hard by) to discover from thence how the men in Towne mounted and dismounted, posted and reposted, drew on and off, what number they were, and how they moved. Hitherto their happen'd no other action then onely firing great and small shott at distances.

But by their movings and drawings up about towne, Bacon understood they intended a sally and accordingly prepares to receive them, drew up his men to the most advantageous places he could, and now expected them (but they observ'd to draw off againe for some tyme) and was resolved to enter the towne with them, as they retreated, as Bacon expected and foretold they would do. In this posture of expectation Bacon's forces continued for a hour till the watchman gave notice that they were drawne off againe in towne, so upon this Bacon's forces did so too. No sooner were they all on the rebells side gone off and squandered but all on a sudden a sally is made by the Governor's party, . . . But we cannot give a better account, nor yet a truer (so far as we are informed) of this action than what this Letter of Bacon's relates: . . .

". . . Yesterday they made a sally with horse and foote in the Van; they came up with a narrow Front, and pressing very close upon one anothers shoulders that the forlorne might be their shelter; our men received them so warmly that they retired in great disorder, throwing downe theire armes, left upon the Bay, as also their drum and dead men, two of which our men brought into our trenches and buried with severall of their armes . . . They shew themselves such pitifull cowards, contemptable as you would admire them. It is said that Hubert Farrell is shot in the belly, Hartwell in the legg, Smith in the head, Mathewes with others, yet as yet we have no certaine account . . ."

After this successless sally the courages and numbers of the Governor's party abated much, and Bacon's men thereby became more bold and daring in so much that Bacon could scarce keepe them from immediately falling to storme and enter the towne; but he (being as wary as they rash) perswaded them from the attempt, bidding them keepe their courages untill such tyme as he found occasion and opportunity to make use of them, telling them that he doubted not to take the towne without losse of a man, and that one of their lives was of more value to him than the whole world.

Having planted his great guns, he takes the wives and female relations of such gentlemen as were in the Governor's service against him (whom he had caused to be brought to the workes) and places them in the face of his enemy, as bulworkes for their battery, by which policy he promised himself (and doubtless had) a goode advantage, yet had the Governor's party by much the odds in number besides the advantage of tyme and place.

But so great was the cowardize and baseness of the generality of Sir William Berkeley's party (being most of them men intent onely upon plunder or compell'd and hired into his service) that of all, at last there were onely some 20 gentlemen willing to stand by him, the rest (whom the hopes or promise of plunder brought thither) being now all in haste to be gone to secure what they had gott; so that Sir Wm. Berkeley himselfe who undoubtedly would rather have dyed on the place than thus deserted it, what with importunate and resistless solicitations of all, was at last over persuaded, now hurryed away against his owne will to Accomack and forced to leave the towne to the mercy of the enemy.

Bacon haveing early intelligence of the Governor and his party's quitting the towne the night before, enters it without any opposition, and soldier like considering of what importance a place of that refuge was, and might againe be to the Governor and his party, instantly resolves to lay it level with the ground, and the same night he became poses'd of it, sett fire to towne, church and state house (wherein were the country's records which Drummond had privately convey'd thense and preserved from burning). The towne consisted of 12 new brick houses besides a considerable number of frame houses with brick chimneys, all which will not be rebuilt (as is computed) for fifteen hundred pounds of tobacco.

Now those who had so lately deserted it, as they rid a little below in the river in the shipps and sloop (to their shame and regret) beheld by night the flames of the towne, which they so basely forsaking, had made a sacrifice to ruine.

• • •

The general condition of so many people in the colonies remained poor and desperate as they watched a small number own huge tracts of land or accumulate fortunes. For instance, in Boston the tax records show that, shortly before the American Revolution, the richest one percent of the property owners owned forty percent of the city's wealth. Poor people in New Hampshire, needing firewood, chopped down trees on the estates of the rich. The British surveyor-general, Daniel Dunbar, found that the local townspeople would not help him in discovering the culprits. He assembled a small force of his own, but when he arrived in the town of Exeter in April 1734, his men were attacked and beaten by a group of local residents. An official report by the New Hampshire legislature follows.

Proclamation of the New Hampshire Legislature on the Mast Tree Riot (1734)[3]

Whereas a great number of ill disposed persons assembled themselves together at Exeter in the Province of New Hampshire, on the 23d of April last past about 9 of the clock at night, and the[n] and there in a riotous, tumultuous and most violent manner came into the house of Captain Samuel Gilman of said Exeter (who kept a public house in said town) and did then fall upon beat wound and terribelly abuse a number of men hired and imployed by the Honorable David Dunbar, Esq. as Surveyor General of his Majesties woods, as assistants to him in the execution of said office, many of which were beat and so abused that they very narrowly escaped with their lives (as appears by examinations taken by power of his Majesties Justices of the Peace for said province) all of which is a very great dishonor to this his Majesties province and contrary to all laws and humanity, and ought to be detested and abhorred by all parts of the legislative power. In order therefore to the finding out and bringing to condign punishment the transgressors and abettors of so vile a piece of disobedience, and in order that so great an odium may not rest upon this province, and to convince his Majestic that such villainies are abhorred by the province in general, Therefore in the House of Representatives voted, that his Excellency the Governor and Council be earnestly desired to order a strict examination into that affaire that the utmost justice may be done to his Majestic and that the persons concerned therein may no longer escape the punishment they have by their actions so justly deserved.

• • •

In the decades before the Revolution, riots against impressments—the drafting of young men in the colonies for the British navy—multiplied throughout the colonies. In Newport, Rhode Island, for instance, five hundred seamen, white and black, rioted after having been impressed for five weeks by the British navy. Here is an account of one of the earliest of these pre-Revolutionary incidents, an uprising against Commodore Knowles, reported in a letter from Governor Shirley of Massachusetts to the Lords of Trade in England.

Letter Written by William Shirley to the Lords of Trade about the Knowles Riot (December 1, 1747)[4]

My Lords,

A riot, and insult upon the King's government lately happen'd here of so extraordinary a nature, that I think it my duty to give your Lordships an account of it.

It was occasion'd by an impress made on the sixteenth of November at night out of all the vessels in this harbour, by order of Commodore Knowles, then on board the Canterbury, for manning his Squadron. . . .

The first notice, I had of the mob, was given me between nine and ten o'clock in the forenoon by the Speaker of the House of Representatives, who had pick'd up in the streets Captain Derby of his Majesty's Ship Alborough, and the Purser of the Canterbury, and brought 'em under his Protection to me for shelter in my house acquainting me at the same time, that the mob consisted of about three hundred seamen, all strangers, (the greatest part Scotch) with cutlasses and clubs, and that they had seiz'd and detain'd in their custody a Lieutenant of the Lark, whom they met with at his lodgins on shoar; The next notice I had was about half an hour after by the Sheriff of the County, who with some of his officers had been in pursuit of the mob in order to recover the Man of War's Lieutenant, and to endeavour to disperse 'em; and who coming up with four of 'em separated from the others, had wrested a cutlass from one and seiz'd two of 'em; but being overtaken by the whole mob, (who were appriz'd of this), as he was carrying those two to goal, was assaulted, and grievously wounded by 'em, and forc'd to deliver up his two prisoners, and leave one of his deputies in their hands, for whose life he assur'd me he was in fear.

Thereupon I immediately sent orders to the Colonel of the Regiment to raise the militia of the town and suppress the mob by force, and, if need was, to fire upon 'em with ball; which were scarcely deliver'd to him, when they appear'd before my gates, and part of 'em advanc'd directly through my court yard up to my door with the Lieutenant, two other sea officers, that part of the mob which stay'd at the outward gate crying out to the party at my door not to give up any of their prisoners to me. Upon this I immediately went out to 'em and demanded the cause of the tumult, to which one of 'em arm'd with a cutlass answer'd me in an insolent manner it was caus'd by my unjustifiable impress warrant; whereupon I told 'em that the impress was not made by my warrant, nor with my knowledge; but that he was a very impudent rascal for his behaviour; and upon his still growing more insolent, my son in law who happen'd to follow me out, struck his hat off his head, asking him if he knew, who he was talking to; this immediately silenced their clamour, when I demanded of 'em, where the King's Officers were, that they had seiz'd; and they being shewn to me, I went up to the Lieutenant and bid him go into my house, and upon his telling me the mob would not suffer him, I took him from among 'em, and putting him before me caus'd him to go in, as I did likewise the other three and follow'd 'em without exchanging more words with the mob, that I might avoid making any promises or terms with 'em; But my son in law, with the Speaker of the Assembly, the Colonel of the Regiment, and Captain of the Massachusetts frigate, who were now come into the house, stood some time at the door parlying and endeavouring to pacify 'em 'till upon the tumult's increasing, and their threatning to recover the sea officers by force, if I did not deliver 'em up again, or the Lieutenant did not come out to 'em and swear that he was not concern'd in the impress, I sent an Under Sheriff, then lately come into my house, to desire the gentlemen to let 'em know that I should consent to neither; and to retire into the house; and arm'd the offi[c]ers, who were now seven or eight in number, to stand upon their defence, in case the mob should be so out-rageous as to attempt to break into the house, and had the door shut against 'em; upon which the mob beset the house round, made some feint appearances of attempting to force the door open, abus'd the under-sheriff in my court yard (whom they beat and at last put in the publick stocks) and after behaving in a tumultuous manner before the House about half an hour, left it. . . .

[T]he mob now increas'd and join'd by some inhabitants came to the Town House (just after candle light) arm'd as in the morning, assaulted the Council Chamber (myself and the Council being then sitting there and the House of Representatives a minute or two before by accident adjourn'd) by throwing stones and brickbatts in at the windows, and having broke all the windows of the lower floor, where a few of the Militia Officers were assembled, forcibly enter'd into it, and oblig'd most of the officers to retire up into the Council Chamber; where the mob was expected soon to follow 'em up; but prevented by some few of the offi-cers below, who behav'd better.

In this confusion two popular members of the Council endeavoured, but in vain, to appease the mob by speaking to 'em from the balcony of the Council Chamber; after which the Speaker of the House and others of the Assembly press'd me much to speak two or three words to 'em, only promising to use my endeav-ours with Mr. Knowles to get the impress'd inhabitants and some of the outward bound seamen discharg'd; which, against my inclinations, and to prevent their charging any bad Consequences, which might happen from this tumult upon my refusal, I yielded to; and in this parley one of the mob, an inhabitant of the town call'd upon me to deliver up the Lieutenant of the Lark, which I refus'd to do; after which among other things he demanded of me, why a boy, one Warren now under sentence of death in goal for being concern'd in a press gang, which kill'd two sailors in this town in the act of impressing, was not executed; and I acquaint'd 'em his exe-cution was suspended by his Majesty's order 'till his pleasure shall be known upon it; whereupon the same person, who was the mob's spokesman ask'd me "if I did not remember Porteous's case who was hang'd upon a sign post in Edinburg." I told 'em very well, and that I hop'd they remember'd what the consequence of that proceeding was to the inhabitants of the city; after which I thought it high time to make an end of parleying with the mob, and retir'd into the Council Chamber: The issue of this was that the mob said they would call again at the Council Chamber the next day to know whether the impressed men were discharg'd; and went off to a dock yard upon proposal made among 'em to burn a twenty gun ship now building there for his Majesty; whereupon I went to my own house accompanied with a party of Officers, Sir William Pepperrell, and the gentlemen of the Council; within a quarter of an Hour after which the mob, who had been diverted from their purpose against the King's ship by the sudden coming to shoar of a barge, which they took to belong to one of Mr. Knowles's squadron, seiz'd and carry'd it in procession through the town with an intention to burn it in my court yard; upon which I order'd a party of officers to go out and oppose their entrance at my outward gate, which about ten of 'em immediately did, and upon the appearance of the mob's preparing to force that gate open, cock'd and presented their musketts at 'em through an open palisade fence, and fir'd upon 'em, if Sir William Pepperrell had not instantly call'd out to the Officers to hold, 'till such, who might only be spectators could be warn'd to separate from among the mob; which they perceiving, and that the windows of the house were likewise lin'd with arm'd officers, desisted and immediately alter'd their scheme to that of burning the barge in an out part of the Common, not discovering, 'till after it was burnt, that it really belong'd to a Master of a Scotch vessell, one of their ringleaders. . . .

The day following Mr. Knowles upon hearing of these outrages wrote me word, that he purpos'd to bring his whole squadron before the town the next morning, but I dissuaded him from it, by an immediate answer to his letter: In the evening the mob forcibly search'd the Navy Hospital upon the Town Common in order to let out what seamen they could find there belonging to the King's ships; and seven or eight private houses for officers, and took four or five petty officers; but soon releas'd 'em without any ill usage, as they did the same day Captain Erskine, whom they had suffer'd to remain in a gentleman's house upon his parole, their chief intent appearing to be, from the beginning, not to use the officers well any otherwise than by detaining 'em, in hopes of obliging Mr. Knowles to give up the impress'd men.

• • •

In this reading, Gottlieb Mittelberger, writing in the mid-eighteenth century, describes in detail the plight of the indentured servant.

Gottlieb Mittelberger, *Gottlieb Mittelberger's Journey to Pennsylvania in the Year 1750 and Return to Germany in the Year 1754* (1754)[5]

Both in Rotterdam and in Amsterdam the people are packed densely, like herrings so to say, in the large sea-vessels. One person receives a place of scarcely 2 feet width and 6 feet length in the bedstead, while many a ship carries four to six hundred souls; not to mention the innumerable implements, tools, provisions, water-barrels and other things which likewise occupy much space.

On account of contrary winds it takes the ships sometimes 2, 3 and 4 weeks to make the trip from Holland to . . . England. But when the wind is good, they get there in 8 days or even sooner. Everything is examined there and the custom-duties paid, whence it comes that the ships ride there 8, 10 to 14 days and even longer at anchor, till they have taken in their full cargoes. During that time every one is compelled to spend his last remaining money and to consume his little stock of provisions which had been reserved for the sea; so that most passengers, finding themselves on the ocean where they would be in greater need of them, must greatly suffer from hunger and want. Many suffer want already on the water between Holland and Old England.

When the ships have for the last time weighed their anchors near the city of Kaupp [Cowes] in Old England, the real misery begins with the long voyage. For from there the ships, unless they have good wind, must often sail 8, 9, 10 to 12 weeks before they reach Philadelphia. But even with the best wind the voyage lasts 7 weeks.

But during the voyage there is on board these ships terrible misery, stench, fumes, horror, vomiting, many kinds of sea-sickness, fever, dysentery, headache, heat, constipation, boils, scurvy, cancer, mouth-rot, and the like, all of which come from old and sharply salted food and meat, also from very bad and foul water, so that many die miserably.

Add to this want of provisions, hunger, thirst, frost, heat, dampness, anxiety, want, afflictions and lamentations, together with other trouble, . . . [and] the lice abound so frightfully, especially on sick people, that they can be scraped off the body. The misery reaches the climax when a gale rages for 2 or 3 nights and days, so that every one believes that the ship will go to the bottom with all human beings on board. In such a visitation the people cry and pray most piteously.

When in such a gale the sea rages and surges, so that the waves rise often like high mountains one above the other, and often tumble over the ship, so that one fears to go down with the ship; when the ship is constantly tossed from side to side by the storm and waves, so that no one can either walk, or sit, or lie, and the closely packed people in the berths are thereby tumbled over each other, both the sick and the well—it will be readily understood that many of these people, none of whom had been prepared for hardships, suffer so terribly from them that they do not survive it.

I myself had to pass through a severe illness at sea, and I best know how I felt at the time. These poor people often long for consolation, and I often entertained and comforted them with singing, praying and exhorting; and whenever it was possible and the winds and waves permitted it, I kept daily prayer-meetings with them on deck. Besides, I baptized five children in distress, because we had no ordained minister on board. I also held divine service every Sunday by reading sermons to the people; and when the dead were sunk in the water, I commended them and our souls to the mercy of God.

Among the healthy, impatience sometimes grows so great and cruel that one curses the other, or himself and the day of his birth, and sometimes come near killing each other. Misery and malice join each other, so that they cheat and rob one another. One always reproaches the other with having persuaded him to undertake the journey. Frequently children cry out against their parents, husbands against their wives and wives against their husbands, brothers and sisters, friends and acquaintances against each other. But most against the soul-traffickers.

Many sigh and cry: "Oh, that I were at home again, and if I had to lie in my pig-sty!" Or they say: "O God, if I only had a piece of good bread, or a good fresh drop of water." Many people whimper, sigh and cry piteously for their homes; most of them get home-sick. Many hundred people necessarily die and perish in such misery, and must be cast into the sea, which drives their relatives, or those who persuaded them to undertake the journey, to such despair that it is almost impossible to pacify and console them.

No one can have an idea of the sufferings which women in confinement have to bear with their innocent children on board these ships. Few of this class escape with their lives; many a mother is cast into the water with her child as soon as she is dead. One day, just as we had a heavy gale, a woman in our ship, who was to give birth and could not give birth under the circumstances, was pushed through a loop-hole [port-hole] in the ship and dropped into the sea, because she was far in the rear of the ship and could not be brought forward.

Children from 1 to 7 years rarely survive the voyage. I witnessed misery in no less than 32 children in our ship, all of whom were thrown into the sea. The parents grieve all the more since their children find no resting-place in the earth, but are devoured by the monsters of the sea.

That most of the people get sick is not surprising, because, in addition to all other trials and hardships, warm food is served only three times a week, the rations being very poor and very little. Such meals can hardly be eaten, on account of being so unclean. The water which is served out on the ships is often very black, thick and full of worms, so that one cannot drink it without loathing, even with the greatest thirst. Toward the end we were compelled to eat the ship's biscuit which had been spoiled long ago; though in a whole biscuit there was scarcely a piece the size of a dollar that had not been full of red worms and spiders nests.

At length, when, after a long and tedious voyage, the ships come in sight of land, so that the promontories can be seen, which the people were so eager and anxious to see, all creep from below on deck to see the land from afar, and they weep for joy, and pray and sing, thanking and praising God. The sight of the land makes the people on board the ship, especially the sick and the half dead, alive again, so that their hearts leap within them; they shout and rejoice, and are content to bear their misery in patience, in the hope that they may soon reach the land in safety. But alas!

When the ships have landed at Philadelphia after their long voyage, no one is permitted to leave them except those who pay for their passage or can give good security; the others, who cannot pay, must remain on board the ships till they are purchased, and are released from the ships by their purchasers. The sick always fare the worst, for the healthy are naturally preferred and purchased first; and so the sick and wretched must often remain on board in front of the city for 2 or 3 weeks, and frequently die, whereas many a one, if he could pay his debt and were permitted to leave the ship immediately, might recover and remain alive.

The sale of human beings in the market on board the ship is carried on thus: Every day Englishmen, Dutchmen and High-German people come from the city of Philadelphia and other places, in part from a great distance, say 20, 30, or 40 hours away, and go on board the newly arrived ship that has brought and offers for sale passengers from Europe, and select among the healthy persons such as they deem suitable for their business, and bargain with them how long they will serve for their passage money, which most of them are still in debt for. When they have come to an agreement, it happens that adult persons bind themselves in writing to serve 3, 4, 5 or 6 years for the amount due by them, according to their age and strength. But very young people, from 10 to 15 years, must serve till they are 21 years old.

Many parents must sell and trade away their children like so many head of cattle; for if their children take the debt upon themselves, the parents can leave the ship free and unrestrained; but as the parents often do not know where and to what people their children are going, it often happens that such parents and children, after leaving the ship, do not see each other again for many years, perhaps no more in all their lives.

It often happens that whole families, husband, wife, and children, are separated by being sold to different purchasers, especially when they have not paid any part of their passage money.

When a husband or wife has died at sea, when the ship has made more than half of her trip, the survivor must pay or serve not only for himself or herself, but also for the deceased.

When both parents have died over half-way at sea, their children, especially when they are young and have nothing to pawn or to pay, must stand for their own and their parents' passage, and serve till they are 21 years old. When one has served his or her term, he or she is entitled to a new suit of clothes at parting; and if it has been so stipulated, a man gets in addition a horse, a woman, a cow.

When a serf has an opportunity to marry in this country, he or she must pay for each year which he or she would have yet to serve, 5 to 6 pounds. But many a one who has thus purchased and paid for his bride, has subsequently repented his bargain, so that he would gladly have returned his exorbitantly dear ware, and lost the money besides.

If some one in this country runs away from his master, who has treated him harshly, he cannot get far. Good provision has been made for such cases, so that a runaway is soon recovered. He who detains or returns a deserter receives a good reward.

If such a runaway has been away from his master one day, he must serve for it as a punishment a week, for a week a month, and for a month half a year.

• • •

In New York, enormous tracts of land were given by the British Crown to the Van Rensselaer family. Tenants on his land were treated like serfs on a feudal estate. Parts of the land claimed by Van Rensselaer were occupied by poor farmers who said that they had bought the land from the Indians. The result was a series of clashes between Van Rensselaer's small army and the local farmers, as described here in newspaper accounts of July 1766.

Account of the New York Tenant Riots (July 14, 1766)[6]

Wednesday an express came to town . . . by whom we had the following particulars. That the inhabitants of a place called Nobletown and a place called Spencer-Town lying west of Sheffield, Great Barrington, and Stock-bridge, who had purchased of the Stockbridge Indians the lands they now possess; by virtue of an order of the General Court of this province, and settled about two hundred families; John Van Renselear [Johannes Van Rensselaer] Esq., pretending a right to said lands, had treated the inhabitants very cruelly, because they would not submit to him as tenants, he claiming a right to said lands by virtue of a patent from the Government of New York; that said Van Renselear some years ago raised a number of men and came upon the poor people, and pulled down some houses killed some people, imprisoned others, and has been constantly vexing and injuring the people. That on the 26th of last month said Renselear came down with between two and three hundred men, all armed with guns, pistols and swords; that upon intelligence that 500 men armed were coming against them, about forty or fifty of the inhabitants went out unarmed, except with sticks, and proceeded to a fence between them and the assailants, in order to compromise the matter between them. That the assailants came up to the fence, and Hermanus Schuyler the Sheriff of the County of Albany, fired his pistol down . . . upon them and three others fired their guns over them. The inhabitants thereupon desired to talk with them, and they would not harken; but the Sheriff, it was said by some who knew him, ordered the men to fire, who thereupon fired, and killed one of their own men, who had got over the fence and one of the inhabitants likewise within the fence. Upon this the chief of the inhabitants, unarmed as aforesaid, retreated most of them into the woods, but twelve betook themselves to the house from whence they set out and there defended themselves with six small arms and some ammunition that were therein. The two parties here fired upon each other. The assailants killed one man in the house, and the inhabitants wounded several of them, whom the rest carried off and retreated, to the number of seven, none of whom at the last accounts were dead. That the Sheriff shewed no paper, nor attempted to execute any warrant, and the inhabitants never offered any provocation at the fence, excepting their continuing there, nor had any one of them a gun, pistol or sword, till they retreated to the house. At the action at the fence one of the inhabitants had a leg broke, whereupon the assailants attempted to seize him and carry him off. He therefore begged they would consider the misery he was in, declaring he had rather die than be carried off, whereupon one of the assailants said "you shall die then" and discharging his pistol upon him as he lay on the ground, shot him to the body, as the wounded man told the informant; that the said wounded man was alive when he left him, but not like to continue long. The affray happened about sixteen miles distant from Hudson's River. It is feared the Dutch will pursue these poor people for thus defending themselves, as murderers; and keep them in great consternation.

CHAPTER FOUR

Preparing the Revolution

Thomas Hutchinson Recounts the Reaction to the Stamp Act in Boston (1765)

Samuel Drowne's Testimony on the Boston Massacre (March 16, 1770)

George Hewes Recalls the Boston Tea Party (1834)

New York Mechanics Declaration of Independence (May 29, 1776)

Thomas Paine, *Common Sense* (1776)

By the year 1760 there had been eighteen uprisings aimed at overthrowing colonial governments. There had also been six black rebellions, from South Carolina to New York, and forty riots of various origins. That rebellious energy soon began to be turned against England by the important people in the colonies who saw great advantages in freedom from British rule.

The Seven Years' War between France and England (known in the colonies as the French and Indian War) ended in 1763, with the French defeated. Now the English could turn their attention to tightening control over the American colonies. Money was needed to pay for the war, and England looked to the colonies for that. Colonial trade had become important to the British economy.

With the French out of the way, the colonial leadership was less in need of English protection. At the same time, the English were now more in need of the colonies' wealth. So the elements were there for conflict. Especially because the war had brought glory for the generals, death to the privates, wealth for the merchants, and unemployment for the poor. The resulting anger could now be turned against England rather than against the rich men of the colonies.

• • •

One notable expression of this anger came in response to the imposition of the Stamp Act. The Stamp Act was a tax laid on the American colonies by the British crown to help alleviate the huge debt that had been accumulated by the costs of the French and Indian War. One of the more explosive reactions to the Stamp Act in 1765 was a series of attacks by a mob in Boston against the home of a rich merchant named Andrew Oliver, one of the officials charged with enforcing the Stamp

Act, and then against the house belonging to the lieutenant governor, Thomas Hutchinson, who here describes the events. William Gordon, who published the first complete history of the American Revolution in 1788, wrote of one of the riots: "Gentlemen of the army, who have seen towns sacked by the enemy, declare they never before saw an instance of such fury." The various violent reactions to the Stamp Act led the British parliament to repeal it.

Thomas Hutchinson Recounts the Reaction to the Stamp Act in Boston (1765)[1]

The distributor of stamps for the colony of Connecticut [Jared Ingersoll] arrived in Boston from London; and, having been agent for that colony, and in other respects of a very reputable character, received from many gentlemen of the town such civilities as were due to him. When he set out for Connecticut, Mr. [Andrew] Oliver, the distributor for Massachusetts Bay, accompanied him out of town. This occasioned murmuring among the people, and an inflammatory piece in the next Boston Gazette. A few days after, early in the morning, a stuffed image was hung upon a tree, called the great tree of the south part of Boston [subsequently called Liberty Tree]. Labels affixed denoted it to be designed for the distributor of stamps. . . .

Before night, the image was taken down, and carried through the townhouse, in the chamber whereof the governor and council were sitting. Forty or fifty tradesmen, decently dressed, preceded; and some thousands of the mob followed down King street to Oliver's dock, near which Mr. Oliver had lately erected a building, which, it was conjectured, he designed for a stamp office. This was laid flat to the ground in a few minutes. From thence the mob proceeded for Fort Hill, but Mr. Oliver's house being in the way, they endeavored to force themselves into it, and being opposed, broke the windows, beat down the doors, entered, and destroyed part of his furniture, and continued in riot until midnight, before they separated. . . .

Several of the council gave it as their opinion, Mr. Oliver being present, that the people, not only of the town of Boston, but of the country in general, would never submit to the execution of the stamp act, let the consequence of an opposition to it be what it would. It was also reported, that the people of Connecticut had threatened to hang their distributor on the first tree after he entered the colony; and that, to avoid it, he had turned aside to Rhode-Island. Despairing of protection, and finding his family in terror and great distress, Mr. Oliver came to a sudden resolution to resign his office before another night. . . .

The next evening, the mob surrounded the house of the lieutenant-governor and chief justice [Hutchinson's own home]. He was at Mr. Oliver's house when it was assaulted, and had excited the sheriff, and the colonel of the regiment, to attempt to suppress the mob. A report was soon spread, that he was a favourer of the stamp act, and had encouraged it by letters to the ministry. Upon notice of the approach of the people, he caused the doors and windows to be barred; and remained in the house. . . .

Certain depositions had been taken, many months before these transactions, by order of the governor, concerning the illicit trade carrying on; and one of them, made by the judge of the admiralty, at the special desire of the governor, had been sworn to before the lieutenant-governor, as chief justice. They had been shewn, at one of the offices in England, to a person who arrived in Boston just at this time, and he had acquainted several merchants, whose names were in some of the depositions as smugglers, with the contents. This brought, though without reason, the resentment of the merchants against the persons who, by their office, were obliged to administer the oaths, as well as against the officers of the customs and admiralty, who had made the depositions; and the leaders of the mob contrived a riot, which, after some small efforts against such officers, was to spend its principal force upon the lieutenant-governor. And, in the evening of the 26th of August, such a mob was collected in King street, drawn there by a bonfire, and well supplied with strong drink. After some annoyance to the house of the registrar of the admiralty, and somewhat greater to that of the comptroller of the customs, whose cellars they plundered of the wine and spirits in them, they came, with intoxicated rage upon the house of the lieutenant-governor. The doors were immediately split to pieces with broad axes, and a way made there, and at the windows, for the entry of the mob; which poured in, and filled, in an instant, every room in the house.

The lieutenant-governor had very short notice of the approach of the mob. He directed his children, and the rest of his family, to leave the house immediately, determining to keep possession himself. His eldest daughter, after going a little way from the house, returned, and refused to quit it, unless her father would do the like.

This caused him to depart from his resolutions, a few minutes before the mob entered. They continued their possessions until day light; destroyed, carried away, or cast into the street, every thing that was in the house; demolished every part of it, except the walls, as far as lay in their power; and had begun to break away from the brickwork.

The damage was estimated at about twenty-five hundred pounds sterling, without any regard to a great collection of the publick as well as private papers, in the possession and the custody of the lieutenant-governor.

The town was, the whole night, under awe of this mob; many of the magistrates, with the field officers of the militia, standing by as spectators; and no body daring to oppose, or contradict.

• • •

Strong feelings against the stationing of British soldiers in Boston formed a background for the Boston Massacre of 1770. The incident itself was instigated by the anger of rope makers against British soldiers taking their jobs. A crowd gathered, British soldiers fired into the crowd, killing five people, including Crispus Attucks, a mulatto worker. John Adams, the defense attorney for the soldiers, described the crowd as "a motley rabble of saucy boys, Negroes and molattoes, Irish teagues and outlandish jack tarrs." When the acquittal of six of the soldiers and light punishment for two others caused more anger, England removed the troops from Boston in the hope of calming things down. Here is a contemporary account of the massacre by a Bostonian.

Samuel Drowne's Testimony on the Boston Massacre (March 16, 1770)[2]

Samuel Drowne of Boston, of lawful age, testifieth and saith, that about nine of the clock of the evening of the fifth day of March current, standing at his own door in Cornhill, saw about 14 or 15 soldiers of the 29th regiment, who came from Murray's barrack, some of whom were armed with naked cutlasses, swords or bayonets, others with clubs, fire-shovels or tongs, and came upon the inhabitants of the town, then standing or walking in Cornhill, and abused some and violently assaulted others as they met them, most of whom were without so much as a stick in their hands to defend themselves, as the deponent very clearly could discern, it being moon-light, and himself being one of the assaulted persons—All of most of the said soldiers he saw go by the way of Cornhill, Crooked-lane and Royal-exchange-lane into King-street, and there followed them, and soon discovered them to be quarrelling and fighting with the people whom they saw there, which the deponent thinks were not more than a dozen, when the soldiers came there first, armed as aforesaid. Of those dozen people, the most of them were gentlemen, standing together a little below the Town-house upon the Exchange. At the appearance of those soldiers so arm'd, the most of the twelve persons went off, some of them being first assaulted—After which the said soldiers were observed by the deponent to go towards the main-guard from whence were at the same time issuing and coming into King-street five soldiers of said guard and a corporal arm'd with firelocks, who call'd out to the fore-mention'd soldiers arm'd with cutlasses, etc. and said to them go away, on which they dispers'd and went out of King-street, some one way and some another—by this time were collected together in King-street about two hundred people, and then the deponent stood upon the steps of the Exchange tavern, being the next house to the Custom-house; and soon after saw Capt. Preston, whom he well knew, with a number of soldiers arm'd with firelocks drawn up near the west corner of the Custom-house; and at that instant the deponent thinks so great a part of the people were dispers'd at the sight of the armed soldiers, as that no more than twenty or thirty remained in King-street; those who did remain being mostly sailors and other persons meanly dressed, called out to the arm'd soldiers and dared them to fire, upon which the deponent heard Capt. Preston say to the soldiers, Damn your bloods! Why don't you fire? The soldiers not regarding those words of their captain, he immediately said FIRE. Upon which they fired irregularly, pointing their guns variously in a part of a circle as they stood; during the time of the soldier firing, the deponent saw the flashes of two guns fired from the Custom-house, one of which was out of a window of the chamber westward of the balcony, and the other from the balcony, the gun which he clearly discerned being pointed through the ballisters, and the person who held the gun in a stooping posture, withdraw himself into the house, having a handkerchief or some kind of cloth over his face. After this the deponent assisted in carrying off the dead and wounded, as soon as the soldiers would permit the people so to do, for at first they were cruel enough to obstruct the carrying them off.

• • •

In debt from its war against France, the British imposed a stiff tax on tea in the American colonies. Tea was a popular drink, so the tax was a broadly unpopular one, symbolizing the fact that the colonies were subjected to "taxation without representation." When the British East India Company started bringing tea to the colonies directly from India, the price fell, but the tax remained. Many advocates for independence began to call for a boycott of British tea. At the end of 1773, a number of British ships carrying tea were headed toward the harbor in Boston. Samuel Adams demanded that three of the ships be sent back to sea, but the Massachusetts governor allowed the ships to enter and insisted that the tariff had to be paid for the shipment. On December 16, 1773, a crowd of men disguising themselves as Native Americans raided the ships and threw the cargo overboard. Here George Hewes, a Boston shoemaker who participated in the Tea Party, describes the event.

George Hewes Recalls the Boston Tea Party (1834)[3]

The tea destroyed was contained in three ships, lying near each other at what was called at that time Griffin's wharf, and were surrounded by armed ships of war, the commanders of which had publicly declared that if the rebels, as they were pleased to style the Bostonians, should not withdraw their opposition to the landing of the tea before a certain day, the 17th day of December, 1773, they should on that day force it on shore, under the cover of their cannon's mouth.

On the day preceding the seventeenth, there was a meeting of the citizens of the county of Suffolk, convened at one of the churches in Boston, for the purpose of consulting on what measures might be considered expedient to prevent the landing of the tea, or secure the people from the collection of the duty. At that meeting a committee was appointed to wait on Governor Hutchinson, and request him to inform them whether he would take any measures to satisfy the people on the object of the meeting.

To the first application of this committee, the Governor told them he would give them a definite answer by five o'clock in the afternoon. At the hour appointed, the committee again repaired to the Governor's house, and on inquiry found he had gone to his country seat at Milton, a distance of about six miles. When the committee returned and informed the meeting of the absence of the Governor, there was a confused murmur among the members, and the meeting was immediately dissolved, many of them crying out, "Let every man do his duty, and be true to his country"; and there was a general huzza for Griffin's wharf.

It was now evening, and I immediately dressed myself in the costume of an Indian, equipped with a small hatchet, which I and my associates denominated the tomahawk, with which, and a club, after having painted my face and hands with coal dust in the shop of a blacksmith, I repaired to Griffin's wharf, where the ships lay that contained the tea. When I first appeared in the street after being thus disguised, I fell in with many who were dressed, equipped and painted as I was, and who fell in with me and marched in order to the place of our destination.

When we arrived at the wharf, there were three of our number who assumed an authority to direct our operations, to which we readily submitted. They divided us into three parties, for the purpose of boarding the three ships which contained the tea at the same time. The name of him who commanded the division to which I was assigned was Leonard Pitt. The names of the other commanders I never knew.

We were immediately ordered by the respective commanders to board all the ships at the same time, which we promptly obeyed. The commander of the division to which I belonged, as soon as we were on board the ship appointed me boatswain, and ordered me to go to the captain and demand of him the keys to the hatches and a dozen candles. I made the demand accordingly, and the captain promptly replied, and delivered the articles; but requested me at the same time to do no damage to the ship or rigging.

We then were ordered by our commander to open the hatches and take out all the chests of tea and throw them overboard, and we immediately proceeded to execute his orders, first cutting and splitting the chests with our tomahawks, so as thoroughly to expose them to the effects of the water.

In about three hours from the time we went on board, we had thus broken and thrown overboard every tea chest to be found in the ship, while those in the other ships were disposing of the tea in the same way, at the same time. We were surrounded by British armed ships, but no attempt was made to resist us.

We then quietly retired to our several places of residence, without having any conversation with each other, or taking any measures to discover who were our associates; nor do I recollect of our having had the knowledge of the name of a single individual concerned in that affair, except that of Leonard Pitt, the commander of my division, whom I have mentioned. There appeared to be an understanding that each individual should volunteer his services, keep his own secret, and risk the consequence for himself. No disorder took place during that transaction, and it was observed at that time that the stillest night ensued that Boston had enjoyed for many months.

During the time we were throwing the tea overboard, there were several attempts made by some of the citizens of Boston and its vicinity to carry off small quantities of it for their family use. To effect that object, they would watch their opportunity to snatch up a handful from the deck, where it became plentifully scattered, and put it into their pockets.

One Captain O'Connor, whom I well knew, came on board for that purpose, and when he supposed he was not noticed, filled his pockets, and also the lining of his coat. But I had detected him and gave information to the captain of what he was doing. We were ordered to take him into custody, and just as he was stepping from the vessel, I seized him by the skirt of his coat, and in attempting to pull him back, I tore it off; but, springing forward, by a rapid effort he made his escape. He had, however, to run a gauntlet through the crowd upon the wharf nine each one, as he passed, giving him a kick or a stroke.

Another attempt was made to save a little tea from the ruins of the cargo by a tall, aged man who wore a large cocked hat and white wig, which was fashionable at that time. He had slightly slipped a little into his pocket, but being detected, they seized him and, taking his hat and wig from his head, threw them, together with the tea, of which they had emptied his pockets, into the water. In consideration of his advanced age, he was permitted to escape, with now and then a slight kick.

The next morning, after we had cleared the ships of the tea, it was discovered that very considerable quantities of it were floating upon the surface of the water; and to prevent the possibility of any of its being saved for use, a number of small boats were manned by sailors and citizens, who rowed them into those parts of the harbor wherever the tea was visible, and by beating it with oars and paddles so thoroughly drenched it as to render its entire destruction inevitable.

• • •

At least ninety state and local declarations of independence, taking various forms, preceded Thomas Jefferson's. Here is one striking example, signed by manual laborers in the Mechanick-Hall, New York, in May 1776. In the resolution, the laborers instruct their representatives in the Provincial Congress to instruct the New York representatives in the Continental Congress to declare independence.

New York Mechanics Declaration of Independence (May 29, 1776)[4]

To the Honourable Representatives of the Province of New-York, in Provincial Congress convened.

The humble Address of the General Committee of Mechanicks in union, of the City and County of New-York, in behalf of themselves and their constituents:

GENTLEMEN: We, as a part of your constituents, and devoted friends to our bleeding country, beg leave, in a dutiful manner, at this time to approach unto you, our Representatives, and request your kind attention to this our humble address.

When we cast a glance upon our beloved continent, where fair freedom, civil and religious, we have long enjoyed, whose fruitful field have made the world glad, and whose trade has filled with plenty of all things, sorrow fills our hearts to behold her now struggling under the heavy load of oppression, tyranny, and death. But when we extend our sight a little farther, and view the iron hand that is lifted up against us, behold it is our King; he who by his oath and station, is bound to support and defend us in the quiet enjoyment of all our glorious rights as freemen, and whose dominions have been supported and made rich by our commerce. Shall we any longer sit silent, and contentedly continue the subjects of such a Prince, who is deaf to our petitions for interposing his Royal authority in our behalf, and for redressing our grievances, but, on the contrary, seems to take pleasure in our destruction? When we see that one whole year is not enough to satisfy the rage of a cruel Ministry, in burning our towns, seizing our vessels, and murdering our precious sons of liberty; making weeping widows for the loss of those who were dearer to them than life, and helpless orphans to bemoan the death of an affectionate father; but who are still carrying on the same bloody pursuit; and for no other reason than this, that we will not become their slaves, and be taxed by them without our consent,—therefore, as we would rather choose to be separate from, than to continue any longer in connection with such oppressors, We, the Committee of Mechanicks in union, do, for ourselves and our constituents, hereby publickly declare that, should you, gentlemen of the honourable Provincial Congress, think proper to instruct our most honourable Delegates in Continental Congress to use their utmost endeavors in that august assembly to cause these United Colonies to become independent of Great Britain, it would give us the highest satisfaction; and we hereby sincerely promise to endeavour to support the same with our lives and fortunes.

Signed by order of the Committee,
Lewis Thibou, Chairman

• • •

Thomas Paine's *Common Sense* appeared in early 1776 and became the most popular pamphlet in the American colonies, going through more than two dozen editions and selling hundreds of thousands of copies. Hundreds of pamphlets had appeared by this time, dealing with the issues between Britain and the colonies, but Paine's words were bold and clear in making the argument for independence, and appealed to a wide range of colonial interests. What follows is an excerpt.

Thomas Paine, *Common Sense* (1776)[5]

In the following pages I offer nothing more than simple facts, plain arguments, and common sense: and have no other preliminaries to settle with the reader, than that he will divest himself of prejudice and prepossession, and suffer his reason and his feelings to determine for themselves that he will put on, or rather that he will not put off, the true character of a man, and generously enlarge his views beyond the present day.

Volumes have been written on the subject of the struggle between England and America. Men of all ranks have embarked in the controversy, from different motives, and with various designs; but all have been ineffectual, and the period of debate is closed. Arms as the last resource decide the contest; the appeal was the choice of the King, and the Continent has accepted the challenge. . . .

Whatever was advanced by the advocates on either side of the question then, terminated in one and the same point, viz. a union with Great Britain; the only difference between the parties was the method of effecting it; the one proposing force, the other friendship; but it hath so far happened that the first hath failed, and the second hath withdrawn her influence.

As much hath been said of the advantages of reconciliation, which, like an agreeable dream, hath passed away and left us as we were, it is but right that we should examine the contrary side of the argument, and enquire into some of the many material injuries which these Colonies sustain, and always will sustain, by being connected with and dependant on Great Britain. To examine that connection and dependence, on the principles of nature and common sense, to see what we have to trust to, if separated, and what we are to expect, if dependant.

I have heard it asserted by some, that as America hath flourished under her former connection with Great Britain, that the same connection is necessary towards her future happiness, and will always have the same effect. Nothing can be more fallacious than this kind of argument. We may as well assert that because a child has thrived upon milk, that it is never to have meat, or that the first twenty years of our lives is to become a precedent for the next twenty. But even this is admitting more than is true, for I answer roundly that America would have flourished as much, and probably much more, had no European power taken any notice of her. The commerce by which she hath enriched herself are the necessaries of life, and will always have a market while eating is the custom of Europe.

But she has protected us, say some. That she hath engrossed us is true, and defended the Continent at our expense as well as her own, is admitted; and she would have defended Turkey from the same motive, viz.—for the sake of trade and dominion. . . .

But Britain is the parent country, say some. Then the more shame upon her conduct. Even brutes do not devour their young, nor savages make war upon their families. Wherefore, the assertion, if true, turns to her reproach; but it happens not to be true, or only partly so, and the phrase parent or mother country hath been jesuitically adopted by the King and his parasites, with a low papistical design of gaining an unfair bias on the credulous weakness of our minds. Europe, and not England, is the parent country of America. This new World hath been the asylum for the persecuted lovers of civil and religious liberty from every part of Europe. Hither have they fled, not from the tender embraces of the mother, but from the cruelty of the monster; and it is so far true of England, that the same tyranny which drove the first emigrants from home, pursues their descendants still. . . .

But, admitting that we were all of English descent, what does it amount to? Nothing. Britain, being now an open enemy, extinguishes every other name and title: And to say that reconciliation is our duty, is truly farcical. The first king of England, of the present line (William the Conqueror) was a Frenchman, and half the peers of England are descendants from the same country; wherefore, by the same method of reasoning, England ought to be governed by France. . . .

I challenge the warmest advocate for reconciliation, to show, a single advantage that this continent can reap by being connected with Great Britain. I repeat the challenge, not a single advantage is derived. Our corn will fetch its price in any market in Europe, and our imported goods must be paid for buy them where we will.

But the injuries and disadvantages which we sustain by that connection, are without number; and our duty to mankind at large, as well as to ourselves, instruct us to renounce the alliance: Because, any submission to, or dependence on, Great Britain, tends directly to involve this Continent in European wars and quarrels, and set us at variance with nations who would otherwise seek our friendship, and against whom we have neither anger nor complaint. As Europe is our market for trade, we ought to form no partial connection with any part of it. It is the true interest of America to steer clear of European contentions, which she never can do, while, by her dependence on Britain, she is made the makeweight in the scale of British politics.

Europe is too thickly planted with Kingdoms to be long at peace, and whenever a war breaks out between England and any foreign power, the trade of America goes to ruin, because of her connection with Britain. The next war may not turn out like the last, and should it not, the advocates for reconciliation now will be wishing for separation then, because neutrality in that case would be a safer convoy than a man of war. Every thing that is right or reasonable pleads for separation. The blood of the slain, the weeping voice of nature cries, 'TIS TIME TO PART. Even the distance at which the Almighty hath placed England and America is a strong and natural proof that the authority of the one over the other, was never the design of Heaven. The time likewise at which the Continent was discovered, adds weight to the argument, and the manner in which it was peopled, increases the force of it. The Reformation was preceded by the discovery of America: As if the Almighty graciously meant to open a sanctuary to the persecuted in future years, when home should afford neither friendship nor safety.

The authority of Great Britain over this continent, is a form of government, which sooner or later must have an end: And a serious mind can draw no true pleasure by looking forward, under the painful and positive conviction that what he calls "the present constitution" is merely temporary. As parents, we can have no joy, knowing that this government is not sufficiently lasting to ensure any thing which we may bequeath to posterity: And by a plain method of argument, as we are running the next generation into debt, we ought to do the work of it, otherwise we use them meanly and pitifully. In order to discover the line of our duty rightly, we should take our children in our hand, and fix our station a few years farther into life; that eminence will present a prospect which a few present fears and prejudices conceal from our sight.

Though I would carefully avoid giving unnecessary offence, yet I am inclined to believe, that all those who espouse the doctrine of reconciliation, may be included within the following descriptions. Interested men, who are not to be trusted; weak men, who cannot see; prejudiced men, who will not see; and a certain set of moderate men, who think better of the European world than it deserves;

and this last class, by an ill-judged deliberation, will be the cause of more calamities to this continent, than all the other three.

It is the good fortune of many to live distant from the scene of sorrow; the evil is not sufficiently brought to their doors to make them feel the precariousness with which all American property is possessed. But let our imaginations transport us for a few moments to Boston, that seat of wretchedness will teach us wisdom, and instruct us for ever to renounce a power in whom we can have no trust. The inhabitants of that unfortunate city, who but a few months ago were in ease and affluence, have now, no other alternative than to stay and starve, or turn out to beg. Endangered by the fire of their friends if they continue within the city, and plundered by the soldiery if they leave it. In their present condition they are prisoners without the hope of redemption, and in a general attack for their relief, they would be exposed to the fury of both armies.

Men of passive tempers look somewhat lightly over the offences of Britain, and, still hoping for the best, are apt to call out, "Come, come, we shall be friends again, for all this." But examine the passions and feelings of mankind, Bring the doctrine of reconciliation to the touchstone of nature, and then tell me, whether you can hereafter love, honor, and faithfully serve the power that hath carried fire and sword into your land? If you cannot do all these, then are you only deceiving yourselves, and by your delay bringing ruin upon posterity. Your future connection with Britain, whom you can neither love nor honor, will be forced and unnatural, and being formed only on the plan of present convenience, will in a little time fall into a relapse more wretched than the first. But if you say, you can still pass the violations over, then I ask, Hath your house been burnt? Hath your property been destroyed before your face? Are your wife and children destitute of a bed to lie on, or bread to live on? Have you lost a parent or a child by their hands, and yourself the ruined and wretched survivor? If you have not, then are you not a judge of those who have? But if you have, and still can shake hands with the murderers, then you are unworthy of the name of husband, father, friend, or lover, and whatever may be your rank or title in life, you have the heart of a coward, and the spirit of a sycophant.

This is not inflaming or exaggerating matters, but trying them by those feelings and affections which nature justifies, and without which, we should be incapable of discharging the social duties of life, or enjoying the felicities of it. I mean not to exhibit horror for the purpose of provoking revenge, but to awaken us from fatal and unmanly slumbers, that we may pursue determinately some fixed object. It is not in the power of Britain or of Europe to conquer America, if she do not conquer herself by delay and timidity. The present winter is worth an age if rightly employed, but if lost or neglected, the whole continent will partake of the misfortune; and there is no punishment which that man will not deserve, be he who, or what, or where he will, that may be the means of sacrificing a season so precious and useful.

It is repugnant to reason, to the universal order of things to all examples from former ages, to suppose, that this continent can longer remain subject to any external power. The most sanguine in Britain does not think so. The utmost stretch of human wisdom cannot, at this time, compass a plan short of separation, which can promise the continent even a year's security. Reconciliation is now a fallacious dream. Nature hath deserted the connection, and Art cannot supply her place. For, as Milton wisely expresses, "never can true reconcilement grow where wounds of deadly hate have pierced so deep."

Every quiet method for peace hath been ineffectual. Our prayers have been rejected with disdain; and only tended to convince us, that nothing flatters vanity, or confirms obstinacy in Kings more than repeated petitioning—and noting hath contributed more than that very measure to make the Kings of Europe absolute: Witness Denmark and Sweden. Wherefore, since nothing but blows will do, for God's sake, let us come to a final separation, and not leave the next generation to be cutting throats, under the violated unmeaning names of parent and child.

To say, they will never attempt it again is idle and visionary, we thought so at the repeal of the stamp act, yet a year or two undeceived us; as well may we suppose that nations, which have been once defeated, will never renew the quarrel.

As to government matters, it is not in the power of Britain to do this continent justice: The business of it will soon be too weighty, and intricate, to be managed with any tolerable degree of convenience, by a power, so distant from us, and so very ignorant of us; for if they cannot conquer us, they cannot govern us. To be always running three or four thousand miles with a tale or a petition, waiting four or five months for an answer, which when obtained requires five or six more to explain it in, will in a few years be looked upon as folly and childishness—There was a time when it was proper, and there is a proper time for it to cease.

Small islands not capable of protecting themselves, are the proper objects for kingdoms to take under their care; but there is something very absurd, in supposing a continent to be perpetually governed by an island. In no instance hath nature made the satellite larger than its primary planet, and as England and America, with respect to each other, reverses the common order of nature, it is evident they belong to different systems: England to Europe, America to itself.

Half a Revolution

Joseph Clarke's Letter about the Rebellion in Springfield (August 30, 1774)

Joseph Plumb Martin, *A Narrative of Some of the Adventures, Dangers and Sufferings of a Revolutionary Soldier* (1830)

Samuel Dewees Recounts the Suppression of Insubordination in the Continental Army after the Mutinies of 1781 (1844)

Henry Knox, Letter to George Washington (October 23, 1786)

"Publius" (James Madison), *Federalist* No. 10 (November 23, 1787)

The American Revolution was a war for independence from England. For a hundred years before the Revolution, the colonies were torn by class conflict: tenants against landlords, riots of the poor. That internal conflict would now be temporarily obscured by the struggle against England. But it was still there, bursting out now and then even during the war, and emerging again after victory over the British Empire.

The Declaration of Independence contained the stirring language of egalitarianism and democracy, that "all men are created equal," and promised the rights to "life, liberty, and the pursuit of happiness." But the reality behind those inspiring words was that a rising class of important people needed to enlist on their side enough Americans to defeat England, without disturbing too much the relations of wealth and power that had developed over 150 years of colonial history.

During the Revolution, mutinies in the Continental Army, and after the war, farmers' uprisings in Massachusetts and other states, were evidence of the continued existence of class anger in the new nation. The Founding Fathers were conscious of that, and worried about future rebellions. The Constitution they framed was designed to control that rebellious spirit and maintain "law and order."

• • •

Here is one striking example of the class anger and spirit of popular rebellion at the time, from a letter that Joseph Clarke, the adopted child of Joseph Hawley, a well-known Massachusetts politician, sent to an unknown friend.

Joseph Clarke's Letter about the Rebellion in Springfield (August 30, 1774)[1]

We arrived in town about noon this day and found all the people gathered before us. A committee from the body of the county had just waited upon the court to demand a satisfactory answer, that is, whether they meant to hold their commissions and exercise their authority according to the new act of parliament for altering the constitution of the province, which being answered in the negative, It was put to vote after the Sd [said] message and answer were read to the people assembled before the meeting house, whether they were willing the Court should sit; it passed in the negative.

Then the people paraded before Mr. Parson's [Landlord Parsons], from thence marched back again to the meeting-house and demanded the appearance of the judges. The judges came according to their desire, and amidst the Crowd in a sandy, sultry place, exposed to the sun as far as they were able in such circumstance gave a reasonable, and, to the major part, a satisfactory answer to such questions as were asked.

It was also demanded of them that they should make a declaration in writing, signed by all the justices and lawyers in the County, renouncing in the most express terms any commission which should be given out to them or either of them under the new arrangement, which was immediately complied with and executed accordingly.

The People then reassembled before Mr. Parson's house. . . . [Major] Catlin falling into a personal quarrel, at length gained the attention of the people. They considered him as an object worthy of their malice, as he was an officer of the court. He was treated with candor and too mildly to make any complaint. His boasted heroism failed him in the day of trial, and vanished like a puf[f] of smo[ke]. He and O[liver] Warner, who came to his assistance in the quarrel, made such declarations as were requested of them, and then were dismissed, unhurt, and in peace. Your uncle may say what he pleases with regard to their abuse of him, but I was an eye witness to the whole, and you I believe will be satisfied that no abuse was intended when I tell you what easy terms they requested and were satisfied with, namely, only a declaration that he would not hold any office under the new act of parliament.

Col. [John] Worthington was next brought upon the board. The sight of him flashed lightening from their eyes. Their spirits were already raised and the sight of this object gave them additional force. He had not refused his new office of counselor. For that reason especially he was very obnoxious. But the people kept their tempers. He attempted to harangue them in mitigation of his conduct, but he was soon obliged to desist. The people were not to be dallied with. Nothing would satisfy them but a renunciation in writing of his office as Counselor and a recantation of his address to Gov. [Thomas] Gage, which last was likewise signed by Jona[than] Bliss and Caleb Strong. . . .

Jonathan Bliss next came upon the floor, he was very humble and the people were very credulous. He asked their pardon for all he had said or done which was contrary to their opinions; and as he depended for his support upon the people, he begged to stand well in their favor.

Mr. Moses Bliss was brought into the ring, but the accusation against him was not well supported, and he passed off in silence. The Sheriff was the next who was demanded; he accordingly appeared. He was charged with saying some imprudent things, but none of them were proved, and he departed. But he was humbled. Col. [Israel] Williams took the next turn. He went round the ring and vindicated himself from some accusations thrown upon him and denied some things that were laid to his charge.

He declared in my hearing that "altho' he had heretofore differed from the people in opinion with regard to the mode of obtaining redress, he would, hereafter, heartily acquiesce in any measures, that they should take for that purpose, and join with them in the common cause. He considered his interest as embarked in the same bottom with theirs, and hoped to leave it in peace to his Children."

Capt. [James] Merrick of Munson was next treated with for uttering imprudent expressions. I thought they would have tarred and feathered him, and I thought he almost deserved it. He was very stubborn, as long as he dare be, but at length he made some concessions. But not till after they had carted him. No man received the least injury, but the strictest order of justice were observed. The people to their honor behaved with the greatest order and regularity, a few individuals excepted, and avoided, as much as possible, confusion.

The people of each town being drawn into separate companies marched with staves and musick. The trumpets sounding, drums beating, fifes playing and Colours flying, struck the passions of the soul into a proper tone, and inspired martial courage into each.

• • •

Joseph Plumb Martin here recalls the hardships soldiers experienced on the line and after they were discharged. Plumb Martin enlisted in the Continental Army in 1776, and served in New York and Connecticut during the American Revolution.

Joseph Plumb Martin, *A Narrative of Some of the Adventures, Dangers and Sufferings of a Revolutionary Soldier* (1830)[2]

When those who engaged to serve during the war enlisted, they were promised a hundred acres of land, each, which was to be in their or the adjoining states. When the country had drained the last drop of service it could screw out of the poor soldiers, they were turned adrift like old worn-out horses, and nothing said about land to pasture them upon. Congress did, indeed, appropriate lands under the denomination of "Soldier's Lands," in Ohio state, or some state, or a future state, but no care was taken that the soldiers should get them. No agents were appointed to see that the poor fellows ever got possession of their lands; no one ever took the least care about it, except a pack of speculators, who were driving about the country like so many evil spirits, endeavoring to pluck the last feather from the soldiers. The soldiers were ignorant of the ways and means to obtain their bounty lands, and there was no one appointed to inform them. The truth was, none cared for them; the country was served, and faithfully served, and that was all that was deemed necessary. It was, soldiers, look to yourselves; we want no more of you. I hope I shall one day find land enough to lay my bones in. If I chance to die in a civilized country, none will deny me that. A dead body never begs a grave;—thanks for that.

They were likewise promised the following articles of clothing per year. One uniform coat, a woolen and a linen waistcoat, four shirts, four pair of shoes, four pair of stockings, a pair of woolen and a pair of linen overalls, a hat or a leather cap, a stock for the neck, a hunting shirt, a pair of shoe buckles, and a blanket. Ample clothing says the reader; and ample clothing says I. But what did we ever realize of all this ample store—why, perhaps a coat (we generally did get that) and one or two shirts, the same of shoes and stockings, and, indeed, the same may be said of every other article of clothing—a few dribbled out in a regiment, two or three times a year, never getting a whole suit at a time, and all of the poorest quality, and blankets of thin baize [woolen], thin enough to have straws shot through without discommoding the threads. How often have I had to lie whole stormy, cold nights in a wood, on a field, or a bleak hill, with such blankets and other clothing like them, with nothing but the canopy of the heavens to cover me. All this too in the heart of winter, when a New England farmer, if his cattle had been in my situation, would not have slept a wink from the sheer anxiety for them. And if I stepped into a house to warm me, when passing, wet to the skin and almost dead with cold, hunger, and fatigue, what scornful looks and hard words have I experienced.

Almost every one has heard of the soldiers of the Revolution being tracked by the blood of their feet on the frozen ground. This is literally true, and the thousandth part of their sufferings has not, nor ever will be told. That the country was young and poor, at that time, I am willing to allow, but young people are generally modest, especially females. Now, I think the country (although of the feminine gender, for we say "she" and "her" of it) showed but little modesty at the time alluded to, for she appeared to think her soldiers had no private parts. For on our march from the Valley Forge, through the Jerseys, and at the boasted Battle of Monmouth, a fourth part of the troops had not a scrap of anything but their ragged shirt flaps to cover their nakedness, and were obliged to remain so long after. I had picked up a few articles of light clothing during the past winter, while among the Pennsylvanian farmers, or I should have been in the same predicament. "Rub and go" was always the Revolutionary soldier's motto.

As to provision of victuals, I have said a great deal already, but ten times as much might be said and not get to the end of the chapter. When we engaged in the service we were promised the following articles for a ration: one pound of good and wholesome fresh or salt beef, or three quarters of a pound of good salt pork, a pound of good flour, soft or hard bread, a quart of salt to every hundred pounds of fresh beef, a quart of vinegar to a hundred rations, a gill [a quarter of a pint] of rum, brandy, or whiskey per day, some little soap and candles, I have forgot how much, for I had so little of these two articles that I never knew the quantity. And as to the article of vinegar, I do not recollect of ever having any except a spoonful at the famous rice and vinegar Thanksgiving in Pennsylvania, in the year 1777. But we never received what was allowed us. Oftentimes have I gone one, two, three, and even four days without a morsel, unless the fields or forests might chance to afford enough to prevent absolute starvation. Often, when I have picked the last grain from the bones of my scanty morsel, have I eat the very bones, as much of them as possibly could be eaten, and then have had to perform some hard and fatiguing duty, when my stomach has been as craving as it was before I had eaten anything at all.

If we had got our full allowance regularly, what was it? A bare pound of fresh beef and a bare pound of bread or flour. The beef, when it had gone through all its divisions and subdivisions, would not be much over three quarters of a pound, and that nearly or quite half bones. The beef that we got in the army was, generally, not many degrees above carrion; it was much like the old Negro's rabbit, it had not much fat upon it and very little lean. When we drew flour, which was much of the time we were in the field or on marches, it was of small value, being eaten half-cooked, besides a deal of it being unavoidably wasted in the cookery.

When in the field, and often while in winter quarters, our usual mode of drawing our provisions, when we did draw any, was as follows: a return being made out for all the officers and men, for seven days, we drew four days of meat and the whole seven days of flour. At the expiration of the four days, the other three days allowance of beef. Now, dear reader, pray consider a moment, how were five men in a mess, five hearty, hungry young men, to subsist four days on twenty pounds of fresh beef (and I might say twelve or fifteen pounds) without any vegetables or any other kind of sauce to eke it out. In the hottest season of the year it was the same. Though there was not much danger of our provisions putrefying, we had none on hand long enough for that, if it did, we obliged to eat it, or go without anything. When General Washington told Congress, "the soldiers eat every kind of horse fodder but hay" he might have gone a little farther and told them that they eat considerable hog's fodder and not a trifle of dog's—when they could get it to eat.

We were, also, promised six dollars and two thirds a month, to be paid us monthly, and how did we fare in this particular? Why, as we did in every other. I received the dollars and two thirds, till (if I remember rightly) the month of August, 1777, when paying ceased. And what was six dollars and sixty-seven cents of this "Continental currency," as it was called, worth? It was scarcely enough to procure a man a dinner. Government was ashamed to tantalize the soldiers any longer with such trash, and wisely gave it up of its own credit. I received one month's pay in specie [in kind] while on the march to Virginia, in the year 1781, and except that, I never received any pay worth the name while I belonged to the army. Had I been paid as I was promised to be at my engaging in the service, I needed not to have suffered as I did, nor would I have done it; there was enough in the country and money would have procured it if I had had it. It is provoking to think of it. The country was rigorous in exacting my compliance to *my* engagements to a punctilio, but equally careless in performing her contracts with me, and why so? One reason was because she had all the power in her own hands and I had none. Such things ought not to be.

The poor soldiers had hardships enough to endure without having to starve; the least that could be done was to give them something to eat. "The laborer is worthy of his meat" at least, and he ought to have it for his interest, if nothing more. How many times have I had to lie down like a dumb animal in the field, and bear "the pelting of the pitiless storm," cruel enough in warm weather, but how much more so in the heart of winter. Could I have had the benefit of a little fire, it would have been deemed a luxury. But, when snow or rain would fall so heavy that it was impossible to keep a spark of fire alive, to have to weather out a long, wet, cold, tedious night in the depth of winter, with scarcely clothes enough to keep one from freezing instantly, how discouraging it must be, I leave to my reader to judge.

It is fatiguing, almost beyond belief, to those that never experienced it, to be obliged to march twenty-four or forty-eight hours (as very many times I have had to) and often more, night and day without rest or sleep, wishing and hoping that some wood or village I could see ahead might prove a short resting place, when, alas, I came to it, almost tired off my legs, it proved no resting place for me. How often have I envied the very swine their happiness, when I have heard them quarreling in their warm dry sties, when I was wet to the skin and wished in vain for that indulgence. And even in dry warm weather, I have often been so beat out with long and tedious marching that I have fallen asleep and not been sensible of it till I have jostled against someone in the same situation; and when permitted to stop and have the superlative happiness to roll myself in my blanket and drop down on the ground in the bushes, briars, thorns, or thistles, and get an hour or two's sleep, O! how exhilarating. . . .

Many murmur now at the apparent good fortune of the poor soldiers. Many I have myself seen, vile enough to say that they never deserved such favor from the country. The only wish I would bestow upon such hardhearted wretches is that they might be compelled to go through just such sufferings and privations as that army did, and then if they did not sing a different tune, I should miss my guess.

But I really hope these people will not go beside themselves. Those men whom they wish to die on a dunghill, men, who, if they had not ventured their lives in battle and faced poverty, disease, and death for their country to gain and maintain that Independence and Liberty, in the sunny beams of which, they, like reptiles, are basking, they would, many or the most of them, be this minute in as much need of help and succor as ever the most indigent soldier was before he experienced his county's beneficence.

The soldiers consider it cruel to be thus vilified, and it is cruel as the grave to any man, when he knows his own rectitude of conduct, to have his hard services not only debased and underrated, but scandalized and vilified. But the Revolutionary soldiers are not the only people that endure obloquy; others, as meritorious and perhaps more deserving than they, are forced to submit to ungenerous treatment.

• • •

Class conflict inside the American Revolution came dramatically alive with mutinies in George Washington's army. In 1781, after enduring five years of war—casualties in the Revolution exceeded, in proportion to population, American casualties in World War II—more than a thousand soldiers in the Pennsylvania line at Morristown, New Jersey, mutinied. They had seen their officers paid handsomely, fed and clothed well, while the privates and sergeants were fed slop, marched in rags without shoes, paid in virtually worthless Continental currency, or not paid at all for months. They were abused, beaten, and whipped by their officers for the smallest breach of discipline. For many, their deepest grievance was that they wanted out of the war, claiming their terms of enlistment had expired and that they were being kept in the army by force. They knew that in the spring of 1780, eleven deserters of the Connecticut line in Morristown were sentenced to death but at the last minute all but one had received a reprieve. (The one who did not was hanged for forging discharge papers for a hundred men.) General Washington, facing nearly two thousand mutineers, a substantial part of his army, assembled at Princeton, New Jersey, decided to make concessions. Many of the rebels were allowed to leave the army, and Washington asked state governors for money to deal with the grievances of the soldiers. The Pennsylvania line quieted down. But when another mutiny broke out in the New Jersey line, involving only a few hundred, Washington ordered harsh measures. He saw the possibility of "this dangerous spirit" spreading. Two of "the most atrocious offenders" were court-martialed on the spot, sentenced to be shot, and their fellow mutineers, some of them weeping as they did so, carried out the executions. In his novel *The Proud and the Free*, Howard Fast tells the story of the mutinies, drawing from the classic historical account by Carl Van Doren, *Mutiny in January*. Fast dramatizes the class conflict inside the Revolutionary Army, as one of his characters, the mutinous soldier Jack Maloney, recalls the words of Thomas Paine and the promise of freedom and says that he is willing to die for that freedom, but "not for that craven Congress in Philadelphia, not for the fine Pennsylvania ladies in their silks and satins, not for the property of every dirty lord and fat patroon in New Jersey." Here is the narrative of this bloody event by Samuel Dewees, a soldier on the Pennsylvania line.

Samuel Dewees Recounts the Suppression of Insubordination in the Continental Army after the Mutinies of 1781 (1844)[3]

Whilst we lay at Lebanon, a circumstance transpired worthy of notice, and which I here record as a prelude to the horridly great tragical event, of which the individual now bearing a part was one of the number that was made to suffer the awful penalty annexed to their crimes, if crimes they may be said to have committed. A sergeant who was known by the appellation of Macaroney Jack, a very intelligent, active, neat and clever fellow, had committed some trivial offense. He had his wife with him in camp who always kept him very clean and neat in his appearance. She was washerwoman to a number of soldiers, myself among the number. She was a very well behaved and good conditioned woman.

The officers, for the purpose of making an impression upon him and to better his conduct, ordered him to be brought from the guard house; which done, he was tied up and the drummers ordered to give him a certain number of lashes upon his bare back. The intention of the officers was not to chastise him.

When he was tied up he looked around and addressed the soldiers, exclaiming at the same time, "Dear brother soldiers, won't you help me?" This in the eyes of the officers savored of mutiny and they called out, "Take him down, take him down!" The order was instantly obeyed and he was taken back to the guardhouse again and handcuffed. At this time there were two deserters confined with him.

On the next or second day after this we were ordered on to York, Pennsylvania, where upon our arrival we encamped upon the common below the town. Upon our arrival, our three prisoners were confined in York jail. In a few days after we arrived at York, a soldier of the name of Jack Smith, and another soldier whose name I do not now remember, were engaged in playing long bullets. Whilst thus engaged, some of the officers were walking along the road where they were throwing the bullets. The bullets passing near to the officers, they used very harsh language to Smith and his comrade, who immediately retorted by using the same kind of indecorous language. A file of men was immediately dispatched with orders to take Smith and his comrade under guard and march them off to York jail.

In three or four days after these arrests were made, a sergeant of the name of Lilly, who was also a very fine fellow and an excellent scholar, so much so, that much of the regimental writing fell to his lot to do, and for which he received a remuneration in some way; this sergeant, having become intoxicated, had quarreled with one or more of his messmates, and upon some of the officers coming around to enquire what the matter was, found him out of his tent. The officers scolded him and bade him to go into his quarters. Lilly, having been much in favor and knowing his own abilities and the services rendered, was (although intoxicated) very much wounded, and could not bear to be thus harshly dealt with, and used language of an unbecoming kind to his superior officers. The officers immediately ordered him to be taken to York jail.

On the next day in the morning we beat up the troop. After roll call we were ordered to beat up the troop again. The whole line was again formed, and I think the orders were for every soldier to appear in line with his knapsack on his back. I suppose that at this time there were parts of three regiments, in all 800 or 1000 men laying at York, the whole of which was commanded by Colonel Butler. The whole body (sentinels, invalids, etc., excepted) when formed were marched to the distance of about half a mile from the camp, and there made to stand under arms. Twenty men were then ordered out of the line and formed into marching order and all the musicians placed at their head. After remaining a short time in a marching posture, the order of forward was given. We were then marched direct to the jail door. The prisoners six in number were then brought out and their sentence (which was death) was read to them.

At this time it was thought that none in the Line save the officers knew for what the provost guard was detached. But it appeared afterwards that previous to the firing which was the means of launching four out of the six into eternity, the matter of rescuing them was whispered among the soldiers; but they did not concert measures in time to prevent the awful catastrophe, which they meditated by an act of insubordination upon their part.

After the sentence of death was read to the condemned soldiers at the jail door, we then marched them out and down below town, playing the "dead march" in front of them. We continued our march full half a mile and halted on a piece of ground (common) adjoining a field of rye, which was then in blossom. This was sometime in the early part of June 1781. After a halt was made, the prisoners were ordered to kneel down with their backs to the rye-field fence. Their eyes were then bandaged or covered over with silk handkerchiefs. The officer in command then divided his force of twenty men into two platoons. The whole was then ordered to load their pieces. This done, ten were ordered to advance, and at the signal given by the officer (which was the wave of his pocket handkerchief) the first platoon of ten fired at one of the six. Macaroney Jack was the first shot at and was instantly killed. The first platoon was then ordered to retire and reload, and the second platoon of ten ordered to advance. When the signal was again given, Smith shared the same fate, but with an awfulness that would have made even devils to have shrunk back and stood appalled. His head was literally blown in fragments from off his body. The second platoon was then ordered to retire and reload, whilst the first was ordered to advance and at the same signal fired at the third man. The second platoon then advanced and fired to order, at Sergeant Lilly, whose brave and noble soul was instantly on the wing to the presence of that Supreme Judge who has pledged himself he will do that which is right. The arms of each had been tied above their elbows with the cords passing behind their backs. Being tied thus enabled them to have the use of their hands. I ventured near and noticed that Macaroney Jack had his hands clasped together in front of his breast, and had both of his thumbs shot off. The distance that the platoons stood from them at the time they fired could not have been more than ten feet. So near did they stand that the handkerchiefs covering the eyes of some of them that were shot were set on fire. The fence and even the heads of rye for some distance within the field were covered over with blood and brains. After four were shot, we musicians with a portion of the twenty men were ordered to march and were then conducted up to the main line of the army. After our arrival there, the whole Line was thrown into marching order and led to this horrid scene of bloody death. When the troops advanced near to the spot they displayed off into double file and were then marched very near to the dead bodies, as also to those still on their knees waiting the awful death that they had every reason to believe still awaited them. The order was for every man to look upon the bodies as he passed; and in order that the soldiers in the Line might behold them more distinctly in passing, they were ordered to countermarch after they had passed and then marched as close to them upon their return.

The two deserters that were still in a kneeling posture were reprieved, the bandages taken from their eyes, then untied, and restored to their respective companies.

A number of men were ordered out to dig a large grave. The bodies of the four dead soldiers were then wrapped up in their blankets and buried together therein. This last sad duty performed, the soldiers were all marched back to their quarters in camp.

My readers may imagine to what a pitch this sad scene was heightened in sorrow when I state that, on our way from the jail to the place of execution, those sentenced were crying, pleading, and praying aloud, women weeping and sobbing over the unhappy fate of the doomed to death, and the wife of Macaroney Jack screaming and almost distracted. On the way she attempted to run into the line, or provost guard, to where her husband was walking, but was hindered by an officer who felled her to the ground with his sword, he having struck her with the side of it.

The execution of these men by Colonel Butler and his officers was undoubtedly brought about by a love of liberty, the good of country, and the necessity of keeping proper subordination in the army, in order to ensure that good ultimately. Mutiny had shewn itself at many of the military posts within the United States. The conduct of the Pennsylvania and Jersey lines in the revolt at Morristown in Jersey had occurred but the year before, and fresh in the memory of all having knowledge of the operations of the army. Still, the destruction of these men seemed like a wanton destruction of human life. The soldiers at York were afraid to say or to do any thing, for so trivial appeared the offenses of these men that were shot that they knew not what in the future was to be made to constitute a crime. I recollect for myself that for some considerable time after this, if I found myself meeting an officer when out of camp, I would avoid coming in contact with him if I possibly could do so by slipping a short distance to one side, not that I was afraid of an officer more than of a private, whilst I done my duty, but fearing lest they might construe my conduct in some way or other into an offense.

All disposition of mutiny was entirely put down by these steps of cruelty. There were no doubt many times during the Revolution that such executions were called for and highly necessary, and perhaps there was an evidence as well as a conviction before the minds of the officers composing the court martial in their case that we know not of, and that demanded the punishment of death. But, to state it in a word, it was a mournful day among the soldiers and hard and stony indeed were the hearts that were not deeply affected in witnessing this distressing execution of their fellow-soldiers.

• • •

The victory over England did not bring domestic peace. The class conflict that had preceded the Revolution, and that continued during the war in the form of mutinies against Washington's army, continued after the war. In a number of the states, small farmers, many of them veterans of the war, felt oppressed by the taxes levied on them by the state governments. In Massachusetts, farmers, seeing land and livestock being taken away for nonpayment of taxes, organized by the thousands. They surrounded courthouses and would not let the selling off of their property continue. This was an armed revolt, taking its name from one of the leaders, Captain Daniel Shays, a veteran of the Revolutionary War. The rebellion was finally suppressed, but a number of rebels had been killed, and a few of the leaders hanged. This event caused deep worry among the Founding Fathers, who, soon after, meeting in Philadelphia to draw up a new constitution, saw the need for a central government strong enough to put down such uprisings. Massachusetts farmer Plough Jogger, speaking about his grievances to one of the illegal conventions where opposition to the legislature was organized, said, "I've labored hard all my days and fared hard. I have been greatly abused, have been obliged to do more than my part in the war; been loaded with class rates, town rates, province rates, Continental rates, and all rates . . . been pulled and hauled by sheriffs, constables and collectors, and had my cattle sold for less than they were worth. I have been obliged to pay and nobody will pay me. I have lost a great deal by this man and that man and t'other man, and the great men are going to get all we have, and I think it is time for us to rise and put a stop to it, and have no more courts, nor sheriffs, nor collectors, nor lawyers, and I know that we are the biggest party, let them say what they will. . . . We've come to relieve the distresses of the people. There will be no court until they have redress of their grievances."

After Shays' Rebellion, Henry Knox, the Revolutionary War artillery commander who became the first U.S. secretary of war, wrote to his former commander, George Washington, to warn him about the goals of the rebels: "[T]hey see the weakness of Government[,] they feel at once their own poverty compared with the opulent, and their own force, and they are determined to make use of the latter in order to remedy the former. Their creed is that that the property of the United States has been protected from the confiscations of Britain by the joint exertions of all, and therefore ought to be the common property of all." This is the full text of his letter.

Henry Knox, Letter to George Washington (October 23, 1786)[4]

My dear sir.

I have long intended myself the pleasure of visiting you at Mount Vernon, and although, I have not given up that hope, and shall probably gratify it in the Course of next month, yet I cannot longer delay presenting myself to the remembrance of my truly respected and beloved general, whose friendship I shall ever esteem among the most valuable circumstances of my existence.

Conscious of affection, and I believing it to be reciprocal in your breast, I have had no apprehensions of my silence being misconstrued. I know the perplexity occasioned by your numerous correspondents and was unwilling to add to it. Besides which, I have lately been once far eastward of Boston, on private business and was no sooner returned here, than the commotions in Massachusetts hurried me back to Boston on a public account.

Our political machine constituted of thirteen independent sovereignties, have been perpetually operating against each other, and against the federal head, ever since the peace—The powers of Congress are utterly inadequate to preserve the balance between the respective States, and oblige them to do those things which are essential for their own welfare, and for the general good. The human mind in the local legislatures seem to be exerted, to prevent the federal constitution from having any beneficial effects. The machine works inversely to the public good in all its parts. Not only is State, against State, and all against the federal head, but the States within themselves possess the name only without having the essential concomitant of government, the power of preserving the peace; the protection of the liberty and property of the citizens.

On the very first impression of Faction and licentiousness the fine theoretic government of Massachusetts has given away and its laws arrested and trampled under foot. Men at a distance, who have admired our systems of government, unfounded in nature, are apt to accuse the rulers, and say that taxes have been assessed too high and collected too rigidly. This is a deception equal to any that has been hitherto entertained. It is indeed a fact, that high taxes are the ostensible cause of the commotions, but that they are the real cause is as far remote from truth as light from darkness. The people who are the insurgents have never paid any, or but very little taxes—But they see the weakness of government; They feel at once their own poverty, compared with the opulent, and their own force, and they are determined to make use of the latter, in order to remedy the former. Their creed is "That the property of the United States has been protected from the confiscations of Britain by the joint exertions of all, and therefore ought to be the common property of all. And he that attempts opposition to this creed is an enemy to equity and justice, and ought to be swept off the face of the earth." In a word they are determined to annihilate all debts public and private and have agrarian Laws which are easily effected by the means of unfunded paper money which shall be a tender in all cases whatever.

The numbers of these people may amount in [M]assachusetts to about one fifth part of several populous counties, and to them may be collected, people of similar sentiments, from the States of Rhode Island, Connecticut and New Hampshire so as to constitute a body of 12 or 15,000 desperate and unprincipled men—They are chiefly of the Young and active part of the community, more easily collected than perhaps Kept together afterwards—But they will probably commit overt acts of treason which will compel them to embody for their own safety—once embodied they will be constrained to submit to discipline for the same reason. Having proceeded to this length for which they are now ripe, we shall have a formidable rebellion against reason, the principles of all government, and against the very name of liberty. This dreadful situation has alarmed every man of principle and property in New England—They start as from a dream, and ask what has been the Cause of our delusion? What is to afford us security against the violence of lawless men? Our government must be braced, changed, or altered to secure our lives and property. We imagined that the mildness of our government and *the virtue* of the people were so correspondent, that we were not as other nations requiring brutal force to support the laws—But we find that we are men, actual men, possessing all the turbulent passions belonging to that animal and that we must have a government proper and adequate for him—The people of Massachusetts for instance, are far advanced in this doctrine, and the men of reflection, and principle, are determined to endeavor to establish a government which shall have the power to protect them in their lawful pursuits, and which will be efficient in all cases of internal commotions or foreign invasions—They mean that liberty shall form the basis, a liberty resulting from the equal and firm administration of the laws. They wish for a general government of unity as they see that the local legislatures, must naturally and necessarily tend to retard general government.

We have arrived at that point of time in which we are forced to see our national humiliation, and that a progression in this line, cannot be productive of happiness either private or public—something is wanting and something must be done or we shall be involved in all the horror of faction and civil war without a prospect of its termination—Every tried friend to the liberties of his country is bound to reflect, and step forward to prevent the dreadful consequences which will result from a government of events—Unless this is done we shall be liable to be ruled by an Arbitrary and Capricious armed tyranny, whose word and will must be Law.

The [I]ndians on the frontiers are giving indisputable evidence of their hostile dispositions. Congress anxiously desirous of averting the evils on the frontiers, have unanimously agreed to augment the troops now in service to a legionary Corps of 2,040 noncommissioned officers and privates—The additionals are to be raised as follows

Connecticut	180	
R[hode] Island	120	
Massachusetts	660	Infantry and artillery
New Hampshire	260	
Maryland	60	Cavalry
Virginia	60	
[Total]	1,340	

This measure is important, and will tend to strengthening the principle of government as well as to defend the frontiers—I mention the idea of strengthening government confidentially but the State of Massachusetts requires the greatest assistance, and Congress are fully impressed with the importance [of] supporting her with great exertions.

• • •

In 1787 and 1788, writing under the pseudonym "Publius," Alexander Hamilton, James Madison, and John Jay wrote a series of articles in support of the ratification of the new Constitution in New York. In *Federalist* No. 10, penned by Madison, we see how his fear of majority "faction" fueled the desire for a strong central government. As the historian Charles Beard notes in his *Economic Interpretation of the Constitution of the United States*, Madison's "wealth consisted principally of plantations and slaves." Using populist language in "appealing to the voters to ratify the Constitution," the authors of the *Federalist Papers* were "by the force of circumstances, compelled to convince large economic groups that safety and strength [would] lie in the adoption of the new system."

"Publius" (James Madison), *Federalist* No. 10 (November 23, 1787)[5]

To the People of the State of New York:

AMONG the numerous advantages promised by a well constructed Union, none deserves to be more accurately developed than its tendency to break and control the violence of faction. The friend of popular governments never finds himself so much alarmed for their character and fate, as when he contemplates their propensity to this dangerous vice. He will not fail, therefore, to set a due value on any plan which, without violating the principles to which he is attached, provides a proper cure for it. The instability, injustice, and confusion introduced into the public councils, have, in truth, been the mortal diseases under which popular governments have everywhere perished; as they continue to be the favorite and fruitful topics from which the adversaries to liberty derive their most specious declamations. The valuable improvements made by the American constitutions on the popular models, both ancient and modern, cannot certainly be too much admired; but it would be an unwarrantable partiality, to contend that they have as effectually obviated the danger on this side, as was wished and expected. Complaints are everywhere heard from our most considerate and virtuous citizens, equally the friends of public and private faith, and of public and personal liberty, that our governments are too unstable, that the public good is disregarded in the conflicts of rival parties, and that measures are too often decided, not according to the rules of justice and the rights of the minor party, but by the superior force of an interested and overbearing majority. However anxiously we may wish that these complaints had no foundation, the evidence, of known facts will not permit us to deny that they are in some degree true. It will be found, indeed, on a candid review of our situation, that some of the distresses under which we labor have been erroneously charged on the operation of our governments; but it will be found, at the same time, that other causes will not alone account for many of our heaviest misfortunes; and, particularly, for that prevailing and increasing distrust of public engagements, and alarm for private rights, which are echoed from one end of the continent to the other. These must be chiefly, if not wholly, effects of the unsteadiness and injustice with which a factious spirit has tainted our public administrations.

By a faction, I understand a number of citizens, whether amounting to a majority or a minority of the whole, who are united and actuated by some common impulse of passion, or of interest, adverse to the rights of other citizens, or to the permanent and aggregate interests of the community.

There are two methods of curing the mischiefs of faction: the one, by removing its causes; the other, by controlling its effects.

There are again two methods of removing the causes of faction: the one, by destroying the liberty which is essential to its existence; the other, by giving to every citizen the same opinions, the same passions, and the same interests.

It could never be more truly said than of the first remedy, that it was worse than the disease. Liberty is to faction what air is to fire, an aliment without which it instantly expires. But it could not be less folly to abolish liberty, which is essential to political life, because it nourishes faction, than it would be to wish the annihilation of air, which is essential to animal life, because it imparts to fire its destructive agency.

The second expedient is as impracticable as the first would be unwise. As long as the reason of man continues [to be] fallible, and he is at liberty to exercise it, different opinions will be formed. As long as the connection subsists between his reason and his self-love, his opinions and his passions will have a reciprocal influence on each other; and the former will be objects to which the latter will attach themselves. The diversity in the faculties of men, from which the rights of property originate, is not less an insuperable obstacle to a uniformity of interests. The protection of these faculties is the first object of government. From the protection of different and unequal faculties of acquiring property, the possession of different degrees and kinds of property immediately results; and from the influence of these on the sentiments and views of the respective proprietors, ensues a division of the society into different interests and parties.

The latent causes of faction are thus sown in the nature of man; and we see them everywhere brought into different degrees of activity, according to the different circumstances of civil society. A zeal for different opinions concerning religion, concerning government, and many other points, as well of speculation as of practice; an attachment to different leaders ambitiously contending for pre-eminence and power; or to persons of other descriptions whose fortunes have been interesting to the human passions, have, in turn, divided mankind into parties, inflamed them with mutual animosity, and rendered them much more disposed to vex and oppress each other than to co-operate for their common good. So strong is this propensity of mankind to fall into mutual animosities, that where no substantial occasion presents itself, the most frivolous and fanciful distinctions have been sufficient to kindle their unfriendly passions and excite their most violent conflicts. But the most common and durable source of factions has been the various and unequal distribution of property. Those who hold and those who are without property have ever formed distinct interests in society. Those who are creditors, and those who are debtors, fall under a like discrimination. A landed interest, a manufacturing interest, a mercantile interest, a moneyed interest, with many lesser interests, grow up of necessity in civilized nations, and divide them into different classes, actuated by different sentiments and views. The regulation of these various and interfering interests forms the principal task of modern legislation, and involves the spirit of party and faction in the necessary and ordinary operations of the government.

No man is allowed to be a judge in his own cause, because his interest would certainly bias his judgment, and, not improbably, corrupt his integrity. With equal, nay with greater reason, a body of men are unfit to be both judges and parties at the same time; yet what are many of the most important acts of legislation, but so many judicial determinations, not indeed concerning the rights of single persons, but concerning the rights of large bodies of citizens? And what are the different classes of legislators but advocates and parties to the causes which they determine? Is a law proposed concerning private debts? It is a question to which the creditors are parties on one side and the debtors on the other. Justice ought to hold the balance between them. Yet the parties are, and must be, themselves the judges; and the most numerous party, or, in other words, the most powerful faction must be expected to prevail. Shall domestic manufactures be encouraged, and in what degree, by restrictions on foreign manufactures? are questions which would be differently decided by the landed and the manufacturing classes, and probably by neither with a sole regard to justice and the public good. The apportionment of taxes on the various descriptions of property is an act which seems to require the most exact impartiality; yet there is, perhaps, no legislative act in which greater opportunity and temptation are given to a predominant party to trample on the rules of justice. Every shilling with which they overburden the inferior number, is a shilling saved to their own pockets.

It is in vain to say that enlightened statesmen will be able to adjust these clashing interests, and render them all subservient to the public good. Enlightened statesmen will not always be at the helm. Nor, in many cases, can such an adjustment be made at all without taking into view indirect and remote considerations, which will rarely prevail over the immediate interest which one party may find in disregarding the rights of another or the good of the whole.

The inference to which we are brought is, that the CAUSES of faction cannot be removed, and that relief is only to be sought in the means of controlling its EFFECTS.

If a faction consists of less than a majority, relief is supplied by the republican principle, which enables the majority to defeat its sinister views by regular vote. It may clog the administration, it may convulse the society; but it will be unable to execute and mask its violence under the forms of the Constitution. When a majority is included in a faction, the form of popular government, on the other hand, enables it to sacrifice to its ruling passion or interest both the public good and the rights of other citizens. To secure the public good and private rights against the danger of such a faction, and at the same time to preserve the spirit and the form of popular government, is then the great object to which our inquiries are directed. Let me add that it is the great desideratum by which this form of government can be rescued from the opprobrium under which it has so long labored, and be recommended to the esteem and adoption of mankind.

By what means is this object attainable? Evidently by one of two only. Either the existence of the same passion or interest in a majority at the same time must be prevented, or the majority, having such coexistent passion or interest, must be rendered, by their number and local situation, unable to concert and carry into effect schemes of oppression. If the impulse and the opportunity be suffered to coincide, we well know that neither moral nor religious motives can be relied on as an adequate control. They are not found to be such on the injustice and violence of individuals, and lose their efficacy in proportion to the number combined together, that is, in proportion as their efficacy becomes needful.

From this view of the subject it may be concluded that a pure democracy, by which I mean a society consisting of a small number of citizens, who assemble and administer the government in person, can admit of no cure for the mischiefs of faction. A common passion or interest will, in almost every case, be felt by a majority of the whole; a communication and concert result from the form of government itself; and there is nothing to check the inducements to sacrifice the weaker party or an obnoxious individual. Hence it is that such democracies have ever been spectacles of turbulence and contention; have ever been found incompatible with personal security or the rights of property; and have in general been as short in their lives as they have been violent in their deaths. Theoretic politicians, who have patronized this species of government, have erroneously supposed that by reducing mankind to a perfect equality in their political rights, they would, at the same time, be perfectly equalized and assimilated in their possessions, their opinions, and their passions.

A republic, by which I mean a government in which the scheme of representation takes place, opens a different prospect, and promises the cure for which we are seeking. Let us examine the points in which it varies from pure democracy, and we shall comprehend both the nature of the cure and the efficacy which it must derive from the Union.

The two great points of difference between a democracy and a republic are: first, the delegation of the government, in the latter, to a small number of citizens elected by the rest; secondly, the greater number of citizens, and greater sphere of country, over which the latter may be extended.

The effect of the first difference is, on the one hand, to refine and enlarge the public views, by passing them through the medium of a chosen body of citizens, whose wisdom may best discern the true interest of their country, and whose patriotism and love of justice will be least likely to sacrifice it to temporary or partial considerations. Under such a regulation, it may well happen that the public voice, pronounced by the representatives of the people, will be more consonant to the public good than if pronounced by the people themselves, convened for the purpose. On the other hand, the effect may be inverted. Men of factious tempers, of local prejudices, or of sinister designs, may, by intrigue, by corruption, or by other means, first obtain the suffrages, and then betray the interests, of the people. The question resulting is, whether small or extensive republics are more favorable to the election of proper guardians of the public weal; and it is clearly decided in favor of the latter by two obvious considerations:

In the first place, it is to be remarked that, however small the republic may be, the representatives must be raised to a certain number, in order to guard against the cabals of a few; and that, however large it may be, they must be limited to a certain number, in order to guard against the confusion of a multitude. Hence, the number of representatives in the two cases not being in proportion to that of the two constituents, and being proportionally greater in the small republic, it follows that, if the proportion of fit characters be not less in the large than in the small republic, the former will present a greater option, and consequently a greater probability of a fit choice.

In the next place, as each representative will be chosen by a greater number of citizens in the large than in the small republic, it will be more difficult for unworthy candidates to practice with success the vicious arts by which elections are too often carried; and the suffrages of the people being more free, will be more likely to centre in men who possess the most attractive merit and the most diffusive and established characters.

It must be confessed that in this, as in most other cases, there is a mean, on both sides of which inconveniences will be found to lie. By enlarging too much the number of electors, you render the representatives too little acquainted with all their local circumstances and lesser interests; as by reducing it too much, you render him unduly attached to these, and too little fit to comprehend and pursue great and national objects. The federal Constitution forms a happy combination in this respect; the great and aggregate interests being referred to the national, the local and particular to the State legislatures.

The other point of difference is, the greater number of citizens and extent of territory which may be brought within the compass of republican than of democratic government; and it is this circumstance principally which renders factious combinations less to be dreaded in the former than in the latter. The smaller the society, the fewer probably will be the distinct parties and interests composing it; the fewer the distinct parties and interests, the more frequently will a majority be found of the same party; and the smaller the number of individuals composing a majority, and the smaller the compass within which they are placed, the more easily will they concert and execute their plans of oppression. Extend the sphere, and you take in a greater variety of parties and interests; you make it less probable that a majority of the whole will have a common motive to invade the rights of other citizens; or if such a common motive exists, it will be more difficult for all who feel it to discover their own strength, and to act in unison with each other. Besides other impediments, it may be remarked that, where there is a consciousness of unjust or dishonorable purposes, communication is always checked by distrust in proportion to the number whose concurrence is necessary.

Hence, it clearly appears, that the same advantage which a republic has over a democracy, in controlling the effects of faction, is enjoyed by a large over a small republic,—is enjoyed by the Union over the States composing it. Does the advantage consist in the substitution of representatives whose enlightened views and virtuous sentiments render them superior to local prejudices and schemes of injustice? It will not be denied that the representation of the Union will be most likely to possess these requisite endowments. Does it consist in the greater security afforded by a greater variety of parties, against the event of any one party being able to outnumber and oppress the rest? In an equal degree does the increased variety of parties comprised within the Union, increase this security. Does it, in fine, consist in the greater obstacles opposed to the concert and accomplishment of the secret wishes of an unjust and interested majority? Here, again, the extent of the Union gives it the most palpable advantage.

The influence of factious leaders may kindle a flame within their particular States, but will be unable to spread a general conflagration through the other States. A religious sect may degenerate into a political faction in a part of the Confederacy; but the variety of sects dispersed over the entire face of it must secure the national councils against any danger from that source. A rage for paper money, for an abolition of debts, for an equal division of property, or for any other improper or wicked project, will be less apt to pervade the whole body of the Union than a particular member of it; in the same proportion as such a malady is more likely to taint a particular county or district, than an entire State.

In the extent and proper structure of the Union, therefore, we behold a republican remedy for the diseases most incident to republican government. And according to the degree of pleasure and pride we feel in being republicans, ought to be our zeal in cherishing the spirit and supporting the character of Federalists.

The Early Women's Movement

Maria Stewart, "An Address Delivered at the African Masonic Hall, Boston," (February 27, 1833)

Angelina Grimké Weld's Speech at Pennsylvania Hall (May 17, 1838)

Harriet Hanson Robinson, "Characteristics of the Early Factory Girls" (1898)

S. Margaret Fuller Ossoli, *Woman in the Nineteenth Century* (1845)

Elizabeth Cady Stanton, "Declaration of Sentiments and Resolutions," Seneca Falls Convention (July 19, 1848)

Sojourner Truth, "Ain't I a Woman?" (1851)

Marriage Protest of Lucy Stone and Henry B. Blackwell (May 1, 1855)

Susan B. Anthony Addresses Judge Ward Hunt in "The United States of America v. Susan B. Anthony" (June 19, 1873)

There was a natural affinity between black women who resisted the bonds of slavery and white women who resented their being consigned to an inferior position in a male-dominated world.

Black women were doubly oppressed, as blacks and as women. White women were seen either as fodder for the new industrial system—factory workers who could be put to work at an early age and literally worked to death—or as obedient helpers of their husbands, servants of a sort who bore children and then took care of them.

In the early part of the nineteenth century, women rebelled on all fronts—mill girls going out on strike, black women speaking out on enslavement, white women joining the anti-slavery movement.

Sarah Grimké, a Southern white woman, and sister of the fiery abolitionist Angelina Grimké, wrote, in the 1830s: "I ask no favors for my sex. I surrender not our claim to equality. All I ask of our brethren, is that they will take their feet from off our necks, and permit us to stand upright on that ground which God designed us to occupy." In another letter, she added, "[To] me it is perfectly clear that whatsoever it is morally right for a man to do, it is morally right for a woman to do."

Women worked in antislavery societies all over the country, gathering thousands of petitions to Congress. In 1840, a World Anti-Slavery Society met in London. After a heated debate on the issue, it was voted to exclude women and that they could attend the meetings only in a curtained enclosure. The women sat in silent protest in the gallery. That experience heightened their determination to continue their struggle for equality.

• • •

Here are the words of the pioneer African-American activist Maria Stewart. Stewart began writing and lecturing against slavery in the early 1830s, despite pressure from peers to keep silent, and became a contributor to William Lloyd Garrison's abolitionist newspaper, *The Liberator*. In this 1833 speech, she advances the cause of abolition, but her comments ("we have planted the vines, they have eaten the fruits of them") speak also to sexism and the degradation of women's work.

Maria Stewart, "An Address Delivered at the African Masonic Hall, Boston," (February 27, 1833)[1]

Most of our color have been taught to stand in fear of the white man, from their earliest infancy, to work as soon as they could walk, and call "master," before they scarce could lisp the name of mother. Continual fear and laborious servitude have in some degree lessened in us that natural force and energy which belong to man; or else, in defiance of opposition, our men, before this, would have nobly and boldly contended for their rights. But give the man of color an equal opportunity with the white from the cradle to manhood, and from manhood to the grave, and you would discover the dignified statesman, the man of science, and the philosopher. But there is no such opportunity for the sons of Africa, and I fear that our powerful one's are fully determined that there never shall be. For bid, ye Powers on high, that it should any longer be said that our men possess no force. O ye sons of Africa, when will your voices be heard in our legislative halls, in defiance of your enemies, contending for equal rights and liberty? How can you, when you reflect from what you have fallen, refrain from crying mightily unto God, to turn away from us the fierceness of his anger, and remember our transgressions against us no more forever. But a God of infinite purity will not regard the prayers of those who hold religion in one hand, and prejudice, sin and pollution in the other; he will not regard the prayers of self-righteousness and hypocrisy. Is it possible, I exclaim, that for the want of knowledge, we have labored for hundreds of years to support others, and been content to receive what they chose to give us in return? Cast your eyes about, look as far as you can see; all, all is owned by the lordly white, except here and there a lowly dwelling which the man of color, midst deprivations, fraud and opposition, has been scarce able to procure. Like king Solomon, who put neither nail nor hammer to the temple, yet received the praise; so also have the white Americans gained themselves a name, like the names of the great men that are in the earth, while in reality we have been their principal foundation and support. We have pursued the shadow, they have obtained the substance; we have performed the labor they have received the profits; we have planted the vines, they have eaten the fruits of them.

• • •

The sisters Sarah and Angelina Grimké were not only outspoken abolitionists, denouncing the evils of slavery, but were early advocates for women's rights. In 1848, Angelina Grimké addressed a crowd at Pennsylvania Hall, in Philadelphia, her last public speech. While she spoke, thousands gathered to protest, and attacked the hall, throwing stones and breaking its windows. Later that night, they burned the hall to the ground.

Angelina E. Grimké Weld's Speech at Pennsylvania Hall (May 17, 1838)[2]

Men, brethren and fathers—mothers, daughters and sisters, what came ye out for to see? A reed shaken with the wind? Is it curiosity merely, or a deep sympathy with the perishing slave, that has brought this large audience together? [A yell from the mob without the building.] Those voices without ought to awaken and call out our warmest sympathies. Deluded beings! "[T]hey know not what they do." They know not that they are undermining their own rights and their own happiness, temporal and eternal. Do you ask, "what has the North to do with slavery?" Hear it—hear it. Those voices without tell us that the spirit of slavery is here, and has been roused to wrath by our abolition speeches and conventions: for surely liberty would not foam and tear herself with rage, because her friends are multiplied daily, and meetings are held in quick succession to set forth her virtues and extend her peaceful kingdom. This opposition shows that slavery has done its deadliest work in the hearts of our citizens. Do you ask, then, "what has the North to do?" I answer, cast out first the spirit of slavery from your own hearts, and then lend your aid to convert the South. Each one present has a work to do, be his or her situation what it may, however limited their means, or insignificant their supposed influence. The great men of this country will not do this work; the church will never do it. A desire to please the world, to keep the favor of all parties and of all conditions, makes them dumb on this and every other unpopular subject. They have become worldly-wise, and therefore God, in his wisdom, employs them not to carry on his plans of reformation and salvation. He hath chosen the foolish things of the world to confound the wise, and the weak to overcome the mighty.

As a Southerner I feel that it is my duty to stand up here tonight and bear testimony against slavery. I have seen it—I have seen it. I know it has horrors that can never be described. I was brought up under its wing: I witnessed for many years its demoralizing influences, and its destructiveness to human happiness. It is admitted by some that the slave is not happy under the worst forms of slavery. But I have never seen a happy slave. I have seen him dance in his chains, it is true; but he was not happy. There is a wide difference between happiness and mirth. Man cannot enjoy the former while his manhood is destroyed, and that part of the being which is necessary to the making, and to the enjoyment of happiness, is completely blotted out. The slaves, however, may be, and sometimes are, mirthful. When hope is extinguished, they say, "let us eat and drink, for tomorrow we die." [Just then stones were thrown at the windows,—a great noise without, and commotion within.] What is a mob? What would the breaking of every window be? What would the leveling of this Hall be? Any evidence that we are wrong, or that slavery is a good and wholesome institution? What if the mob should now burst in upon us, break up our meeting and commit violence upon our persons— would this be any thing compared with what the slaves endure? No, no: and we do not remember them "as bound with them," if we shrink in the time of peril, or feel unwilling to sacrifice ourselves, if need be, for their sake. [Great noise.] I thank the Lord that there is yet life left enough to feel the truth, even though it rages at it—that conscience is not so completely seared as to be unmoved by the truth of the living God.

Many persons go to the South for a season, and are hospitably entertained in the parlor and at the table of the slave-holder. They never enter the huts of the slaves; they know nothing of the dark side of the picture, and they return home with praises on their lips of the generous character of those with whom they had tarried. Or if they have witnessed the cruelties of slavery, by remaining silent spectators they have naturally become callous—an insensibility has ensued which prepares them to apologize even for barbarity. Nothing but the corrupting influence of slavery on the hearts of the Northern people can induce them to apologize for it; and much will have been done for the destruction of Southern slavery when we have so reformed the North that no one here will be willing to risk his reputation by advocating or even excusing the holding of men as property. The South know it, and acknowledge that as fast as our principles prevail, the hold of the master must be relaxed. [Another outbreak of mobocratic spirit, and some confusion in the house.] . . .

Every Southern breeze wafted to me the discordant tones of weeping and wailing, shrieks and groans, mingled with prayers and blasphemous curses. I thought there was no hope; that the wicked would go on in his wickedness, until he had destroyed both himself and his country. My heart sunk within me at the abominations in the midst of which I had been born and educated. What will it avail, cried I in bitterness of spirit, to expose to the gaze of strangers the horrors and pollutions of slavery, when there is no ear to hear nor heart to feel and pray for the slave. The language of my soul was, "Oh tell it not in Gath, publish it not in the streets of Askelon." But how different do I feel now! Animated with hope, nay, with an assurance of the triumph of liberty and good will to man, I will lift up my voice like a trumpet, and show this people their transgression, their sins of omission towards the slave, and what they can do towards affecting Southern mind, and overthrowing Southern oppression.

We may talk of occupying neutral ground, but on this subject, in its present attitude, there is no such thing as neutral ground. He that is not for us is against us, and he that gathereth not with us, scattereth abroad. If you are on what you suppose to be neutral ground, the South look upon you as on the side of the oppressor. And is there one who loves his country willing to give his influence, even indirectly, in favor of slavery—that curse of nations ? God swept Egypt with the besom of destruction, and punished Judea also with a sore punishment, because of slavery. And have we any reason to believe that he is less just now?—or that he will be more favorable to us than to his own "peculiar people?" [Shoutings, stones thrown against the windows, etc.]

There is nothing to be feared from those who would stop our mouths, but they themselves should fear and tremble. The current is even now setting fast against them. If the arm of the North had not caused the Bastille of slavery to totter to its foundation, you would not hear those cries. A few years ago, and the South felt secure, and with a contemptuous sneer asked, "Who are the abolitionists? The abolitionists are nothing?"—Ay, in one sense they were nothing, and they are nothing still. But in this we rejoice, that "God has chosen things that are not to bring to naught things that are." [Mob again disturbed the meeting.]

We often hear the question asked, "What shall we do?" Here is an opportunity for doing something now. Every man and every woman present may do something by showing that we fear not a mob, and, in the midst of threatenings and revilings, by opening our mouths for the dumb and pleading the cause of those who are ready to perish.

To work as we should in this cause, we must know what Slavery is. Let me urge you then to buy the books which have been written on this subject and read them, and then lend them to your neighbors. Give your money no longer for things which pander to pride and lust, but aid in scattering "the living coals of truth" upon the naked heart of this nation,—in circulating appeals to the sympathies of Christians in behalf of the outraged and suffering slave. But, it is said by some, our "books and papers do not speak the truth." Why, then, do they not contradict what we say? They cannot. Moreover the South has entreated, nay commanded us to be silent; and what greater evidence of the truth of our publications could be desired?

Women of Philadelphia! allow me as a Southern woman, with much attachment to the land of my birth, to entreat you to come up to this work. Especially let me urge you to petition. Men may settle this and other questions at the ballot-box, but you have no such right; it is only through petitions that you can reach the Legislature. It is therefore peculiarly your duty to petition. Do you say, "It does no good?" The South already turns pale at the number sent. They have read the reports of the proceedings of Congress, and there have seen that among other petitions were very many from the women of the North on the subject of slavery. This fact has called the attention of the South to the subject. How could we expect to have done more as yet? Men who hold the rod over slaves, rule in the councils of the nation: and they deny our right to petition and to remonstrate against abuses of our sex and of our kind. We have these rights, however, from our God. Only let us exercise them: and though often turned away unanswered, let us remember the influence of importunity upon the unjust judge, and act accordingly. The fact that the South look with jealousy upon our measures shows that they are effectual. There is, therefore, no cause for doubting or despair, but rather for rejoicing.

It was remarked in England that women did much to abolish Slavery in her colonies. Nor are they now idle. Numerous petitions from them have recently been presented to the Queen, to abolish the apprenticeship with its cruelties nearly equal to those of the system whose place it supplies. One petition two miles and a quarter long has been presented. And do you think these labors will be in vain? Let the history of the past answer. When the women of these States send up to Congress such a petition, our legislators will arise as did those of England, and say, "When all the maids and matrons of the land are knocking at our doors we must legislate." Let the zeal and love, the faith and works of our English sisters quicken ours—that while the slaves continue to suffer, and when they shout deliverance, we may feel the satisfaction of having done what we could.

• • •

When Boston capitalists, making use of the new canal system, began building textile mills in Lowell, Massachusetts, in the early nineteenth century, they recruited young women from rural New England as their labor force. They assumed these "girls" would be docile and easily managed. Instead, the young women in the Lowell mills formed reading circles, organized to demand their rights as laborers and as women, and agitated for better workplace conditions. They printed leaflets and published their own newspaper, the *Lowell Offering*. Here, Harriet Hanson Robinson, who started work in the mills when she was only ten, recounts a "turn out," or strike, of the Lowell women, and describes the conditions of women factory workers in the 1830s.

Harriet Hanson Robinson, "Characteristics of the Early Factory Girls" (1898)[3]

When I look back into the factory life of fifty or sixty years ago, I do not see what is called "a class" of young men and women going to and from their daily work, like so many ants that cannot be distinguished one from another; I see them as individuals, with personalities of their own. This one has about her the atmosphere of her early home. That one is impelled by a strong and noble purpose. The other,—what she is, has been an influence for good to me and to all womankind.

Yet they were a class of factory operatives, and were spoken of (as the same class is spoken of now) as a set of persons who earned their daily bread, whose condition was fixed, and who must continue to spin and to weave to the end of their natural existence. Nothing but this was expected of them, and they were not supposed to be capable of social or mental improvement. That they could be educated and developed into something more than work-people, was an idea that had not yet entered the public mind. So little does one class of persons really know about the thoughts and aspirations of another! It was the good fortune of these early mill-girls to teach the people of that time that this sort of labor is not degrading; that the operative is not only "capable of virtue," but also capable of self-cultivation.

At the time the Lowell cotton-mills were started, the factory girl was the lowest among women. In England, and in France particularly, great injustice had been done to her real character; she was represented as subjected to influences that could not fail to destroy her purity and self-respect. In the eyes of her overseer she was but a brute, slave, to be beaten, pinched, and pushed about.

It was to overcome this prejudice that such high wages had been offered to women that they might be induced to become mill-girls, in spite of the opprobrium that still clung to this "degrading occupation." At first only a few came; for, though tempted by the high wages to be regularly paid in "cash," there were many who still preferred to go on working at some more genteel employment at seventy-five cents a week and their board.

But in a short time the prejudice against the factory labor wore away, and the Lowell mills became filled with blooming and energetic New England women. They were naturally intelligent, had mother-wit, and fell easily into the ways of their new life. They soon began to associate with those who formed the community in which they had come to live, and were invited to their houses. They went to the same church, and sometimes married into some of the best families. Or if they returned to their secluded homes again, instead of being looked down upon as "factory girls" by the squire's or lawyer's family, they were more often welcomed as coming from the metropolis, bringing new fashions, new books, and new ideas with them.

In 1831 Lowell was little more than a factory village. Several corporations were started, and the cotton-mills belonging to them were building. Help was in great demand; and the stories were told all over the country of the new factory town, and the high wages that were offered to all classes of work-people,—stories that reached the ears of mechanics' and farmers' sons, and gave new life to lonely and dependent women in distant towns and farmhouses. Into this Yankee El Dorado, these needy people began to pour by the various modes of travel known to those slow old days. The stage-coach and the canal-boat came every day, always filled with the new recruits for this army of useful people. The mechanic and machinist came, each with his home-made chest of tools, and oftentimes his wife and little ones. The widow came with her little flock of scanty housekeeping goods to open a boarding-house or variety store, and so provided a home for her fatherless children. Many farmers' daughters came to earn money to complete their wedding outfit, or buy the bride's share of housekeeping articles.

Women with past histories came, to hide their griefs and their identity, and to earn an honest living in the "sweat of their brow." Single young men came, full of hope and life, to get money for an education, or to lift the mortgage from the home-farm. Troops of young girls came by stages and baggage-wagons, men often being employed to go to other States and to Canada, to collect them at so much a head, and deliver them to the factories. . . .

These country girls had queer names, which added to the singularity of their appearance. Samantha, Triphena, Plumy, Kezia, Aseneth, Elgardy, Leafy, Ruhamah, Lovey, Almaretta, Sarepta, and Florilla were among them.

Their dialect was also very peculiar. On the broken English and Scotch of their ancestors was ingrafted the nasal Yankee twang; so that many of them, when they had just come down, spoke a language almost unintelligible. But the severe discipline and ridicule which met them was as good as a school education, and they were soon taught the "city way of speaking." . . .

One of the first strikes of the cotton-factory operatives that ever took place in this country was that in Lowell, in October, 1836. When it was announced that wages were to be cut down, great indignation was felt, and it was decided to strike, en masse. This was done. The mills were shut down, and the girls went in procession from their several corporations to the "grove" on Chapel Hill, and listened to "incendiary" speeches from early labor reformers.

One of the girls stood on a pump, and gave vent to the feelings of her companions in a neat speech, declaring that it was their duty to resist all attempts at cutting down the wages. This was the first time a woman had spoken in public in Lowell, and the event caused surprise and consternation among her audience.

Cutting down the wages was not their only grievance, nor the only cause of this strike. Hitherto the corporations had paid twenty-five cents a week towards the board of each operative, and now it was their purpose to have the girls pay the sum; and this, in addition to the cut in wages, would make a difference of at least one dollar a week. It was estimated that as many as twelve or fifteen hundred girls turned out, and walked in procession through the streets. . . .

My own recollection of this first strike (or "turn out" as it was called) is very vivid. I worked in a lower room, where I had heard the proposed strike fully, if not vehemently, discussed; I had been an ardent listener to what was said against this attempt at "oppression" on the part of the corporation, and naturally I took sides with the strikers. When the day came on which the girls were to turn out, those in the upper rooms started first, and so many of them left that our mill was at once shut down. Then, when the girls in my room stood irresolute, uncertain what to do, asking each other, "Would you?" or "Shall we turn out?" and not one of them having the courage to lead off, I, who began to think they would not go out, after all their talk, became impatient, and started on ahead, saying, with childish bravado, "I don't care what you do, *I* am going to turn out, whether any one else does or not;" and I marched out, and was followed by the others.

As I looked back at the long line that followed me, I was more proud than I have ever been at any success I may have achieved.

• • •

In 1845, Margaret Fuller published the groundbreaking work *Woman in the Nineteenth Century*, an expanded version of an essay she had written for *The Dial* in 1843, called "The Great Lawsuit—Man versus Men; Woman versus Women." The book, part of which is excerpted here, had a profound impact on the women's rights movement in the United States.

S. Margaret Fuller Ossoli, *Woman in the Nineteenth Century* (1845)[4]

Though the national independence be blurred by the servility of individuals; though freedom and equality have been proclaimed only to leave room for a monstrous display of slave-dealing and slave-keeping; though the free American so often feels himself free, like the Roman, only to pamper his appetites and his indolence through the misery of his fellow-beings; still it is not in vain that the verbal statement has been made, "All men are born free and equal." There it stands, a golden certainty wherewith to encourage the good, to shame the bad. The New World may be called clearly to perceive that it incurs the utmost penalty if it reject or oppress the sorrowful brother. And, if men are deaf, the angels hear. But men cannot be deaf. It is inevitable that an external freedom, an independence of the encroachments of other men, such as has been achieved for the nation, should be so also for every member of it. That which has once been clearly conceived in the intelligence cannot fail, sooner or later, to be acted out. . . .

We sicken no less at the pomp than the strife of words. We feel that never were lungs so puffed with the wind of declamation, on moral and religious subjects, as now. We are tempted to implore these "word-heroes," these word-Catos, word-Christs, to beware of cant above all things; to remember that hypocrisy is the most hopeless as well as the meanest of crimes, and that those must surely be polluted by it, who do not reserve a part of their morality and religion for private use. [Walter Savage] Landor says that he cannot have a great deal of mind who cannot afford to let the larger part of it lie fallow; and what is true of genius is not less so of virtue. The tongue is a valuable member, but should appropriate but a small part of the vital juices that are needful all over the body. We feel that the mind may "grow black and rancid in the smoke" even "of altars." We start up from the harangue to go into our closet and shut the door. There inquires the spirit, "Is this rhetoric the bloom of healthy blood, or a false pigment artfully laid on?" And yet again we know where is so much smoke, must be some fire; with so much talk about virtue and freedom, must be mingled some desire for them; that it cannot be in vain that such have become the common topics of conversation among men, rather than schemes for tyranny and plunder, that the very newspapers see it best to proclaim themselves "Pilgrims," "Puritans," "Heralds of Holiness." The king that maintains so costly a retinue cannot be a mere boast, or Carabbas fiction. We have waited here long in the dust; we are tired and hungry; but the triumphal procession must appear at last.

Of all its banners, none has been more steadily up-held, and under none have more valor and willingness for real sacrifices been shown, than that of the champions of the enslaved African. And this band it is, which, partly from a natural following out of principles, partly because many women have been prominent in that cause, makes, just now, the warmest appeal in behalf of Woman.

Though there has been a growing liberality on this subject, yet society at large is not so prepared for the demands of this party, but that its members are, and will be for some time, coldly regarded as the Jacobins of their day.

"Is it not enough," cries the irritated trader, "that you have done all you could to break up the national union, and thus destroy the prosperity of our country, but now you must be trying to break up family union, to take my wife away from the cradle and the kitchen-hearth to vote at polls, and preach from a pulpit? Of course, if she does such things, she cannot attend to those of her own sphere. She is happy enough as she is. She has more leisure than I have—every means of improvement, every indulgence."

"Have you asked her whether she was satisfied with these indulgences?"

"No, but I know she is. She is too amiable to desire what would make me unhappy, and too judicious to wish to step beyond the sphere of her sex. I will never consent to have our peace disturbed by any such discussions."

"'Consent—you?' it is not consent from you that is in question—it is assent from your wife."

"Am not I the head of my house?"

"You are not the head of your wife. God has given her a mind of her own."

"I am the head, and she the heart."

"God grant you play true to one another, then! I suppose I am to be grateful that you did not say she was only the hand. If the head represses no natural pulse of the heart, there can be no question as to your giving your consent. Both will be of one accord, and there needs but to present any question to get a full and true answer. There is no need of precaution, of indulgence, nor consent. But our doubt is whether the heart does consent with the head, or only obeys its decrees with a passiveness that precludes the exercise of its natural powers, or a repugnance that turns sweet qualities to bitter, or a doubt that lays waste the fair occasions of life. It is to ascertain the truth that we propose some liberating measures."

• • •

In 1848, a historic assembly of women gathered in Seneca Falls, New York, the home of Elizabeth Cady Stanton. Stanton organized the Seneca Falls Convention with Lucretia Mott, who, like her, had been excluded from the World Anti-Slavery Convention in London eight years earlier. Modeling her declaration closely on the Declaration of Independence, Stanton extended it to list the grievances of women. The Declaration also called for the right for women to vote, a radical demand that helped launch the women's suffrage movement, leading, ultimately, to the recognition of voting rights for women in the Nineteenth Amendment, in 1920.

Elizabeth Cady Stanton, "Declaration of Sentiments and Resolutions," Seneca Falls Convention (July 19, 1848)[5]

When, in the course of human events, it becomes necessary for one portion of the family of man to assume among the people of the earth a position different from that which they have hitherto occupied, but one to which the laws of nature and of nature's God entitle them, a decent respect to the opinions of mankind requires that they should declare the causes that impel them to such a course.

We hold these truths to be self-evident: that all men and women are created equal; that they are endowed by their Creator with certain inalienable rights; that among these are life, liberty, and the pursuit of happiness; that to secure these rights governments are instituted, deriving their just powers from the consent of the governed. Whenever any form of government becomes destructive of these ends, it is the right of those who suffer from it to refuse allegiance to it, and to insist upon the institution of a new government, laying its foundation on such principles, and organizing its powers in such form, as to them shall seem most likely to effect their safety and happiness. Prudence, indeed, will dictate that governments long established should not be changed for light and transient causes; and accordingly all experience hath shown that mankind are more disposed to suffer, while evils are sufferable, than to right themselves by abolishing the forms to which they are accustomed. But when a long train of abuses and usurpations, pursuing invariably the same object, evinces a design to reduce them under absolute despotism, it is their duty to throw off such government, and to provide new guards for their future security. Such has been the patient sufferance of the women under this government, and such is now the necessity which constrains them to demand the equal station to which they are entitled.

The history of mankind is a history of repeated injuries and usurpations on the part of man toward woman, having in direct object the establishment of an absolute tyranny over her. To prove this, let facts be submitted to a candid world.

He has never permitted her to exercise her inalienable right to the elective franchise.

He has compelled her to submit to laws, in the formation of which she had no voice.

He has withheld from her rights which are given to the most ignorant and degraded men—both natives and foreigners.

Having deprived her of this first right of a citizen, the elective franchise, thereby leaving her without representation in the halls of legislation, he has oppressed her on all sides.

He has made her, if married, in the eye of the law, civilly dead.

He has taken from her all right in property, even to the wages she earns.

He has made her, morally, an irresponsible being, as she can commit many crimes with impunity, provided they be done in the presence of her husband. In the covenant of marriage, she is compelled to promise obedience to her husband, he becoming, to all intents and purposes, her master—the law giving him power to deprive her of her liberty, and to administer chastisement.

He has so framed the laws of divorce, as to what shall be the proper causes, and in case of separation, to whom the guardianship of the children shall be given, as to be wholly regardless of the happiness of women—the law, in all cases, going upon a false supposition of the supremacy of man, and giving all power into his hands.

After depriving her of all rights as a married woman, if single, and the owner of property, he has taxed her to support a government which recognizes her only when her property can be made profitable to it.

He has monopolized nearly all the profitable employments, and from those she is permitted to follow, she receives but a scanty remuneration. He closes against her all the avenues to wealth and distinction which he considers most honorable to himself. As a teacher of theology, medicine, or law, she is not known.

He has denied her the facilities for obtaining a thorough education, all colleges being closed against her.

He allows her in Church, as well as State, but a subordinate position, claiming Apostolic authority for her exclusion from the ministry, and, with some exceptions, from any public participation in the affairs of the Church.

He has created a false public sentiment by giving to the world a different code of morals for men and women, by which moral delinquencies which exclude women from society, are not only tolerated, but deemed of little account in man.

He has usurped the prerogative of Jehovah himself, claiming it as his right to assign for her a sphere of action, when that belongs to her conscience and to her God.

He has endeavored, in every way that he could, to destroy her confidence in her own powers, to lessen her self-respect, and to make her willing to lead a dependent and abject life.

Now, in view of this entire disfranchisement of one-half the people of this country, their social and religious degradation—in view of the unjust laws above mentioned, and because women do feel themselves aggrieved, oppressed, and fraudulently deprived of their most sacred rights, we insist that they have immediate admission to all the rights and privileges which belong to them as citizens of the United States.

In entering upon the great work before us, we anticipate no small amount of misconception, misrepresentation, and ridicule; but we shall use every instrumentality within our power to effect our object. We shall employ agents, circulate tracts, petition the State and National legislatures, and endeavor to enlist the pulpit and the press in our behalf. We hope this Convention will be followed by a series of Conventions embracing every part of the country.

• • •

Here, the black abolitionist Sojourner Truth, who was freed from slavery in 1827, speaks to a gathering of feminists in Akron in 1851, denouncing the religious arguments commonly made to justify the oppression of women. No exact transcript of the speech, which electrified its audience, exists, but the president of the Akron convention, Frances Gage, later recounted Truth's words.

Sojourner Truth, "Ain't I a Woman?" (1851)[6]

Well, children, where there is so much racket there must be something out of kilter. I think that 'twixt the negroes of the South and the women at the North, all talking about rights, the white men will be in a fix pretty soon. But what's all this here talking about?

That man over there says that women need to be helped into carriages, and lifted over ditches, and to have the best place everywhere. Nobody ever helps me into carriages, or over mud-puddles, or gives me any best place! And ain't I a woman? Look at me! Look at my arm! I have ploughed and planted, and gathered into barns, and no man could head me! And ain't I a woman? I could work as much and eat as much as a man—when I could get it—and bear the lash as well! And ain't I a woman? I have borne thirteen children, and seen most all sold off to slavery, and when I cried out with my mother's grief, none but Jesus heard me! And ain't I a woman?

Then they talk about this thing in the head; what's this they call it? [a member of audience whispers, "intellect"] That's it, honey. What's that got to do with women's rights or negroes' rights? If my cup won't hold but a pint, and yours holds a quart, wouldn't you be mean not to let me have my little half measure full?

Then that little man in black there, he says women can't have as much rights as men, 'cause Christ wasn't a woman! Where did your Christ come from? Where did your Christ come from? From God and a woman! Man had nothing to do with Him.

If the first woman God ever made was strong enough to turn the world upside down all alone, these women together ought to be able to turn it back, and get it right side up again! And now they is asking to do it, the men better let them.

• • •

Lucy Stone was not only the first woman in Massachusetts to earn a college degree, but the first woman in the United States to keep her own name after marriage. When Stone married Henry Blackwell in 1855, she and Blackwell registered the following protest, which was read at the ceremony and then published in abolitionist newspapers.

Marriage Protest of Lucy Stone and Henry B. Blackwell (May 1, 1855)[7]

While we acknowledge our mutual affection by publicly assuming the relationship of husband and wife, yet in justice to ourselves and a great principle, we deem it a duty to declare that this act on our part implies no sanction of, nor promise of voluntary obedience to such of the present laws of marriage, as refuse to recognize the wife as an independent, rational being, while they confer upon the husband an injurious and unnatural superiority, investing him with legal powers which no honorable man would exercise, and which no man should possess. We protest especially against the laws which give to the husband:

1. The custody of the wife's person.

2. The exclusive control and guardianship of their children.

3. The sole ownership of her personal, and use of her real estate, unless previously settled upon her, or placed in the hands of trustees, as in the case of minors, lunatics, and idiots.

4. The absolute right to the product of her industry.

5. Also against laws which give to the widower so much larger and more permanent interest in the property of his deceased wife, than they give to the widow in that of the deceased husband.

6. Finally, against the whole system by which "the legal existence of the wife is suspended during marriage," so that in most States, she neither has a legal part in the choice of her residence, nor can she make a will, nor sue or be sued in her own name, nor inherit property.

We believe that personal independence and equal human rights can never be forfeited, except for crime; that marriage should be an equal and permanent partnership, and so recognized by law; that until it is so recognized, married partners should provide against the radical injustice of present laws, by every means in their power.

• • •

In November 1872, Susan B. Anthony was one of fourteen women who defied the law to cast a ballot in the presidential election. Anthony was arrested for "knowingly voting without having a lawful right to vote," and on June 18, 1873, was found guilty. The next day, when her lawyer appealed the verdict, she addressed the court in response to a question from the judge, Ward Hunt.

Susan B. Anthony Addresses Judge Ward Hunt in *The United States of America v. Susan B. Anthony* (June 19, 1873)[8]

Judge Hunt—(Ordering the defendant to stand up). Has the prisoner anything to say why sentence shall not be pronounced?

Miss Anthony—Yes, your honor, I have many things to say; for in your ordered verdict of guilty you have trampled under foot every vital principle of our government. My natural rights, my civil rights, my political rights, my judicial rights, are all alike ignored. Robbed of the fundamental privilege of citizenship, I am degraded from the status of a citizen to that of a subject; and not only myself individually but all of my sex are, by your honor's verdict, doomed to political subjection under this so-called republican form of government.

Judge Hunt—The Court cannot listen to a rehearsal of argument which the prisoner's counsel has already consumed three hours in presenting.

Miss Anthony—May it please your honor, I am not arguing the question, but simply stating the reasons why sentence can not, in justice, be pronounced against me. Your denial of my citizen's right to vote, is the denial of my right of consent as one of the governed, the denial of my right of representation as one of the taxed, the denial of my right to a trial by a jury of my peers as an offender against law; therefore, the denial of my sacred right to life, liberty, property and—

Judge Hunt—The Court can not allow the prisoner to go on.

Miss Anthony—But your honor will not deny me this one and only poor privilege of protest against this high-handed outrage upon my citizen's rights. May it please the Court to remember that, since the day of my arrest last November, this is the first time that either myself or any person of my disfranchised class has been allowed a word of defense before judge or jury—

Judge Hunt—The prisoner must sit down—the Court can not allow it.

Miss Anthony—Of all of my prosecutors, from the corner grocery politician who entered the complaint, to the United States marshal, commissioner, district attorney, district judge, your honor on the bench—not one is my peer, but each and all are my political sovereigns; and had your honor submitted my case to the jury, as was clearly your duty, even then I should have had just cause of protest, for not one of those men was my peer; but, native or foreign born, white or black, rich or poor, educated or ignorant, sober or drunk, each and every man of them was my political superior; hence, in no sense, my peer. Under such circumstances a commoner of England, tried before a jury of lords, would have far less cause to complain than have I, a woman, tried before a jury of men. Even my counsel, Hon. Henry R. Selden, who has argued my cause so ably, so earnestly, so unanswerably before your honor, is my political sovereign. Precisely as no disfranchised person is entitled to sit upon a jury, and no woman is entitled to the franchise, so none but a regularly admitted lawyer is allowed to practice in the courts, and no woman can gain admission to the bar—hence, jury, judge, counsel, all must be of the superior class.

Judge Hunt—The Court must insist—the prisoner has been tried according to the established forms of law.

Miss Anthony—Yes, your honor, but by forms of law all made by men, interpreted by men, administered by men, in favor of men and against women; and hence your honor's ordered verdict of guilty, against a United States citizen for the exercise of the "citizen's right to vote," simply because that citizen was a woman and not a man. But yesterday, the same man-made forms of law declared it a crime punishable with $1,000 fine and six months' imprisonment to give a cup of cold water, a crust of bread or a night's shelter to a panting fugitive tracking his way to Canada; and every man or woman in whose veins coursed a drop of human sympathy violated that wicked law, reckless of consequences, and was justified in doing so. As then the slaves who got their freedom had to take it over or under or through the unjust forms of law, precisely so now must women take it to get right to a voice in this government; and I have taken mine, and mean to take it at every opportunity.

Judge Hunt—The Court orders the prisoner to sit down. It will not allow another word.

Miss Anthony—When I was brought before your honor for trial, I hoped for a broad and liberal interpretation of the Constitution and its recent amendments, which should declare all United States citizens under its protecting aegis—which should declare equality of rights the national guarantee to all persons born or naturalized in the United States. But failing to get this justice—failing, even, to get a trial by a jury *not* of my peers—I ask not leniency at your hands but rather the full rigors of the law.

Judge Hunt—The Court must insist—(Here the prisoner sat down.) The prisoner will stand up. (Here Miss Anthony arose again.) The sentence of the Court is that you pay a fine of $100 and the costs of the prosecution.

Miss Anthony—May it please your honor, I will never pay a dollar of your unjust penalty. All the stock in trade I possess is a debt of $10,000, incurred by publishing my paper—*The Revolution*—the sole object of which was to educate all women to do precisely as I have done, rebel against your man-made, unjust, unconstitutional forms of law, which tax, fine, imprison and hang women, while denying them the right of representation in the government; and I will work on with might and main to pay every dollar of that honest debt, but not a penny shall go to this unjust claim. And I shall earnestly and persistently continue to urge all women to the practical recognition of the old Revolutionary maxim, "Resistance to tyranny is obedience to God."

CHAPTER SEVEN

Indian Removal

Tecumseh's Speech to the Osages (Winter 1811–1812)

Two Documents on the Cherokee Removal (1829 and 1830)
Cherokee Nation, "Memorial of the Cherokee Indians" (December 1829)
Lewis Ross et al., Address of the Committee and Council of the Cherokee Nation, in General Council Convened, to the People of the United States (July 17, 1830)

Black Hawk's Surrender Speech (1832)

John G. Burnett, "The Cherokee Removal Through the Eyes of a Private Soldier" (December 11, 1890)

Two Statements by Chief Joseph of the Nez Percé (1877 and 1879)
Chief Joseph's Surrender (October 5, 1877)
Chief Joseph Recounts His Trip to Washington, D.C. (1879)

Black Elk, "The End of the Dream" (1932)

The defeat of England in the American Revolution paved the way for the colonists to move westward into Indian territory, because the British had proclaimed in 1763 that they could not settle land beyond a certain line at the Appalachian Mountains.

Thus, by 1840, out of a population in the United States of 13 million, 4,500,000 had crossed the mountains into the Mississippi Valley—that huge expanse of land crisscrossed by rivers flowing into the Mississippi from east and west. In 1820, 120,000 Indians lived east of the Mississippi. By 1844, fewer than 30,000 were left. Most of them had been killed or pushed westward by force. It was an early example of what in the late twentieth century, referring to other countries, would be called "ethnic cleansing."

The Indians of Florida, Alabama, Georgia, and Mississippi resisted "Indian removal," but they were no match (except for the determined resistance of the Seminoles in Florida) for the armed force of the United States. It was an ironic commentary that this brutal treatment of the Indians took place in the time often referred to in history books as the era of "Jacksonian democracy."

• • •

One of the great figures of early Native resistance to colonization was Tecumseh, a Shawnee leader, who earned a reputation for his skills in fighting white settlers and militias in the Midwest. He and his brother worked toward the unification of Indians to struggle collectively against the encroachment on their lands by colonists, as they expanded westward. Here he speaks to the Osages about the struggle against the colonists, arguing that "nothing will satisfy them but the whole of our hunting grounds, from the rising to the setting sun."

Tecumseh's Speech to the Osages (Winter 1811–12)[1]

Brothers,—We all belong to one family; we are all children of the Great Spirit; we walk in the same path; slake our thirst at the same spring; and now affairs of the greatest concern lead us to smoke the pipe around the same council fire!

Brothers,—We are friends; we must assist each other to bear our burdens. The blood of many of our fathers and brothers has run like water on the ground, to satisfy the avarice of the white men. We, ourselves, are threatened with a great evil; nothing will pacify them but the destruction of all the red men.

Brothers,—When the white men first set foot on our grounds, they were hungry; they had no place on which to spread their blankets, or to kindle their fires. They were feeble; they could do nothing for themselves. Our father commiserated their distress, and shared freely with them whatever the Great Spirit had given his red children. They gave them food when hungry, medicine when sick, spread skins for them to sleep on, and gave them grounds, that they might hunt and raise corn.

Brothers,—The white people are like poisonous serpents: when chilled, they are feeble and harmless; but invigorate them with warmth, and they sting their benefactors to death.

The white people came among us feeble; and now we have made them strong, they wish to kill us, or drive us back, as they would wolves and panthers.

Brothers,—The white men are not friends to the Indians: at first, they only asked for land sufficient for a wigwam; now, nothing will satisfy them but the whole of our hunting grounds, from the rising to the setting sun.

Brothers,—The white men want more than our hunting grounds; they wish to kill our warriors; they would even kill our old men, women and little ones.

Brothers,—Many winters ago, there was no land; the sun did not rise and set: all was darkness. The Great Spirit made all things. He gave the white people a home beyond the great waters. He supplied these grounds with game, and gave them to his red children; and he gave them strength and courage to defend them.

Brothers—My people wish for peace; the red men all wish for peace; but where the white people are, there is no peace for them, except it be on the bosom of our mother.

Brothers,—The white men despise and cheat the Indians; they abuse and insult them; they do not think the red men sufficiently good to live.

The red men have borne many and great injuries; they ought to suffer them no longer. My people will not; they are determined on vengeance; they have taken up the tomahawk; they will make it fat with blood; they will drink the blood of the white people.

Brothers,—My people are brave and numerous; but the white people are too strong for them alone. I wish you to take up the tomahawk with them. If we all unite, we will cause the rivers to stain the great waters with their blood.

Brothers,—If you do not unite with us, they will first destroy us, and then you will fall an easy prey to them. They have destroyed many nations of red men because they were not united, because they were not friends to each other.

Brothers,—The white people send runners amongst us; they wish to make us enemies that they may sweep over and desolate our hunting grounds, like devastating winds, or rushing waters.

Brothers,—Our Great Father, over the great waters, is angry with the white people, our enemies. He will send his brave warriors against them; he will send us rifles, and whatever else we want—he is our friend, and we are his children.

Brothers,—Who are the white people that we should fear them? They cannot run fast, and are good marks to shoot at: they are only men; our fathers have killed many of them; we are not squaws, and we will stain the earth red with blood.

Brothers,—The Great Spirit is angry with our enemies; he speaks in thunder, and the earth swallows up villages, and drinks up the Mississippi. The great waters will cover their lowlands; their corn cannot grow; and the Great Spirit will sweep those who escape to the hills from the earth with his terrible breath.

Brothers,—We must be united; we must smoke the same pipe; we must fight each other's battles; and more than all, we must love the Great Spirit: he is for us; he will destroy our enemies, and make all his red children happy.

• • •

In the first half of the nineteenth century, tens of thousands of Native Americans were violently removed from their lands, as the U.S. government led an expansion of its territory and power into the lands of the Cherokee and other Indian nations. In 1823, the Supreme Court ruled that Indian's "right of occupancy" was not as important as the U.S. government's "right of discovery." Four years later, the Cherokees responded by declaring themselves to be a sovereign nation. The state of Georgia, however, did not recognize their sovereign status, but saw them as tenants living on state land. The Cherokee took their case to the Supreme Court, which ruled against them. In 1830, President Andrew Jackson won approval of the Indian Removal Act, gaining the power to negotiate removal treaties with Indian tribes living east of the Mississippi. These two accounts document resistance of the Cherokees to their removal, whether by "direct or by indirect measures."

Two Documents on the Cherokee Removal (1829 and 1830)

CHEROKEE NATION, "MEMORIAL OF THE CHEROKEE INDIANS" (DECEMBER 1829)[2]

To the honorable senate and house of representatives of the United States of America, in congress assembled:

The undersigned memorialists, humbly make known to your honorable bodies, that they are free citizens of the Cherokee nation. Circumstances of late occurrence have troubled our hearts, and induced us at this time to appeal to you, knowing that you are generous and just. As weak and poor children are accustomed to look to their guardians and patrons for protection, so we would come and make our grievances known. Will you listen to us? Will you have pity on us? You are great and renowned—the nation, which you represent, is like a mighty man who stands in his strength. But we are small—our name is not renowned. You are wealthy, and have need of nothing; but we are poor in life, and have not the arm and power of the rich.

By the will of our Father in heaven, the governor of the whole world, the red man of America has become small, and the white man great and renowned. When the ancestors of the people of these United States first came to the shores of America, they found the red man strong—though he was ignorant and savage, yet he received them kindly, and gave them dry land to rest their weary feet. They met in peace, and shook hands in token of friendship. Whatever the white man wanted and asked of the Indian, the latter willingly gave. At that time the Indian was the lord, and the white man the suppliant. But now the scene has changed. The strength of the red man has become weakness. As his neighbors increased in numbers, his power became less, and now, of the many and powerful tribes who once covered these United States, only a few are to be seen—a few whom a sweeping pestilence has left. The northern tribes, who were once so numerous and powerful, are now nearly extinct. Thus it has happened to the red man of America. Shall we, who are remnants, share the same fate?

Brothers—we address you according to usage adopted by our forefathers, and the great and good men who have successfully directed the councils of the nation you represent—we now make known to you our grievances. We are troubled by some of your own people. Our neighbor, the state of Georgia, is pressing hard upon us, and urging us to relinquish our possessions for her benefit. We are told, if we do not leave the country, which we dearly love, and betake ourselves to the western wilds, the laws of the state will be extended over us, and the time, 1st of June, 1830, is appointed for the execution of the edict. When we first heard of this we were grieved and appealed to our father, the president, and begged that protection might be extended over us. But we were doubly grieved when we understood, from a letter of the secretary of war to our delegation, dated March of the present year, that our father the president had refused us protection, and that he had decided in favor of the extension of the laws of the state over us.—This decision induces us to appeal to the immediate representatives of the American people. We love, we dearly love our country, and it is due to your honorable bodies, as well as to us, to make known why we think the country is ours, and why we wish to remain in peace where we are. The land on which we stand, we have received as an inheritance from our fathers, who possessed it from time immemorial, as a gift from our common father in heaven. We have already said, that when the white man came to the shores of America, our ancestors were found in peaceable possession of this very land. They bequeathed it to us as their children, and we have sacredly kept it as containing the remains of our beloved men. This right of inheritance we have *never ceded*, nor ever *forfeited*. Permit us to ask, what better right can a people have to a country, than the right of *inheritance* and *immemorial peaceable possession?* We know it is said of late by the state of Georgia, and by the executive of the United States, that we have forfeited this right—but we think this is said gratuitously. At what time have we made the forfeit? What crime have we committed, whereby we must forever be divested of our country and rights? Was it when we were hostile to the United States, and took part with the king of Great Britain, during the struggle for independence? If so, why was not this forfeiture declared in the first treaty of peace between the United States and our beloved men? Why was not such an article as the following inserted in the treaty: "The United States give peace to the Cherokees, but, for the part they took in the late war, declare them to be but tenants at will, to be removed when the convenience of the states within whose chartered limits they live shall require it." This was the proper time to assume such a position. But it was not thought of, nor would our forefathers have agreed to any treaty, whose tendency was to deprive them of their rights and their country. All that they have conceded and relinquished are inserted in the treaties open to the investigation of all people. We would repeat, then, the right of inheritance and peaceable possession which we claim, we have never ceded nor forfeited.

In addition to that first of all rights, the right of inheritance and peaceable possession, we have the faith and pledge of the U[nited] States, repeated over and over again, in treaties made at various times. By these treaties our rights as a separate people are distinctly acknowledged, and guarantees given that they shall be secured and protected. So we have always understood the treaties. The conduct of the government towards us, from its organization until very lately, the talks given to our beloved men by the presidents of the United States, and the speeches of the agents and commissioners, all concur to show that we are not mistaken in our interpretation.—Some of our beloved men who signed the treaties are still living, and their testimony tends to the same conclusion. We have always supposed that this understanding of the treaties was in accordance with the views of the government; nor have we ever imagined that any body would interpret them otherwise. In what light shall we view the conduct of the United States and Georgia, in their intercourse with us, in urging us to enter into treaties, and cede lands? If we were but tenants at will, why was it necessary that our consent must be obtained before these governments could take lawful possession of our lands? The answer is obvious. These governments perfectly understood our rights—our right to the country, and our right to self government. Our understanding of the treaties is further supported by the intercourse law of the United States, which prohibits all encroachments upon our territory. The undersigned memorialists humbly represent, that if their interpretation of the treaties has been different from that of the government, then they have ever been deceived as to how the government regarded them, and what she asked and promised. Moreover, they have uniformly misunderstood their own acts.

In view of the strong ground upon which their rights are founded, your memorialists solemnly protest against being considered as tenants at will, or as mere occupants of the soil, without possessing the sovereignty. We have already stated to your honorable bodies, that our forefathers were found in possession of this soil in full sovereignty, by the first European settlers; and as we have never ceded nor forfeited the occupancy of the soil and the sovereignty over it, we do solemnly protest against being forced to leave it, either direct or by indirect measures. To the land of which we are now in possession we are attached—it is our fathers' gift—it contains their ashes—it is the land of our nativity, and the land of our intellectual birth. We cannot consent to abandon it, for another far inferior, and which holds out to us no inducements. We do moreover protest against the arbitrary measures of our neighbor, the state of Georgia, in her attempt to extend her laws over us, in surveying our lands without our consent and in direct opposition to treaties and the intercourse law of the United States, and interfering with our municipal regulations in such a manner as to derange the regular operations of our own laws. To deliver and protect them from all these and every encroachment upon their rights, the undersigned memorialists do most earnestly pray your honorable bodies. Their existence and future happiness are at stake—divest them of their liberty and country, and you sink them in degradation, and put a check, if not a final stop, to their present progress in the arts of civilized life, and in the knowledge of the Christian religion. Your memorialists humbly conceive, that such an act would be in the highest degree oppressive. From the people of these United States, who perhaps, of all men under heaven, are the most religious and free, it cannot be expected.—Your memorialists, therefore, cannot anticipate such a result. You represent a virtuous, intelligent and Christian nation. To you they willingly submit their cause for your righteous decision.

• • •

LEWIS ROSS ET AL., ADDRESS OF THE COMMITTEE AND COUNCIL OF THE CHEROKEE NATION, IN GENERAL COUNCIL CONVENED, TO THE PEOPLE OF THE UNITED STATES (JULY 17, 1830)[3]

Before we close this address, permit us to state what we conceive to be our relations with the United States. After the peace of 1783, the Cherokees were an independent people; absolutely so, as much as any people on earth. They had been allies to Great Britain, and as a faithful ally took a part in the colonial war on her side. They had placed themselves under her protection, and had they, without cause, declared hostility against their protector, and had the colonies been subdued, what might not have been their fate? But her [Great Britain's] power on this continent was broken. She acknowledged the independence of the United States, and made peace. The Cherokees therefore stood alone; and, in these circumstances, continued the war. They were then under no obligations to the United States any more than to Great Britain, France or Spain. The United States never subjugated the Cherokees; on the contrary, our fathers remained in possession of their country, and with arms in their hands. . . .

We are aware, that some persons suppose it will be for our advantage to remove beyond the Mississippi. We think otherwise. Our people universally think otherwise. Thinking that it would be fatal to their interests, they have almost to a man sent their memorial to congress, deprecating the necessity of a removal. This question was distinctly before their minds when they signed their memorial. Not an adult person can be found, who has not an opinion on the subject, and if the people were to understand distinctly, that they could be protected against the laws of the neighboring states, there is probably not an adult person in the nation, who would think it best to remove; though possibly a few might emigrate individually. . . .

We are not willing to remove; and if we could be brought to this extremity, it would be not by argument, not because our judgment was satisfied, not because our condition will be improved; but only because we cannot endure to be deprived of our national and individual rights and subjected to a process of intolerable oppression.

We wish to remain on the land of our fathers. We have a perfect and original right to remain without interruption or molestation. The treaties with us, and laws of the United States made in pursuance of treaties, guaranty our residence, and our privileges and secure us against intruders. Our only request is, that these treaties may be fulfilled, and these laws executed.

But if we are compelled to leave our country, we see nothing but ruin before us. The country west of the Arkansas territory is unknown to us. From what we can learn of it, we have no prepossessions in its favor. All the inviting parts of it, as we believe, are preoccupied by various Indian nations, to which it has been assigned. They would regard us as intruders, and look upon us with an evil eye. The far greater part of that region is, beyond all controversy, badly supplied with wood and water; and no Indian tribe can live as agriculturists without these articles. All our neighbors, in case of our removal, though crowded into our near vicinity, would speak a language totally different from ours, and practice different customs. The original possessors of that region are now wandering savages lurking for prey in the neighborhood. They have always been at war, and would be easily tempted to turn their arms against peaceful emigrants. Were the country to which we are urged much better than it is represented to be and were it free from the objections which we have made to it, still it is not the land of our birth, nor of our affections. It contains neither the scenes of our childhood, nor the graves of our fathers.

· · ·

In early 1832, thousands of Native Americans, led by the Sauk chief Black Hawk denounced an 1804 treaty, and moved from Iowa across the Mississippi into Illinois. They were soon attacked by U.S. 6th Infantry, and were eventually defeated, but Black Hawk remained defiant and here, in his surrender speech, explains why he and others fought and why their enemy should be "ashamed" of their actions.

Black Hawk's Surrender Speech (1832)[4]

You have taken me prisoner with all my warriors. I am much grieved, for I expected, if I did not defeat you, to hold out much longer, and give you more trouble before I surrendered. I tried hard to bring you into ambush, but your last general understands Indian fighting. The first one was not so wise. When I saw that I could not beat you by Indian fighting, I determined to rush on you, and fight you face to face. I fought hard. But your guns were well aimed. The bullets flew like birds in the air, and whizzed by our ears like the wind through the trees in the winter. My warriors fell around me; it began to look dismal. I saw my evil day at hand. The sun rose dim on us in the morning, and at night it sunk in a dark cloud, and looked like a ball of fire. That was the last sun that shone on Black Hawk. His heart is dead, and no longer beats quick in his bosom. He is now a prisoner to the white men; they will do with him as they wish. But he can stand torture, and is not afraid of death. He is no coward. Black Hawk is an Indian.

He has done nothing for which an Indian ought to be ashamed. He has fought for his countrymen, the squaws and papooses, against white men, who came, year after year, to cheat them and take away their lands. You know the cause of our making war. It is known to all white men. They ought to be ashamed of it. The white men despise the Indians, and drive them from their homes. But the Indians are not deceitful. The white men speak bad of the Indian, and look at him spitefully. But the Indian does not tell lies; Indians do not steal.

An Indian who is as bad as the white men, could not live in our nation; he would be put to death, and [be] eat[en] up by the wolves. The white men are bad school-masters; they carry false looks, and deal in false actions; they smile in the face of the poor Indian to cheat him; they shake them by the hand to gain their confidence, to make them drunk, to deceive them, and ruin our wives. We told them to let us alone; but they followed on and beset our paths, and they coiled themselves among us like the snake. They poisoned us by their touch. We were not safe. We lived in danger. We were becoming like them, hypocrites and liars, adulterers, lazy drones, all talkers, and no workers.

We looked up to the Great Spirit. We went to our great father. We were encouraged. His great council gave us fair words and big promises, but we got no satisfaction. Things were growing worse. There were no deer in the forest. The opossum and beaver were fled; the springs were drying up, and our squaws and papooses without victuals to keep them from starving; we called a great council and built a large fire. The spirit of our fathers arose and spoke to us to avenge our wrongs or die. . . . We set up the war-whoop, and dug up the tomahawk; our knives were ready, and the heart of Black Hawk swelled high in his bosom when he led his warriors to battle. He is satisfied. He will go to the world of spirits contented. He has done his duty. His father will meet him there, and commend him.

Black Hawk is a true Indian, and disdains to cry like a woman. He feels for his wife, his children and friends. But he does not care for himself. He cares for his nation and the Indians. They will suffer. He laments their fate. The white men do not scalp the head; but they do worse—they poison the heart, it is not pure with them. His countrymen will not be scalped, but they will, in a few years, become like the white men, so that you can't trust them, and there must be, as in the white settlements, nearly as many officers as men, to take care of them and keep them in order.

Farewell, my nation. Black Hawk tried to save you, and avenge your wrongs. He drank the blood of some of the whites. He has been taken prisoner, and his plans are stopped. He can do no more. He is near his end. His sun is setting, and he will rise no more. Farewell to Black Hawk.

• • •

In May 1838, federal militias started to round up Cherokees and move them into stockades in several southern states. They were then forced to march one thousand miles westward. Thousands of Cherokees died as a result of the removal. The journey became known as "The Trail of Tears" or "The Trail Where They Cried." Fifty years later, in 1890, Private John Burnett, who served in the mounted infantry, told his children his memories of the Trail of Tears, which he described as the "execution of the most brutal order in the History of American Warfare."

John G. Burnett, "The Cherokee Removal Through the Eyes of a Private Soldier" (December 11, 1890)[5]

This is my birthday, December 11, 1890. I am eighty years old today. I was born at Kings Iron Works in Sullivan County, Tennessee, December the 11th, 1810. I grew into manhood fishing in Beaver Creek and roaming through the forest hunting the deer and the wild boar and the timber wolf. Often spending weeks at a time in the solitary wilderness with no companions but my rifle, hunting knife, and a small hatchet that I carried in my belt in all of my wilderness wanderings.

On these long hunting trips I met and became acquainted with many of the Cherokee Indians, hunting with them by day and sleeping around their camp fires by night. I learned to speak their language, and they taught me the arts of trailing and building traps and snares. On one of my long hunts in the fall of 1829, I found a young Cherokee who had been shot by a roving band of hunters and who had eluded his pursuers and concealed himself under a shelving rock. Weak from loss of blood, the poor creature was unable to walk and almost famished for water. I carried him to a spring, bathed and bandaged the bullet wound, and built a shelter out of bark peeled from a dead chestnut tree. I nursed and protected him feeding him on chestnuts and toasted deer meat. When he was able to travel I accompanied him to the home of his people and remained so long that I was given up for lost. By this time I had become an expert rifleman and fairly good archer and a good trapper and spent most of my time in the forest in quest of game.

The removal of Cherokee Indians from their life long homes in the year of 1838 found me a young man in the prime of life and a Private soldier in the American Army. Being acquainted with many of the Indians and able to fluently speak their language, I was sent as interpreter into the Smoky Mountain Country in May, 1838, and witnessed the execution of the most brutal order in the History of American Warfare. I saw the helpless Cherokees arrested and dragged from their homes, and driven at the bayonet point into the stockades. And in the chill of a drizzling rain on an October morning I saw them loaded like cattle or sheep into six hundred and forty-five wagons and started toward the west.

One can never forget the sadness and solemnity of that morning. Chief John Ross led in prayer and when the bugle sounded and the wagons started rolling many of the children rose to their feet and waved their little hands goodbye to their mountain homes, knowing they were leaving them forever. Many of these helpless people did not have blankets and many of them had been driven from home barefooted.

On the morning of November the 17th we encountered a terrific sleet and snow storm with freezing temperatures and from that day until we reached the end of the fateful journey on March the 26th, 1839, the sufferings of the Cherokees were awful. The trail of the exiles was a trail of death. They had to sleep in the wagons and on the ground without fire. And I have known as many as twenty-two of them to die in one night of pneumonia due to ill treatment, cold, and exposure. Among this number was the beautiful Christian wife of Chief John Ross [Quatie Ross]. This noble hearted woman died a martyr to childhood, giving her only blanket for the protection of a sick child. She rode thinly clad through a blinding sleet and snow storm, developed pneumonia and died in the still hours of a bleak winter night, with her head resting on Lieutenant Greggs saddle blanket.

I made the long journey to the west with the Cherokees and did all that a Private soldier could do to alleviate their sufferings. When on guard duty at night I have many times walked my beat in my blouse in order that some sick child might have the warmth of my overcoat. I was on guard duty the night Mrs. Ross died. When relieved at midnight I did not retire, but remained around the wagon out of sympathy for Chief Ross, and at daylight was detailed by Captain McClellan to assist in the burial like the other unfortunates who died on the way. Her unconfined body was buried in a shallow grave by the roadside far from her native home, and the sorrowing Cavalcade moved on.

Being a young man, I mingled freely with the young women and girls. I have spent many pleasant hours with them when I was supposed to be under my blanket, and they have many times sung their mountain songs for me, this being all that they could do to repay my kindness. And with all my association with Indian girls from October 1829 to March 26th 1839, I did not meet one who was a moral prostitute. They are kind and tender hearted and many of them are beautiful.

The only trouble that I had with anybody on the entire journey to the west was a brutal teamster by the name of Ben McDonal, who was using his whip on an old feeble Cherokee to hasten him into the wagon. The sight of that old and nearly blind creature quivering under the lashes of a bull whip was too much for me. I attempted to stop McDonal and it ended in a personal encounter. He lashed me across the face, the wire tip on his whip cutting a bad gash in my cheek. The little hatchet that I had carried in my hunting days was in my belt and McDonal was carried unconscious from the scene.

I was placed under guard but Ensign Henry Bullock and Private Elkanah Millard had both witnessed the encounter. They gave Captain McClellan the facts and I was never brought to trial. Years later I met 2nd Lieutenant Riley and Ensign Bullock at Bristol at John Roberson's show, and Bullock jokingly reminded me that there was a case still pending against me before a court martial and wanted to know how much longer I was going to have the trial put off?

McDonal finally recovered, and in the year 1851, was running a boat out of Memphis, Tennessee.

The long painful journey to the west ended March 26th, 1839, with four-thousand silent graves reaching from the foothills of the Smoky Mountains to what is known as Indian territory in the West. And covetousness on the part of the white race was the cause of all that the Cherokees had to suffer. Ever since Ferdinand DeSoto made his journey through the Indian country in the year 1540, there had been a tradition of a rich gold mine somewhere in the Smoky Mountain Country, and I think the tradition was true. At a festival at Echota on Christmas night 1829, I danced and played with Indian girls who were wearing ornaments around their neck that looked like gold.

In the year 1828, a little Indian boy living on Ward creek had sold a gold nugget to a white trader, and that nugget sealed the doom of the Cherokees. In a short time the country was overrun with armed brigands claiming to be government agents, who paid no attention to the rights of the Indians who were the legal possessors of the country. Crimes were committed that were a disgrace to civilization. Men were shot in cold blood, lands were confiscated. Homes were burned and the inhabitants driven out by the gold-hungry brigands.

Chief Junaluska was personally acquainted with President Andrew Jackson. Junaluska had taken 500 of the flower of his Cherokee scouts and helped Jackson to win the battle of the Horse Shoe, leaving 33 of them dead on the field. And in that battle Junaluska had drove his Tomahawk through the skull of a Creek warrior, when the Creek had Jackson at his mercy.

Chief John Ross sent Junaluska as an envoy to plead with President Jackson for protection for his people, but Jackson's manner was cold and indifferent toward the rugged son of the forest who had saved his life. He met Junaluska, heard his plea but curtly said, "Sir, your audience is ended. There is nothing I can do for you." The doom of the Cherokee was sealed. Washington, D.C., had decreed that they must be driven West and their lands given to the white man, and in May 1838, an army of 4000 regulars, and 3000 volunteer soldiers under command of General Winfield Scott, marched into the Indian country and wrote the blackest chapter on the pages of American history.

Men working in the fields were arrested and driven to the stockades. Women were dragged from their homes by soldiers whose language they could not understand. Children were often separated from their parents and driven into the stockades with the sky for a blanket and the earth for a pillow. And often the old and infirm were prodded with bayonets to hasten them to the stockades.

In one home death had come during the night. A little sad-faced child had died and was lying on a bear skin couch and some women were preparing the little body for burial. All were arrested and driven out leaving the child in the cabin. I don't know who buried the body.

In another home was a frail Mother, apparently a widow and three small children, one just a baby. When told that she must go, the Mother gathered the children at her feet, prayed a humble prayer in her native tongue, patted the old family dog on the head, told the faithful creature goodbye, with a baby strapped on her back and leading a child with each hand started on her exile. But the task was too great for that frail Mother. A stroke of heart failure relieved her sufferings. She sunk and died with her baby on her back, and her other two children clinging to her hands.

Chief Junaluska who had saved President Jackson's life at the battle of Horse Shoe witnessed this scene, the tears gushing down his cheeks and lifting his cap he turned his face toward the heavens and said, "Oh my God, if I had known at the battle of the Horse Shoe what I know now, American history would have been differently written."

At this time, 1890, we are too near the removal of the Cherokees for our young people to fully understand the enormity of the crime that was committed against a helpless race. Truth is, the facts are being concealed from the young people of today. School children of today do not know that we are living on lands that were taken from a helpless race at the bayonet point to satisfy the white man's greed.

Future generations will read and condemn the act and I do hope posterity will remember that private soldiers like myself, and like the four Cherokees who were forced by General Scott to shoot an Indian Chief and his children, had to execute the orders of our superiors. We had no choice in the matter. . . .

However, murder is murder whether committed by the villain skulking in the dark or by uniformed men stepping to the strains of martial music.

Murder is murder, and somebody must answer. Somebody must explain the streams of blood that flowed in the Indian country in the summer of 1838. Somebody must explain the 4000 silent graves that mark the trail of the Cherokees to their exile. I wish I could forget it all, but the picture of 645 wagons lumbering over the frozen ground with their Cargo of suffering humanity still lingers in my memory.

Let the Historian of a future day tell the sad story with its sighs, its tears and dying groans. Let the great Judge of all the earth weigh our actions and reward us according to our work.

• • •

The lands of the Nez Percé stretched from Oregon to Idaho, but after the Gold Rush, in the 1860s, the federal government seized millions of acres of their lands, crowding them into a small part of their former lands. Chief Joseph led the resistance to the ongoing encroachment of Nez Percé lands in the 1870s, but his people came under fierce attack in 1877. Chief Joseph was forced to lead a retreat toward the Canadian border. He and his followers were defeated, some forty miles from the border, in Montana, on October 5, 1877. He was sent to the Indian Territories in Oklahoma, where he continued to speak out against the crimes of the U.S. government, as he did in a visit to Washington in 1879.

Two Statements by Chief Joseph of the Nez Percé (1877 and 1879)

CHIEF JOSEPH'S SURRENDER (OCTOBER 5, 1877)[6]

Tell General [Oliver Otis] Howard I know his heart. What he told me before, I have it in my heart. I am tired of fighting. Ta-hool-hool-shute is dead. Looking-Glass is dead. The old men are all dead. It is the young men who say "Yes" or "No." He who led on the young men is dead. It is cold, and we have no blankets; the little children are freezing to death. My people, some of them, have run away to the hills, and have no blankets, no food. No one knows where they are—perhaps freezing to death. I want to have time to look for my children, and see how many of them I can find. Maybe I shall find them among the dead. Hear me, my chiefs! I am tired; my heart is sick and sad. From where the sun now stands I will fight no more forever.

CHIEF JOSEPH RECOUNTS HIS TRIP TO WASHINGTON, D.C. (1879)[7]

At last I was granted permission to come to Washington and bring my friend Yellow Bull and our interpreter with me. I am glad I came. I have shaken hands with a good many friends, but there are some things I want to know which no one seems able to explain. I cannot understand how the Government sends a man out to fight us, as it did General [Nelson] Miles, and then breaks his word. Such a government has something wrong about it. I cannot understand why so many chiefs are allowed to talk so many different ways, and promise so many different things. I have seen the Great Father Chief (President [Rutherford B.] Hayes); the Next Great Chief (Secretary of the Interior [Carl Schurz]); the Commissioner Chief; the Law Chief; and many other law chiefs (Congressmen) and they all say they are my friends, and that I shall have justice, but while all their mouths talk right I do not understand why nothing is done for my people. I have heard talk and talk but nothing is done. Good words do not last long unless they amount to something. Words do not pay for my dead people. They do not pay for my country now overrun by white men. They do not protect my father's grave. They do not pay for my horses and cattle. Good words do not give me back my children. Good words will not make good the promise of your war chief, General Miles. Good words will not give my people good health and stop them from dying. Good words will not give my people a home where they can live in peace and take care of themselves. I am tired of talk that comes to nothing. It makes my heart sick when I remember all the good words and all the broken promises. There has been too much talking by men who had no right to talk. Too many misinterpretations have been made; too many misunderstandings have come up between the white men and the Indians. If the white man wants to live in peace with the Indian he can live in peace. There need be no trouble. Treat all men alike. Give them the same laws. Give them all an even chance to live and grow. All men were made by the same Great Spirit Chief. They are all brothers. The earth is the mother of all people, and all people should have equal rights upon it. You might as well expect all rivers to run backward as that any man who was born a free man should be contented penned up and denied liberty to go where he pleases. If you tie a horse to a stake, do you expect he will grow fat? If you pen an Indian up on a small spot of earth and compel him to stay there, he will not be contented nor will he grow and prosper. I have asked some of the Great White Chiefs where they get their authority to say to the Indian that he shall stay in one place, while he sees white men going where they please. They cannot tell me.

I only ask of the Government to be treated as all other men are treated. If I cannot go to my own home, let me have a home in a country where my people will not die so fast. I would like to go to Bitter Root Valley. There my people would be happy; where they are now they are dying. Three have died since I left my camp to come to Washington.

When I think of our condition, my heart is heavy. I see men of my own race treated as outlaws and driven from country to country, or shot down like animals.

I know that my race must change. We cannot hold our own with the white men as we are. We only ask an even chance to live as other men live. We ask to be recognized as men. We ask that the same law shall work alike on all men. If an Indian breaks the law, punish him by the law. If a white man breaks the law, punish him also.

Let me be a free man, free to travel, free to stop, free to work, free to trade where I choose, free to choose my own teachers, free to follow the religion of my fathers, free to talk, think and act for myself—and I will obey every law or submit to the penalty.

Whenever the white man treats the Indian as they treat each other then we shall have no more wars. We shall be all alike—brothers of one father and mother, with one sky above us and one country around us and one government for all. Then the Great Spirit Chief who rules above will smile upon this land and send rain to wash out the bloody spots made by brothers' hands upon the face of the earth. For this time the Indian race is waiting and praying. I hope no more groans of wounded men and women will ever go to the ear of the Great Spirit Chief above, and that all people may be one people.

Hin-mah-too-yah-lat-kekht has spoken for his people.

• • •

One of the worst massacres of Native Americans occurred on December 29, 1890, and was, as with so many other massacres, reported with indifference and even praised. The massacre followed soon after the killing of the Indian leader Sitting Bull. After his death, the *Saturday Pioneer* in Aberdeen, South Dakota, proclaimed, "The Whites, by law of conquest, by justice of civilization, are masters of the American continent . . . and the best safety of the frontier settlers will be secured by the total annihilation of the few remaining Indians." The editor of the paper was L. Frank Baum, the author of *The Wonderful Wizard of Oz*. This account of the Wounded Knee Massacre is from the Oglala Sioux leader Black Elk, from his oral testimony published as *Black Elk Speaks*.

Black Elk, "The End of the Dream" (1932)[8]

After the soldiers marched away, Red Crow and I started back toward Pine Ridge together, and I took the little baby that I told you about. Red Crow had one too.

We were going back to Pine Ridge, because we thought there was peace back home; but it was not so. While we were gone, there was a fight around the Agency, and our people had all gone away. They had gone away so fast that they left all the tepees standing.

It was nearly dark when we passed north of Pine Ridge where the hospital is now, and some soldiers shot at us, but did not hit us. We rode into the camp, and it was all empty. We were very hungry because we had not eaten anything since early morning, so we peeped into the tepees until we saw where there was a pot with papa [dried meat] cooked in it. We sat down in there and began to eat. While we were doing this, the soldiers shot at the tepee, and a bullet struck right between Red Crow and me. It threw dust in the soup, but we kept right on eating until we had our fill. Then we took the babies and got on our horses and rode away. If that bullet had only killed me, then I could have died with papa in my mouth.

The people had fled down Clay Creek, and we followed their trail. It was dark now, and late in the night we came to where they were camped without any tepees. They were just sitting by little fires, and the snow was beginning to blow. We rode in among them and I heard my mother's voice. She was singing a death song for me, because she felt sure I had died over there. She was so glad to see me that she cried and cried.

Women who had milk fed the little babies that Red Crow and I brought with us.

I think nobody but the little children slept any that night. The snow blew and we had no tepees.

When it was getting light, a war party went out and I went along; but this time I took a gun with me. When I started out the day before to Wounded Knee, I took only my sacred bow, which was not made to shoot with; because I was a little in doubt about the Wanekia religion at that time, and I did not really want to kill anybody because of it.

But I did not feel like that anymore. After what I had seen over there, I wanted revenge; I wanted to kill.

We crossed White Clay Creek and followed it up, keeping on the west side. Soon we could hear many guns going off. So we struck west, following a ridge to where the fight was. It was close to the Mission, and there are many bullets in the Mission yet.

From this ridge we could see that the Lakotas were on both sides of the creek and were shooting at soldiers who were coming down the creek. As we looked down, we saw a little ravine, and across this was a big hill. We crossed and rode up the hillside.

They were fighting right there, and a Lakota cried to me: "Black Elk, this is the kind of a day in which to do something great!" I answered: "How!"

Then I got off my horse and rubbed earth on myself, to show the Powers that I was nothing without their help. Then I took my rifle, got on my horse and galloped up to the top of the hill. Right below me the soldiers were shooting, and my people called out to me not to go down there; that there were some good shots among the soldiers and I should get killed for nothing.

But I remembered my great vision, the part where the geese of the north appeared. I depended upon their power. Stretching out my arms with my gun in the right hand, like a goose soaring when it flies low to turn in a change of weather, I made the sound the geese make—br-r-r-p, br-r-r-p, br-r-r-p; and, doing this, I charged. The soldiers saw, and began shooting fast at me. I kept right on with my buckskin running, shot in their faces when I was near, then swung wide and rode back up the hill.

All this time the bullets were buzzing around me and I was not touched. I was not even afraid. It was like being in a dream about shooting. But just as I had reached the very top of the hill, suddenly it was like waking up, and I was afraid. I dropped my arms and quit making the goose cry. Just as I did this, I felt something strike my belt as though some one had hit me there with the back of an ax. I nearly fell out of my saddle, but I managed to hold on, and rode over the hill.

An old man by the name of Protector was there, and he ran up and held me, for now I was falling off my horse. I will show you where the bullet struck me sidewise across the belly here (showing a long deep scar on the abdomen). My insides were coming out. Protector tore up a blanket in strips and bound it around me so that my insides would stay in. By now I was crazy to kill, and I said to Protector: "Help me on my horse! Let me go over there. It is a good day to die, so I will go over there!" But Protector said: "No, young nephew! You must not die today. That would be foolish. Your people need you. There may be a better day to die." He lifted me into my saddle and led my horse away down hill. Then I began to feel very sick.

By now it looked as though the soldiers would be wiped out, and the Lakotas were fighting harder; but I heard that, after I left, the black Wasichu soldiers came, and the Lakotas had to retreat.

There were many of our children in the Mission, and the sisters and priests were taking care of them. I heard there were sisters and priests right in the battle helping wounded people and praying.

There was a man by the name of Little Soldier who took charge of me and brought me to where our people were camped. While we were over at the Mission Fight, they had fled to the O-ona-gazhee and were camped on top of it where the women and children would be safe from soldiers. Old Hollow Horn was there. He was a very powerful bear medicine man, and he came over to heal my wound. In three days I could walk, but I kept a piece of blanket tied around my belly.

It was now nearly the middle of the Moon of Frost in the Tepee (January). We heard that soldiers were on Smoky Earth River and were coming to attack us in the O-ona-gazhee. They were near Black Feather's place. So a party of about sixty of us started on the war-path to find them. My mother tried to keep me at home, because, although I could walk and ride a horse, my wound was not all healed yet. But I would not stay; for, after what I had seen at Wounded Knee, I wanted a chance to kill soldiers.

We rode down Grass Creek to Smoky Earth, and crossed, riding down stream. Soon from the top of a little hill we saw wagons and cavalry guarding them. The soldiers were making a corral of their wagons and getting ready to fight. We got off our horses and went behind some hills to a little knoll, where we crept up to look at the camp. Some soldiers were bringing harnessed horses down to a little creek to water, and I said to the others: "If you will stay here and shoot at the soldiers, I will charge over there and get some good horses." They knew of my power, so they did this, and I charged on my buckskin while the others kept shooting. I got seven of the horses; but when I started back with these, all the soldiers saw me and began shooting. They killed two of my horses, but I brought five back safe and was not hit. When I was out of range, I caught up a fine bald-faced bay and turned my buckskin loose. Then I drove the others back to our party.

By now more cavalry were coming up the river, a big bunch of them, and there was some hard fighting for a while, because there were not enough of us. We were fighting and retreating, and all at once I saw Red Willow on foot running. He called to me: "Cousin, my horse is killed!" So I caught up a soldier's horse that was dragging a rope and brought it to Red Willow while the soldiers were shooting fast at me. Just then, for a little while, I was a Wanekia myself. In this fight Long Bear and another man, whose name I have forgotten, were badly wounded; but we saved them and carried them along with us. The soldiers did not follow us far into the Badlands, and when it was night we rode back with our wounded to the O-ona-gazhee.

We wanted a much bigger war-party so that we could meet the soldiers and get revenge. But this was hard, because the people were not all of the same mind, and they were hungry and cold. We had a meeting there, and were all ready to go out with more warriors, when Afraid-of-His-Horses came over from Pine Ridge to make peace with Red Cloud, who was with us there.

Our party wanted to go out and fight anyway, but Red Cloud made a speech to us something like this: "Brothers, this is a very hard winter. The women and children are starving and freezing. If this were summer, I would say to keep on fighting to the end. But we cannot do this. We must think of the women and children and that it is very bad for them. So we must make peace, and I will see that nobody is hurt by the soldiers."

The people agreed to this, for it was true. So we broke camp next day and went down from the O-ona-gazhee to Pine Ridge, and many, many Lakotas were already there. Also, there were many, many soldiers. They stood in two lines with their guns held in front of them as we went through to where we camped.

And so it was all over.

I did not know then how much was ended. When I look back now from this high hill of my old age, I can still see the butchered women and children lying heaped and scattered all along the crooked gulch as plain as when I saw them with eyes still young. And I can see that something else died there in the bloody mud, and was buried in the blizzard. A people's dream died there. It was a beautiful dream.

And I, to whom so great a vision was given in my youth,—you see me now a pitiful old man who has done nothing, for the nation's hoop is broken and scattered. There is no center any longer, and the sacred tree is dead.

CHAPTER EIGHT

The War on Mexico

The Diary of Colonel Ethan Allen Hitchcock
(June 30, 1845 to March 26, 1846)

Miguel Barragan, Dispatch on Texas Colonists (October 31, 1835)

Juan Soto, Desertion Handbill (June 6, 1847)

Frederick Douglass, Address to the New England Convention
(May 31, 1849)

North Star Editorial, "The War with Mexico" (January 21, 1848)

Henry David Thoreau, *Civil Disobedience* (1849)

The annexation of Texas, which in 1836 declared its independence from Mexico (with support from the U.S. government), paved the way for the war against Mexico. President James Polk, a Democrat and expansionist elected in 1844, confided to his secretary of the navy on the night of his inauguration in early 1845 that one of his main objectives as president was the acquisition of California, which was part of Mexico.

The *Washington Union*, a newspaper that represented the position of the Democratic Party, wrote: "Let the great measure of annexation be accomplished. . . . For who can arrest the torrents that will pour onward to the West? The road to California will be open to us." In the summer of 1845, John O'Sullivan, editor of the *Democratic Review*, used a phrase that would become famous, saying it was "Our manifest destiny to overspread the continent allotted by providence for the free development of our yearly multiplying millions." Yes, "manifest destiny."

All that was missing in the plan was an incident. A patrol of American troops was sent into territory between the Nueces River and the Rio Grande River that the Mexicans claimed was their land. The patrol was wiped out by Mexican forces. In response, Polk declared, falsely, that "Mexico . . . has invaded our territory and shed American blood upon the American soil."

Even before the incident, he had written in his diary that the United States had "ample cause for war." But Polk immediately asked Congress for a declaration of war. Congress rushed to approve, spending barely thirty minutes discussing the issue.

The Whig Party, which elected Abraham Lincoln to Congress in 1846, after the war had begun, was presumably against the war, but not against expansion.

So they voted overwhelmingly for the war resolution. In Congress, Lincoln challenged Polk with his "spot resolutions," asking Polk to specify the exact spot where American blood was shed "on American soil." But, like the other Whigs, he would not try to end the war by stopping funds. The party voted again and again to appropriate the men and materials for the war.

There was resistance to the war by those Americans who saw expansion as a way of creating more slave territory. But that resistance broadened as the invasion of Mexico became a more and more bloody affair, accompanied by the bombardment of neighborhoods and the killing of women and children. The death toll of American soldiers grew. Volunteer regiments from Virginia, Mississippi, and North Carolina mutinied in northern Mexico against their officers. At least nine thousand soldiers deserted during the war.

Veterans returning home, desperate for money, sold to speculators the land warrants given by the government. The New York *Commercial Advertiser* pointed to the experience of the Revolutionary War, in which "immense fortunes were made out of the poor soldiers who shed their blood," and said the same thing was happening in the war against Mexico.

Mexico surrendered, and was paid $15 million by the U.S. government for the taking of New Mexico and California. A Whig newspaper concluded, "We take nothing by conquest. . . . Thank God."

• • •

In his diary, Colonel Ethan Allen Hitchcock, in the 3rd Infantry Regiment, challenges, as an on-the-scene witness, the rhetoric of politicians who supported the war.

The Diary of Colonel Ethan Allen Hitchcock (June 30, 1845 to March 26, 1846)[1]

Fort Jessup, La., June 30, 1845. Orders came last evening by express from Washington City directing General [Zachary] Taylor to move without any delay to some point on the coast near the Sabine or elsewhere, and as soon as he shall hear of the acceptance by the Texas convention of the annexation resolutions of our Congress he is immediately to proceed with his whole command to the extreme western border of Texas and take up a position on the banks of or near the Rio Grande, and he is to expel any armed force of Mexicans who may cross that river. [William W. S.] Bliss read the orders to me last evening hastily at tattoo. I have scarcely slept a wink, thinking of the needful preparations. I am now noting [writing] at reveille by candlelight and waiting the signal for muster. . . .

Violence leads to violence, and if this movement of ours does not lead to others and bloodshed, I am much mistaken. . . .

29th Aug. Received last evening . . . a letter from Captain Casey and a map of Texas from the Quarter-master-General's office, the latter being the one prepared by Lieutenant Emory; but it has added to it a distinct boundary mark to the Rio Grande. Our people ought to be damned for their impudent arrogance and domineering presumption! It is enough to make atheists of us all to see such wickedness in the world, whether punished or unpunished. . . .

8th Sept. . . . General Taylor talks, whether sincerely or not, of going to the Rio Grande. This is singular language from one who originally and till very lately denounced annexation as both injudicious in policy and wicked in fact! The "claim," so-called, of the Texans to the Rio Grande, is without foundation. The argument of Mr. [Robert J.] Walker passes by the treaty of 1819, by which the United States gave up all west and south of the Sabine, either saying nothing about it or presuming that it was not valid. Yet we took possession of Florida under that treaty. The truth is that the limits of old Louisiana were never settled until by that treaty, so that the treaty of 1819 was really only a treaty of limits or boundary so far as Louisiana was concerned; and to say that the Senate, or treaty-making power, has no authority to determine a question of boundary, is preposterous. Louisiana had no fixed boundaries when Louis XV ceded it to Charles III of Spain and none when it was ceded back to France (to Napoleon), and continued to have none when it was purchased by the United States as much a foreign country as Yucatan, and we have no right whatever to go beyond the treaty.

As for Texas, her original limit was the Nueces and the hills ranging north from its sources, and she has never conquered, possessed, or exercised dominion west of the Nueces, except that a small smuggling company at this place, living here by Mexican sufferance, if not under Mexican protection, has chosen to call itself Texan, and some of the inhabitants have chosen to call themselves Texans. . . .

C.C. [Corpus Christi], Sept. 20. . . . He [Taylor] seems quite to have lost all respect for Mexicans' rights and willing to be an instrument of Mr. Polk for pushing our boundary as far west as possible. When I told him that, if he suggested a movement (which he told me he intended), Mr. Polk would seize upon it and throw the responsibility on him, he at once said he would take it, and added that if the President instructed him to use his discretion, he would ask no orders, but would go upon the Rio Grande as soon as he could get transportation. I think the General wants an additional brevet [medal], and would strain a point to get it. . . .

2nd Nov. Newspapers all seem to indicate that Mexico will make no movement, and the government is magnanimously bent on taking advantage of it to insist upon "our claim" as far as the Rio Grande. I hold this to be monstrous and abominable. But now, I see, the United States of America, as a people, are undergoing changes in character, and the real status and principles for which our forefathers fought are fast being lost sight of. If I could by any decent means get a living in retirement, I would abandon a government which I think corrupted by both ambition and avarice to the last degree. . . .

March 23rd. As to the right of this movement, I have said from the first that the United States are the aggressors. We have outraged the Mexican government and people by an arrogance and presumption that deserve to be punished. For ten years we have been encroaching on Mexico and insulting her. . . . Her people I consider a simple, well disposed, pastoral race, no way inclined to savage usages. . . .

26th March. . . . We have not one particle of right to be here.

Our force is altogether too small for the accomplishment of its errand. It looks as if the government sent a small force on purpose to bring on a war, so as to have a pretext for taking California and as much of this country as it chooses; for, whatever becomes of this army, there it no doubt of a war between the United States and Mexico.

• • •

In an 1819 treaty with Spain, the United States had given up any claim to Texas. But this did not stop politicians in Washington from trying to bribe Mexican officials to sell Texas, and then seeking to colonize the state and annex it. Mexico tried to stop the flow of U.S. immigration into Texas, but colonists continued to come to the state, setting the stage for a conflict over the state's status and for the eventual war against Mexico. Here is a dispatch describing the treatment of Mexicans by the Texas colonists, sent by President Miguel Barragan of Mexico to all Mexican military commanders and governors via his secretary José María Tornel.

Miguel Barragan, Dispatch on Texas Colonists (October 31, 1835)[2]

For a long time the ungrateful Texas colonists have made fun of the national laws of Mexico; disregarding the fact that Mexico gave them a generous welcome and kept them close to our bosom; dispensing to them the same—and even more— benefits than to our own sons.

Every time we have had internal agitation they have thought the Republic weak and impotent to control their excesses. These have multiplied intensely, producing insults again and again against the whole of our National Arms.

When order was finally established in the interior, they hypocritically pretended a bond they did not feel to the institutions of their Stepmother.

Given the slightest opportunity, they returned to their aggressions, throwing insults at our customs employees and even fighting the small detachments which protected them.

To the Texas colonists, the word MEXICAN is, and has been, an execrable word. There has been no insult or violation that our countrymen have not suffered, including being jailed as "foreigners" in their own country.

The Texas colonies have been considered, for a long time, as general quarters for the enemies of the Nation; where all the bums and adventurers from the whole world have been gathered to revolt against the generous nation which has tolerated their insolence.

All this has reached the point where the flag of rebellion has been raised; the Texans aspiring shamelessly to take over one of the most precious parts of our land. Accomplices to this wickedness are adventurers from the State of Louisiana who foment disturbances and give necessary support to the rebels. The civilized world will not delay in pronouncing the judgment they deserve for this infamous and detestable conduct. The Supreme Government knows its duties and knows how to execute them.

But our brave soldiers, so many times victorious over outside and inside enemies, are already marching to maintain in Texas our flag and honor, to punish the traitors and to reward those who remain faithful to their oaths, duties and obligations. In this national war, so unjustly provoked, justice and power are on our side; on the rebel's side crime, usurpation and the torch of discord they intend to use against our Republic in order to humble and vilify it.

Their ideas will be frustrated; our Nation is and will be what it ought to be— a great and glorious country when our laws, property and rights are being violently attacked. Your Excellencies, make a call to the troops under your command that they will produce brilliant testaments of their invincibility in this foreign war as they were in Tepeaca, Cordoba, Azcapozalco, in the Huerta, in Veracruz and Tampico de Tamaulipas.

The Government believes that not one Mexican worthy of his country will favor the treason of foreign rebels, but that if such a misfortunate exists, the power and duty of punishing him lies in your hands.

God and Liberty!

• • •

During the Mexican War, a group of Irish soldiers serving in the U.S. military switched sides to join the Mexican army and take up arms against U.S. expansion into Mexican soil. They were called San Patricio's (St. Patrick's) Battalion. Here is a leaflet they printed explaining their cause, and appealing particularly to Catholics not to fight against others who shared their religion. The unusual capitalization is faithful to the original handbill.

Juan Soto, Desertion Handbill (June 6, 1847)[3]

CATHOLIC Irish, Frenchmen and German of the invading army!

The american nation makes a most unjust war to the mexicans, and has taken all of you as an instrument of their iniquity. You must not fight against a religious people, nor should you be seen in the ranks of those who proclaim slavery of mankind as a constitutive principle. The religious man, he who possesses greatness of mind, must always fight for liberty and liberty is not on the side of those who establish differences in mankind, making an unhappy and innocent people, earn the bread of slavery. Liberty is not on the part of those who desire to be the lords of the world, robbing properties and territories which do not belong to them and shedding so much blood in order to accomplish their views, views in open war with the principles of our holy religion. The mexican people raises every where in order to wage an insurrectionary war, and that american army however large it may become, shall find here a grave. The mexican people wishes not to shed the blood of those who profess their own religion, and I, in the name of inhabitants of the state of Vera Cruz invite you to abandon those ranks to which you must not belong. I have given the necessary orders, so that, should you abandon them, you may be respected in all the towns and places of the states where you happen to go, and all the requisite assistance shall be given to all, till brought before me. Many of your former companions fight now content in our ranks. After this war is over, the magnanimous and generous mexican nation will duly appreciate the services rendered, and you shall remain with us, cultivating our fertile lands. Catholic Irish, French and German!! Long live Liberty!! Long live our holy Religion!!

• • •

In 1829, Mexico abolished slavery, threatening the power of slaveholders who wanted to expand the territory in which slaves could be legally held. For the next two decades a battle would be fought over the status of Texas. In a speech in Belfast, Ireland, in 1846, the fiery abolitionist Frederick Douglass described the U.S. annexation of Texas as a "conspiracy from beginning to end—a most deep and skillfully devised conspiracy—for the purpose of upholding and sustaining one of the darkest and foulest crimes ever committed by man." In this speech, delivered in Boston in 1849, Douglass, speaking to other abolitionists, calls for forcible resistance against the invasion of Mexico—and against slave owners in the South.

Frederick Douglass, Address to the New England Convention (May 31, 1849)[4]

You know as well as I do, that Faneuil Hall has resounded with echoing applause of a denunciation of the Mexican war, as a murderous war—as a war against the free States—as a war against freedom, against the negro, and against the interests of the workingman of this country—and as a means of extending that great evil and damning curse, negro slavery. (Immense applause.) Why may not the oppressed say, when an oppressor is dead, either by disease or by the hand of the foeman on the battlefield, that there is one the less of his oppressors left on earth? For my part, I would not care if, tomorrow, I should hear of the death of every man who engaged in that bloody war in Mexico, and that every man had met the fate he went there to perpetrate upon unoffending Mexicans. (Applause and hisses.)

A word more. There are three millions of slaves in this land, held by the U.S. government, under the sanction of the American Constitution, with all the compromises and guaranties contained in that instrument in favor of the slave system. Among those guaranties and compromises is one by which you, the citizens of Boston, have sworn, before God, that three millions of slaves shall be slaves or die—that your swords and bayonets and arms shall, at any time at the bidding of the slaveholder, through the legal magistrate or governor of a slave State, be at his service in putting down the slaves. With eighteen millions of freemen standing upon the quivering hearts of three millions of slaves, my sympathies, of course, must be with the oppressed. I am among them, and you are treading them beneath your feet. The weight of your influence, numbers, political combinations and religious organizations, and the power of your arms, rest heavily upon them, and serve at this moment to keep them in their chains. When I consider their condition—the history of the American people—how they bared their bosoms to the storm of British artillery, in order to resist simply a three-penny tea tax, and to assert their independence of the mother country—I say, in view of these things, I should welcome the intelligence tomorrow, should it come, that the slaves had risen in the South, and that the sable arms which had been engaged in beautifying and adorning the South, were engaged in spreading death and devastation there. (Marked sensation.) There is a state of war at the South, at this moment. The slaveholder is waging a war of aggression on the oppressed. The slaves are now under his feet. Why, you welcomed the intelligence from France, that Louis Philippe had been barricaded in Paris—you threw up your caps in honor of the victory achieved by

Republicanism over Royalty—you shouted aloud—"Long live the republic!"—and joined heartily in the watchword of "Liberty, Equality, Fraternity"—and should you not hail, with equal pleasure, the tidings from the South, that the slaves had risen, and achieved for himself, against the iron-hearted slaveholder, what the republicans of France achieved against the royalists of France? (Great applause, and some hissing.)

• • •

Here the *North Star*, the abolitionist newspaper edited in Rochester, New York, by Frederick Douglass, argues the case against the war on Mexico, highlighting not only the question of slavery, but the class dimension of the war, as well.

North Star Editorial, "The War with Mexico" (January 21, 1848)[5]

From aught that appears in the present position and movements of the executive and cabinet—the proceedings of either branch of the national Congress,—the several State Legislatures, North and South—the spirit of the public press—the conduct of leading men, and the general views and feelings of the people of the United States at large, slight hope can rationally be predicated of a very speedy termination of the present disgraceful, cruel, and iniquitous war with our sister republic. Mexico seems a doomed victim to Anglo Saxon cupidity and love of dominion. The determination of our slaveholding President to prosecute the war, and the probability of his success in wringing from the people men and money to carry it on, is made evident, rather than doubtful, by the puny opposition arrayed against him. No politician of any considerable distinction or eminence, seems willing to hazard his popularity with his party, or stem the fierce current of executive influence, by an open and unqualified disapprobation of the war. None seem willing to take their stand for peace at all risks; and all seem willing that the war should be carried on, in some form or other. If any oppose the President's demands, it is not because they hate the war, but for want of information as to the aims and objects of the war. The boldest declaration on this point is that of Hon. John P. Hale, which is to the effect that he will not vote a single dollar to the President for carrying on the war, until he shall be fully informed of the purposes and objects of the war. Mr. Hale knows, as well as the President can inform him, for what the war is waged; and yet he accompanies his declaration with that prudent proviso. This shows how deep seated and strongly bulwarked is the evil against which we contend. The boldest dare not fully grapple with it.

Meanwhile, "the plot thickens"—the evil spreads. Large demands are made on the national treasury (to wit: the poor man's pockets)[.] Eloquent and patriotic speeches are made in the Senate, House of Representatives and State Assemblies: Whig as well as Democratic governors stand stoutly up for the war: experienced and hoary-headed statesmen tax their declining strength and ingenuity in devising ways and means for advancing the infernal work: recruiting sergeants and corporals perambulate the land in search of victims for the sword and food for powder. Wherever there is a sink of iniquity, or a den of pollution, these buzzards may be found in search of their filthy prey. They dive into the rum shop, and gambling house, and other sinks too infamous to name, with a swine-like avidity, in pursuit of degraded men to vindicate the insulted honor of our Christian country. Military chieftains and heroes multiply, and towering high above the level of common men, are glorified, if not deified, by the people. The whole nation seems to "wonder after these (bloody) beasts." Grasping ambition, tyrannic usurpation, atrocious aggression, cruel and haughty pride, spread, and pervade the land. The curse is upon us. The plague is abroad. No part of the country can claim entire exemption from its evils. They may be seen as well in the State of New York, as in South Carolina; on the Penobscot, as on the Sabine. The people appear to be completely in the hands of office seekers, demagogues, and political gamblers. Within the bewildering meshes of their political nets, they are worried, confused, and confounded, so that a general outcry is heard—"Vigorous prosecution of the war!"—"Mexico must be humbled!"—"Conquer a peace!"—"Indemnity!"—"War forced upon us!"— "National honor!"—"The whole of Mexico!"—"Our destiny!"—"This continent!"—"Anglo Saxon blood!"—"More territory!"—"Free institutions!"— "Our country!" till it seems indeed "that justice has fled to brutish beasts, and men have lost their reason." The taste of human blood and the smell of powder seem to have extinguished the senses, seared the conscience, and subverted the reason of the people to a degree that may well induce the gloomy apprehension that our nation has fully entered on her downward career, and yielded herself up to the revolting idea of battle and blood. "Fire and sword," are now the choice of our young republic. The loss of thousands of her own men, and the slaughter of tens of thousands of the sons and daughters of Mexico, have rather given edge than dullness to our appetite for fiery conflict and plunder. The civilization of the age, the voice of the world, the sacredness of human life, the tremendous expense, the dangers, hardships, and the deep disgrace which must forever attach to our inhuman course, seem to oppose no availing check to the mad spirit of proud ambition, blood, and carnage, let loose in the land.

We have no preference for parties, regarding this slaveholding crusade. The one is as bad as the other. The friends of peace have nothing to hope from either.

The Democrats claim the credit of commencing, and the Whigs monopolize the glory of voting supplies and carrying on the war; branding the war as dishonorably commenced, yet boldly persisting in pressing it on. If we have any preference of two such parties, that preference inclines to the one whose practice, though wicked, most accords with its professions. We know where to find the so called Democrats. They are the accustomed panderers to slaveholders: nothing is either too mean, too dirty, or infamous for them, when commanded by the merciless man stealers of our country. No one expects any thing honorable or decent from that party, touching human rights. They annexed Texas under the plea of extending the area of freedom. They elected James K. Polk, the slaveholder, as the friend of freedom; and they have backed him up in his Presidential falsehoods. They have used their utmost endeavors to crush the right of speech, abridge the right of petition, and to perpetuate the enslavement of the colored people of this country. But we do not intend to go into any examination of parties just now. That we shall have frequent opportunities of doing hereafter. We wish merely to give our readers a general portrait of the present aspect of our country in regard to the Mexican war, its designs, and its results, as they have thus far transpired.

Of the settled determination to prosecute the war, there can be no doubt: Polk has avowed it; his organs have published it; his supporters have rallied round him; all their actions bend in that direction; and every effort is made to establish their purpose firmly in the hearts of the people, and to harden their hearts for the conflict. All danger must be defied; all suffering despised; all honor eschewed; all mercy dried up; and all the better promptings of the human soul blunted, silenced and repudiated, while all the furies of hell are invoked to guide our hired assassins,— our man-killing machines,—now in and out of Mexico, to the infernal consummation. Qualities of head and heart, principles and maxims, counsels and warnings, which once commanded respect, and secured a nation's reverence, must all now be scouted; sense of decency must be utterly drowned: age nor sex must exercise any humanizing effect upon our gallant soldiers, or restrain their satanic designs. The groans of slaughtered men, the screams of violated women, and the cries of orphan children, must bring no throb of pity from our national heart, but must rather serve as music to inspire our gallant troops to deeds of atrocious cruelty, lust, and blood. The work is thus laid out, commenced, and is to be continued. Where it will end is known only to the Great Ruler of the Universe; but where the responsibility rests, and upon whom retribution will fall, is sure and certain.

In watching the effects of the war spirit, prominent among them, will be seen, not only the subversion of the great principles of Christian morality, but the most horrid blasphemy.

While traveling from Rochester to Victor, a few days ago, we listened to a conversation between two persons of apparent gentility and intelligence, on the subject of the United States' war against Mexico. A wide difference of opinion appeared between them; the one contending for the rightfulness of the war, and the other against it. The main argument in favor of the war was the meanness and wickedness of the Mexican people; and, to cap the climax, he gave it as his solemn conviction, that the hand of the Lord was in the work! that the cup of Mexican iniquity was full; and that God was now making use of the Anglo Saxon race as a rod to chastise them! The effect of this religious outburst was to stun his opponent into silence: he seemed speechless; the ground was too high and holy for him; he did not dare reply to it; and thus the conversation ended. When men charge their sins upon God, argument is idle; rebuke alone is needful; and the poor man, lacking the moral courage to do this, sat silent.

Here, then, we have religion coupled with our murderous designs. We are, in the hands of the great God, a rod to chastise this rebellious people! What say our evangelical clergy to this blasphemy? That clergy seem as silent as the grave; and their silence is the greatest sanction of the crime. They have seen the blood of the innocent poured out like water, and are dumb; they have seen the truth trampled in the dust—right sought by pursuing the wrong—peace sought by prosecuting the war—honor sought by dishonorable means,—and have not raised a whisper against it: they float down with the multitude in the filthy current of crime, and are hand in hand with the guilty. Had the pulpit been faithful, we might have been saved from this withering curse. We sometimes fear, that now our case as a nation is hopeless. May God grant otherwise! Our nation seems resolved to rush on in her wicked career, though the road be ditched with human blood, and paved with human skulls. Well, be it so. But, humble as we are, and unavailing as our voice may be, we wish to warn our fellow countrymen, that they may follow the course which they have marked out for themselves; no barrier may be sufficient to obstruct them; they may accomplish all they desire; Mexico may fall before them; she may be conquered and subdued; her government may be annihilated— her name among the great sisterhood of nations blotted out; her separate existence annihilated; her rights and powers usurped; her people put under the iron arm of a military despotism, and reduced to a condition little better than that endured by the Saxons when vanquished by their Norman invaders; but, so sure as there is a God of justice, we shall not go unpunished; the penalty is certain; we cannot escape; a terrible retribution awaits us. We beseech our countrymen to leave off this horrid conflict, abandon their murderous plans, and forsake the way of blood. Peradventure our country may yet be saved. Let the press, the pulpit, the church, the people at large, unite at once; and let petitions flood the halls of Congress by the million, asking for the instant recall of our forces from Mexico. This may not save us, but it is our only hope.

• • •

One of those who protested the war on Mexico was Henry David Thoreau, who was jailed for refusing to pay a poll tax, on the ground that the tax supported the war effort and, therefore, the extension of slavery.

Henry David Thoreau, *Civil Disobedience* (1849)[6]

I heartily accept the motto,—"That government is best which governs least"; and I should like to see it acted up to more rapidly and systematically. Carried out, it finally amounts to this, which also I believe,—"That government is best which governs not at all"; and when men are prepared for it, that will be the kind of government which they will have. Government is at best but an expedient; but most governments are usually, and all governments are sometimes, inexpedient. The objections which have been brought against a standing army, and they are many and weighty, and deserve to prevail, may also at last be brought against a standing government. The standing army is only an arm of the standing government. The government itself, which is only the mode which the people have chosen to execute their will, is equally liable to be abused and perverted before the people can act through it. Witness the present Mexican war, the work of comparatively a few individuals using the standing government as their tool; for, in the outset, the people would not have consented to this measure. . . .

After all, the practical reason why, when the power is once in the hands of the people, a majority are permitted, and for a long period continue, to rule, is not because they are most likely to be in the right, nor because this seems fairest to the minority, but because they are physically the strongest. But a government in which the majority rule in all cases cannot be based on justice, even as far as men understand it. Can there not be a government in which majorities do not virtually decide right and wrong, but conscience?—in which majorities decide only those questions to which the rule of expediency is applicable? Must the citizen ever for a moment, or in the least degree, resign his conscience to the legislator? Why has every man a conscience, then? I think that we should be men first, and subjects afterward. It is not desirable to cultivate a respect for the law, so much as for the right. The only obligation which I have a right to assume is to do at any time what I think right. It is truly enough said that a corporation has no conscience; but a corporation of conscientious men is a corporation with a conscience. Law never made men a whit more just; and, by means of their respect for it, even the well-disposed are daily made the agents of injustice. A common and natural result of an undue respect for law is, that you may see a file of soldiers, colonel, captain, corporal, privates, powder-monkeys, and all, marching in admirable order over hill and dale to the wars, against their wills, ay, against their common sense and consciences, which makes it very steep marching indeed, and produces a palpitation of the heart. They have no doubt that it is a damnable business in which they are concerned; they are all peaceably inclined. Now, what are they? Men at all? or small movable forts and magazines, at the service of some unscrupulous man in power? . . .

How does it become a man to behave toward this American government today? I answer, that he cannot without disgrace be associated with it. I cannot for an instant recognize that political organization as my government which is the slave's government also.

All men recognize the right of revolution; that is, the right to refuse allegiance to, and to resist, the government, when its tyranny or its inefficiency are great and unendurable. But almost all say that such is not the case now. But such was the case, they think, in the Revolution of [17]75. If one were to tell me that this was a bad government because it taxed certain foreign commodities brought to its ports, it is most probable that I should not make an ado about it, for I can do without them. All machines have their friction; and possibly this does enough good to counterbalance the evil. At any rate, it is a great evil to make a stir about it. But when the friction comes to have its machine, and oppression and robbery are organized, I say, let us not have such a machine any longer. In other words, when a sixth of the population of a nation which has undertaken to be the refuge of liberty are slaves, and a whole country is unjustly overrun and conquered by a foreign army, and subjected to military law, I think that it is not too soon for honest men to rebel and revolutionize. What makes this duty the more urgent is the fact that the country so overrun is not our own, but ours is the invading army. . . .

Practically speaking, the opponents to a reform in Massachusetts are not a hundred thousand politicians at the South, but a hundred thousand merchants and farmers here, who are more interested in commerce and agriculture than they are in humanity, and are not prepared to do justice to the slave and to Mexico, cost what it may. I quarrel not with far-off foes, but with those who, near at home, co-operate with, and do the bidding of those far away, and without whom the latter would be harmless. We are accustomed to say, that the mass of men are unprepared; but improvement is slow, because the few are not materially wiser or better than the many. It is not so important that many should be as good as you, as that there be some absolute goodness somewhere; for that will leaven the whole lump. There are thousands who are in opinion opposed to slavery and to the war, who yet in effect do nothing to put an end to them; who, esteeming themselves children of [George] Washington and [Benjamin] Franklin, sit down with their hands in their pockets, and say that they know not what to do, and do nothing; who even postpone the question of freedom to the question of free-trade, and quietly read the prices-current along with the latest advices from Mexico, after dinner, and, it may be, fall asleep over them both. What is the price-current of an honest man and patriot today? They hesitate, and they regret, and sometimes they petition; but they do nothing in earnest and with effect. They will wait, well disposed, for others to remedy the evil, that they may no longer have it to regret. At most, they give only a cheap vote, and a feeble countenance and Godspeed, to the right, as it goes by them. There are nine hundred and ninety-nine patrons of virtue to one virtuous man; but it is easier to deal with the real possessor of a thing than with the temporary guardian of it.

All voting is a sort of gaming, like checkers or backgammon, with a slight moral tinge to it, a playing with right and wrong, with moral questions; and betting naturally accompanies it. The character of the voters is not staked. I cast my vote, perchance, as I think right; but I am not vitally concerned that that right should prevail. I am willing to leave it to the majority. Its obligation, therefore, never exceeds that of expediency. Even voting for the right is doing nothing for it. It is only expressing to men feebly your desire that it should prevail. A wise man will not leave the right to the mercy of chance, nor wish it to prevail through the power of the majority. There is but little virtue in the action of masses of men. When the majority shall at length vote for the abolition of slavery, it will be because they are indifferent to slavery, or because there is but little slavery left to be abolished by their vote. They will then be the only slaves. Only his vote can hasten the abolition of slavery who asserts his own freedom by his vote. . . .

It is not a man's duty, as a matter of course, to devote himself to the eradication of any, even the most enormous wrong; he may still properly have other concerns to engage him; but it is his duty, at least, to wash his hands of it, and, if he gives it no thought longer, not to give it practically his support. If I devote myself to other pursuits and contemplations, I must first see, at least, that I do not pursue them sitting upon another man's shoulders. I must get off him first, that he may pursue his contemplations too. See what gross inconsistency is tolerated. I have heard some of my townsmen say, "I should like to have them order me out to help put down an insurrection of the slaves, or to march to Mexico;—see if I would go"; and yet these very men have each, directly by their allegiance, and so indirectly, at least, by their money, furnished a substitute. The soldier is applauded who refuses to serve in an unjust war by those who do not refuse to sustain the unjust government which makes the war; is applauded by those whose own act and authority he disregards and sets at naught; as if the state were penitent to that degree that it hired one to scourge it while it sinned, but not to that degree that it left off sinning for a moment. Thus, under the name of Order and Civil Government, we are all made at last to pay homage to and support our own meanness. After the first blush of sin comes its indifference; and from immoral it becomes, as it were, unmoral, and not quite unnecessary to that life which we have made.

CHAPTER NINE

Slavery and Defiance

David Walker's *Appeal* (1830)

Harriet A. Jacobs, *Incidents in the Life of a Slave Girl: Written by Herself* (1861)

James Norcom's Runaway Slave Newspaper Advertisement for Harriet Jacobs (June 30, 1835)

James R. Bradley, Letter to Lydia Maria Child (June 3, 1834)

Reverend Theodore Parker, "Speech of Theodore Parker at the Faneuil Hall Meeting" (May 26, 1854)

Two Letters from Slaves to Their Former Masters (1844 to 1860)
  Henry Bibb, Letter to William Gatewood (March 23, 1844)
  Jermain Wesley Loguen, Letter to Sarah Logue (March 28, 1860)

Frederick Douglass, "The Meaning of July Fourth for the Negro" (July 5, 1852)

John Brown, "John Brown's Last Speech" (November 2, 1859)

Osborne P. Anderson, *A Voice from Harper's Ferry* (1861)

Martin Delany's Advice to Former Slaves (July 23, 1865)

Henry McNeal Turner, "On the Eligibility of Colored Members to Seats in the Georgia Legislature" (September 3, 1868)

Slavery was a brutal institution. It did not originate in any human disposition to cruelty, but in an economic system that required cheap and totally controlled labor—the plantation system of the American South. This system was at first based on the growing of tobacco and rice, and then on the growing of cotton. In 1790, a thousand tons of cotton were being produced every year in the South. By 1860, it was a million tons. In the same period, the number of slaves increased from five hundred thousand to four million.

The South developed a system of controls, backed by the laws, the courts, and the force employed by the slave owners. That system was not challenged by the national government. Indeed, the Tenth Amendment to the Constitution declared that the federal government had certain limited powers, and they did not include the power to do anything about slavery. Indeed, the

Constitution legitimized slavery, providing for the return of escaped slaves to their masters.

Against this system, slaves rebelled again and again, against enormous odds. They ran away, with more success, especially as the anti-slavery movement grew and helped slaves escape through what was called the "Underground Railroad."

The abolitionist movement consisted of white opponents of slavery and free blacks, many of whom had been slaves. They had to deal not only with the Southern governments, but with the federal government, which was cooperating with the slave owners. When the Fugitive Slave Act was passed in 1850, it offered the services of federal marshals and soldiers in capturing escaped slaves and returning them to their masters. Black and white abolitionists defied the law, and helped many slaves to escape.

When slavery was abolished at the end of the Civil War by passage of the Thirteenth Amendment, it did not bring complete freedom. The former slaves, not given land or the resources to become independent farmers, often became serfs tied to their former masters.

Although the Fourteenth and Fifteenth Amendments promised equality and the right to vote, and for a period were enforced by federal troops in the South, that enforcement ended when Northern politicians made a deal with the Southern plantation class. Southern blacks were betrayed, their representatives forced out of the legislatures. Lynch mobs ruled the day. Thousands of blacks fled the deep South to escape violence and poverty. Others waited for the day when they could reclaim their right to equality.

• • •

In 1829, David Walker, a son of a slave, but born free in North Carolina, moved to Boston. The next year he published a pamphlet, *Walker's Appeal to the Colored Citizens of the World*, which became widely read and infuriated southern slaveholders. The state of Georgia offered a reward of $10,000 to anyone who would deliver Walker alive, and $1,000 to anyone who would kill him. Here is an excerpt from his *Appeal*.

David Walker's *Appeal* (1830)[1]

I ask the candid and unprejudiced of the whole world, to search the pages of historians diligently, and see if the Antediluvians—the Sodomites—the Egyptians—the Babylonians—the Ninevites—the Carthaginians—the Persians—the Macedonians—the Greeks—the Romans—the Mahometans—the Jews—or devils, ever treated a set of human beings, as the white Christians of America do us, the blacks, or Africans. I also ask the attention of the world of mankind to the declaration of these very American people, of the United States.

A declaration made July 4, 1776.

It says,

> When in the course of human events, it becomes necessary for one people to dissolve the political bands which have connected them with another, and to assume among the Powers of the earth, the separate and equal station to which the laws of nature and of nature's God entitle them. A decent respect for the opinions of mankind requires, that they should declare the causes which impel them to the separation.—We hold these truths to be self evident—that all men are created equal, that they are endowed by their Creator with certain unalienable rights; that among these, are life, liberty, and the pursuit of happiness; that, to secure these rights, governments are instituted among men, deriving their just powers from the consent of the governed; that when ever any form of government becomes destructive of these ends, it is the right of the people to alter or to abolish it, and to institute a new government laying its foundation on such principles, and organizing its powers in such form, as to them shall seem most likely to effect their safety and happiness. Prudence, indeed, will dictate, that governments long established should not be changed for light and transient causes; and accordingly all experience hath shewn, that mankind are more disposed to suffer, while evils are sufferable, than to right themselves by abolishing the forms to which they are accustomed. But when a long train of abuses and usurpations, pursuing invariably the same object, evinces a design to reduce them under absolute despotism, it is their right, it is their duty to throw off such government, and to provide new guards for their future security.

See your Declaration Americans!!! Do you understand your own language? Hear your language, proclaimed to the world, July 4th, 1776—

> We hold these truths to be self evident—that ALL MEN ARE CREATED EQUAL!! that they are endowed by their Creator with certain unalienable rights; that among these are life, liberty, and the pursuit of happiness!!

Compare your own language above, extracted from your Declaration of Independence, with your cruelties and murders inflicted by your cruel and unmerciful fathers and yourselves on our fathers and on us—men who have never given your fathers or you the least provocation!!!!!!

Hear your language further!

> But when a long train of abuses and usurpation, pursuing invariably the same object, evinces a design to reduce them under absolute despotism, it is their right, it is their duty, to throw off such government, and to provide new guards for their future security.

Now, Americans! I ask you candidly, was your sufferings under Great Britain, one hundredth part as cruel and tyrannical as you have rendered ours under you? Some of you, no doubt, believe that we will never throw off your murderous government and "provide new guards for our future security." If Satan has made you believe it, will he not deceive you? Do the whites say, I being a black man, ought to be humble, which I readily admit? I ask them, ought they not to be as humble as I? or do they think that they can measure arms with Jehovah? Will not the Lord yet humble them? or will not these very colored people whom they now treat worse than brutes, yet under God, humble them low down enough? Some of the whites are ignorant enough to tell us, that we ought to be submissive to them, that they may keep their feet on our throats. And if we do not submit to be beaten to death by them, we are bad creatures and of course must be damned, etc.

If any man wishes to hear this doctrine openly preached to us by the American preachers, let him go into the Southern and Western sections of this country—I do not speak from hear say—what I have written, is what I have seen and heard myself. No man may think that my book is made up of conjecture—I have traveled and observed nearly the whole of those things myself, and what little I did not get by my own observation, I received from those among the whites and blacks, in whom the greatest confidence may be placed.

The Americans may be as vigilant as they please, but they cannot be vigilant enough for the Lord, neither can they hide themselves, where he will not find and bring them out.

$$\bullet \ \bullet \ \bullet$$

In this selection from *Incidents in the Life of a Slave Girl*, first published in 1861 under the pseudonym Linda Brent, Harriet Jacobs explores the relationship between the church and slavery, observing how the teaching "If you disobey your earthly master, you offend your heavenly Master" was used in an attempt to prevent slave rebellion. Religion may have, at times, provided a momentary relief, but in this passage, Jacobs questions whether it could bring a meaningful release from the ills of slavery.

Harriet A. Jacobs, *Incidents in the Life of a Slave Girl: Written by Herself* (1861)[2]

After the alarm caused by Nat Turner's insurrection had subsided, the slaveholders came to the conclusion that it would be well to give the slaves enough of religious instruction to keep them from murdering their masters. The Episcopal clergyman offered to hold a separate service on Sundays for their benefit. His colored members were very few, and also very respectable—a fact which I presume had some weight with him. The difficulty was to decide on a suitable place for them to worship. The Methodist and Baptist churches admitted them in the afternoon, but their carpets and cushions were not so costly as those at the Episcopal church. It was at last decided that they should meet at the house of a free colored man, who was a member.

I was invited to attend, because I could read. Sunday evening came, and, trusting to the cover of night, I ventured out. I rarely ventured out by daylight, for I always went with fear, expecting at every turn to encounter Dr. Flint [James Norcom], who was sure to turn me back, or order me to his office to inquire where I got my bonnet, or some other article of dress. When the Rev. Mr. Pike [John Avery] came, there were some twenty persons present. The reverend gentleman knelt in prayer, then seated himself, and requested all present, who could read, to open their books, while he gave out the portions he wished them to repeat or respond to.

His text was, "Servants, be obedient to them that are your masters according to the flesh, with fear and trembling, in singleness of your heart, as unto Christ."

Pious Mr. Pike brushed up his hair till it stood upright, and, in deep, solemn tones, began: "Hearken, ye servants! Give strict heed unto my words. You are rebellious sinners. Your hearts are filled with all manner of evil. 'Tis the devil who tempts you. God is angry with you, and will surely punish you, if you don't forsake your wicked ways. You that live in town are eye-servants behind your master's back. Instead of serving your masters faithfully, which is pleasing in the sight of your heavenly Master, you are idle, and shirk your work. God sees you. You tell lies. God hears you. Instead of being engaged in worshipping him, you are hidden away somewhere, feasting on your master's substance; tossing coffee-grounds with some wicked fortuneteller, or cutting cards with another old hag. Your masters may not find you out, but God sees you, and will punish you. O, the depravity of your hearts! When your master's work is done, are you quietly together, thinking of the goodness of God to such sinful creatures? No; you are quarrelling, and tying up little bags of roots to bury under the door-steps to poison each other with. God sees you. You men steal away to every grog shop to sell your master's corn, that you may buy rum to drink. God sees you. You sneak into the back streets, or among the bushes, to pitch coppers. Although your masters may not find you out, God sees you; and he will punish you. You must forsake your sinful ways, and be faithful servants. Obey your old master and your young master—your old mistress and your young mistress. If you disobey your earthly master, you offend your heavenly Master. You must obey God's commandments. When you go from here, don't stop at the corners of the streets to talk, but go directly home, and let your master and mistress see that you have come."

The benediction was pronounced. We went home, highly amused at brother Pike's gospel teaching, and we determined to hear him again. I went the next Sabbath evening, and heard pretty much a repetition of the last discourse. At the close of the meeting, Mr. Pike informed us that he found it very inconvenient to meet at the friend's house, and he should be glad to see us, every Sunday evening, at his own kitchen.

I went home with the feeling that I had heard the Reverend Mr. Pike for the last time. Some of his members repaired to his house, and found that the kitchen sported two tallow candles; the first time, I am sure, since its present occupant owned it, for the servants never had any thing but pine knots. It was so long before the reverend gentleman descended from his comfortable parlor that the slaves left, and went to enjoy a Methodist shout. They never seem so happy as when shouting and singing at religious meetings. Many of them are sincere, and nearer to the gate of heaven than sanctimonious Mr. Pike, and other long-faced Christians, who see wounded Samaritans, and pass by on the other side.

The slaves generally compose their own songs and hymns, and they do not trouble their heads much about the measure. They often sing the following verses:

Old Satan is one busy ole man;
    He rolls dem blocks all in my way;
But Jesus is my bosom friend;
    He rolls dem blocks away.

If I had died when I was young,
    Den how my stam'ring tongue would have sung;
But I am ole, and now I stand
    A narrow chance for to tread dat heavenly land.

I well remember one occasion when I attended a Methodist class meeting. I went with a burdened spirit, and happened to sit next a poor, bereaved mother, whose heart was still heavier than mine. The class leader was the town constable—a man who bought and sold slaves, who whipped his brethren and sisters of the church at the public whipping post, in jail or out of jail. He was ready to perform that

Christian office any where for fifty cents. This white-faced, black-hearted brother came near us, and said to the stricken woman, "Sister, can't you tell us how the Lord deals with your soul? Do you love him as you did formerly?"

She rose to her feet, and said, in piteous tones, "My Lord and Master, help me! My load is more than I can bear. God has hid himself from me, and I am left in darkness and misery." Then, striking her breast, she continued, "I can't tell you what is in here! They've got all my children. Last week they took the last one. God only knows where they've sold her. They let me have her sixteen years, and then—O! O! Pray for her brothers and sisters!

I've got nothing to live for now. God make my time short!"

She sat down, quivering in every limb. I saw that constable class leader become crimson in the face with suppressed laughter, while he held up his handkerchief, that those who were weeping for the poor woman's calamity might not see his merriment. Then, with assumed gravity, he said to the bereaved mother, "Sister, pray to the Lord that every dispensation of his divine will may be sanctified to the good of your poor needy soul!"

The congregation struck up a hymn, and sung as though they were as free as the birds that warbled round us,—

Ole Satan thought he had a mighty aim;
He missed my soul, and caught my sins.
Cry Amen, cry Amen, cry Amen to God!

He took my sins upon his back;
Went muttering and grumbling down to hell.
Cry Amen, cry Amen, cry Amen to God!

Ole Satan's church is here below.
Up to God's free church I hope to go.
Cry Amen, cry Amen, cry Amen to God!

Precious are such moments to the poor slaves. If you were to hear them at such times, you might think they were happy. But can that hour of singing and shouting sustain them through the dreary week, toiling without wages, under constant dread of the lash?

• • •

This classified ad, placed by the slave master of Harriet Jacobs, was typical of the newspaper advertisements seeking the return of slaves fleeing their oppression.

Newspapers also commonly ran announcements of auctions of slaves, including young children separated from their parents.

James Norcom's Runaway Slave Newspaper Advertisement for Harriet Jacobs (June 30, 1835)[3]

$100 REWARD

Will be given for the apprehension and delivery of my Servant Girl HARRIET. She is a light mulatto, 21 years of age, about 5 feet 4 inches high, of a thick and corpulent habit, having on her head a thick covering of black hair that curls naturally, but which can be easily combed straight. She speaks easily and fluently, and has an agreeable carriage and address. Being a good seamstress, she has been accustomed to dress well, has a variety of very fine clothes, made in the prevailing fashion, and will probably appear, if abroad, tricked out in gay and fashionable finery. As this girl absconded from the plantation of my son without any known cause or provocation, it is probable she designs to transport herself to the North.

The above reward, with all reasonable charges, will be given for apprehending her, or securing her in any prison or jail within the U[nited] States.

All persons are hereby forewarned against harboring or entertaining her, or being in any way instrumental in her escape, under the most rigorous penalties of the law.

• • •

James R. Bradley, a slave in the Arkansas Territory who worked until he was able to buy his way into freedom, wrote this damning account of his experience of slavery to Lydia Maria Child, the abolitionist author the editor of an antislavery journal, *The Oasis*.

James R. Bradley, Letter to Lydia Maria Child (June 3, 1834)[4]

Dear Madam:

I am now going to try to write a little account of my life as nearly as I can remember. It makes me sorrowful to think of my past days. They have been very dark and full of tears. I always longed and prayed for liberty. I sometimes hoped I should get it and then I would think and pray and study out some way to earn money enough to buy myself by working nights, and then something would fall out and all my hopes would die and it seemed as though I must live and die a slave without anyone to pity me. But I will begin as far back as I can remember. When I was between two and three years old the soul destroyers tore me from my tender mothe[r's] arms somewhere in Africa far back from the sea. They carried me along [a long] distance to the ships. I looked back and wept all the way. The ship was full of men and women loaded down with chains. As I was so small they let me run about on deck. After many long days they brought me to Charlestown [South Carolina]. Then a slave holder bought me and took me up into Pendleton county. I suppose that I stayed with him about six months. Then he sold me to a man whose name was Bradley. Ever since then I have been called by that name. This man was called a wonderfully kind master and he was more kind than most masters. He gave me enough to eat and did not beat me so much as masters g[enera]lly do. But all that was nothing to me. I spent many sleepless nights and bathed my face in tears because I was a slave. I . . . groaned for liberty. . . .

I have said a good deal about my desire for liberty. How strange it is it that any body should believe that a human being could be a slave and feel contented. I don't believe there ever was a slave who did not long for liberty. I know very well that slaveholders take a great deal of pain to make the people of free states believe that this class are happy and contented—and I kn[o]w too that I never knew a slave—no matter how well he was treated—that did not long to be free. There is one thing about this that people of free states don't understand. When they talk with slaves and ask them if they don't want their liberty and if they wouldn't like to be free like the white men—they say no—and very likely they will go on and say that they wouldn't leave their master for the world, when at the same time they have [been] along time laying plans to get free and desire liberty more than anything else in the world. The truth is and every slave knows it—if he should say he wanted to be free and should show any weariness and discontent because he is a slave he is sure to be treated harsher and worked harder for it. So they are always very careful not to show any weariness and particularly when they are asked questions about freedom by white men. When the slaves are together by themselves alone, they are always talking about liberty, liberty is the great thought and feeling that fills the mind full all the time. I could say a great many things more but as you requested in your letter to my dear friend Mr. [Theodore] Weld that I would write a "short account" of my life I am afraid I have written too much already and will say but a few words more. My heart is full and flows over when I hear what is doing for the poor broken hearted slave and free man of color. God will help those who take the part of the oppressed. Yes blessed be his name he will s[u]rely do it. Dear Madam I do not know you personally but I have seen your book on slavery and have read much about you, and I do hope to meet you at the resurrection of the Just. I thank God he has given to the poor bleeding slave and to all the oppressed colored race such a dear friend. May God graciously preserve you—dear Madam, and bless your labors and make you great in this holy cause until you see all the walls of prejudice broke down and all the chains of slavery broken to pieces and all of every color sitting down—together at Jesus' feet, a band of brethren speaking kind words and looking upon each others faces in love and as they expect to love each other and live together in heaven, be willing to love each other and live together on earth.

• • •

There was widespread disobedience to the Fugitive Slave Act of 1850, which enlisted the powers of the national government to return escaped slaves to their masters. Blacks and whites joined in armed resistance. When they were arrested, it often happened that juries, defying the Fugitive Slave Act themselves, would acquit them. In Boston, for instance, in 1851, a man named Shadrack was rescued from a courtroom by 50 blacks, eight of whom were tried and acquitted. That same year, the escaped slave Jerry was rescued from a police station in Syracuse. Eighteen men were indicted, all were acquitted. In 1854, President Franklin Pierce dispatched federal troops, joined by state militia and local police, to capture Anthony Burns, a slave who had escaped to Massachusetts from Virginia. Citing the Fugitive Slave Act, on May 27, 1854, Commissioner Edward G. Loring ordered Burns be returned to slavery in Virginia. The night before, black and white abolitionists used a battering ram against the courthouse doors but were repulsed. On June 2, Burns was marched to the waterfront, through streets draped with black cloth and lined with thousands of his supporters, to the sound of church bells tolling, and was forcibly sent back to slavery. On the eve of Burns's sentencing, the Unitarian abolitionist minister Theodore Parker, a supporter of the rebel John Brown, gave this rousing address to a packed meeting house in Boston. That night thirteen people were arrested and one marshal killed.

Reverend Theodore Parker, "Speech of Theodore Parker at the Faneuil Hall Meeting" (May 26, 1854)[5]

Fellow-citizens, a deed which Virginia commands has just been done in the city of John Hancock, and the "brace of Adamses." It was done by a Boston hand. It was a Boston man who issued the warrant; it was a Boston Marshal who put it in execution; they are Boston men who are seeking to kidnap a citizen of Massachusetts, and send him into slavery for ever and ever. It is our fault that it is so. Eight years ago, a merchant of Boston "kidnapped a man on the high road between Faneuil Hall and old Quincy," at 12 o'clock—at the noon of day; and the next day mechanics of this city exhibited the half-eagles that they had received for their share of the spoils, in enslaving a brother man. You called a meeting in this hall. It was as crowded as it is now. I stood side by side with my friend and former neighbor, your honorable and noble chairman tonight [loud cheers], and that man who had fought for the cause of liberty in Greece, and been imprisoned for that sacred cause in the dungeons of Poland (Dr. Samuel G. Howe), stood here and introduced to the audience that "old man eloquent," John Quincy Adams [loud cheers]. It was the last time he ever stood in Faneuil Hall. He came to defend the inalienable rights of a friendless negro slave, kidnapped in Boston. There is even no picture of JOHN QUINCY ADAMS tonight! A Suffolk grand jury could find no indictment against the Boston merchant for kidnapping that man ["shame," "shame"]. If Boston had spoken then, we should not have been here tonight. We should have had no Fugitive Slave Bill. When that bill passed, we fired a hundred guns. Don't you remember the Union meeting, held in this very hall? A man stood on this platform—he is a Judge of the Supreme Court now—and he said, "When a certain 'reverend gentleman' is indicted for perjury, I should like to ask him how he will answer the charge?" And, when that "reverend gentleman" rose, and asked, "Do you want an answer now to your question?" Faneuil Hall cried out, "No," "no,"—"Throw him over!" Had Faneuil Hall spoken then on the side of truth and freedom, we should not now be the subjects of Virginia. Yes, we are the *vassals* of Virginia. It reaches its arm over the graves of our mothers, and it kidnaps men in the city of the Puritans, over the graves of Samuel Adams and John Hancock [cries of "shame"]. Shame! So I say; but who is to blame? "There is no North," said Mr. [Daniel] Webster. There is none. The South goes clear up to the Canada line. No, gentlemen, there is no Boston today. There *was* a Boston once. Now, there is a north suburb to the city of Alexandria; that is what Boston is [laughter]. And you and I, fellow-subjects of the State of Virginia [cries of "no," "no"]. I will take it back when you show me the fact is not so. Men and brothers (brothers, at any rate), I am an old man; I have heard hurrahs and cheers for liberty many times; I have not seen a great many *deeds* done for liberty. I ask you, are we to have *deeds* as well as words? ["yes," "yes," and loud cheers.]

Now, brethren,—you are brothers at any rate, whether citizens of Massachusetts or subjects of Virginia,—(I am a minister), and, fellow-citizens of Boston, there are two great laws in this country; one of them is the LAW OF SLAVERY; that law is declared to be a "finality." Once the Constitution was formed "to establish justice, promote tranquility, and secure the blessings of liberty to ourselves and our posterity." *Now*, the Constitution is *not* to secure liberty; it is to *extend slavery* into Nebraska; and, when slavery is established there, in order to show what it is, there comes a sheriff from Alexandria to kidnap a man in the city of

Boston, and he gets a Judge of Probate, in the county of Suffolk, to issue a writ, and a Boston man to execute that writ! [cries of "shame," "shame."]

Slavery tramples on the Constitution; it treads down State rights. Where are the rights of Massachusetts? A Fugitive Slave Law Commissioner has got them all in his pocket. Where is the trial by jury? Watson Freeman has it under his Marshal's staff. Where is the great right of personal replevin [a legal remedy in which a court requires the return of specific goods], which our fathers wrested, several hundred years ago, from the tyrants who once lorded it over Great Britain? Judge [Peleg] Sprague trod it under his feet! Where is the sacred right of *habeas corpus*? Deputy Marshal Riley can crush it in his hands, and Boston does not say anything against it. Where are the laws of Massachusetts forbidding state edifices to be used as prisons for the incarceration of fugitives? They, too, are trampled under foot. "Slavery is a finality."

These men came from Virginia to kidnap a man here. Once, this was Boston; now, it is a northern suburb of Alexandria. At first, when they carried a fugitive slave from Boston, they thought it was a difficult thing to do it. They had to get a Mayor to help them; they bad to put chains round the Court House; they bad to call out the "Sims' Brigade"; it took nine days to do it. Now, they are so confident that we are subjects of Virginia that they do not even put chains round the Court House; the police have nothing to do with it. I was told, today, that one of the officers of the city said to twenty-eight policemen, if any man in the employment of the city meddles in this business, he will be discharged from service without a hearing [great applause]. Well, gentlemen, how do you think they received that declaration? They shouted, and hurrahed, and gave three cheers [renewed applause]. My friend here would not have the honor of presiding over you tonight, if application had been made a little sooner to the Mayor. Another gentleman told me that, when he was asked to preside at this meeting, he said that he regretted that all his time tonight was previously engaged. If he had known it earlier, he said, he might have been able to make arrangements to preside. When the man was arrested, he told the Marshal he regretted it, and that his sympathies were wholly with the slave [loud applause]. Fellow-citizens, remember that word. Hold Your Mayor to it, and let it be seen that he has got a background, and a foreground, which will authorize him to repeat that word in public, and act it out in Faneuil Hall. I say, so confident are the slave agents now that they can carry off their slave, in the day-time, that they do not put chains round the Court House; they have got no soldiers billeted in Faneuil Hall, as in 1851. They think they can carry this man off tomorrow morning in a cab [voices—"they can't do it"—"let's see them try"].

I say, there are two great laws in this country. One is the slave law: that is the law of the President of the United States; it is Senator [Stephen A.] Douglas's law; it is the law of the Supreme Court of the United States; it is the law of the

Commissioner; it is the law of every Marshal, and of every meanest ruffian whom the Marshal hires to execute his behests. There is another law, which my friend, Mr. [Wendell] Phillips, has described in language such as I cannot equal, and therefore shall not try; I only state it in its plainest terms. It is the law of the people, when they are sure they are right and determined to go ahead [cheers].

Now, gentlemen, there was a Boston once, and you and I had fathers—brave fathers; and mothers who stirred up those fathers to manly deeds. Well, gentlemen, once it came to pass that the British Parliament enacted a "law"—*they* called it a law—issuing stamps here. What did your fathers do on that occasion? They said, in the language of Algernon Sydney, quoted in your resolutions, "That which is not just is not law, and that which is not law ought not to be obeyed" [cheers]. They did not obey the stamp act. They did not call it a *law*, and the man that did call it a law here, eighty years ago, would have had a very warm coat of tar and feathers on him. They called it an "act," and they took the Commissioner who was here to execute it, took him solemnly, manfully,—*they didn't harm a hair of his head,* they were non-resistants of a very potent sort [laughter],—and made him take a solemn oath that he would not issue a single stamp. He was brother-in-law of the Governor of the State, the servant of a royal master, exceedingly respectable, of great wealth, and once very popular; but they took him, and made him swear not to execute his commission; and he kept his oath, and the stamp act went to its own place, and you know what that was [cheers]. That was an instance of the people going behind a wicked law to enact absolute justice into their justice, and making it common law. You know what they did with the tea.

Well, gentlemen, in the South there is a public opinion (it is a very wicked public opinion), which is stronger than law. When a colored seaman goes to Charleston from Boston, he is clapped instantly into jail, and kept there until the vessel is ready to sail, and the Boston merchant or master must pay the bill, and the Boston black man must feel the smart. That is a wicked example, set by the State of South Carolina. When Mr. [Samuel] Hoar, one of our most honored and respected fellow-citizens, was sent to Charleston, to test the legality of this iniquitous law, the citizens of Charleston ordered him off the premises, and he was glad to escape, to save himself from further insult. There was no violence, no guns fired. This is an instance of the *strength of public opinion*—of a most unjust and iniquitous public opinion.

Well, gentlemen, I say there is one law—slave law; it is everywhere. There is another law, which also is a finality; and that law, it is in your hands and your arms, and you can put that in execution just when you see fit. Gentlemen, I am a clergyman and a man of peace; I love peace. But there is a means, and there is an end; liberty is the end, and sometimes peace is not the means towards it [applause]. Now I want to ask you what you are going to do [a voice—"shoot,

shoot"]. There are ways of managing this matter, without shooting anybody. Be sure that these men who have kidnapped a man in Boston are cowards, every mother's son of them; and, if we stand up there resolutely, and declare that this man shall not go out of the city of Boston, *without shooting a gun*—[cries of "that's it," and great applause],—then he won't go back. Now, I am going to propose that when you adjourn, it be to meet in *Court Square tomorrow morning at 9 o'clock*. As many as are in favor of that motion will raise their hands [a large number of hands were raised, but many voices cried out, "Let's go tonight," "let's pay a visit to the slave-catchers at the Revere House," etc., etc.]. Do you propose to go to the Revere House tonight? then show your hands [some hands were held up]. It is not a vote. We shall meet in *Court Square at 9 o'clock tomorrow morning.*

• • •

Freed slaves and fugitive slaves played a vital role in building the Underground Railroad and organizing for abolition. As slaves began to tell their stories, some wrote private, or in some cases public, letters to their former owners, defying their attempt to return them to slavery. Here are two of these letters. The first is from Henry Bibb, who was born a slave to a Kentucky state senator and fought for years until he eventually won his freedom in 1841. The second is from Jermain Wesley Loguen, who was pivotal to the underground railroad in Syracuse.

Two Letters from Slaves to Their Former Masters (1844 to 1860)

HENRY BIBB, LETTER TO WILLIAM GATEWOOD (MARCH 23, 1844)[6]

Dear Sir:—I am happy to inform you that you are not mistaken in the man whom you sold as property, and received pay for as such. But I thank God that I am not property now, but am regarded as a man like yourself, and although I live far north, I am enjoying a comfortable living by my own industry. If you should ever chance to be traveling this way, and will call on me, I will use you better than you did me while you held me as a slave. Think not that I have any malice against you, for the cruel treatment which you inflicted on me while I was in your power. As it was the custom of your country, to treat your fellow men as you did me and my little family, I can freely forgive you.

I wish to be remembered in love to my aged mother, and friends; please tell her that if we should never meet again in this life, my prayer shall be to God that we may meet in Heaven, where parting shall be no more.

You wish to be remembered to King and Jack. I am pleased, sir, to inform you that they are both here . . . and doing well. They are both living in Canada West. They are now the owners of better farms than the men are who once owned them.

You may perhaps think hard of us for running away from slavery, but as to myself, I have but one apology to make for it, which is this: I have only to regret that I did not start at an earlier period. I might have been free long before I was. I think it is very probable that I should have been a toiling slave on your property today, if you had treated me differently.

To be compelled to stand by and see you whip and slash my wife without mercy, when I could afford her no protection, not even by offering myself to suffer the lash in her place, was more than I felt it to be the duty of a slave husband to endure, while the way was open to Canada. My infant child was also frequently flogged by Mrs. [William] Gatewood, for crying, until its skin was bruised literally purple. This kind of treatment was what drove me from home and family, to seek a better home for them. But I am willing to forget the past. I should be pleased to hear from you again, on the reception of this and should also be very happy to correspond with you often, if it should be agreeable to yourself. I subscribe myself a friend to the oppressed, and Liberty forever.

JERMAIN WESLEY LOGUEN, LETTER TO SARAH LOGUE (MARCH 28, 1860)[7]

Mrs. Sarah Logue: Yours of the 20th of February is duly received, and I thank you for it. It is a long time since I heard from my poor old mother, and I am glad to know that she is yet alive, and, as you say, "as well as common." What that means, I don't know. I wish you had said more about her.

You are a woman; but, had you a woman's heart, you never could have insulted a brother by telling him you sold his only remaining brother and sister, because he put himself beyond your power to convert him into money.

You sold my brother and sister, Abe and Ann, and twelve acres of land, you say, because I ran away. Now you have the unutterable meanness to ask me to return and be your miserable chattel, or in lieu thereof, send you $1000 to enable you to redeem the land, but not to redeem my poor brother and sister! If I were to send you money, it would be to get my brother and sister, and not that you should get land. You say you are a cripple, and doubtless you say it to stir my pity, for you knew I was susceptible in that direction. I do pity you from the bottom of my heart. Nevertheless, I am indignant beyond the power of words to express, that you should be so sunken and cruel as to tear the hearts I love so much all in pieces; that you should be willing to impale and crucify us all, out of compassion for your poor foot or leg. Wretched woman! Be it known to you that I value my freedom, to say nothing of my mother, brothers and sisters, more than your whole body;

more, indeed, than my own life; more than all the lives of all the slaveholders and tyrants under heaven.

You say you have offers to buy me, and that you shall sell me if I do not send you $1000, and in the same breath and almost in the same sentence, you say, "You know we raised you as we did our own children." Woman, did you raise your own children for the market? Did you raise them for the whipping-post? Did you raise them to be driven off, bound to a coffle [a group of slaves being driven to market] in chains? Where are my poor bleeding brothers and sisters? Can you tell? Who was it that sent them off into sugar and cotton fields, to be kicked and cuffed, and whipped, and to groan and die; and where no kin can hear their groans, or attend and sympathize at their dying bed, or follow in their funeral? Wretched woman! Do you say you did not do it? Then I reply, your husband did, and you approved the deed—and the very letter you sent me shows that your heart approves it all. Shame on you!

But, by the way, where is your husband? You don't speak of him. I infer, therefore, that he is dead; that he has gone to his great account, with all his sins against my poor family upon his head. Poor man! gone to meet the spirits of my poor, outraged and murdered people, in a world where Liberty and Justice are Masters.

But you say I am a thief, because I took the old mare along with me. Have you got to learn that I had a better right to the old mare, as you call her, than Mannasseth Logue had to me? Is it a greater sin for me to steal his horse, than it was for him to rob my mother's cradle, and steal me? If he and you infer that I forfeit all my rights to you, shall not I infer that you forfeit all your rights to me? Have you got to learn that human rights are mutual and reciprocal, and if you take my liberty and life, you forfeit your own liberty and life? Before God and high heaven, is there a law for one man which is not a law for every other man?

If you or any other speculator on my body and rights, wish to know how I regard my rights, they need but come here, and lay their hands on me to enslave me. Did you think to terrify me by presenting the alternative to give my money to you, or give my body to slavery? Then let me say to you, that I meet the proposition with unutterable scorn and contempt. The proposition is an outrage and an insult. I will not budge one hair's breadth. I will not breathe a shorter breath, even to save me from your persecutions. I stand among a free people, who, I thank God, sympathize with my rights, and the rights of mankind; and if your emissaries and venders come here to re-enslave me, and escape the unshrinking vigor of my own right arm, I trust my strong and brave friends, in this city and State, will be my rescuers and avengers.

• • •

July Fourth is held up as a day to celebrate the struggle for freedom and independence. But the great abolitionist Frederick Douglass, himself a former slave and the editor of the abolitionist newspaper *The North Star*, dared to challenge the exaltation of the holiday. Here is part of his remarkable address to the Rochester (New York) Ladies' Anti-Slavery Society.

Frederick Douglass, "The Meaning of July Fourth for the Negro" (July 5, 1852)[8]

Mr. President, Friends and Fellow Citizens:

He who could address this audience without a quailing sensation, has stronger nerves than I have. I do not remember ever to have appeared as a speaker before any assembly more shrinkingly, nor with greater distrust of my ability, than I do this day. A feeling has crept over me quite unfavorable to the exercise of my limited powers of speech. The task before me is one which requires much previous thought and study for its proper performance. I know that apologies of this sort are generally considered flat and unmeaning. I trust, however, that mine will not be so considered. Should I seem at ease, my appearance would much misrepresent me. The little experience I have had in addressing public meetings, in country school houses, avails me nothing on the present occasion.

The papers and placards say, that I am to deliver a Fourth of July Oration. This certainly sounds large, and out of the common way, for me. It is true that I have often had the privilege to speak in this beautiful Hall, and to address many who now honor me with their presence. But neither their familiar faces, nor the perfect gage I think I have of Corinthian Hall seems to free me from embarrassment.

The fact is, ladies and gentlemen, the distance between this platform and the slave plantation, from which I escaped, is considerable—and the difficulties to be overcome in getting from the latter to the former are by no means slight. That I am here today is, to me, a matter of astonishment as well as of gratitude. You will not, therefore, be surprised, if in what I have to say I evince no elaborate preparation, nor grace my speech with any high sounding exordium. With little experience and with less learning, I have been able to throw my thoughts hastily and imperfectly together; and trusting to your patient and generous indulgence, I will proceed to lay them before you. . . .

[Y]our fathers, who had not adopted the fashionable idea of this day, of the infallibility of government, and the absolute character of its acts, presumed to differ from the home government in respect to the wisdom and the justice of some of those burdens and restraints. They went so far in their excitement as to pronounce the measures of government unjust, unreasonable, and oppressive, and altogether such as ought not to be quietly submitted to. I scarcely need say, fellow-citizens, that my opinion of those measures fully accords with that of your fathers. Such a declaration of agreement on my part would not be worth much to anybody. It would, certainly, prove nothing as to what part I might have taken, had I lived during the great controversy of 1776. To say now that America was right, and England wrong, is exceedingly easy. Everybody can say it; the dastard, not less than the noble brave, can flippantly descant on the tyranny of England towards the American Colonies. It is fashionable to do so; but there was a time when to pronounce against England, and in favor of the cause of the colonies, tried men's souls. They who did so were accounted in their day plotters of mischief, agitators and rebels, dangerous men. To side with the right against the wrong, with the weak against the strong, and with the oppressed against the oppressor! here lies the merit, and the one which, of all others, seems unfashionable in our day. The cause of liberty may be stabbed by the men who glory in the deeds of your fathers. . . .

Fellow Citizens, I am not wanting in respect for the fathers of this republic. The signers of the Declaration of Independence were brave men. They were great men too—great enough to give frame to a great age. It does not often happen to a nation to raise, at one time, such a number of truly great men. The point from which I am compelled to view them is not, certainly, the most favorable; and yet I cannot contemplate their great deeds with less than admiration. They were statesmen, patriots and heroes, and for the good they did, and the principles they contended for, I will unite with you to honor their memory. . . .

They were peace men; but they preferred revolution to peaceful submission to bondage. They were quiet men; but they did not shrink from agitating against oppression. They showed forbearance; but that they knew its limits. They believed in order; but not in the order of tyranny. With them, nothing was "settled" that was not right. With them, justice, liberty and humanity were "final"; not slavery and oppression. You may well cherish the memory of such men. They were great in their day and generation. Their solid manhood stands out the more as we contrast it with these degenerate times. . . .

Fellow-citizens, pardon me, allow me to ask, why am I called upon to speak here today? What have I, or those I represent, to do with your national independence? Are the great principles of political freedom and of natural justice, embodied in that Declaration of Independence, extended to us? and am I, therefore, called upon to bring our humble offering to the national altar, and to confess the benefits and express devout gratitude for the blessings resulting from your independence to us?

Would to God, both for your sakes and ours, that an affirmative answer could be truthfully returned to these questions! Then would my task be light, and my burden easy and delightful. For who is there so cold, that a nation's sympathy could not warm him? Who so obdurate and dead to the claims of gratitude, that would not thankfully acknowledge such priceless benefits? Who so stolid and selfish, that would not give his voice to swell the hallelujahs of a nation's jubilee, when the chains of servitude had been torn from his limbs? I am not that man. In a case like that, the dumb might eloquently speak, and the "lame man leap as an hart."

But such is not the state of the case. I say it with a sad sense of the disparity between us. I am not included within the pale of this glorious anniversary! Your high independence only reveals the immeasurable distance between us. The blessings in which you, this day, rejoice, are not enjoyed in common.—The rich inheritance of justice, liberty, prosperity and independence, bequeathed by your fathers, is shared by you, not by me. The sunlight that brought light and healing to you, has brought stripes and death to me. This Fourth July is yours, not mine. You may rejoice, I must mourn. To drag a man in fetters into the grand illuminated temple of liberty, and call upon him to join you in joyous anthems, were inhuman mockery and sacrilegious irony. Do you mean, citizens, to mock me, by asking me to speak today? If so, there is a parallel to your conduct. And let me warn you that it is dangerous to copy the example of a nation whose crimes, towering up to heaven, were thrown down by the breath of the Almighty, burying that nation in irrevocable ruin! I can today take up the plaintive lament of a peeled and woe-smitten people! . . .

Fellow-citizens, above your national, tumultuous joy, I hear the mournful wail of millions! whose chains, heavy and grievous yesterday, are, today, rendered more intolerable by the jubilee shouts that reach them. If I do forget, if I do not faithfully remember those bleeding children of sorrow this day, "may my right hand forget her cunning, and may my tongue cleave to the roof of my mouth!" To forget them, to pass lightly over their wrongs, and to chime in with the popular theme, would be treason most scandalous and shocking, and would make me a reproach before God and the world. My subject, then fellow-citizens, is American slavery. I shall see this day, and its popular characteristics from the slave's point of view. Standing there identified with the American bondman, making his wrongs mine, I do not hesitate to declare, with all my soul, that the character and conduct of this nation never looked blacker to me than on this 4th of July! Whether we turn to the declarations of the past, or to the professions of the present, the conduct of the nation seems equally hideous and revolting. America is false to the past, false to the present, and solemnly binds herself to be false to the future. Standing with God and the crushed and bleeding slave on this occasion, I will, in the name of humanity which is outraged, in the name of liberty which is fettered, in the name of the constitution and the Bible which are disregarded and trampled upon, dare to call in question and to denounce, with all the emphasis I can command, everything that serves to perpetuate slavery—the great sin and shame of America! "I will not equivocate; I will not excuse"; I will use the severest language I can command; and yet not one word shall escape me that any man, whose judgment is not blinded by prejudice, or who is not at heart a slaveholder, shall not confess to be right and just. . . .

What, am I to argue that it is wrong to make men brutes, to rob them of their liberty, to work them without wages, to keep them ignorant of their relations to their fellow men, to beat them with sticks, to flay their flesh with the lash, to load their limbs with irons, to hunt them with dogs, to sell them at auction, to sunder their families, to knock out their teeth, to burn their flesh, to starve them into obedience and submission to their masters? Must I argue that a system thus marked with blood, and stained with pollution, is wrong? No! I will not. I have better employment for my time and strength, than such arguments would imply. . . .

At a time like this, scorching irony, not convincing argument, is needed. O! had I the ability, and could reach the nation's ear, I would, today, pour out a fiery stream of biting ridicule, blasting reproach, withering sarcasm, and stern rebuke. For it is not light that is needed, but fire; it is not the gentle shower, but thunder. We need the storm, the whirlwind, and the earthquake. The feeling of the nation must be quickened; the conscience of the nation must be roused; the propriety of the nation must be startled; the hypocrisy of the nation must be exposed; and its crimes against God and man must be proclaimed and denounced.

What, to the American slave, is your 4th of July? I answer; a day that reveals to him, more than all other days in the year, the gross injustice and cruelty to which he is the constant victim. To him, your celebration is a sham; your boasted liberty, an unholy license; your national greatness, swelling vanity; your sounds of rejoicing are empty and heartless; your denunciations of tyrants, brass fronted impudence; your shouts of liberty and equality, hollow mockery; your prayers and hymns, your sermons and thanksgivings, with all your religious parade and solemnity, are, to him, mere bombast, fraud, deception, impiety, and hypocrisy—a thin veil to cover up crimes which would disgrace a nation of savages. There is not a nation on the earth guilty of practices more shocking and bloody than are the people of the United States, at this very hour.

Go where you may, search where you will, roam through all the monarchies and despotisms of the Old World, travel through South America, search out every abuse, and when you have found the last, lay your facts by the side of the everyday practices of this nation, and you will say with me, that, for revolting barbarity and shameless hypocrisy, America reigns without a rival.

• • •

On October 16, 1859, John Brown and nearly two dozen comrades seized the armory at Harper's Ferry in West Virginia, hoping to use its massive arsenal in the struggle to forcibly end slavery. Captured and brought to trial at nearby Charles Town, Brown was found guilty of treason. One month before his execution, John Brown addressed a courtroom in Charlestown, West Virginia, defending his role in the action at Harper's Ferry. Henry David Thoreau, although he himself did not favor violence, praised John Brown, and when the fiery preacher was sentenced to death, Ralph Waldo Emerson said: "He will make the gallows holy as the cross."

John Brown, "John Brown's Last Speech" (November 2, 1859)[9]

I have, may it please the Court, a few words to say.

In the first place, I deny every thing but what I have all along admitted—the design on my part to free the slaves. I intended certainly to have made a clear thing of that matter, as I did last winter, when I went into Missouri, and there took slaves without the snapping of a gun on either side, moved them through the country, and finally left them in Canada. I designed to have done the same thing again, on a larger scale. That was all I intended. I never did intend murder, or treason, or the destruction of property, or to excite or incite slaves to rebellion, or to make insurrection.

I have another objection: and that is, it is unjust that I should suffer such a penalty. Had I interfered in the manner which I admit, and which I admit has been fairly proved—(for I admire the truthfulness and candor of the greater portion of the witnesses who have testified in this case)—had I so interfered in behalf of the rich, the powerful, the intelligent, the so-called great, or in behalf of any of their friends, either father, mother, brother, sister, wife, or children, or any of that class, and suffered and sacrificed what I have in this interference, it would have been all right, and every man in this Court would have deemed it an act worthy of reward rather than punishment.

This Court acknowledges, as I suppose, the validity of the Law of God. I see a book kissed here which I suppose to be the Bible, or, at least, the New Testament. That teaches me that all things "whatsoever I would that men should do unto me, I should do even so to them." It teaches me, further, to "remember them that are in bonds as bound with them." I endeavored to act up to that instruction. I say, I am yet too young to understand that God is any respecter of persons. I believe that to have interfered as I have done, as I have always freely admitted I have done, in behalf of His despised poor, was not wrong, but right. Now, if it is deemed necessary that I should forfeit my life for the furtherance of the ends of justice, and mingle my blood further with the blood of my children, and with the blood of millions in this slave country whose rights are disregarded by wicked, cruel, and unjust enactments, I submit: so let it be done!

Let me say one word further.

I feel entirely satisfied with the treatment I have received on my trial. Considering all the circumstances, it has been more generous than I expected. But I feel no consciousness of guilt. I have stated from the first what was my intention and what was not. I never had any design against the life of any person, nor any disposition to commit treason, or excite slaves to rebel, or make any general insurrection. I never encouraged any man to do so, but always discouraged any idea of that kind.

Let me say, also, a word in regard to the statements made by some of those connected with me. I hear it has been stated by some of them that I have induced them to join me. But the contrary is true. I do not say this to injure them, but as regretting their weakness. There is not one of them but joined me of his own accord, and the greater part of them at their own expense. A number of them I never saw, and never had a word of conversation with, till the day they came to me, and that was for the purpose I have stated.

Now I have done.

• • •

Seventeen whites and five blacks participated in John Brown's raid on Harper's Ferry. Osborne Anderson was the only black person who survived to write about the experience. Here is an excerpt from his narrative of the raid.

Osborne P. Anderson, *A Voice from Harper's Ferry* (1861)[11]

Of the various contradictory reports made by slaveholders and their satellites about the time of the Harper's Ferry conflict, none were more untruthful than those relating to the slaves. There was seemingly a studied attempt to enforce the belief that the slaves were cowardly, and that they were really more in favor of Virginia masters and slavery, than of their freedom. As a party who had an intimate knowledge of the conduct of the colored men engaged, I am prepared to make an emphatic denial of the gross imputation against them. They were charged specially with being unreliable, with deserting Captain Brown [at] the first opportunity, and going back to their masters; and with being so indifferent to the work of their salvation from the yoke, as to have to be forced into service by the Captain, contrary to their will.

On the Sunday evening of the outbreak, when we visited the plantations and acquainted the slaves with our purpose to effect their liberation, the greatest enthusiasm was manifested by them—joy and hilarity beamed from every countenance. One old mother, white-haired from age, and borne down with the labors of many years in bonds, when told of the work in hand, replied: "God bless you! God bless you!" She then kissed the party at her house, and requested all to kneel, which we did, and she offered prayer to God for His blessing on the enterprise, and our success. At the slaves' quarters, there was apparently a general jubilee, and they stepped forward manfully, without impressing or coaxing. In one case, only, was there any hesitation. A dark-complexioned free-born man refused to take up arms. He showed the only want of confidence in the movement, and far less courage than any slave consulted about the plan. In fact, so far as I could learn, the free blacks [of the] South are much less reliable than the slaves, and infinitely more fearful. In Washington City, a party of free colored persons offered their services to the Mayor, to aid in suppressing our movement. Of the slaves who followed us to the Ferry, some were sent to help remove stores, and the others were drawn up in a circle around the engine-house, at one time, where they were, by Captain Brown's order, furnished by me with pikes, mostly, and acted as a guard to the prisoners to prevent their escape, which they did.

As in the war of the American Revolution, the first blood shed was a black man's, Crispus Attucks's, so at Harper's Ferry, the first blood shed by our party, after the arrival of the United States troops, was that of a slave. In the beginning of the encounter, and before the troops had fairly emerged from the bridge, a slave was shot. I saw him fall. . . . Of the men shot on the rocks, when [John Henry] Kagi's party were compelled to take to the river, some were slaves, and they suffered death before they would desert their companions, and their bodies fell into the waves beneath. Captain Brown, who was surprised and pleased by the promptitude with which they volunteered, and with their manly bearing at the scene of violence, remarked to me, on that Monday morning, that he was agreeably disappointed in the behavior of the slaves; for he did not expect one out of ten to be willing to fight. The truth of the Harper's Ferry "raid," as it has been called, in regard to the part taken by the slaves, and the aid given by colored men generally, demonstrates clearly: first, that the conduct of the slaves is a strong guarantee of the weakness of the institution, should a favorable opportunity occur; and, secondly, that the colored people, as a body, were well represented by numbers, both in the fight, and in the number who suffered martyrdom afterward.

The first report of the number of "insurrectionists" killed was seventeen, which showed that several slaves were killed; for there were only ten of the men that belonged to the Kennedy Farm who lost their lives at the Ferry, namely: John Henri Kagi, Jerry Anderson, Watson Brown, Oliver Brown, Stewart Taylor,

Adolphus Thompson, William Thompson, William Leeman, all eight whites, and Dangerfield Newby and Sherrard Lewis Leary, both colored. The rest reported dead, according to their own showing, were colored. Captain Brown had but seventeen with him, belonging to the Farm, and when all was over, there were four besides himself taken to Charlestown, prisoners, viz.: A. D. Stevens, Edwin Coppic, white; John A. Copeland and Shields Green, colored. It is plain to be seen from this, that there was a proper percentage of colored men killed at the Ferry, and executed at Charlestown. Of those that escaped from the fangs of the human bloodhounds of slavery, there were four whites, and one colored man, myself being the sole colored man of those at the Farm.

That hundreds of slaves were ready, and would have joined in the work, had Captain Brown's sympathies not been aroused in favor of the families of his prisoners, and that a very different result would have been seen, in consequence, there is no question. There was abundant opportunity for him and the party to leave a place in which they held entire sway and possession, before the arrival of the troops. And so cowardly were the slaveholders, proper, that from Colonel Lewis Washington, the descendant of the Father of his Country, General George Washington, they were easily taken prisoners. They had not pluck enough to fight, nor to use the well-loaded arms in their possession, but were concerned rather in keeping a whole skin by parleying, or in spilling cowardly tears, to excite pity, as did Colonel Washington, and that way escape merited punishment. No, the conduct of the slaves was beyond all praise; and could our brave old Captain have steeled his heart against the entreaties of his captives, or shut up the fountain of his sympathies against their families—could he, for the moment, have forgotten them, in the selfish thought of his own friends and kindred, or, by adhering to the original plan, have left the place, and thus looked forward to the prospective freedom of the slave—hundreds ready and waiting would have been armed before twenty-four hours had elapsed. As it was, even the noble old man's mistakes were productive of great good, the fact of which the future historian will record, without the embarrassment attending its present narration. John Brown did not only capture and hold Harper's Ferry for twenty hours, but he held the whole South. He captured President [James] Buchanan and his Cabinet, convulsed the whole country, killed Governor [Henry] Wise, and dug the mine and laid the train which will eventually dissolve the union between Freedom and Slavery. The rebound reveals the truth. So let it be!

• • •

In this fiery speech Martin Robinson Delany, the son of free blacks and a leading African-American officer in the Union army, speaks to a congregation of several hundred at St. Helena Island, South Carolina, about the struggle against slavery and the struggle for freedom after the Emancipation Proclamation. Delany was employed by the Freedmen's Bureau at the end of the Civil War, but the bureau, worried about his politics, sent Lieutenant Edward M. Stoeber to listen to his address at the Brick Church at St. Helena Island. His account is the only existing text of this speech. Stoeber noted, "The excitement with the congregation was immense" and "cheers were given to some particular sentence of the speech." Afterward congregants told Stoeber, "they would get rid of the Yankee employer" and that Delany "is the only man who ever told them the truth."

Martin Delany's Advice to Former Slaves (July 23, 1865)[11]

It was only a War policy of the Government, to declare the slaves of the South free, knowing that the whole power of the South, laid in the possession of the Slaves.

But I want you to *understand*, that we would not have become free, had we not armed ourselves and fought out our independence. . . .

If I had been a slave, I would have been most troublesome and not to be conquered by any threat or punishment. I would not have worked, and no one would have dared to come near me, I would have struggled for life or death, and would have thrown fire and sword between them. I know *you* have been good, only too good. I was told by a friend of mine that when owned by a man and put to work on the field, he laid quietly down, and just looked out for the overseer to come along, when he pretended to work very hard. But he confessed to me, that he never had done a fair day's work for his master. And so he was right, so I would have done the same, and all of you ought to have done the same.

People say that you are too lazy to work, that you have no intelligence to get on for yourselves, without being guided and driven to the work by overseers. I say it is a lie, and a blasphemous lie, and I will prove it to be so.

I am going to tell you now, what you are worth. As you know Christopher Columbus landed here in 1492. They came here only for the purpose to dig gold, gather precious pearls, diamonds and all sorts of jewels, only for the "proud Aristocracy of White Spaniards" and Portuguese, to adorn their persons, to have brooches for their breasts, earrings for their ears, Bracelets for their ankles and rings for their limbs and fingers. They found here . . . Indians whom they obliged to dig and work and slave for them—but they found out that they died away too fast and cannot stand the work. In course of time they had taken some blacks . . . along with them and put them to work— they could not stand it—and yet the Whites say they are superior to our race, though they could not stand it. . . .

The work was so profitable which those poor blacks did, that in the year 1502

Charles the V gave permission to import into America yearly 4,000 blacks. The profit of these sales was so immense, that afterwards even the Virgin Queen of England and James the II took part in the Slave trade and were accumulating great wealth for the Treasury of the Government. And so you always have been the means of riches.

I tell you I have been all over Africa (I was born there) and I tell you (as I told to the Geographical Faculty of London) that those people there, are a well-driving class of cultivators, and I never saw or heard of one of our brethren there to travel without taking seeds with him as much as he can carry and to sow it wherever he goes to, or to exchange it with his brethren.

So you ought further to know, that all the spices, cotton, rice, and coffee has only been brought over by you, from the land of our brethren.

Your masters who lived in opulence, kept you to hard work by some contemptible being called overseer—who chastised and beat you whenever he pleased—while your master lived in some Northern town or in Europe to squander away the wealth only you acquired for him. He never earned a single Dollar in his life. You men and women, every one of you around me, made thousands and thousands of dollars for your master. Only you were the means for your masters to lead the ideal and inglorious life, and to give his children the education, which he denied to you, for fear you may awake to conscience. If I look around me, I tell you all the houses of this Island and in Beaufort, they are all familiar to my eye, they are the same structures which I have met with in Africa. They have all been made by the Negroes, you can see it by such exteriors.

I tell you they cannot teach you anything, and they could not make them because they have not the brain to do it. At least I mean the Southern people; Oh the Yankees they are smart. Now tell me from all you have heard from me, are you not worth anything? Are you those men whom they think, God only created as a curse and for a slave? Whom they do not consider their equals? As I said before the Yankees are smart; there are good ones and bad ones. The good ones, if they are good they are very good, if they are bad, they are very bad. But the worst and most contemptible, and even worse than even your masters were, are those Yankees, who hired themselves as overseers.

Believe not in these School teachers, Emissaries, Ministers, and agents, because they never tell you the truth, and I particularly warn you against those Cotton Agents, who come honey mouthed unto you, their only intent being to make profit by your inexperience.

If there is a man who comes to you, who will meddle with your affairs, send him to one of your more enlightened brothers, who shall ask him who he is, what business he seeks with you, etc.

Believe none but those Agents who are sent out by Government, to enlighten and guide you. I am an officer in the service of the U.S. Government, and ordered to aid Gen[era]l [Rufus] Saxton, who has been only lately appointed Ass[istan]t Com[missione]r from South Carolina. So is Gen[era]l [Edward A.] Wild Ass[istan]t Com[missione]r for Georgia.

When Chief Justice [Salmon P.] Chase was down here to speak to you, some of those malicious and abominable New York papers derived from it that he only seeks to be elected by you as President. I have no such ambition, I let them have for a President a white or a black one. I don't care who it be—it may be who has a mind to. I shall not be intimidated whether by threats or imprisonment, and no power will keep me from telling you the truth. So I expressed myself even at Charleston, the hotbed of those scoundrels, your old masters, without fear or reluctance.

So I will come to the main purpose for which I have come to see you. As before the whole *South* depended upon you, now the *whole country* will depend upon you. I give you an advice how to get along. Get up a community and get all the lands you can—if you cannot get any singly.

Grow as much vegetables, etc., as you want for your families; on the other part of the land you cultivate Rice and Cotton. Now for instance one acre will grow a crop of Cotton of $90—now a land with ten acres will bring $900 every year: if you cannot get the land all yourself,—the community can, and so you can divide the profit. There is Tobacco for instance (Virginia is the great place for Tobacco). There are whole squares at Dublin and Liverpool named after some place of Tobacco notoriety, so you see of what enormous value your labor was to the benefits of your masters. Now you understand that I want you to be the producers of this country. It is the wish of the Government for you to be so. We will send friends to you, who will further instruct you how to come to the end of our wishes. You see that by so adhering to our views, you will become a wealthy and powerful population.

Now I look around me and notice a man, barefooted, covered with rags and dirt. Now I ask, what is that man doing, for whom is he working. I hear that he works for that and that farmer for 30 cents a day. I tell you that must not be. That would be cursed slavery over again. I will not have it, the Government will not have it, and the Government shall hear about it. *I* will tell the Government.

I tell you slavery is over, and shall never return again. We have now 200,000 of our men well drilled in arms and used to War fare, and I tell you . . . that slavery shall not come back again, if you are determined it will not return again.

Now go to work, and in a short time I will see you again, and other friends will come to show you how to begin.

Have your fields in good order and well tilled and planted, and when I pass the fields and see a land well planted and well cared for, then I may be sure from the look of it, that it belongs to a free Negro, and when I see a field thinly planted and little cared for, then I may think it belongs to some man who works it with slaves.

• • •

After helping to organize the First U.S. Colored Troops, which he later joined as chaplain, Henry McNeal Turner became a delegate to the state constitutional convention in Atlanta and was elected as a representative to the Georgia state legislature in 1868. But soon after, he was among two dozen legislators expelled for the "crime" of being black. Here is an excerpt of his address to his fellow legislators denouncing the expulsions.

Henry McNeal Turner, "On the Eligibility of Colored Members to Seats in the Georgia Legislature" (September 3, 1868)[12]

Before proceeding to argue this question upon its intrinsic merits, I wish the members of this House to understand the position that I take. I hold that I am a member of this body. Therefore, sir, I shall neither fawn or cringe before any party, nor stoop to *beg* them for my rights. Some of my colored fellow members, in the course of their remarks, took occasion to appeal to the *sympathies* of Members on the opposite side, and to eulogize their character for magnanimity. It reminds me very much, sir, of slaves begging under the lash. I am here to demand my rights, and to hurl thunderbolts at the men who would dare to cross the threshold of my manhood. There is an old aphorism which says, "Fight the Devil with fire," and if I should observe the rule in this instance, I wish gentlemen to understand that it is but fighting them with their own weapon.

The scene presented in this House, today, is one unparalleled in the history of the world. From this day, back to the day when God breathed the breath of life into Adam, no analogy for it can be found. Never, in the history of the world, has a man been arraigned before a body clothed with legislative, judicial or executive functions, charged with the offence of being of a darker hue than his fellowmen. I know that questions have been before the Courts of this country, and of other countries, involving topics not altogether dissimilar to that which is being discussed here today. But, sir, never in all the history of the great nations of this world—never before—has a man been arraigned, charged with an offence committed by the God of Heaven Himself. Cases may be found where men have been deprived of their rights for crimes and misdemeanors; but it has remained for the State of Georgia, in the very heart of the nineteenth century, to call a man before the bar, and there charge him with an act for which he is no more responsible than for the head which he carries upon his shoulders. The Anglo-Saxon race, sir, is a most surprising one. No man has ever been more deceived in that race than I have been for the last three weeks. I was not aware that there was in the character of that race so much cowardice, or so much pusillanimity. The treachery which has been exhibited in it by gentlemen belonging to that race has shaken my confidence in it more than anything that has come under my observation from the day of my birth.

What is the question at issue? Why, sir, this Assembly, today, is discussing and deliberating on a judgment; there is not a Cherubim that sits around God's eternal Throne, today, that would not tremble—even were an order issued by the Supreme God Himself—to come down here and sit in judgment on my manhood. Gentlemen may look at this question in whatever light they choose, and with just as much indifference as they may think proper to assume, but I tell you, sir, that this is a question which will not die today. This event shall be remembered by posterity for ages yet to come, and while the sun shall continue to climb the hills of heaven.

Whose Legislature is this? Is it a white man's Legislature, or is it a black man's Legislature? Who voted for a Constitutional Convention, in obedience to the mandate of the Congress of the United States? Who first rallied around the standard of Reconstruction? Who set the ball of loyalty rolling in the State of Georgia? And whose voice was heard on the hills and in the valleys of this State? It was the voice of the brawny-armed Negro, with the few humanitarian-hearted white men who came to our assistance. I claim the honor, sir, of having been the instrument of convincing hundreds—yea, thousands—of white men, that to reconstruct under the measures of the United States Congress was the safest and the best course for the interest of the State. . . .

[T]here are persons in this Legislature today, who are ready to spit their poison in my face, while they themselves opposed, with all their power, the ratification of this Constitution. They question my right to a seat in this body, to represent the people whose legal votes elected me. This objection, sir, is an unheard of monopoly of power. No analogy can be found for it, except it be the case of a man who should go into my house, take possession of my wife and children, and then tell me to walk out. I stand very much in the position of a criminal before your bar, because I dare to be the exponent of the views of those who sent me here. Or, in other words, we are told that if black men want to speak, they must speak through white trumpets; if black men want their sentiments expressed, they must be adulterated and sent through white messengers, who will quibble, and equivocate, and evade, as rapidly as the pendulum of a clock. If this be not done, then the black men have committed an outrage, and their Representatives must be denied the right to represent their constituents.

The great question, sir, is this: Am I a man? If I am such, I claim the rights of a man. Am I not a man because I happen to be of a darker hue than honorable gentlemen around me? . . .

But Mr. Speaker, I do not regard this movement as a thrust at me, it is a thrust at the Bible—a thrust at the God of the Universe, for making a man and not finishing him; it is simply calling the Great Jehovah a fool. Why, sir, though we are not white, we have accomplished much. We have pioneered civilization here; we have built up your country; we have worked in your fields, and garnered your harvests, for two hundred and fifty years! And what do we ask of you in return? Do we ask you for compensation for the sweat our fathers bore for you—for the tears you have caused, and the hearts you have broken, and the lives you have curtailed, and the blood you have spilled? Do we ask retaliation? We ask it not. We are willing to let the dead past bury its dead; but we ask you now for our *rights*. You have all the elements of superiority upon your side; you have our money and your own; you have our education and your own; and you have your land and our own, too. We, who number hundreds of thousands in Georgia, including our wives and families, with not a foot of land to call our own—strangers in the land of our birth; without money, without education, without aid, without a roof to cover us while we live, nor sufficient clay to cover us when we die! It is extraordinary that a race such as yours, professing gallantry, and chivalry, and education, and superiority, living in a land where ringing chimes call child and sire to the Church of God—a land where Bibles are read and Gospel truths are spoken, and where courts of justice are presumed to exist; it is extraordinary, I say, that, with all these advantages on your side, you can make war upon the poor defenseless black man.

Civil War and Class Conflict

An Eyewitness Account of the Flour Riot in New York (February 1837)

Hinton Rowan Helper, *The Impending Crisis of the South* (1857)

"Mechanic" (Unknown), "Voting by Classes" (October 13, 1863)

Joel Tyler Headley, *The Great Riots of New York* (1873)

Four Documents on Disaffection in the South During the Civil War
(1864 to 1865)
  Report on a Bread Riot in Savannah, Georgia (April 1864)
  "Exempt" (Unknown), "To Go, Or Not to Go" (June 28, 1864)
  O.G.G. (Unknown), Letter to the Editor (February 17, 1865)
  Columbus Sun, "The Class That Suffer" (February 17, 1865)

J. A. Dacus, *Annals of the Great Strikes in the United States* (1877)

Most histories of the Civil War have concentrated on the military struggle between the North and South, in a war that took six hundred thousand lives (the equivalent of more than three million dead in today's population), however something important has been overlooked: the conflict between rich and poor on both sides of the conflict.

In the North, as the industrial system grew, men and women trapped in the factories began to rebel against their employers, against the conditions of their lives. The coming of the war muted this conflict, but did not eliminate it. There were strikes all over the country during the war. The war itself was seen in class terms. Because the rich could escape the draft by paying $300, it was the poor, as in any war, who died in battle. The draft riots in New York and other places were directed both against the rich and against black people, whom they saw as responsible for the onset of the war.

In the South, only a minority of white people were slave owners, but many poor whites were persuaded that their future also depended on the maintenance of slavery. Some Southern whites volunteered, and others were drafted. But as the war went on, desertion grew in the Confederate army. At home, Southern women rioted when they saw their husbands and sons suffering and dying in the war while plantation owners grew cotton instead of food because cotton was more profitable.

Thus, while forces in the North and South both demanded "unity" to fight the war, class conflict continued. The unity was artificial, created by the rhetoric of politicians—and enforced by arms. Working people in the North would be attacked by soldiers if they dared to strike. Indians would be massacred in Colorado by the U.S. Army. And those daring to criticize Lincoln's policies would be put in jail without trial—perhaps thirty thousand political prisoners suffered this fate.

It was a classic situation, the onset of war spurring demands for national unity, though in reality the nation was divided between rich and poor. When the war ended, that division would assert itself forcefully, dramatically.

• • •

Here is one account of unrest in the North, from an unsympathetic observer. It describes the actions of six thousand New Yorkers who, before the Civil War, assaulted local flour merchants who were hoarding flour in order to drive up prices.

An Eyewitness Account of the Flour Riot in New York (February 1837)[1]

There were . . . speakers . . . who came directly to the business of the meeting, and, in the most exciting manner, denounced the landlords, and the holders of flour, for the prices of rents and provisions. One of these orators, in the course of his address, after working upon the passions of his audience until they were fitted for the work of spoil and outrage, is reported to have expressly directed the popular vengeance against Mr. Eli Hart, who is one of our most extensive flour dealers on commission. "Fellow-citizens!" he exclaimed, "Mr. Hart has now 53,000 barrels of flour in his store; let us go and offer him eight dollars a barrel, and if he does not take it"— here some person touched the orator on the shoulder, and he suddenly lowered his voice, and finished his sentence by saying, "we shall depart from him in peace."

The hint was sufficient; and a large body of the meeting moved off in the direction of Mr. Hart's store, in Washington, between Dey and Courtlandt streets. The store is a very large brick building, having three wide but strong iron doors upon the street. Being apprised of the approach of the mob, the clerks secured the doors and windows; but not until the middle door had been forced, and some twenty or thirty barrels of flour or more, rolled into the street, and the heads staved in. At this point of time Mr. Hart himself arrived on the ground, with a posse of officers from the police. The officers were assailed by a portion of the mob in Dey street, their staves wrested from them, and shivered to pieces. The number of the mob not being large at this time, the officers succeeded in entering the store, and for a short time interrupted the work of destruction.

The mayor next arrived at the scene of waste and riot, and attempted to remonstrate with the infatuated multitude on the folly of their conduct—but to no purpose; their numbers were rapidly increasing, and his honor was assailed with missiles of all sorts at hand, and with such fury that he was compelled to retire. Large reinforcements of the rioters having arrived, the officers were driven from the field, and the store carried by assault—the first iron door torn from its hinges, being used as a battering ram against the others. The *destructives* at once rushed in, and the windows and doors of the lofts were broken open. And now again commenced the work of destruction.

Barrels of flour, by dozens, fifties and hundreds were tumbled into the street from the doors, and thrown in rapid succession from the windows, and the heads of those which did not break in falling, were instantly staved in. Intermingled with the flour, were sacks of wheat by the hundred, which were cast into the street, and their contents thrown upon the pavement. About one thousand bushels of wheat, and four or five hundred barrels of flour, were thus wantonly and foolishly as well as wickedly destroyed. The most active of the *destructionists* were foreigners—indeed the greater part of the assemblage was of exotic origin; but there were probably five hundred or a thousand others, standing by and abetting their incendiary labors.

Amidst the falling and bursting of the barrels and sacks of wheat, numbers of women were engaged, like the crones who strip the dead in battle, filling the boxes and baskets with which they were provided, and their aprons, with flour, and making off with it. One of the destructives, a boy named James Roach, was seen upon one of the upper window sills, throwing barrel after barrel into the street, and crying out with every throw—"here goes flour at eight dollars a barrel!" Early in the assault, Mr. Hart's counting room was entered, his books and papers seized and scattered to the winds. And herein, probably, consists his greatest loss.

Night had now closed upon the scene, but the work of destruction did not cease until strong bodies of police arrived, followed, soon afterward, by detachments of troops. The store was then cleared by justices Lownds and Bloodgood, and several of the rioters were arrested, and dispatched to Bridewell, under charge of Bowyer, of the police. On his way to the prison, he and his assistants were assailed, his coat torn from his back, and several of the prisoners were rescued. Several more, however, were afterwards captured and secured.

Before the close of the proceedings at Hart's store, however, the cry of "Meech" was raised—whereupon a detachment of the rioters crossed over to Coenties slip, for the purpose of attacking the establishment of Meech and Co., but the store of S. H. Herrick and Co. coming first in their way, they commenced an attack upon that. The windows were first smashed in with a shower of brick-bats, and the doors immediately afterwards broken. Some twenty or thirty barrels of flour were then rolled into the street, and the heads of ten or a dozen knocked in.

The numbers of the rioters engaged in this work was comparatively small and they soon desisted from their labors—probably from an intimation that a strong body of the police were on the way thither. Another account is that they were induced to desist from the work of mischief, by an assurance from the owner, that if they would spare the flour, he would give it all to the poor today. Be this, however, as it may, the officers were promptly on the spot, and by the aid of the citizens who collected rapidly, the wretched rabble was dispersed—some thirty or forty of them having been taken and secured at the two points of action. Unfortunately, however, the ringleaders escaped almost if not quite to a man.

• • •

Disaffection in the South took many forms during the Civil War, including desertions from the Confederate Army and resentment of poor whites against the Southern plantation owners and the Southern political establishment. Some of that class consciousness, present in the South long before the Civil War, was articulated in 1857 by the writer Hilton Rowman Helper, whose book *The Impending Crisis of the South* was banned by Southern states opposed to its message.

Hinton Rowan Helper, *The Impending Crisis of the South* (1857)[2]

We have not breathed away seven and twenty years in the South, without becoming acquainted with the demagogical maneuverings of the oligarchy. Their intrigues and tricks of legerdemain are as familiar to us as household words; in vain might the world be ransacked for a more precious junta of flatterers and cajolers. It is amusing to ignorance, amazing to credulity, and insulting to intelligence, to hear them in their blathering efforts to mystify and pervert the sacred principles of liberty, and turn the curse of slavery into a blessing. To the illiterate poor whites—made poor and ignorant by the system of slavery—they hold out the idea that slavery is the very bulwark of our liberties, and the foundation of American independence! For hours at a time, day after day, will they expatiate upon the inexpressible beauties and excellencies of this great, free and independent nation; and finally, with the most extravagant gesticulations and rhetorical flourishes, conclude their nonsensical ravings, by attributing all the glory and prosperity of the country, from Maine to Texas, and from Georgia to California, to the "invaluable institutions of the South!" With what patience we could command, we have frequently listened to the incoherent and truth-murdering declamations of these champions of slavery, and, in the absence of a more politic method of giving vent to our disgust and indignation, have involuntarily bit our lips into blisters.

The lords of the lash are not only absolute masters of the blacks, who are bought and sold, and driven about like so many cattle, but they are also the oracles and arbiters of all non-slaveholding whites, whose freedom is merely nominal, and whose unparalleled illiteracy and degradation is purposely and fiendishly perpetuated. How little the "poor white trash," the great majority of the Southern people, know of the real condition of the country is, indeed, sadly astonishing. The truth is, they know nothing of public measures, and little of private affairs, except what their imperious masters, the slave-drivers, condescend to tell, and that is but precious little, and even that little, always garbled and one-sided, is never told except in public harangues; for the haughty cavaliers of shackles and handcuffs will not degrade themselves by holding private converse with those who have neither dimes nor hereditary rights in human flesh.

Whenever it pleases, and to the extent it pleases, a slaveholder to become communicative, poor whites may hear with fear and trembling, but not speak. They must be as mum as dumb brutes, and stand in awe of their august superiors, or be crushed with stern rebukes, cruel oppressions, or downright violence. If they dare to think for themselves, their thoughts must be forever concealed. The expression of any sentiment at all conflicting with the gospel of slavery, dooms them at once in the community in which they live, and then, whether willing or unwilling, they are obliged to become heroes, martyrs, or exiles. They may thirst for knowledge, but there is no Moses among them to smite it out of the rocks of Horeb. The black veil, through whose almost impenetrable meshes light seldom gleams, has long been pendent over their eyes, and there, with fiendish jealousy, the slave-driving ruffians sedulously guard it. Non-slaveholders are not only kept in ignorance of what is transpiring at the North, but they are continually misinformed of what is going on even in the South. Never were the poorer classes of a people, and those classes so largely in the majority, and all inhabiting the same country, so basely duped, so adroitly swindled, or so damnably outraged.

It is expected that the stupid and sequacious [malleable] masses, the white victims of slavery, will believe, and, as a general thing, they do believe, whatever the slaveholders tell them; and thus it is that they are cajoled into the notion that they are the freest, happiest and most intelligent people in the world, and are taught to look with prejudice and disapprobation upon every new principle or progressive movement. Thus it is that the South, woefully inert and inventionless, has lagged behind the North, and is now weltering in the cesspool of ignorance and degradation.

We have already intimated that the opinion is prevalent throughout the South that the free States are quite sterile and unproductive, and that they are mainly dependent on us for breadstuffs and other provisions. So far as the cereals, fruits, garden vegetables and esculent [edible] roots are concerned, we have . . . shown the utter falsity of this opinion; and we now propose to show that it is equally erroneous in other particulars, and very far from the truth in the general reckoning. We can prove, and we intend to prove, from facts in our possession, that the hay crop of the free States is worth considerably more in dollars and cents than all the cotton, tobacco, rice, hay and hemp produced in the fifteen slave States. This statement may strike some of our readers with amazement, and others may, for the moment, regard it as quite incredible; but it is true, nevertheless, and we shall soon proceed to confirm it. The single free State of New-York produces more than three times the quantity of hay that is produced in all the slave States. Ohio produces a larger number of tons than all the Southern and Southwestern States, and so does Pennsylvania. Vermont, little and unpretending as she is, does the same thing, with the exception of Virginia. Look at the facts . . . and let your own eyes, physical and intellectual, confirm you in the truth.

And yet, forsooth, the slave-driving oligarchy would whip us into the belief that agriculture is not one of the leading and lucrative pursuits of the free States, that the soil there is an uninterrupted barren waste, and that our Northern brethren, having the advantage in nothing except wealth, population, inland and foreign commerce, manufactures, mechanism, inventions, literature, the arts and sciences, and their concomitant branches of profitable industry,—miserable objects of charity—are dependent on us for the necessaries of life.

• • •

In this letter, sent to the editor of the Columbus, Georgia, *Daily Sun*, an unknown laborer challenges an editorial from a competing newspaper, the *Enquirer*. The letter provides a window on the class consciousness of workers in the Confederacy and also the resentment at the broken promises about the gains that ordinary people would receive from the war.

"Mechanic" (Unknown), "Voting by Classes" (October 13, 1863)[3]

Editor *Daily Sun:*—I notice in the Enquirer, of Friday evening, an article complaining bitterly of the people voting by classes, in which both classes are accused of clannishness, but the burden of his complaint seems to rest on mechanics and workingmen. He says, "there is certainly no ground for any antagonism in the city." In this the Enquirer is mistaken, for any man, woman or child can see that the people are dividing into two classes, just as fast as the pressure of the times can force them on. As for example: class No. 1, in their thirst for gain, in their worship of Mammon, and in their mighty efforts to appropriate every dollar on earth to their own account, have lost sight of every principle of humanity, patriotism, and virtue itself, and seem to have forgotten that the very treasures they are now heaping up are the price of blood, and unless this mania ceases, will be the price of liberty itself; for we know something of the feeling which now exists in the army, as well as in our work-shops at home. The men know well enough that their helpless families are not cared for, as they were promised at the beginning of the war. They know that the depreciation of our currency is only a trick of our enemies at home, else why should they strive so hard to secure it all? They know, too, that every day they remain from home, reduces them more and more in circumstances, and that by the close of the war a large majority of the soldiery will be unable to live, in fact, many of them are ruined now, as many of their homes and other effects are passing into the hands of speculators and extortioners, for subsistence to their families. Thus you see, that all the capital, both in money and property, in the South, is passing into the hands of class No. 1 while class No. 2 are traveling down, soon to take their station among the descendants of Ham. You can easily perceive who are class No. 2. The soldiery, the mechanics, and the workingmen, not only of Columbus, but of all the Confederate States. In view of these things, is it not time that our class should awake to a sense of their danger, and in the mildest possible manner begin the work of self-defense, and endeavor to escape a bondage more servile than that imposed by the Aristocracy of England on their poor peasantry? Then we claim the right, as the first alternative, to try and avert the great calamity, by electing such men to the councils of the nation as we think will best represent our interests. If this should fail, we must then try more potent remedies.

As the Enquirer is ignorant of the evils we complain of, and the cause of our alienation, I will briefly enumerate some of them, though we thought they were plain enough to all who wish to see.

In the first place, there has been an effort made to fix a price on labor without the consent of the mechanics or workingmen, whilst the producers of the necessaries of life, and the speculators, are left to extortion without stint or limit, until nothing less that fifteen hundred per cent profit will satisfy the most of them.

Let us compare a few figures before we close, and you can see that we have justifiable cause of complaint. I once could get 75 pounds of flour for a day's work. What do I get now? I once got 25 pounds of bacon for a day's work. What do I get now? *Only two.* I once could get 50 pounds of beef for a day's work. What do I get now? *Only six.* I once could get eight bushels of sweet potatoes for a day's work. What can I get now? *Not one.* And at the same rate through the whole catalogue of family supplies. Thus you see the Enquirer is again mistaken, when he says that "labor is independent of capital, and always commands *remunerative* prices." Wonder if he would work for three dollars per day, and board himself, at the present prices of provisions?

But, notwithstanding the mechanics and working men can barely sustain animal life, their condition is much better than the poor soldiers', who are fighting the rich man's fight, for they suffer all of the privations and hardships incident to the life of a soldier, with a perfect knowledge of the sufferings of their families at home, who are (many of them) without a comfortable shelter; many of them refugees in a strange land, despised, persecuted and insulted, because a merciless foe has driven them into exile, and because their husbands, brothers and natural protectors are engaged in the noble cause of liberty. True, they are sometimes offered assistance at the sacrifice of their honor, and that by men who occupy high places both in church and State. Then is there not an "organization of hostility" against the interests of our class, which justice and honor demand that we should guard with unceasing vigilance? The Enquirer speaks of equality, which is denied us by class No. 1, in the doctrine of property qualification, or disenfranchisement, which is gradually working its way (secretly) into the circles of the rich, which I, for one, have heard strongly advocated.

• • •

The institution of a draft during the Civil War caused widespread resentment throughout the North, leading to a number of violent protests in 1863, particularly in New York. Many working-class Irish immigrants in New York pointed to the fact that the rich could buy their way out the draft, but also turned their anger against black people, seeing the war as a war against slavery in which poor whites were dying. They blamed blacks for their own misery, especially when blacks, desperate for work themselves, were used as strikebreakers. On July 13, 1863, a number of draft resisters burned down a New York City draft office, setting off four days of violence, most of it targeted against blacks. In this account of the riots, historian Joel Tyler Headley describes some of the genuine grievances of the Northern draft resisters, but also reveals his fears of sweeping change.

Joel Tyler Headley, *The Great Riots of New York* (1873)[4]

Meanwhile, events were assuming an alarming aspect in the western part of the city. Early in the morning men began to assemble here in separate groups, as if in accordance with a previous arrangement, and at last moved quietly north along the various avenues. Women, also, like camp followers, took the same direction in crowds. They were thus divided into separate gangs, apparently to take each avenue in their progress, and make a clean sweep. The factories and workshops were visited, and the men compelled to knock off work and join them, while the proprietors were threatened with the destruction of their property, if they made any opposition. The separate crowds were thus swelled at almost every step, and armed with sticks, and clubs, and every conceivable weapon they could lay hands on, they moved north towards some point which had evidently been selected as a place of rendezvous. This proved to be a vacant lot near Central Park, and soon the living streams began to flow into it, and a more wild, savage, and heterogeneous-looking mass could not be imagined. After a short consultation they again took up the line of march, and in two separate bodies, moved down Fifth and Sixth Avenues, until they reached Forty-sixth and Forty-seventh Streets, when they turned directly east.

The number composing this first mob has been so differently estimated, that it would be impossible from reports merely, to approximate the truth. A pretty accurate idea, however, can be gained of its immense size, from a statement made by Mr. King, son of President [Charles] King, of Columbia College. Struck by its magnitude, he had the curiosity to get some estimate of it by timing its progress, and he found that although it filled the broad street from curbstone to curbstone, and was moving rapidly, it took between twenty and twenty-five minutes for it to pass a single point.

A ragged, coatless, heterogeneously weaponed army, it heaved tumultuously along toward Third Avenue. Tearing down the telegraph poles as it crossed the Harlem and New Haven Railroad track, it surged angrily up around the building where the drafting was going on. The small squad of police stationed there to repress disorder looked on bewildered, feeling they were powerless in the presence of such a host. Soon a stone went crashing through a window, which was the signal for a general assault on the doors. These giving way before the immense pressure, the foremost rushed in, followed by shouts and yells from those behind, and began to break up the furniture. The drafting officers, in an adjoining room, alarmed, fled precipitately through the rear of the building. The mob seized the wheel in which were the names, and what books, papers, and lists were left, and tore them up, and scattered them in every direction. A safe stood on one side, which was supposed to contain important papers, and on this they fell with clubs and stones, but in vain. Enraged at being thwarted, they set fire to the building, and hurried out of it. As the smoke began to ascend, the onlooking multitude without sent up a loud cheer. Though the upper part of the building was occupied by families, the rioters, thinking that the officers were concealed there, rained stones and brick-bats against the windows, sending terror into the hearts of the inmates. Deputy Provost Marshal Vanderpoel, who had mingled in the crowd, fearing for the lives of the women and children, boldly stepped to the front, and tried to appease the mob, telling them the papers were all destroyed, and begged them to fall back, and let others help the inmates of the building, or take hold themselves. The reply was a heavy blow in the face. Vanderpoel shoved the man who gave it aside, when he was assailed with a shower of blows and curses. Fearing for his life, he broke through the crowd, and hastened to the spot where the police were standing, wholly powerless in the midst of this vast, excited throng.

In the meantime, the flames, unarrested, made rapid way, and communicating to the adjoining building, set it on fire. The volumes of smoke, rolling heavenward, and the crackling and roaring of the flames, seemed for a moment to awe the mob, and it looked silently on the ravaging of a power more terrible and destructive than its own.

At this time Superintendent [of Police John A.] Kennedy was quietly making his way across the town toward the office of the provost marshal, [Marshal] Jenkins. But noticing a fire as he approached, he left his wagon at the corner of Forty-sixth Street and Lexington Avenue, and walked over toward Third Avenue. The street was blocked with people, but they seemed quiet and orderly as any gathering in presence of a fire, and differed from it only in that the countenances of all seemed to wear a pleased, gratified look. As he unsuspiciously edged his way forward toward the fire, he heard some one cry out, "There's Kennedy!" "Which is him?" asked a second; and he was pointed out.

Kennedy was dressed in ordinary citizen's clothes, and carried only a slight bamboo cane. Thinking the allusion to him was prompted only by curiosity, he kept on, when suddenly he felt himself violently pushed against. Turning around, he encountered a man in a soldier's old uniform, and sternly demanded what he meant by that. The words had hardly escaped his lips, when a heavy blow was planted full in his face. Instantly the crowd closed around him, and rained blows in rapid succession on him, until he fell over and down the graded street, some six feet, into a vacant lot. The crowd, with yells, poured after him. Kennedy, springing to his feet, started on a run across the lot towards Forty-seventh Street, distancing his pursuers. But as he reached Forty-seventh Street, and attempted to ascend the embankment, another crowd, which had witnessed the pursuit, rushed upon him, and knocked him back again in front of his pursuers. He quickly sprang up, though bleeding and stunned, for he knew his only chance for life was in keeping his feet. But the crowd closing around on both sides gave him no chance to run. One huge fellow, armed with a heavy club, endeavored to break in his skull, but Kennedy dodged his blows. Careful only for his head, he let them beat his body, while he made desperate efforts to break through the mass, whose demoniacal yells and oaths showed that they intended to take his life. In the struggle the whole crowd, swaying to and fro, slowly advanced toward Lexington Avenue, coming, as they did so, upon a wide mud-hole. "Drown him! drown him!" arose at once on every side, and the next moment a heavy blow, planted under his ear, sent him headforemost into the water.

Falling with his face amid the stones, he was kicked and trampled on, and pounded, till he was a mass of gore. Still struggling desperately for life, he managed to get to his feet again, and made a dash for the middle of the pond. The water was deep, and his murderers, disliking to get wet, did not follow him, but ran around to the other side, to meet him as he came out. But Kennedy was ahead of them, and springing up the bank into Lexington Avenue, saw a man whom he knew, and called out: "John Eagan, come here and save my life!" Mr. Eagan, who was a well-known and influential resident of that vicinity, immediately rushed forward to his assistance, and arrested his pursuers. But the Superintendent was so terribly bruised and mangled, that Eagan did not recognize him. He, however, succeeded in keeping the mob back, who, seeing the horrible condition their victim was in, doubtless thought they had finished him. Other citizens now coming forward, a passing feed wagon was secured, into which Kennedy was lifted, and driven to police headquarters. Acton, who was in the street as the wagon approached, saw the mangled body within, but did not dream who it was. The driver inquired where he should take him. "Around to the [police] station," carelessly replied Acton. The driver hesitated, and inquired again, "Where to?" Acton, supposing it was some drunkard, bruised in a brawl, replied rather petulantly, "Around to the station." The man then told him it was Kennedy. Acton, scanning the features more closely, saw that it indeed was the Superintendent himself in this horrible condition. As the officers gathered around the bleeding, almost unconscious form, a murmur of wrath was heard, a sure premonition what work would be done when the hour of vengeance should come.

• • •

In April 1863, there was a bread riot in Richmond, Virginia. That summer, draft riots occurred in various southern cities. In September, another bread riot broke out in Mobile, Alabama. Georgia Lee Tatum, in her study *Disloyalty in the Confederacy*, writes, "Before the end of the war, there was much disaffection in every state, and many of the disloyal had formed into bands—in some states into well-organized, active societies." Acts of resistance took place not only among soldiers, but also among women forced to deal with the growing costs of the war. These articles from Southern newspapers show the ferment of the time.

Four Documents on Disaffection in the South During the Civil War (1864 to 1865)

REPORT ON A BREAD RIOT IN SAVANNAH, GEORGIA (APRIL 1864)[5]

A small "bread riot" occurred in Savannah [Georgia] on Tuesday last [April 17, 1864]. The News says that a combination of women numbering from fifty to one hundred, appeared at a grocery store on Whitaker street, when their demand for provisions being made, the proprietor was in the act of distributing bacon among them, when others of the party made a rush into the store and helped themselves to whatever they wanted. The same crowd also went to two other places on the same mission, where they obtained bacon, etc. Three of the women were arrested and taken to the guard house, and would be brought before the Mayor Thursday morning.

In relation to this affair, the News says:

> That the present high prices of provisions have provided distress no one can doubt, and it is probable that some who participated in the riotous proceedings of yesterday were goaded to their course by pressure of want, but if we are rightly informed many if not the majority of them, had not even that excuse for the commission of acts of lawlessness. Be this as it may, there can be no necessity or justification for such acts of outrage and robbery. It is not generally the truly worthy deserving poor who resort to such measures, and those who thus set the laws and public propriety at defiance forfeit the sympathy of the community. If there is indeed want and suffering let the sufferers make their condition known in the right quarter, and a community that has never turned a deaf ear to the appeals of the helpless and needy will give them relief.
>
> We trust that our city authorities will investigate this matter, ascertain who they are that truly need assistance, and take the proper steps for their relief. Such action is not only due to the wives and children of soldiers in the service, to the helpless poor, and to the peaceful and good name of our community, but also to the best interests of our city. While the mob spirit should be met with firmness, we should, in these times, act in accordance with the maxim of "help one another." Let the turbulent be rebuked, but let not the worthy and law abiding poor suffer.

"EXEMPT" (UNKNOWN), "TO GO, OR NOT TO GO" (JUNE 28, 1864)[6]

To go or not to go, that is the question:
Whether it pays best to suffer pestering
By idle girls and garrulous old women,
Or to take up arms against a host of Yankees,
And by opposing get killed—To die, to sleep,
(Git eout) and in this sleep to say we "sink
To rest by all our Country's wishes blest"
And live forever—(that's a consummation
Just what I'm after). To march, to fight—
To fight! perchance to die, aye ther's the rub!
For while I'm asleep, who'll take care of Mary
And the babes—when Billy's in the low ground,
Who'll feed 'em, hey! There's the respect
I have for them that makes life sweet;
For who would bear the bag to mill,
Plough Dobbin, cut the wheat, dig taters,
Kill hogs, and do all sorts of drudgery
If I am fool enough to get a Yankee
Bullet on my brain! Who'll cry for me!
Would patriotism pay my debts, when dead?
But oh! The dread of something after death—
That undiscovered fellow who'll court Mary,
And do my huggin—that's agony,
And makes me want to stay home,
Specially as I aint mad with nobody.
Shells and bullets make cowards of us all,
And blam'd my skin if snortin steeds,
And pomp and circumstance of War
Are to be compared with feather beds
And Mary by my side.

O.G.G. (UNKNOWN), LETTER TO THE EDITOR (FEBRUARY 17, 1865)[7]

Mr. Editor: On Thursday last, about fifty women in Miller county, claiming to be soldiers' wives, made a raid upon the tithe depot at Colquit, in said county, and with axes, forced open the door, and abstracted therefrom about fifty sacks of government corn—about one hundred bushels. At last accounts from them, another raid of the same character was apprehended. Wonder why it is that soldiers' wives are reduced to the necessity of providing from themselves? Would not the proper authorities do well to look into the matter? If these women were forced by necessity to commit the depredation above alluded to—and even the wives of soldiers, absent in the defense of their country, their wants should be relieved at once.

Truly yours,

O.G.G.

COLUMBUS SUN, "THE CLASS THAT SUFFER" (FEBRUARY 17, 1865)[8]

Upon poor women and children, upon soldiers who are toiling and bleeding for liberty, upon salaried men who have not the time, or who desire to speculate, the whole weight of this fearful struggle falls. Men of wealth, who are hoarding thousands, put up the piteous cry of exorbitant rates—more bitterly than ever just after increasing the prices one thousand fold, while upon ragged blood drenched soldiers, upon weary despairing, heart sick women, and those whose only dependence is a pitiful yearly sum must be made to bitterly suffer.

Non producers alone feel the war. Others can meet high rates with the same—those who speculate not, must shift as best they can. What matters life or death so avarice can be gratified? What is honor unattended by wealth? What is liberty, unless money can be hoarded by millions? What, if the country be ruined, its women ravished, its homes desolated, its altars violated and freedom forever perish—what matters all so the almighty dollar may be amassed in piles? What care men of the present day whether their country sinks so property may be secured, and the price at which liberty is bought rests as light as possible upon their patriotic shoulders?

That is right. Pile up wealth—no matter whether bread be drawn from the mouth of the soldier's orphan or the one-armed, one limbed hero who hungry walks your streets—take every dollar you can, pay out as little as possible, deprive your noble warriors of every comfort and luxury, increase in every way the necessaries of life, make everybody but yourself and non producers bear the taxes of the war; but be very careful to parade everything you give before the public—talk boldly on the street corners of your love of country, be a grand home general—and, when the war is over, point to your princely palace and its magnificent surroundings and exclaim with pompous swell "These are the results of my patriotism."

• • •

Class conflict continued to find expression after the end of the Civil War. The year 1877 saw the nation deep in an economic crisis. That summer, in the hot cities where poor families lived in cellars and drank dirty water, children became sick in large numbers. That same year, railroad workers went on strike throughout the

East, reacting against wage cuts, long working hours, profiteering by the railroad companies, and deaths and injuries resulting from the absence of safety precautions. The strike spread quickly, and violence escalated as the National Guard and then federal troops (withdrawn from the South) were brought in against the strikers. When the strikes were over, a hundred people were dead, one thousand had been jailed, and one hundred thousand workers had gone on strike. Here, St. Louis journalist J. A. Dacus describes the dynamic of the railway strike.

J. A. Dacus, *Annals of the Great Strikes in the United States* (1877)[9]

And here we find the immediate, potent cause of the Great Strikes. Depression in business, but more important still, depression in transportation rates brought about by the jealousies and hostility of each other of Thomas A. Scott, John W. Garrett, and William H. Vanderbilt, rendering it necessary to reduce operating expenses in order to "make something,"—that is ten per cent on their largely increased amount of stock. The lower orders of laborers were first to feel the weight of this curtailment of income. Meanwhile the higher grades of employe[e]s were still receiving salaries not much less than were obtained ten years ago, when the whole country was enjoying unparalleled prosperity. The higher officers of companies received higher salaries in 1876 than they obtained in 1866, notwithstanding the immense change in values which had taken place.

The reduction of ten per cent in the wages of laborers, which was made by a majority of the railway companies throughout the country during the first half of the year 1877, was sufficient to evoke the earnest protests of the men affected by the curtailment of their income. Had the reduction on all the roads which have cut the wages of their employe[e]s, taken effect at the same time, it is probable that a general strike would have taken place earlier in the season. But the date of reduction was not the same on any considerable number of the roads. Petitions and remonstrances from employe[e]s of railroad companies were received by their employers, but were wholly disregarded. A feeling of discontent was engendered, while the burden of "hard times" weighed more heavily upon workingmen.

The mine was already prepared, a spark only was necessary to cause an explosion. That was supplied by the action of the managers of the Baltimore and Ohio Railroad. The pressure put upon their employe[e]s elicited the spark, and the explosion followed. Commencing at Martinsburg, West Virginia, in less than three hours the strike was fully inaugurated, and had already reached Baltimore. The line of the Baltimore and Ohio Railway was completely invested by the strikers in less than twenty hours. From the Baltimore and Ohio Railway the strikes extended first to the Connellsville branch, then to the Pennsylvania system, Pittsburgh and Fort Wayne, and other railways. In an incredibly short space of time, strikes had taken place in Maryland, Pennsylvania, West Virginia, Ohio, New York, New Jersey, Indiana, Michigan, Illinois, Kentucky, and Missouri. Fifteen thousand men were engaged in the strikes.

The whole country was profoundly agitated. The uprising had assumed a dangerous aspect. A feeling of alarm and dread quickly succeeded the first impulsive feeling of sympathy entertained by the masses for the strikers. The vast numbers engaged in the strikes against the railroads, their apparent determination, the general belief that they were well organized and prepared, produced a dangerous effect upon the idle and vicious classes in all the large cities. Labor unions were suddenly aroused into unwonted activity, and displayed alarming vigor. "The Workingmen's Party of the United States," which is but another name for the "International Association of Workingmen," which has caused so much anxiety to the governments of Europe, came forth from its shadowy coverts, and what had been regarded as a phantom party, assumed a realistic attitude that caused a thrill of astonishment and terror to fall upon the urban populations of the country. Nothing to compare with the demonstrations of the Internationalists in all the larger cities, by day and by night, had, at any time, been witnessed in this country.

In less than four days after the commencement of the strike on the Baltimore and Ohio Railroad, no inconsiderable portion of the territory of the United States was in the hands of the strikers; transportation was embargoed; shops closed, factories deserted, and the great marts which but a few days before had been so noisy, had become silent as "banquet halls deserted." Men remembered France, and the scenes of 1789–93, and trembled as they heard the tumult increase, and saw the mighty masses of strange, grimy men, excited by passions, dark and fearful, surging along the streets. . . .

It was the first time in the history of the country that a labor strike had become so formidable as to require the intervention of the general Government to preserve order. It was nine o'clock at night when the armed battalion of regulars filed through the streets of Washington on the way to the station of the Baltimore and Ohio Railway to embark on the train to proceed to Martinsburg. A vast concourse of people had assembled to witness their departure. The scene was not unlike some of those which characterized the early days of the year 1861. The train moved away from the station at ten o'clock in the evening, bound for the scene of the disturbance.

Meanwhile bands of strikers had taken possession of the railway stations at Cumberland, Grafton, Keyser, and other points, and refused to allow any freight trains to pass. Emissaries were dispatched from the headquarters of the strikers at Martinsburg and Wheeling, to induce the firemen and brakemen; along the

Connellsville Branch, the Pennsylvania road, the Pittsburgh and Chicago, and other railroads in that section of the country to join in the strike. During the day the strikers at Wheeling made a demonstration of a rather threatening character. The single company of militia at that place paraded for action. But it was evident that it was not strong enough to effect anything, and so the citizen-soldiers allowed themselves to be quietly disarmed by the striking workingmen.

The strikers at Martinsburg received the President's proclamation with indifference or positive disrespect. No attention whatever was paid to the injunction to disperse. On the contrary, with constant accessions to their numbers, they became more demonstrative and threatening in their bearing.

During the day, a committee of strikers at Baltimore prepared and caused to be printed and circulated a statement of the causes which impelled them to pursue the course which they had adopted. They declared that they had submitted to three reductions of wages in three years; that they would have acquiesced in a moderate reduction; that they were frequently sent out on a trip to Martinsburg, and there detained four days at the discretion of the company, for which detention they were allowed pay for but two day's time; that they were compelled to pay their board during the time they were detained, which was more than the wages they received; that they had nothing left with which to support their families; that it was a question of bread with them; that when times were dull on the road they could not get more than fifteen day's work in a month; that many sober, steady, economical men became involved in debt last winter; that honest men had their wages attached because they could not meet their expenses; that by a rule of the company any man who had his wages attached should be discharged; that this was a tyranny to which no rational being should submit, and that it was utterly impossible for a man with a family to support himself and family at the reduced rate of wages.

These statements of the striking employe[e]s were not without effect in awakening sympathy for them among the great mass of the people. . . .

It was formally announced that the Baltimore and Ohio Railroad Company would make no further efforts to run trains on their line for the time being.

Thus, the efforts of a gigantic corporation, supplemented by the whole power of the Government to protect and aid it, were ineffective to raise a blockade on one of the great thoroughfares of the nation, when that blockade was enforced only by a number of stokers and brakemen without financial credit or political patronage. Thus the movement had gone on until the National Government found itself powerless for the time being to suppress it. The strikers had now become a mighty power. With a purpose of revolution, with organization and leadership, it was within the grasp of the railroad employe[e]s and other classes of laborers to have taken absolute possession of every commercial center in the nation; aye! even to have overturned the Government itself!

CHAPTER ELEVEN

Strikers and Populists in the Gilded Age

Henry George, *The Crime of Poverty* (April 1, 1885)

August Spies, "Address of August Spies" (October 7, 1886)

Anonymous, "Red-Handed Murder: Negroes Wantonly Killed at Thibodaux, La." (November 26, 1887)

Reverend Ernest Lyon et al., Open Letter from the New Orleans Mass Meeting (August 22, 1888)

Two Speeches by Mary Elizabeth Lease (circa 1890)
  "Wall Street Owns the Country" (circa 1890)
  Speech to the Women's Christian Temperance Union (1890)

The Omaha Platform of the People's Party of America (1892)

Reverend J. L. Moore on the Colored Farmers' Alliance (March 7, 1891)

Ida B. Wells-Barnett, "Lynch Law" (1893)

Statement from the Pullman Strikers (June 15, 1894)

Edward Bellamy, *Looking Backward: 2000–1887* (1888)

In the period between the Civil War and the end of the nineteenth century the United States became a great industrial power. Steam and electricity replaced human muscle, iron replaced wood, and steel replaced iron. Machines could now drive steel tools and change the nature of farming. Oil could lubricate machines and light homes, streets, factories. People and goods could move by railroad, propelled by steam along steel rails. By 1900, there were 193,000 miles of railroad.

All of this industrial progress had an enormous human cost. In the year 1889, twenty-two thousand railroad workers were killed or injured, according to the records of the Interstate Commerce Commission. Thousands of others died or were crippled in the mines, in the steel mills, in the textile mills. Workers often were forced to live in company towns.

Waves of immigrants were pouring into the cities from Europe, after suffering the harrowing ocean voyage of the poor. They worked on the railroads, in the garment factories, in the mines, long hours, at puny wages. Their families were crowded into city slums.

People rebelled against these conditions. The farmers formed Granges, then the People's Party. Workers went on strike for the eight-hour day. Radicalism grew. Anarchism and socialism took root. Millions of people began to imagine that there might be a different kind of society, a different way of sharing the wealth of the nation, their ideas often put into words by writers like Henry George and Edward Bellamy.

• • •

Henry George was an itinerant typesetter and newspaper editor who became a skilled lecturer and critic of the economic system. His book *Progress and Poverty* made him famous, and he ran, unsuccessfully, for mayor of New York several times in the 1880s and 1890s. In this address, delivered in an opera house in Burlington, Iowa, George examines the social roots of poverty in the United States in the nineteenth century, challenging the myth of individual blame.

Henry George, "The Crime of Poverty" (April 1, 1885)[1]

I propose to talk to you tonight of the Crime of Poverty. I cannot, in a short time, hope to convince you of much; but the thing of things I should like to show you is that poverty is a crime. I do not mean that it is a crime to be poor. Murder is a crime; but it is not a crime to be murdered; and a man who is in poverty, I look upon, not as a criminal in himself, so much as the victim of a crime for which others, as well perhaps as himself, are responsible. That poverty is a curse, the bitterest of curses, we all know. [Thomas] Carlyle was right when he said that the hell of which Englishmen are most afraid is the hell of poverty; and this is true, not of Englishmen alone, but of people all over the civilized world, no matter what their nationality. It is to escape this hell that we strive and strain and struggle; and work on oftentimes in blind habit long after the necessity for work is gone.

The curse born of poverty is not confined to the poor alone; it runs through all classes, even to the very rich. They, too, suffer; they must suffer; for there cannot be suffering in a community from which any class can totally escape. The vice, the crime, the ignorance, the meanness born of poverty, poison, so to speak, the very air which rich and poor alike must breathe.

I walked down one of your streets this morning, and I saw three men going along with their hands chained together. I knew for certain that those men were not rich men; and, although I do not know the offence for which they were carried in chains through your streets, this I think I can safely say, that, if you trace it up you will find it in some way to spring from poverty. Nine tenths of human misery, I think you will find, if you look, to be due to poverty. . . . And it seems to me clear that the great majority of those who suffer from poverty are poor not from their own particular faults, but because of conditions imposed by society at large. Therefore I hold that poverty is a crime—not an individual crime, but a social crime, a crime for which we all, poor as well as rich, are responsible. . . .

I hold, and I think no one who looks at the facts can fail to see, that poverty is utterly unnecessary. It is not by the decree of the Almighty, but it is because of our own injustice, our own selfishness, our own ignorance, that this scourge, worse than any pestilence, ravages our civilization, bringing want and suffering and degradation, destroying souls as well as bodies. Look over the world, in this heyday of nineteenth century civilization. In every civilized country under the sun you will find men and women whose condition is worse than that of the savage: men and women and little children with whom the veriest savage could not afford to exchange. Even in this new city of yours with virgin soil around you, you have had this winter to institute a relief society. Your roads have been filled with tramps, fifteen, I am told, at one time taking shelter in a round-house here. As here, so everywhere; and poverty is deepest where wealth most abounds. . . .

Poverty necessary! Why, think of the enormous powers that are latent in the human brain! Think how invention enables us to do with the power of one man what not long ago could not be done by the power of a thousand. Think that in England alone the steam machinery in operation is said to exert a productive force greater than the physical force of the population of the world, were they all adults. And yet we have only begun to invent and discover. We have not yet utilized all that has already been invented and discovered. And look at the powers of the earth. They have hardly been touched. In every direction as we look new resources seem to open. Man's ability to produce wealth seems almost infinite—we can set no bounds to it. Look at the power that is flowing by your city in the current of the Mississippi that might be set at work for you. So in every direction energy that we might utilize goes to waste; resources that we might draw upon are untouched. . . .

I read in the New York papers a while ago that the girls at the Yonkers factories had struck. The papers said that the girls did not seem to know why they had struck, and intimated that it must be just for the fun of striking. Then came out the girls' side of the story and it appeared that they had struck against the rules in force. They were fined if they spoke to one another, and they were fined still more heavily if they laughed. There was a heavy fine for being a minute late. I visited a lady in Philadelphia who had been a forewoman in various factories, and I asked her, "Is it possible that such rules are enforced?" She said it was so in Philadelphia. There is a fine for speaking to your next neighbor, a fine for laughing; and she told me that the girls in one place where she was employed were fined ten cents a minute for being late, though many of them had to come for miles in winter storms. She told me of one poor girl who really worked hard one week and made $3.50; but the fines against her were $5.25. That seems ridiculous; it is ridiculous, but it is pathetic and it is shameful.

But take the cases of those even who are comparatively independent and well off. Here is a man working hour after hour, day after day, week after week, in doing one thing over and over again, and for what? Just to live! He is working ten hours a day in order that he may sleep eight and may have two or three hours for himself when he is tired out and all his faculties are exhausted. That is not a reasonable life; that is not a life for a being possessed of the powers that are in man, and I think every man must have felt it for himself. I know that when I first went to my trade I thought to myself that it was incredible that a man was created to work all day long just to live. I used to read the *Scientific American*, and as invention after invention was heralded in that paper I used to think to myself that when I became a man it would not be necessary to work so hard. But on the contrary, the struggle for existence has become more and more intense. People who want to prove the contrary get up masses of statistics to show that the condition of the working classes is improving. Improvement that you have to take a statistical microscope to discover does not amount to anything. But there is not improvement. . . .

I say that all this poverty and the ignorance that flows from it is unnecessary; I say that there is no natural reason why we should not all be rich, in the sense, not of having more than each other, but in the sense of all having enough to completely satisfy all physical wants; of all having enough to get such an easy living that we could develop the better part of humanity. . . . There is enough and to spare. The trouble is that, in this mad struggle, we trample in the mire what has been provided in sufficiency for us all; trample it in the mire while we tear and rend each other.

There is a cause for this poverty; and, if you trace it down, you will find its root in a primary injustice. Look over the world today—poverty everywhere. The cause must be a common one. You cannot attribute it to the tariff, or to the form of government, or to this thing or to that in which nations differ; because, as deep poverty is common to them all the cause that produces it must be a common cause. What is that common cause? There is one sufficient cause that is common to all nations; and that is the appropriation as the property of some of that natural element on which and from which all must live. . . .

Did you ever think of the utter absurdity and strangeness of the fact that, all over the civilized world, the working classes are the poor classes? Go into any city in the world, and get into a cab and ask the man to drive you where the working people live. He won't take you to where the fine houses are. He will take you, on the contrary, into the squalid quarters, the poorer quarters. Did you ever think how curious that is? Think for a moment how it would strike a rational being who had never been on the earth before, if such an intelligence could come down, and you were to explain to him how we live on earth, how houses and food and clothing, and all the many things we need were all produced by work, would he not think that the working people would be the people who lived in the finest houses and had most of everything that work produces? Yet, whether you took him to London or Paris or New York, or even to Burlington, he would find that those called the working people were the people who live in the poorest houses.

• • •

On the evening of May 4, 1886, a meeting was called for Haymarket Square in Chicago to protest the killing of four strikers at the McCormick Harvester Works the day before. It was a peaceful meeting, and had dwindled from several thousand to a few hundred when a detachment of 180 policemen asked the crowd to disperse. The speaker said that the meeting was almost over and then a bomb exploded in the midst of the police, wounding sixty-six policemen, of whom seven later died. The police fired into the crowd, killing several people, wounding two hundred. Although there was no evidence of who threw the bomb, eight Chicago anarchists were arrested, tried, and sentenced to death. This became known worldwide as the Haymarket Affair. Four of the eight were executed, among them August Spies, who here addresses the court in his own defense. Just before his execution Spies said: "There will be a time when our silence will be more powerful than the voices you strangle today."

August Spies, "Address of August Spies" (October 7, 1886)[2]

Your Honor: In addressing this court I speak as the representative of one class to the representative of another. I will begin with the words uttered five hundred years ago on a similar occasion, by the Venetian Doge Faheri, who addressing the court, said: "MY DEFENSE IS YOUR ACCUSATION." "The causes of my alleged crime your history!" I have been indicted on the charge of murder, as an accomplice or accessory. Upon this indictment I have been convicted. There was no evidence produced by the State to show or even indicate that I had any knowledge of the man who threw the bomb, or that I myself had anything to do with the throwing of the missile, unless, of course, you weigh the testimony of the accomplices of the State's Attorney [Julius Grinnell] and [James] Bonfield, the testimony of [Malvern] Thompson and [Harry] Gilmer, BY THE PRICE THEY WERE PAID FOR IT.

If there was no evidence to show that I was legally responsible for the deed, then my conviction and the execution of the sentence is nothing less than willful, malicious, and deliberate murder, as foul a murder as may be found in the annals of religious, political, or any other sort of persecution. There have been many judicial murders committed where the representatives of the State were acting in good faith, believing their victims to be guilty of the charge accused of. In this case the representatives of the State cannot shield themselves with a similar excuse. For they themselves have fabricated most of the testimony which was used as a pretense to convict us; to convict us by a jury picked out to convict! Before this court, and before the public, which is supposed to be the State, I charge the State's Attorney and Bonfield with the heinous CONSPIRACY TO COMMIT MURDER. . . .

If the opinion of the court given this morning is good law, then there is no person in this country who could not lawfully be hanged. I vouch that, upon the very laws you have read, there is no person in this courtroom now who could not be "fairly, impartially and lawfully" hanged! [Joseph] Fouche, Napoleon's right bower, once said to his master: "Give me a line that any one man has ever written, and I will bring him to the scaffold." And this court has done essentially the same. Upon that law every person in this country can be indicted for conspiracy, and, as the case may be, for murder. Every member of a trade union, Knights of Labor, or any other labor organization, can then be convicted of conspiracy, and in cases of violence, for which they may not be responsible at all, of murder, as we have been. This precedent once established, and you force the masses who are now agitating in a peaceable way into open rebellion! You thereby shut off the last safety valve—and the blood which will be shed, the blood of the innocent— it will come upon your heads!

"Seven policemen have died," said Grinnell, suggestively winking at the jury. You want a life for a life, and have convicted an equal number of men, of whom it cannot be truthfully said that they had anything whatsoever to do with the killing of Bonfield's victims. The very same principle of jurisprudence we find among various savage tribes. Injuries among them are equalized, so to speak. The Chinooks and the Arabs, for instance, would demand the life of an enemy for every death that they had suffered at their enemy's hands. They were not particular in regard to the persons, just so long as they had a life for a life. This principle also prevails today among the natives of the Sandwich Islands. If we are to be hanged on this principle then let us know it, and let the world know what a CIVILIZED AND CHRISTIAN COUNTRY, it is in which the Goulds, the Vanderbilts, the Stanfords, the Fields, Armours, and other local money hamsters have come to the rescue of liberty and justice!

Grinnell has repeatedly stated that our country is an enlightened country[.] (Sarcastically.) The verdict fully corroborates the assertion! This verdict against us is THE ANATHEMA OF THE WEALTHY CLASSES over their despoiled victims—the vast army of wage workers and farmers. If your honor would not have these people believe this; if you would not have them believe that we have once more arrived at the Spartan Senate, the Athenian Areopagus, the Venetian Council of Ten, etc., then sentence should not be pronounced. But, if you think that by hanging us, you can stamp out the labor movement—the movement from which the downtrodden millions, the millions who toil and live in want and misery—the wage slaves—expect salvation—if this is your opinion, then hang us! Here you will tread upon a spark, but there, and there, and behind you and in front of you, and everywhere, flames will blaze up. It is a subterranean fire. You cannot put it out.

• • •

Black and white sugar workers in Louisiana began organizing with the Knights of Labor in 1886. Several strikes were broken by violence and the use of imported strike breakers. In 1887, ten thousand workers, most of them black, walked off the sugar plantations when the planters refused to meet their demands for wages of $1.25 a day. The governor called out the militia, angry at the sight of black and white workers on strike together. He said: "God Almighty has himself drawn the color line." Militia men killed four blacks. The black settlement at Thibodaux was then attacked by militia, and at least twenty people were killed. Two strike leaders were arrested, then lynched. What follows is a report on the strike from an African-American newspaper in Louisiana.

Anonymous, "Red-Handed Murder: Negroes Wantonly Killed at Thibodaux, La." (November 26, 1887)[3]

Murder, foul murder has been committed and the victims were inoffensive and law-abiding Negroes. Assassins more cruel, more desperate, more wanton than any who had hitherto practiced their nefarious business in Louisiana have been shooting down, like so many cattle, the Negroes in and around Thibodaux, Lafourche parish, La.

For three weeks past the public has been regaled, daily, with garbled reports of the troubles existing between the laborers and planters in the sugar district. Strange to say not one of these reports, excepting two, exculpated the Negroes from any desire, or any intention so far as their actions could be judged, of resorting to violence and bloodshed in order to secure the just and equable demand made by them for an increase of wages. Militia from different portions of the State have been on duty in the threatened section, and during all of this time the only acts and crimes of an outrageous character committed were so committed by either the troops, sugar planters or those in their hire. The Negroes during all of the time behaving peaceably, quietly and within the limits of the law, desiring only to secure what they asked and demanding what they had and have a perfect right to do—an increase of wages.

The planters refused to accede to their requests and at the same time ordered them from the plantations. At this juncture, and especially was it the case at both Thibodaux and Houma, the Knights of Labor, to which organization most of the laborers belong, hired all the empty houses in the above towns they could, and there quartered the homeless blacks. Such unexpected action maddened the planters and their followers, (some excepted) and as a [con]sequence they resorted to arms and every other devilish device which the ingenuity of a few chosen spirits could devise in order to force the Negroes to work for the wages offered.

With an obstinacy worthy of the righteousness of their cause the Negroes quartered in Thibodaux refused to accede to the planters.

Such being the case, the planters determined to kill a number of them, thus endeavoring to force the balance into submission. The militia was withdrawn to better accomplish this purpose, and no sooner had they departed for home than the preparation for the killing of the Negroes began. Last Sunday night, about 11 o'clock, plantation wagons containing strange men fully armed were driven into Thibodaux and to Frost's restaurant and hotel and there the strangers were quartered. Who they were and where they came from, no one, with the exception of the planters and Judge Taylor Beattie, seemed to know; but it is a fact that next day, Monday, [martial] law was declared and these cavalcades of armed men put on patrol duty and no Negro allowed to either leave or enter the town without shooters, insolent and overbearing toward the Negroes, doing all in their power to provoke a disturbance. . . . Finding that the Negroes could not be provoked from their usual quiet, it was resolved that some pretext or other should be given so that a massacre might ensue.

It came: Tuesday night the patrol shot two of their number, Gorman and Molaison, and the cry went forth "to arms, to arms! the Negroes are killing the whites!" This was enough. The unknown men who by this time had turned out to be Shreveport guerrillas, well versed in the Ouachita and Red River plan of killing "niggers," assisted by Lafourche's oldest and best, came forth and fired volley after volley, into the houses, the churches, and wherever a Negro could be found.

"Six killed and five wounded" is what the daily papers here say, but from an eye witness to the whole transaction we learn that no less than thirty-five Negroes were killed outright. Lame men and blind women shot; children and hoary-headed grandsires ruthlessly swept down! The Negroes offered no resistance; they could not, as the killing was unexpected. Those of them not killed took to the woods, a majority of them finding refuge in this city.

Such is a true tale of affairs as enacted at Thibodaux. To read it makes the blood of every man, black or white, tingle if his system is permeated with one spark of manhood. To even think that such disregard of human life is permitted in this portion of the United States makes one question whether or not the war was a failure?

Citizens of the United States killed by a mob directed by a State judge, and no redress for the same! Laboring men seeking an advance in wages, treated as if they were dogs! Black men whose equality before the law was secured at the point of the bayonet shown less consideration than serfs? This is what is being enacted in Louisiana today, all of which is due to the Monroe speeches of Gov. [Samuel Douglas] McEnery and Senator [James] Eustis.

At such times and upon such occasions, words of condemnation fall like snow-flakes upon molten lead. The blacks should defend their lives, and if they needs must die, die with their faces toward their persecutors fighting for their homes, their children and their lawful rights.

• • •

A year after the massacre at Thibodaux, blacks in Louisiana gathered to protest the "reign of terror" of the Ku Klux Klan, police, and employers against African Americans. Here is their declaration.

Reverend Ernest Lyon et al., Open Letter from the New Orleans Mass Meeting (August 22, 1888)[4]

To the people of the United States:

We, citizens of New Orleans, as well as of neighboring parishes, from which we have been driven away without warrant or law, assembled in mass meeting at New Orleans, La., on Wednesday, August 22 [1888], at Geddes Hall, declare and assert: That a reign of terror exists in many parts of the state; that the laws are suspended and the officers of the government, from the governor down, afford no protection to the lives and property of the people against armed bodies of whites, who shed innocent blood and commit deeds of savagery unsurpassed in the dark ages of mankind.

For the past twelve years we have been most effectively disfranchised and robbed of our political rights. While denied the privilege in many places of voting for the party and candidates of our choice, acts of violence have been committed to compel us to vote against the dictates of our conscience for the Democratic party, and the Republican ballots cast by us have been counted for the Democratic candidates. The press, the pulpit, the commercial organizations, and executive authority of the State have given both open and silent approval of all these crimes. In addition to these methods, there seems to be a deep laid scheme to reduce the Negroes of the State to a condition of abject serfdom and peonage.

It is being executed by armed bodies of men, styling themselves regulators, all of whom are white, except when a Negro is occasionally forced to join them to give color to the pretense that they represent the virtue of their communities in the suppression impartially of vicious and immoral persons. With that pretense as a cloak these lawless bands make night hideous with their unblushing outrages and murders of inoffensive colored citizens. They go out on nightly raids, order peaceable citizens away never to return, whip some, fire into houses of others—endangering the defenseless lives of women and children—and no attempt is being made to indict them. No virtuous element in the State is found among the whites to rise up in their might and sternly repress these outrageous crimes.

These acts are done in deliberate defiance of the Constitution and laws of the United States, which are so thoroughly nullified that the Negroes who bore arms in defense of the Union have no protection or shelter from them within the borders of Louisiana. During the past twelve months our people have suffered from the lawless regulators as never before since the carnival of bloodshed conducted by the Democratic party in 1868. . . .

Fully aware of their utter helplessness, unarmed and unable to offer resistance to an overpowering force which varies from a "band of whites" to a "sheriff's posse" or the "militia," but which in reality is simply the Democratic party assembled with military precision and armed with rifles of the latest improved patents, toilers forbidden to follow occupations of their choice, compelled to desist from the discussing of labor questions, and being whipped and butchered when in a defenseless condition.

In the instances where the Negroes have attempted to defend themselves, as at Pattersonville and Thibodeaux, they have been traduced in a spirit of savage malignity, the governor of the State, with scarce an observance of the forms of the law has hastened his mercenaries or militia to the scene with cannon and rifles ostensibly to preserve the peace, but actually to re-enforce the already too well fortified Negro murderers falsely assuming to be lawful posses.

A single volume would scarcely afford sufficient space to enumerate the outrages our people have suffered, and are daily suffering at the hand of their oppressors. They are flagrantly deprived of every right guaranteed them by the Constitution; in many parts of the State they are free only in name; they cannot assemble in place to indicate and discuss an equitable rate of wages for their labor; they do not feel safe as property holders and tax-payers, and are permitted to enjoy but very few public conveniences. . . .

We have exhausted all means in our power to have our wrongs redressed by those whose sworn duty it is to impartially execute the laws, but all in vain, until now, because of our murdered fellow-citizens, and apprehensive for our own safety, we appeal to the awakened conscience, the sense of justice and sympathy of the civilized world, and of the American people in particular, to assist us with such moral and material support, as to secure the removal of our people, penniless as many of them are under the feudal system under which they live, to the public lands and other places of the northwest where they can enjoy some security for their persons and property.

To this end we have organized a bureau of immigration. . . .

To our people we advise calmness and a strict regard for law and order. If your homes are invaded expect no mercy, for none will be shown, and if doomed to die, then die defending your life and home to the best of your ability. If convinced that you will not be permitted to live where you are in peace and perfect security quietly go away. If you are without other means to travel take to the public roads or through the swamps and walk away.

Steamboats and railroads are inventions of recent years; your forefathers dared the bloodhounds, the patrollers, and innumerable obstacles, lived in the woods on roots and berries in making their way to Canadian borders.

Invoking the guiding favor of Almighty God and the sympathy of mankind, we are your brethren in affliction and the common bond of humanity.

• • •

The mechanization of farming in the late nineteenth century forced small farmers to borrow money to pay for their equipment. When they could not pay, their farms were taken away. They began to organize, first in farmers' alliances. North and South, black and white, and then came together in the Populist movement of the 1880s and 1890s, to fight the banks and railroads that they saw as their enemies. Populism became a powerful force, involving several million farmers, black and white. Its Lecture Bureau sent 35,000 lecturers throughout the country, and there were more than a thousand Populist journals. The movement ultimately fell apart after it threw its support in the 1896 election to the Democratic candidate, William Jennings Bryan. But its influence lasted long after that, and its program was partly realized in the New Deal farm programs of the 1930s. Here, one of its most respected leaders, Mary Elizabeth Lease, also known as Mary Ellen Lease, of Kansas, presents the ideas of the movement.

Two Speeches by Mary Elizabeth Lease (circa 1890)

"WALL STREET OWNS THE COUNTRY" (CIRCA 1890)[5]

This is a nation of inconsistencies. The Puritans fleeing from oppression became oppressors. We fought England for our liberty and put chains on four million of blacks. We wiped out slavery and our tariff laws and national banks began a system of white wage slavery worse than the first. Wall Street owns the country. It is no longer a government of the people, by the people, and for the people, but a government of Wall Street, by Wall Street, and for Wall Street. The great common people of this country are slaves, and monopoly is the master. The West and South are bound and prostrate before the manufacturing East. Money rules, and our Vice-President [Levi Parsons Morton] is a London banker. Our laws are the output of a system which clothes rascals in robes and honesty in rags. The parties lie to us and the political speakers mislead us. We were told two years ago to go to work and raise a big crop, that was all we needed. We went to work and plowed and planted; the rains fell, the sun shone, nature smiled, and we raised the big crop that they told us to; and what came of it? Eight-cent corn, ten-cent oats, two-cent beef and no price at all for butter and eggs—that's what came of it. Then the politicians said we suffered from over-production. Over-production, when 10,000 little children, so statistics tell us, starve to death every year in the United States, and over 100,000 shop-girls in New York are forced to sell their virtue for the bread their niggardly wages deny them. . . . We want money, land and transportation. We want the abolition of the National Banks, and we want the power to make loans direct from the Government. We want the accursed foreclosure system wiped out. . . . We will stand by our homes and stay by our fireside by force if necessary, and we will not pay our debts to the loan-shark companies until the Government pays its debts to us. The people are at bay, [so] let the bloodhounds of money who dogged us thus far beware.

SPEECH TO THE WOMEN'S CHRISTIAN TEMPERANCE UNION (1890)[6]

Madame President and Fellow Citizens:—If God were to give me my choice to live in any age of the world that has flown, or in any age of the world yet to be, I would say, O God, let me live here and now, in this day and age of the world's history.

For we are living in a grand and wonderful time—a time when old ideas, traditions and customs have broken loose from their moorings and are hopelessly adrift on the great shoreless, boundless sea of human thought—a time when the gray old world begins to dimly comprehend that there is no difference between the brain of an intelligent woman and the brain of an intelligent man; no difference between the soul-power or brainpower that nerved the arm of Charlotte Corday to deeds of heroic patriotism and the soul-power or brain-power that swayed old John Brown behind his death dealing barricade at Ossawattomie. We are living in an age of thought. The mighty dynamite of thought is upheaving the social and political structure and stirring the hearts of men from center to circumference. Men, women and children are in commotion, discussing the mighty problems of the day. The agricultural classes, loyal and patriotic, slow to act and slow to think, are today thinking for themselves; and their thought has crystallized into action. Organization is the key-note to a mighty movement among the masses which is the protest of the patient burden-bearers of the nation against years of economic and political superstition. . . .

Yet, after all our years of toil and privation, dangers and hardships upon the Western frontier, monopoly is taking our homes from us by an infamous system of mortgage foreclosure, the most infamous that has ever disgraced the statutes of a civilized nation. It takes from us at the rate of five hundred a month the homes that represent the best years of our life, our toil, our hopes, our happiness. How did it happen? The government, at the bid of Wall Street, repudiated its contracts with the people; the circulating medium was contracted in the interest of Shylock from $54 per capita to less than $8 per capita; or, as Senator [Preston] Plumb tells us, "Our debts were increased, while the means to pay them was decreased"; or as grand Senator [William Morris] Stewart puts it, "For twenty years the market value of the dollar has gone up and the market value of labor has gone down, till today the American laborer, in bitterness and wrath, asks which is the worst—the black slavery that has gone or the white slavery that has come?"

Do you wonder the women are joining the Alliance? I wonder if there is a woman in all this broad land who can afford to stay out of the Alliance. Our loyal, white-ribbon women should be heart and hand in this Farmers' Alliance movement, for the men whom we have sent to represent us are the only men in the councils of this nation who have not been elected on a liquor platform; and I want to say here, with exultant pride, that the five farmer Congressmen and the United States Senator we have sent up from Kansas—the liquor traffic, Wall Street, "nor the gates of hell shall not prevail against them."

It would sound boastful were I to detail to you the active, earnest part the Kansas women took in the recent campaign. A Republican majority of 82,000 was reduced to less than 8,000 when we elected 97 representatives, 5 out of 7 Congressmen, and a United States Senator, for to the women of Kansas belongs the credit of defeating John J. Ingalls; He is feeling badly about it yet, too, for he said today that "women and Indians were the only class that would scalp a dead man." I rejoice that he realizes that he is politically dead.

I might weary you to tell you in detail how the Alliance women found time from cares of home and children to prepare the tempting, generous viands for the Alliance picnic dinners; where hungry thousands and tens of thousands gathered in the forests and groves to listen to the words of impassioned oratory, ofttimes from woman's lips, that nerved the men of Kansas to forget their party prejudice and vote for "Mollie and the babies." And not only did they find their way to the voters' hearts, through their stomachs, but they sang their way as well. I hold here a book of Alliance songs, composed and set to music by an Alliance woman, Mrs. Florence Olmstead of Butler County, Kan., that did much toward moulding public sentiment. Alliance Glee Clubs composed of women, gave us such stirring melodies as the nation has not heard since the Tippecanoe [William Henry Harrison] and [John] Tyler campaign of 1840. And while I am individualizing, let me call your attention to a book written also by an Alliance woman. I wish a copy of it could be placed in the hands of every woman in this land. "The Fate of a Fool" is written by Mrs. Emma G. Curtis of Colorado. This book in the hands of women would teach them to be just and generous toward women, and help them to forgive and condone in each other the sins so sweetly forgiven when committed by men.

Let no one for a moment believe that this uprising and federation of the people is but a passing episode in politics. It is a religious as well as a political movement, for we seek to put into practical operation the teachings and precepts of Jesus of Nazareth. We seek to enact justice and equity between man and man. We seek to bring the nation back to the constitutional liberties guaranteed us by our forefathers. The voice that is coming up to day from the mystic chords of the American heart is the same voice that Lincoln heard blending with the guns of Fort Sumter and the Wilderness, and it is breaking into a clarion cry today that will be heard around the world.

Crowns will fall, thrones will tremble, kingdoms will disappear, the divine right of kings and the divine right of capital will fade away like the mists of the morning when the Angel of Liberty shall kindle the fires of justice in the hearts of men. "Exact justice to all, special privileges to none." No more millionaires, and no more paupers; no more gold kings, silver kings and oil kings, and no more little waifs of humanity starving for a crust of bread. No more gaunt faced, hollow-eyed girls in the factories, and no more little boys reared in poverty and crime for the penitentiaries and the gallows. But we shall have the golden age of which Isaiah sang and the prophets have so long foretold; when the farmers shall be prosperous and happy, dwelling under their own vine and fig tree; when the laborer shall have that for which he toils; when occupancy and use shall be the only title to land, and every one shall obey the divine injunction, "In the sweat of thy face shalt thou eat bread." When men shall be just and generous, little less than gods, and women shall be just and charitable toward each other, little less than angels;

when we shall have not a government of the people by capitalists, but a government of the people, by the people.

• • •

The Populist Party held its first convention in Omaha, Nebraska, in July 1892, and passed the so-called Omaha Platform, initially drafted by Minnesota politician Ignatius Donnelly. Here is an excerpt.

The Omaha Platform of the People's Party of America (July 4, 1892)[7]

The conditions which surround us best justify our cooperation: we meet in the midst of a nation brought to the verge of moral, political, and material ruin. Corruption dominates the ballot-box, the legislatures, the Congress, and touches even the ermine of the bench. The people are demoralized; most of the States have been compelled to isolate the voters at the polling places to prevent universal intimidation or bribery. The newspapers are largely subsidized or muzzled, public opinion silenced, business prostrated, our homes covered with mortgages, labor impoverished, and the land concentrating in the hands of the capitalists. The urban workmen are denied the right of organization for self protection. Imported pauperized labor beats down their wages; a hireling standing army, unrecognized by our laws, is established to shoot them down, and they are rapidly degenerating into European conditions. The fruits of the toil of millions are boldly stolen to build up colossal fortunes for a few unprecedented in the history of mankind, and the possessors of these, in turn, despise the republic and endanger liberty. From the same prolific womb of governmental injustice we breed the two great classes—tramps and millionaires.

The national power to create money is appropriated to enrich bondholders; a vast public debt payable in legal tender currency has been funded into gold bearing bonds, thereby adding millions to the burdens of the people.

Silver, which has been accepted as coin since the dawn of history, has been demonetized to add to the purchasing power of gold by decreasing the value of all forms of property as well as human labor, and the supply of currency is purposely abridged to fatten usurers, bankrupt enterprise, and enslave industry. A vast conspiracy against mankind has been organized on two continents, and it is rapidly taking possession of the world. If not met and overthrown at once it forebodes terrible social convulsions, the destruction of civilization, or the establishment of an absolute despotism. We have witnessed for more than a quarter of a century the struggles of the two great political parties for power and plunder, while grievous wrongs have been inflicted upon the suffering people. We charge that the controlling influences dominating both these parties have permitted the existing dreadful conditions to develop without serious effort to prevent or restrain them.

Neither do they now promise us any substantial reform. They have agreed together to ignore, in the coming campaign, every issue but one. They propose to drown the outcries of a plundered people with the uproar of a sham-battle over the tariff, so that capitalists, corporations, national banks, rings, trusts, watered stock, the demonetization of silver, and the oppressions of the usurers may all be lost sight of. They propose to sacrifice our homes, lives and children on the altar of mammon; to destroy the multitude in order to secure corruption funds from the millionaires. Assembled on the anniversary of the birthday of the nation and filled with the spirit of the grand general chief, who established our independence, we seek to restore the government of the republic to the hands of "the plain people" with whose class it originated. We assert our purposes to be identical with the purposes of the national Constitution, to form a more perfect union and establish justice, insure domestic tranquility, provide for the common defense, promote the general welfare, and secure the blessings of liberty for ourselves and our posterity.

We declare that this republic can only endure as a free government while built upon the love of the whole people for each other and for the nation; that it cannot be pinned together by bayonets; that the civil war is over and that every passion and resentment which grew out of it must die with it, and that we must be in fact, as we are in name, one united brotherhood of freedmen.

• • •

Here is an early argument for the idea of an alliance between white and black farmers. In this letter to a Florida newspaper, Reverend J. L. Moore, a leader of the Florida Colored Farmers' Alliance, argues that "the laboring colored man's interests and the laboring white man's interests are one and the same," urging the formation of political parties that serve the needs of farmers and working people.

Reverend J. L. Moore on the Colored Farmers' Alliance (March 7, 1891)[8]

In all the discussions of the whites in all the various meetings they attend and the different resolutions, remarks, and speeches they make against the Negro, I never hear you, Mr. Editor, nor any of the other leading journals, once criticize their action or say they are antagonizing the races, neither do you ever call a halt. But let the Negro speak once, and what do you hear? Antagonizing races, Negro uprising, Negro domination, etc. Anything to keep the reading public hostile toward the Negro, not allowing him the privilege to speak his opinion, and if that opinion be wrong show him by argument, and not at once make it a race issue. . . .

[A]s members of the Colored Farmers' Alliance we avowed that we were going to vote with and for the man or party that will secure for the farmer or laboring man his just rights and privileges, and in order that he may enjoy them without experiencing a burden.

We want protection at the ballot box, so that the laboring man may have an equal showing, and the various labor organizations to secure their just rights, we will join hands with them irrespective of party, "and those fellows will have to walk." We are aware of the fact that the laboring colored man's interests and the laboring white man's interests are one and the same. Especially is this true at the South. Anything that can be brought about to benefit the workingman, will also benefit the Negro more than any other legislation that can be enacted. . . .

So I for one have fully decided to vote with and work for that party, or those who favor the workingman, let them belong to the Democratic, or Republican, or the People's Party. I know I speak the sentiment of that convention, representing as we do one-fifth of the laborers of this country, seven-eighths of our race in this country being engaged in agricultural pursuits.

Can you wonder why we have turned our attention from the few pitiful offices a few of our members could secure, and turned our attention toward benefiting the mass of our race, and why we are willing to legislate that this must be benefited? And we ask Congress to protect the ballot box, so they may be justly dealt with in their effort to gain that power. We know and you know that neither of the now existing parties is going to legislate in the interest of the farmers or laboring men except so far as it does not conflict with their interest to do so. . . .

Now, Mr. Editor, I wish to say, if the laboring men of the United States will lay down party issues and combine to enact laws for the benefit of the laboring man, I, as county superintendent of Putnam County Colored Farmers' Alliance, and member of the National Colored Farmers, know that I voice the sentiment of that body, representing as we did 750,000 votes, when I say we are willing and ready to lay down the past, take hold with them irrespective of party, race, or creed, until the cry shall be heard from the Heights of Abraham of the North, to the Everglades of Florida, and from the rock-bound coast of the East, to the Golden Eldorado of the West, that we can heartily endorse the motto, "Equal rights to all and special privileges to none."

• • •

With the betrayal of the former slaves by the national administration in 1877, violence against black people became widespread in the South, and also in parts of the North. Between 1880 and 1920, at least 5,000 blacks were the victims of lynch mobs, with local and national governments looking the other way. In 1892, after learning of a triple lynching in Memphis, Tennessee, the African-American journalist Ida B. Wells-Barnett began to document the way lynchings were used as a means of terrorizing and repressing Blacks.

Ida B. Wells-Barnett, "Lynch Law" (1893)[9]

"Lynch Law," says the Virginia Lancet, "as known by that appellation, had its origin in 1780 in a combination of citizens of Pittsylvania County, Virginia, entered into for the purpose of suppressing a trained band of horse-thieves and counterfeiters whose well concocted schemes had bidden defiance to the ordinary laws of the land, and whose success encouraged and emboldened them in their outrages upon the community. Col. W[illiam] Lynch drafted the constitution for this combination of citizens, and hence 'Lynch Law' has ever since been the name given to the summary infliction of punishment by private and unauthorized citizens."

This law continues in force today in some of the oldest states of the Union, where courts of justice have long been established, whose laws are executed by white Americans. It flourishes most largely in the states which foster the convict lease system, and is brought to bear mainly, against the Negro. The first fifteen years of his freedom he was murdered by masked mobs for trying to vote. Public opinion having made lynching for that cause unpopular, a new reason is given to justify the murders of the past 15 years. The Negro was first charged with attempting to rule white people, and hundreds were murdered on that pretended supposition. He is now charged with assaulting or attempting to assault white women. This charge, as false as it is foul, robs us of the sympathy of the world and is blasting the race's good name.

The men who make these charges encourage or lead the mobs which do the lynching. They belong to the race which holds Negro life cheap, which owns the telegraph wires, newspapers, and all other communication with the outside world. They write the reports which justify lynching by painting the Negro as black as possible, and those reports are accepted by the press associations and the world without question or investigation. The mob spirit had increased with alarming frequency and violence. Over a thousand black men, women and children have been thus sacrificed the past ten years. Masks have long since been thrown aside and the lynchings of the present day take place in broad daylight. The sheriffs, police, and state officials stand by and see the work done well. The coroner's jury is often formed among those who took part in the lynching and a verdict, "Death at the hands of parties unknown to the jury" is rendered. As the number of lynchings have increased, so has the cruelty and barbarism of the lynchers. Three human beings [were] burned alive in civilized America during the first six months of this year (1893). Over one hundred have been lynched in this half year. They were hanged, then cut, shot and burned.

The following table published by the *Chicago Tribune* January, 1892, is submitted for thoughtful consideration.

1882:	52	Negroes murdered by mobs
1883:	39	[Negroes murdered by mobs]
1884:	53	[Negroes murdered by mobs]
1885:	77	[Negroes murdered by mobs]
1886:	73	[Negroes murdered by mobs]
1887:	70	[Negroes murdered by mobs]
1888:	72	[Negroes murdered by mobs]
1889:	95	[Negroes murdered by mobs]
1890:	100	[Negroes murdered by mobs]
1891:	169	[Negroes murdered by mobs]

Of this number

269	were charged with rape
253	[were charged with] murder
44	[were charged with] robbery
37	[were charged with] incendiarism
4	[were charged with] burglary
27	[were charged with] race prejudice
13	[were charged with] quarreling with white men
10	[were charged with] making threats
7	[were charged with] rioting
5	[were charged with] miscegenation
32	[were charged with] no reason given

This table shows (1) that only one-third of nearly a thousand murdered black persons have been even charged with the crime of outrage. This crime is only so punished when white women accuse black men, which accusation is never proven. The same crime committed by Negroes against Negroes, or by white men against black women is ignored even in the law courts.

(2) That nearly as many were lynched for murder as for the above crime, which the world believes is the cause of all the lynchings. The world affects to believe that white womanhood and childhood, surrounded by their lawful protectors, are not safe in the neighborhood of the black man who protected and cared for them during the four years of civil war. The husbands, fathers and brothers of those white women were away for four years, fighting to keep the Negro in slavery, yet not one case of assault has ever been reported!

(3) That "robbery, incendiarism, race prejudice, quarreling with white men, making threats, rioting, miscegenation (marrying a white person), and burglary," are capital offences punishable by death when committed by a black against a white person. Nearly as many blacks were lynched for these charges (and unproven) as for the crime of rape.

(4) That for nearly fifty of these lynchings no reason is given. There is no demand for reasons, or need of concealment for what no one is held responsible. The simple word of any white person against a Negro is sufficient to get a crowd of white men to lynch a Negro. Investigation as to the guilt or innocence of the accused is never made. Under these conditions, white men have only to blacken their faces, commit crimes against the peace of the community, accuse some Negro, nor rest till he is killed by a mob. Will Lewis, an 18 year old Negro youth was lynched at Tullahoma, Tennessee, August, 1891, for being "drunk and saucy to white folks."

• • •

In the 1880s, George Pullman built the company town of Pullman, outside of Chicago. He slashed his workers' wages, forced them to pay high rents for the dwellings he owned, and controlled every aspect of their lives, treating them like serfs on a feudal estate. Workers struck Pullman on May 11, 1894. To support them, the American Railway Union, led by Eugene Debs, organized a nationwide boycott of the railroads. Soon all traffic on the twenty-four railroad lines leading out of Chicago could not move. The strike was broken by court injunctions and federal troops sent by President Grover Cleveland. Debs went to prison for six months, and came out a socialist. Here is a statement the Pullman workers delivered at the union's convention at Uhlich Hall in Chicago.

Statement from the Pullman Strikers (June 15, 1894)[10]

Mr. President and Brothers of the American Railway Union: We struck at Pullman because we were without hope. We joined the American Railway Union because it gave us a glimmer of hope. Twenty thousand souls, men, women, and little ones, have their eyes turned toward this convention today, straining eagerly through dark despondency for a glimmer of the heaven-sent message you alone can give us on this earth.

In stating to this body our grievances it is hard to tell where to begin. You all must know that the proximate cause of our strike was the discharge of two members of our grievance committee the day after George M. Pullman, himself, and Thomas H. Wickes, his second vice-president, had guaranteed them absolute immunity. The more remote causes are still imminent. Five reductions in wages, in work, and in conditions of employment swept through the shops at Pullman between May and December, 1893. The last was the most severe, amounting to nearly 30 percent, and our rents had not fallen. We owed Pullman $70,000 when we struck May 11. We owe him twice as much today. He does not evict us for two reasons: One, the force of popular sentiment and public opinion; the other because he hopes to starve us out, to break through in the back of the American Railway Union, and to deduct from our miserable wages when we are forced to return to him the last dollar we owe him for the occupancy of his houses.

Rents all over the city in every quarter of its vast extent have fallen, in some cases to one-half. Residences, compared with which ours are hovels, can be had a few miles away at the prices we have been contributing to make a millionaire a billionaire. What we pay $15 for in Pullman is leased for $8 in Roseland; and remember that just as no man or woman of our 4,000 toilers has ever felt the friendly pressure of George M. Pullman's hand, so no man or woman of us all has ever owned or can ever hope to own one inch of George M. Pullman's land. Why, even the very streets are his. . . . And do you know what their names are? Why, Fulton, Stephenson, Watt, and Pullman. . . .

When we went to tell him our grievances he said we were all his "children." Pullman, both the man and the town, is an ulcer on the body politic. He owns the houses, the schoolhouses, and churches of God in the town he gave his once humble name. The revenue he derives from these, the wages he pays out with one hand—the Pullman Palace Car Company, he takes back with the other—the Pullman Land Association. He is able by this to bid under any contract car shop in this country. His competitors in business, to meet this, must reduce the wages of their men. This gives him the excuse to reduce ours to conform to the market. His business rivals must in turn scale down; so must he. And thus the merry war—the dance of skeletons bathed in human tears—goes on, and it will go on, brothers, forever, unless you, the American Railway Union, stop it; end it; crush it out.

Our town is beautiful. In all these thirteen years no word of scandal has arisen against one of our women, young or old. What city of 20,000 persons can show the like? Since our strike, the arrests, which used to average four or five a day, have dwindled down to less than one a week. We are peaceable; we are orderly, and but for the kindly beneficence of kindly-hearted people in and about Chicago we would be starving. We are not desperate today, because we are not hungry, and our wives and children are not begging for bread. But George M. Pullman, who ran away from the public opinion that has arisen against him, like the genie from the bottle in the Arabian Nights, is not feeding us. He is patiently seated beside his millions waiting for what? To see us starve. We have grown better acquainted with the American Railway Union these convention days, and as we have heard sentiments of the noblest philanthropy fall from the lips of our general officers—your officers and ours—we have learned that there is a balm for all our troubles, and that the box containing it is in your hands today only awaiting opening to disseminate its sweet savor of hope.

George M. Pullman, you know, has cut our wages from 30 to 70 percent. George M. Pullman has caused to be paid in the last year the regular quarterly dividend of 2 percent on his stock and an extra slice of 1 1/2 percent, making 9 1/2 percent on $30,000,000 of capital. George M. Pullman, you know, took three contracts on which he lost less than $5,000. Because he loved us? No. Because it was cheaper to lose a little money in his freight car and his coach shops than to let his workingmen go, but that petty loss, more than made up by us from money we needed to clothe our wives and little ones, was his excuse for effecting a gigantic reduction of wages in every department of his great works, of cutting men and boys and girls; with equal zeal, including everyone in the repair shops of the Pullman Palace cars on which such preposterous profits have been made. . . .

We will make you proud of us, brothers, if you will give us the hand we need. Help us make our country better and more wholesome. Pull us out of our slough of despond. Teach arrogant grinders of the faces of the poor that there is still a God in Israel, and if need be a Jehovah—a God of battles. Do this, and on that last great day you will stand, as we hope to stand, before the great white throne "like gentlemen unafraid."

• • •

One reaction to the poverty and violence of capitalism in the nineteenth century was to dream of a different kind of world. Edward Bellamy's novel *Looking Backward* imagined a man waking up in the year 2000 in a society based on equality and justice. His book sold a million copies in a few years, and over a hundred groups were organized around the country to work toward Bellamy's vision.

Edward Bellamy, *Looking Backward: 2000–1887* (1888)[11]

"And, in heaven's name, who are the public enemies?" exclaimed Dr. Leete. "Are they France, England, Germany, or hunger, cold, and nakedness? In your day governments were accustomed, on the slightest international misunderstanding, to seize upon the bodies of citizens and deliver them over by hundreds of thousands to death and mutilation, wasting their treasures the while like water; and all this oftenest for no imaginable profit to the victims. We have no war now, and our governments no war powers, but in order to protect every citizen against hunger, cold, and nakedness, and provide for all his physical and mental needs, the function is assumed of directing his industry for a term of years. No, Mr. West, I am sure on reflection you will perceive that it was in your age, not in ours, that the extension of the functions of governments was extraordinary. Not even for the best ends would men now allow their governments such powers as were then used for the most maleficent."

"Leaving comparisons aside," I said, "the demagoguery and corruption of our public men would have been considered, in my day, insuperable objections to any assumption by government of the charge of the national industries. We should have thought that no arrangement could be worse than to entrust the politicians with control of the wealth-producing machinery of the country. Its material interests were quite too much the football of parties as it was."

"No doubt you were right," rejoined Dr. Leete, "but all that is changed now. We have no parties or politicians, and as for demagoguery and corruption, they are words having only an historical significance."

"Human nature itself must have changed very much," I said.

"Not at all," was Dr. Leete's reply, "but the conditions of human life have changed, and with them the motives of human action. The organization of society with you was such that officials were under a constant temptation to misuse their power for the private profit of themselves or others. Under such circumstances it seems almost strange that you dared entrust them with any of your affairs. Nowadays, on the contrary, society is so constituted that there is absolutely no way in which an official, however ill-disposed, could possibly make any profit for himself or anyone else by a misuse of his power. Let him be as bad an official as you please, he cannot be a corrupt one. There is no motive to be. The social system no longer offers a premium on dishonesty. But these are matters which you can only understand as you come, with time, to know us better."

"But you have not yet told me how you have settled the labor problem. It is the problem of capital which we have been discussing," I said. "After the nation had assumed conduct of the mills, machinery, railroads, farms, mines, and capital in general of the country, the labor question still remained. In assuming the responsibilities of capital the nation had assumed the difficulties of the capitalist's position."

"The moment the nation assumed the responsibilities of capital those difficulties vanished," replied Dr. Leete. "The national organization of labor under one direction was the complete solution of what was, in your day and under your system, justly regarded as the insoluble labor problem. When the nation became the sole employer, all the citizens, by virtue of their citizenship, became employees, to be distributed according to the needs of industry."

"That is," I suggested, "you have simply applied the principle of universal military service, as it was understood in our day, to the labor question."

"Yes," said Dr. Leete, "that was something which followed as a matter of course as soon as the nation had become the sole capitalist. The people were already accustomed to the idea that the obligation of every citizen, not physically disabled, to contribute his military services to the defense of the nation was equal and absolute. That it was equally the duty of every citizen to contribute his quota of industrial or intellectual services to the maintenance of the nation was equally evident, though it was not until the nation became the employer of labor that citizens were able to render this sort of service with any pretense either of universality or equity. No organization of labor was possible when the employing power was divided among hundreds or thousands of individuals and corporations, between which concert of any kind was neither desired, nor indeed feasible. It constantly happened then that vast numbers who desired to labor could find no opportunity, and on the other hand, those who desired to evade a part or all of their debt could easily do so."

"Service, now, I suppose, is compulsory upon all," I suggested.

"It is rather a matter of course than of compulsion," replied Dr. Leete. "It is regarded as so absolutely natural and reasonable that the idea of its being compulsory has ceased to be thought of." . . .

"Is the term of service in this industrial army for life?"

"Oh, no; it both begins later and ends earlier than the average working period in your day. Your workshops were filled with children and old men, but we hold the period of youth sacred to education, and the period of maturity, when the physical forces begin to flag, equally sacred to ease and agreeable relaxation. The period of industrial service is twenty-four years, beginning at the close of the course of education at twenty-one and terminating at forty-five. After forty-five, while discharged from labor, the citizen still remains liable to special calls, in case of emergencies causing a sudden great increase in the demand for labor, till he reaches the age of fifty-five, but such calls are rarely, in fact almost never, made."

CHAPTER TWELVE

The Expansion of the Empire

Calixto Garcia's Letter to General William R. Shafter (July 17, 1898)

Three Documents on African-American Opposition to Empire
(1898 to 1899)

Lewis H. Douglass on Black Opposition to McKinley
(November 17, 1899)

Missionary Department of the Atlanta, Georgia, A.M.E. Church, "The
Negro Should Not Enter the Army" (May 1, 1899)

I. D. Barnett et al., Open Letter to President McKinley by Colored
People Of Massachusetts (October 3, 1899)

Samuel Clemens, "Comments on the Moro Massacre"
(March 12, 1906)

Smedley D. Butler, War Is a Racket (1935)

From the end of the Revolutionary War on, the history of the United States is one of continuous expansion. First, it was the march across the continent, initiating a war with Mexico, driving Indians off their land through the breaking of treaties and the use of military force. The culmination of this came in 1890 with the massacre of Indians in the village of Wounded Knee.

With the country now stretching from the Atlantic to the Pacific, the nation looked southward into the Caribbean and westward to Hawaii, the Philippines, Japan, and China.

There were 103 military interventions in other countries between 1798 and 1895, according to records of the State Department. (Ironically, the list was provided to Congress in 1962 to show precedent for the attempt to invade Cuba the year before.)

By the 1890s, political leaders and newspaper editors were hailing the idea of "manifest destiny." Senator Henry Cabot Lodge of Massachusetts wrote in a magazine article that "in the interests of our commerce . . . we should build the Nicaragua canal, and for the protection of that canal and for the sake of our commercial supremacy in the Pacific we should control the Hawaiian Islands and maintain our influence in Samoa," adding that "when the Nicaraguan canal is built, the island of Cuba . . . will become a necessity."

An editorial in the Washington Post declared: "A new consciousness seems to have come upon us—the consciousness of strength, and with it a new appetite, the yearning to show our strength. . . . The taste of Empire is in the mouth of the people even as the taste of blood in the jungle."

Even before he was elected president in 1896, William McKinley said, "We want a foreign market for our surplus products." Senator Albert Beveridge of Indiana spoke of the need to sell surplus products abroad: "Fate has written our policy for us; the trade of the world must and shall be ours."

In 1893, a number of U.S. officials initiated a failed attempt to annex Hawaii to the United States, supporting the overthrow of the Hawaiian government. Although an investigation found the intervention illegal, President William McKinley arranged for another annexation treaty on June 16, 1897. Under the pressure of a formal letter of protest delivered by Queen Lili'uokalani in Washington, D.C., and the opposition of more than 20,000 Hawaiians who signed petitions against the annexation, the Senate did not ratify the arrangement. But, using the pretext of the Spanish-American War, the United States annexed Hawaii through fiat, this time a congressional joint resolution on July 7, 1898, that seized its land for use as a military base needed to fight the Spanish in Guam and the Philippines.

The United States also turned Puerto Rico into a "protectorate" under the pretense of freeing it. But in 1898, writing in the *New York Times*, the businessman Amos K. Fiske laid out a remarkably honest assessment of the value Puerto Rico would have for the United States: "Of the commercial value of Puerto Rico as a possession there is no possibility of doubt."

The same year, the United States invaded Cuba. The Cuban people had been rebelling against Spanish rule for a long time before 1898. But their cruel treatment by the Spanish was used by the U.S. government to justify going to war with Spain. The blowing up of the battle ship *Maine* in Havana harbor, leading to the deaths of 268 men, was used to inflame public sentiment against Spain, although there was never any evidence that the Spanish were responsible for that disaster.

It was a short victorious war in Cuba. Secretary of State John Hay called it "a splendid little war." The rule of Spain was ended, but Cuba was not free, because now the United States was taking over the country. It was not officially a colony, but U.S. corporations rushed in to dominate the economy, and the new Cuban Constitution was reworked to allow U.S. military intervention any time the United States was so inclined.

The Cuban rebels, who had done a great deal of the fighting against Spain, were shunted aside. The United States was not going to allow the Cubans to run their own country.

Now the nation turned to the Pacific, and invaded another Spanish colony, the Philippines. Unlike the Cuban war, this was a long and bloody affair, lasting for years, in which an American army fought against the Filipino independence movement.

Atrocities were committed by U.S. forces in the course of winning the war. At least five hundred thousand Filipinos died.

In the United States, there was opposition to the war in the Philippines. An Anti-Imperialist League was formed, of which Mark Twain was a leading member. Twain wrote: "We have pacified some thousands of the islanders and buried them. . . . And so by these Providences of God—and the phrase is the government's not mine—we are a World Power."

There was bitter irony for the black population of the United States, whose sons were sent to fight against the people of the Philippines. Black people were lynched in great numbers during those years of the war, while "patience, industry, and moderation" was being preached to blacks and "patriotism" was being preached to whites.

• • •

Here are the words of General Calixto Garcia, writing to General William R. Shafter, head of the American Expeditionary Army, about the U.S. seizure of power in Cuba.

Calixto Garcia's Letter to General William R. Shafter (July 17, 1898)[1]

Sir: On May 12 the government of the Republic of Cuba ordered me, as commander of the Cuban army in the east to cooperate with the American army following the plans and obeying the orders of its commander. I have done my best, sir, to fulfill the wishes of my government, and I have been until now one of your most faithful subordinates, honoring myself in carrying out your orders as far as my powers have allowed me to do it.

The city of Santiago surrendered to the American army, and news of that important event was given to me by persons entirely foreign to your staff. I have not been honored with a single word from yourself informing me about the negotiations for peace or the terms of the capitulation by the Spaniards. The important ceremony of the surrender of the Spanish army and the taking possession of the city by yourself took place later on, and I only knew of both events by public reports.

I was neither honored, sir, with a kind word from you inviting me or any officer of my staff to represent the Cuban army on that memorable occasion.

Finally, I know that you have left in power in Santiago the same Spanish authorities that for three years I have fought as enemies of the independence of Cuba. I beg to say that these authorities have never been elected at Santiago by the residents of the city; but were appointed by royal decrees of the Queen of Spain.

I would agree, sir, that the army under your command should have taken possession of the city, the garrison and the forts.

I would give my warm cooperation to any measure you may have deemed best under American military law to hold the city for your army and to preserve public order until the time comes to fulfill the solemn pledge of the people of the United States to establish in Cuba a free and independent government. But when the question arises of appointing authorities in Santiago de Cuba under the special circumstances of our thirty years strife against Spanish rule, I cannot see but with the deepest regret that such authorities are not elected by the Cuban people, but are the same ones selected by the Queen of Spain, and hence are ministers appointed to defend Spanish sovereignty against the Cubans.

A rumor, too absurd to be believed, General, describes the reason of your measure and of the orders forbidding my army to enter Santiago for fear of massacres and revenge against the Spaniards. Allow me, sir, to protest against even the shadow of such an idea. We are not savages ignoring the rules of civilized warfare. We are a poor, ragged army as ragged and poor as was the army of your forefathers in their noble war for independence, but like the heroes of Saratoga and Yorktown, we respect our cause too deeply to disgrace it with barbarism and cowardice.

In view of all these reasons, I sincerely regret being unable to fulfill any longer the orders of my government, and, therefore, I have tendered today to the commander-in-chief of the Cuban army, Maj. Gen. Máximo Gómez, my resignation as commander of this section of our army.

Awaiting his resolution, I have retired with all my forces to Jiguaní.

I am respectfully yours,

Calixto Garcia

• • •

The expansion of the U.S. empire fueled significant opposition among African Americans, who opposed the racism and the violence of these ventures. In 1903, in *The Souls of Black Folk*, the writer and agitator W. E. B. Du Bois wrote of Black revulsion to "the recent course of the United States toward weaker and darker peoples in the West Indies, Hawaii, and the Philippines." Here are three accounts of antiwar sentiment among blacks at the time.

Three Documents on African-American Opposition to Empire (1898 to 1899)

LEWIS H. DOUGLASS ON BLACK OPPOSITION TO MCKINLEY (NOVEMBER 17, 1899)[2]

President [William] McKinley, in the course of his speech at Minneapolis, said of the Filipinos under American sovereignty: "They will not be governed as vassals, or serfs, or slaves. They will be given a government of liberty, regulated by law, honestly administered, without oppressing exaction, taxation without tyranny, justice without bribe, education without distinction of social conditions, freedom of religious worship, and protection of life, liberty, and pursuit of happiness."

I do not believe that President McKinley has any confidence in the statement above. It cannot be successfully asserted that the great tariff statesman is blind to the fact of the race and color prejudice that dominates the greater percentage of the soldiers who are killing Filipinos in the name of freedom and civilization.

President McKinley knows that brave, loyal, black American soldiers, who fight and die for their country, are hated, despised, and cruelly treated in that section of the country from which this administration accepts dictation and to the tastes of which the President, undoubtedly, caters. The President of the United States knows that he dare not station a regiment of black heroes in the State of Arkansas. He knows that at the race hating command of a people who sought destruction of the nation his administration rescinded an order to send black soldiers to Little Rock. The administration lacks the courage to deal with American citizens without regard to race or color, as is clearly demonstrated in the weak and contemptibly mean act of yielding to the demands of those who hold that this is a white man's government and that dark races have no rights which white men are bound to respect.

It is a sorry, though true, fact that whatever this government controls, injustice to dark races prevails. The people of Cuba, Porto Rico, Hawaii and Manila know it well as do the wronged Indian and outraged black man in the United States. . . .

The question will Be asked: How is it that such promises are made to Filipinos thousands of miles away while the action of the administration in protecting dark citizens at home does not even extend to a promise of any attempt to rebuke the outlawry which kills American citizens of African descent for the purpose of gratifying blood-thirstiness and race hatred? . . .

It is hypocrisy of the most sickening kind to try to make us believe that the killing of Filipinos is for the purpose of good government and to give protection to life and liberty and the pursuit of happiness. . . .

When the United States learns that justice should be blind as to race and color, then may it undertake to, with some show of propriety, expand. Now its expansion means extension of race hate and cruelty, barbarous lynchings and gross injustice to dark people.

MISSIONARY DEPARTMENT OF THE ATLANTA, GEORGIA, A.M.E. CHURCH, "THE NEGRO SHOULD NOT ENTER THE ARMY" (MAY 1, 1899)[3]

It is about time for the ministers of the A.M.E. Church, who, in the aggregate, are the most progressive, enlightened and racial of the Africanite ministry of the world, with the highest regard for all other denominations, to begin to tell the young men of our race to stay out of the United States army. If it is a white man's government, and we grant it is, let him take care of it. The Negro has no flag to defend. There is not a star in the flag of this nation, out of the forty odd, that the colored race can claim, nor is there any symbol signalized in the colors of the flag that he can presume to call his, unless it would be the stripes, and the stripes are now too good for him. . . . He has no civil, social, political, judicial or existing rights any longer. He may exist, be or live till the lynchers say he must die, and when they get ready to demand his life, the nation, from President McKinley down, down and down to the most contemptible white riff-raff, says well done! If not in words, they say it by their silence; and those who did enlist some months ago, were abused, misrepresented and vilified when they even passed through the country, worse than brutes would have been. If they came out of the cars and walked about the depot, they were charged with trying to kill men, women and children, and fire the cities and villages. If they sat in the cars and failed to get out, the newspapers branded them with cowardice, and said they were afraid, they knew what would follow, while one town would telegraph to the next that Negro soldiers would pass through. "Have your armed police at the railroad station, armed to the teeth and ready to shoot them down upon the slightest provocation." Yet the same towns and villages were ready to supply them with all the rot-gut whiskey they were able to purchase, to transform them into maniacs and human devils, if these soldiers were low enough to drink the infernal drug. We now ask, in the face of these facts, and they are not half told, what does the Negro want to enlist[,] lay his life upon the alter of the nation[,] and die for? What is to be gained? Where is the credit? Who will accord it to him? In what particular will the race be benefited? Suppose the Negro should enlist in great numbers and go to the Spanish islands and help to subjugate the territory now in dispute, and subordinate it to the dictatorial whim of the United States. What right, what privilege, what immunity, what enjoyment, what possession will he be the recipient of? A Cuban from Havana who was compelled to ride with us in a jim-crow car a week ago, and who was as mad as vengeance at this restriction of his manhood, told us that the diabolical prejudice of the United States was being exhibited there, and his curse-words were sulphuretic vengeance itself. He said "This valuing a man by his color was unknown in Cuba until the scoundrels and villains of this country went there." He showed us papers which represented him as a great business man, dealing in the finest tobacco and cigars, yet he was compelled to ride in the jim-crow car or be mobbed at every station, and this Cuban was not a black man. We ask the young men of the Negro race if you have got any life to throw away for such a country as this? If you have a spare life on hand, that you wish to dispose of by sacrifice, for mercy's sake, for honor's sake, for manhood's sake, and for common sense sake throw it away for a better purpose, in a nobler act, in doing something that will perpetuate your memory, to say the least. While we are the first Africanite Chaplain in the history of the nation, and have once been proud of the flag of this nation as it waved and flaunted in the air, as a Negro we regard it a worthless rag. It is the symbol of liberty, of manhood sovereignty and of national independence to the white man, we grant, and he should justly be proud of it, but to the colored man, that has any sense, any honor, and is not a scullionized fool, it is a miserable dirty rag. We repeat that the A.M.E. ministry, yes, and the Negro ministry of the country should fight the enlistment of colored men in the United States army, as they would liquor brothels, thievery, breaking the Sabbath, or any crime even in the catalogue of villainy. The Negro minister of the gospel who would encourage enlistment in the United States army, in the conditions things are now, encourages murder and the shedding of innocent blood for nothing, as the foolish young men do not know what steps they are taking. Moreover, the bulk of the white people do not want colored soldiers. Our own governor disapproves of it. The majority of the white press is against it. They regard the black soldiers as monstrosities, and we regard them monstrosities also. Again we say to the colored men, stay out of the United States army. Take no oath to protect any flag that offers no protection to its sable defenders. If we had the voice of seven thunders, we would sound a protest against Negro enlistment till the very ground shook below our feet.

I. D. BARNETT ET AL., OPEN LETTER TO PRESIDENT MCKINLEY BY COLORED PEOPLE OF MASSACHUSETTS (OCTOBER 3, 1899)[4]

Sir:—We, colored people of Massachusetts in mass meeting assembled to consider our oppressions and the state of the country relative to the same, have resolved to address ourselves to you in an open letter, notwithstanding your extraordinary, your incomprehensible silence on the subject of our wrongs in your annual and other messages to Congress, as in your public utterances to the country at large. We address ourselves to you, sir, not as suppliants, but as of right, as

American citizens, whose servant you are, and to whom you are bound to listen, and for whom you are equally bound to speak, and upon occasion to act, as for any other body of your fellow-countrymen in like circumstances. We ask nothing for ourselves at your hands, as chief magistrate of the republic, to which all American citizens are not entitled. We ask for the enjoyment of life, liberty and the pursuit of happiness equally with other men. We ask for the free and full exercise of all the rights of American freemen, guaranteed to us by the Constitution and laws of the Union, which you were solemnly sworn to obey and execute. We ask you for what belongs to us by the high sanction of Constitution and law, and the Democratic genius of our institutions and civilization. These rights are everywhere throughout the South denied to us, violently wrested from us by mobs, by lawless legislatures, and nullifying conventions, combinations, and conspiracies, openly, defiantly, under your eyes, in your constructive and actual presence. And we demand, which is a part of our rights, protection, security in our life, our liberty, and in the pursuit of our individual and social happiness under a government, which we are bound to defend in war, and which is equally bound to furnish us in peace protection, at home and abroad.

We have suffered, sir,—God knows how much we have suffered!—since your accession to office, at the hands of a country professing to be Christian, but which is not Christian, from the hate and violence of a people claiming to be civilized, but who are not civilized, and you have seen our sufferings, witnessed from your high place our awful wrongs and miseries, and yet you have at no time and on no occasion opened your lips in our behalf. Why? we ask. Is it because we are black and weak and despised? Are you silent because without any fault of our own we were enslaved and held for more than two centuries in cruel bondage by your forefathers? Is it because we bear the marks of those sad generations of Anglo-Saxon brutality and wickedness, that you do not speak? Is it our fault that our involuntary servitude produced in us widespread ignorance poverty and degradation? Are we to be damned and destroyed by the whites because we have only grown the seeds which they planted? Are we to be damned by bitter laws and destroyed by the mad violence of mobs because we are what white men made us? And is there no help in the federal arm for us, or even one word of audible pity, protest and remonstrance in your own breast, Mr. President, or in that of a single member of your Cabinet? Black indeed we are, sir, but we are also men and American citizens. . . .

Had, eighteen months ago, the Cuban revolution to throw off the yoke of Spain, or the attempt of Spain to subdue the Cuban rebellion, any federal aspect? We believe that you and the Congress of the United States thought that they had, and therefore used, finally, the armed force of the nation to expel Spain from that island. Why? Was it because "the people of the Island of Cuba are, and of right ought to be free and independent?" You and the Congress said as much, and may we fervently pray, sir, in passing, that the freedom and independence of that brave people shall not much longer be denied them by our government? But to resume, there was another consideration which, in your judgment, gave to the Cuban question a federal aspect, which provoked at last the armed interposition of our government in the affairs of that island, and this was "the chronic condition of disturbance in Cuba so injurious and menacing to our interests and tranquility, as well as shocking to our sentiments of humanity." Wherefore you presently fulfilled "a duty to humanity by ending a situation, the indefinite prolongation of which had become insufferable."

Mr. President, had that "chronic condition of disturbance in Cuba so injurious and menacing to our interest and tranquility as well as shocking to our sentiments of humanity," which you wished to terminate and did terminate, a federal aspect, while that not less "chronic condition of disturbance" in the South, which is a thousand times more "injurious and menacing to our interests and tranquility," as well as far more "shocking to our sentiments of humanity," or ought to be, none whatever? Is it better to be Cuban revolutionists fighting for Cuban independence than American citizens striving to do their simple duty at home? Or is it better only in case those American citizens doing their simple duty at home happen to be negroes residing in the Southern States?

Are crying national transgressions and injustices more "injurious and menacing" to the Republic, as well as "shocking to its sentiments of humanity," when committed by a foreign state, in foreign territory, against a foreign people, than when they are committed by a portion of our own people at home? There were those of our citizens who did not think that the Cuban question possessed any federal aspect, while there were others who thought otherwise; and these, having the will and power eventually found a way to suppress a menacing danger to the country and a wrong against humanity at the same time. Where there is a will among constitutional lawyers and rulers, Mr. President, there is ever a way; but where there is no will, there is no way. Shall it be said that the federal government, with arms of Briareus, reaching to the utmost limits of the habitable globe for the protection of its citizens, for the liberation of alien islanders and the subjugation of others, is powerless to guarantee to certain of its citizens at home their inalienable right to life, liberty and the pursuit of happiness, because those citizens happen to be negroes residing in the Southern section of our country? Do the colored people of the United States deserve equal consideration with the Cuban people at the hands of your administration, and shall they, though late, receive it?

• • •

At the end of the nineteenth century, the United States moved to expand its formal empire, annexing lands in Hawaii, Guam, Cuba, Puerto Rico, Samoa, and the Philippines following the end of the Spanish-American War. But this expansionism produced political opposition at home. The anti-imperialist movement counted among its members leading writers and intellectuals, including the satirist Samuel Clemens, known by his pen name Mark Twain. Twain is remembered for his novels *Huckleberry Finn* and *Tom Sawyer*. Far less well known are his scathing writings against the expansion of the U.S. empire. Moved to public opposition against the bloody invasion and occupation of the Philippines in 1899—which President George W. Bush cited in 2003 as a "model" for the occupation of Iraq— Twain returned after ten years of living abroad to become the vice president of the recently formed Anti-Imperialist League in 1900. Upon his return, he declared "I am an anti-imperialist. I am opposed to having the eagle put its talons on any other land." Here is part of his bitter essay about a massacre of some six hundred Moros in the Philippines.

Samuel Clemens, "Comments on the Moro Massacre" (March 12, 1906)[5]

This incident burst upon the world last Friday in an official cablegram from the commander of our forces in the Philippines to our Government at Washington. The substance of it was as follows:

A tribe of Moros, dark-skinned savages, had fortified themselves in the bowl of an extinct crater not many miles from Jolo; and as they were hostiles, and bitter against us because we have been trying for eight years to take their liberties away from them, their presence in that position was a menace. Our commander, Gen. Leonard Wood, ordered a reconnaissance. It was found that the Moros numbered six hundred, counting women and children; that their crater bowl was in the summit of a peak or mountain twenty-two hundred feet above sea level, and very difficult of access for Christian troops and artillery. Then General Wood ordered a surprise, and went along himself to see the order carried out. Our troops climbed the heights by devious and difficult trails, and even took some artillery with them. The kind of artillery is not specified, but in one place it was hoisted up a sharp acclivity by tackle a distance of some three hundred feet. Arrived at the rim of the crater, the battle began. Our soldiers numbered five hundred and forty. They were assisted by auxiliaries consisting of a detachment of native constabulary in our pay—their numbers not given—and by a naval detachment, whose numbers are not stated. But apparently the contending parties were about equal as to number— six hundred men on our side, on the edge of the bowl; six hundred men, women and children in the bottom of the bowl. Depth of the bowl, 50 feet.

Gen. Wood's order was, "Kill or capture the six hundred."

The battle began—it is officially called by that name—our forces firing down into the crater with their artillery and their deadly small arms of precision; the savages furiously returning the fire, probably with brickbats—though this is merely a surmise of mine, as the weapons used by the savages are not nominated in the cablegram. Heretofore the Moros have used knives and clubs mainly; also ineffectual trade-muskets when they had any.

The official report stated that the battle was fought with prodigious energy on both sides during a day and a half, and that it ended with a complete victory for the American arms. The completeness of the victory is established by this fact: that of the six hundred Moros not one was left alive. The brilliancy of the victory is established by this other fact, to wit: that of our six hundred heroes only fifteen lost their lives.

General Wood was present and looking on. His order had been, "Kill or capture those savages." Apparently our little army considered that the "or" left them authorized to kill or capture according to taste, and that their taste had remained what it has been for eight years, in our army out there—the taste of Christian butchers.

The official report quite properly extolled and magnified the "heroism" and "gallantry" of our troops; lamented the loss of the fifteen who perished, and elaborated the wounds of thirty-two of our men who suffered injury, and even minutely and faithfully described the nature of the wounds, in the interest of future historians of the United States. It mentioned that a private had one of his elbows scraped by a missile, and the private's name was mentioned. Another private had the end of his nose scraped by a missile. His name was also mentioned—by cable, at one dollar and fifty cents a word.

Next day's news confirmed the previous day's report and named our fifteen killed and thirty-two wounded again, and once more described the wounds and gilded them with the right adjectives.

Let us now consider two or three details of our military history. In one of the great battles of the Civil War ten per cent of the forces engaged on the two sides were killed and wounded. At Waterloo, where four hundred thousand men were present on the two sides, fifty thousand fell, killed and wounded, in five hours, leaving three hundred and fifty thousand sound and all right for further adventures. Eight years ago, when the pathetic comedy called the Cuban War was played, we summoned two hundred and fifty thousand men. We fought a number of showy battles, and when the war was over we had lost two hundred and sixty-eight men out of our two hundred and fifty thousand, in killed and wounded in the field, and just fourteen times as many by the gallantry of the army doctors in the hospitals and camps. We did not exterminate the Spaniards—far from it. In each engagement we left an average of two per cent of the enemy killed or crippled on the field.

Contrast these things with the great statistics which have arrived from that Moro crater! There, with six hundred engaged on each side, we lost fifteen men killed outright, and we had thirty-two wounded—counting that nose and that elbow. The enemy numbered six hundred—including women and children—and we abolished them utterly, leaving not even a baby alive to cry for its dead mother. This is incomparably the greatest victory that was ever achieved by the Christian soldiers of the United States.

Now then, how has it been received? The splendid news appeared with splendid display-heads in every newspaper in this city of four million and thirteen thousand inhabitants, on Friday morning. But there was not a single reference to it in the editorial columns of any one of those newspapers. The news appeared again in all the evening papers of Friday, and again those papers were editorially silent upon our vast achievement. Next day's additional statistics and particulars appeared in all the morning papers, and still without a line of editorial rejoicing or a mention of the matter in any way. These additions appeared in the evening papers of that same day (Saturday) and again without a word of comment. In the columns devoted to correspondence, in the morning and evening papers of Friday and Saturday, nobody said a word about the "battle." Ordinarily those columns are teeming with the passions of the citizen; he lets no incident go by, whether it be large or small, without pouring out his praise or blame, his joy or his indignation about the matter in the correspondence column. But, as I have said, during those two days he was as silent as the editors themselves. So far as I can find out, there was only one person among our eighty millions who allowed himself the privilege of a public remark on this great occasion—that was the President of the United States. All day Friday he was as studiously silent as the rest. But on Saturday he recognized that his duty required him to say something, and he took his pen and performed that duty. If I know President Roosevelt—and I am sure I do—this utterance cost him more pain and shame than any other that ever issued from his pen or his mouth. I am far from blaming him. If I had been in his place my official duty would have compelled me to say what he said. It was a convention, an old tradition, and he had to be loyal to it. There was no help for it. This is what he said:

Washington, March 10.

Wood, Manila:—I congratulate you and the officers and men of your command upon the brilliant feat of arms wherein you and they so well upheld the honor of the American flag.

(Signed) Theodore Roosevelt.

His whole utterance is merely a convention. Not a word of what he said came out of his heart. He knew perfectly well that to pen six hundred helpless and weaponless savages in a hole like rats in a trap and massacre them in detail during a stretch of a day and a half, from a safe position on the heights above, was no brilliant feat of arms—and would not have been a brilliant feat of arms even if Christian America, represented by its salaried soldiers, had shot them down with Bibles and the Golden Rule instead of bullets. He knew perfectly well that our uniformed assassins had not upheld the honor of the American flag, but had done as they have been doing continuously for eight years in the Philippines—that is to say, they had dishonored it.

The next day, Sunday,—which was yesterday—the cable brought us additional news—still more splendid news—still more honor for the flag. The first display-head shouts this information at us in the stentorian capitals: "WOMEN SLAIN IN MORO SLAUGHTER."

"Slaughter" is a good word. Certainly there is not a better one in the Unabridged Dictionary for this occasion.

The next display line says:

"With Children They Mixed in Mob in Crater, and All Died Together."

They were mere naked savages, and yet there is a sort of pathos about it when that word children falls under your eye, for it always brings before us our perfectest symbol of innocence and helplessness; and by help of its deathless eloquence color, creed and nationality vanish away and we see only that they are children—merely children. And if they are frightened and crying and in trouble, our pity goes out to them by natural impulse. We see a picture. We see the small forms. We see the terrified faces. We see the tears. We see the small hands clinging in supplication to the mother; but we do not see those children that we are speaking about. We see in their places the little creatures whom we know and love.

The next heading blazes with American and Christian glory like to the sun in the zenith:

"Death List is Now 900."

I was never so enthusiastically proud of the flag till now!

• • •

Smedley Butler was a prominent U.S. Marine Corps major general who joined the army in 1898 to fight in the Spanish-American War. After that he was involved in military interventions in China, the Philippines, Nicaragua, Panama, Honduras, Mexico, and Haiti, twice winning the Congressional Medal of Honor. However, Butler came to see his actions in a new light. Butler wrote, "It may seem odd for me, a military man to adopt such a comparison. Truthfulness compels me to. I spent thirty-three years and four months in active military service as a member of this country's most agile military force, the Marine Corps. I served in all commissioned ranks from Second Lieutenant to Major-General. And during that period, I spent most of my time being a high class muscle-man for Big Business, for Wall Street and for the Bankers. In short, I was a racketeer, a gangster for capitalism. . . . I helped make Mexico, especially Tampico, safe for American oil interests in 1914. I helped make Haiti and Cuba a decent place for the National City Bank boys to collect revenues in. I helped in the raping of half a dozen Central American republics for the benefits of Wall Street. The record of racketeering is long. I helped purify Nicaragua for the international banking house of Brown Brothers in 1909–1912 (where have I heard that name before?). I brought light to the Dominican Republic for American sugar interests in 1916. In China I helped to see to it that Standard Oil went its way unmolested. . . . During those years, I had, as the boys in the back room would say, a swell racket. Looking back on it, I feel that I could have given Al Capone a few hints. The best he could do was to operate his racket in three districts. I operated on three continents." In 1935, Butler published a powerful condemnation of the business interests he served in those imperialist ventures, *War Is a Racket*. The section printed here is from the chapter "Who Makes the Profits?"

Smedley D. Butler, *War Is a Racket* (1935)[6]

War is a racket. It always has been. It is possibly the oldest, easily the most profitable, surely the most vicious. It is the only one international in scope. It is the only one in which the profits are reckoned in dollars and the losses in lives.

A racket is best described, I believe, as something that is not what it seems to the majority of the people. Only a small "inside" group knows what it is about. It is conducted for the benefit of the very few, at the expense of the very many. Out of war a few people make huge fortunes.

In the World War a mere handful garnered the profits of the conflict. At least 21,000 new millionaires and billionaires were made in the United States during the World War. That many admitted their huge blood gains in their income tax returns. How many other war millionaires falsified their tax returns no one knows.

How many of these war millionaires shouldered a rifle? How many of them dug a trench? How many of them knew what it meant to go hungry in a rat-infested dug-out? How many of them spent sleepless, frightened nights, ducking shells and shrapnel and machine gun bullets? How many of them parried a bayonet thrust of an enemy? How many of them were wounded or killed in battle?

Out of war nations acquire additional territory, if they are victorious. They just take it. This newly acquired territory promptly is exploited by the few—the self-same few who wrung dollars out of blood in the war. The general public shoulders the bill.

And what is this bill?

This bill renders a horrible accounting. Newly placed gravestones. Mangled bodies. Shattered minds. Broken hearts and homes. Economic instability. Depression and all its attendant miseries. Back-breaking taxation for generations and generations.

For a great many years, as a soldier, I had a suspicion that war was a racket; not until I retired to civil life did I fully realize it. Now that I see the international war clouds gathering, as they are today, I must face it and speak out.

Again they are choosing sides. France and Russia met and agreed to stand side by side. Italy and Austria hurried to make a similar agreement. Poland and Germany cast sheep's eyes at each other, forgetting for the nonce [one unique occasion], their dispute over the Polish Corridor.

The assassination of King Alexander [I] of Yugoslavia complicated matters. Yugoslavia and Hungary, long bitter enemies, were almost at each other's throats. Italy was ready to jump in. But France was waiting. So was Czechoslovakia. All of them are looking ahead to war. Not the people—not those who fight and pay and die—only those who foment wars and remain safely at home to profit.

There are 40,000,000 men under arms in the world today, and our statesmen and diplomats have the temerity to say that war is not in the making.

Hell's bells! Are these 40,000,000 men being trained to be dancers?

Not in Italy, to be sure. Premier [Benito] Mussolini knows what they are being trained for. He, at least, is frank enough to speak out. Only the other day, Il Duce in "International Conciliation," the publication of the Carnegie Endowment for International Peace, said:

> And above all, Fascism, the more it considers and observes the future and the development of humanity quite apart from political considerations of the moment, believes neither in the possibility nor the utility of perpetual peace. . . . War alone brings up to its highest tension all human energy and puts the stamp of nobility upon the people who have the courage to meet it.

Undoubtedly Mussolini means exactly what he says. His well-trained army, his great fleet of planes, and even his navy are ready for war—anxious for it, apparently. His recent stand at the side of Hungary in the latter's dispute with Yugoslavia showed that. And the hurried mobilization of his troops on the Austrian border after the assassination of [Austrian chancellor Engelbert] Dollfuss [on July 25, 1934] showed it too. There are others in Europe too whose saber-rattling presages war, sooner or later.

Herr Hitler, with his rearming Germany and his constant demands for more and more arms, is an equal if not greater menace to peace. France only recently increased the term of military service for its youth from a year to eighteen months.

Yes, all over, nations are camping in their arms. The mad dogs of Europe are on the loose.

In the Orient the maneuvering is more adroit. Back in 1904, when Russia and Japan fought, we kicked out our old friends the Russians and backed Japan. Then our very generous international bankers were financing Japan. Now the trend is to poison us against the Japanese. What does the "open door" policy to China mean to us? Our trade with China is about $90,000,000 a year. Or the Philippine Islands? We have spent about $600,000,000 in the Philippines in thirty-five years and we (our bankers and industrialists and speculators) have private investments there of less than $200,000,000.

Then, to save that China trade of about $90,000,000, or to protect these private investments of less than $200,000,000 in the Philippines, we would be all stirred up to hate Japan and go to war—a war that might well cost us tens of billions of dollars, hundreds of thousands of lives of Americans, and many more hundreds of thousands of physically maimed and mentally unbalanced men.

Of course, for this loss, there would be a compensating profit—fortunes would be made. Millions and billions of dollars would be piled up. By a few. Munitions makers. Bankers. Ship builders. Manufacturers. Meat packers. Speculators. They would fare well.

Yes, they are getting ready for another war. Why shouldn't they? It pays high dividends.

But what does it profit the masses?

What does it profit the men who are killed? What does it profit the men who are maimed? What does it profit their mothers and sisters, their wives and their sweethearts? What does it profit their children?

What does it profit anyone except the very few to whom war means huge profits?

Yes, and what does it profit the nation?

Take our own case. Until 1898 we didn't own a bit of territory outside the mainland of North America. At that time our national debt was a little more than $1,000,000,000. Then we became "internationally minded." We forgot, or shunted aside, the advice of the Father of our country. We forgot George Washington's warning about "entangling alliances." We went to war. We acquired outside territory. At the end of the World War period, as a direct result of our fiddling in international affairs, our national debt had jumped to over $25,000,000,000. Our total favorable trade balance during the twenty-five-year period was about $24,000,000,000. Therefore, on a purely bookkeeping basis, we ran a little behind year for year, and that foreign trade might well have been ours without the wars.

It would have been far cheaper (not to say safer) for the average American who pays the bills to stay out of foreign entanglements. For a very few this racket, like bootlegging and other underworld rackets, brings fancy profits, but the cost of operations is always transferred to the people—who do not profit.

CHAPTER THIRTEEN

Socialists and Wobblies

Mother Jones, "Agitation: The Greatest Factor for Progress" (March 24, 1903)

Upton Sinclair, *The Jungle* (1906)

W. E. B. Du Bois, *The Souls of Black Folk* (1903)

Emma Goldman, "Patriotism: A Menace to Liberty" (1908)

"Proclamation of the Striking Textile Workers of Lawrence" (1912)

Arturo Giovannitti's Address to the Jury (November 23, 1912)

Woody Guthrie, "Ludlow Massacre" (1946)

Julia May Courtney, "Remember Ludlow!" (May 1914)

Joe Hill, "My Last Will" (November 18, 1915)

The overseas wars, the bitter conditions of workers, the misery of the poor in the crowded cities—these factors contributed to the rise of radicalism in the early part of the twentieth century.

One important expression of the radicalism of this period was the anarchist-influenced labor union called the Industrial Workers of the World—the IWW, popularly known as the "Wobblies." When the IWW was formed in 1905, on the platform with labor leader "Big Bill" Haywood were the Socialist Party leader Eugene Debs and the seventy-five-year-old organizer of miners, Mary "Mother" Jones.

The IWW preamble of 1908 spoke of the class struggle: "The working class and the employing class have nothing in common. There can be no peace so long as hunger and want are found among millions of the working people and the few, who make up the employing class, have all the good things of life. . . . By organizing industrially we are forming the structure of the new society within the shell of the old."

The socialist movement was another powerful movement born of the grievances of this era. Eugene Debs had become a socialist while in prison for his participation in the Pullman strike of 1894. He became a leader of the party, running as its presidential candidate five times. The Socialist Party at one time had one hundred thousand members and 1,200 office holders in 340 municipalities. Distinguished writers of the time such as Upton Sinclair, Helen Keller, and Jack London were socialists. This period was the high water mark for the idea of socialism in the history of this country.

• • •

One of the most extraordinary organizers of the labor movement in the early twentieth century was Mary Harris, who took the name "Mother Jones." Born in Ireland, she became an organizer for the United Mine Workers, and, in her eighties, organized miners in West Virginia and Colorado. In 1905, she helped form the IWW. Upton Sinclair was so inspired by her that he used her as a model for one of his characters in his novel *The Coal War*, which chronicled the Ludlow strike and massacre. "All over the country she had roamed, and wherever she went, the flame of protest had leaped up in the hearts of men; her story was a veritable Odyssey of revolt." Here is a selection from an address Mother Jones gave to a mass audience in Toledo's Memorial Hall in 1903, as reported by the *Toledo Bee*.

Mother Jones, "Agitation—The Greatest Factor for Progress" (March 24, 1903)[1]

"Mother" Jones, known throughout the country and in fact throughout the world as "The Miners' Angel," addressed a motley gathering of about 1,200 persons in Memorial hall last night. The lower hall was packed. The gallery was full to overflowing and some even crowded the steps leading to the building.

It was truly a motley gathering. The society woman, attracted by mere curiosity to see and hear the woman who has won such fame as the guardian spirit of the miners; the factory girl, the wealthy man and his less fortunate brothers, the black man and the white man, old and young, sat side by side and each came in for a share of criticism.

"Mother" Jones is an eloquent speaker. There is just enough of the down-east accent to her words to make it attractive and she has the faculty of framing pathetic and beautiful word pictures. Despite her sixty years and her gray hairs, she is hale and hearty; has a voice that reaches to the furthermost corner of almost any hall but it is nevertheless anything but harsh. . . .

"Fellow workers," she began, " 'tis well for us to be here. Over a hundred years ago men gathered to discuss the vital questions and later fought together for a principle that won for us our civil liberty. Forty years ago men gathered to discuss a growing evil under the old flag and later fought side by side until chattel slavery was abolished. But, by the wiping out of this black stain upon our country another great crime—wage slavery—was fastened upon our people. I stand on this platform ashamed of the conditions existing in this country. I refused to go to England and lecture only a few days ago because I was ashamed, first of all, to make the conditions existing here known to the world and second, because my services were needed here. I have just come from a God-cursed country, known as West Virginia; from a state which has produced some of our best and brightest statesmen; a state where conditions are too awful for your imagination.

"I shall tell you some things tonight that are awful to contemplate; but, perhaps, it is best that you to know of them. They may arouse you from your lethargy if there is any manhood, womanhood or love of country left in you. I have just come from a state which has an injunction on every other foot of ground. Some months ago the president of the United Mine Workers [John Mitchell] asked me to take a look into the condition of the men in the mines of West Virginia. I went. I would get a gathering of miners in the darkness of the night up on the mountain side. Here I would listen to their tale of woe; here I would try to encourage them. I did not dare to sleep in one of those miner's houses. If I did the poor man would be called to the office in the morning and would be discharged for sheltering old Mother Jones.

"I did my best to drive into the downtrodden men a little spirit, but it was a task. They had been driven so long that they were afraid. I used to sit through the night by a stream of water. I could not go to the miners' hovels so in the morning I would call the ferryman and he would take me across the river to a hotel not owned by the mine operators.

"The men in the anthracite district finally asked for more wages. They were refused. A strike was called. I stayed in West Virginia; held meetings and one day as I stood talking to some break-boys two injunctions were served upon me. I asked the deputy if he had more. We were arrested but we were freed in the morning. I objected to the food in the jail and to my arrest. When I was called up before the judge I called him a czar and he let me go. The other fellows were afraid and they went to jail. I violated injunction after injunction but I wasn't re-arrested. Why? The courts themselves force you to have no respect for that court.

"A few days later that awful wholesale murdering in the quiet little mining camp of Stamford took place. I know those people were law-abiding citizens. I had been there. And their shooting by United States deputy marshals was an atrocious and cold-blooded murder. After the crimes had been committed the marshals— the murderers—were banqueted by the operators in the swellest hotel in Pennsylvania. You have no idea of the awfulness of that wholesale murder. Before daylight broke in the morning in that quiet little mining camp deputies and special officers went into the homes, shot the men down in their beds, and all because the miners wanted to try to induce 'black-legs' [strike-breakers] to leave the mines.

"I'll tell you how the trouble started. The deputies were bringing these strike-breakers to the mines. The men wanted to talk with them and at last stepped on ground loaded down with an injunction. There were thirty-six or seven in the party of miners. They resisted arrest. They went home finally without being arrested. One of the officials of the miners' unions telegraphed to the men. 'Don't resist. Go to jail. We will bail you out.' A United States marshal . . . sent back word that the operators would not let them use the telephone to send the message to the little mining camp and that he could not get there before hours had passed. The miners' officials secured the names of the men and gave their representatives authority to bail them out of jail the next morning. But when the next morning arrived they were murdered in cold blood.

"These federal judges, who continue granting injunctions, are appointed by men who have their political standing through the votes of you labor union fellows! You get down on your knees like a lot of Yahoos when you want something. At the same time you haven't sense enough to take peaceably what belongs to you through the ballot. You are chasing a will-o'-the-wisp, you measly things, and the bullets which should be sent into your own measly, miserable, dirty carcasses, shoot down innocent men. Women are not responsible because they have no vote. You'd all better put on petticoats. If you like those bullets vote to put them into your own bodies. Don't you think it's about time you began to shoot ballots instead of voting for capitalistic bullets.

"I hate your political parties, you Republicans and Democrats. I want you to deny if you can what I am going to say. You want an office and must necessarily get into the ring. You must do what that ring says and if you don't you won't be elected. There you are. Each time you do that you are voting for a capitalistic bullet and you get it. I want you to know that this man [Samuel Milton] Jones who is running for mayor of your beautiful city is no relative of mine; no, sir. He belongs to that school of reformers who say capital and labor must join hands. He may be all right. He prays a good deal. But, I wonder if you would shake hands with me if I robbed you. He builds parks to make his workmen contented. But a contented workman is no good. All progress stops in the contented man. I'm for agitation. It's the greater factor for progress[.]"

Here the speaker changed her attention to the society woman. "I see a lot of society women in this audience, attracted here out of a mere curiosity to see 'that old Mother Jones.' I know you better than you do yourselves. I can walk down the aisle and pick every one of you out. You probably think I am crazy but I know you. And you society dudes—poor creatures. You wear high collars to support your jaw and keep your befuddled brains from oozing out of your mouths. While this commercial cannibalism is reaching into the cradle; pulling girls into the factory to be ruined; pulling children into the factory to be destroyed; you, who are doing all in the name of Christianity, you are at home nursing your poodle dogs. It's high time you got out and worked for humanity. Christianity will take care of itself. I started in a factory. I have traveled through miles and miles of factories and there is not an inch of ground under that flag that is not stained with the blood of children."

• • •

The influence and wide appeal of socialist ideas in the early part of the twentieth century can be measured, in part, by the impact of Upton Sinclair's novel *The Jungle*. Sinclair, who joined the Socialist Party in 1902, was a contributor to the influential socialist magazine *Appeal to Reason*, which first serialized the chapters of the book (dedicated to "the workingmen of America") starting in 1905. The novel's detailed description of the exploitation of workers in the meatpacking factories in Chicago sparked widespread calls for reform, and led to the passage of the Meat Inspection Act of 1906. In this selection, from Chapter 31, Sinclair offers a vision of a socialist alternative to the injustices of capitalism.

Upton Sinclair, *The Jungle* (1906)[2]

Mr. Maynard, the editor, took occasion to remark, somewhat naively, that he had always understood that Socialists had a cut-and-dried program for the future of civilization; whereas here were two active members of the party, who, from what he could make out, were agreed about nothing at all. Would the two, for his enlightenment, try to ascertain just what they had in common, and why they belonged to the same party? This resulted, after much debating, in the formulating of two carefully worded propositions: First, that a Socialist believes in the common ownership and democratic management of the means of producing the necessities of life; and, second, that a Socialist believes that the means by which this is to be brought about is the class conscious political organization of the wage-earners. Thus far they were at one; but no farther. To Lucas, the religious zealot, the co-operative commonwealth was the New Jerusalem, the kingdom of Heaven, which is "within you." To the other, Socialism was simply a necessary step toward a far-distant goal, a step to be tolerated with impatience. Schliemann called himself a "philosophic anarchist"; and he explained that an anarchist was one who believed that the end of human existence was the free development of every personality, unrestricted by laws save those of its own being. Since the same kind of match would light every one's fire and the same-shaped loaf of bread would fill every one's stomach, it would be perfectly feasible to submit industry to the control of a majority vote. There was only one earth, and the quantity of material things was limited. Of intellectual and moral things, on the other hand, there was no limit, and one could have more without another's having less; hence "Communism in material production, anarchism in intellectual," was the formula of modern proletarian thought. As soon as the birth agony was over, and the wounds of society had been healed, there would be established a simple system whereby each man was credited with his labor and debited with his purchases; and after that the processes of production, exchange, and consumption would go on automatically, and without our being conscious of them, any more than a man is conscious of the beating of his heart. And then, explained Schliemann, society would break up into independent, self-governing communities of mutually congenial persons; examples of which at present were clubs, churches, and political parties. After the revolution, all the intellectual, artistic, and spiritual activities of men would be cared for by such "free associations"; romantic novelists would be supported by those who liked to read romantic novels, and impressionist painters would be supported by those who liked to look at impressionist pictures—and the same with preachers and scientists, editors and actors and musicians. If any one wanted to work or paint or pray, and could find no one to maintain him, he could support himself by working part of the time. That was the case at present, the only difference being that the competitive wage system compelled a man to work all the time to live, while, after the abolition of privilege and exploitation, any one would be able to support himself by an hour's work a day. Also the artist's audience of the present was a small minority of people, all debased and vulgarized by the effort it had cost them to win in the commercial battle; of the intellectual and artistic activities which would result when the whole of mankind was set free from the nightmare of competition, we could at present form no conception whatever.

And then the editor wanted to know upon what ground Dr. Schliemann asserted that it might be possible for a society to exist upon an hour's toil by each of its members. "Just what," answered the other, "would be the productive capacity of society if the present resources of science were utilized, we have no means of ascertaining; but we may be sure it would exceed anything that would sound reasonable to minds inured to the ferocious barbarities of capitalism. After the triumph of the international proletariat, war would of course be inconceivable; and who can figure the cost of war to humanity—not merely the value of the lives and the material that it destroys, not merely the cost of keeping millions of men in idleness, of arming and equipping them for battle and parade, but the drain upon the vital energies of society by the war attitude and the war terror, the brutality and ignorance, the drunkenness, prostitution, and crime it entails, the industrial impotence and the moral deadness? Do you think that it would be too much to say that two hours of the working time of every efficient member of a community goes to feed the red fiend of war?"

And then Schliemann went on to outline some of the wastes of competition: the losses of industrial warfare; the ceaseless worry and friction; the vices—such as drink, for instance, the use of which had nearly doubled in twenty years, as a consequence of the intensification of the economic struggle; the idle and unproductive members of the community, the frivolous rich and the pauperized poor; the law and the whole machinery of repression; the wastes of social ostentation, the milliners and tailors, the hairdressers, dancing masters, chefs and lackeys. "You understand," he said, "that in a society dominated by the fact of commercial competition, money is necessarily the test of prowess, and wastefulness the sole criterion of power. So we have, at the present moment, a society with, say, thirty per cent of the population occupied in producing useless articles, and one per cent occupied in destroying them. And this is not all; for the servants and panders of the parasites are also parasites, the milliners and the jewelers and the lackeys have also to be supported by the useful members of the community. And bear in mind also that this monstrous disease affects not merely the idlers and their menials, its poison penetrates the whole social body. Beneath the hundred thousand women of the elite are a million middle-class women, miserable because they are not of the elite, and trying to appear of it in public; and beneath them, in turn, are five million farmers' wives reading 'fashion papers' and trimming bonnets, and shop-girls and serving-maids selling themselves into brothels for cheap jewelry and imitation seal-skin robes. And then consider that, added to this competition in display, you have, like oil on the flames, a whole system of competition in selling! You have manufacturers contriving tens of thousands of catchpenny devices, storekeepers displaying them, and newspapers and magazines filled up with advertisements of them!" . . .

"So long as we have wage-slavery," answered Schliemann, "it matters not in the least how debasing and repulsive a task may be, it is easy to find people to perform it. But just as soon as labor is set free, then the price of such work will begin to rise. So one by one the old, dingy, and unsanitary factories will come down—it will be cheaper to build new; and so the steamships will be provided with stoking machinery, and so the dangerous trades will be made safe, or substitutes will be found for their products. In exactly the same way, as the citizens of our Industrial Republic become refined, year by year the cost of slaughterhouse products will increase; until eventually those who want to eat meat will have to do their own killing—and how long do you think the custom would survive then?— To go on to another item—one of the necessary accompaniments of capitalism in a democracy is political corruption; and one of the consequences of civic administration by ignorant and vicious politicians, is that preventable diseases kill off half our population. And even if science were allowed to try, it could do little, because the majority of human beings are not yet human beings at all, but simply machines for the creating of wealth for others. They are penned up in filthy houses and left to rot and stew in misery, and the conditions of their life make them ill faster than all the doctors in the world could heal them; and so, of course, they remain as centers of contagion, poisoning the lives of all of us, and making happiness impossible for even the most selfish. For this reason I would seriously maintain that all the medical and surgical discoveries that science can make in the future will be of less importance than the application of the knowledge we already possess, when the disinherited of the earth have established their right to a human existence."

• • •

In *The Souls of Black Folk*, the black sociologist, activist, and socialist W. E. B. Du Bois set out to describe "the strange meaning of being black here in the dawning of the Twentieth Century," stating prophetically that "the problem of the Twentieth Century is the problem of the color-line." In this classic study, Du Bois foreshadowed the growth of the civil rights movement in the twentieth century. Here is a reading from the first chapter, "Of Our Spiritual Strivings."

W. E. B. Du Bois, *The Souls of Black Folk* (1903)[3]

Between me and the other world there is ever an unasked question: unasked by some through feelings of delicacy; by others through the difficulty of rightly framing it. All, nevertheless, flutter round it. They approach me in a half-hesitant sort of way, eye me curiously or compassionately, and then, instead of saying directly, How does it feel to be a problem? they say, I know an excellent colored man in my town; or, I fought at Mechanicsville; or, Do not these Southern outrages make your blood boil? At these I smile, or am interested, or reduce the boiling to a simmer, as the occasion may require. To the real question, How does it feel to be a problem? I answer seldom a word.

And yet, being a problem is a strange experience,—peculiar even for one who has never been anything else, save perhaps in babyhood and in Europe. It is in the early days of rollicking boyhood that the revelation first bursts upon one, all in a day, as it were. I remember well when the shadow swept across me. I was a little thing, away up in the hills of New England, where the dark Housatonic winds between Hoosac and Taghkanic to the sea. In a wee wooden schoolhouse, something put it into the boys' and girls' heads to buy gorgeous visiting-cards—ten cents a package—and exchange. The exchange was merry, till one girl, a tall newcomer, refused my card,—refused it peremptorily, with a glance. Then it dawned upon me with a certain suddenness that I was different from the others; or like, mayhap, in heart and life and longing, but shut out from their world by a vast veil. I had thereafter no desire to tear down that veil, to creep through; I held all beyond it in common contempt, and lived above it in a region of blue sky and great wandering shadows. That sky was bluest when I could beat my mates at examination-time, or beat them at a foot-race, or even beat their stringy heads. Alas, with the years all this fine contempt began to fade; for the worlds I longed for, and all their dazzling opportunities, were theirs, not mine. But they should not keep these prizes, I said; some, all, I would wrest from them. Just how I would do it I could never decide: by reading law, by healing the sick, by telling the wonderful tales that swam in my head,—some way. With other black boys the strife was not so fiercely sunny: their youth shrunk into tasteless sycophancy, or into silent hatred of the pale world about them and mocking distrust of everything white; or wasted itself in a bitter cry, Why did God make me an outcast and a stranger in mine own house? The shades of the prison-house closed round about us all: walls strait and stubborn to the whitest, but relentlessly narrow, tall, and unscalable to sons of night who must plod darkly on in resignation, or beat unavailing palms against the stone, or steadily, half hopelessly, watch the streak of blue above.

After the Egyptian and Indian, the Greek and Roman, the Teuton and Mongolian, the Negro is a sort of seventh son, born with a veil, and gifted with second-sight in this American world,—a world which yields him no true self-consciousness, but only lets him see himself through the revelation of the other world. It is a peculiar sensation, this double-consciousness, this sense of always looking at one's self through the eyes of others, of measuring one's soul by the tape of a world that looks on in amused contempt and pity. One ever feels his two-ness,—an American, a Negro; two souls, two thoughts, two unreconciled strivings; two warring ideals in one dark body, whose dogged strength alone keeps it from being torn asunder.

The history of the American Negro is the history of this strife,—this longing to attain self-conscious manhood, to merge his double self into a better and truer self. In this merging he wishes neither of the older selves to be lost. He would not Africanize America, for America has too much to teach the world and Africa. He would not bleach his Negro soul in a flood of white Americanism, for he knows that Negro blood has a message for the world. He simply wishes to make it possible for a man to be both a Negro and an American, without being cursed and spit upon by his fellows, without having the doors of Opportunity closed roughly in his face.

This, then, is the end of his striving: to be a co-worker in the kingdom of culture, to escape both death and isolation, to husband and use his best powers and his latent genius. These powers of body and mind have in the past been strangely wasted, dispersed, or forgotten. The shadow of a mighty Negro past flits through the tale of Ethiopia the Shadowy and of Egypt the Sphinx. Throughout history, the powers of single black men flash here and there like falling stars, and die some-times before the world has rightly gauged their brightness. Here in America, in the few days since Emancipation, the black man's turning hither and thither in hesitant and doubtful striving has often made his very strength to lose effectiveness, to seem like absence of power, like weakness. And yet it is not weakness,—it is the contradiction of double aims. The double-aimed struggle of the black artisan—on the one hand to escape white contempt for a nation of mere hewers of wood and drawers of water, and on the other hand to plough and nail and dig for a poverty-stricken horde—could only result in making him a poor craftsman, for he had but half a heart in either cause. By the poverty and ignorance of his people, the Negro minister or doctor was tempted toward quackery and demagogy; and by the criticism of the other world, toward ideals that made him ashamed of his lowly tasks. The would-be black savant was confronted by the paradox that the knowledge his people needed was a twice-told tale to his white neighbors, while the knowledge which would teach the white world was Greek to his own flesh and blood. The innate love of harmony and beauty that set the ruder souls of his people a-dancing and a-singing raised but confusion and doubt in the soul of the black artist; for the beauty revealed to him was the soul-beauty of a race which his larger audience despised, and he could not articulate the message of another people. This waste of double aims, this seeking to satisfy two unreconciled ideals, has wrought sad havoc with the courage and faith and deeds of ten thousand thousand people,—has sent them often wooing false gods and invoking false means of salvation, and at times has even seemed about to make them ashamed of themselves.

Away back in the days of bondage they thought to see in one divine event the end of all doubt and disappointment; few men ever worshipped Freedom with half such unquestioning faith as did the American Negro for two centuries. To him, so far as he thought and dreamed, slavery was indeed the sum of all villainies, the cause of all sorrow, the root of all prejudice; Emancipation was the key to a promised land of sweeter beauty than ever stretched before the eyes of wearied Israelites. . . .

The Nation has not yet found peace from its sins; the freedman has not yet found in freedom his promised land. Whatever of good may have come in these years of change, the shadow of a deep disappointment rests upon the Negro people,—a disappointment all the more bitter because the unattained ideal was unbounded save by the simple ignorance of a lowly people.

The first decade was merely a prolongation of the vain search for freedom, the boon that seemed ever barely to elude their grasp,—like a tantalizing will-o'-the-wisp, maddening and misleading the headless host. The holocaust of war, the terrors of the Ku-Klux Klan, the lies of carpet-baggers, the disorganization of industry, and the contradictory advice of friends and foes, left the bewildered serf with no new watchword beyond the old cry for freedom. As the time flew, however, he began to grasp a new idea. The ideal of liberty demanded for its attainment powerful means, and these the Fifteenth Amendment gave him. The ballot, which before he had looked upon as a visible sign of freedom, he now regarded as the chief means of gaining and perfecting the liberty with which war had partially endowed him. And why not? Had not votes made war and emancipated millions? Had not votes enfranchised the freedmen? Was anything impossible to a power that had done all this? A million black men started with renewed zeal to vote themselves into the kingdom. So the decade flew away, the revolution of 1876 came, and left the half-free serf weary, wondering, but still inspired. Slowly but steadily, in the following years, a new vision began gradually to replace the dream of political power,—a powerful movement, the rise of another ideal to guide the unguided, another pillar of fire by night after a clouded day. It was the ideal of "book-learning"; the curiosity, born of compulsory ignorance, to know and test the power of the cabalistic letters of the white man, the longing to know. Here at last seemed to have been discovered the mountain path to Canaan; longer than the highway of Emancipation and law, steep and rugged, but straight, leading to heights high enough to overlook life.

Up the new path the advance guard toiled, slowly, heavily, doggedly; only those who have watched and guided the faltering feet, the misty minds, the dull understandings, of the dark pupils of these schools know how faithfully, how piteously, this people strove to learn. It was weary work. The cold statistician wrote down the inches of progress here and there, noted also where here and there a foot had slipped or some one had fallen. To the tired climbers, the horizon was ever dark, the mists were often cold, the Canaan was always dim and far away. If, however, the vistas disclosed as yet no goal, no resting-place, little but flattery and criticism, the journey at least gave leisure for reflection and self-examination; it changed the child of Emancipation to the youth with dawning self-consciousness, self-realization, self-respect. In those somber forests of his striving his own soul rose before him, and he saw himself,—darkly as through a veil; and yet he saw in himself some faint revelation of his power, of his mission. He began to have a dim feeling that, to attain his place in the world, he must be himself, and not another. For the first time he sought to analyze the burden he bore upon his back, that dead-weight of social degradation partially masked behind a half-named Negro problem. He felt his poverty; without a cent, without a home, without land, tools, or savings, he had entered into competition with rich, landed, skilled neighbors. To be a poor man is hard, but to be a poor race in a land of dollars is the very bottom of hardships. He felt the weight of his ignorance,—not simply of letters, but of life, of business, of the humanities; the accumulated sloth and shirking and awkwardness of decades and centuries shackled his hands and feet. Nor was his burden all poverty and ignorance. The red stain of bastardy, which two centuries of systematic legal defilement of Negro women had stamped upon his race, meant not only the loss of ancient African chastity, but also the hereditary weight of a mass of corruption from white adulterers, threatening almost the obliteration of the Negro home.

A people thus handicapped ought not to be asked to race with the world, but rather allowed to give all its time and thought to its own social problems. But alas! while sociologists gleefully count his bastards and his prostitutes, the very soul of the toiling, sweating black man is darkened by the shadow of a vast despair. Men call the shadow prejudice, and learnedly explain it as the natural defence of culture against barbarism, learning against ignorance, purity against crime, the "higher" against the "lower" races. To which the Negro cries Amen! and swears that to so much of this strange prejudice as is founded on just homage to civilization, culture, righteousness, and progress, he humbly bows and meekly does obeisance. But before that nameless prejudice that leaps beyond all this he stands helpless, dismayed, and well-nigh speechless; before that personal disrespect and mockery, the ridicule and systematic humiliation, the distortion of fact and wanton license of fancy, the cynical ignoring of the better and the boisterous welcoming of the worse, the all-pervading desire to inculcate disdain for everything black, from Toussaint [L'Ouverture] to the devil,—before this there rises a sickening despair that would disarm and discourage any nation save that black host to whom "discouragement" is an unwritten word.

But the facing of so vast a prejudice could not but bring the inevitable self-questioning, self-disparagement, and lowering of ideals which ever accompany repression and breed in an atmosphere of contempt and hate. Whisperings and portents came borne upon the four winds: Lo! we are diseased and dying, cried the dark hosts; we cannot write, our voting is vain; what need of education, since we must always cook and serve? And the Nation echoed and enforced this self-criticism, saying: Be content to be servants, and nothing more; what need of higher culture for half-men? Away with the black man's ballot, by force or fraud,—and behold the suicide of a race! Nevertheless, out of the evil came something of good,—the more careful adjustment of education to real life, the clearer perception of the Negroes' social responsibilities, and the sobering realization of the meaning of progress.

So dawned the time of Sturm und Drang: storm and stress today rocks our little boat on the mad waters of the world-sea; there is within and without the sound of conflict, the burning of body and rending of soul; inspiration strives with doubt, and faith with vain questionings. The bright ideals of the past,—physical freedom, political power, the training of brains and the training of hands,—all these in turn have waxed and waned, until even the last grows dim and overcast. Are they all wrong,—all false? No, not that, but each alone was over-simple and incomplete,—the dreams of a credulous race-childhood, or the fond imaginings of the other world which does not know and does not want to know our power. To be really true, all these ideals must be melted and welded into one. The training of the schools we need today more than ever,—the training of deft hands, quick eyes and ears, and above all the broader, deeper, higher culture of gifted minds and pure hearts. The power of the ballot we need in sheer self-defence,—else what shall save us from a second slavery? Freedom, too, the long-sought, we still seek,—the freedom of life and limb, the freedom to work and think, the freedom to love and aspire. Work, culture, liberty,—all these we need, not singly but together, not successively but together, each growing and aiding each, and all striving toward that vaster ideal that swims before the Negro people, the ideal of human brotherhood, gained through the unifying ideal of Race; the ideal of fostering and developing the traits and talents of the Negro, not in opposition to or contempt for other races, but rather in large conformity to the greater ideals of the American Republic, in order that some day on American soil two world-races may give each to each those characteristics both so sadly lack. We the darker ones come even now not altogether empty-handed: there are today no truer exponents of the pure human spirit of the Declaration of Independence than the American Negroes; there is no true American music but the wild sweet melodies of the Negro slave; the American fairy tales and folk-lore are Indian and African; and, all in all, we black men seem the sole oasis of simple faith and reverence in a dusty desert of dollars and smartness. Will America be poorer if she replace her brutal dyspeptic blundering with light-hearted but determined Negro humility? or her coarse and cruel wit with loving jovial good-humor? or her vulgar music with the soul of the Sorrow Songs?

Merely a concrete test of the underlying principles of the great republic is the Negro Problem, and the spiritual striving of the freedmen's sons is the travail of souls whose burden is almost beyond the measure of their strength, but who bear it in the name of an historic race, in the name of this the land of their fathers' fathers, and in the name of human opportunity.

• • •

A Lithuanian immigrant, Emma Goldman was an anarchist and feminist orator, agitator, and organizer. She was jailed many times for her speeches. An outspoken critic of war, Goldman, after the outbreak of World War I in Europe, worked to launch the No-Conscription League. When she and her fellow anarchist Alexander Berkman spoke out against the draft in June 1917 they were imprisoned, and after the war deported to their country of origin, Russia (which had become Soviet Russia). She gave this speech in San Francisco, in the period leading up to the outbreak of the first world war.

Emma Goldman, "Patriotism: A Menace to Liberty" (1908)[4]

What is patriotism? Is it love of one's birthplace, the place of childhood's recollections and hopes, dreams and aspirations? Is it the place where, in childlike naivety, we would watch the fleeting clouds, and wonder why we, too, could not run so swiftly? The place where we would count the milliard [billion] glittering stars, terror-stricken lest each one "an eye should be," piercing the very depths of our little souls? Is it the place where we would listen to the music of the birds, and long to have wings to fly, even as they, to distant lands? Or the place where we would sit at mother's knee, enraptured by wonderful tales of great deeds and conquests? In short, is it love for the spot, every inch representing dear and precious recollections of a happy, joyous, and playful childhood?

If that were patriotism, few American men of today could be called upon to be patriotic, since the place of play has been turned into factory, mill, and mine, while deafening sounds of machinery have replaced the music of the birds. Nor can we longer hear the tales of great deeds, for the stories our mothers tell today are but those of sorrow, tears, and grief.

What, then, is patriotism? "Patriotism, sir, is the last resort of scoundrels," said Dr. [Samuel] Johnson. Leo Tolstoy, the greatest anti-patriot of our times, defines patriotism as the principle that will justify the training of wholesale murderers; a trade that requires better equipment for the exercise of man-killing than the making of such necessities of life as shoes, clothing, and houses; a trade that guarantees better returns and greater glory than that of the average workingman. . . .

Indeed, conceit, arrogance, and egotism are the essentials of patriotism. Let me illustrate. Patriotism assumes that our globe is divided into little spots, each one surrounded by an iron gate. Those who have had the fortune of being born on some particular spot, consider themselves better, nobler, grander, more intelligent than the living beings inhabiting any other spot. It is, therefore, the duty of everyone living on that chosen spot to fight, kill, and die in the attempt to impose his superiority upon all the others.

The inhabitants of the other spots reason in like manner, of course, with the result that, from early infancy, the mind of the child is poisoned with blood-curdling stories about the Germans, the French, the Italians, Russians, etc. When the child has reached manhood, he is thoroughly saturated with the belief that he is chosen by the Lord himself to defend his country against the attack or invasion of any foreigner. It is for that purpose that we are clamoring for a greater army and navy, more battleships and ammunition. . . .

An army and navy represents the people's toys. To make them more attractive and acceptable, hundreds and thousands of dollars are being spent for the display of these toys. That was the purpose of the American government in equipping a fleet and sending it along the Pacific coast, that every American citizen should be made to feel the pride and glory of the United States. The city of San Francisco spent one hundred thousand dollars for the entertainment of the fleet; Los Angeles, sixty thousand; Seattle and Tacoma, about one hundred thousand. To entertain the fleet, did I say? To dine and wine a few superior officers, while the "brave boys" had to mutiny to get sufficient food. Yes, two hundred and sixty thousand dollars were spent on fireworks, theater parties, and revelries, at a time when men, women, and children through the breadth and length of the country were starving in the streets; when thousands of unemployed were ready to sell their labor at any price.

Two hundred and sixty thousand dollars! What could not have been accomplished with such an enormous sum? But instead of bread and shelter, the children of those cities were taken to see the fleet, that it may remain, as one of the newspapers said, "a lasting memory for the child."

A wonderful thing to remember, is it not? The implements of civilized slaughter. If the mind of the child is to be poisoned with such memories, what hope is there for a true realization of human brotherhood?

We Americans claim to be a peace-loving people. We hate bloodshed; we are opposed to violence. Yet we go into spasms of joy over the possibility of projecting dynamite bombs from flying machines upon helpless citizens. We are ready to hang, electrocute, or lynch anyone, who, from economic necessity, will risk his own life in the attempt upon that of some industrial magnate. Yet our hearts swell with pride at the thought that America is becoming the most powerful nation on earth, and that it will eventually plant her iron foot on the necks of all other nations.

Such is the logic of patriotism. . . .

Thinking men and women the world over are beginning to realize that patriotism is too narrow and limited a conception to meet the necessities of our time. The centralization of power has brought into being an international feeling of solidarity among the oppressed nations of the world; a solidarity which represents a greater harmony of interests between the workingman of America and his brothers abroad than between the American miner and his exploiting compatriot; a solidarity which fears not foreign invasion, because it is bringing all the workers to the point when they will say to their masters, "Go and do your own killing. We have done it long enough for you."

This solidarity is awakening the consciousness of even the soldiers, they, too, being flesh of the great human family. A solidarity that has proven infallible more than once during past struggles, and which has been the impetus inducing the Parisian soldiers, during the Commune of 1871, to refuse to obey when ordered to shoot their brothers. It has given courage to the men who mutinied on Russian warships during recent years. It will eventually bring about the uprising of all the oppressed and downtrodden against their international exploiters. . . .

When we have undermined the patriotic lie, we shall have cleared the path for that great structure wherein all nationalities shall be united into a universal brotherhood,—a truly FREE SOCIETY.

• • •

One of the most dramatic labor struggles in American history took place in Lawrence, Massachusetts, in 1912 when textile workers, mostly women, European immigrants speaking a dozen different languages, carried on a strike during the bitterly cold months of January to March 1912. Despite police violence and hunger, they persisted, and were victorious against the powerful textile mill owners. Borrowing from the U.S. Declaration of Independence, the following strike declaration, issued by the workers of Lawrence, was translated into the many languages of the immigrant textile workers in Massachusetts and circulated around the world.

"Proclamation of the Striking Textile Workers of Lawrence" (1912)[5]

We, the 20,000 textile workers of Lawrence, are out on strike for the right to live free from slavery and starvation; free from overwork and underpay; free from a state of affairs that had become so unbearable and beyond our control, that we were compelled to march out of the slave pens of Lawrence in united resistance against the wrongs and injustice of years and years of wage slavery.

In our fight we have suffered and borne patiently the abuse and calumnies of the mill owners, the city government, police, militia, State government, legislature, and the local police court judge. We feel that in justice to our fellow workers we should at this time make known the causes which compelled us to strike against the mill owners of Lawrence. We hold that as useful members of society and as wealth producers we have the right to lead decent and honorable lives; that we ought to have homes and not shacks; that we ought to have clean food and not adulterated food at high prices; that we ought to have clothes suited to the weather and not shoddy garments. That to secure sufficient food, clothing and shelter in a society made up of a robber class on the one hand and a working class on the other hand, it is absolutely necessary for the toilers to band themselves together and form a union, organizing its powers in such form as to them seem most likely to effect their safety and happiness.

Prudence, indeed, will dictate that conditions long established should not be changed for light or transient causes, and accordingly all experience has shown that the workers are more disposed to suffer, while evils are sufferable, than to right themselves, by striking against the misery to which they are accustomed. But when a long train of abuses and ill treatment, pursuing invariably the same object, evinces a design to reduce them to a state of beggary, it is their duty to resist such tactics and provide new guards for their future security. Such has been the patient sufferance of these textile workers, and such is now the necessity which compels them to fight the mill-owning class.

The history of the present mill owners is a history of repeated injuries, all having in direct object the establishment of an absolute tyranny over these textile workers. To prove this let facts be submitted to all right-thinking men and women of the civilized world. These mill owners have refused to meet the committees of the strikers. They have refused to consider their demands in any way that is reasonable or just. They have, in the security of their sumptuous offices, behind stout mill gates and serried rows of bayonets and policemen's clubs, defied the State, city, and public. In fact, the city of Lawrence and the government of Massachusetts have become the creatures of the mill owners. They have declared that they will not treat with the strikers till they return to the slavery against which they are in rebellion. They have starved the workers and driven them to such an extent that their homes are homes no longer, inasmuch as the mothers and children are driven by the low wages to work side by side with the father in the factory for a wage that spells bare existence and untimely death. To prove this to the world the large death rate of children under one year of age in Lawrence proves that most of these children perish because they were starved before birth. And those who survive the starving process grow up the victims of malnutrition. . . .

The brutality of the police in dealing with the strikers has aroused them to a state of rebellious opposition to all such methods of maintaining order. The crimes of the police during this trouble are almost beyond human imagination. They have dragged young girls from their beds at midnight. They have clubbed the strikers at every opportunity. They have dragged little children from their mothers' arms and with their clubs they have struck women who are in a state of pregnancy. They have placed people under arrest for no reason whatsoever. They have prevented mothers from sending their children out of the city and have laid hold of the children and the mothers violently and thr[own] the children into waiting patrol wagons like so much rubbish. They have caused the death of a striker by clubbing the strikers into a state of violence. They have arrested and clubbed young boys and placed under arrest innocent girls for no offense at all. . . .

The city government has denied the strikers the right to parade through the streets. They have abridged public assemblage by refusing the strikers the use of the city hall and public grounds for public meetings. They have turned the public buildings of the city into so many lodging houses for an army of hirelings and butchers. They have denied the strikers the right to use the Common for mass meetings, and they have ordered the police to take little children away from their parents, and they are responsible for all the violence and brutality on the part of the police.

The Massachusetts Legislature has refused to use any of the money of the State to help the strikers. They have voted $150,000 to maintain an army of 1,500 militiamen to be ready to shoot down innocent men, women, and children who are out on strike for a living wage. They have refused to use the powers of the State for the workers. They have appointed investigation committees, who declare, after perceiving the signs of suffering on the part of the strikers on every side, that there is no trouble with these people.

All the nations of the world are represented in this fight of the workers for more bread. The flaxen-haired son of the North marches side by side with his dark-haired brother of the South. They have toiled together in the factory for one boss. And now they have joined together in a great cause, and they have cast aside all racial and religious prejudice for the common good, determined to win a victory over the greed of the corrupt, unfeeling mill owners, who have ruled these people so long with the whip of hunger and the lash of the unemployed.

Outlawed, with their children taken away from them, denied their rights before the law, surrounded by bayonets of the militia, and driven up and down the streets of the city by an overfed and arrogant body of police, these textile workers, sons and daughters of the working class, call upon the entire civilized world to witness what they have suffered at the hands of the hirelings of the mill-owning class. These men and women can not suffer much longer; they will be compelled to rise in armed revolt against their oppressors if the present state of affairs is allowed to continue in Lawrence.

• • •

Among the many Wobblies who came to Massachusetts to show solidarity with the Lawrence textile strikers was Arturo Giovannitti, an Italian born poet and labor organizer. Soon after their arrival, Giovannitti and his friend Joseph Ettor were accused by the mill owners of inciting violence. After a soldier in the Massachusetts state militia killed an Italian woman, Ana LoPizzo, during the strike, local authorities charged an Italian striker and arrested Giovannitti and Ettor as "accessories to the murder." An international campaign was organized to support the three defendants, who were finally acquitted in November 1912, eight months after the textile strike had ended in victory. Here is Giovannitti's address to the jury before the verdict.

Arturo Giovannitti's Address to the Jury (November 23, 1912)[6]

Mr. Foreman and Gentlemen of the Jury:

It is the first time in my life that I speak publicly in your wonderful language, and it is the most solemn moment in my life. I know not if I will go to the end of my remarks. The District Attorney and the other gentlemen here who are used to measure all human emotions with the yardstick may not understand the tumult that is going on in my soul in this moment. . . .

There has been brought only one side of this great industrial question, only the method and only the tactics. But what about, I say, the ethical part of this question? What about the human and humane part of our ideas? What about the grand condition of tomorrow as we see it, and as we foretell it now to the workers at large, here in this same cage where the felon has sat, in this same cage where the drunkard, where the prostitute, where the hired assassin has been?

What about the ethical side of that? What about the better and nobler humanity where there shall be no more slaves, where no man will ever be obliged to go on strike in order to obtain fifty cents a week more, where children will not have to starve any more, where women no more will have to go and prostitute themselves—let me say, even if there are women in this courtroom here, because the truth must out at the end—where at last there will not be any more slaves, any more masters, but just one great family of friends and brothers.

It may be, gentlemen of the jury, that you do not believe in that. It may be that we are dreamers. It may be that we are fanatics, Mr. District Attorney. We are fanatics. But yet so was Socrates a fanatic, who instead of acknowledging the philosophy of the aristocrats of Athens, preferred to drink the poison. And so was Jesus Christ a fanatic, who instead of acknowledging that Pilate, or that Tiberius was emperor of Rome, and instead of acknowledging his submission to all the rulers of the time and all the priest craft of the time, preferred the cross between two thieves.

And so were all the philosophers and all the dreamers and all the scholars of the Middle Ages, who preferred to be burned alive by one of these very same churches concerning which you reproach me now of having said that no one of our membership should belong to them. Yes, gentlemen of the jury, you are judges. You must deal with facts. You must not deal with ideas. . . .

If there was any violence in Lawrence it was not Joe Ettor's fault. It was not my fault. If you must go back to the origin of all the trouble, gentlemen of the jury, you will find that the origin and reason was the wage system. It was the infamous rule of domination of one man by another man. It was the same reason that forty years ago impelled your great martyred President, Abraham Lincoln, by an illegal act, to issue the Proclamation of Emancipation—a thing which was beyond his powers as the Constitution of the United States expressed before that time.

I say it is the same principle now, the principle that made a man at that time a chattel slave, a soulless human being, a thing that could be bought and bartered and sold, and which now, having changed the term, makes the same man—but a white man—the slave of the machine.

They say you are free in this great and wonderful country. I say that politically you are, and my best compliments and congratulations for it. But I say you cannot be half free and half slave, and economically all the working class in the United States are as much slaves now as the negroes were forty and fifty years ago; because the man that owns the tool wherewith another man works, the man that owns the house where this man lives, the man that owns the factory where this man wants to go to work—that man owns and controls the bread that that man eats and therefore owns and controls his mind, his body, his heart and his soul. . . .

But I say and I repeat, that we have been working in something that is dearer to us than our lives and our liberty. We have been working in what are our ideas, our ideals, our aspirations, our hopes—you may say our religion, gentlemen of the jury. . . .

But I say, whether you want it or not, we are now the heralds of a new civilization. We have come here to proclaim a new truth. We are the apostles of a new evangel, of a new gospel, which is now at this very same moment being proclaimed and heralded from one side of the earth to the other.

Comrades of our same faith, while I am speaking in this case, are addressing a different crowd, a different forum, a different audience in other parts of the world, in every known tongue, in every civilized language, in every dialect, in Russia as in Italy, in England as in France, in China as in South Africa—everywhere this message of socialism, this message of brotherhood, this message of love, is being proclaimed in this same manner, gentlemen of the jury, and it is in the name of that that I want to speak and for nothing else. . . .

Gentlemen of the jury, I have finished. After this comes your verdict. I do not ask you to acquit us. It is not in my power to do so after my attorney has so nobly and ably pleaded for me. I say, though, that there are two ways open. If we are responsible, we are responsible in full. If what the District Attorney has said about us is true, then we ought to pay the extreme penalty, for if it is true it was a premeditated crime. If what he said is true, it means that we went to Lawrence specifically for that purpose and that for years and years we had been studying and maturing our thoughts along that line; then we expect from you a verdict of guilty.

But we do not expect you to soothe your conscience and at the same time to give a helping hand to the other side—simply to go and reason and say, "Well, something has happened there and somebody is responsible; let us balance the scales and do half and half." No, gentlemen. We are young. I am twenty-nine years old—not quite, yet; I will be so two months from now. I have a woman that loves me and that I love. I have a mother and father that are waiting for me. I have an ideal that is dearer to me than can be expressed or understood. And life has so many allurements and it is so nice and so bright and so wonderful that I feel the passion of living in my heart and I do want to live.

I don't want to pose to you as a hero. I don't want to pose as a martyr. No, life is dearer to me than it is probably to a good many others. But I say this, that there is something dearer and nobler and holier and grander, something I could never come to terms with, and that is my conscience and that is my loyalty to my class and to my comrades who have come here in this room, and to the working class of the world, who have contributed with a splendid hand penny by penny to my defense and who have all over the world seen that no injustice and no wrong was done to me.

Therefore, I say, weigh both sides and then judge. And if it be, gentlemen of the jury, that your judgment shall be such that this gate will be opened and we shall pass out of it and go back into the sunlit world, then let me assure you what you are doing. Let me tell you that the first strike that breaks again in this Commonwealth or any other place in America where the work and the help and the intelligence of Joseph J. Ettor and Arturo Giovannitti will be needed and necessary, there we shall go again regardless of any fear and of any threat.

We shall return again to our humble efforts, obscure, humble, unknown, misunderstood—soldiers of this mighty army of the working class of the world, which out of the shadows and the darkness of the past is striving towards the destined goal, which is the emancipation of human kind, which is the establishment of love and brotherhood and justice for every man and every woman in this earth.

On the other hand, if your verdict shall be the contrary,—if it be that we who are so worthless as to deserve neither the infamy nor the glory of the gallows—if it be that these hearts of ours must be stilled on the same death chair and by the same current of fire that has destroyed the life of the wife murderer and the parricide, then I say, gentlemen of the jury, that tomorrow we shall pass into a greater judgment, that tomorrow we shall go from your presence into a presence where history shall give its last word to us.

Whichever way you judge, gentlemen of the jury, I thank you.

• • •

In September 1913, angered by a series of mine explosions and the feudal conditions of the mining camps where they lived, 11,000 miners went on strike. Evicted from their hovels in the mine canyons, they trekked with their wives and children and belongings to the tent colonies set up by the United Mine Workers. They were challenging the power of the mine operators, especially the Colorado Fuel and Iron Corporation, owned by the Rockefeller family. The mine owners hired the Baldwin-Felts Detective Agency to attack the tent colonies with rifles and Gatling guns. When the miners still held out, the governor called out the National Guard. On April 20, 1914, two companies of the National Guard were stationed in the hills above the largest tent colony at Ludlow, which housed a thousand people. They began pouring machine-gun fire into the tents, killing a number of miners, including a young boy. Then they moved down from the hills and set fire to the tents. The next morning, a telephone linesman going through the burned tents found the charred bodies of eleven children and two women who had been trapped in a pit under one of the tents. This became known as the "Ludlow Massacre." The miners reacted furiously with violent attacks on mine property and then the federal government sent troops into the area. The strike was lost. Thirty-three years later, Woody Guthrie told the story in a dark, haunting song.

Woody Guthrie, "Ludlow Massacre" (1946)[7]

It was early springtime when the strike was on,
They drove us miners out of doors,
Out from the houses that the Company owned,
We moved into tents up at old Ludlow.

I was worried bad about my children,
Soldiers guarding the railroad bridge,
Every once in a while a bullet would fly,
Kick up gravel under my feet.

We were so afraid you would kill our children,
We dug us a cave that was seven foot deep,
Carried our young ones and pregnant women
Down inside the cave to sleep.

That very night your soldiers waited,
Until all us miners were asleep,
You snuck around our little tent town,
Soaked our tents with your kerosene.

You struck a match and in the blaze that started,
You pulled the triggers of your Gatling guns,
I made a run for the children but the fire wall stopped me.
Thirteen children died from your guns.

I carried my blanket to a wire fence corner,
Watched the fire till the blaze died down,
I helped some people drag their belongings,
While your bullets killed us all around.

I never will forget the look on the faces
Of the men and women that awful day,
When we stood around to preach their funerals,
And lay the corpses of the dead away.

We told the Colorado Governor to call the President,
Tell him to call off his National Guard,
But the National Guard belonged to the Governor,
So he didn't try so very hard.

Our women from Trinidad they hauled some potatoes,
Up to Walsenburg in a little cart,
They sold their potatoes and brought some guns back,
And they put a gun in every hand.

The state soldiers jumped us in a wire fence corners,
They did not know we had these guns,
And the Red-neck Miners mowed down these troopers,
You should have seen those poor boys run.

We took some cement and walled that cave up,
Where you killed these thirteen children inside,
I said, "God bless the Mine Workers' Union,"
And then I hung my head and cried.

• • •

The Colorado anarchist Julia May Courtney penned this account of the Ludlow massacre for Emma Goldman's magazine *Mother Earth*.

Julia May Courtney, "Remember Ludlow!" (May 1914)[8]

"REMEMBER LUDLOW" the battle cry of the crushed, downtrodden, despised miners stifled at Calumet, in West Virginia, in Cripple Creek, has echoed from coal camp to coal camp in southern Colorado, and has served again to notify the world that Labor will not down.

Peaceful Colorado, slumbering in her eternal sunshine, has been rudely awakened. And her comfortable citizens, tremendously busy with their infinitely important little affairs, have been shocked into a mental state wavering between terror and hysteria. And the terrified and hysterical community, like the individual, has grabbed for safety at the nearest straw. The federal troops are called to the strike zone in the vain hope that their presence would intimidate the striking miners into submission, and the first spasm of the acute attack has subsided. But the end is not yet.

In September the coal miners in the southern Colorado district went out on strike. Immediately the word went forth from No. 26 Broadway, the Rockefeller headquarters in New York City, and the thugs and gunmen of the Felts-Baldwin agency were shipped from the Virginia and Texas fields and sent by hundreds, into the coal camps. With their wives and children the miners were evicted from their huts on the company's ground, and just as the heavy winter of the mountains settled down, the strikers put up their tents and prepared for the long siege. It was then that the puerile, weak-kneed Governor [Elias] Ammons, fawning on the representatives of the coal companies, at the request of the Colorado Fuel and Iron Co., called out the militia to "keep order."

And the climax came when the first spring winds blew over the hills and the snows melted from the mountain sides. On the 20th of April the cry was heard "Remember Ludlow!"—the battle cry that every workingman in Colorado and in America will not forget. For on that day the men of the tent colony were shot in the back by soft-nosed bullets, and their women and children were offered in burning sacrifice on the field of Ludlow.

The militia had trained the machine guns on the miners' tent colony. At a ball game on Sunday between two teams of strikers the militia interfered, preventing the game; the miners resented, and the militia—with a sneer and a laugh—*fired the machine guns directly into the tents*, knowing at the time that the strikers' wives and children were in them. Charging the camp, they fired the two largest buildings—the strikers' stores—and going from tent to tent, poured oil on the flimsy structures, setting fire to them.

From the blazing tents rushed the women and children, only to be beaten back into the fire by the rain of bullets from the militia. The men rushed to the assistance of their families; and as they did so, they were dropped as the whirring messengers of death sped surely to the mark. Louis Tikas, leader of the Greek colony, fell a victim to the mine guards' fiendishness, being first clubbed, then shot in the back while he was their prisoner. Fifty-two bullets riddled his body.

Into the cellars—the pits of hell under their blazing tents—crept the women and children, less fearful of the smoke and flames than of the nameless horror of the spitting bullets. One man counted the bodies of nine little children, taken from one ashy pit, their tiny fingers burned away as they held to the edge in their struggle to escape. As the smoking ruins disclosed the charred and suffocated bodies of the victims of the holocaust, thugs in State uniform hacked at the lifeless forms, in some instances nearly cutting off heads and limbs to show their contempt for the strikers.

Fifty-five women and children perished in the fire of the Ludlow tent colony. Relief parties carrying the Red Cross flag were driven back by the gunmen, and for twenty-four hours the bodies lay crisping in the ashes, while rescuers vainly tried to cross the firing line. And the Militiamen and gunmen laughed when the miners petitioned "Czar Chase" [General John Chase] and Governor Ammons for the right to erect their homes and live in them. . . .

[F]or the first time in the history of the labor war in America the people are with the strikers—they glory in their success. The trainmen have refused to carry the militia—entire companies of the National Guard have mutinied—nearly every union in the State has offered funds and support of men and arms to the strikers—and the governor has asked for federal troops.

The federal troops are here—the women who forced the governor to ask for them believe they have secured Peace—but it is a dead hope. For Peace can never be built on the foundation of Greed and Oppression. And the federal troops cannot change the system—only the strikers can do that. And though they may lay down their arms for a time—they will "Remember Ludlow!"

• • •

The labor troubadour Joe Hill was executed by the state of Utah on November 19, 1915, accused of murdering two shopkeepers. Five years earlier, while working on the docks in California, Hill met members of the IWW and became an active

Wobbly. Soon his humorous and biting political songs, like "The Preacher and the Slave," were being sung on picket lines across the country. From his jail cell in Utah, Hill wrote to "Big Bill" Haywood in a telegram, "Don't waste time mourning. Organize!"—a line that became a slogan of the U.S. labor movement. On the eve of his execution, Hill penned these words.

Joe Hill, "My Last Will" (November 18, 1915)[9]

My Will is easy To decide,
For there is nothing To divide
My kin don't need To fuss and moan—
"Moss does not cling to rolling stone["]
My body?—Oh!—If I could choose
I would want To ashes it reduce,
And let The merry breezes blow
My dust To where some flowers grow

Perhaps some fading flower Then
Would come to life and bloom again

This is my Last and Final Will.—
Good Luck to All of you

Joe Hill

Protesting the First World War

Helen Keller, "Strike Against War" (January 5, 1916)

John Reed, "Whose War?" (April 1917)

"Why the IWW Is Not Patriotic to the United States" (1918)

Emma Goldman, Address to the Jury in *U.S. v. Emma Goldman and Alexander Berkman* (July 9, 1917)

Two Antiwar Speeches by Eugene Debs (1918)
  "The Canton, Ohio, Speech" (June 16, 1918)
  Statement to the Court (September 18, 1918)

Randolph Bourne, "The State" (1918)

e. e. cummings, "i sing of Olaf glad and big" (1931)

John Dos Passos, "The Body of an American" (1932)

Dalton Trumbo, *Johnny Got His Gun* (1939)

In the war between the Allied Powers (England, France, Russia, and later the United States) and Germany, Italy, Austria-Hungary, and Turkey, between 1914 and 1918, ten million men died on the battlefields of Europe. They died often for a hundred yards of land, for a line of trenches. Many who didn't die ended up without arms or legs, or blinded, or simply driven out of their minds (it was called "shell shock"). One memorable photograph of the war shows soldiers, walking in a single line, each with a hand on the shoulder of the soldier in front of him—all of them blind.

When it was all over, no one could explain what the war had been about. No wonder, then, that there had been widespread opposition in the United States to the country's entrance into that war. No wonder also that the government had passed legislation allowing it to put anti-war protesters in prison.

A huge propaganda effort had been launched by the Wilson administration, backed up by punitive laws, the Espionage Act of 1917, and the Sedition Act of 1918. Using those laws, the government had sent to prison close to a thousand people for speaking out against the war, many of them labor activists and radicals, including the Socialist leader Eugene Debs, who had been sentenced to ten years in prison. The anarchists Emma Goldman and Alexander Berkman would be deported.

After the war, as the wartime atmosphere of hysterical patriotism dissipated, a powerful anti-war literature appeared: by Ernest Hemingway, John Dos Passos, Irwin Shaw, Dalton Trumbo.

• • •

One of the most important—and earliest—voices against the war was Helen Keller. In our schools we learn about Helen Keller, the deaf and blind girl who became a famous writer, but we do not learn that she was a socialist and an agitator. Here is the text of a speech Keller delivered before U.S. entry into the war in 1917.

Helen Keller, "Strike Against War" (January 5, 1916)[1]

To begin with, I have a word to say to my good friends, the editors, and others who are moved to pity me. Some people are grieved because they imagine I am in the hands of unscrupulous persons who lead me astray and persuade me to espouse unpopular causes and make me the mouthpiece of their propaganda. Now, let it be understood once and for all that I do not want their pity; I would not change places with one of them. I know what I am talking about. My sources of information are as good and reliable as anybody else's. I have papers and magazines from England, France, Germany and Austria that I can read myself. Not all the editors I have met can do that. Quite a number of them have to take their French and German second hand. No, I will not disparage the editors. They are an over-worked, misunderstood class. Let them remember, though, that if I cannot see the fire at the end of their cigarettes, neither can they thread a needle in the dark. All I ask, gentlemen, is a fair field and no favor. I have entered the fight against [war] preparedness and against the economic system under which we live. It is to be a fight to the finish, and I ask no quarter.

The future of the world rests in the hands of America. The future of America rests on the backs of 80,000,000 working men and women and their children. We are facing a grave crisis in our national life. The few who profit from the labor of the masses want to organize the workers into an army which will protect the interests of the capitalists. You are urged to add to the heavy burdens you already bear the burden of a larger army and many additional warships. It is in your power to refuse to carry the artillery and the dread-noughts and to shake off some of the burdens, too, such as limousines, steam yachts and country estates. You do not need to make a great noise about it. With the silence and dignity of creators you can end wars and the system of selfishness and exploitation that causes wars. All you need to do to bring about this stupendous revolution is to straighten up and fold your arms.

We are not preparing to defend our country. Even if we were as helpless as Congressman [Augustus] Gardner says we are, we have no enemies foolhardy enough to attempt to invade the United States. The talk about attack from Germany and Japan is absurd. Germany has its hands full and will be busy with its own affairs for some generations after the European war is over.

With full control of the Atlantic Ocean and the Mediterranean Sea, the allies failed to land enough men to defeat the Turks at Gallipoli; and then they failed again to land an army at Salonica in time to check the Bulgarian invasion of Serbia. The conquest of America by water is a nightmare confined exclusively to ignorant persons and members of the Navy League.

Yet, everywhere, we hear fear advanced as argument for armament. It reminds me of a fable I read. A certain man found a horseshoe. His neighbor began to weep and wail because, as he justly pointed out, the man who found the horseshoe might someday find a horse. Having found the shoe, he might shoe him. The neighbor's child might some day go so near the horse's heels as to be kicked, and die. Undoubtedly the two families would quarrel and fight, and several valuable lives would be lost through the finding of the horseshoe. You know the last war we had we quite accidentally picked up some islands in the Pacific Ocean which may some day be the cause of a quarrel between ourselves and Japan. I'd rather drop those islands right now and forget about them than go to war to keep them. Wouldn't you?

Congress is not preparing to defend the people of the United States. It is planning to protect the capital of American speculators and investors in Mexico, South America, China, and the Philippine Islands. Incidentally this preparation will benefit the manufacturers of munitions and war machines.

Until recently there were uses in the United States for the money taken from the workers. But American labor is exploited almost to the limit now, and our national resources have all been appropriated. Still the profits keep piling up new capital. Our flourishing industry in implements of murder is filling the vaults of New York's banks with gold. And a dollar that is not being used to make a slave of some human being is not fulfilling its purpose in the capitalistic scheme. That dollar must be invested in South America, Mexico, China, or the Philippines.

It was no accident that the Navy League came into prominence at the same time that the National City Bank of New York established a branch in Buenos Aires. It is not a mere coincidence that six business associates of J. P. Morgan are officials of defense leagues. And chance did not dictate that Mayor [John] Mitchel should appoint to his Committee of Safety a thousand men that represent a fifth of the wealth of the United States. These men want their foreign investments protected.

Every modern war has had its root in exploitation. The Civil War was fought to decide whether the slaveholders of the South or the capitalists of the North should exploit the West. The Spanish-American War decided that the United States should exploit Cuba and the Philippines. The South African War decided that the British should exploit the diamond mines. The Russo-Japanese War decided that Japan should exploit Korea. The present war is to decide who shall exploit the Balkans, Turkey, Persia, Egypt, India, China, Africa. And we are whetting our sword to scare the victors into sharing the spoils with us. Now, the workers are not interested in the spoils; they will not get any of them anyway.

The preparedness propagandists have still another object, and a very important one. They want to give the people something to think about besides their own unhappy condition. They know the cost of living is high, wages are low, employment is uncertain and will be much more so when the European call for munitions stops. No matter how hard and incessantly the people work, they often cannot afford the comforts of life; many cannot obtain the necessities.

Every few days we are given a new war scare to lend realism to their propaganda. They have had us on the verge of war over the Lusitania, the Gulflight, the Ancona, and now they want the workingmen to become excited over the sinking of the Persia. The workingman has no interest in any of these ships. The Germans might sink every vessel on the Atlantic Ocean and the Mediterranean Sea, and kill Americans with every one—the American workingman would still have no reason to go to war.

All the machinery of the system has been set in motion. Above the complaint and din of the protest from the workers is heard the voice of authority.

"Friends," it says, "fellow workmen, patriots; your country is in danger! There are foes on all sides of us. There is nothing between us and our enemies except the Pacific Ocean and the Atlantic Ocean. Look at what has happened to Belgium. Consider the fate of Serbia. Will you murmur about low wages when your country, your very liberties, are in jeopardy? What are the miseries you endure compared to the humiliation of having a victorious German army sail up the East River? Quit your whining, get busy and prepare to defend your firesides and your flag. Get an army, get a navy; be ready to meet the invaders like the loyal-hearted freemen you are."

Will the workers walk into this trap? Will they be fooled again? I am afraid so. The people have always been amenable to oratory of this sort. The workers know they have no enemies except their masters. They know that their citizenship papers are no warrant for the safety of themselves or their wives and children. They know that honest sweat, persistent toil and years of struggle bring them nothing worth holding on to, worth fighting for. Yet, deep down in their foolish hearts they believe they have a country. Oh blind vanity of slaves!

The clever ones, up in the high places know how childish and silly the workers are. They know that if the government dresses them up in khaki and gives them a rifle and starts them off with a brass band and waving banners, they will go forth to fight valiantly for their own enemies. They are taught that brave men die for their country's honor. What a price to pay for an abstraction—the lives of millions of young men; other millions crippled and blinded for life; existence made hideous for still more millions of human beings; the achievement and inheritance of generations swept away in a moment—and nobody better off for all the misery! This terrible sacrifice would be comprehensible if the thing you die for and call country fed, clothed, housed and warmed you, educated and cherished your children. I think the workers are the most unselfish of the children of men; they toil and live and die for other people's country, other people's sentiments, other people's liberties and other people's happiness! The workers have no liberties of their own; they are not free when they are compelled to work twelve or ten or eight hours a day. They are not free when they are ill paid for their exhausting toil. They are not free when their children must labor in mines, mills and factories or starve, and when their women may be driven by poverty to lives of shame. They are not free when they are clubbed and imprisoned because they go on strike for a raise of wages and for the elemental justice that is their right as human beings.

We are not free unless the men who frame and execute the laws represent the interests of the lives of the people and no other interest. The ballot does not make a free man out of a wage slave. There has never existed a truly free and democratic nation in the world. From time immemorial men have followed with blind loyalty the strong men who had the power of money and of armies. Even while battlefields were piled high with their own dead they have tilled the lands of the rulers and have been robbed of the fruits of their labor. They have built palaces and pyramids, temples and cathedrals that held no real shrine of liberty.

As civilization has grown more complex the workers have become more and more enslaved, until today they are little more than parts of the machines they operate. Daily they face the dangers of railroad, bridge, skyscraper, freight train, stokehold, stockyard, lumber raft and mine. Panting and training at the docks, on the railroads and underground and on the seas, they move the traffic and pass from land to land the precious commodities that make it possible for us to live. And what is their reward? A scanty wage, often poverty, rents, taxes, tributes and war indemnities.

The kind of preparedness the workers want is reorganization and reconstruction of their whole life, such as has never been attempted by statesmen or governments. The Germans found out years ago that they could not raise good soldiers in the slums so they abolished the slums. They saw to it that all the people had at least a few of the essentials of civilization—decent lodging, clean streets, wholesome if scanty food, proper medical care and proper safeguards for the workers in their occupations. That is only a small part of what should be done, but what wonders that one step toward the right sort of preparedness has wrought for Germany! For eighteen months it has kept itself free from invasion while carrying on an extended war of conquest, and its armies are still pressing on with unabated vigor. It is your business to force these reforms on the Administration. Let there be no more talk about what a government can or cannot do. All these things have been done by all the belligerent nations in the hurly-burly of war. Every fundamental industry has been managed better by the governments than by private corporations.

It is your duty to insist upon still more radical measure. It is your business to see that no child is employed in an industrial establishment or mine or store, and that no worker in needlessly exposed to accident or disease. It is your business to make them give you clean cities, free from smoke, dirt and congestion. It is your business to make them pay you a living wage. It is your business to see that this kind of preparedness is carried into every department in the nation, until everyone has a chance to be well born, well nourished, rightly educated, intelligent and serviceable to the country at all times.

Strike against all ordinances and laws and institutions that continue the slaughter of peace and the butcheries of war. Strike against war, for without you no battles can be fought. Strike against manufacturing shrapnel and gas bombs and all other tools of murder. Strike against preparedness that means death and misery to millions of human beings. Be not dumb, obedient slaves in an army of destruction. Be heroes in an army of construction.

• • •

The radical journalist John Reed of Portland, Oregon, is best remembered for his detailed reportage of the Russian revolution in October 1917, *Ten Days That Shook the World*. But before then, in spring 1917, he wrote a series of articles describing World War I as an imperialist venture: "War means an ugly mob-madness, crucifying the truth-tellers, choking the artists, side-tracking reforms, revolutions, and the working of social forces."

John Reed, "Whose War?" (April 1917)[2]

By the time this goes to press the United States may be at war. The day the German note arrived, Wall Street flung the American flag to the breeze, the brokers on the floor of the Stock Exchange sang "The Star Spangled Banner" with tears rolling down their cheeks, and the stock market went up. In the theaters they are singing "patriotic" ballads of the George M. Cohan–Irving Berlin variety, playing the national anthem, and flashing the flag and the portrait of long-suffering Lincoln—while the tired suburbanite who has just been scalped by a ticket-speculator goes into hysterics. Exclusive ladies whose husbands own banks are rolling bandages for the wounded, just like they do in Europe; a million-dollar fund for ice in field-hospitals has been started; and the Boston Budget for Conveying Virgins Inland has grown enormously. The directors of the British, French and Belgian Permanent Blind Relief Fund have added "American" to the name of the organization, in gruesome anticipation. Our soldier boys, guarding the aqueducts and bridges, are shooting each other by mistake for Teutonic spies. There is talk of "conscription," "war-brides," and "On to Berlin." . . .

I know what war means. I have been with the armies of all the belligerents except one, and I have seen men die, and go mad, and lie in hospitals suffering hell; but there is a worse thing than that. War means an ugly mob-madness, crucifying the truth-tellers, choking the artists, side-tracking reforms, revolutions, and the working of social forces. Already in America those citizens who oppose the entrance of their country into the European melee are called "traitors," and those who protest against the curtailing of our meager rights of free speech are spoken of as "dangerous lunatics." We have had a forecast of the censorship—when the naval authorities in charge of the Sayville wireless cut off American news from Germany, and only the wildest fictions reached Berlin via London, creating a perilous situation. . . . The press is howling for war. The church is howling for war. Lawyers, politicians, stock-brokers, social leaders are all howling for war. Roosevelt is again recruiting his thrice-thwarted family regiment.

But whether it comes to actual hostilities or not, some damage has been done. The militarists have proved their point. I know of at least two valuable social movements that have suspended functioning because no one cares. For many years this country is going to be a worse place for free men to live in; less tolerant, less hospitable. Maybe it is too late, but I want to put down what I think about it all.

Whose war is this? Not mine. I know that hundreds of thousands of American workingmen employed by our great financial "patriots" are not paid a living wage. I have seen poor men sent to jail for long terms without trial, and even without any charge. Peaceful strikers, and their wives and children, have been shot to death, burned to death, by private detectives and militiamen. The rich have steadily become richer, and the cost of living higher, and the workers proportionally poorer· These toilers don't want war—not even civil war. But the speculators, the employers, the plutocracy—they want it, just as they did in Germany and in

England; and with lies and sophistries they will whip up our blood until we are savage—and then we'll fight and die for them.

I am one of a vast number of ordinary people who read the daily papers, and occasionally *The New Republic*, and want to be fair. We don't know much about international politics; but we want our country to keep off the necks of little nations, to refuse to back up American beasts of prey who invest abroad and get their fingers burned, and to stay out of quarrels not our own. We've got an idea that international law is the crystallized common-sense of nations, distilled from their experiences with each other, and that it holds good for all of them, and can be understood by anybody.

We are simple folk. Prussian militarism seemed to us insufferable; we thought the invasion of Belgium a crime; German atrocities horrified us, and also the idea of German submarines exploding ships full of peaceful people without warning. But then we began to hear about England and France jailing, fining, exiling and even shooting men who refused to go out and kill; the Allied armies invaded and seized a part of neutral Greece, and a French admiral forced upon her an ultimatum as shameful as Austria's to Serbia; Russian atrocities were shown to be more dreadful than German; and hidden mines sown by England in the open sea exploded ships full of peaceful people without warning.

Other things disturbed us. For instance, why was it a violation of international law for the Germans to establish a "war-zone" around the British Isles, and perfectly legal for England to close the North Sea? Why is it we submitted to the British order forbidding the shipment of non-contraband to Germany, and insisted upon our right to ship contraband to the Allies? If our "national honor" was smirched by Germany's refusal to allow war materials to be shipped to the Allies, what happened to our national honor when England refused to let us ship non-contraband food and even *Red Cross hospital supplies* to Germany? Why is England allowed to attempt the avowed starvation of German civilians, in violation of international law, when the Germans cannot attempt the same thing without our horrified protest? How is it that the British can arbitrarily regulate our commerce with neutral nations, while we raise a howl whenever the Germans "threaten to restrict our merchant ships going about their business?" Why does our Government insist that Americans should not be molested while traveling on Allied ships armed against submarines?

We have shipped and are shipping vast quantities of war materials to the Allies, we have floated the Allied loans. We have been strictly neutral toward the Teutonic powers only. Hence the inevitable desperation of the last German note. Hence this war we are on the brink of.

Those of us who voted for Woodrow Wilson did so because we felt his mind and his eyes were open, because he had kept us out of the mad-dogfight of Europe, and because the plutocracy opposed him. We had learned enough about the war to lose some of our illusions, and we wanted to be neutral. We grant that the President, considering the position he'd got himself into, couldn't do anything else but answer the German note as he did—but if we had been neutral, that note wouldn't have been sent. The President didn't ask us; he won't ask us if we want war or not. The fault is not ours. It is not our war.

• • •

From its founding in 1905, the IWW had organized workers around the country—in the mines and lumber camps, the textile mills, and ironworks—uniting them by their workplace, including the skilled, unskilled, black, white, native-born, and foreign-born, into "One Big Union." It was militant, fearless, and determinedly class-conscious, and although it had only 100,000 members at its peak, its influence went far beyond that. Its opposition to World War I gave the government an opportunity to put its leaders in prison. Here is one of its members addressing the court, pointing to the class character of the war the IWW was opposing.

"Why the IWW Is Not Patriotic to the United States" (1918)[3]

You ask me why the IWW is not patriotic to the United States. If you were a bum without a blanket; if you had left your wife and kids when you went west for a job, and had never located them since; if your job had never kept you long enough in a place to qualify you to vote; if you slept in a lousy, sour bunkhouse, and ate food just as rotten as they could give you and get by with it; if deputy sheriffs shot your cooking cans full of holes and spilled your grub on the ground; if your wages were lowered on you when the bosses thought they had you down; if there was one law for [Herman] Ford, [Blackie] Suhr and [Tom] Mooney, and another for Harry Thaw; if every person who represented law and order and the nation beat you up, railroaded you to jail, and the good Christian people cheered and told them to go to it, how in hell do you expect a man to be patriotic? This war is a business man's war and we don't see why we should go out and get shot in order to save the lovely state of affairs which we now enjoy.

• • •

In 1917, after declaring war, President Woodrow Wilson imposed a draft to build up U.S. fighting forces. To openly advocate draft resistance was to risk immediate arrest and, for some, deportation. After the 1917 draft began, Emma Goldman and Alexander Berkman helped found the No-Conscription League. They were both tried and convicted for conspiracy to obstruct the draft, a crime under the Espionage Act, and were sentenced to two years in prison. Goldman was sent to a state penitentiary in Missouri, and Berkman served in a federal penitentiary in Atlanta. After their release in December 1919, using the expanded powers of the Alien Act of 1918, which allowed deportation of "alien" anarchists, the U.S. government deported Goldman (whose husband had been denaturalized as a U.S. citizen in 1908) and Berkman (a Russian émigré), along with 247 other noncitizens. The deportations presaged the anti-immigrant and anti-radical Palmer Raids and "Red Scare" that soon followed. Here are excerpts of Goldman's words to the jury at their July 1917 anti-conscription trial, held in New York City.

Emma Goldman, Address to the Jury in *U.S. v. Emma Goldman and Alexander Berkman* (July 9, 1917)[4]

I wish to say emphatically that no such expression as "We believe in violence and we will use violence" was uttered at the meeting of May 18th, or at any other meeting. I could not have employed such a phrase, as there was no occasion for it. If for no other reason, it is because I want my lectures and speeches to be coherent and logical. The sentence credited to me is neither.

I have read to you my position toward political violence from a lengthy essay called "The Psychology of Political Violence."

But to make that position clearer and simpler, I wish to say that I am a social student. It is my mission in life to ascertain the cause of our social evils and of our social difficulties. As a student of social wrongs it is my aim to diagnose a wrong. To simply condemn the man who has committed an act of political violence, in order to save my skin, would be as unpardonable as it would be on the part of the physician, who is called to diagnose a case, to condemn the patient because the patient has tuberculosis, cancer, or some other disease. The honest, earnest, sincere physician does not only prescribe medicine, he tries to find out the cause of the disease. And if the patient is at all capable as to means, the doctor will say to him, "Get out of this putrid air, get out of the factory, get out of the place where your lungs are being infected." He will not merely give him medicine. He will tell him the cause of the disease. And that is precisely my position in regard to acts of violence. That is what I have said on every platform. I have attempted to explain the cause and the reason for acts of political violence.

It is organized violence on top which creates individual violence at the bottom. It is the accumulated indignation against organized wrong, organized crime, organized injustice which drives the political offender to his act. To condemn him means to be blind to the causes which make him. I can no more do it, nor have I the right to, than the physician who were to condemn the patient for his disease. You and I and all of us who remain indifferent to the crimes of poverty, of war, of human degradation, are equally responsible for the act committed by the political offender. May I therefore be permitted to say, in the words of a great teacher: "He who is without sin among you, let him cast the first stone." Does that mean advocating violence? You might as well accuse Jesus of advocating prostitution, because He took the part of the prostitute, Mary Magdalene.

Gentlemen of the jury, the meeting of the 18th of May was called primarily for the purpose of voicing the position of the conscientious objector and to point out the evils of conscription. Now, who and what is the conscientious objector? Is he really a shirker, a slacker, or a coward? To call him that is to be guilty of dense ignorance of the forces which impel men and women to stand out against the whole world like a glittering lone star upon a dark horizon. The conscientious objector is impelled by what President Wilson in his speech of February 3, 1917, called "the righteous passion for justice upon which all war, all structure of family, State and of mankind must rest as the ultimate base of our existence and our liberty." The righteous passion for justice which can never express itself in human slaughter—that is the force which makes the conscientious objector. Poor indeed is the country which fails to recognize the importance of that new type of humanity as the "ultimate base of our existence and liberty." It will find itself barren of that which makes for character and quality in its people. . . .

Gentlemen of the jury, we have been in public life for twenty-seven years. We have been hauled into court, in and out of season—we have never denied our position. Even the police know that Emma Goldman and Alexander Berkman are not shirkers. You have had occasion during this trial to convince yourselves that we do not deny. We have gladly and proudly claimed responsibility, not only for what we ourselves have said and written, but even for things written by others and with which we did not agree. Is it plausible, then, that we would go through the ordeal, trouble and expense of a lengthy trial to escape responsibility in this instance? A thousand times no! But we refuse to be tried on a trumped-up charge, or to be convicted by perjured testimony, merely because we are Anarchists and hated by the class whom we have openly fought for many years. . . .

Whatever your verdict, gentlemen, it cannot possibly affect the rising tide of discontent in this country against war which, despite all boasts, is a war for conquest and military power. Neither can it affect the ever increasing opposition to conscription which is a military and industrial yoke placed upon the necks of the American people. Least of all will your verdict affect those to whom human life is sacred, and who will not become a party to the world slaughter.

Your verdict can only add to the opinion of the world as to whether or not justice and liberty are a living force in this country or a mere shadow of the past.

Your verdict may, of course, affect us temporarily, in a physical sense—it can have no effect whatever upon our spirit. For even if we were convicted and found guilty and the penalty were that we be placed against a wall and shot dead, I should nevertheless cry out with the great Luther: "Here I am and here I stand and I cannot do otherwise."

And gentlemen, in conclusion let me tell you that my co-defendant, Mr. Berkman, was right when he said the eyes of America are upon you. They are upon you not because of sympathy for us or agreement with Anarchism. They are upon you because it must be decided sooner or later whether we are justified in telling people that we will give them democracy in Europe, when we have no democracy here? Shall free speech and free assemblage, shall criticism and opinion—which even the espionage bill did not include—be destroyed? Shall it be a shadow of the past, the great historic American past? Shall it be trampled underfoot by any detective, or policeman, anyone who decides upon it? Or shall free speech and free press and free assemblage continue to be the heritage of the American people?

Gentlemen of the jury, whatever your verdict will be, as far as we are concerned, nothing will be changed. I have held ideas all my life. I have publicly held my ideas for twenty-seven years. Nothing on earth would ever make me change my ideas except one thing; and that is, if you will prove to me that our position is wrong, untenable, or lacking in historic fact. But never would I change my ideas because I am found guilty. I may remind you of two great Americans, undoubtedly not unknown to you, gentlemen of the jury; Ralph Waldo Emerson and Henry David Thoreau. When Thoreau was placed in prison for refusing to pay taxes, he was visited by Ralph Waldo Emerson and Emerson said: "David, what are you doing in jail?" and Thoreau replied: "Ralph, what are you doing outside, when honest people are in jail for their ideals?"

• • •

One of the most eloquent and uncompromising voices against war was that of Eugene Debs, the railroad union organizer and leader of the Socialist Party. On June 18, 1918, he addressed a mass rally of workers in Ohio, knowing very well that his words could lead, as they did, to his arrest and imprisonment. Speaking to the jury before it began its deliberations, he said: "I have been accused of obstructing the war. I admit it. Gentlemen, I abhor war. I would oppose the war if I stood alone." He was found guilty by the jury of violating the Espionage Act, which made it a crime to "obstruct the recruitment or enlistment service." His sentence of ten years was upheld by a unanimous Supreme Court. Here is the speech that led to his arrest, and then his statement to the court before sentencing.

Two Antiwar Speeches by Eugene Debs (1918)

"THE CANTON, OHIO, SPEECH" (JUNE 16, 1918)[5]

Sam Johnson declared that "patriotism is the last refuge of the scoundrel." He must have had . . . [the] Wall Street gentry in mind, or at least their prototypes, for in every age it has been the tyrant, the oppressor and the exploiter who has wrapped himself in the cloak of patriotism, or religion, or both to deceive and over-awe the people.

They would have you believe that the Socialist Party consists in the main of dis-loyalists and traitors. It is true in a sense not at all to their discredit. We frankly admit that we are disloyalists and traitors to the real traitors of this nation; to the gang that on the Pacific coast are trying to hang Tom Mooney and Warren Billings in spite of their well-known innocence and the protest of practically the whole civilized world. . . .

Every solitary one of these aristocratic conspirators and would-be murderers claims to be an arch-patriot; every one of them insists that the war is being waged to make the world safe for democracy. What humbug! What rot! What false pre-tense! These autocrats, these tyrants, these red-handed robbers and murderers, the "patriots," while the men who have the courage to stand face to face with them, speak the truth, and fight for their exploited victims—they are the disloy-alists and traitors. If this be true, I want to take my place side by side with the trai-tors in this fight. . . .

Max Eastman has been indicted and his paper [*The Masses*] suppressed, just as the papers with which I have been connected have all been suppressed. What a won-derful compliment they pay us! They are afraid that we may mislead and con-taminate you. You are their wards; they are your guardians and they know what is best for you to read and hear and know. They are bound to see to it that our vicious doctrines do not reach your ears. And so in our great democracy, under our free institutions, they flatter our press by suppression; and they ignorantly imag-ine that they have silenced revolutionary propaganda in the United States. What an awful mistake they make for our benefit! As a matter of justice to them we should respond with resolutions of thanks and gratitude. Thousands of people who had never before heard of our papers are now inquiring for and insisting upon seeing them. They have succeeded only in arousing curiosity in our litera-ture and propaganda. And woe to him who reads Socialist literature from curiosity! He is surely a goner. I have known of a thousand experiments but never one that failed. . . .

How stupid and shortsighted the ruling class really is! Cupidity is stone blind. It has no vision. The greedy, profit-seeking exploiter cannot see beyond the end of his nose. He can see a chance for an "opening"; he is cunning enough to know what graft is and where it is, and how it can be secured, but vision he has none—not the slightest. He knows nothing of the great throbbing world that spreads out in all directions. He has no capacity for literature; no appreciation of art; no soul for beauty. That is the penalty the parasites pay for the violation of the laws of life. The Rockefellers are blind. Every move they make in their game of greed but hastens their own doom. Every blow they strike at the Socialist movement reacts upon themselves. Every time they strike at us they hit themselves. It never fails. Every time they strangle a Socialist paper they add a thousand voices proclaiming the truth of the principles of socialism and the ideals of the Socialist movement. They help us in spite of themselves. . . .

Wars throughout history have been waged for conquest and plunder. In the Middle Ages when the feudal lords who inhabited the castles whose towers may still be seen along the Rhine concluded to enlarge their domains, to increase their power, their prestige and their wealth they declared war upon one another. But they themselves did not go to war any more than the modern feudal lords, the barons of Wall Street go to war. The feudal barons of the Middle Ages, the economic predecessors of the capitalists of our day, declared all wars. And their miserable serfs fought all the battles. The poor, ignorant serfs had been taught to revere their masters; to believe that when their masters declared war upon one another, it was their patriotic duty to fall upon one another and to cut one another's throats for the profit and glory of the lords and barons who held them in contempt. And that is war in a nutshell. The master class has always declared the wars; the subject class has always fought the battles. The master class has had all to gain and nothing to lose, while the subject class has had nothing to gain and all to lose—especially their lives.

They have always taught and trained you to believe it to be your patriotic duty to go to war and to have yourselves slaughtered at their command. But in all the history of the world you, the people, have never had a voice in declaring war, and strange as it certainly appears, no war by any nation in any age has ever been declared by the people.

And here let me emphasize the fact—and it cannot be repeated too often—that the working class who fight all the battles, the working class who make the supreme sacrifices, the working class who freely shed their blood and furnish the corpses, have never yet had a voice in either declaring war or making peace. It is the ruling class that invariably does both. They alone declare war and they alone make peace.

Yours not to reason why;
Yours but to do and die.

That is their motto and we object on the part of the awakening workers of this nation.

If war is right let it be declared by the people. You who have your lives to lose, you certainly above all others have the right to decide the momentous issue of war or peace.

STATEMENT TO THE COURT (SEPTEMBER 18, 1918)[6]

Your Honor, years ago I recognized my kinship with all living beings, and I made up my mind that I was not one bit better than the meanest on earth. I said then, and I say now, that while there is a lower class, I am in it, and while there is a criminal element I am of it, and while there is a soul in prison, I am not free. . . .

I believe, Your Honor, in common with all Socialists, that this nation ought to own and control its own industries. I believe, as all Socialists do, that all things that are jointly needed and used ought to be jointly owned—that industry, the basis of our social life, instead of being the private property of a few and operated for their enrichment, ought to be the common property of all, democratically administered in the interest of all. . . .

I am opposing a social order in which it is possible for one man who does absolutely nothing that is useful to amass a fortune of hundreds of millions of dollars, while millions of men and women who work all the days of their lives secure barely enough for a wretched existence.

This order of things cannot always endure. I have registered my protest against it. I recognize the feebleness of my effort, but, fortunately, I am not alone. There are multiplied thousands of others who, like myself, have come to realize that before we may truly enjoy the blessings of civilized life, we must reorganize society upon a mutual and cooperative basis; and to this end we have organized a great economic and political movement that spreads over the face of all the earth.

There are today upwards of sixty millions of Socialists, loyal, devoted adherents to this cause, regardless of nationality, race, creed, color, or sex. They are all making common cause. They are spreading with tireless energy the propaganda of the new social order. They are waiting, watching, and working hopefully through all the hours of the day and the night. They are still in a minority. But they have learned how to be patient and to bide their time. They feel—they know, indeed—that the time is coming, in spite of all opposition, all persecution, when this emancipating gospel will spread among all the peoples, and when this minority will become the triumphant majority and, sweeping into power, inaugurate the greatest social and economic change in history.

In that day we shall have the universal commonwealth—the harmonious cooperation of every nation with every other nation on earth. . . .

Your Honor, I ask no mercy and I plead for no immunity. I realize that finally the right must prevail. I never so clearly comprehended as now the great struggle between the powers of greed and exploitation on the one hand and upon the other the rising hosts of industrial freedom and social justice.

I can see the dawn of the better day for humanity. The people are awakening. In due time they will and must come to their own.

• • •

The writer and social critic Randolph Bourne broke with his friends Charles Beard and John Dewey over their support for World War I. Here is a section of an unpublished essay on "The State," discovered at the time of his early death, in 1918. In it Bourne exposes the way in which war expands the repressive power of the state against its people.

Randolph Bourne, "The State" (1918)[7]

The moment war is declared . . . the mass of the people, through some spiritual alchemy, become convinced that they have willed and executed the deed themselves. They then, with the exception of a few malcontents, proceed to allow themselves to be regimented, coerced, deranged in all the environments of their lives, and turned into a solid manufactory of destruction toward whatever other people may have, in the appointed scheme of things, come within the range of the Government's disapprobation. The citizen throws off his contempt and indifference to Government, identifies himself with its purposes, revives all his military memories and symbols, and the State once more walks, an august presence, through the imaginations of men. Patriotism becomes the dominant feeling, and produces immediately that intense and hopeless confusion between the relations which the individual bears and should bear toward the society of which he is a part. . . .

Wartime brings the ideal of the State out into very clear relief, and reveals attitudes and tendencies that were hidden. In times of peace the sense of the State flags in a republic that is not militarized. For war is essentially the health of the State. The ideal of the State is that within its territory its power and influence should be universal. As the Church is the medium for the spiritual salvation of man, so the

State is thought of as the medium for his political salvation. Its idealism is a rich blood flowing to all the members of the body politic. And it is precisely in war that the urgency for union seems greatest, and the necessity for universality seems most unquestioned. The State is the organization of the herd to act offensively or defensively against another herd similarly organized. The more terrifying the occasion for defense, the closer will become the organization and the more coercive the influence upon each member of the herd. War sends the current of purpose and activity flowing down to the lowest level of the herd, and to its most remote branches. All the activities of society are linked together as fast as possible to this central purpose of making a military offensive or a military defense, and the State becomes what in peacetimes it has vainly struggled to become—the inexorable arbiter and determinant of men's business and attitudes and opinions. The slack is taken up, the crosscurrents fade out, and the nation moves lumberingly and slowly, but with ever accelerated speed and integration, toward the great end, toward the "peacefulness of being at war," of which L. P. Jacks has so unforgettably spoken. . . .

War is the health of the State. It automatically sets in motion throughout society those irresistible forces for uniformity, for passionate cooperation with the Government in coercing into obedience the minority groups and individuals which lack the larger herd sense. The machinery of government sets and enforces the drastic penalties; the minorities are either intimidated into silence, or brought slowly around by a subtle process of persuasion which may seem to them really to be converting them. Of course, the ideal of perfect loyalty, perfect uniformity is never really attained. The classes upon whom the amateur work of coercion falls are unwearied in their zeal, but often their agitation instead of converting, merely serves to stiffen their resistance. Minorities are rendered sullen, and some intellectual opinion bitter and satirical. But in general, the nation in wartime attains a uniformity of feeling, a hierarchy of values culminating at the undisputed apex of the State ideal, which could not possibly be produced through any other agency than war. Loyalty—or mystic devotion to the State—becomes the major imagined human value. Other values, such as artistic creation, knowledge, reason, beauty, the enhancement of life, are instantly and almost unanimously sacrificed, and the significant classes who have constituted themselves the amateur agents of the State are engaged not only in sacrificing these values for themselves but in coercing all other persons into sacrificing them.

War—or at least modern war waged by a democratic republic against a powerful enemy—seems to achieve for a nation almost all that the most inflamed political idealist could desire. Citizens are no longer indifferent to their Government, but each cell of the body politic is brimming with life and activity. We are at last on the way to full realization of that collective community in which each individual somehow contains the virtue of the whole. In a nation at war, every citizen identifies himself with the whole, and feels immensely strengthened in that identification. The purpose and desire of the collective community live in each person who throws himself wholeheartedly into the cause of war. The impeding distinction between society and the individual is almost blotted out. At war, the individual becomes almost identical with his society. He achieves a superb self-assurance, an intuition of the rightness of all his ideas and emotions, so that in the suppression of opponents or heretics he is invincibly strong; he feels behind him all the power of the collective community. The individual as social being in war seems to have achieved almost his apotheosis. Not for any religious impulse could the American nation have been expected to show such devotion en masse, such sacrifice and labor. Certainly not for any secular good, such as universal education or the subjugation of nature, would it have poured forth its treasure and its life, or would it have permitted such stern coercive measures to be taken against it, such as conscripting its money and its men. But for the sake of a war of offensive self-defense, undertaken to support a difficult cause to the slogan of "democracy," it would reach the highest level ever known of collective effort. . . .

The members of the working classes, that portion at least which does not identify itself with the significant classes and seek to imitate it and rise to it, are notoriously less affected by the symbolism of the State, or, in other words, are less patriotic than the significant classes. For theirs is neither the power nor the glory. The State in wartime does not offer them the opportunity to regress, for, never having acquired social adulthood, they cannot lose it. If they have been drilled and regimented, as by the industrial regime of the last century, they go out docilely enough to do battle for their State, but they are almost entirely without that filial sense and even without that herd-intellect sense which operates so powerfully among their "betters." They live habitually in an industrial serfdom, by which, though nominally free, they are in practice as a class bound to a system of machine-production the implements of which they do not own, and in the distribution of whose product they have not the slightest voice, except what they can occasionally exert by a veiled intimidation which draws slightly more of the product in their direction. From such serfdom, military conscription is not so great a change. But into the military enterprise they go, not with those hurrahs of the significant classes whose instincts war so powerfully feeds, but with the same apathy with which they enter and continue in the industrial enterprise. . . .

Thus arises conflict within the State. War becomes almost a sport between the hunters and the hunted. The pursuit of enemies within outweighs in psychic attractiveness the assault on the enemy without. The whole terrific force of the State is brought to bear against the heretics. The nation boils with a slow insistent fever. A white terrorism is carried on by the Government against pacifists, socialists, enemy aliens, and a milder unofficial persecution against all persons or movements that can be imagined as connected with the enemy. War, which should be the health of the State, unifies all the bourgeois elements and the common people, and outlaws the rest. The revolutionary proletariat shows more resistance to this unification, is, as we have seen, psychically out of the current. Its vanguard, as the IWW, is remorselessly pursued, in spite of the proof that it is a symptom, not a cause, and its persecution increases the disaffection of labor and intensifies the friction instead of lessening it. . . .

It cannot be too firmly realized that war is a function of States and not of nations, indeed that it is the chief function of States. War is a very artificial thing. It is not the naïve spontaneous outburst of herd pugnacity; it is no more primary than is formal religion. War cannot exist without a military establishment, and a military establishment cannot exist without a State organization. War has an immemorial tradition and heredity only because the State has a long tradition and heredity. But they are inseparably and functionally joined. We cannot crusade against war without crusading implicitly against the State. And we cannot expect, or take measures to ensure, that this war is a war to end war, unless at the same time we take measures to end the State in its traditional form. The State is not the nation, and the State can be modified and even abolished in its present form, without harming the nation. On the contrary, with the passing of the dominance of the State, the genuine life-enhancing forces of the nation will be liberated. If the State's chief function is war, then the State must suck out of the nation a large part of its energy for its purely sterile purposes of defense and aggression. It devotes to waste or to actual destruction as much as it can of the vitality of the nation. No one will deny that war is a vast complex of life-destroying and life-crippling forces. If the State's chief function is war, then it is chiefly concerned with coordinating and developing the powers and techniques which make for destruction. And this means not only the actual and potential destruction of the enemy, but of the nation at home as well. For the very existence of a State in a system of States means that the nation lies always under a risk of war and invasion, and the calling away of energy into military pursuits means a crippling of the productive and life-enhancing processes of the national life. . . .

All of which goes to show that the State represents all the autocratic, arbitrary, coercive, belligerent forces within a social group, it is a sort of complexus of everything most distasteful to the modern free creative spirit, the feeling for life, liberty, and the pursuit of happiness. War is the health of the State. Only when the State is at war does the modern society function with that unity of sentiment, simple uncritical patriotic devotion, cooperation of services, which have always been the ideal of the State lover. With the ravages of democratic ideas, however, the modern republic cannot go to war under the old conceptions of autocracy and death-dealing belligerency. If a successful animus for war requires a renaissance of State ideals, they can only come back under democratic forms, under this retrospective conviction of democratic control of foreign policy, democratic desire for war, and particularly of this identification of the democracy with the State. How unregenerate the ancient State may be, however, is indicated by the laws against sedition, and by the Government's unreformed attitude on foreign policy. One of the first demands of the more farseeing democrats in the democracies of the Alliance was that secret diplomacy must go. The war was seen to have been made possible by a web of secret agreements between States, alliances that were made by Governments without the shadow of popular support or even popular knowledge, and vague, half-understood commitments that scarcely reached the stage of a treaty or agreement, but which proved binding in the event. Certainly, said these democratic thinkers, war can scarcely be avoided unless this poisonous underground system of secret diplomacy is destroyed, this system by which a nation's power, wealth, and manhood may be signed away like a blank check to an allied nation to be cashed in at some future crisis. Agreements which are to affect the lives of whole peoples must be made between peoples and not by Governments, or at least by their representatives in the full glare of publicity and criticism.

• • •

On November 11, 1918, World War I ended. Ten million people were dead, including more than one hundred thousand Americans. Disillusionment quickly set in, and was reflected in a burst of anti-war literature, as in the poems of Wilfred Owen and Siegfried Sassoon, Erich Maria Remarque's *All Quiet on the Western Front*, Ernest Hemingway's *A Farewell to Arms*, and Ford Maddox Ford's *No More Parades*. The rebellious and anti-authoritarian poet e. e. cummings, who served in an ambulance group in France in World War I, here writes of a conscientious objector to the war.

e. e. cummings, "i sing of Olaf glad and big" (1931)[8]

i sing of Olaf glad and big
whose warmest heart recoiled at war:
a conscientious object-or

his wellbeloved colonel(trig
westpointer most succinctly bred)
took erring Olaf soon in hand;
but—though an honest of overjoyed

noncoms(first knocking on the head
him)do through icy waters roll
that helplessness which others stroke
with brushes recently employed,
anent this muddy toiletbowl,
while kindred intellects evoke
allegiance per blunt instruments—
Olaf(being to all intents
a corpse and wanting any rag
upon what God unto him gave)
responds, without getting annoyed
"I will not kiss your fucking flag."

straightaway the silver bird looked grave
(departing hurriedly to shave)

but—though all kinds of officers
(a yearning nation's blueeyed pride)
their passive prey did kick and curse
until for wear their clarion
voices and boots were much the worse,
and egged the firstclassprivates on
his rectum wickedly to tease
by means of skilfully applied
bayonets roasted hot with heat—
Olaf(upon what were once knees)
does almost ceaselessly repeat
"there is some shit I will not eat"

our president, being of which
assertions duly notified
threw the yellowsonofabitch
into a dungeon,where he died

Christ(of His mercy infinite)
i pray to see;and Olaf,too.

preponderatingly because
unless statistics lie he was
more brave than me:more blond than you.

. . .

John Dos Passos wrote a trilogy, *USA*, which expressed a horror of war. Here is a section from a passage called "The Body of an American," from *Nineteen-Nineteen*, the second volume of *USA*, published in 1932.

John Dos Passos, "The Body of an American" (1932)[9]

John Doe
and Richard Roe and other person or persons unknown
drilled hiked, manual of arms, ate slum, learned to salute, to soldier, to loaf in the latrines, forbidden to smoke on deck, overseas guard duty, forty men and eight horses, shortarm inspection and the ping of shrapnel and the shrill bullets combing the air and the sorehead woodpeckers the machineguns mud cooties gasmasks and the itch.
Say feller tell me how I can get back to my outfit.

John Doe had a head
for twentyodd years intensely the nerves of the eyes the ears the palate the tongue the fingers the toes the armpits, the nerves warmfeeling under the skin charged the coiled brain with hurt sweet warm cold mine must don't sayings print headlines:
Thou shalt not the multiplication table long division, Now is the time for all good men knocks but once at a young man's door, It's a great life if Ish gebibbel, The first five years'll be the Safety First, Suppose a hun tried to rape you're my country right or wrong, Catch 'em young, What he don't know wont treat 'em rough, Tell 'm nothing, He got what was coming to him he got his, This is a white man's country, Kick the bucket, Gone west, If you don't like it you can croaked him
Say buddy cant you tell me how I can get back to my outfit?

Cant help jumpin when them things go off, give me the trots them things do. I lost my identification tag swimmin in the Marne, roughhousin with a guy while we was waitin to be deloused, in bed with a girl name Jeanne (Love moving picture wet French postcard dream began with saltpeter in the coffee and ended at the propho station);—
Say soldier for chrissake cant you tell me how I can get back to my outfit?

John Doe's
heart pumped blood:
alive thudding silence of blood in your ears
    down in the clearing in the Oregon forest where the punkins were punk-incolor pouring into the blood through the eyes and the fallcolored trees and the bronze hoopers were hopping through the dry grass, where tiny striped snails hung on the underside of the blades and the flies hummed, wasps droned, bumble-bees buzzed, and the woods smelt of wine and mushrooms and apples, homey smell of fall pouring into the blood,
    and I dropped the tin hat and the sweaty pack and lay flat with the dogday sun licking my throat and adamsapple and the tight skin over the breastbone.
The shell had his number on it.

The blood ran into the ground.

The service record dropped out of the filing cabinet when the quartermaster sergeant got blotto that time they had to pack up and leave the billets in a hurry.
The identification tag was in the bottom of the Marne.

The blood ran into the ground, the brains oozed out of the cracked skull and were licked up by the trenchrats, the belly swelled and raised a generation of blue-bottle flies.
    and the incorruptible skeleton,
    and the scraps of dried viscera and skin bundled in khaki

they took to Chalons-sur-Marne
and laid it out neat in a pine coffin

and took it home to God's Country on a battleship
    and buried in a sarcophagus in the Memorial Amphitheatre in the Arlington National Cemetery
    and draped the Old Glory over it
    and the bugler played taps
    and Mr. Harding prayed to God and the diplomats and the generals and the admirals and the brasshats and the politicians and the handsomely dressed ladies out of the society column of the Washington Post stood up solemn
    and thought how beautiful sad Old Glory God's Country it was go have the bugler play taps and the three volleys made their ears ring.

Where his chest ought to have been they pinned
the Congressional Medal, the D.S.C., the Medaille Militaire, the Belgian
Croix de Guerre, the Italian gold medal, the Vitutea Militara sent by Queen Marie
of Rumania, the Czechoslovak war cross, the Virtuti Militari of the Poles, a wreath
sent by Hamilton Fish, Jr., of New York, and a little wampum presented by a dep-
utation of Arizona redskins in warpaint and feathers. All the Washingtonians
brought flowers.

Woodrow Wilson brought a bouquet of poppies.

• • •

Two decades after the end of World War I, on the eve of yet another world war, one
of the most damning indictments of the realities of war was written by the screen-
writer Dalton Trumbo. A few years after the release of the book, which became an
international bestseller, Trumbo was blacklisted as one of the Hollywood Ten.
Johnny Got His Gun is written from the point of view of Joe Bonham, a World
War I soldier found on the battlefield with all his limbs severed, blind—a torso and
a brain all that was left of him.

Dalton Trumbo, *Johnny Got His Gun* (1939)[10]

Take me along country roads and stop by every farmhouse and every field and ring
a dinner gong so that the farmers and their wives and their children and their
hired men and women can see me. Say to the farmers here is something I'll bet
you haven't seen before. Here is something you can't plow under. Here is something that will never grow and flower. The manure you plow into your fields is filthy
enough but here is something less than manure because it won't die and decay
and nourish even a weed. Here is something so terrible that if it were born to a
mare or a heifer or a sow or a ewe you would kill it on the spot but you can't kill
this because it is a human being. It has a brain. It is thinking all the time. Believe
it or not this thing thinks and it is alive and it goes against every rule of nature
although nature didn't make it so. You know what made it so. Look at it medals
real medals probably of solid gold. Lift up the top of the case and you'll know
what made it so. It stinks of glory.

Take me into the places where men work and make things. Take me there and
say boys here is a cheap way to get by. Maybe times are bad and your salaries are low.
Don't worry boys because there is always a way to cure things like that. Have a war
and then prices go up and wages go up and everybody makes a hell of a lot of money.

There'll be one along pretty soon boys so don't get impatient. It'll come and then you'll have your chance. Either way you win. If you don't have to fight why you stay at home and make sixteen bucks a day working in the shipyards. And if they draft you why you've got a good chance of coming back without so many needs. Maybe you'll need only one shoe instead of two that's saving money. Maybe you'll be blind and if you are why then you never need worry about the expense of glasses. Maybe you'll be lucky like me. Look at me close boys I don't need anything. A little broth or something three times a day and that's all. No shoes no socks no underwear no shirt no gloves no hat no necktie no collar-buttons no vest no coat no movies no vaudeville no football not even a shave. Look at me boys I have no expenses at all. You're suckers boys. Get on the gravy train. I know what I'm talking about. I used to need all the things that you need right now. I used to be a consumer. I've consumed a lot in my time. I've consumed more shrapnel and gunpowder than any living man. So don't get blue boys because you'll have your chance there'll be another war along pretty soon and then maybe you'll be lucky like me.

Take me into the schoolhouses all the school-houses in the world. Suffer little children to come unto me isn't that right? They may scream at first and have nightmares at night but they'll get used to it because they've got to get used to it and its best to start them young. Gather them around my case and say here little girl here little boy come and take a look at your daddy. Come and look at yourself. You'll be like that when you grow up to be great big strong men and women. You'll have a chance to die for your country. And you may not die you may come back like this. Not everybody dies little kiddies.

Closer please. You over there against the blackboard what's the matter with you? Quit crying you silly little girl come over here and look at the nice man the nice man who was a soldier boy. You remember him don't you? Don't you remember little crybaby how you waved flags and saved tinfoil and put your savings in thrift stamps? Of course you do you silly. Well here's the soldier you did it for.

Come on youngsters take a nice look and then we'll go into our nursery rhymes. New nursery rhymes for new times. Hickory dickory dock my daddy's nuts from shellshock. Humpty dumpty thought he was wise till gas came along and burned out his eyes. A diller a dollar a ten o'clock scholar blow off his legs and then watch him holler. Rockabye baby in the treetop don't stop a bomb or you'll probably flop. Now I lay me down to sleep my bombproof cellar's good and deep but if I'm killed before I wake remember god it's for your sake amen.

Take me into the colleges and universities and academies and convents. Call the girls together all the healthy beautiful young girls. Point down to me and say here girls is your father. Here is that boy who was strong last night. Here is your little son your baby son the fruit of your love the hope of your future. Look down on him girls so you won't forget him. See that red gash there with mucus hanging to it? That was his face girls. Here girls touch it don't be afraid. Bend down and kiss it. You'll have to wipe your lips afterward because they will have a strange rotten stuff on them but that's all right because a lover is a lover and here is your lover.

Call all the young men together and say here is your brother here is your best friend here you are young men. This is a very interesting case young men because we know there is a mind buried down there. Technically this thing is living meat like that tissue we kept alive all last summer in the lab. But this is a different cut of meat because it also contains a brain. Now listen to me closely young gentlemen. That brain is thinking. Maybe it's thinking about music. Maybe it has a great symphony all thought out or a mathematical formula that would change the world or a book that would make people kinder or the germ of an idea that would save a hundred million people from cancer. This is a very interesting problem young gentlemen because if this brain does hold such secrets how in the world are we ever going to find out? In any event there you are young gentlemen breathing and thinking and dead like a frog under chloroform with its stomach laid open so that its heartbeat may be seen so quiet so helpless but yet alive. There is your future and your sweet wild dreams there is the thing your sweethearts loved and there is the thing your leaders urged it to be. Think well young gentlemen. Think sharply young gentlemen and then we will go back to our studies of the barbarians who sacked Rome.

Take me wherever there are parliaments and diets and congresses and chambers of statesmen. I want to be there when they talk about honor and justice and making the world safe for democracy and fourteen points and the self determination of peoples. I want to be there to remind them I haven't got a tongue to stick into the cheek I haven't got either. But the statesmen have tongues. The statesmen have cheek. Put my glass case upon the speaker's desk and every time the gavel descends let me feel its vibration through my little jewel case. Then let them speak of trade policies and embargoes and new colonies and old grudges. Let them debate the menace of the yellow race and the white man's burden and the course of empire and why should we take all this crap off Germany or whoever the next Germany is. Let them talk about the South American market and why so-and-so is beating us out of it and why our merchant marine can't compete and oh what the hell let's send a good stiff note. Let them talk more munitions and airplanes and battleships and tanks and gases why of course we've got to have them we can't get along without them how in the world could we protect the peace if we didn't have them? Let them form blocs and alliances and mutual assistance pacts and guarantees of neutrality. Let them draft notes and ultimatums and protests and accusations.

But before they vote on them before they give the order for all the little guys to start killing each other let the main guy rap his gavel on my case and point down at me and say here gentlemen is the only issue before this house and that is are you for this thing here or are you against it. And if they are against it why goddam them let them stand up like men and vote. And if they are for it let them be hanged and drawn and quartered and paraded through the streets in small chopped up little bits and thrown out into the fields where no clean animal will touch them and let their chunks rot there and may no green thing ever grow where they rot.

Take me into your churches your great towering cathedrals that have to be rebuilt every fifty years—because they are destroyed by war. Carry me in my glass box down the aisles where kings and priests and brides and children at their confirmation have gone so many times before to kiss a splinter of wood from a true cross on which was nailed the body of a man who was lucky enough to die. Set me high on your altars and call on god to look down upon his murderous little children his dearly beloved little children. Wave over me the incense I can't smell. Swill down the sacramental wine I can't taste. Drone out the prayers I can't hear. Go through the old old holy gestures for which I have no legs and no arms. Chorus out the hallelujas I can't sing. Bring them out loud and strong for me your hallelujas all of them for me because I know the truth and you don't you fools. You fools you fools you fools. . . .

From the Jazz Age to the Uprisings of the 1930s

F. Scott Fitzgerald, "Echoes of the Jazz Age" (1931)

Yip Harburg, "Brother, Can You Spare a Dime?" (1932)

Paul Y. Anderson, "Tear-Gas, Bayonets, and Votes" (August 17, 1932)

Mary Licht, "I Remember the Scottsboro Defense" (February 15, 1997)

Ned Cobb ("Nate Shaw"), *All God's Dangers* (1969)

Billie Holiday, "Strange Fruit" (1937)

Two Poems by Langston Hughes (1934 and 1940)
 "Ballad of Roosevelt" (1934)
 "Ballad of the Landlord" (1940)

Bartolomeo Vanzetti, Speech to the Court (April 9, 1927)

Vicky Starr ("Stella Nowicki"), "Back of the Yards" (1973)

Sylvia Woods, "You Have to Fight for Freedom" (1973)

Rose Chernin on Organizing the Unemployed in the Bronx in the 1930s (1949)

Genora (Johnson) Dollinger, *Striking Flint: Genora (Johnson) Dollinger Remembers the 1936–37 GM Sit-Down Strike* (February 1995)

John Steinbeck, *The Grapes of Wrath* (1939)

Woody Guthrie, "This Land Is Your Land" (February 1940)

There are a number of historical myths around the 1920s and 1930s that deserve to be re-examined.

The 1920s are often described as the "Jazz Age," the "Age of Prosperity," suggesting the era was a delightful time, broken only by the Great Depression of the 1930s. Despite a surface "prosperity" enjoyed by the upper class, though, there was widespread hardship among city-dwellers and farmers, anti-foreign and anti-radical hysteria, and brutality against the nation's African-Americans, as the Ku Klux Klan became a national force.

Another myth is that the reforms of the New Deal in the 1930s were the product of the benevolence of the Roosevelt administration. This view ignores the tumultuous rebellions of the decade, starting with the Bonus March of 1932 and continuing into widespread strikes and protests that threatened the capitalist system. The result of this agitation—often involving anarchists, socialists—was a series of unprecedented reforms: social security, unemployment insurance, subsidies for low-cost housing, protection for labor unions. Perhaps the most striking, and never duplicated since that time, was the program that gave work to people in the arts: to writers, musicians, actors and directors, painters and sculptors.

In the following pages, we attempt to present voices that challenge some of the leading myths about this important period.

• • •

Even before the stock market crash of October 24, 1929, which sparked the Great Depression, there were signs of cultural and social decay. One of the great chroniclers of the excesses of the "Roaring Twenties" was the novelist F. Scott Fitzgerald, author of *The Great Gatsby*. Here is part of an essay he wrote for *Scribner's Magazine* looking back at this period.

F. Scott Fitzgerald, "Echoes of the Jazz Age" (1931)[1]

It is too soon to write about the Jazz Age with perspective, and without being suspected of premature arteriosclerosis. Many people still succumb to violent retching when they happen upon any of its characteristic words—words which have since yielded in vividness to the coinages of the underworld. It is as dead as were the Yellow Nineties in 1902. Yet the present writer already looks back to it with nostalgia. It bore him up, flattered him and gave him more money than he had dreamed of, simply for telling people that he felt as they did, that something had to be done with all the nervous energy stored up and unexpended in the War.

The ten-year period that, as if reluctant to die outmoded in its bed, leaped to a spectacular death in October, 1929, began about the time of the May Day riots in 1919. When the police rode down the demobilized country boys gaping at the orators in Madison Square, it was the sort of measure bound to alienate the more intelligent young men from the prevailing order. We didn't remember anything about the Bill of Rights until [H. L.] Mencken began plugging it, but we did know that such tyranny belonged in the jittery little countries of South Europe. If goose-livered business men had this effect on the government, then maybe we had gone to war for J. P. Morgan's loans after all. But, because we were tired of Great Causes, there was no more than a short outbreak of moral indignation. . . .

Scarcely had the staider citizens of the republic caught their breaths when the wildest of all generations, the generation which had been adolescent during the confusion of the War, brusquely shouldered my contemporaries out of the way and danced into the limelight. This was the generation whose girls dramatized themselves as flappers, the generation that corrupted its elders and eventually overreached itself less through lack of morals than through lack of taste. May one offer in exhibit the year 1922! That was the peak of the younger generation, for though the Jazz Age continued, it became less and less an affair of youth.

The sequel was like a children's party taken over by the elders, leaving the children puzzled and rather neglected and rather taken aback. By 1923 their elders, tired of watching the carnival with ill-concealed envy, had discovered that young liquor will take the place of young blood, and with a whoop the orgy began. They younger generation was starred no longer.

A whole race going hedonistic, deciding on pleasure. The precocious intimacies of the younger generation would have come about with or without prohibition—they were implicit in the attempt to adapt English customs to American conditions. (Our South, for example, is tropical and early maturing—it has never been part of the wisdom of France and Spain to let young girls go unchaperoned at sixteen and seventeen.) But the general decision to be amused that began with the cocktail parties of 1921 had more complicated origins.

The word jazz in its progress toward respectability has meant first sex, then dancing, then music. It is associated with a state of nervous stimulation, not unlike that of big cities behind the lines of a war. . . .

But it was not to be. Somebody had blundered and the most expensive orgy in history was over.

It ended two years ago, because the utter confidence which was its essential prop received an enormous jolt and it didn't take long for the flimsy structure to settle earthward. And after two years the Jazz Age seems as far away as the days before the War. It was borrowed time anyhow—the whole upper tenth of a nation living with the insouciance of grand dukes and the casualness of chorus girls. But moralizing is easy now and it was pleasant to be in one's twenties in such a certain and unworried time. Even when you were broke you didn't worry about money, because it was in such profusion around you. Toward the end one had a struggle to pay one's share; it was almost a favor to accept hospitality that required any traveling. Charm, notoriety, mere good manners, weighed more than money as a social asset. This was rather splendid but things were getting thinner and thinner as the eternal necessary human values tried to spread over all that expansion. Writers were geniuses on the strength of one respectable book or play; just as during the War officers of four months' experience commanded hundreds of men, so there were now many little fish lording it over great big bowls. In the theatrical world extravagant productions were carried by a few second-rate stars, and so on up the scale into politics where it was difficult to interest good men in positions of the highest importance and responsibility, importance and responsibility far exceeding that of business executives but which paid only five or six thousand a year.

Now once more the belt is tight and we summon the proper expression of horror as we look back on our wasted youth. Sometimes, though, there is a ghostly rumble among the drums, an asthmatic whisper in the trombones that swings me back into the early twenties when we drank wood alcohol and every day in every way grew better and better, and there was the first abortive shortening of skirts, and girls all looked alike in sweater dresses, and people you didn't want to know said "Yes, we have no bananas" and it seemed only a question of a few years before the older people would step aside and let the world be run by those who saw things as they were—and it all seems so rosy and romantic to us who were young then, because we will never feel quite so intensely about our surroundings any more.

• • •

One of best known songs of the Depression era was written by E. Y. ("Yip") Harburg, the son of Jewish immigrants from Russia who lived in the Lower East Side of New York City. Working with composer Jay Gorney, Harburg wrote "Brother, Can You Spare a Dime?" in 1932. Franklin Delano Roosevelt soon adopted it as the theme song of his presidential campaign.

Yip Harburg, "Brother, Can You Spare a Dime" (1932)[2]

They used to tell me I was building a dream, and so I followed the mob,
When there was earth to plow or guns to bear, I was always there, right there on the job.
They used to tell me I was building a dream, with peace and glory ahead.
Why should I be standing in line, just waiting for bread?

Once I built a railroad, made it run, made it race against time.
Once I built a railroad. Now it's done. Brother, can you spare a dime?
Once I built a tower, to the sun, brick, and rivet, and lime.
Once I built a tower, now it's done. Brother, can you spare a dime?

Once in khaki suits, gee, we looked swell,
Full of that Yankee Doodle-de-Dum.

Half a million boots went sloggin' through Hell,
And I was the kid with the drum.

Say, don't you remember, they called me Al.
It was Al all the time.
Say, don't you remember, I'm your pal!
Buddy, can you spare a dime?

• • •

Returning soldiers from World War I had been issued a "bonus" in 1924, in the form of government bonds that would be paid out in 1945. But with the onset of the Depression, many veterans were hard hit. They were without jobs, and their families were going hungry. They began to organize, demanding immediate payment of the bonds. They gathered all over the country and came to Washington, with wives and children or alone, in broken-down autos, stealing rides on freight trains, hitchhiking. Twenty thousand came. They called themselves the "Bonus Expeditionary Force" or "The Bonus Army." They set up camp across the Potomac River from the Capitol on Anacostia Flats. But Congress refused to act, and when the veterans remained in their encampment, President Herbert Hoover ordered the army to evict them. The officers in charge of the operation included Douglas MacArthur, Dwight Eisenhower, and George Patton. The veterans were attacked with tear gas and bayonets. Their tents were burned down. Here is a first-hand account of the Bonus Army march by Paul Anderson, a Missouri journalist who was an organizer of the American Newspaper Guild and had come to national prominence through his coverage of the East St. Louis massacre.

Paul Y. Anderson, "Tear-Gas, Bayonets, and Votes" (August 17, 1932)[3]

Hoover's campaign for reelection was launched Thursday, July 28, at Pennsylvania Avenue and Third Street, with four troops of cavalry, four companies of infantry, a mounted machine-gun squadron, six whippet tanks, 300 city policemen and a squad of Secret Service men and Treasury agents. Among the results immediately achieved were the following:

Two veterans of the World War shot to death; one eleven-weeks-old baby in a grave condition from gas, shock, and exposure; one eight-year-old boy partially blinded by gas; two policemen's skulls fractured; one bystander shot through the shoulder; one veteran's ear severed with a cavalry saber; one veteran stabbed in the hip with a bayonet; more than a dozen veterans, policemen, and soldiers injured by bricks and clubs; upward of 1,000 men, women, and children gassed, including policemen, reporters, ambulance drivers, and residents of Washington; and approximately $10,000 worth of property destroyed by fire, including clothing, food, and temporary shelters of the veterans and a large amount of building material owned by a government contractor.

The political results are less impressive. Indeed, among high officials of the Administration there is fast-growing apprehension that the great exploit was planned and executed with more daring than judgment, and that, as a campaign effort, it may prove to be one of the deadliest boomerangs in political history. That fear already has found expression in two public statements by the gallant Secretary of War, Pat Hurley, seeking to justify the employment of gas bombs, tanks, sabers, bayonets, and fire against unarmed men, women, and children. One of them, as I shall presently show, is such a tissue of known and demonstrable falsehoods that utter panic must have prompted it.

The circumstances surrounding the use of troops and modern implements of war to evict these people from then-miserable hovels and to drive them from the capital force me to the reluctant conclusion that the whole affair was deliberately conceived and carried out for a political purpose—namely, to persuade the American people that their government was threatened with actual overthrow, and that the courage and decisiveness of Herbert Hoover had averted revolution. It is no secret that Mr. Hoover and his advisers hope to make "Hoover versus radicalism" the leading issue of the campaign. The presence of the unemployed veterans and their families in the capital presented an opportunity to show the country that the danger of "insurrection" was real and that the Administration had prepared to meet it. To accomplish this object it was necessary to provoke actual conflict, and that is what the Administration proceeded to do. A simple review of the salient facts would seem to make this apparent.

For several weeks the men and their families had been encamped in Washington, some occupying abandoned and partially wrecked buildings and shacks on downtown plots owned by the government, but a large majority existing in crude shelters erected by themselves on a large government-owned field on the opposite bank of the Anacostia River. Excepting a small unit of Communists, which the main body promptly outlawed, the behavior of the men was characterized by extraordinary discipline and restraint. To one who visited their camps many times and talked to scores of them, any suggestion that they constituted a threat against the government is preposterous. Even the Communist gestures were confined mainly to two futile attempts to parade before the White House, which got them nothing but broken heads, jail sentences, and fines. The attitude of the great majority was one of good-humored and patient fortitude under incredibly primitive conditions of existence. In a thousand ways they exhibited the instinct to make comedy out of their own vicissitudes—an instinct as characteristic now as it was in France. The so-called "bonus army" in actuality was an army of unemployed men who believed they had a special claim on the government and came here asking the government to give them relief unless it was ready to provide work. Bonus or no bonus, they would not have come if they had had jobs. Any assertion to the contrary is ridiculous.

Save for the feeble gestures of the isolated Communist group there was no trouble until that fatal Thursday, due in part to the remarkable tact and common sense of General [Pelham] Glassford, the chief of police, in part to the discipline enforced by the leaders of the camps, and in part to the essentially law-abiding instincts of the men themselves. The worthy Hurley mouths indignant phrases about "panhandling" and "forced tribute from citizens," but in all my visits to the camps I was never asked for anything more valuable than a cigarette—and I am a fairly prosperous looking citizen. As soon as Congress adjourned there was a steady exodus of the campers, as attested by the daily statements of the Veterans' Bureau, dutifully reported by the Associated Press and Administration newspapers. Responsible officials repeatedly declared it was only a matter of days until all would be gone.

But suddenly someone high in authority decided the government must have immediate possession of the partially razed block bounded by Third and Fourth Streets and Pennsylvania and Missouri Avenues, where about 1,500 were existing in abandoned buildings and makeshift huts. Most of these people were from Texas, California, the Carolinas, Nebraska, West Virginia, and Florida, which are not exactly hotbeds of "radicalism." Instructions went from the Treasury to the District commissioners to have the police evict the squatters. On two occasions Glassford convinced the commissioners that the police had no authority to conduct such evictions, and pointed out that the procedure for eviction is definitely prescribed by law. On Wednesday there was a conference at the White House attended by Hurley, Attorney General [William] Mitchell, and General Douglas MacArthur, chief of staff of the army. On Thursday morning Glassford was informed that Treasury agents would begin evacuation of a part of the block, and that if anyone resisted eviction he was to be arrested for disorderly conduct. This meant that the actual eviction would be done by the police, and so it worked out. Someone had devised a technicality for getting around the law. Glassford's protests were unavailing. It was obvious that irresistible pressure had been applied to the commissioners. . . .

The trouble was that someone in authority had determined to force the issue. Two District commissioners reported to President Hoover that the civil authorities were "unable to maintain order," and within a few minutes infantry, cavalry, machine-gunners, and tanks were on their way from Fort Myer and Fort Washington. . . .

When the troops arrived they actually were cheered by the veterans on the south sidewalk of Pennsylvania Avenue. A cavalry officer spurred up to the curb and shouted: "Get the hell out of here." Infantrymen with fixed bayonets and trench helmets deployed along the south curb, forcing the veterans back into the contested block. Cavalry deployed along the north side, riding their horses up on the sidewalk and compelling policemen, reporters, and photographers to climb on automobiles to escape being trampled. A crowd of three or four thousand spectators had congregated in the vacant lot on the north side of the avenue. A command was given and the cavalry charged the crowd with drawn sabers. Men, women, and children fled shrieking across the broken ground, falling into excavations as they strove to avoid the rearing hoofs and saber points. Meantime, the infantry on the south side had adjusted gas masks and were hurling tear bombs into the block into which they had just driven the veterans. Secretary Hurley states that "the building occupied by the women and children was protected, and no one was permitted to molest them."

What he means by "the building" I do not know, because scores of shanties and tents in the block were occupied by women and children. I know that I saw dozens of women grab their children and stagger out of the area with streaming, blinded eyes while the bombs fizzed and popped all around them. I saw a woman stand on the Missouri Avenue side and plead with a non-commissioned officer to let her rescue a suitcase which, she told him, contained all the spare clothing of herself and her child, and I heard him reply: "Get out of here, lady, before you get hurt," as he calmly set fire to her shanty.

"No one was injured after the coming of the troops," declares the veracious Mr. Hurley. I saw one of his own blood-splashed cavalrymen put into an ambulance, apparently unconscious, as several of his comrades pursued a fugitive into a filling station, trampling a woman in their charge. Simultaneously an ear was shorn from the head of a Tennessee veteran by a cavalry saber. As a matter of fact, there was hardly a minute when an ambulance did not dash in and dash off with a victim. I was in that hapless mass of policemen, reporters, and spectators at Third and C Streets a few minutes later when an order was given from a staff officer's car, and a company of infantry came up on the double quick, tossing gas bombs right and left. Some exploded on the sidewalk. Some fell in front yards jammed with Negro women and children. One appeared to land on the front porch of a residence. Two small girls fell to the sidewalk, choking and screaming. . . .

Secretary Hurley defiantly announced that "statements made to the effect that the billets of the marchers were fired by troops is a falsehood." On the day when he first made this declaration it appeared in dozens of newspapers which also published a graphic Underwood and Underwood photograph of an infantryman applying a torch to a veteran's shanty. I am only one of numerous reporters who stood by while the soldiers set fire to many such shelters. In the official apologia, the Secretary asserts that "the shacks and tents at Anacostia were set on fire by the bonus marchers before the troops crossed the Anacostia Bridge." I was there when the troops crossed. They celebrated their arrival at the Anacostia terminus of the bridge by tossing gas bombs into a throng of spectators who booed and refused to "get back" as soon as ordered. About fifteen minutes after their arrival in the camp the troops set fire to two improvised barracks. These were the first fires. Prior to this General MacArthur had summoned all available reporters and told them that "operations are completely suspended," that "our objective has been accomplished," that "the camp is virtually abandoned," and that it would "not be burned." Soon after making that statement he departed for the White House. When the two barracks ignited by the soldiers had been burning fiercely for at least thirty minutes, the veterans began firing their own shelters as they abandoned them. On the high embankment which bounds the plain opposite the Anacostia River, thousands of veterans had gathered, and with them mingled thousands of Anacostia residents, all intent on the lurid spectacle below. Promptly at midnight (General MacArthur had gone to the White House more than an hour earlier) a long and shadowy line of infantry and cavalry advanced across the fiery plain toward the embankment. Sabers and bayonets gleamed in the red light cast by the flames. Virtually everyone had deserted the camp; it seemed incredible that the offensive would be pushed still further. It seemed so to the veterans and the residents of Anacostia—but an officer had told me earlier in the evening that the strategy was to drive all the campers "into the open country of Maryland." . . .

For many blocks along the embankment similar scenes were being enacted. With "unparalleled humanity and kindliness," the troops tossed scores of gas bombs into the vast crowds lining the hillside, driving them back to the main thoroughfare of Anacostia. Automobilists, unable either to turn or back up, abandoned their vehicles and ran from the stinging fumes and menacing bayonets. Within five yards of the main business corner a veteran carrying an American flag failed to move rapidly enough, and I saw a gleaming blade sink into his hip. Moaning, he staggered toward a drug store, still clutching his flag.

Chief Glassford, who was in the best position to know, has said that it was "unnecessary." But, although a brilliant soldier and an even more brilliant policeman, he is not a politician. The politicians had decided it was necessary. It was necessary to dramatize the issue of "Hoover versus radicalism." One hitch has developed. The President has asserted that less than half of the campers were men who had actually served under the flag, and Hurley assures us that the disorders were led by "reds" and "agitators." How unfortunate, then, that those killed were bona fide veterans of The World War, entitled to honorable burial in Arlington! But how much more tragic it is that, in a crisis like this, the United States

Government should be under the control of such a trio of adventurers as Hoover, Hurley, and Mills!

• • •

In March 1931, a group of nine black youths were pulled off a freight train in Point Rock, Alabama, and charged with assault, soon followed by charges of rape of two white women. Within five days, all nine were indicted by a federal grand jury. Within another nine days, eight of the "Scottsboro Boys," as the group was called, were sentenced to death. The case aroused outrage around the world, symbolizing the lack of justice for African Americans in the U.S. legal system. Even after Ruby Bates testified in court in 1933 that the rapes never took place, the nine continued to be imprisoned. With protests continuing, twice the Supreme Court called for new trials, ruling that their counsel was inadequate and noting that the jury selection was limited to whites. But they were tried again, found guilty, and sentenced to long prison terms ranging from twenty to ninety-nine years, with one of them given the death penalty. The Supreme Court refused to hear their case, but agitation continued around the country and after many years in prison, the one death sentence was commuted and the others eventually were released from prison. The Communist Party was a leading force in demanding justice for the Scottsboro Boys. Here one of its organizers recalls the case.

Mary Licht, "I Remember the Scottsboro Defense" (February 15, 1997)[4]

On March 25, 1931, an armed mob stopped a freight train at Paint Rock, Alabama, and rounded up nine African American youths, the youngest of whom was 13. Two young white women and one white man were also taken off the train. ("Hoboing" or hitching rides on freight trains, the original pretext for stopping the train, was illegal.)

Sheriff's deputies arrested the nine young men, loaded them onto a flatbed truck and took them to the Jackson County jail in Scottsboro. There they were charged with a second offense: "having raped the white girls in a freight car passing through Alabama."

When a crowd gathered at the jail, the sheriff called the governor who, in turn, called out the National Guard and the mob dispersed. Twelve days later, all were put on trial and in four days, four separate all-white, all-male juries convicted eight and sentenced them to death.

In the years since, many people have asked how I become involved in the case—an involvement that makes it possible for me to categorically deny Denton L. Watson's crude lies about the role of the Communist Party in building the campaign to defend the Nine.

Yes, we did embarrass the Klan, white supremacists and Alabama authorities. And yes, we plucked a few tail feathers from Jim Crow. But our first—and only—goal was to save the lives of nine innocent young African American youth. I'm proud to say that we accomplished that task and that I had a role in it.

I lived in Chattanooga, Tennessee, at that time, as did four of the nine. I first heard of the case while I was in jail awaiting trial for "sedition."

I considered the arrest of the Scottsboro "boys" and my arrest as two sides of the same coin: They were riding the rails in search of work and I was working to organize the unemployed who had been thrown out of work.

For me, the arrest, trial and conviction of these unemployed Black youth was a symbol of the inequality of the then 12 million African Americans in America. I believed their trial was a legal lynching—that they had been framed and sentenced to death under the pretext of "rape."

During the Hoover administration of the early 1930s, America found itself in the midst of a devastating economic depression, with millions out of work. Although things were hard in the North, they were desperate in the South where the Depression had really begun in 1927.

But by 1931 a mass fight back had begun. Throughout the country Unemployed Councils, led by the Trade Union Unity League and the Communist Party, were organizing. Petitions with more than a million signatures demanding relief and unemployment insurance had been presented to the White House in December 1930. I was a leader of the Unemployed Council in Chattanooga.

The councils called mass demonstrations across the country for March 6 to demand that Congress pass the Lundeen Bill for relief, unemployment insurance and Social Security.

Our demonstration in Chattanooga was attended by many Black and white workers but even before the rally started, the three scheduled speakers—I was one of them—were arrested. We were indicted for sedition and held without bail while awaiting trial. Nothing like this happened anywhere else in the country—but it gives one a taste of the South at that time.

When I read about the conviction of the Scottsboro youth, I told my co-worker that when we were released I would secure the International Labor Defense (ILD) for this case. I said the way the ILD had conducted our trial convinced me that it was the only organization that would mobilize the kind of campaign that would overturn the savage death sentences given these youngsters.

Our lawyers didn't just depend on arguing the fine points of the law or on the "impartiality" of the courts. They said we had to pack the courtroom with our supporters and appeal to the public for support. And they were right.

Our trial was held in a courtroom packed with Black and white unemployed workers and we were freed after a three-day trial, thanks in part to the eloquence of Joe Brodsky, the ILD lawyer who helped us defeat the city's sedition charge.

A half hour after my release I was visiting Sherman Bell, who was affectionately called the "Mayor" of Chattanooga's Black community. He had been a delegate to the convention of the American Negro Labor Congress (ANLC) in St. Louis that issued a "Bill of Negro Rights" with the aim of developing a movement to enact legislation for African American rights and to suppress lynching. The ANLC changed their name at this convention to the League of Struggle for Negro Rights and became active participants in the Scottsboro case.

Bell and I visited Mrs. [Ada] Wright and Mrs. [Janie] Patterson, mothers of three of the Scottsboro defendants. We told them about how our trial had been conducted—a packed courtroom and a team of eloquent lawyers who believed in our program of equality for African American people.

We explained that the case of the Scottsboro Nine was not a case that could be won in a southern court room. We said that a mass protest movement capable of rallying millions of people from around the world was required if there was to be a stay of the execution scheduled for July 10. We said that without that stay, nothing else mattered.

Wright and Patterson told us that they had been visited by representatives of the NAACP [the National Association for the Advancement of Colored People] that morning who would, most likely, return. And they did. But, after 10 days of visits and discussion with these two mothers, we secured their agreement that the ILD would represent their sons. Shortly after, the other parents agreed to representation by the ILD.

Immediately after the trial and sentencing, the ILD went to court, demanding a stay of execution and a new trial, since the defendants had not had counsel of their choice during their trial. The rest is history. Demonstrations were organized in major cities across the country and American embassies became the target of angry demonstrators abroad as millions supported the ILD demand.

The militant defense of the Scottsboro Nine became a catalyst that helped bring union organization to thousands of Southern workers. Sharecroppers in Alabama and Arkansas joined the Sharecroppers Union, while workers employed by Tennessee Coal and Iron and miners in Harlan County, Kentucky, joined unions and laid the base for the Congress of Industrial Organization that loomed just over the horizon.

The Scottsboro defense by the Communist Party and the International Labor Defense was not a bolt from the blue. Nor was it a liberal humanitarian gesture limited to the plight of nine unemployed Black youth. To the contrary. The decision to represent and fight for the Scottsboro Nine was preceded by years of activity led by the Communist Party and its predecessor organizations.

The founding convention of the Workers Party in 1921 adopted a program of Black equality, at that time a more advanced program than that of any organization. At its 1922 convention, the Party adopted a program for economic, political and social equality that was carried out side-by-side with a struggle against the racism that had oppressed African Americans for centuries.

* * *

While the suffering of the poor was felt by both black and white, there was a special oppression felt by blacks, who had to confront economic and racial oppression. Here are the words of Ned Cobb (named "Nate Shaw" in the book *All God's Dangers* by Theodore Rosengarten). Cobb was born in Alabama in 1885, and in the 1930s became a leader of the Alabama Sharecropper's Union (SCU), a radical union that organized thousands of black sharecroppers, as well as small number of white farmers, during the Great Depression. With the help of organizers from the Communist Party, the SCU organized in the face of threats against blacks who dared to engage in union activity. Meetings had to be held in secret, sometimes disguised as Bible readings.

Ned Cobb ("Nate Shaw"), *All God's Dangers* (1969)[5]

A heap of families, while I was livin on the Tucker place down on Sitimachas, was leavin goin north. Some of my neighbors even picked up and left. . . .

I knowed I was in a bad way of life here but I didn't intend to get out—that never come in my mind. I thought somehow, some way, I'd overcome it. I was a farmin man at that time and I knowed more about this country than I knowed about the northern states. I've always been man enough to stick up for my family, and love them, and try to support em, and I just thought definitely I could keep it up. In other words, I was determined to try.

And durin of the pressure years, a union begin to operate in this country, called it the Sharecroppers Union—that was a nice name, I thought—and my first knowin about this union, this organization, that riot come off at Crane's Ford in '31. I looked deep in that thing, too—I heard more than I seed and I taken that in consideration. And I knowed what was goin on was a turnabout on the southern man, white and colored; it was somethin unusual. And I heard about it bein a organization for the poor class of people—that's just what I wanted to get into, too; I wanted to know the secrets of it enough that I could become in the knowledge of it. Now I heard talk about trucks comin into this country deliverin guns to the colored people but I decided all that was talk, tryin to accuse the niggers of gettin into somethin here that maybe they weren't—and maybe they were. But didn't no trucks haul no guns to nobody. Colored people hadn't been armed up for nothin; it was told like that just to agitate the thing further. Of course, some of these colored folks in here had some good guns—you know a Winchester rifle is a pretty good gun itself. But they didn't have nothin above that. It weren't nothin that nobody sent in here for em to use, just their own stuff.

Well, they killed a man up there, colored fellow; his name was Adam Cole. And they tell me—I didn't see it but I heard lots about it and I never did hear nothin about it that backed me off—Kurt Beall, the High Sheriff for Tukabahchee County, got shot in the stomach. He run up there to break up this meetin business amongst the colored people and someone in that crowd shot him. That kind of broke him up from runnin in places like that.

And these white folks woke up and stretched themselves and commenced a runnin around meddlin with niggers about this organization. And it's a close thing today. One old man—and he was as big a skunk as ever sneaked in the woods— old man Mac Sloane, come up to me one day—he didn't come to my home, he met me on the outside—old man Mac Sloane come to me hot as a stove iron, "Nate, do you belong to that mess they carryin on in this country?"

I just cut him off short. I didn't belong to it at that time, but I was eager to join and I was aimin to join, just hadn't got the right opportunity.

"No, I don't belong to nothin."

Mac Sloane, white man, said, "You stay out of it. That damn thing will get you killed. You stay out of it. These niggers runnin around here carryin on some kind of meetin—you better stay out of it."

I said to myself, "You a fool if you think you can keep me from joinin." I went right on and joined it, just as quick as the next meetin come. Runnin around and givin me orders—he suspected I might be the kind of man to belong to such a organization; put the finger on me before I ever joined. And he done just the thing to push me into it—gived me orders not to join.

The teachers of this organization begin to drive through this country—they couldn't let what they was doin be known. One of em was a colored fella; I disremember his name but he did tell us his name. He wanted us to organize and he was with us a whole lot of time, holdin meetins with us—that was part of his job. We colored farmers would meet and the first thing we had to do was join the organization. And it was said, we didn't want no bad men in it at all, no weakhearted fellows that would be liable to give the thing away. It was secret with them all that joined it; they knowed to keep their mouths shut and meet the meetins. And this teacher said—don't know where his home was; he had a different way of talkin than we did—"I call em stool pigeons if they broadcast the news about what's happenin." And said, if a nigger, like myself, went and let out any secrets to the white folks about the organization, the word was, "Do away with him."

Had the meetins at our houses or anywhere we could have em where we could keep a look and a watch-out that nobody was comin in on us. Small meetins, sometimes there'd be a dozen, sometimes there'd be more, sometimes there'd be less—niggers was scared, niggers was scared, that's tellin the truth. White folks in this country didn't allow niggers to have no organization, no secret meetins. They kept up with you and watched you, didn't allow you to associate in a crowd, unless it was your family or your church. It just worked in a way that the nigger wasn't allowed to have nothin but church services and, O, they liked to see you goin to church, too. Sometimes white people would come into the Negro church and set there and listen at the meetin. Of course, it weren't nothin but a church service goin on. But if a nigger walked into a white church, he'd just be driven out, if they didn't kill him. But if a Negro was a servant for white people, then they'd carry him to church with em, accept him to come in and take a seat on the back seat and listen at the white people. But if you was a independent Negro you better stay away from there. But if you was a white man's dear flunky, doin what he said do, or even on the woman's side, if they was maids for the white people, well thought of, they'd take em out to their home churches, dupe em up in a way. They knowed they weren't goin to cause no trouble—and if they did, they'd just been knocked out of the box and called in close question. But they never did act disorderly; just set there and listened at the white folks' meetin quiet as a lamb. And when the white folks would come in the colored churches, good God, the niggers would get busy givin em first class seats—if there was any in that buildin the white folks got em. They was white people; they classed theirselves over the colored and the colored people never did do nothin but dance to what the white people said and thought. White people was their bosses and their controllers and the colored people went along with it. White men, white women—I been there—go in colored churches and be seated. Nigger aint got nothin to do but run around there and give em the nicest seats.

First thing the organization wanted for the colored people was the privilege to have a organization. That's one of the best things they ever could fight for and get on foot. From my boy days comin along, ever since I been in God's world, I've never had no rights, no voice in nothin that the white man didn't want me to have— even been cut out of education, book learnin, been deprived of that. How could I favor such rulins as have been the past? . . .

I never tried to beat nobody out of nothin since I been in this world, never has, but I understands that there's a whole class of people tries to beat the other class of people out of what they has. I've had it put on me; I've seen it put on others, with these eyes. O, it's plain: if every man thoroughly got his rights, there wouldn't be so many rich people in the world—I spied that a long time ago. And I've looked deep in that angle. How can one man get out there and labor for his own way of life and get to be a rich man? Where is his earnins comin from that he's palmin off and stickin it behind? It come out of the poor little farmers and other laborin men. O, it's desperately wrong. There's many a man today aint able to support his family. There's many a man aint able to wear the clothes that he should wear and accumulate nothin that he should have, and accomplish nothin that he should do. And who is the backbone of the world? It's the laborin man, it's the laborin man. My God, the big man been on him with both foots all these years and now don't want to get off him. I found out all of that because they tried to take I don't know what all away from me.

I've gotten along in this world by studyin the races and knowin that I was one of the underdogs. I was under many rulins, just like the other Negro, that I knowed was injurious to man and displeasin to God and still I had to fall back. I got tired of it but no help did I know; weren't nobody to back me up. I've taken every kind of insult and went on. In my years past, I'd accommodate anybody; but I didn't believe in this way of bowin to my knees and doin what any white man said do. Still, I always knowed to give the white man his time of day or else he's ready to knock me in the head. I just aint goin to go nobody's way against my own self. First thing of all—I care for myself and respect myself. . . .

I come into the world with this against me: that if a man comes to take away what I have and he don't have a fair claim against me, I'll die before I stand quiet as a fence post and let him do it. If I die tryin to defend myself, why, let me go. I'm goin to try, definitely.

• • •

In 1937, a Bronx schoolteacher, Abel Meeropol, saw a gruesome picture of two black teenagers, Thomas Shipp and Abram Smith, who had been lynched in Marion, Indiana, seven years earlier. Afterwards he wrote the haunting poem "Bitter Fruit." Meeropol, who was a member of the Communist Party, published the words to the song in the New York Teacher and New Masses. But fame for the song came after Meeropol showed it to the extraordinary blues singer Billie Holiday. Though her record company refused to record the song, she released it through a specialty label under the title "Strange Fruit" and performed it live (crediting the lyrics to "Lewis Allan," Meeropol's pseudonym). It was Meeropol and his wife who later adopted the two sons of Ethel Rosenberg and Julius Rosenberg after their execution in 1953.

Billie Holiday, "Strange Fruit" (1937)[6]

Southern trees bear a strange fruit,
    (Blood on the leaves and blood at the root,)
Black body swinging in the southern breeze,
    Strange fruit hanging from the poplar trees.

Pastoral scene of the gallant South,
    (The bulging eyes and the twisted mouth,)
Scent of magnolia, sweet and fresh,
    (And the sudden smell of burning flesh.)

Here is a fruit for the crows to pluck,
    For the rain to gather, for the wind to suck,
For the sun to rot, for a tree to drop,
    Here is a strange and bitter crop.

• • •

The "Harlem Renaissance" of the 1920s and 1930s produced an extraordinary group of black writers and artists. There were the novelists Zora Neale Hurston and Nella Larsen, the painters Jacob Lawrence and Aaron Douglas, the poets Gwendolyn Bennett, Claude McKay, and Countee Cullen, and many others. One of the most challenging of these voices was that of poet Langston Hughes, who speaks in these two poems of the social conditions of African Americans, the poor, the working people. Hughes captures the feeling of being "damn tired" of waiting for rescue from the political leadership of the country.

Two Poems by Langston Hughes (1934 and 1940)

"BALLAD OF ROOSEVELT" (1934)[7]

The pot was empty,
The cupboard was bare.
I said, Papa,
What's the matter here?
       I'm waitin' on Roosevelt, son,
       Roosevelt, Roosevelt,
       Waitin' on Roosevelt, son.

The rent was due,
And the lights was out.
I said, Tell me, Mama,
What's it all about?
    We're waitin' on Roosevelt, son,
    Roosevelt, Roosevelt,
    Just waitin' on Roosevelt.

Sister got sick
And the doctor wouldn't come
Cause we couldn't pay him
The proper sum—
    A-waitin' on Roosevelt,
    Roosevelt, Roosevelt,
    A-waitin' on Roosevelt.

Then one day
They put us out o' the house.
Ma and Pa was
Meek as a mouse
    Still waitin' on Roosevelt,
    Roosevelt, Roosevelt.

But when they felt those
Cold winds blow
And didn't have no
Place to go
    Pa said, I'm tired
    O' waitin' on Roosevelt,
    Roosevelt, Roosevelt.
    Damn tired o' waitin' on Roosevelt.

I can't git a job
And I can't git no grub.
Backbone and navel's
Doin' the belly-rub—
    A-waitin' on Roosevelt,
    Roosevelt, Roosevelt.

And a lot o' other folks
What's hungry and cold
Done stopped believin'
What they been told
     By Roosevelt,
     Roosevelt, Roosevelt—

Cause the pot's still empty,
And the cupboard's still bare,
And you can't build a bungalow
Out o' air—
     Mr. Roosevelt, listen!
     What's the matter here?

"BALLAD OF THE LANDLORD" (1940)[8]

Landlord, landlord
My roof has sprung a leak
Don't you 'member I told you about it
Way last week?

Landlord, landlord,
These steps is broken down.
When you come up yourself
It's a wonder you don't fall down.

Ten Bucks you say I owe you?
Ten Bucks you say is due?
Well, that's Ten Bucks more'n I'll pay you
Till you fix this house up new.

What? You gonna get eviction orders?
You gonna cut off my heat?
You gonna take my furniture and
Throw it in the street?

Um-huh! You talking high and mighty.
Talk on—till you get through.
You ain't gonna be able to say a word
If I land my fist on you.

Police! Police!
Come and get this man!
He's trying to ruin the government
And overturn the land!

Copper's whistle!
Patrol bell!
Arrest.

Precinct Station
Iron cell.
Headlines in press:

MAN THREATENS LANDLORD

   •

 •   •

TENANT HELD NO BAIL

   •

 •   •

JUDGE GIVES NEGRO 90 DAYS IN COUNTY JAIL.

• • •

In 1921, Nicola Sacco, a shoemaker, and Bartolomeo Vanzetti, a fish peddler, both Italian immigrants and anarchists, were arrested and charged with a murder and holdup in South Braintree, Massachusetts. Their trial took place before a jury contemptuous of foreigners and a judge who referred to them privately as "anarchist bastards," in an atmosphere still filled with wartime patriotism, the bodies of soldiers still being returned from Europe. They were found guilty and sentenced to death. During the next six years their case became famous throughout the world, but all appeals, pointing to tainted evidence and judicial bias, were turned down. Their guilt was affirmed by a special panel consisting of the president of Harvard, the president of M.I.T., and a retired judge. The prominent journalist Heywood Broun wrote bitterly, "What more can the immigrants from Italy expect? It is not every person who has a president of Harvard University throw the switch for him. If this is lynching, at least the fish-peddler and his friend, the factory hand, may take unction to their souls that they will die at the hands of men in dinner jackets or academic gowns." On August 23, 1927—as police broke up protests with arrests and beatings, and troops surrounded Charlestown Prison—they were electrocuted. What follows is the voice of Vanzetti, from his trial in 1927.

Bartolomeo Vanzetti, Speech to the Court (April 9, 1927)[9]

CLERK WORTHINGTON: Bartolomeo Vanzetti, have you anything to say why sentence of death should not be passed upon you?

BARTOLOMEO VANZETTI: Yes. What I say is that I am innocent, not only of the Braintree crime, but also of the Bridgewater crime. That I am not only innocent of these two crimes, but in all my life I have never stolen and I have never killed and I have never spilled blood. That is what I want to say. And it is not all. Not only am I innocent of these two crimes, not only in all my life I have never stolen, never killed, never spilled blood, but I have struggled all my life, since I began to reason, to eliminate crime from the earth. . . .

[T]he jury were hating us because we were against the war, and the jury don't know that it makes any difference between a man that is against the war because he believes that the war is unjust, because he hate no country, because he is a cosmopolitan, and a man that is against the war because he is in favor of the other country that fights against the country in which he is, and therefore a spy, an enemy, and he commits any crime in the country in which he is in behalf of the other country in order to serve the other country. We are not men of that kind. Nobody can say that we are German spies or spies of any kind. . . . [W]e were against the war because we did not believe in the purpose for which they say that the war was fought. We believed that the war is wrong, and we believe this more now after ten years that we studied and observed and understood it day by day,—the consequences and the result of the after war. We believe more now than ever that the war was wrong, and we are against war more now than ever, and I am glad to be on the doomed scaffold if I can say to mankind, "Look out; you are in a catacomb of the flower of mankind. For what? All that they say to you, all that they have promised to you—it was a lie, it was an illusion, it was a cheat, it was a fraud, it was a crime. They promised you liberty. Where is liberty? They promised you prosperity. Where is prosperity? They have promised you elevation. Where is the elevation?"

From the day that I went in Charlestown, the misfortunate, the population of Charlestown, has doubled in number. Where is the moral good that the war has given to the world? Where is the spiritual progress that we have achieved from the war? Where are the security of life, the security of the things that we possess for our necessity? Where are the respect for human life? Where are the respect and the admiration for the good characteristics and the good of the human nature? Never before the war as now have there been so many crimes, so much corruption, so much degeneration as there is now. . . .

What I want to say is this: Everybody ought to understand that the first beginning of our defense has been terrible. My first lawyer did not try to defend us. He has made no attempt to collect witnesses and evidence in our favor. The record in the Plymouth court is a pity. I am told that they are part or almost one-half lost. So that later on the defense have had a tremendous work to do in order to collect some evidence, to collect some testimony to offset and to learn what the testimony of the State had been. . . .

Well, I have already say that I not only am not guilty of these two crimes, but I never committed a crime in my life,—I have never stolen and I have never killed and I have never spilt blood, and I have fought against crime, and I have fought and I have sacrificed myself even to eliminate the crimes that the law and the church legitimate and sanctify.

This is what I say: I would not wish to a dog or to a snake, to the most low and misfortunate creature of the earth—I would not wish to any of them what I have had to suffer for things that I am not guilty of. I am suffering because I am a radical and indeed I am a radical; I have suffered because I was an Italian, and indeed I am an Italian; I have suffered more for my family and for my beloved than for myself; but I am so convinced to be right that you can only kill me once but if you could execute me two times, and if I could be reborn two other times, I would live again to do what I have done already.

· · ·

The economic crisis of the 1930s led to a wave of union organizing and strikes all over the country. "Stella Nowicki" was the assumed name of Vicky Starr, a rank-and-file activist who was active in the campaign to organize unions in the meatpacking factories of Chicago. Years later, she spoke to Alice and Staughton Lynd, the labor historians and activists, about the conditions in the plants and the tactics radicals used to organize meatpacking and other workers.

Vicky Starr ("Stella Nowicki"), "Back of the Yards" (1973)[10]

I ran away from home at age 17. I had to because there was not enough money to feed the family in 1933 during the Depression. . . .

I was not really introduced to socialism until I came to Chicago and the Marches began telling me about it. I lived with them at 59th and Ashland. They lived on the second floor and on the third floor they had bedrooms and an attic room. Anyone who didn't have some place to live could always find room there.

It was near the streetcar intersection and when there were meetings blacks could come. (This was a real problem at that time.) The Marches would have meetings of the YCL [Young Communist League] in the attic and they'd ask me to sit in. The terminology was like a foreign language. I thought that I better join this out-fit so that I would know what they were talking about.

They pointed out things to me that, in my very unsophisticated and farm-like way, I saw. There was so much food being dumped—the government bought it up—and people were hungry and didn't have enough to eat. (There were days when I didn't have anything to eat. That's when I picked up smoking. Somebody said, "Here, smoke. It'll kill your appetite." And it did.) I realized that there was this tremendous disparity. The people in our YCL group told me that the government was set up to keep it this way. They thought that instead of just thinking about ourselves we should be thinking about other people and try to get them together in a union and organize and then maybe we would have socialism where there would not be hunger, war, etc. They initiated me into a lot of political ideas and gave me material to read. We had classes and we would discuss industrial unionism, the craft unions and the history of the labor move-ment in this country. We talked about Debs, we talked about the eight hour day, many things.

I was doing housework for $4 a week and I hated it. I would cry and cry. I was horribly homesick because I hated the restraint of being in a house all the time. I was used to being out a lot on the farm. So Herb suggested that I get a job in the stockyards.

Herb was working at Armour's at the time. He bought me a steel, with which one sharpens a knife, and I took it with me. He took me down to the stock yards and I said, "Those beautiful cows! They can't kill those beautiful cows!" At home we just had cows for milking. But here were all these cows and they were going to be killed and they were crying, mooing, as they were going to be killed. But one had to get a job!

One of the ways to get a job was to go down to the employment office. Every morning you got there by six or six-thirty. There were just so many benches and they would all be filled early. They would only need one, maybe two people. This woman, Mrs. McCann, women's hiring director, would look around for the biggest and brawniest person. At seventeen I weighed 157 pounds coming from the farm, rosy-cheeked and strong. "Have you had experience?" I said, "Well not in the stock yards but we used to butcher our own hogs at home." I carried this big steel and that impressed her. Mrs. McCann hired me.

I was in the cook room. At that time the government bought up drought cat-tle and they were killed, canned, and given to people on relief to eat. The meat would be cut into big hunks and steamed. Then it would come on a rail and be dumped out on the table. The women would be all around the table and we would cut the meat up, remove the gristle and bad parts, and make hash out of it. The government inspector would come around to see that bad meat wasn't being thrown into the hash. But as soon as his back would be turned, the foreman would push this stuff right down the chute to go into the cans—all this stuff we had put aside to be thrown away he would push right down in, including gloves, cockroaches, anything. The company didn't give a damn.

The meat would be so hot and steamy your fingers almost blistered but you just stayed on. In 1933–34 we worked six hour shifts at 37 1/2 cents an hour. We would have to work at a high rate of speed. It was summer. It would be so hot that women used to pass out. The ladies' room was on the floor below and I would help carry these women down almost vertical stairs into the washroom.

We started talking union. The thing that precipitated it is that on the floor below they used to make hotdogs and one of the women, in putting the meat into the chopper, got her fingers caught. There were no safety guards. Her fingers got into the hotdogs and they were chopped off. It was just horrible.

Three of us "colonizers" had a meeting during our break and decided this was the time to have a stoppage and we did. . . . All six floors went on strike. We said, "Sit, stop." And we had a sit-down. We just stopped working right inside the building, protesting the speed and the unsafe conditions. We thought that people's fingers shouldn't go into the machine, that it was an outrage. The women got interested in the union.

We got the company to put in safety devices. Soon after the work stoppage the supervisors were looking for the leaders because people were talking up the action. They found out who was involved and we were all fired. I was blacklisted.

I got a job doing housework again and it was just horrible. Here I was taking care of this family with a little spoiled brat and I had to pick up after them—only Thursday afternoon off and every other Sunday—and all for four dollars a week of which I sent two dollars home. I just couldn't stand it. I would rather go back and work in a factory, any day or night.

A friend of mine who had been laid off told me that she got called to go back to work. Meanwhile she had a job in an office and she didn't want to go back to the stockyards, so she asked me if I wanted to go in her place. She had used the name Helen Ellis. I went down to the stockyards and it was the same department, exactly the same job on the same floor where I had been fired. But it was the afternoon and Mrs. McCann wasn't there. Her assistant was there. Her assistant said, "Can you do this work?" I said, "Oh yes, I can. I've done it." She told me that I would start work the following afternoon.

I came home and talked with Herb and Jane [March]. We decided that I would have to go to the beauty shop. I got my hair cut really short and hennaed. I thinned my eyebrows and penciled them, wore a lot of lipstick and painted my nails. Because I hadn't been working, I had a suntan. I wore sandals and I had my toenails painted, which I would never have done before. I came in looking sharp and not like a country girl, so I passed right through and I was hired as Helen Ellis on the same job, the same forelady!

After several days the forelady, Mary, who was also Polish, came around and said, "OK, Helen, I know you're Stella. I won't say anything but just keep quiet" if I wanted to keep the job. I answered her in Polish that I knew that the job wouldn't last long and I thanked her. She knew I was pro-union and I guess she was too, so I kept the job as Helen Ellis until I got laid off. (Later on I was blacklisted under the name Ellis.) . . .

[I]f you even talked union you were fired. Jobs were at a premium. You didn't have the law which guaranteed people the right to organize. So we actually had secret meetings. Everybody had to vouch for anyone that they brought to the meeting, that they were people that we could trust, because as soon as the company found out that people were trying to organize, they would try to send in stool pigeons. They paid people to come in and try to get information. . . .

When I look back now, I really think we had a lot of guts. But I didn't even stop to think about it at the time. It was something that had to be done. We had a goal. That's what we felt had to be done and we did it.

We got into sending people all over to different groups and into different shops so that when union organization picked up we would have people everywhere. . . .

Women had an awfully tough time in the union because the men brought their prejudices there. The fellows couldn't believe that women in the union were there for the union's sake. They thought that they were there to get a guy or something else. Some thought that we were frivolous. I would be approached by men for dates and they would ask me why I was in the union, so I would tell them that I was for socialism and I thought that this was the only way of bringing it about.

Some of my brothers, who believed in equality and that women should have rights, didn't crank the mimeograph, didn't type. I did the shit work, until all hours, as did the few other women who didn't have family obligations. And then when the union came around giving out jobs with pay, the guys got them. I and the other women didn't. It was the men who got the organizing jobs. Men who worked in plants got paid for their time loss—women didn't. I never did. But we were a dedicated group. We worked in coolers and from there I would go to the union hall and get out leaflets, write material for shop papers, turn in dues, etc., get home and make supper, get back. These guys had wives to do this but there was nobody to do mine. Sometimes I'd be up until eleven, twelve, or one o'clock and then have to get up early and be punched in by quarter to seven and be working on the job by seven. . . .

We organized women's groups, young women's groups. They liked to dance and I loved to dance so we went dancing together and I talked to them about the union. The women were interested after a while when they saw that the union could actually win things for them, bread and butter things. . . .

Later on, during the war, there was one department where I got the women but couldn't get the guys in. They hung out in the tavern and so I went there and started talking with them. I didn't like beer, but I'd drink ginger ale and told them to show me how to play pool. I learned to play pool and I got the men into the union. I did what they did. I went into the taverns. I became a bowler and I joined the league. The only thing I didn't do is rejoin the Catholic Church. . . .

If you are an honest leader, recognized and supported by the workers, you could raise and talk about issues. You couldn't talk about socialism and what it meant in an abstract sense. You had to talk about it in terms of what it would mean for that person. We learned that you can't manipulate people but that you really had to be concerned with the interests and needs of the people. However, you also had to have a platform—a projection of where you were going.

At certain times we felt that the union wasn't enough. We worked in the stockyards with blacks but when we came home, we went to lily-white neighborhoods and the blacks went to their ghetto. How were we going to bridge that? There was unemployment and people were being laid off. There were many young people who didn't get jobs. There was no concern on the part of anyone, the city fathers, the church, the union and others, about the needs of young people and places to play. What are unemployed young people going to do?

• • •

Another of the rank-and-file leaders interviewed by the Lynds was Sylvia Woods, a pioneer in the struggle of African-American and women trade unionists. Here she describes how she and others confronted racism and sexism and organized under the difficult conditions of the depression.

Sylvia Woods, "You Have to Fight for Freedom" (1973)[11]

I was born March 15, 1909. My father was a roofer. In those days they put slates on the roofs and he was a slater. It was a very skilled job. You had to nail the slate. They used to make a fancy diamond with different colors. . . .

And he was a union man. There was a dual union—one for whites and one for blacks. He said we should have one big union but a white and a black is better than none. He was making big money—eight dollars a day. I used to brag that "My father makes eight dollars a day." But he taught me that "You got to belong to the union, even if it's a black union. If I wasn't in the union I wouldn't make eight dollars a day." . . .

When I was maybe ten years old, I changed schools. On the way to school, I had to go through a park that was for white people only. We could walk through the park but we couldn't stop at all, just pass through it. There were swings in this park and, oh, I so much wanted sometimes to just stop and swing a little while, but we couldn't because we were black. I would walk through this park to my school where there weren't any swings.

Every morning all the kids would line up according to classrooms and we would have prayers and sing the Star Spangled Banner and then we'd march to our respective groups after this business.

I decided I wasn't going to sing the Star Spangled Banner. I just stood there every morning and I didn't sing it. One morning, one of the teachers noticed that I wasn't doing it. So she very quietly called me over and asked me why didn't I sing the Star Spangled Banner. I said I just didn't feel like singing it. So she said, "Well then you have to go in to the principal and explain that to him. All of the children in the school take part and you've got to do it too." OK, I went in to the principal and he asked me why I wasn't singing the Star Spangled Banner. . . .

Finally I told him. "Because it says 'The land of the free and the home of the brave' and this is not the land of the free. I don't know who's brave but I'm not going to sing it any more." Then he said, "Why you've been singing it all the time haven't you? How come you want to stop now?" And I told him about coming through the park and if I could not swing in those swings in the park, and I couldn't sit in the park, and I could only walk in Shakespeare Park, then it couldn't be the land of the free. "Who's free?" He didn't say anything.

Then he said, "Well, you could pledge allegiance to your flag." I said, "It's not my flag. The flag is with freedom. If the land is free and the flag is mine, then how come I can't do like the white kids?" . . . .

[Later on] I [moved to Chicago and] got this job in a laundry. The first morning I went there, this guy asked me, "Did you ever work in a laundry before?" I said, "No." He said, "Well there's no point in your coming here because we only hire people who know how to work in a laundry." I said "OK" and I left. The next morning I went back because I didn't know any place else to go. "Weren't you here yesterday?" "Yes." He said, "Well, I told you that we don't hire people who don't know how to work in a laundry." I said, "Well, maybe you'll need somebody one day. I'll come back tomorrow." So the next day I came back. When I walked in the door he said, "Come with me." He took me upstairs and he said to the foreman, "Teach her how to shake out."

You had to shake these clothes out and put them on long poles. You know how things look when they come out of a wringer. You had to shake them out so that they could run them through the mangle. Two girls put the things through the mangle. One girl did the sheets and the other did the small things like towels and pillow slips. I worked really hard. I kept those poles full. The women would say, "You mean you never worked before?" I'd say, "I never had a job before." . . .

One day [a friend] . . . called me up at home. "Hurry up and come on over here. There's a man here says he'll hire you." We always thought that this guy had some connection with the Communist Party. He hired everything black that came in. Martina went to him and she said, "I have a friend who wants to work in the factory and she's been coming and coming and they never will hire her." He said, "Tell her to come. I'll hire her." So he hired me. When I walked in the door of the plant I said, "I'm going to make you sorry for every day that I walked around to this shop hoping to get hired!"

I worked on the carburetors. I was on an assembly line that had two sides and a belt ran down the center and I was burring—taking all of the burrs off the carburetor. Right across from me was a young Polish woman named Eva. She was going to show me how to do it. We did about ten of them. Then I said, "You don't have to help me any more." She said, "Do you think that you can keep up with the line?" "I can keep up with the line." So I did. Eva and I became real good friends because when she got stuck I would reach over and help her.

One night she said, "There's a union meeting tonight. Will you go with me to the union meeting?" And I said, "Ahh, I'm tired." She said, "Aw, come on and go." She said, "I want to buy you a drink anyway," because I had helped her. I said, "OK, you can buy me a drink but I don't want to go to a union meeting."

So we went to this tavern and then we started talking union. I got kind of high, you know, and "OK, we'll go to the union meeting."

This was United Automobile Workers. I was the only black there. All the stewards were coming in and saying how they couldn't organize the workers: "I can't get anybody to join"; "So-and-So said the union is no good. . . ."

I said, "You know why you can't get anybody to join? Because you don't have anything to sell them. You aren't selling them union. You're letting them sell you non-union from what I hear you saying here. You'll never get the workers to join the union if you let them tell you the union isn't any good. I wouldn't join a union that's no good either." A steward must sell the union, telling the workers how much strength they have when they are organized.

I looked at this guy who was the organizer and his face was just lighting up. "Union! What do you mean? I'll bet you if I was the steward I could sign them up." The next day I was elected steward of my department. Two nights later everybody in that department was signed up.

I only joined the union for what it could do for black people. I didn't care anything about whites. I didn't care if they lined them all up and shot them down—I wished they would! I had no knowledge of the unity of white and black. I had no knowledge that you can't go any place alone. The only thing that I was interested in was what happened to black people. . . .

Every night I would have departmental meetings. The women were coming off the night shift at three o'clock in the morning. They didn't have to go home, so this was some recreation for them. We'd have beer and sandwiches and coffee and cake or whatever. We'd sit there and eat and talk. People would voice their grievances about the shop, home, family or whatever. They'd love to come. Every night we met, department by department. This kept us organized.

We had good union meetings too. We would have speakers. Either I would speak or Mamie [Harris] would speak or we would invite a speaker to come in. We would talk about trade unionism. How were trade unions organized? What was the very beginning? How come they were organized? We would talk about the structure of the international union, how it was set up and how it worked and why it worked like it did, how the CIO was born. We would have a question period where the workers could ask questions. We would discuss current events. . . .

Two years after the plant closed up, we still had union meetings. We would have full crowds. We were fighting for [unemployment] compensation. We made ninety cents an hour and some, of course, made more. You would go to get your compensation and they'd offer you a job. You weren't supposed to take a job that was less than the rate you had been getting. We would fight these cases. They would throw them out and we would go down to the arbitration board and fight the cases and win them. We could call a union meeting and bring in maybe 75 percent of our plant two years after it closed down. We had representation in the international because we still had the workers together.

The main thing that I would say is that you have to have faith in people. You know, I had very little faith in white people. I think that I had faith in black people. But you have to have faith in people, period. The whites, probably a lot of them feel towards blacks like I felt. But people, as a rule, come through.

You have to tell people things that they can see. Then they'll say, "Oh, I never thought of that," or "I have never seen it like that." I have seen it done. Like Tennessee. He hated black people. A poor sharecropper who only came up here to earn enough money to go back and buy the land he had been renting. After the plant closed he went back there with a different outlook on life. He danced with a black woman. He was elected steward and you just couldn't say anything to a black person. So, I have seen people change. This is the faith you've got to have in people.

The big job is teaching them. And I was not patient. That is another thing, you must be patient. I just didn't have any patience. If a worker did something, "To hell with you. You didn't come to the last union meeting, so don't tell me when you have a grievance. You just handle it the best way you can by yourself." But you can't do that. "You better go talk to Mamie Harris because I don't talk to non-union people and folks who don't come to the union meeting. Don't talk to me." This I learned was wrong. You have to be patient with people. People have to learn and they can't learn unless we give them a chance.

• • •

In the 1930s, tens of thousands of laid off and discouraged workers formed councils to fight for the rights of unemployed workers. These unemployed councils marched, supported strikes, and also supported anti-eviction struggles, like the one recounted here by the essayist and activist Kim Chernin, whose mother, Rose Chernin, became active in anti-eviction protests in the Bronx, and told her the story of their efforts.

Rose Chernin on Organizing the Unemployed in the Bronx in the 1930s (1949)[12]

The things we take for granted now, part of the American way of life, these were revolutionary ideas when we began to demand them in the thirties. We wanted unemployment insurance; we wanted home relief, hot meals for children in schools, and housing for the destitute people living in the city dumps.

In that time, who heard of the eight-hour day? If a man would be hurt on the job, you think the employer would pay a cent to him? Why should he care? There was always another poor man to take his place. Even the idea of a union was in this time a new concept in the world. No one expected decent wages. The others, with the privilege, were born up there. But we were on the bottom. To us, the idea that we had the right to strike was something hard even to imagine.

So what could be done about all this? How could a person, a woman not even five feet tall, change the world?

I'll tell you. It's a good story, because in those days we began to organize. We formed Unemployed Councils. They were spontaneous peoples' organizations and I want you to know about them because I helped to organize them from the first days. In this activity I was already involved before I joined the Communist Party.

We would open an office in the middle of a neighborhood. We'd come in during the morning, make coffee, people would bring doughnuts and we would talk. Suddenly another person would come in and we'd say, "Hi, who are you?"

"I was just laid off."

And you should have heard the shout: "Hooray! Another one laid off. Wonderful."

He would look at us as though we were crazy. Why should we celebrate that he was laid off? For him it meant no wages, no rent, no place to sleep, nothing to eat. So why were we excited? We said, "We're glad you're here. We'll have one more person to distribute leaflets."

This was the way we changed the terrible thing that was happening to this man, and to all of us, into productive action. We got into control of our lives. We were no longer victims.

It's so simple. I used to wonder why other people didn't see it, too. You cannot fail. Basically, failure is impossible; already, just in being together, you have changed the personal tragedy, this despair, this hopelessness, into a collective endeavor.

Our main task was to try to get a congressman to introduce a bill for unemployment insurance. We circulated a petition, house to house, in the tenements of the Bronx.

A typical encounter would go like this: I and another person would enter the building and knock on the first door we came to. Someone, usually a man, would open the door. Just a crack at first. Then, when he saw we were not the landlord, he'd open it wider. I'd say, "We're here circulating a petition asking a congressman to introduce a bill in Congress. We want unemployment insurance and we think we can get the government to give it to us. Is there anybody unemployed in this family?"

"Are you kidding? Everybody is unemployed in this family." Or they'd say, "Most of us are unemployed, one is working but he expects to be laid off by the end of the week."

We told them, "We, too, are unemployed workers and we want Congress to pass a bill giving us either jobs or wages."

So they'd say, not believing, "You're asking the government to give us money without working?" People just couldn't believe we were asking for this.

And we'd answer, "Yes, we're asking the government to give us jobs. If they can't give us jobs, they have to support us."

"But you're asking for socialism."

"We're asking for jobs or money."

We organized around our basic needs. We could speak very easily to people because we also were working people. I always found it strange when people didn't join us. I used to think about this because to me organization seemed so essential. You wonder, maybe, why I became a Communist. But I used to wonder why everyone did not. Basically, I felt that those who failed to join us had no confidence in themselves or in the fact that we could change the system. They are the ones who say, "We're just poor people. What can we do?" We would hear this when we went about knocking on the doors.

I, on the other hand, when I talked to people, could convince them to struggle against their conditions. I believed in this struggle. That is all it takes to be an organizer. Belief in our power.

Take an example: We felt the one thing the system feared was angry women. We wanted milk for the children. So, we would get twenty or thirty women together. We'd go out early in the morning. We would come into the borough hall. We would demand to speak to an alderman. Each one of us came with a child in the carriage. Nina was three or four years old; she always came with me.

Who could forget it, a sight like this? There was a woman in a red sweater, rolled up at the sleeves. Another one with a kerchief on the head. The faces with a look of determination. And the children, this one in a blue cap the grandma knitted. Nina had a little open face with merry eyes. And we would go stepping together, all the women on the left foot, then all on the right. Singing, chanting: "We want milk. Milk for the children."

We would go about the streets advertising the neighborhood councils. We'd ask people to come and told them to bring whatever they could spare. There was always something to eat in the councils. People would drop in, we'd get them to work on a pamphlet, we would involve them in a conversation. Coming off the street in those days, out of that despair, you can imagine the impact the council made upon them.

The women were organized to monitor the prices of food all the time. If an item became too expensive in a particular store, we immediately went on strike. Again, we came with the children in the carriage. We picketed with the sign: DON'T PATRONIZE THIS GROCERY. THEY ARE CHARGING TOO MUCH FOR BREAD.

These strikes were very successful. Nobody would cross our picket lines.

The same things were happening in Brooklyn, in Manhattan, in Harlem. In Harlem the starvation was legion and soup kitchens couldn't supply the people with enough food. We used to move whatever we could from the council to Harlem.

This struggle of people against their conditions, that is where you find the meaning in life. In the worst situations, you are together with people. If there were five apples, we cut them ten ways and everybody ate. If somebody had a quarter, he went down to the corner and bought some bread and brought it back into the council.

Life changes when you are together in this way, when you are united. You lose the fear of being alone. You cannot solve these problems when you are alone. They become overwhelming. When you are standing, one to one, with an employer, he has all the power and you have none. But together, we felt our strength, and we could laugh. Someone who knew how to sing would start singing. Others would know how to dance. There we were, unemployed people, but we were dancing.

In those years I was happy. Happy, you say? With the unemployment, the evictions, the high prices of food? But that's how it was. And why? In those years I became what I have been all my life since then. And from this maybe comes happiness, what else?

If you're an organizer and you see how successfully people are coming together you feel fulfilled. We were very successful in our activities. We kept prices down, we kept pressure on the congressmen, we were making people conscious of their identity as workers, and we were winning rent strikes. . . .

By that time the Unemployed Councils were well known: our workers were everywhere, leading demonstrations, circulating petitions, speaking on street corners. So we would go into a building, introduce ourselves, and ask the people to organize. We said, "As long as we strike we certainly don't pay rent. Let's say we're striking for three months. That rent will never be paid."

The people listened, the idea appealed to them. We promised that we would fight the evictions and help take care of the people who were thrown out. In those days you would walk down the street and see whole families with their children sitting on the sidewalk surrounded by furniture.

When an entire building was organized and willing to participate in a strike, we formed negotiating committees for the tenants, put up large signs in every window facing the street, and picketed the house. The signs read: RENT STRIKE. DON'T RENT APARTMENTS IN THIS BUILDING.

The landlord, of course, would rather die than give in to the tenants' demands. So the strike began. We knew that one day he would give some eviction notices. But he could never evict everyone. It cost too much.

On the day of the eviction we would tell all the men to leave the building. We knew that the police were rough and would beat them up. It was the women who remained in the apartments, in order to resist. We went out onto the fire escapes and spoke through bullhorns to the crowd that gathered below.

In the Bronx you could get two hundred people together if you just looked up at the sky. As soon as the police came to begin the eviction, we roped off the street and people gathered. The police put machine guns on the roofs, they pointed them down at the people in the street.

We, meanwhile, were standing out on the balcony. I would address the crowd gathered in the street below: "People, fellow workers. We are the wives of unemployed men and the police are evicting us. Today we are being evicted. Tomorrow it will be you. So stand by and watch. What is happening to us will happen to you. We have no jobs. We can't afford food. Our rents are too high. The marshal has brought the police to carry out our furniture. Are you going to let it happen?"

Or sometimes we would address the workers who had been brought to take the furniture: "We are talking to you, you men who have come here to throw out the furniture of unemployed workers. Who are you? You, too, are unemployed men who have had to take this job in order to eat. We don't blame you. You are one of us. We represent the Unemployed Council and last night we made a collection among the unemployed. We have enough money to pay you off. How much are you going to get for evicting an unemployed worker? Five dollars? Six dollars? We have the money for you. Come up here without the police and without the marshal and we will pay you off. Look at the marshal standing there. Is he working? Let him do the work."

And so we would harangue. We could see the men hesitating. We would continue: "We women are standing here with the furniture that is to be evicted. The water is hot in our kettles. The doors are locked. We're not letting you in."

Often, the hired men would come up anyway. Our doors were locked but they would break them in. We were behind those doors, with our kettles. They would grab a piece of furniture on one side and we would grab it on the other. And both would start pulling. Meanwhile we would say: "Here, here is the money. Leave the furniture."

Some would take the money and go. Sometimes we poured the hot water on the men. Sometimes they would hit us. And then we would run out onto the fire escape, grab the bullhorn, and shout to the crowd: "They're hitting us. They're big men and they're hitting us. But we're not going to let them move the furniture. They can't overcome us. We shall win."

Sometimes, they'd get so disgusted with all this fighting and hollering they'd take the furniture from the apartment but leave it on the landing. That was a victory. We'd stay there and wait for the husbands to return and then we'd put the furniture back into the apartment. We'd put a new lock on the door and the landlord would have to get a new eviction notice. He'd call the marshal and the whole thing would start all over again.

Our fight was successful. The rents came down, the evicted families returned to their apartments, the landlord would stop fighting us. Sometimes we failed and the furniture was carried into the street. Immediately we would cover it with a tarpaulin so it wouldn't get spoiled, and then we'd hold a mass meeting on the furniture, using it as a platform. We were only waiting for the police to leave. As soon as they were gone, the people standing around would pick up the furniture and carry it right back into the building. We'd break the lock, put back the furniture, install a new lock, and the landlord would have to go through the whole procedure another time.

Within two years we had rent control in the Bronx. That's the way it was in those days.

• • •

In the mid-1930s, a wave of sit-down strikes spread across the country. Workers figured out that if they sat down and occupied the factories, they could not only stop production, they could prevent strikebreakers from coming in to replace them. Tens of thousands of workers in various industries joined the strike wave, usually demanding better working conditions and recognition of new industrial unions, like the United Auto Workers (UAW). One of the most important of these sit-downs took place in the auto factories of Flint, Michigan, in 1937. Workers in Flint held out for weeks and won a major victory against General Motors, which was forced to recognize the UAW as the sole bargaining representative of workers in its plants. Decades after the strike, the socialist Genora (Johnson) Dollinger described the sit-downs and their impact.

Genora (Johnson) Dollinger, *Striking Flint: Genora (Johnson) Dollinger Remembers the 1936–37 GM Sit-Down Strike* (February 1995)[13]

Conditions in Flint before the strike were very, very depressing for working people. We had a large influx of workers come into the city from the deep South. They came north to find jobs, because there was no work back home. They came with their furniture strapped on old jalopies and they'd move into the cheapest housing that they could find. Usually these were just little one or two-room structures with no inside plumbing and no inside heating arrangements. They just had kerosene heaters to heat their wash water, their bath water, and their homes. You could smell kerosene all over their clothing. They were very poor.

One woman came from a small section of Flint around Fenton Road, where many of these poor southerners settled. She would walk the picket line in the snow in tennis shoes with no gloves. She was a wonderful person. She was there every day, and we'd have to make sure she got warmed up in the union headquarters before she went out on the picket line again.

Before the strike, the women didn't have the opportunity to participate in any activities. The small neighborhood churches were the only places they had to go to. They knew some of their neighbors and they would go to some of these little churches, but that's all. The men frequented the beer gardens and talked to other men about shop problems or whatever. They got to be shop buddies.

When you worked in the factory in those days, no one cared what your name was. You became "Whitey" if you happened to be blonde. Or you might be

"Blacky" if you had black hair. If you asked, "Well, who is he?" you'd get, "I don't know, he works in department so-and-so, Plant 4, on the line half way down." It was just "Blacky" or "Shorty" or some nickname. They were wage slaves with a complete loss of identity and rights inside the plant.

At first, when these workers were approached to join the union, they were afraid they might lose this job that was so very valuable to them. At that time, men working in the auto plants were getting around forty-five cents an hour. The younger girls that worked in the A.C. Sparkplug division of General Motors, were being paid twelve-and-a-half cents an hour to make minor car instruments. That was the only plant that employed women. . . .

They used to say, "Once you pass the gates of General Motors, forget about the United States Constitution." Workers had no rights when they entered that plant. If a foreman didn't like the way you parted your hair—or whatever he didn't like about you—you may have looked at him the wrong way, or said something that rubbed him the wrong way—he could fire you. No recourse, no nothing. And practically all foremen expected workers to bring them turkeys on Thanksgiving and gifts for Christmas and repair their motor cars and even paint their houses. The workers were kept intimidated because if they didn't comply with what the foreman told them to do, they would lose their jobs and their families would starve. You can see what a feeling of slavery and domination workers felt inside the GM plants.

Not only that, but when workers started talking about organizing, management hired lip-readers to watch the men talk to each other, even when they were right close to each other, so they could tell if they were talking union. One of our friends who was a member of the Socialist Party wore the first UAW button into the Chevrolet plant. He was fired immediately. He didn't even get to his job. They spotted the button and that was it. If you went into a beer garden or other place like that and began to talk about unions, very often you didn't get home without getting an awful beating by GM-hired thugs.

That was the condition inside the plants. Combined with the bad conditions on the outside: poor living conditions, lack of proper food, lack of proper medical attention and everything else, the auto workers came to the conclusion that there was no way they could ever escape any of this injustice without joining a union. But they didn't all decide at one time. . . .

A considerable amount of preparatory work was done before the strike. That preparatory work was done by radical parties. We had several very active organizations in Flint and Detroit: the Communist Party, the Proletarian Party, the Socialist Labor Party, the Socialist Party and the International Workers of the World (IWW). And, with the exception of the Communist Party, we all had our headquarters in the Pengelly Building, a very old building that became the major strike headquarters of the whole United Automobile Workers Union of Flint. Even as the strike was going on, we still had our rooms on the second floor, while the main activities in the auditorium were on the third floor.

Two years before the strike broke out, the Socialist Party in Flint organized the League for Industrial Democracy (LID). We held meetings in garages and in basements, secret meetings, so the people wouldn't get caught and beaten up.

As we got bigger, the Socialist Party started sending us their speakers from New York. Many of them were from the Brookwood Labor College. We put out leaflets and sold tickets for these meetings, which were held in the basement of the biggest Methodist church and in the Masonic Temple.

We held lectures in socialism mainly, plus labor history and current events, focusing on what was happening politically. Those were very popular meetings. We would get three and four hundred people at some of our meetings.

This was all before the strike, in preparation for when the struggle actually broke out, when the workers couldn't take any more and rebelled. A core of socialists understood that this would eventually happen. . . .

The first sit-down was on December 30 in the small Fisher Body Plant 2 over a particularly big grievance that had occurred. The workers were at the point where they had just had enough, and under a militant leadership, they sat down. When the UAW leaders in the big Fisher Body Plant 1 heard about the sit-down in Fisher 2, they sat down, also. That took real guts, and it took political leadership. The leaders of the political parties knew what they had to do because they'd studied labor history and the ruthlessness of the corporations. . . .

After the first sit-down started, I went down to see what I could do to help. I was either on the picket lines or up at the Pengelly Building all the time, but some of the strike leaders didn't know who I was and didn't know that I had been teaching classes in unionism and so on. So they said, "Go to the kitchen. We need a lot of help out there." They didn't know what else to tell a woman to do. I said, "You've got a lot of little, skinny men around here who can't stand to be out on the cold picket lines for very long. They can peel potatoes as well as women can." I turned down the idea of kitchen duty.

Instead, I organized a children's picket line. I got Bristol board and paints, and I was painting signs for this children's picket line. One of my socialist comrades came up and said, "Hey, Genora, what are you doing here?" I said, "I'm doing your job." Since he was a professional sign painter, I turned the sign-painting project over to him and that was the beginning of the sign-painting department.

We could only do the children's picket line once because it was too dangerous, but we got an awful lot of favorable publicity from it, much of it international. The picture of my two-year-old son, Jarvis, holding a picket sign saying, "My daddy strikes for us little tykes," went all over the nation, and people sent me articles from French newspapers and from Germany and from other European countries. I thought it was remarkable that the news traveled so far. . . .

The company decided they had to break the strike. On January 11, they attacked the smaller Fisher Body Plant 2. I happened to be on the picket line that day, and I was amazed to see what was happening. The plant guards prevented the men from getting any food for about 24 hours. It was very cold, and they turned off the heat in the building. The men inside were very angry.

Then the company police and the city police started shooting. At first they were shooting tear gas inside the plant, but that was too difficult, so they decided to tear-gas and shoot this huge mass of picketers that had formed in front of the plant. The police were using rifles, buckshot, fire-bombs, and tear-gas canisters. It was a shock to a lot of people. We had thought that General Motors would try to freeze us out or do something in the plants, but never open fire on us right in the middle of the city.

The union picketers took their own cars and barricaded off a section so that the police couldn't get us from both ends. Then, over the radio came the equivalent of saying that there was a revolution starting in Flint. With all the propaganda saying, "The communists are coming into the city to take over the union," people gathered in vast numbers on both sides of this battle. When the police misfired, tear-gas and bullets went over our heads into the crowds which had came out to watch. It was very frightening. People would run away and dart into restaurants up the street.

The battle continued for quite some time. Workers overturned police cars to make barricades. They ran to pick up the fire bombs thrown at them and hurl them back at the police. It was very, very cold. The men in the plant were using fire hoses against the police, and when the water ran down, it would quickly ice over.

I saw one of our Socialist Party members, Fred Stevens, jump over a gutter where there was icy water flowing down. A little stream of blood spurted down his leg into the water. I couldn't get my wits together for a moment.

The men wanted to get me out of the way. You know that old "protect the women and children" business. If there are any women or children around, usher them right out, protect them. I told them, "Get away from me. I've got as many weapons as you have." I was the only woman who stayed.

The battle went on for hours. Throughout the whole time, the sound car was giving instructions and trying to bolster the courage of the men inside the plant as well as the picketers on the outside. Victor Reuther spoke for a while and then other men substituted for him, giving him relief. But there were only the voices of men. At one point, Victor came over and told us that the batteries in the sound car were running down.

Lights went on in my head. I thought, "I've never used a loudspeaker to address a large crowd of people, but I've got to tell them that there are women down here." So I asked him, "Victor, can I take the loudspeaker?" He said, "We've got nothing to lose."

The first thing I did was attack the police. I called to them, "Cowards! Cowards! Shooting into the bellies of unarmed men and firing at the mothers of children." Then everything became quiet. There was silence on both sides of the line. I thought, "The women can break this up." So I appealed to the women in the crowd, "Break through those police lines and come down here and stand beside your husbands and your brothers and your uncles and your sweethearts."

In the dusk, I could barely see one woman struggling to come forward. A cop had grabbed her by the back of her coat. She just pulled out of that coat and started walking down to the battle zone. As soon as that happened there were other women and men who followed. The police wouldn't shoot people in the back as they were coming down, so that was the end of the battle. When those spectators came into the center of the battle and the police retreated, there was a big roar of victory. That battle became known as the Battle of Bulls Run because we made the cops run. . . .

Following the strike, the auto worker became a different human being. The women that had participated actively became a different type of woman, a different type from any we had ever known anywhere in the labor movement and certainly not in the city of Flint. They carried themselves with a different walk, their heads were high, and they had confidence in themselves. They were not only mentally different, but physically different. If you saw one of those women in the beginning and then saw her just a short period after going through this experience, learning and feeling that she had things she could fit together in her life, it would be an entirely different woman.

• • •

John Steinbeck's novel *The Grapes of Wrath* sold out its first printing in April 1939, and was soon selling 10,000 copies a week. The story of migrant farm workers—trekking across the country from Oklahoma to California in search of work—symbolized for many the situation of workers around the country. It not only encouraged a belief in unionism, but prompted thinking about more fundamental change. In this scene, from Chapter 28, the novel's protagonist, Tom Joad, talks about "people livin' like pigs, an' the good rich lan' layin' fallow, or maybe one fella with a million acres, while a hunderd thousan' good farmers is starvin'."

John Steinbeck, *The Grapes of Wrath* (1939)[14]

Ma went down on her hands and knees. She felt sand under her, and then the black inside of the mound no longer touched her, and she felt Tom's blanket on the ground. He arranged the vines in place again. It was lightless in the cave.

"Where are you, Ma?"

"Here. Right here. Talk soft, Tom."

"Don't worry. I been livin' like a rabbit some time."

She heard him unwrap his tin plate.

"Pork chops," she said. "And fry potatoes."

"God Awmighty, an' still warm."

Ma could not see him at all in the blackness, but she could hear him chewing, tearing at the meat and swallowing.

"It's a pretty good hide-out," he said.

Ma said uneasily, "Tom—Ruthie tol' about you." She heard him gulp.

"Ruthie? What for?"

"Well, it wasn' her fault. Got in a fight, an' says her brother'll lick that other girl's brother. You know how they do. An' she tol' that her brother killed a man an' was hidin'."

Tom was chuckling. "With me I was always gonna get Uncle John after 'em, but he never would do it. That's jus' kid talk, Ma. That's awright."

"No, it ain't," Ma said. "Them kids'll tell it aroun' an' then the folks'll hear, an' they'll tell aroun', an' pretty soon, well, they liable to get men out to look, jus' in case. Tom, you got to go away."

"That's what I said right along. I was always scared somebody'd see you put stuff in that culvert, an' then they'd watch."

"I know. But I wanted you near. I was scared for you. I ain't seen you. Can't see you now. How's your face?"

"Gettin' well quick."

"Come clost, Tom. Let me feel it. Come clost." He crawled near. Her reaching hand found his head in the blackness and her fingers moved down to his nose, and then over his left cheek. "You got a bad scar, Tom. An' your nose is all crooked."

"Maybe that's a good thing. Nobody wouldn't know me, maybe. If my prints wasn't on record, I'd be glad." He went back to his eating.

"Hush," she said. "Listen!"

"It's the wind, Ma. Jus' the wind." The gust poured down the stream, and the trees rustled under its passing.

She crawled close to his voice. "I wanta touch ya again, Tom. It's like I'm blin', it's so dark. I wanta remember, even if it's on'y my fingers that remember. You got to go away, Tom."

"Yeah! I knowed it from the start."

"We made purty good," she said. "I been squirrelin' money away. Hol' out your han', Tom. I got seven dollars here."

"I ain't gonna take ya money," he said. "I'll get 'long all right."

"Hol' out ya han', Tom. I ain't gonna sleep none if you got no money. Maybe you got to take a bus, or somepin. I want you should go a long ways off, three-four hunderd miles."

"I ain't gonna take it."

"Tom," she said sternly. "You take this money. You hear me? You got no right to cause me pain."

"You ain't playin' fair," he said.

"I thought maybe you could go to a big city. Los Angeles, maybe. They wouldn' never look for you there."

"Hm-m," he said. "Lookie, Ma. I been all day an' all night hidin' alone. Guess who I been thinkin' about? Casy! He talked a lot. Used ta bother me. But now I been thinkin' what he said, an' I can remember—all of it. Says one time he went out in the wilderness to find his own soul, an' he foun' he didn' have no soul that was his'n. Says he foun' he jus' got a little piece of a great big soul. Says a wilderness ain't no good, 'cause his little piece of a soul wasn't no good 'less it was with the rest, an' was whole. Funny how I remember. Didn' think I was even listenin'. But I know now a fella ain't no good alone."

"He was a good man," Ma said.

Tom went on, "He spouted out some Scripture once, an' it didn' soun' like no hell-fire Scripture. He tol' it twicet, an' I remember it. Says it's from the Preacher."

"How's it go, Tom?"

"Goes, 'Two are better than one, because they have a good reward for their labor. For if they fall, the one will lif' up his fellow, but woe to him that is alone when he falleth, for he hath not another to help him up.' That's part of her."

"Go on," Ma said. "Go on, Tom."

"Jus' a little bit more. 'Again, if two lie together, then they have heat: but how can one be warm alone? And if one prevail against him, two shall withstand him, and a three-fold cord is not quickly broken.'"

"An' that's Scripture?"

"Casy said it was. Called it the Preacher."

"Hush—listen."

"On'y the wind, Ma. I know the wind. An' I got to thinkin', Ma—most of the preachin' is about the poor we shall have always with us, an' if you got nothin', why, jus' fol' your hands an' to hell with it, you gonna git ice cream on gol' plates when you're dead. An' then this here Preacher says two get a better reward for their work."

"Tom," she said. "What you aimin' to do?"

He was quiet for a long time. "I been thinkin' how it was in that gov'ment camp, how our folks took care a theirselves, an' if they was a fight they fixed it theirself; an' they wasn't no cops wagglin' their guns, but they was better order than them cops ever give. I been a-wonderin' why we can't do that all over. Throw out the cops that ain't our people. All work together for our own thing— all farm our own lan'."

"Tom," Ma repeated, "what you gonna do?"

"What Casy done," he said.

"But they killed him."

"Yeah," said Tom. "He didn' duck quick enough. He wasn' doing nothin' against the law, Ma. I been thinkin' a hell of a lot, thinkin' about our people livin' like pigs, an' the good rich lan' layin' fallow, or maybe one fella with a million acres, while a hunderd thousan' good farmers is starvin'. An' I been wonderin' if all our folks got together an' yelled, like them fellas yelled, only a few of 'em at the Hooper ranch—"

Ma said, "Tom, they'll drive you, an' cut you down like they done to young Floyd."

"They gonna drive me anyways. They drivin' all our people."

"You don't aim to kill nobody, Tom?"

"No. I been thinkin', long as I'm a outlaw anyways, maybe I could—Hell, I ain't thought it out clear, Ma. Don' worry me now. Don' worry me."

They sat silent in the coal-black cave of vines. Ma said, "How'm I gonna know 'bout you? They might kill ya an' I wouldn' know. They might hurt ya. How'm I gonna know?"

Tom laughed uneasily, "Well, maybe like Casy says, a fella ain't got a soul of his own, but on'y a piece of a big one—an' then—"

"Then what, Tom?"

"Then it don' matter. Then I'll be all aroun' in the dark. I'll be ever'where— wherever you look. Wherever they's a fight so hungry people can eat, I'll be there. Wherever they's a cop beatin' up a guy, I'll be there. If Casy knowed, why, I'll be in the way guys yell when they're mad an'—I'll be in the way kids laugh when they're hungry an' they know supper's ready. An' when our folks eat the stuff they raise an' live in the houses they build—why, I'll be there. See? God, I'm talkin' like Casy. Comes of thinkin' about him so much. Seems like I can see him sometimes."

"I don' un'erstan'," Ma said. "I don' really know."

"Me neither," said Tom. "It's jus' stuff I been thinkin' about. Get thinkin' a lot when you ain't movin' aroun'. You got to get back, Ma."

"You take the money then."

He was silent for a moment. "Awright," he said.

"An', Tom, later—when it's blowed over, you'll come back. You'll find us?"

"Sure," he said. "Now you better go. Here, gimme your han'." He guided her toward the entrance. Her fingers clutched his wrist. He swept the vines aside and followed her out. "Go up to the field till you come to a sycamore on the edge, an' then cut acrost the stream. Good-by."

"Good-by," she said, and she walked quickly away. Her eyes were wet and burning, but she did not cry.

• • •

Woody Guthrie, born in Oklahoma in 1912 in a poor and troubled family, was one of the great folk singers of the twentieth century, a model for the socially conscious singer-songwriters of the 1960s like Bob Dylan, Joan Baez, Pete Seeger, and Phil Ochs. In 1940, Guthrie penned a response to the patriotic song "God Bless America" by Irving Berlin. "This Land Is Your Land," though quite radical in its spirit, became a patriotic anthem in its own right, and has been printed in textbooks and sung in schools around the country. But in many cases, the song's fourth and sixth stanzas, which speak to Guthrie's sense of social justice, have been suppressed.

Woody Guthrie, "This Land Is Your Land" (February 1940)[15]

This land is your land, this land is my land
From California to the New York Island,
From the Redwood Forest, to the Gulf stream waters,
This land was made for you and me.

As I went walking that ribbon of highway
And saw above me that endless skyway,
And saw below me the golden valley, I said:
This land was made for you and me.

I roamed and rambled and followed my footsteps
To the sparkling sands of her diamond deserts,
And all around me, a voice was sounding:
This land was made for you and me.

Was a high wall there that tried to stop me
A sign was painted said: Private Property,
But on the back side it didn't say nothing—
That side was made for you and me.

When the sun come shining, then I was strolling
In wheat fields waving and dust clouds rolling;
The voice was chanting as the fog was lifting:
This land was made for you and me.

One bright sunny morning in the shadow of the steeple
By the Relief Office I saw my people—
As they stood hungry, I stood there wondering if
This land was made for you and me.

World War II and McCarthyism

Paul Fussell, "'Precision Bombing Will Win the War'" (1989)

Yuri Kochiyama, "Then Came the War" (1991)

Yamaoka Michiko, "Eight Hundred Meters from the Hypocenter" (1992)

United States Strategic Bombing Survey, Summary Report (Pacific War) (July 1, 1946)

Admiral Gene Larocque Speaks to Studs Terkel About "The Good War" (1985)

Kurt Vonnegut, *Slaughterhouse-Five* (1969)

Paul Robeson's Unread Statement before the House Committee on Un-American Activities (June 12, 1956)

Peter Seeger, "Thou Shall Not Sing" (1989)

I. F. Stone, "But It's Not Just Joe McCarthy" (March 15, 1954)

The Final Letter from Ethel and Julius Rosenberg to Their Children (June 19, 1953)

World War I had given war a bad name. But World War II had a moral core absent in the previous conflict. This was the "good war." It was a war against great evils: the Nazi system, the invasion of European countries, the Holocaust against the Jews, the Japanese cruelties in China. Despite the initial reluctance of Americans to enter the war, the attack on Pearl Harbor brought a surge of support for military action. It was probably the most popular war the United States had ever fought.

And yet, when it was over, although no one questioned the evils of Nazism, there were questions to be raised about the moral purity of the Allies, racial segregation in the U.S. army, putting Japanese Americans in concentration camps. There was the ruthless bombing of civilian populations in Germany and Japan: the devastation of Dresden, the firebombing of Tokyo, and the atomic bombs killing hundreds of thousands in Hiroshima and Nagasaki. Altogether the bombings killed more than a million civilians.

In the years that followed the war, the promise of a new world free of militarism and war, or racism and inequality, was not fulfilled. Instead, there were now two great powers, the Soviet Union and the United States, possessing thousands of nuclear weapons, threatening the world with destruction in what was called a "cold war."

In the United States, a hysterical fear of communism led to the suppression of free speech: jailing of dissidents, inquisition by congressional committees, surveillance of ordinary citizens by the FBI—a phenomenon which came to be known as McCarthyism.

But there were Americans who insisted on speaking their minds, and who kept alive the idea of democracy.

$$\bullet \; \bullet \; \bullet$$

Very few writers have dared to question the purity of the "good war." One of them is Paul Fussell. As he writes in the preface to his book *Wartime*, "For the past fifty years the Allied war has been sanitized and romanticized almost beyond recognition by the sentimental, the loony patriotic, the ignorant, and the bloodthirsty." Here Fussell dismantles the myths about "precision bombing," repeated again and again since World War II.

Paul Fussell, "'Precision Bombing Will Win the War'" (1989)[1]

A panacea was the natural thing for the audience at home to believe in, since for years it had been lulled into comfort by the conviction that the war could be won by shrewd Yankee technological expedients, like, for example, bombing from costly airplanes flying at safe altitudes. This misapprehension had been in large part promoted by the American government itself. Witness a popular official pamphlet designating the bomber as The Weapon of Ultimate Victory. It bears no date, but its insisting that "America cannot lose this war!" suggests the end of 1942, when the issue seemed rather in doubt. The weapon of ultimate victory is specifically the B-17 Flying Fortress, "the mightiest bomber ever built." It is a precision instrument, "equipped with the incredibly accurate Norden bomb sight, which hits a 25-foot circle from 20,000 feet." And the safety of the crew is strongly stressed. One picture caption reads: "Safe within the strong fuselage of his bomber, this master-gunner aims his heavy [50-caliber] weapon." It is as if no such thing as flak had been invented. (During 1942 the U.S. Army Air Corps had called on the War Writers Board to produce materials which might "remove the false impression that the tail gunner's job, which is a hazardous one, is necessarily a shortcut to suicide.") The great height ("seven miles") from which it operates enables the Flying Fortress to "make daylight raids with a greater margin of safety than any other bombing plane." The altitudes at which it will fly guarantee that this bomber will constitute "the poorest target yet developed." Confronted with this advertising, only a deep cynic or sadist could have predicted in 1942 that before the war ended the burnt and twisted bits of almost 22,000 of these Allied bombers would strew the fields of Europe and Asia, attended by the pieces of almost 110,000 airmen. In 1942 it was impossible to imagine the future multitudes empowered to say with the bomber crewmen in Randall Jarrell's "Losses,"

> our bodies lay among
> The people we had killed and never seen.

The fact was that bombing proved so grossly inaccurate that the planes had to fly well within anti-aircraft range to hit anywhere near the target, and even then they very often missed it entirely. As the war went on, "precision bombing" became a comical oxymoron relished by bomber crews with a sense of black humor. It became obvious to everyone except the home folks reading *Life* and *The Saturday Evening Post* that although you could destroy lots of things with bombs, they weren't necessarily the things you had in mind. Navigation through winds and clouds and turbulence presented such problems that as early as August, 1941, it was clear to even the most naive in RAF [the British Royal Air Force] Bomber Command that on a typical mission "only one in ten of the bombers found its way to within five miles of the assigned target." In the first German raids on London, when 500 tons of bombs were dropped, only half fell on the land at all, and only 30 tons hit London. The popular broadcaster J. B. Priestley imagined egotistically that one of the main German targets in this raid was Broadcasting House, where he performed, when actually the Germans were lucky to hit anything in London at all.

One memorable ironic action occurred on May 10, 1940, when a Luftwaffe squadron, setting out to bomb Dijon, by some error dropped its load on its own civilians in Freiburg-im-Breisgau, killing fifty-seven of them. In instantly imputing this atrocity (as it seemed then) to the French, and later to the British, the German propagandists were exploiting the wide public belief that bombers could hit what they aimed at. Even in the air forces some people were very slow to catch on. They were those who had read, and credited, optimistic books like *The Command of the Air* (1921), by the Italian general Giulio Douhet, which asserted that bombing alone would win future wars. The assumption behind this book was that human beings could do without gross error anything they rationally proposed to do, regardless of natural forces like wind and weather and psychological disruptions of purpose like boredom, terror, and self-destructiveness. At the beginning of the war it was widely believed that poison gas would be used against civilians and that it would be dropped in bombs from aircraft. That it never was indicates less that humane considerations prevailed than that aerial bombing gradually revealed its limitations, reminding the rationalists that man did not control wind direction and force. Diehards like Sir Arthur Harris, head of RAF Bomber Command, never retreated from their stubborn position that bombing alone could force the surrender of Germany. A virtual sacred text supporting this belief was Alexander Seversky's *Victory through Air Power* (1942). When the Allies bombed the Italians on the island of Pantelleria in June, 1943, General [Carl] Spaatz, of the United States Air Corps, concluded that bombing "can reduce to the point of surrender any first-class nation now in existence, within six months. . . ."

Thus one staff officer at an RAF Group Headquarters, presented with evidence that an attack had entirely missed its mark, "scrawled across it in red, 'I do not accept this report.'" It was the grave inaccuracy of the bombers that led finally to the practice of "area bombing," whose effect was, in [Winston] Churchill's memorable euphemism, to "dehouse" the enemy population. And area bombing led inevitably, as intensification overrode scruples, to Hiroshima and Nagasaki. And yet it was not until the war was half over that the presumed accuracy of the bomber was abandoned as a propaganda ploy. The RAF flyer Robert Kee records in his diary in 1941: "I've now been on many raids where owing to total cloud it's been impossible to do anything but fling the bombs out somewhere near the flak and the searchlights, and yet I have invariably read the next morning of 'attacks on rail communications or industrial premises.'"

• • •

The Japanese-American civil rights activist, feminist, and author Yuri Kochiyama was born and raised in San Pedro, California. She and her family were among the 120,000 Japanese Americans on the West Coast who were rounded up in a wave of anti-Japanese hysteria that followed the bombing of Pearl Harbor. President Franklin D. Roosevelt signed Executive Order 9066 on February 19, 1942, giving the army the power—without warrants, indictments, or hearings—to arrest all Japanese Americans (three-fourths of them children born in the United States and therefore citizens), take them from their homes, transport them to camps far into the interior, and keep them there under prison conditions. The Supreme Court upheld this on grounds of military necessity. Not until the 1980s did the federal courts concede that a wrong had been committed. Yuri Kochiyama describes here the conditions in the detention camps.

Yuri Kochiyama, "Then Came the War" (1991)[2]

I was red, white and blue when I was growing up. I taught Sunday school, and was very, very American. But I was also very provincial. We were just kids rooting for our high school. . . .

I was nineteen at the time of the evacuation. I had just finished junior college. I was looking for a job, and didn't realize how different the school world was from the work world. In the school world, I never felt racism. But when you got into the work world, it was very difficult. This was 1941, just before the war. I finally did get a job at a department store. But for us back then, it was a big thing, because I don't think they had ever hired an Asian in a department store before. I tried, because I saw a Mexican friend who got a job there. . . .

Everything changed for me on the day Pearl Harbor was bombed. On that very day—December 7, the FBI came and they took my father. He had just come home from the hospital the day before. For several days we didn't know where they had taken him. Then we found out that he was taken to the federal prison at Terminal Island. Overnight, things changed for us. They took all men who lived near the Pacific waters, and had anything to do with fishing. A month later, they took every fisherman from Terminal Island, sixteen and over, to places—not the regular concentration camps—but to detention centers in places like South Dakota, Montana, and New Mexico. They said that all Japanese who had given money to any kind of Japanese organization would have to be taken away. At that time, many people were giving to the Japanese Red Cross. The first group was thirteen hundred Isseis—my parent's generation. They took those who were leaders of the community, or Japanese school teachers, or were teaching martial arts, or who were Buddhist priests. Those categories which would make them very "Japanesey," were picked up. This really made a tremendous impact on our lives. My twin brother was going to the University at Berkeley. He came rushing back. All of our classmates were joining up, so he volunteered to go into the service. And it seemed strange that here they had my father in prison, and there the draft board okayed my brother. He went right into the army. My other brother, who was two years older, was trying to run my father's fish market. But business was already going down, so he had to close it. He had finished college at the University of California a couple of years before.

They took my father on December 7th. The day before, he had just come home from the hospital. He had surgery for an ulcer. We only saw him once on December 13. On December 20th they said he could come home. By the time they brought him back, he couldn't talk. He made guttural sounds and we didn't know if he could hear. He was home for twelve hours. He was dying. The next morning, when we got up, they told us that he was gone. He was very sick. And I think the interrogation was very rough. My mother kept begging the authorities to let him go to the hospital until he was well, then put him back in the prison. They did finally put him there, a week or so later. But they put him in a hospital where they were bringing back all these American Merchant Marines who were hit on Wake Island. So he was the only Japanese in that hospital, so they hung a sheet around him that said, Prisoner of War. The feeling where he was was very bad.

You could see the hysteria of war. There was a sense that war could actually come to American shores. Everybody was yelling to get the "Japs" out of California. In Congress, people were speaking out. Organizations such as the Sons and Daughters of the Golden West were screaming "Get the 'Japs' out." So were the real estate people, who wanted to get the land from the Japanese farmers. The war had whipped up such a hysteria that if there was anyone for the Japanese, you didn't hear about it. I'm sure they were afraid to speak out, because they would be considered not only just "Jap" lovers, but unpatriotic.

Just the fact that my father was taken made us suspect to people. But on the whole, the neighbors were quite nice, especially the ones adjacent to us. There was already a six a.m. to six p.m. curfew and a five mile limit on where we could go from our homes. So they offered to do our shopping for us, if we needed.

Most Japanese Americans had to give up their jobs, whatever they did, and were told they had to leave. The edict for 9066—President Roosevelt's edict for evacuation—was in February 1942. We were moved to a detention center that April. By then the Japanese on Terminal Island were just helter skelter, looking for anywhere they could go. They opened up the Japanese school and Buddhist churches, and families just crowded in. Even farmers brought along their chickens and chicken coops. They just opened up the places for people to stay until they could figure out what to do. Some people left for Colorado and Utah. Those who had relatives could do so. The idea was to evacuate all the Japanese from the coast. But all the money was frozen, so even if you knew where you wanted to go, it wasn't that simple. By then, people knew they would be going into camps, so they were selling what they could, even though they got next to nothing for it. . . .

We were sent to an assembly center in Arcadia, California, in April. It was the largest assembly center on the West Coast having nearly twenty thousand people. There were some smaller centers with about six hundred people. All along the West Coast—Washington, Oregon, California—there were many, many assembly centers, but ours was the largest. Most of the assembly centers were either fairgrounds, or race tracks. So many of us lived in stables and they said you could take what you could carry. We were there until October.

Even though we stayed in a horse stable, everything was well organized. Every unit would hold four to six people. So in some cases, families had to split up, or join others. We slept on army cots, and for mattresses they gave us muslin bags, and told us to fill them with straw. And for chairs, everybody scrounged around for carton boxes, because they could serve as chairs. You could put two together and it could be a little table. So it was just makeshift. But I was amazed how, in a few months, some of those units really looked nice. Japanese women fixed them up. Some people had the foresight to bring material and needles and thread. But they didn't let us bring anything that could be used as weapons. They let us have spoons, but no knives. For those who had small children or babies, it was rough. They said you could take what you could carry. Well, they could only take their babies in their arms, and maybe the little children could carry something, but it was pretty limited.

I was so red, white and blue, I couldn't believe this was happening to us. America would never do a thing like this to us. This is the greatest country in the world. So I thought this is only going to be for a short while, maybe a few weeks or something, and they will let us go back. At the beginning no one realized how long this would go on. I didn't feel the anger that much because I thought maybe this was the way we could show our love for our country, and we should not make too much fuss or noise, we should abide by what they asked of us. I'm a totally different person now than I was back then. I was naive about so many things. The more I think about, the more I realize how little you learn about American history. It's just what they want you to know.

At the beginning, we didn't have any idea how temporary or permanent the situation was. We thought we would be able to leave shortly. But after several months they told us this was just temporary quarters, and they were building more permanent quarters elsewhere in the United States. All this was so unbelievable. A year before we would never have thought anything like this could have happened to us—not in this country. As time went by, the sense of frustration grew. Many families were already divided. The fathers, the heads of the households, were taken to other camps. In the beginning, there was no way for the sons to get in touch with their families. Before our group left for the detention camp, we were saying goodbye almost every day to other groups who were going to places like Arizona and Utah. Here we finally had made so many new friends—people who we met, lived with, shared the time, and gotten to know. So it was even sad on that note and the goodbyes were difficult. Here we had gotten close to these people, and now we had to separate again. I don't think we even thought about where they were going to take us, or how long we would have to stay there. When we got on the trains to leave for the camps, we didn't know where we were going. None of the groups knew. It was later on that we learned so and so ended up in Arizona, or Colorado, or some other place. We were all at these assembly centers for about seven months. Once they started pushing people out, it was done very quickly. By October, our group headed out for Jerome, Arkansas, which is on the Tex-Arkana corner. . . .

When we got to Jerome, Arkansas, we were shocked because we had never seen an area like it. There was forest all around us. And they told us to wait till the rains hit. This would not only turn into mud, but Arkansas swamp lands. That's where they put us—in swamp lands, surrounded by forests. It was nothing like California.

I'm speaking as a person of twenty who had good health. Up until then, I had lived a fairly comfortable life. But there were many others who didn't see the whole experience the same way. Especially those who were older and in poor health and had experienced racism. One more thing like this could break them. I was at an age where transitions were not hard; the point where anything new could even be considered exciting. But for people in poor health, it was hell.

There were army-type barracks, with two hundred to two hundred and five people to each block and every block had its own mess hall, facility for washing clothes, showering. It was all surrounded by barbed wire, and armed soldiers. I think they said only seven people were killed in total, though thirty were shot, because they went too close to the fence. . . .

When we first arrived, there were some things that weren't completely fixed. For instance, the roofers would come by, and everyone would hunger for information from the outside world. We wanted to know what was happening with the war. We weren't allowed to bring radios; that was contraband. And there were no televisions then. So we would ask the workers to bring us back some papers, and they would give us papers from Texas or Arkansas, so for the first time we would find out about news from the outside.

Just before we went in to the camps, we saw that being a Japanese wasn't such a good thing, because everybody was turning against the Japanese, thinking we were saboteurs, or linking us with Pearl Harbor. But when I saw the kind of work they did at camp, I felt so proud of the Japanese, and proud to be Japanese, and wondered why I was so white, white when I was outside, because I was always with white folks. Many people had brothers or sons who were in the military and Japanese American servicemen would come into the camp to visit the families, and we felt so proud of them when they came in their uniforms. We knew that it would only be a matter of time before they would be shipped overseas. . . .

We always called the camps "relocation centers" while we were there. Now we feel it is apropos to call them concentration camps. It is not the same as the concentration camps of Europe; those we feel were death camps. Concentration camps were a concentration of people placed in an area, and disempowered and disenfranchised. So it is apropos to call what I was in a concentration camp. After two years in the camp, I was released. . . .

I returned in October of 1945. It was very hard to find work, at least for me. I wasn't expecting to find anything good, just something to tie me over until my boyfriend came back from New York. The only thing I was looking for was to work in a restaurant as a waitress. But I couldn't find anything. I would walk from one end of the town to the other, and down every main avenue. But as soon as they found out I was Japanese, they would say no. Or they would ask me if I was in the union, and of course I couldn't be in the union because I had just gotten there. Anyway, no Japanese could be in the union, so if the answer was no I'm not in the union, they would say no. So finally what I did was go into the rough area of San Pedro—there's a strip near the wharf—and I went down there. I was determined to keep the jobs as long as I could. But for a while, I could last maybe two hours, and somebody would say "Is that a 'Jap?'" And as soon as someone would ask that, the boss would say, "Sorry, you gotta go. We don't want trouble here." . . .

Historically, Americans have always been putting people behind walls. First there were the American Indians who were put on reservations, Africans in slavery, their lives on the plantations, Chicanos doing migratory work, and the kinds of camps they lived in, and even too, the Chinese when they worked on the railroad camps where they were almost isolated, dispossessed people—disempowered. And I feel those are the things we should fight against so they won't happen again. It wasn't so long ago—in 1979—that the feeling against the Iranians was so strong because of the takeover of the U.S. embassy in Iran, where they wanted to deport Iranian students. And that is when a group called Concerned Japanese Americans organized, and that was the first issue we took up, and then we connected it with what the Japanese had gone through. This whole period of what the Japanese went through is important. If we can see the connections of how often this happens in history, we can stem the tide of these things happening again by speaking out against them.

• • •

The United States and its allies used horrific violence in the war. The fire bombing of Dresden killed more than one hundred thousand people. The dropping of two atomic bombs on Japan in August 1945 killed two hundred thousand more. Here Yamaoka Michiko, a survivor of the bombing, describes the awful morning, August 6, 1945, when a Boeing B-29 bomber, the Enola Gay, dropped "Little Boy," an enriched uranium bomb, on Hiroshima. On August 9, a plutonium bomb, "Fat Boy," was dropped on Nagasaki.

Yamaoka Michiko, "Eight Hundred Meters from the Hypocenter" (1992)[3]

That year, on August 6 [1945], I was in the third year of girls' high school, fifteen years old. I was an operator at the telephone exchange. We had been mobilized from school for various work assignments for more than a year. My assigned place of duty was civilian, but we, too, were expected to protect the nation. We were tied by strong bonds to the country, We'd heard the news about the Tokyo and Osaka bombings, but nothing had dropped on Hiroshima. Japan was winning. So we still believed. We only had to endure. I wasn't particularly afraid when B-29s flew overhead.

That morning I left the house at about seven forty-five. I heard that the B-29s had already gone home. Mom told me, "Watch out, the B-29s might come again." My house was one point three kilometers from the hypocenter. My place of work was five hundred meters from the hypocenter. I walked toward the hypocenter in an area where all the houses and buildings had been deliberately demolished for fire breaks. There was no shade. I had on a white shirt and *monpe* [pants]. As I walked there, I noticed middle-school students pulling down houses at a point about eight hundred meters away from the hypocenter. I heard the faint sound of planes as I approached the river. The planes were tricky. Sometimes they only pretended to leave. I could still hear the very faint sound of planes. Today, I have no hearing in my left ear because of damage from the blast. I thought, how strange, so I put my right hand above my eyes and looked up to see if I could spot them. The sun was dazzling. That was the moment.

There was no sound. I felt something strong. It was terribly intense. I felt colors. It wasn't heat. You can't really say it was yellow, and it wasn't blue. At that moment I thought I would be the only one who would die. I said to myself, "Goodbye, Mom."

They say temperatures of seven thousand degrees centigrade hit me. You can't really say it washed over me. It's hard to describe. I simply fainted. I remember my body floating in the air. That was probably the blast, but I don't know how far I was blown. When I came to my senses, my surroundings were silent. There was no wind. I saw a slight threadlike light, so I felt I must be alive. I was under stones. I couldn't move my body. I heard voices crying, "Help! Water!" It was then I realized I wasn't the only one. I couldn't really see around me. I tried to say something, but my voice wouldn't come out.

"Fire! Run away! Help! Hurry up!" They weren't voices but moans of agony and despair. "I have to get help and shout," I thought. The person who rescued me was Mom, although she herself had been buried under our collapsed house. Mom knew the route I'd been taking. She came, calling out to me. I heard her voice and cried for help. Our surroundings were already starting to burn. Fires burst out from just the light itself. It didn't really drop. It just flashed.

It was beyond my mother's ability. She pleaded, "My daughter's buried here, she's been helping you, working for the military." She convinced soldiers nearby to help her and they started to dig me out. The fire was now blazing. "Woman, hurry up, run away from here," soldiers called. From underneath the stones I heard the crackling of flames. I called to her, "It's all right. Don't worry about me. Run away." I really didn't mind dying for the sake of the nation. Then they pulled me out by my legs.

Nobody there looked like human beings. Until that moment I thought incendiary bombs had fallen. Everyone was stupefied. Humans had lost the ability to speak. People couldn't scream, "It hurts!" even when they were on fire. People didn't say, "It's hot!" They just sat catching fire.

My clothes were burnt and so was my skin. I was in rags. I had braided my hair, but now it was like a lion's mane. There were people, barely breathing, trying to push their intestines back in. People with their legs wrenched off. Without heads. Or with faces burned and swollen out of shape. The scene I saw was a living hell.

Mom didn't say anything when she saw my face and I didn't feel any pain. She just squeezed my hand and told me to run. She was going to go rescue my aunt. Large numbers of people were moving away from the flames. My eyes were still able to see, so I made my way towards the mountain, where there was no fire, toward Hijiyama. On this flight I saw a friend of mine from the phone exchange. She'd been inside her house and wasn't burned. I called her name, but she didn't respond. My face was so swollen she couldn't tell who I was. Finally, she recognized my voice. She said, "Miss Yamaoka, you look like a monster!" That's the first time I heard that word. I looked at my hands and saw my own skin hanging down and the red flesh exposed. I didn't realize my face was swollen up because I was unable to see it.

The only medicine was tempura oil. I put it on my body myself. I lay on the concrete for hours. My skin was now flat, not puffed up anymore. One or two layers had peeled off. Only now did it become painful. A scorching sky was overhead. The flies swarmed over me and covered my wounds, which were already festering. People were simply left lying around. When their faint breathing became silent, they'd say, "This one's dead," and put the body in a pile of corpses. Some called for water, and if they got it, they died immediately.

Mom came looking for me again. That's why I'm alive today. I couldn't walk anymore. I couldn't see anymore. I was carried on a stretcher as far as Ujina, and then from there to an island where evacuees were taken. On the boat there I heard voices saying, "Let them drink water if they want. They'll die either way." I drank a lot of water.

I spent the next year bedridden. All my hair fell out. When we went to relatives' houses later they wouldn't even let me in because they feared they'd catch the disease. There was neither treatment nor assistance for me. Those people who had money, people who had both parents, people who had houses, they could go to the Red Cross Hospital or the Hiroshima City Hospital. They could get operations. But we didn't have any money. It was just my Mom and I. Keloids [scar tissue] covered my face, my neck. I couldn't even move my neck. One eye was hanging down. I was unable to control my drooling because my lip had been burned off. I couldn't get any treatments at a hospital, so my mother gave me massages. Because she did that for me, my keloids aren't as bad as they would have been. My fingers were all stuck together. I couldn't move them. The only thing I could do was sew shorts, since I only needed to sew a straight line. I had to do something to earn money.

The Japanese government just told us we weren't the only victims of the war. There was no support or treatment. It was probably harder for my Mom. Once she told me she tried to choke me to death. If a girl has terrible scars, a face you couldn't be born with, I understand that even a mother could want to kill her child. People threw stones at me and called me Monster. That was before I had my many operations. I only showed this side of my face, the right hand side, when I had to face someone. Like I'm sitting now.

A decade after the bomb, we went to America. I was one of the twenty-five selected by Norman Cousins [the editor of the *Saturday Review*] to be brought to America for treatment and plastic surgery. We were called the Hiroshima Maidens. The American government opposed us, arguing that it would be acknowledging a mistake if they admitted us to America, but we were supported by many civilian groups. We went to Mount Sinai Hospital in New York and spent about a year and a half undergoing treatment. I improved tremendously. I've now had thirty-seven operations, including efforts at skin grafts.

When I went to America I had a deep hatred toward America. I asked myself why they ended the war by a means which destroyed human beings. When I talked about how I suffered, I was often told, "Well, you attacked Pearl Harbor!" I didn't understand much English then, and it's probably just as well. From the American point of view, they dropped that bomb in order to end the war faster, in order to create more damage faster. But it's inexcusable to harm human beings in this way. I wonder what kind of education there is now in America about atomic bombs. They're still making them, aren't they?

• • •

Some historians, and many politicians, claimed the atomic bombing of Japan was "necessary" to "save lives" and end the war. But the internal assessment of the U.S. Strategic Bombing Survey, excerpted here, reached a different conclusion: "Japan would have surrendered even if the atomic bombs had not been dropped, even if Russia had not entered the war, and even if no invasion had been planned or contemplated." It seems that the U.S. government was determined to use the bomb, even if the Japanese were on the verge of surrender. Its motive may have been to demonstrate to the world—and particularly to the Soviet Union—the military power of the United States in the post-war period, as suggested by the exhaustive research of Gar Alperovitz. In the words of British scientist P. M. S. Blackett, an adviser to Winston Churchill, "[T]he dropping of the atomic bombs was not so much the last military act of the second World War as the first major operation of the cold diplomatic war with Russia."

United States Strategic Bombing Survey, Summary Report (Pacific War) (July 1, 1946)[4]

On 6 August and 9 August 1945, the first two atomic bombs to be used for military purposes were dropped on Hiroshima and Nagasaki respectively. One hundred thousand people were killed, 6 square miles or over 50 percent of the built-up areas of the two cities were destroyed. The first and crucial question about the atomic bomb thus was answered practically and conclusively; atomic energy had been mastered for military purposes and the overwhelming scale of its possibilities had been demonstrated. A detailed examination of the physical, economic, and morale effects of the atomic bombs occupied the attention of a major portion of the Survey's staff in Japan in order to arrive at a more precise definition of the present capabilities and limitations of this radically new weapon of destruction.

Eyewitness accounts of the explosion all describe similar pictures. The bombs exploded with a tremendous flash of blue-white light, like a giant magnesium flare. The flash was of short duration and accompanied by intense glare and heat. It was followed by a tremendous pressure wave and the rumbling sound of the explosion. This sound is not clearly recollected by those who survived near the center of the explosion, although it was clearly heard by others as much as fifteen miles away. A huge snow-white cloud shot rapidly into the sky and the scene on the ground was obscured first by a bluish haze and then by a purple-brown cloud of dust and smoke.

Such eyewitness accounts reveal the sequence of events. At the time of the explosion, energy was given off in the forms of light, heat, radiation, and pressure. The complete band of radiations, from X- and gamma-rays, through ultraviolet and light rays to the radiant heat of infra-red rays, traveled with the speed of light. The shock wave created by the enormous pressures built up almost instantaneously at the point of explosion but moved out more slowly, that is at about the speed of sound. The superheated gases constituting the original fire ball expanded outward and upward at a slower rate.

The light and radiant heat rays accompanying the flash traveled in a straight line and any opaque object, even a single leaf of a vine, shielded objects lying behind it. The duration of the flash was only a fraction of a second, but it was sufficiently intense to cause third degree burns to exposed human skin up to a distance of a mile. Clothing ignited, though it could be quickly beaten out, telephone poles charred, thatch roofed houses caught fire. Black or other dark-colored surfaces of combustible material absorbed the heat and immediately charred or burst into flames; white or light-colored surfaces reflected a substantial portion of the rays and were not consumed. Heavy black clay tiles which are an almost universal feature of the roofs of Japanese houses bubbled at distances up to a mile. Test of samples of this tile by the National Bureau of Standards in Washington indicates that temperatures in excess of $1,800°$ C[entigrade]. must have been generated in the surface of the tile to produce such an effect. The surfaces of granite blocks exposed to the flash scarred and spalled at distances up to almost a mile. In the immediate area of ground zero (the point on the ground immediately below the explosion), the heat charred corpses beyond recognition.

Penetrating rays such as gamma-rays exposed X-ray films stored in the basement of a concrete hospital almost a mile from ground zero. Symptoms of their effect on human beings close to the center of the explosion, who survived other effects thereof, were generally delayed for two or three days. The bone marrow and as a result the process of blood formation were affected. The white corpuscle count went down and the human processes of resisting infection were destroyed. Death generally followed shortly thereafter.

The majority of radiation cases who were at greater distances did not show severe symptoms until 1 to 4 weeks after the explosion. The first symptoms were loss of appetite, lassitude and general discomfort. Within 12 to 48 hours, fever became evident in many cases, going as high as $104°$ to $105°$ F[ahrenheit], which in fatal cases continued until death. If the fever subsided, the patient usually showed a rapid disappearance of other symptoms and soon regained his feeling of good health. Other symptoms were loss of white blood corpuscles, loss of hair, and decrease in sperm count.

Even though rays of this nature have great powers of penetration, intervening substances filter out portions of them. As the weight of the intervening material increases the percentage of the rays penetrating goes down. It appears that a few feet of concrete, or a somewhat greater thickness of earth, furnished sufficient protection to humans, even those close to ground zero, to prevent serious after effects from radiation.

The blast wave which followed the flash was of sufficient force to press in the roofs of reinforced concrete structures and to flatten completely all less sturdy structures. Due to the height of the explosion, the peak pressure of the wave at ground zero was no higher than that produced by a near miss of a high-explosive bomb, and decreased at greater distances from ground zero. Reflection and shielding by intervening hills and structures produced some unevenness in the pattern. The blast wave, however, was of far greater extent and duration than that of a high-explosive bomb and most reinforced-concrete structures suffered structural damage or collapse up to 700 feet at Hiroshima and 2,000 feet at Nagasaki. Brick buildings were flattened up to 7,300 feet at Hiroshima and 8,500 feet at Nagasaki. Typical Japanese houses of wood construction suffered total collapse up to approximately 7,300 feet at Hiroshima and 8,200 feet at Nagasaki. Beyond these distances structures received less serious damage to roofs, wall partitions, and the like. Glass windows were blown out at distances up to 5 miles. The blast wave, being of longer duration than that caused by high-explosive detonations, was accompanied by more flying debris. Window frames, doors, and partitions which would have been shaken down by a near-miss of a high-explosive bomb were hurled at high velocity through those buildings which did not collapse. Machine tools and most other production equipment in industrial plants were not directly damaged by the blast wave, but were damaged by collapsing buildings or ensuing general fires.

The above description mentions all the categories of the destructive action by the atomic-bomb explosions at Hiroshima and Nagasaki. There were no other types of action. Nothing was vaporized or disintegrated; vegetation is growing again immediately under the center of the explosions; there are no indications that radio-activity continued after the explosion to a sufficient degree to harm human beings.

Let us consider, however, the effect of these various types of destructive action on the cities of Hiroshima, and Nagasaki and their inhabitants.

Hiroshima is built on a broad river delta; it is flat and little above sea level. The total city area is 26 square miles but only 7 square miles at the center were densely built up. The principal industries, which had been greatly expanded during the war, were located on the periphery of the city. The population of the city had been reduced from approximately 340,000 to 245,000 as a result of a civilian defense evacuation program. The explosion caught the city by surprise. An alert had been sounded but in view of the small number of planes the all-clear had been given. Consequently, the population had not taken shelter. The bomb exploded a little northwest of the center of the built-up area. Everyone who was out in the open and was exposed to the initial flash suffered serious burns where not protected by clothing. Over 4 square miles in the center of the city were flattened to the ground with the exception of some 50 reinforced concrete buildings, most of which were internally gutted and many of which suffered structural damage. Most of the people in the flattened area were crushed or pinned down by the collapsing buildings or flying debris. Shortly thereafter, numerous fires started, a few from the direct heat of the flash, but most from overturned charcoal cooking stoves or other secondary causes. These fires grew in size, merging into a general conflagration fanned by a wind sucked into the center of the city by the rising heat. The civilian-defense organization was overwhelmed by the completeness of the destruction, and the spread of fire was halted more by the air rushing toward the center of the conflagration than by efforts of the fire-fighting organization.

Approximately 60,000 to 70,000 people were killed, and 50,000 were injured. Of approximately 90,000 buildings in the city, 65,000 were rendered unusable and almost all the remainder received at least light superficial damage. The underground utilities of the city were undamaged except where they crossed bridges over the rivers cutting through the city. All of the small factories in the center of the city were destroyed. However, the big plants on the periphery of the city were almost completely undamaged and 94 percent of their workers unhurt. These factories accounted for 74 percent of the industrial production of the city. It is estimated that they could have resumed substantially normal production within 30 days of the bombing, had the war continued. The railroads running through the city were repaired for the resumption of through traffic on 8 August, 2 days after the attack.

Nagasaki was a highly congested city built around the harbor and up into the ravines and river valleys of the surrounding hills. Spurs of these hills coming down close to the head of the bay divide the city roughly into two basins. The built-up area was 3.4 square miles of which 0.6 square miles was given over to industry. The peak wartime population of 285,000 had been reduced to around 230,000 by August 1945, largely by pre-raid evacuations. Nagasaki had been attacked sporadically prior to 9 August by an aggregate of 136 planes which dropped 270 tons of high explosives and 53 tons of incendiary bombs. Some 2 percent of the residential buildings had been destroyed or badly damaged; three of the large industrial plants had received scattered damage. The city was thus comparatively intact at the time of the atomic bombing.

The alarm was improperly given and therefore few persons were in shelters. The bomb exploded over the northwest portion of the city; the intervening hills protected a major portion of the city lying in the adjoining valley. The heat radiation and blast actions of the Nagasaki bomb were more intense than those of the bomb dropped over Hiroshima. Reinforced-concrete structures were structurally damaged at greater distances; the heavy steel-frame industrial buildings of the Mitsubishi steel works and the arms plant were pushed at crazy angles away from the center of the explosion. Contrary to the situation at Hiroshima, the majority of the fires that started immediately after the explosion resulted from direct ignition by the flash.

Approximately 40,000 persons were killed or missing and a like number injured. Of the 52,000 residential buildings in Nagasaki 14,000 were totally destroyed and a further 5,400 badly damaged. Ninety-six percent of the industrial output of Nagasaki was concentrated in the large plants of the Mitsubishi Co. which completely dominated the town. The arms plant and the steel works were located within the area of primary damage. It is estimated that 58 percent of the yen value of the arms plant and 78 percent of the value of the steel works were destroyed. The main plant of the Mitsubishi electric works was on the periphery of the area of greatest destruction. Approximately 25 percent of its value was destroyed. The dockyard, the largest industrial establishment in Nagasaki and one of the three plants previously damaged by high-explosive bombs, was located down the bay from the explosion. It suffered virtually no new damage. The Mitsubishi plants were all operating, prior to the attack, at a fraction of their capacity because of a shortage of raw materials. Had the war continued, and had the raw material situation been such as to warrant their restoration, it is estimated that the dockyard could have been in a position to produce at 80 percent of its full capacity within 3 to 4 months; that the steel works would have required a year to get into substantial production; that the electric works could have resumed some production within 2 months and been back at capacity within 6 months; and that restoration of the arms plant to 60 to 70 percent of former capacity would have required 15 months.

Some 400 persons were in the tunnel shelters in Nagasaki at the time of the explosion. The shelters consisted of rough tunnels dug horizontally into the sides of hills with crude, earth-filled blast walls protecting the entrances. The blast walls were blown in but all the occupants back from the entrances survived, even in those tunnels almost directly under the explosion. Those not in a direct line with the entrance were uninjured. The tunnels had a capacity of roughly 100,000 persons. Had the proper alarm been sounded, and these tunnel shelters been filled to capacity, the loss of life in Nagasaki would have been substantially lower.

The Survey has estimated that the damage and casualties caused at Hiroshima by the one atomic bomb dropped from a single plane would have required 220 B-29s carrying 1,200 tons of incendiary bombs, 400 tons of high-explosive bombs, and 500 tons of anti-personnel fragmentation bombs, if conventional weapons, rather than an atomic bomb, had been used. One hundred and twenty-five B-29s carrying 1,200 tons of bombs would have been required to approximate the damage and casualties at Nagasaki. This estimate pre-supposed bombing under conditions similar to those existing when the atomic bombs were dropped and bombing accuracy equal to the average attained by the Twentieth Air Force during the last 3 months of the war.

As might be expected, the primary reaction of the populace to the bomb was fear, uncontrolled terror, strengthened by the sheer horror of the destruction and suffering witnessed and experienced by the survivors. Prior to the dropping of the atomic bombs, the people of the two cities had fewer misgivings about the war than people in other cities and their morale held up after it better than might have been expected. Twenty-nine percent of the survivors interrogated indicated that after the atomic bomb was dropped they were convinced that victory for Japan was impossible. Twenty-four percent stated that because of the bomb they felt personally unable to carry on with the war. Some 40 percent testified to various degrees of defeatism. A greater number (24 percent) expressed themselves as being impressed with the power and scientific skill which underlay the discovery and production of the atomic bomb than expressed anger at its use (20 percent). In many instances, the reaction was one of resignation.

The effect of the atomic bomb on the confidence of the Japanese civilian population outside the two cities was more restricted. This was in part due to the effect of distance, lack of understanding of the nature of atomic energy, and the impact of other demoralizing experiences. The role of the atomic bomb in the surrender must be considered along with all the other forces which bore upon that question with Japan. . . .

On 6 August the atomic bomb was dropped on Hiroshima, and on 9 August Russia entered the war. In the succeeding meetings of the Supreme War Direction Council, the differences of opinion previously existing as to the Potsdam terms persisted exactly as before. By using the urgency brought about through fear of further atomic bombing attacks, the Prime Minister found it possible to bring the Emperor directly into the discussions of the Potsdam terms. Hirohito, acting as arbiter, resolved the conflict in favor of unconditional surrender.

The public admission of defeat by the responsible Japanese leaders, which constituted the political objective of the United States offensive begun in 1943, was thus secured prior to invasion and while Japan was still possessed of some 2,000,000 troops and over 9,000 planes in the home islands. Military defeats in the air, at sea and on the land, destruction of shipping by submarines and by air, and direct air attack with conventional as well as atomic bombs, all contributed to this accomplishment.

There is little point in attempting precisely to impute Japan's unconditional surrender to any one of the numerous causes which jointly and cumulatively were responsible for Japan's disaster. The time lapse between military impotence and political acceptance of the inevitable might have been shorter had the political structure of Japan permitted a more rapid and decisive determination of national policies. Nevertheless, it seems clear that, even without the atomic bombing attacks, air supremacy over Japan could have exerted sufficient pressure to bring about unconditional surrender and obviate the need for invasion.

Based on a detailed investigation of all the facts, and supported by the testimony of the surviving Japanese leaders involved, it is the Survey's opinion that certainly prior to 31 December 1945, and in all probability prior to 1 November 1945, Japan would have surrendered even if the atomic bombs had not been dropped, even if Russia had not entered the war, and even if no invasion had been planned or contemplated.

• • •

Years after the war, Admiral Gene Larocque, who had served for years in the navy and been bombed at Pearl Harbor, shared these thoughts on the war with the great people's historian and radio pioneer, Studs Terkel.

Admiral Gene Larocque Speaks to Studs Terkel About "The Good War" (1985)[5]

In the summer of '41 I asked to be sent to Pearl Harbor. The Pacific fleet was there and it sounded romantic. I was attached to the U.S.S. MacDonough when the Japanese attacked. We got under way about ten o'clock looking for the Japanese fleet. It's lucky we didn't find them; they would probably have sunk us. I spent the whole war in the Pacific, four years.

At first I thought the U.S. Army Air Corps was accidentally bombing us. We were so proud, so vain, and so ignorant of Japanese capability. It never entered our consciousness that they'd have the temerity to attack us. We knew the Japanese didn't see well, especially at night—we knew this as a matter of fact. We knew they couldn't build good weapons, they made junky equipment, they just imitated us. All we had to do was get out there and sink 'em. It turns out they could see better than we could and their torpedoes, unlike ours, worked.

We'd thought they were little brown men and we were the great big white men. They were of a lesser species. The Germans were well known as tremendous fighters and builders, whereas the Japanese would be a pushover. We used nuclear weapons on these little brown men. We talked about using them in Vietnam. We talked about using our military force to get our oil in the Middle East from a sort of dark-skinned people. I never hear about us using the military to get our oil from Canada. We still think we're a great super-race.

It took a long time to realize how good these fellows were. We couldn't believe it. One time I was down in a South Pacific atoll that we'd captured. There were still a few Japanese ships in the harbor. We ran into two Japanese who hanged themselves right in front of us rather than be captured. We hated them during the war. They were Japs. They were subhuman.

I hated the boredom of four years in the Pacific, even though I had been in thirteen battle engagements, had sunk a submarine, and was the first man ashore in the landing at Roi. In that four years, I thought, What a hell of a waste of a man's life. I lost a lot of friends. I had the task of telling my roommate's parents about our last days together. You lose limbs, sight, part of your life—for what? Old men send young men to war. Flags, banners, and patriotic sayings.

I stayed in the navy because I believed the United States could really make the world safe for democracy. I went around to high schools in uniform, telling the kids that I thought war was stupid, to ignore all this baloney that shows up in poetry and novels and movies about gallantry and heroism and beauty. I told them it's just a miserable, ugly business.

After the war, we were the most powerful nation in the world. Our breadbasket was full. We enjoyed being the big shots. We were running the world. We were the only major country that wasn't devastated. France, Britain, Italy, Germany had all felt it. The Soviet Union, our big ally, was on its knees. Twenty million dead.

We are unique in the world, a nation of thirty million war veterans. We're the only country in the world that's been fighting a war since 1940. Count the wars—Korea, Vietnam—count the years. We have built up in our body politic a group of old men who look upon military service as a noble adventure. It was the big excitement of their lives and they'd like to see young people come along and share that excitement. We are unique.

We've always gone somewhere else to fight our wars, so we've not really learned about its horror. Seventy percent of our military budget is to fight somewhere else.

We've institutionalized militarism. This came out of World War Two. In 1947, we passed the National Security Act. You can't find that term—national security—in any literature before that year. It created the Department of Defense. Up till that time, when you appropriated money for the War Department, you knew it was for war and you could see it clearly. Now it's for the Department of Defense. Everybody's for defense. Otherwise you're considered unpatriotic. So there's absolutely no limit to the money you must give to it. So they've captured all the Christians: the right of self-defense. Even the "just war" thing can be wrapped into it.

We never had a Joint Chiefs of Staff before. In World War Two, there was a loose coalition, but there was no institution. It gave us the National Security Council. It gave us the CIA, that is able to spy on you and me this very moment. For the first time in the history of man, a country has divided up the world into military districts. No nation in the world has done that before or has done it since. They have a military solution for everything that happens in their area. They write up contingency plans—a euphemism for war plans. General Bernie Rogers has intelligence, has logistics, has airplanes, has people, has an international staff. There is not one U.S. ambassador in Europe who makes any significant move without checking with Bernie Rogers. He's the most important man in Europe and he has tenure. You can't fire him.

Our military runs our foreign policy. The State Department simply goes around and tidies up the messes the military makes. The State Department has become the lackey of the Pentagon. Before World War Two, this never happened. You had a War Department, you had a Navy Department. Only if there was a war did they step up front. The ultimate control was civilian. World War Two changed all this.

I don't think I've changed. I was a good ship captain. I was tough. I worked like the devil to see that my ship and my men were the best. I loved the sea and still do. I think the United States has changed. It got away from the idea of trying to settle differences by peaceful means. Since World War Two, we began to use military force to get what we wanted in the world. That's what military is all about. Not long ago, the Pentagon proudly announced that the U.S. had used military force 215 times to achieve its international goals since World War Two. The Pentagon likes that: military force to carry out national will. Of course, there are nuclear weapons now.

Nuclear weapons have become the conventional weapons. We seriously considered using them in Vietnam. I was in the Pentagon myself trying to decide what targets we could use. We explored every way we could to win that war, believe me. We just couldn't find a good enough target. We were not concerned about the opprobrium attached to the use of nuclear weapons.

I was in Vietnam. I saw the senseless waste of human beings. I saw this bunch of marines come off this air-conditioned ship. Nothing was too good for our sailors, soldiers, and marines. We send 'em ashore as gung ho young nineteen-year-old husky nice-looking kids and bring 'em back in black rubber body bags. There are a few little pieces left over, some entrails and limbs that don't fit in the bags. Then you take a fire hose and you hose down the deck and push that stuff over the side.

I myself volunteered to go to Vietnam and fight. I didn't question whether it was in the nation's interest. I was a professional naval officer and there was a war. I hope as we get older, we get smarter. You could argue World War Two had to be fought. Hitler had to be stopped. Unfortunately, we translate it unchanged to the situation today. I met some Russians during World War Two, officers from ships. They looked to me like human beings. I had been burned before, having been taught to hate the Japanese with such fervor. I saw no good reason, at that point, to hate the Russians, who I knew had fought valiantly in World War Two.

I think they want to be accepted as a world power and perhaps spread their hegemony around the world. I think we have to compete with communism wherever it appears. Our mistake is trying to stem it with guns. It alienates the very people we're trying to win over. The Russians really have influence only in the buffer areas around their country. They've been a flop in other countries. Yet the Russian bear determines just about everything we do. I wonder how much of my whole life and my generation has been influenced to hate the Russians. Even when I didn't even know where it was. I remember a Tom Swift book when I was thirteen: beware the Russian bear.

World War Two has warped our view of how we look at things today. We see things in terms of that war, which in a sense was a good war. But the twisted memory of it encourages the men of my generation to be willing, almost eager, to use military force anywhere in the world.

For about twenty years after the war, I couldn't look at any film on World War Two. It brought back memories that I didn't want to keep around. I hated to see how they glorified war. In all those films, people get blown up with their clothes and fall gracefully to the ground. You don't see anybody being blown apart. You don't see arms and legs and mutilated bodies. You see only an antiseptic, clean, neat way to die gloriously. I hate it when they say, "He gave his life for his country." Nobody gives their life for anything. We steal the lives of these kids. We take it away from them. They don't die for the honor and glory of their country. We kill them.

• • •

In the afterglow of righteousness about World War II, that went on for years, it seemed that only in fiction was it possible to challenge the smug confidence in "the good war." Kurt Vonnegut did it in *Slaughterhouse-Five*, his novel on the bombing of Dresden, where he had been held as a prisoner of war. Joseph Heller, who had flown bombing missions over France and Italy, wrote an outrageously comic novel about the war, titled *Catch-22*. It was turned down by twenty-five publishers, but when finally published it was read by millions of people. Here is a selection from *Slaughterhouse-Five*.

Kurt Vonnegut, *Slaughterhouse-Five* (1969)[6]

Eight Dresdeners crossed the steel spaghetti of the railroad yard. They were wearing new uniforms. They had been sworn into the army the day before. They were boys and men past middle age, and two veterans who had been shot to pieces in Russia. Their assignment was to guard one hundred American prisoners of war, who would work as contract labor. A grandfather and his grandson were in the squad. The grandfather was an architect.

The eight were grim as they approached the boxcars containing their wards. They knew what sick and foolish soldiers they themselves appeared to be. One of them actually had an artificial leg, and carried not only a loaded rifle but a cane. Still—

they were expected to earn obedience and respect from tall, cocky, murderous American infantrymen who had just come from all the killing at the front.

And then they saw bearded Billy Pilgrim in his blue toga and silver shoes, with his hands in a muff. He looked at least sixty years old. Next to Billy was little Paul Lazzaro with a broken arm. He was fizzing with rabies. Next to Lazzaro was the poor old high school teacher, Edgar Derby, mournfully pregnant with patriotism and middle age and imaginary wisdom. And so on.

The eight ridiculous Dresdeners ascertained that these hundred ridiculous creatures really *were* American fighting men fresh from the front. They smiled, and then they laughed. Their terror evaporated. There was nothing to be afraid of. Here were more crippled human beings, more fools like themselves. Here was light opera.

So out of the gate of the railroad yard and into the streets of Dresden marched the light opera. Billy Pilgrim was the star. He led the parade. Thousands of people were on the sidewalks, going home from work. They were watery and putty-colored, having eaten mostly potatoes during the past two years. They had expected no blessings beyond the mildness of the day. Suddenly—here was fun.

Billy did not meet many of the eyes that found him so entertaining. He was enchanted by the architecture of the city. Merry amoretti wove garlands above windows. Roguish fauns and naked nymphs peeked down at Billy from festooned cornices. Stone monkeys frisked among scrolls and seashells and bamboo.

Billy, with his memories of the future, knew that the city would be smashed to smithereens and then burned—in about thirty more days. He knew, too, that most of the people watching him would soon be dead. So it goes.

And Billy worked his hands in his muff as he marched. His fingertips, working there in the hot darkness of the muff, wanted to know what the two lumps in the lining of the little impresario's coat were. The fingertips got inside the lining. They palpated the lumps, the pea-shaped thing and the horseshoe-shaped thing. The parade had to halt by a busy corner. The traffic light was red.

There at the corner, in the front rank of pedestrians, was a surgeon who had been operating all day. He was a civilian, but his posture was military. He had served in two world wars. The sight of Billy offended him, especially after he learned from the guards that Billy was an American. It seemed to him that Billy was in abominable taste, supposed that Billy had gone to a lot of silly trouble to costume himself just so.

The surgeon spoke English, and he said to Billy, "I take it you find war a very comical thing."

Billy looked at him vaguely. Billy had lost track momentarily of where he was or how he had gotten there. He had no idea that people thought he was clowning. It was Fate, of course, which had costumed him—Fate, and a feeble will to survive.

"Did you expect us to *laugh?*" the surgeon asked him.

The surgeon was demanding some sort of satisfaction. Billy was mystified. Billy wanted to be friendly, to help, if he could, but his resources were meager. His fingers now held the two objects from the lining of the coat. Billy decided to show the surgeon what they were.

"You thought we would enjoy being mocked?" the surgeon said. "And do you feel proud to represent America as you do?"

Billy withdrew a hand from his muff, held it under the surgeon's nose. On his palm rested a two-carat diamond and a partial denture. The denture was an obscene little artifact—silver and pearl and tangerine. Billy smiled.

• • •

At the end of World War II, the House Committee on Un-American Activities (known commonly as HUAC), set up in 1938 to investigate "subversive" activity in the United States, called before it Hollywood writers, actors, and directors, presumably to find evidence of Communist influence in the movie industry. A number of these artists, who became known as the "Hollywood Ten," were sent to prison for refusing to answer the Committee's questions about ties with the Communist Party. The Committee also interrogated folk singer Pete Seeger, playwright Arthur Miller, and many others. This was part of a general attack on civil liberties in the atmosphere of the "Cold War" against the Soviet Union: loyalty oaths for government employees instituted by President Harry Truman, hearings before a Senate panel chaired by Senator Joseph McCarthy (giving the events of that period its name "McCarthyism"). The FBI accumulated lists of hundreds of thousands of Americans who had signed certain petitions, attended certain meetings. The leaders of the Communist Party were imprisoned. One of the artists singled out for attack was the great singer and actor Paul Robeson, who had been a fierce opponent of racism and the foreign policy of the United States. Here is a statement Robeson intended to present before HUAC, but which he was not allowed to read.

Paul Robeson's Unread Statement before the House Committee on Un-American Activities (June 12, 1956)[7]

It is a sad and bitter commentary on the state of civil liberties in America that the very forces of reaction, typified by Representative Francis Walter and his Senate counterparts, who have denied me access to the lecture podium, the concert hall, the opera house, and the dramatic stage, now hale me before a committee of inquisition in order to hear what I have to say. It is obvious that those who are trying to gag me here and abroad will scarcely grant me the freedom to express myself fully in a hearing controlled by them.

It would be more fitting for me to question Walter, [James] Eastland and [John Foster] Dulles than for them to question me, for it is they who should be called to account for their conduct, not I. Why does Walter not investigate the truly "un-American" activities of Eastland and his gang, to whom the Constitution is a scrap of paper when invoked by the Negro people and to whom defiance of the Supreme Court is a racial duty? And how can Eastland pretend concern over the internal security of our country while he supports the most brutal assaults on fifteen million Americans by the White Citizens' Councils and the Ku Klux Klan? When will Dulles explain his reckless irresponsible "brink of war" policy by which the world might have been destroyed?

And specifically, why is Dulles afraid to let me have a passport, to let me travel abroad to sing, to act, to speak my mind? This question had been partially answered by State Department lawyers who have asserted in court that the State Department claims the right to deny me a passport because of what they called my "recognized status as a spokesman for large sections of Negro Americans" and because I have "been for years extremely active in behalf of independence of colonial peoples of Africa." The State Department has also based its denial of a passport to me on the fact that I sent a message of greeting to the Bandung Conference, convened by [Jawaharwal] Nehru, Sukarno, and other great leaders of the colored people of the world. Principally, however, Dulles objects to speeches I have made abroad against the oppression suffered by my people in the United States.

I am proud that those statements can be made about me. It is my firm intention to continue to speak out against injustices to the Negro people, and I shall continue to do all within my power in behalf of independence of colonial peoples of Africa. It is for Dulles to explain why a Negro who opposes colonialism and supports the aspirations of Negro Americans should for those reasons be denied a passport.

My fight for a passport is a struggle for freedom—freedom to travel, freedom to earn a livelihood, freedom to speak, freedom to express myself artistically and culturally. I have been denied these freedoms because Dulles, Eastland, Walter, and their ilk oppose my views on colonial liberation, my resistance to oppression of Negro Americans, and my burning desire for peace with all nations. But these are views which I shall proclaim whenever given the opportunity, whether before this committee or any other body.

President [Dwight D.] Eisenhower has strongly urged the desirability of international cultural exchanges. I agree with him. The American people would welcome artistic performances by the great singers, actors, ballet troupes, opera companies, symphony orchestras and virtuosos of South America, Europe, Africa, and Asia, including the folk and classic art of African peoples, the ancient culture of China, as well as the artistic works of the western world. I hope the day will come soon when Walter will consent to lowering the cruel bars which deny the American people the right to witness performances of many great foreign artists. It is certainly high time for him to drop the ridiculous "Keystone Kop" antics of fingerprinting distinguished visitors.

I find no such restrictions placed upon me abroad as Walter has had placed upon foreign artists whose performances the American people wish to see and hear. I have been invited to perform all over the world, and only the arbitrary denial of a passport has prevented realization of this particular aspect of the cultural exchange which the President favors.

I have been invited by Leslie Linder Productions to play the title role in a production of *Othello* in England. British actors' Equity Association has unanimously approved of my appearance and performance in England.

I have been invited by Workers' Music Association Ltd. to make a concert tour of England under its auspices. The invitation was signed by all of the vice-presidents, including Benjamin Britten, and was seconded by a personal invitation of R. Vaughan Williams.

I have been invited by Adam Holender, impresario, to make a concert tour of Israel, and he has tendered to me a proposed contract for that purpose.

Mosfilm, a Soviet moving-picture producing company, has invited me to play the title role in a film version of *Othello*, assuring me "of the tremendous artistic joy which association with your wonderful talent will bring us."

The British Electrical Trades Union requested me to attend their annual policy conference, recalling my attendance at a similar conference held in 1949 at which, they wrote me, "you sang and spoke so movingly."

The British Workers' Sports Association, erroneously crediting a false report that I would be permitted to travel, wrote me, "We view the news with very great happiness." They invited me "to sing to our members in London, Glasgow, Manchester or Cardiff, or all four, under the auspices of our International Fund, and on a financial basis favorable to yourself, and to be mutually agreed." They suggested a choice of three different halls in London, seating, respectively, 3,000, 4,500, and 7,000.

The Australian Peace Council invited me to make a combined "singing and peace tour" of the dominion.

I have received an invitation from the Education Committee of the London Co-operative Society to sing at concerts in London under their auspices.

A Swedish youth organization called "Democratic Youth" has invited me to visit Sweden "to give some concerts here, to get to know our culture and our people." The letter of invitation added, "Your appearance here would be greeted with the greatest interest and pleasure, and a tour in Sweden can be arranged either by us or by our organization in cooperation with others, or by any of our cultural societies or artist's bureaus, whichever you may prefer."

I have an invitation from the South Wales Miners to sing at the Miners' Singing Festival on October 6, 1956, and in a series of concerts in the mining valley thereafter.

In Manchester, England, a group of people called the "Let Paul Robeson Sing Committee" has asked me to give a concert at the Free Trade Hall in that city either preceding or following my engagement in Wales.

I have been requested by the Artistic and Literary Director of the Agence Littéraire et Artistique Parisienne pour les Échanges Culturels to sign a contract with the great French concert organizer, M. Marcel de Valmalette, to sing in a series of concerts at the Palais de Chaillot in Paris.

There is no doubt that the governments of those countries and many others where I would be invited to sing if I could travel abroad would have no fear of what I might sing or say while there, whether such governments be allies and friends of America or neutrals or those others whose friendship for the American people is obstructed by Dulles and Walter and like-minded reactionaries.

My travels abroad to sing and act and speak cannot possibly harm the American people. In the past I have won friends for the real America among the millions before whom I have performed—not for Walter, not for Dulles, not for Eastland, not for the racists who disgrace our country's name—but friends for the American Negro, our workers, our farmers, our artists.

By continuing the struggle at home and abroad for peace and friendship with all of the world's people, for an end to colonialism, for full citizenship for Negro Americans, for a world in which art and culture may abound, I intend to continue to win friends for the best in American life.

• • •

On September 4, 1949, I took my wife and two-year-old daughter to a concert given in an outdoor area near the town of Peekskill, New York. The concert artist was Paul Robeson. A week before, on August 27, racists had violently prevented Robeson from performing. This night, protected by unionists and others, he defiantly sang under the open sky to an audience of thousands. Meanwhile, a shouting, angry crowd gathered around the field. When the concert was over and we drove off the grounds, the cars moving in a long slow line, we saw the sides of the road filled with cursing, jeering men and women. Then the rocks began to fly. My wife was pregnant at the time. She ducked and pushed our daughter down near the floor of our car. All four side windows and the rear window were smashed by rocks. Sitting in the back seat was a young woman, a stranger, to whom we had given a lift. A flying rock fractured her skull. There were dozens of casualties that day. Here the folksinger Pete Seeger describes that night's terrible events. Seeger would go on to write a song with Lee Hays, "Hold the Line," that proclaimed, "As we held the line in Peekskill, we hold it everywhere!"

Peter Seeger, "Thou Shall Not Sing" (1989)[8]

The Peekskill riot was in September 1949. From the conversations I've had with various people, it now seems pretty clear it was organized by the Ku Klux Klan, which had members in the local police departments. When Paul Robeson made the statement in Paris that American Blacks would not fight against the Soviet Union, the one country that had outlawed race discrimination, they were outraged. He touched America's Achilles' heel, and when he was going to give a concert in Peekskill, they said, "Let's go get him."

The mob came to the site of the concert, overturned the stage, beat up the people who were setting up the public address system, and the police didn't do a thing to stop it. The police just stood there and made sure that the Ku Kluxers did what they wanted to do. But then they were surprised because Robeson got on the radio and said, "I've got a right to sing anywhere I want to. I'm going to sing in Peekskill next week."

The next week ten thousand people came to hear him. The field was surrounded by a thousand or more union members, shoulder to shoulder, to see that no mob would get in to disrupt the concert. There were people with eagle eyes standing next to Robeson.

There was an opposition crowd of maybe one hundred to one hundred and fifty at the gate. They were hollering things like "Go back to Russia! Kikes! Nigger lovers!" There were about three or four policemen, though, who kept the gate open. The ten thousand or more people drove their cars in, parked them, and then sat down and enjoyed a wonderful concert. I was among the singers in the first half. Robeson did me the honor. I was very unknown and very unskilled, but I sang three or four songs, including the song "If I Had a Hammer." Then Robeson took over the second half. At the end of the concert, the crowd moved very slowly out the gate. It must have been an hour and a half at least before my family and I finally got our car through.

I wanted to turn left because my home was north of Peekskill. A policeman said,

"No, all cars go here." He pointed south, along the road which is ironically called Division Street. We hadn't gone but a hundred yards when I saw glass on the road. My wife and two baby children, my father-in-law, and two friends were all in a little jeep station wagon. I said, "Oh-oh, I see glass. You better be prepared to duck. Somebody may want to throw a stone."

Ha! What an understatement. There were young men with piles of stones waist high waiting around each bend. Each stone was about as big as a baseball. Wham! Into every car that passed they would throw a stone at close range with all their strength. There must have been fifteen or twenty of these piles.

We ran a gauntlet. Every window but the rear window was broken. Two stones came through completely, and I later cemented them into the fireplace in my house so I would never forget them. At one point there was a policeman standing not more than a hundred feet from a man throwing stones. I stopped, and I said, "Officer, aren't you going to do something?" He said, "Move on, move on." I looked around. The man in back of me couldn't move because I was in front of him, and he was getting stone after stone. He was a sitting duck. So I moved on.

When we got back home, we put our children in the shower and washed the broken glass out of their hair. No one in our car was hurt, but others were. One person at the concert lost his eyesight. Robeson himself was saved by people who put their bodies on top of his.

In Peekskill there were signs in many windows, bumper stickers on many cars, and more signs in barrooms saying, "Wake up, America! Peekskill did." They were quite frankly calling for the rest of the country to start a wave of terror against anybody who could be suspected of being a Communist or a Communist sympathizer.

Following Peekskill, there were many people who said this was the beginning of fascism in America. This was the way Hitler started in Germany. The police were going to stand by and watch the fascists lynch and murder and kill. However, I was not convinced. And I remember not being convinced. I knew some relatively well-to-do people who were leaving the country, going to Mexico or England or Canada. I knew some people who were burning their books. I did participate in a project to microfilm our song library, which is a priceless collection of labor songs. But I wasn't convinced that things were going to be as bad as some of my friends said they were going to be.

About a month or six weeks after the Peekskill affair, many of those "Wake up, America" signs disappeared. Although I don't have any proof, I'm personally convinced that in many a family there was an argument. It might have been a grandmother who said, "You mean you threw stones at women and children? Well, I don't like these people either, but still, you don't throw stones at women and children." There is a strain of decency in America. I bet there were people saying, "Well, is this what Thomas Jefferson was talking about? Is this what Abe Lincoln was talking about? I mean, we've heard of lynchings down South. Do we really like them?" And so while there was terror in many places during the 1950s, Peekskill actually wasn't repeated.

•   •   •

The journalist I. F. Stone, who for years edited the invaluable *I. F. Stone's Weekly*, was a rare voice of journalistic integrity, speaking out on the lies behind the wars in Korea and Vietnam. In this essay, he challenges not just Joe McCarthy but the entire anti-Communist hysteria and Cold War framework accepted by many of McCarthy's liberal critics.

I. F. Stone, "But It's Not Just Joe McCarthy" (March 15, 1954)[9]

Buds are beginning to appear on the forsythia, and welts on Joe McCarthy. The early arrival of spring and a series of humiliations for our would-be Führer have made this a most pleasant week in the capital.

The events of the week are worth savoring. Blunt Charlie Wilson called McCarthy's charges against the army "tommyrot" and for once Joe had no comeback. Next day came the ignominious announcement that he was dropping that $2,000,000 suit against former Senator [William] Benton for calling McCarthy a crook and a liar; the lame excuse promised to launch a nationwide "I Believe Benton" movement. [Adlai] Stevenson followed with a speech calculated to impress those decent conservatives who had grown disgusted with the Eisenhower Administration's cowardice in the [General Ralph] Zwicker affair.

When McCarthy sought to answer Stevenson, the Republican National Committee turned up in Ike's [Dwight D. Eisenhower's] corner and grabbed the radio and TV time away from him. [Richard] Nixon was to reply, and McCarthy was out (unless somebody smuggled him into the program in place of Checkers [Nixon's dog]). While McCarthy fumed and threatened, his own choice for the Federal Communications Commission, Robert E. Lee, ungratefully declared he thought the networks had done enough in making time available to Nixon. Next day a Republican, albeit a liberal Republican, [Ralph] Flanders of Vermont, actually got up on the floor of the Senate and delivered a speech against McCarthy. That same night Ed Murrow telecast a brilliant TV attack on McCarthy.

Under Stevenson's leadership, Eisenhower rallied. At a press conference he endorsed the Flanders attack, said he concurred heartily in the decision to have

Nixon reply to Stevenson, asserted that he saw no reason why the networks should also give time to McCarthy. Like an escaped prisoner, flexing cramped muscles in freedom, the President also made it clear he had no intention of turning Indo-China into another Korea and even had the temerity to suggest that it might be a good idea to swap butter and other surplus farm commodities with Russia.

The White House conference was no sooner over than Senator [Homer] Ferguson as chairman of the Senate Republican Policy Committee released a set of suggested rules for Senate investigating committees which are no great shakes at reform but would, if adopted, make it impossible for McCarthy any longer to operate his subcommittee as a one-man show. These may be small enough gains in the fight against McCarthyism, but they were bitter pills for McCarthy to swallow.

So far McCarthy's colleagues on both sides of the aisle have been lying low. When Flanders attacked McCarthy, the Senate was as silent as it was some weeks earlier when [Allen] Ellender of Louisiana made a lone onslaught and [James] Fulbright of Arkansas cast the sole vote against his appropriation. Only [Herbert] Lehman of New York and John Sherman Cooper (R[epublican]) of Kentucky rose to congratulate Flanders. Nobody defended McCarthy, but nobody joined in with those helpful interjections which usually mark a Senate speech. When the Democratic caucus met in closed session, the Stevenson speech was ignored. Lyndon Johnson of Texas, the Democratic floor leader, is frightened of McCarthy's Texas backers.

Great issues are rarely resolved by frontal assault; for every abolitionist prepared to challenge slavery as a moral wrong, there were dozens of compromising politicians (including Lincoln) who talked as if the real issue were states' rights or the criminal jurisdiction of the Federal courts or the right of the people in a new territory to determine their own future. In the fight against the witch mania in this country and in Europe, there were few enough to defend individual victims but fewer still who were willing to assert publicly that belief in witchcraft was groundless. So today in the fight against "McCarthyism." It is sometimes hard to draw a line of principles between McCarthy and his critics. If there is indeed a monstrous and diabolic conspiracy against world peace and stability, then isn't McCarthy right? If "subversives" are at work like termites here and abroad, are they not likely to be found in the most unlikely places and under the most unlikely disguises? How talk of fair procedure if dealing with a protean and Satanic enemy?

To doubt the power of the devil, to question the existence of witches, is again to read oneself out of respectable society, to brand oneself a heretic, to incur suspicion of being oneself in league with the powers of evil. So all the fighters against McCarthyism are impelled to adopt its premises. This was true even of the Stevenson speech, but was strikingly so of Flanders.

The country is in a bad way indeed when as feeble and hysterical a speech is hailed as an attack on McCarthyism. Flanders talked of "a crisis in the age-long warfare between God and the Devil for the souls of men." He spoke of Italy as "ready to fall into Communist hands," of Britain "nibbling at the drugged bait of trade profits." There are passages of sheer fantasy, like this one: "Let us look to the South. In Latin America there are sturdy strongpoints of freedom. But there are likewise, alas, spreading infections of Communism. Whole countries are being taken over . . ." What "whole countries"? and what "sturdy strongpoints of freedom"? Flanders pictured the Iron Curtain drawn tight about the U.S. and Canada, the rest of the world captured "by infiltration and subversion." Flanders told the Senate, "We will be left with no place to trade and no place to go except as we are permitted to trade and to go by the Communist masters of the world."

The center of gravity in American politics has been pushed so far right that such childish nightmares are welcomed as the expression of liberal statesmanship. Nixon becomes a middle-of-the-road spokesman and conservative papers like the *Washington Star* and *New York Times* find themselves classified more and more as parts of the "left-wing press." In this atmosphere the Senate Republican reply to McCarthy's silly "Communist coddling" charges against the army is to launch a formal investigation of their own through [Senator Leverett] Saltonstall and the Armed Services Committee. This will be the Republican and army analogue of the [Senator Millard] Tydings inquiry into the charges against the State Department and will be greeted with the same cry of whitewash by the growing lunatic fringe behind McCarthy.

There are some charges which must be laughed off or brushed off. They cannot be disproved. If a man charges that he saw Eisenhower riding a broomstick over the White House, he will never be convinced to the contrary by sworn evidence that the President was in bed reading a Western at the time. Formal investigations like Saltonstall's merely pander to paranoia and reward demagogy. What if McCarthy were next to attack the President and the Supreme Court? Are they, too, to be investigated? Is America to become a country in which any adventurer flanked by two ex-Communist screwballs will put any institution on the defensive?

McCarthy is personally discomfited, but McCarthyism is still on the march. [Dean] Acheson fought McCarthy, but preached a more literate variation of the Bogeyman Theory of History. Eisenhower fights McCarthy, but his Secretary of State in Caracas is pushing hard for a resolution which would spread McCarthyism throughout the hemisphere, pledging joint action for "security" and against "subversion." Nowhere in American politics is there evidence of any important figure (even Stevenson) prepared to talk in sober, mature and realistic terms of the real problems which arise in a real world where national rivalries, mass aspirations and ideas clash as naturally as the waves of the sea. The premises of free society and of liberalism find no one to voice them, yet McCarthyism will not be ended until someone has the nerve to make this kind of a fundamental attack on it.

What are the fundamentals which need to be recognized? The first is that there can be no firm foundation for freedom in this country unless there is real peace. There can be no real peace without a readiness for live-and-let-live, i.e. for coexistence with Communism. The fear cannot be extirpated without faith in man and freedom. The world is going "socialist" in one form or another everywhere; Communism is merely the extreme form this movement takes when and where blind and backward rulers seek by terror and force to hold back the tide, as the Tsar did and as Chiang Kai-shek did.

There must be renewed recognition that societies are kept stable and healthy by reform, not by thought police; this means that there must be free play for so-called "subversive" ideas—every idea "subverts" the old to make way for the new. To shut off "subversion" is to shut off peaceful progress and to invite revolution and war. American society has been healthy in the past because there has been a constant renovating "subversion" of this kind. Had we operated on the Bogeyman Theory of History, America would have destroyed itself long ago. It will destroy itself now unless and until a few men of stature have the nerve to speak again the traditional language of free society.

The business of saying, "Of course there are witches and their power is dreadfully pervasive and they are all around us, but we must treat suspects fairly . . ." is not good enough. To acquiesce in the delusions which create a panic is no way to stem it.

• • •

One of the darkest moments of the anti-Communist hysteria of the Cold War was the execution of Ethel and Julius Rosenberg on June 19, 1953. They were accused of delivering atomic secrets to the Soviet Union, and the controversy has continued over the years about that charge. Julius Rosenberg may have been involved in passing some kind of military information to the Soviet Union, which at the time was a wartime ally of the United States. His wife Ethel Rosenberg was certainly innocent (and known to be innocent by her accusers), but she was imprisoned with the hope of using her to get her husband to confess, even though their deaths would leave their two boys without parents. Both maintained their innocence to the very end. Their trial had been ridden with prejudice, taking place in the heated anti-Communist atmosphere of the Cold War. Their judge held secret meetings with the Justice Department promising to give them the death sentence if found guilty. There was an international campaign to save them, and several Supreme Court justices granted stays, but ultimately the entire Supreme Court was flown back from their summer vacations to get a majority to approve carrying out the execution. Here is their final letter, written to their six-year-old son Robert and their ten-year-old son Michael, on the day of their execution.

The Final Letter from Ethel and Julius Rosenberg to Their Children (June 19, 1953)[10]

Dearest Sweethearts, my most precious children,

Only this morning it looked like we might be together again after all. Now that this cannot be, I want so much for you to know all that I have come to know.

Unfortunately, I may write only a few simple words; the rest your own lives must teach you, even as mine taught me.

At first, of course, you will grieve bitterly for us, but you will not grieve alone. That is our consolation and it must eventually be yours.

Eventually, you too must come to believe that life is worth living. Be comforted that even now, with the end of ours slowly approaching, that we know this with a conviction that defeats the executioner!

Your lives must teach you, too, that good cannot flourish in the midst of evil; that freedom and all the things that go to make up a truly satisfying and worthwhile life, must sometime be purchased very dearly. Be comforted then that we were serene and understood with the deepest kind of understanding, that civilization had not as yet progressed to the point where life did not have to be lost for the sake of life; and that we were comforted in the sure knowledge that others would carry on after us.

We wish we might have had the tremendous joy and gratification of living our lives out with you. Your Daddy who is with me in the last momentous hours, sends his heart and all the love that is in it for his dearest boys. Always remember that we were innocent and could not wrong our conscience.

We press you close and kiss you with all our strength.

Lovingly,

Daddy and Mommy

CHAPTER SEVENTEEN

The Black Upsurge Against Racial Segregation

Richard Wright, *12 Million Black Voices* (1941)

Langston Hughes, *Montage of a Dream Deferred* (1951)

Anne Moody, *Coming of Age in Mississippi* (1968)

John Lewis, Original Text of Speech to Be Delivered at the Lincoln Memorial (August 28, 1963)

Malcolm X, "A Message to the Grass Roots" (November 10, 1963)

Martha Honey, Letter from Mississippi Freedom Summer (August 9, 1964)

Testimony of Fannie Lou Hamer (August 22, 1964)

Testimony of Rita L. Schwerner (1964)

Alice Walker, "Once" (1968)

Sandra A. West, "Riot!—A Negro Resident's Story" (July 24, 1967)

Martin Luther King, Jr., "Where Do We Go from Here?" (August 16, 1967)

For almost a hundred years after the passage of the Fourteenth and Fifteenth Amendments to the Constitution, those amendments, guaranteeing the right to vote, proclaiming equal rights for all, were left unenforced by the federal government. In short, for all that time, black people in the South were abandoned by the U.S. government, ignoring the Constitutional rights won after the Civil War. The result was disfranchisement, racial segregation, beatings, and murders.

But under the surface, there was resentment, indignation, and anger. And little forays against the system, most of them unsuccessful and unnoticed.

In 1955, this surface silence was broken with the extraordinary effort by black people in Montgomery, Alabama, to boycott the buses in that city in protest against racial segregation. The boycott was won, and the simmerings of protest grew. In early 1960, the sit-in of four black college students in a five-and-dime in Greensboro, North Carolina, led to violence and arrests. But it inspired a wave of sit-ins throughout the South. Out of those sit-ins was born a remarkable organization of young activists, the Student Nonviolent Coordinating Committee.

The following year, black and white activists joined in the Freedom Rides, on buses going through the South. The riders were attacked and beaten, but now there was national attention on the struggle for civil rights. In the next several years, demonstrations throughout the South grew, culminating in Birmingham, Alabama, in 1963, when thousands marched for racial equality. In the first three months of 1963, the Department of Justice recorded more than 1,400 demonstrations.

Now the whole world was taking notice. Congress was pressured to pass civil rights legislation in 1964 and 1965, finally ending legal racial segregation and enforcing the right of black people in the South to vote. But this did not really address the plight of poor black people in the ghettos of the country, and in 1964 and 1965 there were racial explosions in Harlem and in Los Angeles, followed by the Detroit rebellion of 1967.

Poverty, desperation, and police brutality persisted despite the gains in civil rights. Malcolm X was one expression of black anger, speaking to the inadequacy of what had been accomplished. He was assassinated in 1965.

Groups such as the Black Panthers, the Dodge Revolutionary Union (DRUM), and the Young Lords explored revolutionary forms of organization and protest. In their final years, Martin Luther King, Jr., and Malcolm X also drew more radical conclusions.

In the year before his assassination in 1968, King recognized that the fundamental problem of economic justice had not been solved. He spoke to his staff about the limitations of the capitalist system and set out to organize a "Poor People's March" on Washington, which he did not live to observe.

• • •

The roots of the civil rights movement can be traced to the long years of repression under the "Jim Crow" system in the South and to the experiences of blacks in the North, where millions of blacks had come hoping to escape racism. Blacks who migrated North often came with expectations that they could find better living and working conditions. Instead, they found unemployment, dangerous and underpaid work, continued segregation, and persistent discrimination, police brutality. Here the novelist Richard Wright, who himself migrated from Mississippi to Chicago in 1927, describes the crisis blacks confronted when they arrived in the cities of the North.

Richard Wright, *12 Million Black Voices* (1941)[1]

The train and the auto move north, ever north, and from 1916 to 1928, 1,200,000 of us were moving from the South to the North and we kept leaving. Night and day, in rain and in sun, in winter and in summer, we leave the land. Already, as we sit and look broodingly out over the turning fields, we notice with attention and hope that the dense southern swamps give way to broad, cultivated wheat farms. The spick-and-span farmhouses done in red and green and white crowd out the casual, unpainted gingerbread shacks. Silos take the place of straggling piles of hay. Macadam highways now wind over the horizon instead of dirt roads. The cheeks of the farm people are full and ruddy, not sunken and withered like soda crackers. The slow southern drawl, which in legend is so sweet and hospitable but which in fact has brought down on our black bodies suffering untold, is superseded by clipped Yankee phrases, phrases spoken with such rapidity and neutrality that we, with our slow ears, have difficulty in understanding. And the foreigners—Poles, Germans, Swedes, and Italians—we never dreamed that there were so many in the world! Yes, coming north for a Negro sharecropper involves more strangeness than going to another country. It is the beginning of living on a new and terrifying plane of consciousness.

We see white men and women get on the train, dressed in expensive new clothes. We look at them guardedly and wonder will they bother us. Will they ask us to stand up while they sit down? Will they tell us to go to the back of the coach? Even though we have been told that we need not be afraid, we have lived so long in fear of all white faces that we cannot help but sit and wait. We look around the train and we do not see the old familiar signs: FOR COLORED and FOR WHITE. The train speeds north and we cannot sleep. Our heads sink in a doze, and then we sit bolt-upright, prodded by the thought that we must watch these strange surroundings. But nothing happens; these white men seem impersonal and their very neutrality reassures us—for a while. Almost against our deeper judgment, we try to force ourselves to relax, for these brisk men give no sign of what they feel. They are indifferent. O sweet and welcome indifference!

The miles click behind us. Into Chicago, Indianapolis, New York, Cleveland, Buffalo, Detroit, Toledo, Philadelphia, Pittsburgh, and Milwaukee we go, looking for work. We feel freer than we have ever felt before, but we are still a little scared. It is like a dream. Will we wake up suddenly and find that none of this is really true, that we are merely daydreaming behind the barn, snoozing in the sun, waiting to hear the hoarse voice of the riding boss saying: "Nigger, where do you think you are? Get the hell up from there and move on!"

Timidly, we get off the train. We hug our suitcases, fearful of pickpockets, looking with unrestrained curiosity at the great big brick buildings. We are very reserved, for we have been warned not to act "green," that the city people can spot a "sucker" a mile away. Then we board our first Yankee street car to go to a cousin's home, a brother's home, a sister's home, a friend's home, an uncle's home, or an aunt's home. We pay the conductor our fare and look about apprehensively for a seat. We have been told that we can sit where we please, but we are still scared. We cannot shake off three hundred years of fear in three hours. We ease into a seat and look out of the window at the crowded streets. A white man or a white woman comes and sits beside us, not even looking at us, as though this were a normal thing to do. The muscles of our bodies tighten. Indefinable sensations crawl over our skins and our blood tingles. Out of the corners of our eyes we try to get a glimpse of the strange white face that floats but a few inches from ours. The impulses to laugh and to cry clash in us; we bite our lips and stare out of the window.

There are so many people. For the first time in our lives we feel human bodies, strangers whose lives and thoughts are unknown to us, pressing always close about us. We cannot see or know a man because of the thousands upon thousands of men. The apartments in which we sleep are crowded and noisy, and soon enough we learn that the brisk, clipped men of the North, the Bosses of the Buildings, are not at all indifferent. They are deeply concerned about us, but in a new way. It seems as though we are now living inside of a machine; days and events move with a hard reasoning of their own. We live amid swarms of people, yet there is a vast distance between people, a distance that words cannot bridge. No longer do our lives depend upon the soil, the sun, the rain, or the wind; we live by the grace of jobs and the brutal logic of jobs. We do not know this world, or what makes it move. In the South life was different; men spoke to you, cursed you, yelled at you, or killed you. The world moved by signs we knew. But here in the North cold forces hit you and push you. It is a world of things.

Our defenseless eyes cloud with bewilderment when we learn that there are not enough houses for us to live in. And competing with us for shelter are thousands of poor migrant whites who have come up from the South, just as we have come. The cost of building a house is high, and building activities are on the downgrade. It is wartime; no new labor is coming in from the old countries across the seas. The only district we can live in is the area just beyond the business belt, a transition area where a sooty conglomeration of factories and mills belches smoke that stains our clothes and lungs.

We black folk are not the only ones who move into this so-called transition area; it is the first port of call for that incoming horde of men who float continuously into cities. The tenements we live in are old; they are rarely repaired or replaced. On most of our buildings are signs: THIS PROPERTY IS FOR SALE. Any day we can be told to move, that our home is to be torn down to make way for a new factory or a new mill.

So, under the black mourning pall of smoke from the stacks of American industry, our observing Negro eyes watch a thousand rivulets of blood melt, fuse, blend, and flow in a common stream of human unity as it merges with the great American tide. But we never mix with that stream; we are not allowed to.

• • •

After World War II, blacks returned from the war to face continued racism, Jim Crow segregation, unemployment, and poverty. The rhetoric they'd heard about fighting for democracy abroad stood in sharp contrast to the lack of democracy at home. In *Montage of a Dream Deferred*, excerpted here, Langston Hughes gave expression to the idea that the "dream deferred" might soon "explode." His words were prescient.

Langston Hughes, *Montage of a Dream Deferred* (1951)

"DREAM BOOGIE" (1951)[2]

Good morning, daddy!
Ain't you heard
The boogie-woogie rumble
Of a dream deferred?

Listen closely:
You'll hear their feet
Beating out and beating out a—

You think
It's a happy beat?

Listen to it closely:
Ain't you heard
something underneath
like a—

What did I say?

Sure,
I'm happy!
Take it away!

Hey, pop!
Re-bop!
Mop!

Y-e-a-h!

"HARLEM" (1951)[3]

What happens to a dream deferred?

Does it dry up
like a raisin in the sun?
Or fester like a sore—
And then run?
Does it stink like rotten meat?
Or crust and sugar over—
like a syrupy sweet?

Maybe it just sags
like a heavy load.

Or does it explode?

• • •

At great personal risk to themselves, blacks began to physically challenge the boundaries of segregation through civil disobedience. In December 1955, Rosa Parks was arrested when she refused to give up her seat to a white passenger in Montgomery, Alabama, helping spark a bus boycott that lasted 381 days before ending in a victory. In the early 1960s, students began a campaign to desegregate lunch counters in the South. One of the most important of these sit-ins took place on May 23, 1963, in Jackson, Mississippi, at a Woolworth's department store. Here the civil rights activist and author Anne Moody—who at the time was a student at Tougaloo College—recalls the sit-in.

Anne Moody, *Coming of Age in Mississippi* (1968)[4]

I had become very friendly with my social science professor, John Salter, who was in charge of NAACP activities on campus. All during the year, while the NAACP conducted a boycott of the downtown stores in Jackson, I had been one of Salter's most faithful canvassers and church speakers. During the last week of school, he told me that sit-in demonstrations were about to start in Jackson and that he wanted me to be the spokesman for a team that would sit-in at Woolworth's lunch counter. The two other demonstrators would be classmates of mine, Memphis [Norman] and Pearlena [Lewis]. Pearlena was a dedicated NAACP worker, but Memphis had not been very involved in the Movement on campus. It seemed that the organization had had a rough time finding students who were in a position to go to jail. I had nothing to lose one way or the other. Around ten o'clock the morning of the demonstrations, NAACP headquarters alerted the news services. As a result, the police department was also informed, but neither the policemen nor the newsmen knew exactly where or when the demonstrations would start. They stationed themselves along Capitol Street and waited.

To divert attention from the sit-in at Woolworth's, the picketing started at J. C. Penney's a good fifteen minutes before. The pickets were allowed to walk up and down in front of the store three or four times before they were arrested. At exactly 11 a.m., Pearlena, Memphis, and I entered Woolworth's from the rear entrance. We separated as soon as we stepped into the store, and made small purchases from various counters. Pearlena had given Memphis her watch. He was to let us know when it was 11:14. At 11:14 we were to join him near the lunch counter and at exactly 11:15 we were to take seats at it.

Seconds before 11:15 we were occupying three seats at the previously segregated Woolworth's lunch counter. In the beginning the waitresses seemed to ignore us, as if they really didn't know what was going on. Our waitress walked past us a couple of times before she noticed we had started to write our own orders down and realized we wanted service. She asked us what we wanted. We began to read to her from our order slips. She told us that we would be served at the back counter, which was for Negroes.

"We would like to be served here," I said.

The waitress started to repeat what she had said, then stopped in the middle of the sentence. She turned the lights out behind the counter, and she and the other waitresses almost ran to the back of the store, deserting all their white customers. I guess they thought that violence would start immediately after the whites at the counter realized what was going on. There were five or six other people at the counter. A couple of them just got up and walked away. A girl sitting next to me finished her banana split before leaving. A middle-aged white woman who had not yet been served rose from her seat and came over to us. "I'd like to stay here with you," she said, "but my husband is waiting."

The newsmen came in just as she was leaving. They must have discovered what was going on shortly after some of the people began to leave the store. One of the newsmen ran behind the woman who spoke to us and asked her to identify herself. She refused to give her name, but said she was a native of Vicksburg and a former resident of California. When asked why she had said what she had said to us, she replied, "I am in sympathy with the Negro movement." By this time a crowd of cameramen and reporters had gathered around us taking pictures and asking questions, such as Where were we from? Why did we sit-in? What organization sponsored it? Were we students? From what school? How were we classified?

I told them that we were all students at Tougaloo College, that we were represented by no particular organization, and that we planned to stay there even after the store closed. "All we want is service," was my reply to one of them. After they had finished probing for about twenty minutes, they were almost ready to leave.

At noon, students from a nearby white high school started pouring in to Woolworth's. When they first saw us they were sort of surprised. They didn't know how to react. A few started to heckle and the newsmen became interested again. Then the white students started chanting all kinds of anti-Negro slogans. We were called a little bit of everything. The rest of the seats except the three we were occupying had been roped off to prevent others from sitting down. A couple of the boys took one end of the rope and made it into a hangman's noose. Several attempts were made to put it around our necks. The crowds grew as more students and adults came in for lunch.

We kept our eyes straight forward and did not look at the crowd except for occasional glances to see what was going on. All of a sudden I saw a face I remembered—the drunkard from the bus station sit-in. My eyes lingered on him just long enough for us to recognize each other. Today he was drunk too, so I don't think he remembered where he had seen me before. He took out a knife, opened it, put it in his pocket, and then began to pace the floor. At this point, I told Memphis and Pearlena what was going on. Memphis suggested that we pray. We bowed our heads, and all hell broke loose. A man rushed forward, threw Memphis from his seat, and slapped my face. Then another man who worked in the store threw me against an adjoining counter.

Down on my knees on the floor, I saw Memphis lying near the lunch counter with blood running out of the corners of his mouth. As he tried to protect his face, the man who'd thrown him down kept kicking him against the head. If he had worn hard-soled shoes instead of sneakers, the first kick probably would have killed Memphis. Finally a man dressed in plain clothes identified himself as a police officer and arrested Memphis and his attacker.

Pearlena had been thrown to the floor. She and I got back on our stools after Memphis was arrested. There were some white Tougaloo teachers in the crowd. They asked Pearlena and me if we wanted to leave. They said that things were getting too rough. We didn't know what to do. While we were trying to make up our minds, we were joined by Joan Trumpauer. Now there were three of us and we were integrated. The crowd began to chant, "Communists, Communists, Communists." Some old man in the crowd ordered the students to take us off the stools.

"Which one should I get first?" a big husky boy said.

"That white nigger," the old man said.

The boy lifted Joan from the counter by her waist and carried her out of the store. Simultaneously, I was snatched from my stool by two high school students. I was dragged about thirty feet toward the door by my hair when someone made them turn me loose. As I was getting up off the floor, I saw Joan coming back inside. We started back to the center of the counter to join Pearlena. Lois Chaffee, a white Tougaloo faculty member, was now sitting next to her. So Joan and I just climbed across the rope at the front end of the counter and sat down. There were now four of us, two whites and two Negroes, all women. The mob started smearing us with ketchup, mustard, sugar, pies, and everything on the counter. Soon Joan and I were joined by John Salter, but the moment he sat down he was hit on the jaw with what appeared to be brass knuckles. Blood gushed from his face and someone threw salt into the open wound. Ed King, Tougaloo's chaplain, rushed to him.

At the other end of the counter, Lois and Pearlena were joined by George Raymond, a CORE [Congress of Racial Equality] field worker and a student from Jackson State College. Then a Negro high school boy sat down next to me. The mob took spray paint from the counter and sprayed it on the new demonstrators. The high school student had on a white shirt; the word "nigger" was written on his back with red spray paint.

We sat there for three hours taking a beating when the manager decided to close the store because the mob had begun to go wild with stuff from other counters. He begged and begged everyone to leave. But even after fifteen minutes of begging, no one budged. They would not leave until we did. Then Dr. [A. Daniel] Beittel, the president of Tougaloo College, came running in. He said he had just heard what was happening.

About ninety policemen were standing outside the store; they had been watching the whole thing through the windows, but had not come in to stop the mob or do anything. President Beittel went outside and asked Captain Ray to come and escort us out. The captain refused, stating the manager had to invite him in before he could enter the premises, so Dr. Beittel himself brought us out. He had told the police that they had better protect us after we were outside the store. When we got outside, the policemen formed a single line that blocked the mob from us. However, they were allowed to throw at us everything they had collected. Within ten minutes, we were picked up by Reverend [Edwin] King in his station wagon and taken to the NAACP headquarters on Lynch Street.

After the sit-in, all I could think of was how sick Mississippi whites were. They believed so much in the segregated Southern way of life, they would kill to preserve it. I sat there in the NAACP office and thought of how many times they had killed when this way of life was threatened. I knew that the killing had just begun. "Many more will die before it is over with," I thought. Before the sit-in, I had always hated the whites in Mississippi. Now I knew it was impossible for me to hate sickness. The whites had a disease, an incurable disease in its final stage.

• • •

On August 28, 1963, the historic March on Washington for Jobs and Freedom brought more than 200,000 demonstrators to the steps of the Lincoln Memorial to fight for civil rights. While the rally is best remembered for being the occasion of Martin Luther King, Jr.'s historic "I Have Dream Speech," perhaps the most militant speech of the day was delivered by John Lewis, a young SNCC leader from Alabama. But pressured by King and other established civil rights leaders, Lewis had toned down the text, which spoke of "revolution" and argued that President John F. Kennedy's proposed civil rights legislation was "too little, too late." Here is the text of the original speech he had hoped to deliver that day.

John Lewis, Original Text of Speech to Be Delivered at the Lincoln Memorial (August 28, 1963)[5]

We march today for jobs and freedom, but we have nothing to be proud of. For hundreds and thousands of our brothers are not here. They have no money for their transportation, for they are receiving starvation wages . . . or no wages, at all.

In good conscience, we cannot support the administration's civil rights bill, for it is too little, and too late. There's not one thing in the bill that will protect our people from police brutality.

This bill will not protect young children and old women from police dogs and fire hoses, [for] engaging in peaceful demonstrations. . .

The voting section of this bill will not help thousands of black citizens who want to vote. It will not help the citizens of Mississippi, of Alabama, and Georgia, who are qualified to vote, but lack a 6th Grade education. "One man, one vote," is the African cry. It is ours, too. (It must be ours.)

We are now involved in . . . revolution. This nation is still a place of cheap political leaders who build their careers on immoral compromise and ally themselves with open forms of political, economic and social exploitation. What political leader here can stand up and say, "My party is the party of principles"? The party of Kennedy is also the party of [James] Eastland. The party of [Jacob] Javits is also the party of [Barry] Goldwater. Where is our party?

In some parts of the South we work in the fields from sun-up to sun-down for $12 a week. In Albany, Georgia, nine of our leaders have been indicted not by Dixiecrats but by the Federal Government for peaceful protest. But what did the Federal Government do when Albany's Deputy Sheriff [Cull Campbell] beat Attorney C. B. King and left him half dead? What did the Federal Government do when local police officials kicked and assaulted the pregnant wife [Marion] of Slater King, and she lost her baby?

It seems to me that the Albany indictment is part of a conspiracy on the part of the Federal Government and local politicians in the interest of expediency.

I want to know, which side is the Federal Government on?

The revolution is at hand, and we must free ourselves of the chains of political and economic slavery. The non-violent revolution is saying, "We will not wait for the courts to act, for we have been waiting for hundreds of years. We will not wait for the President, the Justice Department, nor Congress, but we will take matters into our own hands and create a source of power, outside any national structure that could and would assure us a victory."

To those who have said, "Be Patient and Wait," we must say that, "Patience is a dirty and nasty word." We cannot be patient, we do not want to be free gradually, we want our freedom, and we want it now. We cannot depend on any political party, for both the Democrats and Republicans have betrayed the basic principles of the Declaration of Independence.

We all recognize the fact that if any radical social, political and economic changes are to take place in our society, the people, the masses, must bring them about. In the struggle we must seek more than civil rights; we must work for the community of love, peace and true brotherhood. Our minds, souls, and hearts cannot rest until freedom and justice exist for all the people.

The revolution is a serious one. Mr. Kennedy is trying to take the revolution out of the street and put in the courts. Listen, Mr. Kennedy, Listen, Mr. Congressman, listen, fellow citizens, the black masses are on the march for jobs and freedom, and we must say to the politicians that there won't be a "cooling-off" period.

We won't stop now. All the forces of Eastland, [Ross] Barnett, [George] Wallace, and [Strom] Thurmond won't stop this revolution. The time will come when we will not confine our marching to Washington. We will march through the South, through the Heart of Dixie, the way [General William] Sherman did. We shall pursue our own "scorched earth" policy and burn Jim Crow to the ground—non-violently. We shall fragment the South into a thousand pieces and put them back together in the image of democracy. We will make the action of the past few months look petty. And I say to you, WAKE UP AMERICA!

• • •

While some civil rights leaders urged a more cautious approach to winning civil rights, Malcolm X expressed the feelings of many blacks that more uncompromising methods of struggle were needed. Like members of the Black Panther Party for Self-Defense, Malcolm X advocated the right of armed self-defense for blacks and other oppressed groups who lived in so violently racist a society as the United States. Here is an excerpt of a speech Malcolm X delivered in Detroit, Michigan. Two years after giving this speech, on February 21, 1965, he was assassinated in New York City.

Malcolm X, "Message to the Grass Roots" (November 10, 1963)[6]

We want to have just an off-the-cuff chat between you and me, us. We want to talk right down to earth in a language that everybody here can easily understand. We all agree tonight, all of the speakers have agreed, that America has a very serious problem. Not only does America have a very serious problem, but our people have a very serious problem. America's problem is us. We're her problem. The only reason she has a problem is she doesn't want us here. And every time you look at yourself, be you black, brown, red or yellow, a so-called Negro, you represent a person who poses such a serious problem for America because you're not wanted. Once you face this as a fact, then you can start plotting a course that will make you appear intelligent, instead of unintelligent.

What you and I need to do is learn to forget our differences. When we come together, we don't come together as Baptists or Methodists. You don't catch hell because you're a Baptist, and you don't catch hell because you're a Methodist. You don't catch hell because you're a Methodist or Baptist, you don't catch hell because you're a Democrat or a Republican, you don't catch hell because you're a Mason or an Elk, and you sure don't catch hell because you're an American; because if you were an American, you wouldn't catch hell. You catch hell because you're a black man. You catch hell, all of us catch hell, for the same reason.

So we're all black people, so-called Negroes, second-class citizens, ex-slaves. You're nothing but an ex-slave. You don't like to be told that. But what else are you? You are ex-slaves. You didn't come here on the "Mayflower." You came here on a slave ship. In chains, like a horse, or a cow, or a chicken. And you were brought here by the people who came here on the "Mayflower," you were brought here by the so-called Pilgrims, or Founding Fathers. They were the ones who brought you here.

We have a common enemy. We have this in common: We have a common oppressor, a common exploiter, and a common discriminator. But once we all realize that we have a common enemy, then we unite on the basis of what we have in common. And what we have foremost in common is that enemy—the white man. He's an enemy to all of us. I know some of you all think that some of them aren't enemies. Time will tell. . . .

I would like to make a few comments concerning the difference between the black revolution and the Negro revolution. Are they both the same? And if they're not, what is the difference? What is the difference between a black revolution and a Negro revolution? First, what is a revolution? Sometimes I'm inclined to believe that many of our people are using this word "revolution" loosely, without taking careful consideration of what this word actually means, and what its historic characteristics are. When you study the historic nature of revolutions, the motive of a revolution, the objective of a revolution, the result of a revolution, and the methods used in a revolution, you may change words. You may devise another program, you may change your goal and you may change your mind.

Look at the American Revolution in 1776. That revolution was for what? For land. Why did they want land? Independence. How was it carried out? Bloodshed. Number one, it was based on land, the basis of independence. And the only way they could get it was bloodshed. The French Revolution—what was it based on? The landless against the landlord. What was it for? Land. How did they get it? Bloodshed. Was no love lost, was no compromise, was no negotiation. I'm telling you—you don't know what a revolution is. Because when you find out what it is, you'll get back in the alley, you'll get out of the way.

The Russian Revolution—what was it based on? Land; the landless against the landlord. How did they bring it about? Bloodshed. You haven't got a revolution that doesn't involve bloodshed. And you're afraid to bleed. I said, you're afraid to bleed.

As long as the white man sent you to Korea, you bled. He sent you to Germany, you bled. He sent you to the South Pacific to fight the Japanese, you bled. You bleed for white people, but when it comes to seeing your own churches being bombed and little black girls murdered; you haven't got any blood. You bleed when the white man says bleed; you bite when the white man says bite; and you bark when the white man says bark. I hate to say this about us, but it's true. How are you going to be nonviolent in Mississippi, as violent as you were in Korea? How can you justify being nonviolent in Mississippi and Alabama, when your churches are being bombed, and your little girls are being murdered, and at the same time you are going to get violent with Hitler, and Tojo, and somebody else you don't even know?

If violence is wrong in America, violence is wrong abroad. If it is wrong to be violent defending black women and black children and black babies and black men, then it is wrong for America to draft us and make us violent abroad in defense of her. And if it is right for America to draft us, and teach us how to be violent in defense of her, then it is right for you and me to do whatever is necessary to defend our own people right here in this country.

• • •

One of the most important new organizations to come out of the civil rights movement was the Student Nonviolent Coordinating Committee (SNCC), or "Snick" as it was usually called. SNCC was established in 1960, growing out of the student sit-ins in the south. In 1964, the group issued a call for young people to come to Mississippi to join in voter registration, "freedom schools," and other projects. Here is a letter from one of the volunteers, activist and author Martha Honey, then a first-year student at Oberlin College, writing to a classmate, Blake Alcott.

Martha Honey, Letter from Mississippi Freedom Summer (August 9, 1964)[7]

Mileston, August 9 [1964]

Dear Blake,

. . . . Dave finally broke down and couldn't finish and the Chaney family was moaning and much of the audience and I were also crying. It's such an impossible thing to describe but suddenly again, as I'd first realized when I heard the three men [James Chaney, Andrew Goodman, and Michael Schwerner] were missing when we were still training up at Oxford [Ohio], I felt the sacrifice the Negroes have been making for so long. How the Negro people are able to accept all the abuses of the whites—all the insults and injustices which make me ashamed to be white—and then turn around and say they want to love us, is beyond me. There are Negros who want to kill whites and many Negros have much bitterness but still the majority seem to have the quality of being able to look for a future in which whites will love the Negroes. Our kids talk very critically of all the whites around here and still they have a dream of freedom in which both races understand and accept each other. There is such an overpowering task ahead of these kids that sometimes I can't do anything but cry for them. I hope they are up to the task, I'm not sure I would be if I were a Mississippi Negro. As a white northerner I can get involved whenever I feel like it and run home whenever I get bored or frustrated or scared. I hate the attitude and position of the Northern whites and despise myself when I think that way.

Lately I've been feeling homesick and longing for pleasant old Westport and sailing and swimming and my friends. I don't quite know what to do because I can't ignore my desire to go home and yet I feel I am a much weaker person than I like to think I am because I do have these emotions. I've always tried to avoid situations which aren't so nice, like arguments and dirty houses and now maybe Mississippi. I asked my father if I could stay down here for a whole year and I was almost glad when he said "no" that we couldn't afford it because it would mean supporting me this year in addition to three more years of college. I have a desire to go home and to read a lot and go to Quaker meetings and be by myself so I can think about all this rather than being in the middle of it all the time. But I know if my emotions run like they have in the past, that I can only take that pacific sort of life for a little while and then I get the desire to be active again and get involved with knowing other people.

I guess this all sounds crazy and I seem to always think out my problems as I write to you. I am angry because I have a choice as to whether or not to work in the Movement and I am playing upon that choice and leaving here. I wish I could talk with you 'cause I'd like to know if you ever felt this way about anything. I mean have you ever despised yourself for your weak conviction or something. And what is making it worse is that all those damn northerners are thinking of me as a brave hero.

• • •

The civil rights activist Fannie Lou Hamer was born in Montgomery County, Mississippi, daughter of two sharecroppers. In 1962, after attending a local meeting with James Forman of the Student Nonviolent Coordinating Committee (SNCC) and James Bevel of the Southern Christian Leadership Conference (SCLC), she joined a group of eighteen blacks who traveled to the courthouse in Indianola to register to vote. At the time, fewer than seven percent of blacks were registered to vote in Mississippi. But Mississippi required that potential voters pass a literacy test before they could register, and Hamer and the others were told they had failed the test, and so could not register. Returning to Ruleville, the group was harassed and later she was arrested. Here, Hamer, who later became a field secretary for SNCC and a leader of the Mississippi Freedom Democratic Party (MFDP), describes to the Credentials Committee of the Democratic National Convention in Washington in 1964 the treatment she received for trying to vote in Mississippi. She was part of a Mississippi delegation that asked the Convention to let black delegates, in proportion to their part of the population of Mississippi, represent the state at the Convention. The Democratic Party leaders, including Lyndon Johnson and Hubert Humphrey, rejected this, and the Mississippi delegation remained all-white.

Testimony of Fannie Lou Hamer (August 22, 1964)[8]

Mr. Chairman, and the Credentials Committee, my name is Mrs. Fannie Lou Hamer, and I live at 626 East Lafayette Street, Ruleville, Mississippi, Sunflower County, the home of Senator James O. Eastland, and Senator [John] Stennis.

It was the 31st of August in 1962 that eighteen of us traveled twenty-six miles to the country courthouse in Indianola to try to register to try to become first-class citizens.

We was met in Indianola by Mississippi men, Highway Patrolmens[,] and they only allowed two of us in to take the literacy test at the time. After we had taken this test and started back to Ruleville, we was held up by the City Police and the State Highway Patrolmen and carried back to Indianola where the bus driver was charged that day with driving a bus the wrong color.

After we paid the fine among us, we continued on to Ruleville, and Reverend Jeff Sunny carried me four miles in the rural area where I had worked as a timekeeper and sharecropper for eighteen years. I was met there by my children, who told me the plantation owner was angry because I had gone down to try to register.

After they told me, my husband came, and said that the plantation owner was raising cain because I had tried to register, and before he quit talking the plantation owner came, and said, "Fannie Lou, do you know—did Pap tell you what I said?"

And I said, "Yes, sir."

He said, "I mean that," he said, "If you don't go down and withdraw your registration, you will have to leave. . . because we are not ready for that in Mississippi."

And I addressed him and told him and said, "I didn't try to register for you. I tried to register for myself."

I had to leave that same night.

On the 10th of September, 1962, sixteen bullets was fired into the home of Mr. and Mrs. Robert Tucker for me. That same night two girls were shot in Ruleville, Mississippi. Also Mr. Joe McDonald's house was shot in.

And in June the 9th, 1963, I had attended a voter registration workshop, was returning back to Mississippi. Ten of us was traveling by the Continental Trailway bus. When we got to Winona, Mississippi, which is Montgomery County, four of the people got off to use the washroom, and two of the people—to use the restaurant—two of the people wanted to use the washroom.

The four people that had gone in to use the restaurant was ordered out. During this time I was on the bus. But when I looked through the window and saw they had rushed out I got off of the bus to see what had happened, and one of the ladies said, "It was a State Highway Patrolman and a Chief of Police ordered us out."

I got back on the bus and one of the persons had used the washroom got back on the bus, too.

As soon as I was seated on the bus, I saw when they began to get the four people in a highway patrolman's car, I stepped off of the bus to see what was happening and somebody screamed from the car that the four workers was in and said, "Get that one there," and when I went to get in the car, when the man told me I was under arrest, he kicked me.

I was carried to the county jail, and put in the booking room. They left some of the people in the booking room and began to place us in cells. I was placed in a cell with a young woman called Miss [Euvester] Simpson. After I was placed in the cell I began to hear the sounds of kicks and screams. I could hear somebody say, "Can you say, yes, sir, nigger? Can you say yes, sir?"

And they would say other horrible names.

She would say, "Yes, I can say yes, sir."

"So say it."

She says, "I don't know you well enough."

They beat her, I don't know how long, and after a while she began to pray, and asked God to have mercy on those people.

And it wasn't too long before three white men came to my cell. One of these men was a State Highway Patrolman and he asked me where I was from, and I told him Ruleville, [and he] said, "We are going to check this."

And they left my cell and it wasn't too long before they came back. He said, "You are from Ruleville all right," and he used a curse word, and he said, "We are going to make you wish you was dead."

I was carried out of that cell into another cell where they had two Negro prisoners. The State Highway Patrolmen ordered the first Negro to take the blackjack.

The first Negro prisoner ordered me, by orders from the State Highway Patrolman for me, to lay down on a bunk bed on my face, and I laid on my face.

The first Negro began to beat, and I was beat by the first Negro until he was exhausted, and I was holding my hands behind me at that time on my left side because I suffered from polio when I was six years old.

After the first Negro had beat until he was exhausted the State Highway Patrolman ordered the second Negro to take the blackjack.

The second Negro began to beat and I began to work my feet, and the State Highway Patrolman ordered the first Negro who had beat me to set on my feet to keep me from working my feet. I began to scream and one white man got up and began to beat me in my head and tell me to hush.

One white man—my dress had worked up high, he walked over and pulled my dress down—and he pulled my dress back, back up.

I was in jail when Medgar Evers was murdered.

All of this is on account we want to register, to become first-class citizens, and if the [Mississippi] Freedom Democratic Party is not seated now, I question America, is this America, the land of the free and the home of the brave where we have to sleep with our telephones off of the hooks because our lives be threatened daily because we want to live as decent human beings, in America?

• • •

During the Mississippi Freedom Summer of 1964 over a thousand white college students from the North traveled South to challenge racial segregation and the disenfranchisement of black voters. On June 21, 1964, at the start of the Freedom Summer, a young black Mississippian, James Chaney, and two whites from the North, Michael Schwerner and Andrew Goodman, drove to Philadelphia, Mississippi, to look into the bombing of a black church. They never returned, and pleas to the Justice Department to take immediate action were met with coldness. Chaney, Goodman, and Schwerner had been arrested by local police, then released. In a plan participated in by the sheriff and deputy sheriff of the county, they were then followed by a group of white men who blockaded their car, took them to a deserted farm, beat them with chains, shot them to death, and buried their bodies. Not until forty-four days after their arrest were the bodies of the three young men found. Schwerner's wife, Rita, made this statement before the discovery of the three bodies.

Testimony of Rita L. Schwerner (1964)[9]

I am 22 years old and the wife of Michael H. Schwerner, one of the three civil rights workers who have been missing in or near Philadelphia, Mississippi, since June 21, 1964. Michael and I came to Mississippi on about January 16 this year as field staff workers for the Congress of Racial Equality, assigned to the Council of Federated Organizations. On about January 21 we went to Meridian, Mississippi, with the purpose of establishing a community center in that city which would provide such services which the state and local authorities would not provide for Negro citizens. From that time until June 21, 1964, we worked continually in and around the area of Meridian and other counties in the eastern half of the Fourth Congressional District. To my knowledge, the only times that Michael left the state in those six and a half months were for a four-day conference in New Orleans in February, a one-day trip the two of us took to New York in March, and the Oxford orientation session in Oxford, Ohio, immediately prior to his disappearance. The only additional time that I was out of the state was for a ten-day visit to New York City from May 24 to June 2.

Shortly after we arrived in Meridian in January, we met Mr. James E. Chaney, a 21-year-old Negro man who worked with us and eventually became part of the Congress of Racial Equality staff. From about the middle of February to the end of March, James was out of Meridian, working first in Canton and then, for a short time, in Greenwood. At the end of March, he returned to Meridian to work with us.

In the first few weeks that Michael and I were in Meridian, we had to change our place of residence some three or four times, because the Negro families who took us in received intimidating phone calls and became afraid to house us. In February we were able to rent a house from a Negro, Mr. Albert Jones, which he rented from a white woman, Mrs. Roy Cunningham. We lived in that house until the beginning of June, when Mrs. Cunningham insisted that we leave. Prior to our eviction, we had had our rent raised by her.

In the first few weeks that we were in Meridian, we received no threats, nor did we suffer harassment at the hands of the local authorities. However, as people came to know us better, to recognize us, and to know what we were attempting to do, the tension increased. On several occasions my husband was picked up by the local police and taken to the police station, where he was questioned as to our activities, asked to show proof of ownership of our car, etc. They never did pick me up for questioning.

As we achieved some success in establishing the community center, the threats and intimidation began to increase. By May we received so many phone calls at late hours of the night that in order to get some sleep we were forced to remove our telephone receiver before going to bed. We finally resolved this problem by obtaining an unpublished telephone number when we moved to our new apartment after being evicted. The phone calls at the office during the day and evenings continued. They were of several forms. Some were extremely unpleasant in that when I picked up the phone the party at the other end of the line would use extremely offensive language towards me. Other calls we received were threats of violence, such as someone calling and telling me that he was planning to kill my husband, or that my husband was already dead. Michael received anonymous calls telling him that they intended to kill me or that I was already dead. . . .

Michael started making trips into Neshoba County in February and, in all, made about 30 such expeditions. Every time he went into that county to work, I remained in the office in Meridian to receive his phone calls when he checked in, or in the event that anything went wrong and he needed to contact someone. The only times that I did not serve in that capacity were the few trips he made into Neshoba County when I was out of the state. Because the county was known to be so dangerous, I insisted on assuming that job myself, out of obvious concern for my husband's safety. When James Chaney returned to Meridian at the end of

March, the two of them usually traveled to Neshoba together, although there were one or two occasions when one of them went alone or with another person. Neshoba County has had a reputation for being so volatile that it has been nicknamed "Bloody Neshoba," and many experienced civil rights workers, for very good reason, declined to work in that territory.

My husband believed very strongly in security precautions, such as phoning in one's whereabouts, and on several occasions I heard him reprimand others who did not call in to the office when they were supposed to. I remember only one incident prior to his disappearance when Michael was two hours late returning from Neshoba County and did not call to tell me why. I was frantic and at the point of calling the jails, but refrained because I knew that if he had not been picked up, this would inform the authorities of his whereabouts and make the situation far graver. When he and James returned that particular evening, they said that they had been detained in talking with a contact who had no telephone, and that they were fearful of stopping on the road to call in and advise me of their delay. . . .

On one or more occasions, James told me that the car had been followed in Neshoba County by white persons in cars with the license plates either covered or removed. On one occasion he said he had been followed by an official car, either that of police or sheriff's department, but I don't know which.

On June 21, 1964, Michael and James made another trip to Philadelphia, this time accompanied by Andrew Goodman, one of the volunteer COFO summer workers. I was in Oxford, Ohio, at the time, but before my husband left Oxford at 3 a.m., Saturday, June 20, he told me of his intention to go on Sunday to Philadelphia to investigate the burning of the Mt. Zion Church in the Longdale community. The three men never returned to Meridian, nor did they call in their whereabouts. All knowledge I have of my husband's habits and training indicates that, given the opportunity, he certainly would have called in. It is foolish to assert that he would have turned down the opportunity to do so. The information from officials is vague and contradictory, and all knowledge of the situation in Neshoba County would lead me to believe that the three men have been murdered.

On June 25, at about 3 p.m., I went to the State Capitol building in Jackson with John Robert Zellner, a Student Nonviolent Coordinating Committee field secretary, and Reverend Edwin King, the Tougaloo College chaplain. I attempted to see Governor [Paul B.] Johnson [Jr.] to ask for his promise of help in the search for the three men. We were told by Senator Barbour that the governor was out for the afternoon and could not be contacted. He was extremely rude in his treatment of me. We then walked over to the Governor's Mansion, arriving just as Governor Johnson walked up the steps with Governor [George] Wallace of Alabama. We followed them up the steps and Mr. Zellner introduced himself by name to Governor

Johnson and they shook hands. Mr. Zellner then turned towards me and introduced me as the wife of Michael Schwerner, one of the three missing men. He said that I would like to speak for a moment with the Mississippi governor. The moment Johnson heard who I was, he turned and bolted for the door of the Mansion. The door was locked behind him and a group of Mississippi highway patrolmen surrounded the three of us. An officer with the name plate "Harper" refused to allow us to request an appointment with the governor. Harper said that he would not convey our request to Johnson.

On June 26, 1964, when I went to Neshoba County to speak with Sheriff [Lawrence] Rainey, the car which I was in was followed by a blue, late-model pick-up truck without license plates. There were two white men in the truck. At one point the truck blocked us off in front and a white, late-model car blocked us from behind. We turned our automobile around and were able to get by the white car; the pick-up truck followed us awhile farther. We reported this to the FBI agents who were working in Philadelphia on the investigation. After I spoke with Sheriff Rainey, who denied knowledge of the circumstances of the disappearance of the three men, we obtained permission from Rainey and the FBI to follow the sheriff's car to the garage where the station wagon (which the men had driven on June 21) was being kept, in order that I could see it. Several young white men, who I believe were workers at the garage, laughed and made screams which are usually referred to as rebel yells when they realized who I was. When we left the garage the sheriff's car was close behind ours, and the blue pick-up truck once more followed after us to the outskirts of town, with the sheriff making no attempt to stop it or question the occupants about the lack of license plates.

• • •

Alice Walker grew up in Eatonton, Georgia, in a family of sharecroppers. She started reading at an early age, attended Spelman College and then Sarah Lawrence College, and soon was turning out volumes of poetry and novels. Her novel *The Color Purple* won the American Book Award and the Pulitzer Prize, and sold several million copies. While at Spelman College, she became active in the student movement against racial segregation, was arrested, and through all the following years remained a powerful voice for peace and social justice. The following poems, which reflect her experiences in the southern movement and speak to the dynamism of the struggle for civil rights, appear in her first volume of poetry, *Once*.

Alice Walker, "Once" (1968)[10]

I
Green lawn
a picket fence
flowers—
My friend smiles
she had heard
that Southern
jails
were drab.

Looking up I see
a strong arm
raised
the Law
Someone in America
is being
protected
(from me.)

In the morning
there was
a man in grey
but the sky
was blue.

II
"Look at that
nigger with those
white folks!"
        My dark
Arrogant friend
turns calmly, curiously
helpfully,
                "Where?" he
                        asks.

It was the fifth
arrest
In as many
        days
How glad I am
that I can
look
surprised
        still.

III
Running down
Atlanta
        streets
With my sign
I see heads
        turn
Eyes
        goggle
"a nice girl
        like her!"

A Negro cook
assures
        her mistress—

But I had seen
the fingers
near her eyes
        wet with
        tears.

IV
One day in
Georgia
Working around

the Negro section
My friend got a
letter
in
the mail
—the letter
said
        "I hope you're
having a good
time
fucking all
        the niggers."

"Sweet," I winced.
        "Who
        wrote it?"

"mother."
        she
                said.

That day she sat
        a long time
a little black girl
in pigtails
on her lap

Her eyes were very
Quiet.

She used to tell the big colored ladies
her light eyes just
the same
"I am alone
my mother died."
Though no other
letter
came.

V

It is true—
I've always loved
the daring
        ones
Like the black young
man
Who tried
to crash
All barriers
at once,
        wanted to
swim
At a white
beach (in Alabama)
Nude.

VI

Peter always
thought
the only
way to
"enlighten"
southern towns
was to
introduce
        himself
to
the county
sheriff
        first thing.

Another thing
Peter wanted—
was to be
cremated
        but we
couldn't
        find him
when he needed it.

But he was just a yid
seventeen.

VII
I
never liked
white folks
really
it
happened quite
suddenly
one
day
A pair of
amber
eyes
I
think
he
had.

VIII
I don't think
integration
entered
into it
officer

You see
there was
this little
Negro
girl
Standing here
alone
and her
mother
went into
that store
there

then—
there came by
this little boy
here
without his
mother
& eating
an
ice cream cone
—see there it is—
strawberry

Anyhow

and the little
girl was
hungry
and
stronger
than
the little
boy—

Who is too
fat
really,

anyhow.

IX
Someone said
to
me
that
if
the South
rises
again
it will do so

"from
the grave."

Someone
        else
        said
if the South
rises
        again
he would
        "step on
                it."

Dick Gregory
        said that
        if the
        South
        rises
        again
        there is
        a
        secret
        plan.

But I say—
        if the
        South
rises
        again
It will not
        do
        so
in my presence.

X
"but I don'
really
        give a fuck
Who
        my daughter

marries—"
the lady
was
adorable—
it was in a
tavern
i remember
her daughter
sat there
beside her
tugging
at
her arm
sixteen—
very shy
        and
very pim
        pled.

XI
Then there
Was the charming
        half-wit
who told
the judge
re: indecent exposure
"but when I
step out
of the
tub
I look
        Good—
just because
my skin
is black
don't mean
it ain't
pretty
        you old bastard!)
what will we

finally do
with
prejudice

some people like
to take a walk
after a bath.

XII
"look, honey
said
the
blond
amply
boobed
babe
in the
green

     g
string

"i like you
sure
i ain't
prejudiced

but the
lord didn't
give me
legs
like
these
because
he
wanted
to see'm
dangling
from a
poplar!"

"But they're so
    much
prettier
than mine.

Would you really mind?"
he asked
wanting her to dance.

XIII
I remember
seeing
a little girl,
dreaming—perhaps,
hit by
a
van truck
"That nigger was
in the way!" the
man
    said
    to
understanding cops.

    But was she?
    She was
    just eight
    her mother
    said
    and little
    for
    her age.

XIV
then there was
the
picture of
the
bleak-eyed
little black

girl
waving the
american
flag
holding it
gingerly
with
the very
tips
of her
fingers.

• • •

Despite the victories of the civil rights movement, resentment against continued poverty and police brutality remained. Dramatic proof of this came in the Watts Riot of August 13, 1965, in Los Angeles, just as President Lyndon B. Johnson was signing the Voting Rights Act, providing for federal registration of black voters. This was the most violent urban outbreak since World War II. It was provoked by the arrest of a young African-American driver, the clubbing of a bystander by police, and the seizure of a young black woman falsely accused of spitting on the police. After five days of rioting, thirty-four people were dead, most of them black. Two years after Watts, in July 1967, resentment over the high levels of racism, poverty, and police brutality boiled over into an urban rebellion that lasted three days in Detroit, Michigan. That summer, urban rebellions also took place in New York, Cleveland, Atlanta, and Chicago, and Newark, New Jersey. (A year later, many of these same cities would erupt in anger over the assassination of Martin Luther King, Jr.) Here is journalist Sandra A. West's account from the *Detroit News* about the events in Detroit, in which more than forty African Americans were killed and more than seven thousand were arrested.

Sandra A. West, "Riot!—A Negro Resident's Story" (July 24, 1967)[11]

Negroes moved into Detroit's near west side because it was "a nice neighborhood."
    Yesterday they cried with fear as burning and looting raged all around them.
    I have lived in the area since 1954.
    Yesterday I saw sights I never dreamed possible. I saw things I had only read about or seen on television.

Raging fires burned out of control for blocks and blocks. Thick black smoke and cinders rained down, at times so heavily they blocked out the vision of homes 20 feet away.

Looters drove pickup trucks loaded with everything from floor mops to new furniture. Price tags still dangled from the merchandise.

Youngsters no more than eight or nine years old rode two on a bicycle with loot under their shirts and clutched in their arms.

There was agony on the faces of those who lived close to the burnings, afraid their homes would be burned, too.

Friends of ours, in and out of the area, set up telephone relay systems with us to pass on any new information. Rumors spread as fast as the flames and it was hard to know what was true.

By 5 p.m. it was necessary to close our home to keep the smoke from saturating the house.

At 6:30 p.m. the electricity went out. We couldn't use our electric fan and were forced to open the house again.

We walked to 12th street where the riots began. There we watched as arsonists touched off fires at two establishments within a one-block area.

Burglar alarms wailed out of control. They went unanswered. Negro-owned stores sported hastily printed signs that read "Soul Brother."

A 12-year-old boy flashed a diamond ring that he said he found on his lawn.

On Linwood, three blocks west of 12th, smoke was so thick it was impossible to see one block away.

Some of the families on the blocks between 12th and Linwood packed their belongings and prepared to leave during the night if it became necessary. We were one of those families.

At the height of the rampage, several homes caught fire from the burning stores.

A man, his wife and two small children stumbled along the street with a suitcase and a bedsheet filled with the few belongings they could grab. Tears streamed down the mother's face.

The acrid odor of smoke burned our lungs and as the sun set we began rummaging around for candles and flashlights. Neighbors told us they planned to sit up on their porches all night.

By the 9 p.m. curfew, the streets were relatively quiet, but fear remained etched on the faces of those of us who had to spend the night there.

Nothing stirred on the streets at 10 p.m. except an occasional police car and jeeps and trucks loaded with national guardsmen. But the residents of "this nice neighborhood" were afraid that the riot wasn't over.

And it wasn't.

. . .

Reverend Martin Luther King, Jr.'s eloquence as a leader of the black struggle was unparalleled. He gave dozens of speeches, and led many more actions, that defined an era. In this speech, which has received less attention than some of his others, he raises some of his most profound criticisms of U.S. society, pointing to the economic roots of racism and raising the issue of the fundamental transformation of U.S. capitalism. The speech was delivered, to rousing response, as King's Annual Report at the convention of the Southern Christian Leadership Conference in Atlanta, Georgia.

Martin Luther King, Jr., "Where Do We Go from Here?" (August 16, 1967)[12]

[O]ver the last ten years the Negro decided to straighten his back up, realizing that a man cannot ride your back unless it is bent. We made our government write new laws to alter some of the cruelest injustices that affected us. We made an indifferent and unconcerned nation rise from lethargy and subpoenaed its conscience to appear before the judgment seat of morality on the whole question of civil rights. We gained manhood in the nation that had always called us "boy." It would be hypocritical indeed if I allowed modesty to forbid my saying that SCLC stood at the forefront of all of the watershed movements that brought these monumental changes in the South. For this, we can feel a legitimate pride. But in spite of a decade of significant progress, the problem is far from solved. The deep rumbling of discontent in our cities is indicative of the fact that the plant of freedom has grown only a bud and not yet a flower. . . .

With all the struggle and all the achievements, we must face the fact, however, that the Negro still lives in the basement of the Great Society. He is still at the bottom, despite the few who have penetrated to slightly higher levels. Even where the door has been forced partially open, mobility for the Negro is still sharply restricted. There is often no bottom at which to start, and when there is there's almost no room at the top. In consequence, Negroes are still impoverished aliens in an affluent society. They are too poor even to rise with the society, too impoverished by the ages to be able to ascend by using their own resources. And the Negro did not do this himself; it was done to him. For more than half of his American history, he was enslaved. Yet, he built the spanning bridges and the grand mansions, the sturdy docks and stout factories of the South. His unpaid labor made cotton "King" and established America as a significant nation in international commerce. Even after his release from chattel slavery, the nation grew over him, submerging him. It became the richest, most powerful society in the history of man, but it left the Negro far behind.

And so we still have a long, long way to go before we reach the promised land of freedom. Yes, we have left the dusty soils of Egypt, and we have crossed a Red Sea that had for years been hardened by a long and piercing winter of massive resistance, but before we reach the majestic shores of the promised land, there will still be gigantic mountains of opposition ahead and prodigious hilltops of injustice. . . .

Now, in order to answer the question, "Where do we go from here?" which is our theme, we must first honestly recognize where we are now. When the Constitution was written, a strange formula to determine taxes and representation declared that the Negro was sixty percent of a person. Today another curious formula seems to declare he is fifty percent of a person. Of the good things in life, the Negro has approximately one half those of whites. Of the bad things of life, he has twice those of whites. Thus, half of all Negroes live in substandard housing. And Negroes have half the income of whites. When we turn to the negative experiences of life, the Negro has a double share: There are twice as many unemployed; the rate of infant mortality among Negroes is double that of whites; and there are twice as many Negroes dying in Vietnam as whites in proportion to their size in the population.

In other spheres, the figures are equally alarming. In elementary schools, Negroes lag one to three years behind whites, and their segregated schools receive substantially less money per student than the white schools. One-twentieth as many Negroes as whites attend college. Of employed Negroes, seventy-five percent hold menial jobs. This is where we are. . . .

I want to say to you as I move to my conclusion, as we talk about "Where do we go from here?" that we must honestly face the fact that the movement must address itself to the question of restructuring the whole of American society. There are forty million poor people here, and one day we must ask the question, "Why are there forty million poor people in America?" And when you begin to ask that question, you are raising a question about the economic system, about a broader distribution of wealth. When you ask that question, you begin to question the capitalistic economy. And I'm simply saying that more and more, we've got to begin to ask questions about the whole society. We are called upon to help the discouraged beggars in life's marketplace. But one day we must come to see that an edifice which produces beggars needs restructuring. It means that questions must be raised. And you see, my friends, when you deal with this you begin to ask the question, "Who owns the oil?" You begin to ask the question, "Who owns the iron ore?" You begin to ask the question, "Why is it that people have to pay water bills in a world that's two-thirds water?" These are words that must be said. . . .

Now, when I say questioning the whole society, it means ultimately coming to see that the problem of racism, the problem of economic exploitation, and the problem of war are all tied together. These are the triple evils that are interrelated.

And if you will let me be a preacher just a little bit. One day, one night, a juror came to Jesus and he wanted to know what he could do to be saved. Jesus didn't get bogged down on the kind of isolated approach of what you shouldn't do. Jesus didn't say, "Now Nicodemus, you must stop lying." He didn't say, "Nicodemus, now you must not commit adultery." He didn't say, "Now Nicodemus, you must stop cheating if you are doing that." He didn't say, "Nicodemus, you must stop drinking liquor if you are doing that excessively." He said something altogether different, because Jesus realized something basic: that if a man will lie, he will steal. And if a man will steal, he will kill. So instead of just getting bogged down on one thing, Jesus looked at him and said, "Nicodemus, you must be born again."

In other words, "Your whole structure must be changed." A nation that will keep people in slavery for 244 years will "thingify" them and make them things. And therefore, they will exploit them and poor people generally economically. And a nation that will exploit economically will have to have foreign investments and everything else, and it will have to use its military might to protect them. All of these problems are tied together.

What I'm saying today is that we must go from this convention and say, "America, you must be born again!"

And so, I conclude by saying today that we have a task, and let us go out with a divine dissatisfaction.

Let us be dissatisfied until America will no longer have a high blood pressure of creeds and an anemia of deeds.

Let us be dissatisfied until the tragic walls that separate the outer city of wealth and comfort from the inner city of poverty and despair shall be crushed by the battering rams of the forces of justice.

Let us be dissatisfied until those who live on the outskirts of hope are brought into the metropolis of daily security.

Let us be dissatisfied until slums are cast into the junk heaps of history, and every family will live in a decent, sanitary home.

Let us be dissatisfied until the dark yesterdays of segregated schools will be transformed into bright tomorrows of quality integrated education.

Let us be dissatisfied until integration is not seen as a problem but as an opportunity to participate in the beauty of diversity.

Let us be dissatisfied until men and women, however black they may be, will be judged on the basis of the content of their character, not on the basis of the color of their skin. Let us be dissatisfied.

Let us be dissatisfied until every state capitol will be housed by a governor who will do justly, who will love mercy, and who will walk humbly with his God.

Let us be dissatisfied until from every city hall, justice will roll down like waters, and righteousness like a mighty stream.

Let us be dissatisfied until that day when the lion and the lamb shall lie down together, and every man will sit under his own vine and fig tree, and none shall be afraid.

Let us be dissatisfied, and men will recognize that out of one blood God made all men to dwell upon the face of the earth.

Let us be dissatisfied until that day when nobody will shout, "White Power!" when nobody will shout, "Black Power!" but everybody will talk about God's power and human power.

And I must confess, my friends, that the road ahead will not always be smooth. There will still be rocky places of frustration and meandering points of bewilderment. There will be inevitable setbacks here and there. And there will be those moments when the buoyancy of hope will be transformed into the fatigue of despair. Our dreams will sometimes be shattered and our ethereal hopes blasted. We may again, with tear-drenched eyes, have to stand before the bier of some courageous civil rights worker whose life will be snuffed out by the dastardly acts of bloodthirsty mobs. But difficult and painful as it is, we must walk on in the days ahead with an audacious faith in the future. . . .

When our days become dreary with low-hovering clouds of despair, and when our nights become darker than a thousand midnights, let us remember that there is a creative force in this universe working to pull down the gigantic mountains of evil, a power that is able to make a way out of no way and transform dark yesterdays into bright tomorrows.

Let us realize that the arc of the moral universe is long, but it bends toward justice. Let us realize that William Cullen Bryant is right: "Truth, crushed to earth, will rise again." Let us go out realizing that the Bible is right: "Be not deceived. God is not mocked. Whatsoever a man soweth, that shall he also reap." This is our hope for the future, and with this faith we will be able to sing in some not too distant tomorrow, with a cosmic past tense, "We have overcome! We have overcome! Deep in my heart, I did believe we would overcome."

Vietnam and Beyond: The Historic Resistance

Mississippi Freedom Democratic Party, McComb, Mississippi, Petition Against the War in Vietnam (July 28, 1965)

Martin Luther King, Jr., "Beyond Vietnam" (April 4, 1967)

Student Nonviolent Coordinating Committee, Position Paper on Vietnam (January 6, 1966)

Bob Dylan, "Masters of War" (1963)

Muhammad Ali Speaks Out Against the Vietnam War (1966)

Jonathan Schell, *The Village of Ben Suc* (1967)

Larry Colburn, "They Were Butchering People" (2003)

Haywood T. "The Kid" Kirkland, from *Bloods: An Oral History of the Vietnam War by Black Veterans* (1984)

Loung Ung, "People Just Disappeared and You Didn't Say Anything" (2003)

Tim O'Brien, "The Man I Killed" (1990)

Maria Herrera-Sobek, Two Poems on Vietnam (1999)

Daniel Ellsberg, *Secrets: A Memoir of Vietnam and the Pentagon Papers* (2003)

After World War II, when the French failed to retake their colony of Indochina (which included Laos, Cambodia, and Vietnam) in a long war that ended in 1954, the United States moved in to replace them. The treaty ending the war between the French and the Vietminh (the independence movement led by Ho Chi Minh, a Communist) had provided for an election in 1954 to establish a unified Vietnam. But the United States obstructed that path, and instead set up a government in South Vietnam.

Rebellion spread against the South Vietnamese government, and the United States sent more and more troops in to suppress the rebellion. In 1964, an incident was manufactured in the Gulf of Tonkin that became an excuse for the United States to initiate a full-scale war in Vietnam against the Viet Cong rebels of the South and its supporters in the Communist government of North Vietnam.

The protest against the war in the United States began slowly, but grew into a great national movement. Blacks in the South were among the first to refuse to be drafted, but this refusal became widespread all over the country. It soon became clear that the United States was committing atrocities in Vietnam. It was bombing peasant villages, rounding up women and children, destroying the rice fields, killing large numbers of civilians.

In 1966, two-thirds of the American people supported the war. By the early 1970s, two-thirds of the population opposed the war. Resistance in the armed forces, veterans returning and speaking out against the war, acts of civil disobedience, and draft refusal all contributed to an unprecedented national movement that played an important part in finally bringing the war to an end.

• • •

In McComb, Mississippi, in July 1965, civil rights activists in the Mississippi Freedom Democratic Party circulated and published this petition. It was one of the first petitions against the war in Vietnam.

Mississippi Freedom Democratic Party, McComb, Mississippi, Petition Against the War in Vietnam (July 28, 1965)[1]

Here are five reasons why Negroes should not be in any war fighting for America:

1. No Mississippi Negroes should be fighting in Vietnam for the White Man's freedom, until all the Negro People are free in Mississippi.

2. Negro Boys should not honor the draft here in Mississippi. Mothers should encourage their sons not to go.

3. We will gain respect and dignity as a race only by forcing the U.S. Government and the Mississippi Government to come with guns, dogs and trucks to take our sons away to fight and be killed protecting Mississippi, Alabama, Georgia, and Louisiana.

4. No one has a right to ask us to risk our lives and kill other Colored People in Santo Domingo and Vietnam, so that the White American can get richer. We will be looked upon as traitors by all the Colored People of the world if the Negro people continue to fight and die without a cause.

5. Last week a white soldier from New Jersey was discharged from the Army because he refused to fight in Vietnam; he went on a hunger strike. Negro boys can do the same thing. We can write and ask our sons if they know what they are fighting for. If he answers Freedom, tell him that's what we are fighting for here

in Mississippi. And if he says Democracy, tell him the truth—we don't know anything about Communism, Socialism, and all that, but we do know that Negroes have caught hell right here under this American Democracy.

• • •

A number of civil rights leaders urged Martin Luther King, Jr., not to speak out on the growing intervention of the United States in Vietnam, but he said he could not separate the issues of economic injustice, racism, war, and militarism. In a speech he gave in the Riverside Church in New York, exactly one year before his assassination, King articulated his opposition. A section of this historic speech is included here.

Martin Luther King, Jr., "Beyond Vietnam" (April 1, 1967)[2]

I come to this magnificent house of worship tonight because my conscience leaves me no other choice. I join you in this meeting because I am in deepest agreement with the aims and work of the organization which has brought us together, Clergy and Laymen Concerned About Vietnam. The recent statements of your executive committee are the sentiments of my own heart, and I found myself in full accord when I read its opening lines: "A time comes when silence is betrayal." That time has come for us in relation to Vietnam.

The truth of these words is beyond doubt, but the mission to which they call us is a most difficult one. Even when pressed by the demands of inner truth, men do not easily assume the task of opposing their government's policy, especially in time of war. Nor does the human spirit move without great difficulty against all the apathy of conformist thought within one's own bosom and in the surrounding world. Moreover, when the issues at hand seem as perplexing as they often do in the case of this dreadful conflict, we are always on the verge of being mesmerized by uncertainty. But we must move on.

Some of us who have already begun to break the silence of the night have found that the calling to speak is often a vocation of agony, but we must speak. We must speak with all the humility that is appropriate to our limited vision, but we must speak. And we must rejoice as well, for surely this is the first time in our nation's history that a significant number of its religious leaders have chosen to move beyond the prophesying of smooth patriotism to the high grounds of a firm dissent based upon the mandates of conscience and the reading of history. Perhaps a new spirit is rising among us. If it is, let us trace its movement, and pray that our own inner being may be sensitive to its guidance. For we are deeply in need of a new way beyond the darkness that seems so close around us.

Over the past two years, as I have moved to break the betrayal of my own silences and to speak from the burnings of my own heart, as I have called for radical departures from the destruction of Vietnam, many persons have questioned me about the wisdom of my path. At the heart of their concerns, this query has often loomed large and loud: "Why are you speaking about the war, Dr. King? Why are you joining the voices of dissent?" "Peace and civil rights don't mix," they say. "Aren't you hurting the cause of your people?" they ask. And when I hear them, though I often understand the source of their concern, I am nevertheless greatly saddened, for such questions mean that the inquirers have not really known me, my commitment, or my calling. Indeed, their questions suggest that they do not know the world in which they live. In the light of such tragic misunderstanding, I deem it of signal importance to try to state clearly, and I trust concisely, why I believe that the path from Dexter Avenue Baptist Church—the church in Montgomery, Alabama, where I began my pastorate—leads clearly to this sanctuary tonight. . . .

Since I am a preacher by calling, I suppose it is not surprising that I have seven major reasons for bringing Vietnam into the field of my moral vision. There is at the outset a very obvious and almost facile connection between the war in Vietnam and the struggle I and others have been waging in America. A few years ago there was a shining moment in that struggle. It seemed as if there was a real promise of hope for the poor, both black and white, through the poverty program. There were experiments, hopes, new beginnings. Then came the buildup in Vietnam, and I watched this program broken and eviscerated as if it were some idle political plaything of a society gone mad on war. And I knew that America would never invest the necessary funds or energies in rehabilitation of its poor so long as adventures like Vietnam continued to draw men and skills and money like some demonic, destructive suction tube. So I was increasingly compelled to see the war as an enemy of the poor and to attack it as such.

Perhaps a more tragic recognition of reality took place when it became clear to me that the war was doing far more than devastating the hopes of the poor at home. It was sending their sons and their brothers and their husbands to fight and to die in extraordinarily high proportions relative to the rest of the population. We were taking the black young men who had been crippled by our society and sending them eight thousand miles away to guarantee liberties in Southeast Asia which they had not found in southwest Georgia and East Harlem. So we have been repeatedly faced with the cruel irony of watching Negro and white boys on TV screens as they kill and die together for a nation that has been unable to seat them together in the same schools. So we watch them in brutal solidarity burning the huts of a poor village, but we realize that they would hardly live on the same block in Chicago. I could not be silent in the face of such cruel manipulation of the poor.

My third reason moves to an even deeper level of awareness, for it grows out of my experience in the ghettos of the North over the last three years, especially the last three summers. As I have walked among the desperate, rejected, and angry young men, I have told them that Molotov cocktails and rifles would not solve their problems. I have tried to offer them my deepest compassion while maintaining my conviction that social change comes most meaningfully through nonviolent action. But they asked, and rightly so, "What about Vietnam?" They asked if our own nation wasn't using massive doses of violence to solve its problems, to bring about the changes it wanted. Their questions hit home, and I knew that I could never again raise my voice against the violence of the oppressed in the ghettos without having first spoken clearly to the greatest purveyor of violence in the world today: my own government. For the sake of those boys, for the sake of this government, for the sake of the hundreds of thousands trembling under our violence, I cannot be silent. . . .

Somehow this madness must cease. We must stop now. I speak as a child of God and brother to the suffering poor of Vietnam. I speak for those whose land is being laid waste, whose homes are being destroyed, whose culture is being subverted. I speak for the poor of America who are paying the double price of smashed hopes at home, and dealt death and corruption in Vietnam. I speak as a citizen of the world, for the world as it stands aghast at the path we have taken. I speak as one who loves America, to the leaders of our own nation: The great initiative in this war is ours; the initiative to stop it must be ours. . . .

We must continue to raise our voices and our lives if our nation persists in its perverse ways in Vietnam. We must be prepared to match actions with words by seeking out every creative method of protest possible.

As we counsel young men concerning military service, we must clarify for them our nation's role in Vietnam and challenge them with the alternative of conscientious objection. I am pleased to say that this is a path now chosen by more than seventy students at my own alma mater, Morehouse College, and I recommend it to all who find the American course in Vietnam a dishonorable and unjust one. Moreover, I would encourage all ministers of draft age to give up their ministerial exemptions and seek status as conscientious objectors. These are the times for real choices and not false ones. We are at the moment when our lives must be placed on the line if our nation is to survive its own folly. Every man of humane convictions must decide on the protest that best suits his convictions, but we must all protest.

Now there is something seductively tempting about stopping there and sending us all off on what in some circles has become a popular crusade against the war in Vietnam. I say we must enter that struggle, but I wish to go on now to say something even more disturbing.

The war in Vietnam is but a symptom of a far deeper malady within the American spirit, and if we ignore this sobering reality . . . we will find ourselves organizing "clergy and laymen concerned" committees for the next generation. They will be concerned about Guatemala and Peru. They will be concerned about Thailand and Cambodia. They will be concerned about Mozambique and South Africa. We will be marching for these and a dozen other names and attending rallies without end unless there is a significant and profound change in American life and policy. So such thoughts take us beyond Vietnam, but not beyond our calling as sons of the living God. . . .

I am convinced that if we are to get on the right side of the world revolution, we as a nation must undergo a radical revolution of values. We must rapidly begin . . . the shift from a thing-oriented society to a person-oriented society. When machines and computers, profit motives and property rights, are considered more important than people, the giant triplets of racism, extreme materialism, and militarism are incapable of being conquered.

A true revolution of values will soon cause us to question the fairness and justice of many of our past and present policies. On the one hand we are called to play the Good Samaritan on life's roadside, but that will be only an initial act. One day we must come to see that the whole Jericho Road must be transformed so that men and women will not be constantly beaten and robbed as they make their journey on life's highway. True compassion is more than flinging a coin to a beggar. It comes to see that an edifice which produces beggars needs restructuring.

A true revolution of values will soon look uneasily on the glaring contrast of poverty and wealth. With righteous indignation, it will look across the seas and see individual capitalists of the West investing huge sums of money in Asia, Africa, and South America, only to take the profits out with no concern for the social betterment of the countries, and say, "This is not just." It will look at our alliance with the landed gentry of South America and say, "This is not just." The Western arrogance of feeling that it has everything to teach others and nothing to learn from them is not just.

A true revolution of values will lay hand on the world order and say of war, "This way of settling differences is not just." This business of burning human beings with napalm, of filling our nation's homes with orphans and widows, of injecting poisonous drugs of hate into the veins of peoples normally humane, of sending men home from dark and bloody battlefields physically handicapped and psychologically deranged, cannot be reconciled with wisdom, justice, and love. A nation that continues year after year to spend more money on military defense than on programs of social uplift is approaching spiritual death.

America, the richest and most powerful nation in the world, can well lead the way in this revolution of values. There is nothing except a tragic death wish to prevent us from reordering our priorities so that the pursuit of peace will take precedence over the pursuit of war. There is nothing to keep us from molding a recalcitrant status quo with bruised hands until we have fashioned it into a brotherhood.

● ● ●

The Student Nonviolent Coordinating Committee (SNCC) also spoke out in early 1966 against the war in Vietnam in this statement, seeking to connect the issues of racism at home and the war in Asia.

Student Nonviolent Coordinating Committee, Position Paper on Vietnam (January 6, 1966)[3]

The Student Nonviolent Coordinating Committee assumes its right to dissent with United States foreign policy on any issue, and states its opposition to Untied States involvement in Vietnam on these grounds:

We believe the United States government has been deceptive in claims of concern for the freedom of the Vietnamese people, just as the government has been deceptive in claiming concern for the freedom of colored people in such other countries as the Dominican Republic, the Congo, South Africa, Rhodesia, and in the United States itself.

We, the Student Nonviolent Coordinating Committee, have been involved in the black people's struggle for liberation and self-determination in this country for the past five years. Our work, particularly in the South, taught us that the United States government has never guaranteed the freedom of oppressed citizens and is not yet truly determined to end the rule of terror and oppression within its own borders.

We ourselves have often been victims of violence and confinement executed by U.S. government officials. We recall the numerous persons who have been murdered in the South because of their efforts to secure their civil and human rights, and whose murderers have been allowed to escape penalty for their crimes. The murder of Samuel Younge in Tuskegee, Alabama[,] is no different than the murder of people in Vietnam, for both Younge and the Vietnamese sought and are seeking to secure the rights guaranteed them by law. In each case, the U.S. government bears a great part of the responsibility for these deaths.

Samuel Younge was murdered because U.S. law is not being enforced.

Vietnamese are murdered because the United States is pursuing an aggressive policy in violation of international law. The U.S. is no respecter of persons or law when such persons or laws run counter to its needs and desires. We recall the indifference, suspicion and outright hostility with which our reports of violence have been met in the past by government officials.

We know that for the most part, elections in this country, in the North as well as the South, are not free. We have seen that the 1965 Voting Rights Act and the 1964 Civil Rights Act have not yet been implemented with full federal power and concern. We question then the ability and even the desire of the U.S. government to guarantee free elections abroad. We maintain that our country's cry of "Preserve freedom in the world" is a hypocritical mask behind which it squashed liberation movements which are not bound and refuse to be bound by the expediency of the U.S. cold war policy.

We are in sympathy with and support the men in this country who are unwilling to respond to a military draft which would compel them to contribute their lives to U.S. aggression in the name of the "freedom" we find so false in this country. We recoil with horror at the inconsistency of a supposedly free society where responsibility to freedom is equated with the responsibility to lend oneself to military aggression. We take note of the fact that 16 percent of the draftees from this country are Negro, called on to stifle the liberation of Vietnam, to preserve a "democracy" which does not exist for them at home

We ask: Where is the draft for the Freedom fight in the United States?

We therefore encourage those Americans who prefer to use their energy in building democratic forms within the country. We believe that work in the civil rights movement and other human relations organizations is a valid alternative to the draft. We urge all Americans to seek this alternative knowing full well that it may cost them their lives, as painfully as in Vietnam.

• • •

The songs of Minnesota-born Robert Zimmerman, who reinvented himself as Bob Dylan, were an unmistakable part of the radicalization of the 1960s and the Vietnam era. His 1963 protest song "Masters of War" remains the strongest indictment of war in popular music and came during a period when Dylan also penned songs like "With God on Our Side" and "Blowin' in the Wind," and turned his attention to racism and injustice at home, in songs like "Only a Pawn in Their Game" and "The Lonesome Death of Hattie Carroll," based on a real murder by a child of the Baltimore elite, William Zantzinger.

Bob Dylan, "Masters of War" (1963)[4]

Come you masters of war
You that build all the guns
You that build the death planes
You that build the big bombs
You that hide behind walls
You that hide behind desks
I just want you to know
I can see through your masks

You that never done nothin'
But build to destroy
You play with my world
Like it's your little toy
You put a gun in my hand
And you hide from my eyes
And you turn and run farther
When the fast bullets fly

Like Judas of old
You lie and deceive
A world war can be won
You want me to believe
But I see through your eyes
And I see through your brain
Like I see through the water
That runs down my drain

You fasten the triggers
For the others to fire
Then you set back and watch
When the death count gets higher
You hide in your mansion
As young people's blood
Flows out of their bodies
And is buried in the mud

You've thrown the worst fear
That can ever be hurled

Fear to bring children
Into the world
For threatening my baby
Unborn and unnamed
You ain't worth the blood
That runs in your veins

How much do I know
To talk out of turn
You might say that I'm young
You might say I'm unlearned
But there's one thing I know
Though I'm younger than you
Even Jesus would never
Forgive what you do

Let me ask you one question
Is your money that good
Will it buy you forgiveness
Do you think that it could
I think you will find
When your death takes its toll
All the money you made
Will never buy back your soul

And I hope that you die
And your death'll come soon
I will follow your casket
In the pale afternoon
And I'll watch while you're lowered
Down to your deathbed
And I'll stand o'er your grave
'Til I'm sure that you're dead

• • •

In 1964, shortly after becoming the world heavyweight boxing champion, the boxer Cassius Marcellus Clay (named after a white abolitionist by that name) took the name Muhammad Ali, renouncing what he called his slave name. Two years later, the outspoken fighter caused outrage in the media when he petitioned for exemption from military service in Vietnam and then, when denied, refused to be drafted. As a result of his protest against the war, Ali's title was revoked and he was sentenced to a five-year prison term. Ali's battle against the sentence went to the U.S. Supreme Court and was not reversed until 1971. In 1966, Ali spoke in Louisville, Kentucky, his home town, about the reasons for not fighting in Vietnam.

Muhammad Ali Speaks Out Against the Vietnam War (1966)[5]

Why should they ask me to put on a uniform and go ten thousand miles from home and drop bombs and bullets on brown people in Vietnam while so-called Negro people in Louisville are treated like dogs and denied simple human rights? No, I am not going ten thousand miles from home to help murder and burn another poor nation simply to continue the domination of white slave masters of the darker people the world over. This is the day when such evils must come to an end. I have been warned that to take such a stand would put my prestige in jeopardy and could cause me to lose millions of dollars which should accrue to me as the champion. But I have said it once and I will say it again. The real enemy of my people is right here. I will not disgrace my religion, my people or myself by becoming a tool to enslave those who are fighting for their own justice, freedom and equality. . . .

If I thought the war was going to bring freedom and equality to twenty-two million of my people, they wouldn't have to draft me, I'd join tomorrow. But I either have to obey the laws of the land or the laws of Allah. I have nothing to lose by standing up for my beliefs. So I'll go to jail. We've been in jail for four hundred years.

• • •

The journalist Jonathan Schell was one of the first journalists to expose the reality of the war in Vietnam. *The Village of Ben Suc*, his first book, began as a series of articles for *The New Yorker* magazine. Unlike so much reporting of the time, Schell gave voice to the people of Vietnam, in whose name the war was allegedly being fought.

Jonathan Schell, *The Village of Ben Suc* (1967)[6]

During the Phu Loi camp's first week, I spent several afternoons there interviewing villagers from Ben Suc through an interpreter. Before I asked them any questions,

I would say that I was a reporter, not connected with the Army. They clearly disbelieved me. At first, they would nod understandingly, but later they would ask me for salt, cooking oil, or rice, or for permission to leave the camp, and I would have to explain again that I had no authority in these matters. They would nevertheless ask several more times for food or privileges, as though my claim to be a journalist were part of a game they had played with many interrogators before me. They refused to believe that this young man—the latest in a long procession of young men, of many political colorations, in their lives—did not want to persuade them of something or use them for his own ends. As we spoke, it was difficult to hear each other above the din of loud, enthusiastic taped voices coming over the public-address system.

When I ducked, with an interpreter, into a section of one canopy and asked a young man who was holding the hand of his three-year-old son if we could talk with him for a minute, he leaned down, smiled at the boy, and told him to go to his mother, a young woman with a broad, open face and large, dark eyes, who was standing nearby. The young man came forward to meet us with an unruffled composure that I encountered again and again in the Ben Suc villagers, as though nothing in the world could be more natural for them than to have a talk with an American. He stood before us with a faint smile of amusement. After introducing myself in my usual way, I asked what he thought about coming to the camp. Through the interpreter he said, "I realize now that there is a war going on and that I have to leave to be defended by the government troops and the Americans. Here it is safe—there will be no bombs and artillery. The crops in my field have all been destroyed by chemicals, and my elder brother was killed by a bomb. Many people were killed when the center of the village was bombed last year. Here we are protected by the American troops."

I asked him what he had enjoyed most in his life at Ben Suc.

With a laugh at being asked such a question, he answered, "I play the guitar, and I liked to sing at night and drink with friends—to eat fish and drink until the sun came up. I am thirty-one now, and was married when I was twenty-three. I have three children. I believe in Confucius and pray to Confucius to keep me from misfortune, to send me good luck, and for peace. On most days, I would get up at six o'clock, eat, have a bath, and then go out to the fields. At midday, I would come back, have another bath, and eat, and I would have a bath again when I stopped working at night. I haven't had a bath in four days now. Do you think we'll be able to have one soon?"

I expressed surprise at his taking so many baths, and told him that most Americans take only one bath a day.

"I don't believe it!" he answered. "We always take three baths a day—four when we are sick. After a bath, you feel healthy and feel like eating a lot. We have become very tired here waiting for food, and for water for a bath."

Outside another canopy, I approached a middle-aged man with long, mussed-up hair who sat cross-legged on a straw mat in front of his compartment, scowling frankly while his wife, squatting next to him, tried to blow life into a small twig fire. It was late afternoon, and a chilly breeze had picked up as the sun moved lower in the sky. The thin, scowling man, who wore only a black shirt and green short pants, was shivering slightly. "I have a stomach ache," he told me, pressing his hands over his belly. "I got here yesterday morning on a boat, but we couldn't bring anything with us. All our things are still in Ben Suc—our oxen, our rice, our oxcarts, our farming tools, and our furniture." He related this without looking at me, in a restrained but disgruntled tone. "Now we have only plain rice to eat—nothing to flavor it, not even salt. They don't bring any food. And there's not enough water to take a bath."

I asked him how he felt about leaving his village.

"Anybody would be sad to leave his village," he said. Then, quoting the loudspeakers, he added, "But we have to be protected by the government and American troops."

At this, his wife turned and said furiously, "We have nothing! I have no cooking oil, no rice! We have to beg from the people next to us!"

I asked her if she knew about the rice distribution by the Revolutionary Development workers.

Now losing all control of her temper, she snatched a green meal ticket out of her pocket and waved it at me. "They gave me a ticket a day ago, but they never have enough rice. We couldn't even bring blankets or clothes. My son is naked. Look!" She pointed to a little naked boy of about four, who stood watching his angry mother. "It's no good for children here. Not good for their health. They get cold at night, and there is nowhere for them to go to play." Abruptly, she turned her back and began trying again to get her fire going.

Her sick husband continued to look at the ground. After a minute or so, he said, "I am actually from Mi Hung, but we moved to Ben Suc six months ago, after Mi Hung was bombed."

I asked how long he thought he would be made to stay in the camp.

"I don't know. I was just put here. I can't do anything about it. I can't speak English. How should I know what they are going to do next? I can't understand what they are saying. Many of the old women were weeping when they were taken away."

At another place, addressing myself to a mother holding a baby, I was immediately surrounded by three mothers. They all wore rolled-up black pants with white or blue shirts—dirty now, since the camp had no washing facilities. At first, only one replied when I asked how they liked life at the camp.

"Everybody was taken away from Ben Suc," she said. "We couldn't bring our rice, and we brought only a few possessions. We ran into the bomb shelters when the bombing started."

When I asked the women about their husbands, they all began talking excitedly:

"My husband was out plowing, but I don't know where he is now."

"We don't know where they are."

"They were taken away."

"I don't know if he is still alive or not."

"I saw people dead in the fields, but I didn't know who they were."

One of the women moved forward, and the others grew silent. "We want to go back, but they are going to destroy everything." She was not supposed to know this yet, but she looked at me evenly as she said it.

I asked her whether she was from Ben Suc.

"I am actually from Yao Tin, and was at Ben Suc only for the harvest, to help my parents. I left all my money and things at Yao Tin. I couldn't even go back to my parents' house after coming to the center of the village. My sister is still at Ben Suc, I think."

Having heard that Vietnamese villages often rely on a group of elders to make decisions on village matters, and thinking that it would be interesting to talk with them, I asked the three women if they could tell me who the village elders of Ben Suc were. As this was translated, a hint of mischievous amusement appeared on the face of one of the women, and with sudden cheerful recklessness she declared, "We didn't have any village elders." Her little smile was contagious, and the three women exchanged conspiratorial glances, like schoolgirls with a secret. Emboldened, the first speaker added, "Nobody was important. Everyone was equal." All three watched my face closely to see how I would react to this gambit.

I asked if anyone had collected taxes.

"No, there were no taxes," another of the women answered. "We used what we grew for ourselves."

The first then said, "There was no government. And no government troops." All three struggled with suppressed amusement.

I asked them how they had liked having no government and no government troops.

At this, they all broke into girlish laughter, hardly even trying to cover their smiles with their hands. No one answered the question. Instead, one of them said, "Anyway, now we must be protected by the government and the American troops." She still could not wholly suppress her rebellious smile. As though to say something calculated to please me even more, she added, "Last year, government troops and Americans came just to give out medicine, and no one was killed."

Another woman said, "This time, many were wounded, killed, or taken away."

In one compartment, an old man sitting on a mat told me, "I was born in Ben Suc, and I have lived there for sixty years. My father was born there also, and so was his father. Now I will have to live here for the rest of my life. But I am a farmer. How can I farm here? What work will I do? There were many killed, but luckily I came safely with my three daughters. They have given us rice here, but I can't eat it. The American rice is for pigs. And we have no cooking oil." (After the first handout of rice, in several places around the camp I noticed pigs with their snouts deep in piles of American rice that had been dumped out by the Vietnamese. Like most East Asians, the Vietnamese are extremely particular about the color, texture, size, and flavor of their rice. Rice also has ritual meanings for them that go beyond matters of taste and nutrition. The Vietnamese welcomed the long-grained, brownish, American-grown rice about the way an American would welcome a plate of dog food—as a dish that was adequately nutritious, and perhaps not even bad-tasting, but psychologically repellent.)

The old man had an idea for his future. "I have relatives in Phu Cuong who will help me and my daughters. Won't you let me go out of here and build a new house in Phu Cuong, where I can farm?"

Once more I tried to explain that I was not from the government. The old man obviously didn't believe me.

In the morning of the fourth day, there was a high wind, which blew clouds of dust so thick that you couldn't see from one end to the other of the aisles between the canopies. Under one of the canopies, an old man with a wispy goatee and a mild, gracious smile sat on a mat, holding a baby in his arms, in the lee of a pile of possessions and several mats that his family had hung from the bamboo framework to protect themselves from the wind and dust. He smiled down at the baby as it played with a twig. Answering my questions, he said, "I have two sons, but I don't know where they are now. They went into the government Army, and I haven't heard anything about them for several years. Now I live with my daughter." The baby became agitated, beat its arms, and threw away the twig. Shifting the baby into one arm, the old man drew a tobacco pouch from his pocket and gave it to the baby to play with. In the pouch, along with a small box for tobacco and paper for roll-your-own cigarettes, was his newly issued identification card, which already had a slight tear in the center. The baby's interest lit on the I.D. card, and, grasping it tightly in both hands, it widened the tear until the card ripped in two and it was left holding a piece in each hand. The old man, who was delighted with everything the baby did, laughed warmly at its latest deed and smiled at the people around him. Then he put the two pieces back in the pouch and put the pouch in his pocket. . . .

Under another canopy, a woman with a blank, lonely gaze sat holding a tiny baby. She hardly seemed to notice me as I approached her. When I addressed her, she talked as though she were thinking out loud, and didn't answer any questions directly. She said, "The helicopters came early in the morning while I was on my way to the field. My husband is in Saigon now. I think he's in Saigon. The loud-speakers came overhead, but how could I hear them? The bombs were exploding everywhere. My father is deaf, so how could he hear the voices from the helicopter? Now I don't know where he is. All I could bring was my children and my clothes. My father is very old. Maybe he is dead."

The demolition teams arrived in Ben Suc on a clear, warm day after the last boatload of animals had departed down the river for Phu Cuong. G.I.s moved down the narrow lanes and into the sunny, quiet yards of the empty village, pouring gasoline on the grass roofs of the houses and setting them afire with torches. Columns of black smoke boiled up briefly into the blue sky as the dry roofs and walls burned to the ground, exposing little indoor tableaux of charred tables and chairs, broken cups and bowls, an occasional bed, and the ubiquitous bomb shelters. Before the flames had died out in the spindly black frames of the houses, bull-dozers came rolling through the copses of palms, uprooting the trees as they proceeded and lowering their scoops to scrape the packed-mud foundations bare. When the bulldozers hit the heavy walls of the bomb shelters, they whined briefly at a higher pitch but continued to press ahead, unchecked. There were very few dwellings in Ben Suc to make a bulldozer pause. The bulldozers cut their own paths across the backyard fences, small graveyards, and ridged fields of the village, ignoring the roads and lanes. When the demolition teams withdrew, they had flattened the village, but the original plan for the demolition had not yet run its course. Faithful to the initial design, Air Force jets sent their bombs down on the deserted ruins, scorching again the burned foundations of the houses and pulverizing for a second time the heaps of rubble, in the hope of collapsing tunnels too deep and well hidden for the bulldozers to crush—as though, having once decided to destroy it, we were now bent on annihilating every possible indication that the village of Ben Suc had ever existed.

• • •

On March 16, 1968, a company of U.S. infantry entered the village of My Lai, and although they did not receive a single round of hostile fire, methodically slaughtered some five hundred Vietnamese peasants, mostly women and children. The freelance journalist Seymour Hersh heard the story, but the major media ignored his efforts to publicize it. Finally, in December 1969 *Life* magazine carried Ronald Haeberle's horrendous photos of GIs pouring automatic rifle fire into trenches where Vietnamese women, babies in their arms, crouched in fear. The military arrested Lieutenant William Calley, a platoon leader at My Lai, who had ordered the shootings. Many officers were involved in the incident and then the cover-up, however, only Calley received a jail sentence. His life sentence was diminished to five years by the intervention of President Nixon. He served three and a half years under house arrest and was then released. In the following recollection, Larry Colburn, a helicopter door-gunner, who, with his pilot, Hugh Thompson, came upon the scene and stopped some of the killing, tells his story.

Larry Colburn, "They Were Butchering People" (2003)[7]

We weren't pacifists. We did our job and when we had to kill people we did. But we didn't do it for sport. We didn't randomly shoot people. In our gun company it was very important to capture weapons, not just to legitimize your kill, but psychologically it was easier when you could say, "If I didn't do that, he was going to shoot me."

We flew an OH-23—a little gasoline-engine bubble helicopter. We were aerial scouts—a new concept. Instead of just sending assault helicopters they'd use our small aircraft as bait and have a couple gunships cover us. Basically we'd go out and try to get into trouble. We'd fly real low and if we encountered anything we'd mark it with smoke, return fire, and let the gunships work out. We also went on "snatch missions," kidnapping draft-age males to take back for interrogation. We did that a lot in 1968.

On March 16, we came on station a little after seven a.m. The only briefing I got was that they were going to put a company on the ground to sweep through this village. Normally we'd go in beforehand to see if we could find enemy positions or entice people to shoot at us. It was clear and warm and the fog was lifting off the rice paddies. On our first pass we saw a man in uniform carrying a carbine and a pack coming out of a tree line. Thompson said, "Who wants him?" I said, "I'll take him." So he aimed the aircraft at him and got it down low and started toward the suspect. He was obviously Viet Cong. He was armed, evading, and heading for the next tree line. I couldn't hit him to save my life. We worked that area a little more but that was the only armed Vietnamese I saw that day.

After that we just started working the perimeter of My Lai–4, –5, and –6 and I remember seeing the American troops come in on slicks [helicopters]. We got ahead of them to see if they were going to encounter anything and we still didn't receive any fire. It was market day and we saw a lot of women and children leaving the hamlet. They were moving down the road carrying empty baskets. As we went further around the perimeter we saw a few wounded women in the rice fields south of My Lai–4. We marked their bodies with smoke grenades expecting that medics would give them medical assistance.

When we came back to the road we started seeing bodies, the same people that were walking to the market. They hadn't even gotten off the road. They were in piles, dead. We started going through all the scenarios of what might have happened. Was it artillery? Gunships? Viet Cong? The American soldiers on the ground were just walking around in a real nonchalant sweep. No one was crouching, ducking, or hiding.

Then we saw a young girl about twenty years old lying on the grass. We could see that she was unarmed and wounded in the chest. We marked her with smoke because we saw a squad not too far away. The smoke was green, meaning it's safe to approach. Red would have meant the opposite. We were hovering six feet off the ground not more than twenty feet away when Captain [Ernest] Medina came over, kicked her, stepped back, and finished her off. He did it right in front of us. When we saw Medina do that, it clicked. It was our guys doing the killing.

The bodies we marked with smoke—you find yourself feeling that you indirectly killed them. I'll never forget one lady who was hiding in the grass. She was crouched in a fetal position. I motioned to her—stay down, be quiet, stay there. We flew off on more reconnaissance. We came back later and she was in the same position, right where I'd told her to stay. But someone had come up behind her and literally blew her brains out. I'll never forget that look of bewilderment on her face.

Around ten a.m. [Hugh] Thompson spotted a group of women and children running toward a bunker northeast of My Lai–4 followed by a group of U.S. soldiers. When we got overhead, [Glenn] Andreotta spotted some faces peeking out of an earthen bunker. Thompson knew that in a matter of seconds they were going to die, so he landed the aircraft in between the advancing American troops and the bunker. He went over and talked to a Lieutenant [Stephen] Brooks. Thompson said, "These are civilians. How do we get them out of the bunker?" Brooks said, "I'll get them out with hand grenades." The veins were sticking out on Thompson's neck and I thought they were actually going to fight. Thompson came back and said to Andreotta and me, "If they open up on these people when I'm getting them out of the bunker, shoot 'em." Then he walked away leaving us standing there looking at each other. Thompson went over to the bunker and motioned for the people to come out. There were nine or ten of them.

We had a staredown going with the American soldiers. About half of them were sitting down, smoking and joking. I remember looking at one fellow and waving. He waved back and that's when I knew we were okay, that these guys weren't doing anything to us. No one pointed weapons at us and we didn't point any weapons at them.

Thompson called Dan Millians, a gunship pilot friend of his, and said, "Danny, I've got a little problem down here, can you help out?" Millians said sure and did something unheard of. You don't land a gunship to use it as a medevac, but he did. He got those people a couple of miles away and let 'em go. I think he had to make two trips.

We flew over the ditch where more than a hundred Vietnamese had been killed. Andreotta saw movement so Thompson landed again. Andreotta went directly into that ditch. He literally had to wade waist deep through people to get to a little child. I stood there in the open. Glenn came over and handed me the child, but the ditch was so full of bodies and blood he couldn't get out. I gave him the butt of my rifle and pulled him out. We took the little one to an orphanage. We didn't know if he was a little boy or little girl. Just a cute little child. I felt for broken bones or bullet holes and he appeared to be fine. He wasn't crying, but he had this blank stare on his face and he was covered with blood.

The only thing I remember feeling back then was that these guys were really out for revenge. They'd lost men to booby traps and snipers and they were ready to engage. They were briefed the night before and I've heard it said that they were going in there to waste everything. They didn't capture any weapons. They didn't kill any draft-age males. I've seen the list of dead and there were a hundred and twenty some humans under the age of five. It's something I've struggled with my whole adult life, how people can do that. I know what it's like to seek revenge, but we would look for a worthy opponent. These were elders, mothers, children, and babies. The fact that the VC [Viet Cong] camped out there at night is no justification for killing everyone in the hamlet.

Compare it to a little town in the United States. We're at war with someone on our own soil. They come into a town and rape the women, kill the babies, kill everyone. How would we feel? And it wasn't just murdering civilians. They were butchering people. The only thing they didn't do is cook 'em and eat 'em. How do you get that far over the edge?

• • •

In an article in the *New York Times Magazine* on March 24, 1968, reporter Sol Stern observed, "In Vietnam between 1961 and 1964, Negroes accounted for more than 20 percent of Army fatalities, even though they represented only 12.6 percent of Army personnel in Vietnam" and even less in the general U.S. population. "Simply put, the statistics show that the Negro in the army was more likely than his white buddy to be sent to Vietnam in the first place; once there, he was more likely to wind up in a front-line combat unit; and within the combat unit was more likely than the white to be killed or wounded." Black Vietnam vets who were not killed in Vietnam returned from the war to encounter persistent racism and wide-spread unemployment. Many became openly critical of the war and joined organizations fighting against war and for civil rights. Stern quotes one returned Black veteran from Vietnam as saying, "I would never fight on a foreign shore for America again. . . . The only place I would fight is right here." Here Haywood Kirkland describes the Vietnam war and its aftermath from the standpoint of a Black GI.

Haywood T. "The Kid" Kirkland, from *Bloods: An Oral History of the Vietnam War by Black Veterans* (1984)[8]

I got drafted on November 22, 1966. I had been working for a book distributor and as a stock boy in some stores coming out of high school. A lot of dudes were trying to do things to get deferments. One of my brothers put some kind of liquid in his eye and said he had an eye problem at the physical. He never went.

I didn't try anything. I knew when I got drafted I was going to Vietnam, no matter what I did. I knew because of the vision I had when I was twelve.

As soon as I hit boot camp in Fort Jackson, South Carolina, they tried to change your total personality. Transform you out of that civilian mentality to a military mind.

Right away they told us not to call them Vietnamese. Call everybody gooks, dinks.

Then they told us when you go over in Vietnam, you gonna be face to face with Charlie, the Viet Cong. They were like animals, or something other than human. They ain't have no regard for life. They'd blow up little babies just to kill one GI. They wouldn't allow you to talk about them as if they were people. They told us they're not to be treated with any type of mercy or apprehension. That's what they engraved into you. That killer instinct. Just go away and do destruction.

Even the chaplains would turn the thing around in the Ten Commandments. They'd say, "Thou shall not murder," instead of "Thou shall not kill." Basically, you had a right to kill, to take and seize territory, or to protect the lives of each other. Our conscience was not to bother us once we engaged in that kind of killing. As long as we didn't murder, it was like the chaplain would give you his blessings. But you knew all of that was murder anyway.

On May 15, 1967, I came into Vietnam as a replacement in the Third Brigade of the Twenty-Fifth Division. The Cacti Green. It was the task-force brigade that went anywhere there was trouble. The division was down in Cu Chi, but we operated all over II Corps and Eye Corps.

At the time I basically had a gung ho attitude about being a soldier. But could

I get in the best situation and not get hurt was a legitimate concern of mine. So I checked out that the line companies—ones making all the heavy contact—are the ones who are getting overran. I thought maybe I should avoid that and volunteer for one of these long-range recon patrols. It was a smaller group, and I had an opportunity to share my ideas and help make some decisions. With a line company, you're really just a pin on the map for sure.

The recon unit was basically to search out the enemy and call in air strikes or a larger military force to engage the enemy. Most of our activities was at night. We was hide by day, and out by night.

The politics of the war just had not set in when I got there. They told us not to fire unless fired upon. But once we enter into a village, we literally did anything that we wanted to do. There was no rules at all. I began to see a lot of the politics. . . .

You would see the racialism in the base-camp area. Like rednecks flying rebel flags from their jeeps. I would feel insulted, intimated. The brothers they was calling quote unquote troublemakers, they would send to the fields. A lot of brothers who had supply clerk or cook MOS [Military Occupational Specialties] when they came over ended up in the field. And when the brothers who was shot came out of the field, most of them got the jobs burning shit in these 50-gallon drums. Most of the white dudes got jobs as supply clerks or in the mess hall.

So we began to talk to each other, close our ranks, and be more organized amongst ourselves to deal with some of this stuff. The ones like me from the field would tell the brothers in base camp, "Look man, you know how to use grenades. If you run into any problems, throw a grenade in their hootch."

When I came home, I really got upset about the way my peers would relate to me. They called me a crazy nigger for going to the war. And I was still dealing with Vietnam in my head.

Well, they sent me to Fort Carson in Colorado to do the six months I had left. I really didn't want to give no more of myself to the Army. So I played crazy.

I told people I ain't know what rank I was. I told them I was busted in Vietnam. I didn't wear no emblems. I was a buck private. I don't know where the papers at.

They made me cut my bush. What I did, I did not get another size hat. So the hat was falling all over my eyes.

Then I convinced the doctor that my feet was bad. I had jungle rot. I couldn't run, couldn't stand for a long time. I couldn't wear boots. All I could do was wear these Ho Chi Minh sandals I had.

And I would fall out in formation in my sandals, my big hat, and my shades.

I rode them right to the point they was about ready to kick me out of the military.

Then on my twenty-first birthday they said they was going to the Democratic convention. Our unit was going to Chicago to be the riot squadron. I told them I'm not going there holding no weapon in front of my brothers and sisters. The captain said, "Kirkland, you going to Chicago if I have to carry you myself." But I went to the doctor and told him I had a relapse of malaria. He said he couldn't really tell me anything. I would have to stay in the hospital for the weekend. He thought he was getting me. I said, "That's fine."

I was successful playing crazy. I got an honorable discharge.

Because I was a veteran with medals and an honorable discharge, Washington city had a job offer for me. The police force or the post office. The police force had too much military connected to it. My whole thing was to get the military out of my system. I chose the post office. Basically I was sitting on a stool sorting mail. Stuffing mail, sorting mail, do it faster. The supervisors were like the first sergeants. Six months later I resigned. I just got tired of it.

I was also enrolled in a computer-operations school. They fulfilled . . . none of their promises. It was a $2,200 rip-off of the VA [Veterans' Administration] money I got for school. They folded at the graduation of my class.

Well, I was getting more of a revolutionary, militant attitude. It had begun when I started talking with friends before leaving 'Nam about being a part of the struggle of black people. About contributing in the world since Vietnam was doing nothin' for black people. They killed Dr. [Martin Luther] King just before I came home. I felt used.

• • •

The U.S. bombing of Vietnam spread in the late 1960s and early 1970s to include a "secret war" against Cambodia and Laos, in which millions more Asians would die. The U.S. war on Cambodia led to profound destabilization, helping to create the conditions that allowed Cambodia's brutal Khmer Rouge to rise to power in 1975. Millions would die in Cambodia's "killing fields" under the reign of terror of the Khmer Rouge. In this passage, Cambodian refugee Loung Ung describes the forced evacuation of Phnom Penh and some of the horrific events that followed.

Loung Ung, "People Just Disappeared and You Didn't Say Anything" (2003)[9]

I was playing hopscotch on the street when all these trucks roared into the city, every one of them filled with soldiers. I ran upstairs and asked my father who they were. He said they were Khmer Rouge and that they were destroyers. But why was everybody cheering and giving them food and flowers? He said it was just that everyone was happy the war was over. I started cheering with everybody else. The soldiers were so elated. When I came back upstairs my father and mother were packing up the house.

Everybody had to evacuate to Phnom Penh—two million people. The Khmer Rouge soldiers weren't happy anymore. They were scowling and shooting in the air and screaming into their bullhorns for us to get out. They said, "You can come back in three days, but you've got to leave now because the U.S. is going to bomb." I remember sitting in the back of a truck. When it ran out of gas we walked. I had to carry a rice pot and it kept banging my shins. I was crying the whole time and kept asking my father when we were going home. Finally, he got down to my level, looked me in the eyes, and told me we weren't going back, that the Khmer Rouge had lied and I had to stop thinking about it.

We just kept walking and walking. At a military base the Khmer Rouge separated people into two lines. In one line they called for all the former Lon Nol soldiers, civil servants, and professionals. They said they needed all those people to help rebuild the country. But when people started to move into that line my father gathered the family around and quietly said with such urgency that he was going to tell them he was just a porter and that my mother had sold old clothes in the market. We were never to talk about our family or say anything that would permit people to know we were from the city. I was really confused but there was no time to explain. So we got in the line with all the poor people. The next day my brother said the people who went in the other line had all been killed.

I have a very sharp memory of arriving in a village and someone spitting at my father. I was so angry—I idolized my father—but he said nothing and told me to keep quiet. There were probably three or four hundred people in the town square who had just arrived. The soldiers started taking people's bags and emptying the clothes into a pile. Then they started preaching about how bad it was to have colorful clothing—how it was vain and Western and from now on everybody would wear the same black clothes, the same shoes, the same haircut, and eat the same amount of rice. When they got to our family, a soldier reached into my mother's bag and pulled out a little fluffy red dress my mother had made for me. The soldier threw it in the pile. Then he took out a match and burned everything.

Eventually they separated the children from their parents to allow the soldiers more control over us. I worked at a child labor camp in the fields every day from sunrise to sunset. They told us we were the saviors of society because we were pure. Unlike the adults, we had not been tainted by foreign powers, greed, and capitalism. Every day in the camps they taught us how to use guns or knives or sticks. We were encouraged to be the eyes and ears of the Khmer Rouge. We were told to look for traitors and inform on anybody who looked, acted, or spoke against the Khmer Rouge whether they were older, younger, neighbors, aunts, fathers, or mothers. It was like a witch-hunt spread over the whole country. When you pointed your finger at someone it didn't matter if the allegations were true. If the soldiers believed them, the person was shot or bludgeoned to death.

Many executions were done out of sight. People just disappeared and you didn't say anything. You didn't know if they had died or were killed or working somewhere else. Disappearance mixed hope with horror. It was psychologically unbearable.

I was so afraid the Khmer Rouge would find out I was from the urban elite I just stopped talking. I always knew if they found out more about me they would kill me, so I really never believed their propaganda. But there were many children who did and some were more brutal than the soldiers. My survival really depended on a lot of luck. There were millions of land mines underground and every time I went looking for berries or animals I could have stepped on one. I was also very resourceful. I knew where to find food, how to keep secrets, and I was a good thief.

We were living in complete terror every day. Hunger and sadness were all around. My fourteen-year-old sister died from starvation. You rarely saw people smile. Laughter was so uncommon, if you heard it you would be shocked.

When I was about thirteen and going to school in Vermont I always had nightmares about being chased by people trying to kill me. Once I told some classmates about a dream in which I was having trouble cutting the throat of a man who was chasing me because I only had a butter knife and the edge wasn't sharp enough. They all stared at me and their jaws completely dropped open. That's when I realized they didn't have dreams like mine.

• • •

After being drafted, Tim O'Brien served in the army from 1969 to 1970. In 1990, he published a damning account of the war, *The Things They Carried*. Here is a section of the chapter "The Man I Killed."

Tim O'Brien, "The Man I Killed" (1990)[10]

His jaw was in his throat, his upper lip and teeth were gone, his one eye was shut, his other eye was a star-shaped hole, his eyebrows were thin and arched like a woman's, his nose was undamaged, there was a slight tear at the lobe of one ear, his clean black hair was swept upward into a cowlick at the rear of the skull, his forehead was lightly freckled, his fingernails were clean, the skin at his left cheek was peeled back in three ragged strips, his right cheek was smooth and hairless, there was a butterfly on his chin, his neck was open to the spinal cord and the blood there was thick and shiny and it was this wound that had killed him. He lay face-up in the center of the trail, a slim, dead, almost dainty young man. He had bony legs, a narrow waist, long shapely fingers. His chest was sunken and poorly muscled—a scholar, maybe. His wrists were the wrists of a child. He wore a black shirt, black pajama pants, a gray ammunition belt, a gold ring on the third finger of his right hand. His rubber sandals had been blown off. One lay beside him, the other a few meters up the trail. He had been born, maybe, in 1946 in the village of My Khe near the central coastline of Quang Ngai Province, where his parents farmed, and where his family had lived for several centuries, and where, during the time of the French, his father and two uncles and many neighbors had joined in the struggle for independence. He was not a Communist. He was a citizen and a soldier. In the village of My Khe, as in all of Quang Ngai, patriotic resistance had the force of tradition, which was partly the force of legend, and from his earliest boyhood the man I killed would have listened to stories about the heroic Trung sisters and Iran Hung Dao's famous rout of the Mongols and Le Loi's final victory against the Chinese at Tot Dong. He would have been taught that to defend the land was a man's highest duty and highest privilege. He had accepted this. It was never open to question. Secretly, though, it also frightened him. He was not a fighter. His health was poor, his body small and frail. He liked books. He wanted someday to be a teacher of mathematics. At night, lying on his mat, he could not picture himself doing the brave things his father had done, or his uncles, or the heroes of the stories. He hoped in his heart that he would never be tested. He hoped the Americans would go away. Soon, he hoped. He kept hoping and hoping, always, even when he was asleep.

"Oh, man, you fuckin' trashed the fucker," Azar said. "You scrambled his sorry self, look at that, you did, you laid him out like Shredded fuckin' Wheat."

"Go away," Kiowa said.

"I'm just saying the truth. Like oatmeal."

"Go," Kiowa said.

"Okay, then, I take it back," Azar said. He started to move away, then stopped and said, "Rice Krispies, you know? On the dead test, this particular individual gets A-plus."

Smiling at this, he shrugged and walked up the trail toward the village behind the trees.

Kiowa kneeled down.

"Just forget that crud," he said. He opened up his canteen and held it out for a while and then sighed and pulled it away. "No sweat, man. What else could you do?"

Later, Kiowa said, "I'm serious. Nothing anybody could do. Come on, stop staring."

The trail junction was shaded by a row of trees and tall brush. The slim young man lay with his legs in the shade. His jaw was in his throat. His one eye was shut and the other was a star-shaped hole.

Kiowa glanced at the body.

"All right, let me ask a question," he said. "You want to trade places with him? Turn it all upside down—you want that? I mean, be honest."

The star-shaped hole was red and yellow. The yellow part seemed to be getting wider, spreading out at the center of the star. The upper lip and gum and teeth were gone. The man's head was cocked at a wrong angle, as if loose at the neck, and the neck was wet with blood.

"Think it over," Kiowa said.

Then later he said, "Tim, it's a war. The guy wasn't Heidi—he had a weapon, right? It's a tough thing, for sure, but you got to cut out that staring."

Then he said, "Maybe you better lie down a minute."

Then after a long empty time he said, "Take it slow. Just go wherever the spirit takes you."

The butterfly was making its way along the young man's forehead, which was spotted with small dark freckles. The nose was undamaged. The skin on the right cheek was smooth and fine-grained and hairless. Frail-looking, delicately boned, the young man would not have wanted to be a soldier and in his heart would have feared performing badly in battle. Even as a boy growing up in the village of My Khe, he had often worried about this. He imagined covering his head and lying in a deep hole and closing his eyes and not moving until the war was over. He had no stomach for violence. He loved mathematics. His eyebrows were thin and arched like a woman's, and at school the boys sometimes teased him about how pretty he was, the arched eyebrows and long shapely fingers, and on the playground they mimicked a woman's walk and made fun of his smooth skin and his love for mathematics. The young man could not make himself fight them. He often wanted to, but he was afraid, and this increased his shame. If he could not fight little boys, he thought, how could he ever become a soldier and fight the Americans with their airplanes and helicopters and bombs? It did not seem possible. In the presence of his father and uncles, he pretended to look forward to doing his patriotic duty, which was also a privilege, but at night he prayed with his mother that the war might end soon. Beyond anything else, he was afraid of disgracing himself, and therefore his family and village. But all he could do, he thought, was wait and pray and try not to grow up too fast.

"Listen to me," Kiowa said. "You feel terrible, I know that."

Then he said, "Okay, maybe I don't know."

Along the trail there were small blue flowers shaped like bells. The young man's head was wrenched sideways, not quite facing the flowers, and even in the shade a single blade of sunlight sparkled against the buckle of his ammunition belt. The left cheek was peeled back in three ragged strips. The wounds at his neck had not yet clotted, which made him seem animate even in death, the blood still spreading out across his shirt.

Kiowa shook his head.

There was some silence before he said, "Stop staring."

The young man's fingernails were clean. There was a slight tear at the lobe of one ear, a sprinkling of blood on the forearm. He wore a gold ring on the third finger of his right hand. His chest was sunken and poorly muscled—a scholar, maybe. His life was now a constellation of possibilities. So, yes, maybe a scholar. And for years, despite his family's poverty, the man I killed would have been determined to continue his education in mathematics. The means for this were arranged, perhaps, through the village liberation cadres, and in 1964 the young man began attending classes at the university in Saigon, where he avoided politics and paid attention to the problems of calculus. He devoted himself to his studies. He spent his nights alone, wrote romantic poems in his journal, took pleasure in the grace and beauty of differential equations. The war, he knew, would finally take him, but for the time being he would not let himself think about it. He had stopped praying; instead, now, he waited. And as he waited, in his final year at the university, he fell in love with a classmate, a girl of seventeen, who one day told him that his wrists were like the wrists of a child, so small and delicate, and who admired his narrow waist and the cowlick that rose up like a bird's tail at the back of his head. She liked his quiet manner; she laughed at his freckles and bony legs. One evening, perhaps, they exchanged gold rings.

Now one eye was a star.

"You okay?" Kiowa said.

The body lay almost entirely in shade. There were gnats at the mouth, little flecks of pollen drifting above the nose. The butterfly was gone. The bleeding had stopped except for the neck wounds.

Kiowa picked up the rubber sandals, clapping off the dirt, then bent down to search the body. He found a pouch of rice, a comb, a fingernail clipper, a few soiled piasters, a snapshot of a young woman standing in front of a parked motorcycle. Kiowa placed these items in his rucksack along with the gray ammunition belt and rubber sandals.

Then he squatted down.

"I'll tell you the straight truth," he said. "The guy was dead the second he stepped on the trail. Understand me? We all had him zeroed. A good kill—weapon, ammunition, everything." Tiny beads of sweat glistened at Kiowa's forehead. His eyes moved from the sky to the dead man's body to the knuckles of his own hands. "So listen, you best pull your shit together. Can't just sit here all day."

Later he said, "Understand?"

Then he said, "Five minutes, Tim. Five more minutes and we're moving out."

The one eye did a funny twinkling trick, red to yellow. His head was wrenched sideways, as if loose at the neck, and the dead young man seemed to be staring at some distant object beyond the bell-shaped flowers along the trail. The blood at the neck had gone to a deep purplish black. Clean fingernails, clean hair—he had been a soldier for only a single day. After his years at the university, the man I killed returned with his new wife to the village of My Khe, where he enlisted as a common rifleman with the 48th Vietcong Battalion. He knew he would die quickly. He knew he would see a flash of light. He knew he would fall dead and wake up in the stories of his village and people.

Kiowa covered the body with a poncho.

"Hey, you're looking better," he said. "No doubt about it. All you needed was time—some mental R&R."

Then he said, "Man, I'm sorry."

Then later he said, "Why not talk about it?"

Then he said, "Come on, man, talk."

He was a slim, dead, almost dainty young man of about twenty. He lay with one leg bent beneath him, his jaw in his throat, his face neither expressive nor inexpressive. One eye was shut. The other was a star-shaped hole.

"Talk," Kiowa said.

• • •

In these two poems, the poet Maria Herrera-Sobek writes about the much-neglected experience of Chicanos and Latinos in the Vietnam war. Like blacks and other people of color, Chicanos faced racism from their officers, and were often assigned the most dangerous positions. They also were among those most active opponents of the war, pointing out the hypocrisy of the U.S. government's claim to be bringing "democracy" to Vietnam.

Maria Herrera-Sobek, Two Poems on Vietnam (1999)[11]

"UNTITLED"

We saw them coming
in funeral black bags
body bags they called them
eyes locked forever
they were our

brown men
shot
in a dishonest war
Vietnam taught us
not to trust
anyone over thirty
for they had the guns
and the power
to send our boyfriends
fathers, brothers
off to war
while they sauntered
in lily white
segregated
country clubs
a bomb was planted
in our minds
a bomb exploded
in 1969
Watts, East Los
Black Panthers
Brown Berets
Drank the night
and lighted up the sky
with homemade
fireworks
the war had come
to roost
in our own backyard
made in the USA guns
turned inward
and shot our young
Dead in the streets
Dead in the battlefields
Dead in the schools
and yet a plaintive song
Crashing against the crackling explosion
of a Molotov cocktail.
insisted
"We shall overcome."

"VIETNAM—A FOUR-LETTER WORD"

Vietnam
Was a four-letter word
The stench of napalm
In the air
seared our nightmares
California palm trees
Waving fronds of anti-patriotism
"Hell no, we won't go"
Was not a T.V. jingle
It was the chant
Of those who marched
To a different tune
Of those who wore peace
On their foreheads
Love on their sleeves
And American flags
On their behinds

• • •

In 1969, Daniel Ellsberg, a strategic analyst at the RAND Corporation and a former government official, began work on a secret study authorized by Secretary of Defense Robert McNamara, "U.S. Decision-making in Vietnam, 1945–68." But Ellsberg, increasingly outraged by the lies being told to support the war, began secretly to copy thousands of pages of the document. In 1971, he leaked the Pentagon Papers, as they came to be known, to the *New York Times*, *Washington Post*, and other newspapers that published excerpts of them despite the attempt of the government to prevent them from doing so. Millions more now saw the gap between the internal government discussion about Vietnam and the reality that was well understood by those in Washington. Here is the preface to Ellsberg's memoir, which discusses his motivations for releasing the papers.

Daniel Ellsberg, *Secrets: A Memoir of Vietnam and the Pentagon Papers* (2003)[12]

On the evening of October 1, 1969, I walked out past the guards' desk at the Rand Corporation in Santa Monica, carrying a briefcase filled with Top Secret documents, which I planned to photocopy that night. The documents were part of a 7,000-page Top Secret study of U.S. decision-making in Vietnam, later known as the Pentagon Papers. The rest of the study was in a safe in my office. I had decided to copy it all and make it public: perhaps through Senate hearings, or the press if necessary. I believed this course, especially the latter possibility, would probably put me in prison for the rest of my life. . . .

For eleven years, from mid-1964 to the end of the war in May 1975, I was, like a great many other Americans, preoccupied with our involvement in Vietnam. In the course of that time I saw it first as a problem, next as a stalemate, then as a moral and political disaster, a crime. . . . My own personal commitment and subsequent actions eased along with these changing perspectives. When I saw the conflict as a problem, I tried to help solve it; when I saw it as a stalemate, I tried to help extricate ourselves, without harm to other national interests; when I saw it as a crime, I tried to expose and resist it—and above all, to help end it immediately. Throughout all of these phases, even the first, I sought in various ways to avoid further escalation of the conflict. But as late as early 1973, as I entered a federal criminal trial for my actions starting in late 1969, I would have said that none of these aims or efforts—neither my own nor anyone else's—had met with any success. Efforts to end the conflict—whether it was seen as a failed test, a quagmire, or a moral misadventure—seemed to have been no more rewarded than efforts to win it. Why?

As I saw it then, the war needed not only to be resisted; it remained to be understood. Thirty years later, I still believe that is true. . . .

For three years starting in mid-1964, with the highest civil servant grade, I had helped prosecute a war I felt at the outset to be doomed. Working in Washington under top decision-makers in 1964–65, I watched them secretly maneuver the country into a full-scale war with no real promise of success. My pessimism during those years was not unbroken, and for about a year—from the spring of 1965 to the spring of 1966—I hoped and worked toward some sort of success, once the President, despite many misgivings, including his own, had committed us to war. Once we were fully committed, I volunteered in mid-1965 to serve in Vietnam as a State Department civilian. My job came to be evaluating "pacification" in the countryside. In this I drew on my earlier training as a Marine infantry commander to observe the war up close. Whether we had a right—any more than the French before us—to pursue by fire and steel in Indochina the objectives our leaders had chosen was a question that never occurred to me. But during two years in Vietnam, its people and plight became real to me, as real as the U.S. troops I walked with, as real as my own hands, in a way that made continuing the hopeless war intolerable.

Knocked out of the field with hepatitis and back in the U.S. in mid-1967, I began to do everything I could imagine to help free our country from the war. For

two years I did this as an insider, briefing high officials, advising presidential candidates, and eventually, in early 1969, helping the president's national security
advisor, Henry Kissinger, discover uncertainties and alternatives. But later that
same year I felt called on to go beyond this approach, and so to end my career as
a government insider.

One of these actions risked my own freedom. In 1969 and 1970, with the help
of my friend Anthony Russo, a former Rand associate, I secretly photocopied the
entire forty-seven-volume Pentagon Papers, a top secret study of U.S. decision-making in Vietnam from 1945 to 1968, which were then in my authorized possession,
and gave them to Senator William Fulbright, Chairman of the Senate Foreign
Relations Committee. In 1971 I also gave copies to the *New York Times*, the
Washington Post, and ultimately, in the face of four unprecedented federal injunctions, to some seventeen other newspapers, all of whom defied the government in
printing them for the public to read.

I wasn't wrong about the personal risks. Shortly, I was indicted in a federal
court, with Russo later joining me in a second, superseding indictment. Eventually
I faced twelve federal felony charges totaling a possible 115 years in prison, with
the prospect of several further trials for me beyond that first one. But I was not
wrong, either, to hope that exposing secrets five presidents had withheld and the
lies they told might have benefits for our democracy that were worthy of the risks.
This truth-telling set in motion a train of events—including criminal White
House efforts to silence or incapacitate me—that led to dismissal of the charges
against me and my codefendant. Much more importantly, these particular Oval
Office crimes helped topple the president, which was crucial to ending the war.

Women, Gays, and Other Voices of Resistance

Allen Ginsberg, "America" (January 17, 1956)

Martin Duberman, *Stonewall* (1993)

Wamsutta (Frank B.) James, Suppressed Speech on the 350th Anniversary of the Pilgrim's Landing at Plymouth Rock (September 10, 1970)

Adrienne Rich, *Of Woman Born* (1977)

Abbey Lincoln, "Who Will Revere the Black Woman?" (September 1966)

Susan Brownmiller, "Abortion Is a Woman's Right" (1999)

Assata Shakur (Joanne Chesimard), "Women in Prison: How We Are" (April 1978)

Kathleen Neal Cleaver, "Women, Power, and Revolution" (October 16, 1998)

The movements of the 1960s—against racial segregation, against the Vietnam War—generated radically different ideas about how people should live their lives. A woman's liberation movement grew. Men and women who were discriminated against because they were gay or lesbian began to speak up and fight back. Native Americans occupied Alcatraz Island in California and the massacre ground of Wounded Knee in South Dakota to register their anger at what had been done to them historically and what was being done in the present.

The United States experienced a general revolt in the culture against oppressive, artificial, previously unquestioned ways of living. This revolt touched every aspect of personal life: childbirth, childhood, love, sex, marriage, dress, music, art, sports, language, food, housing, religion, literature, education, death. What was called "the Sixties" might end, but the cultural revolution continued.

• • •

Allen Ginsberg, one of the great rebel poets of our time, burst onto the national scene as one of the Beat Generation poets of the 1950s when he read his poem "Howl" in San Francisco. It was then published by fellow poet Lawrence Ferlinghetti, founder of City Lights Books. Ginsberg knew Jack Kerouac, Gregory Corso, and William Burroughs. At one point the U.S. Customs Service seized 520 copies of "Howl," calling it "obscene and indecent." Ginsberg became an important figure in the counterculture movement of the 1960s, deeply involved in the movement against the war in Vietnam. This poem, written just a few months after *Howl*, gives voice to his critique of the nation's establishment. It expresses his homosexuality, his refusal to go along with orthodoxy on any level, and presaged many of the countercultural, gay rights, and other liberation movements that erupted in the 1960s and 1970s.

Allen Ginsberg, "America" (January 17, 1956)[1]

America I've given you all and now I'm nothing.
America two dollars and twentyseven cents January 17, 1956.
I can't stand my own mind.
America when will we end the human war?
Go fuck yourself with your atom bomb.
I don't feel good don't bother me.
I won't write my poem till I'm in my right mind.
America when will you be angelic?
When will you take off your clothes?
When will you look at yourself through the grave?
When will you be worthy of your million Trotskyites?
America why are your libraries full of tears?
America when will you send your eggs to India?
I'm sick of your insane demands.
When can I go into the supermarket and buy what I need with my good looks?
America after all it is you and I who are perfect not the next world.
Your machinery is too much for me.
You made me want to be a saint.
There must be some other way to settle this argument.
Burroughs is in Tangiers I don't think he'll come back it's sinister.
Are you being sinister or is this some form of practical joke?
I'm trying to come to the point.
I refuse to give up my obsession.
America stop pushing I know what I'm doing.

America the plum blossoms are falling.

I haven't read the newspapers for months, everyday somebody goes on trial for
   murder.

America I feel sentimental about the Wobblies.

America I used to be a communist when I was a kid I'm not sorry.

I smoke marijuana every chance I get.

I sit in my house for days on end and stare at the roses in the closet.

When I go to Chinatown I get drunk and never get laid.

My mind is made up there's going to be trouble.

You should have seen me reading Marx.

My psychoanalyst thinks I'm perfectly right.

I won't say the Lord's Prayer.

I have mystical visions and cosmic vibrations.

America I still haven't told you what you did to Uncle Max after he came over
   from Russia.

I'm addressing you.

Are you going to let your emotional life be run by Time Magazine?

I'm obsessed by Time Magazine.

I read it every week.

Its cover stares at me every time I slink past the corner candystore.

I read it in the basement of the Berkeley Public Library.

It's always telling me about responsibility. Businessmen are serious. Movie
   producers are serious. Everybody's serious but me.

It occurs to me that I am America.

I am talking to myself again.

Asia is rising against me.

I haven't got a chinaman's chance.

I'd better consider my national resources.

My national resources consist of two joints of marijuana millions of genitals an
   unpublishable private literature that goes 1400 miles an hour and twenty-
   five-thousand mental institutions.

I say nothing about my prisons nor the millions of underprivileged who live
   in my flowerpots under the light of five hundred suns.

I have abolished the whorehouses of France, Tangiers is the next to go.

My ambition is to be President despite the fact that I'm a Catholic.

America how can I write a holy litany in your silly mood?

I will continue like Henry Ford my strophes are as individual as his automobiles more so they're all different sexes.

America I will sell you strophes $2500 apiece $500 down on your old strophe
America free Tom Mooney
America save the Spanish Loyalists
America Sacco & Vanzetti must not die
America I am the Scottsboro boys.

America when I was seven momma took me to Communist Cell meetings they
    sold us garbanzos a handful per ticket a ticket costs a nickel and the speeches
    were free everybody was angelic and sentimental about the workers it was
    all so sincere you have no idea what a good thing the party was in 1835
    Scott Nearing was a grand
old man a real mensch Mother Bloor made me cry I once saw Israel Amter
    plain. Everybody must have been a spy.
America you don't really want to go to war.
America it's them bad Russians.
Them Russians them Russians and them Chinamen. And them Russians.
The Russia wants to eat us alive. The Russia's power mad. She wants to take our
    cars from out our garages.
Her wants to grab Chicago. Her needs a Red *Readers' Digest.* Her wants our auto
    plants in Siberia. Him big bureaucracy running our fillingstations.
That no good. Ugh. Him make Indians learn read. Him need big black nig-
    gers. Hah. Her make us all work sixteen hours a day. Help.
America this is quite serious.
America this is the impression I get from looking in the television set.
America is this correct?
I'd better get right down to the job.
It's true I don't want to join the Army or turn lathes in precision parts facto-
    ries, I'm nearsighted and psychopathic anyway.
America I'm putting my queer shoulder to the wheel.

• • •

One of the most important moments of resistance from the 1960s was the
Stonewall Rebellion. On the night of June 27–28, 1969, a multiracial group of gays
who had gathered at the Stonewall Inn on Christopher Street in New York City's
Greenwich Village resisted when police sought to shut down the bar (allegedly for
serving alcohol without a license) and to arrest patrons. They fought back, as the
historian Martin Duberman recounts here, and, in doing so, helped spur a new, more
militant phase of the struggle for gay liberation.

Martin Duberman, *Stonewall* (1993)[2]

As the police, amid a growing crowd and mounting anger, continued to load prisoners into the van, Martin Boyce, an eighteen-year-old scare drag queen, saw a leg
in nylons and sporting a high heel shoot out of the back of the paddy wagon into
the chest of a cop, throwing him backward. Another queen then opened the door
on the side of the wagon and jumped out. The cops chased and caught her, but
Blond Frankie [Frank Esselourne] quickly managed to engineer another escape from
the van; several queens successfully made their way out with him and were swal-
lowed up in the crowd. Tammy Novak was one of them; she ran all the way to Joe
Tish's apartment, where she holed up throughout the weekend. The police handcuffed subsequent prisoners to the inside of the van, and succeeded in driving
away from the scene to book them at the precinct house. Deputy Inspector
Seymour Pine, the ranking officer, nervously told the departing police to "just
drop them off at the Sixth Precinct and hurry back."

From this point on, the melee broke out in several directions and swiftly
mounted in intensity. The crowd, now in full cry, started screaming epithets at the
police—"Pigs!" "Faggot cops!" Sylvia [(Ray) Rivera] and Craig [Rodwell] enthusiastically joined in, Sylvia shouting her lungs out, Craig letting go with a full-
throated "Gay power!" One young gay Puerto Rican went fearlessly up to a
policeman and yelled in his face, "What you got against faggots? We don't do you
nuthin'!" Another teenager started kicking at a cop, frequently missing as the cop
held him at arm's length. One queen mashed an officer with her heel, knocked him
down, grabbed his handcuff keys, freed herself, and passed the keys to another queen
behind her.

By now, the crowd had swelled to a mob, and people were picking up and
throwing whatever loose objects came to hand—coins, bottles, cans, bricks from
a nearby construction site. Someone even picked up dog shit from the street
and threw it in the cops' direction. As the fever mounted, Zucchi [Zookie
Zarfas] was overheard nervously asking Mario what the hell the crowd was upset
about: the Mafia or the police? The police, Mario reassured him. Zucchi gave a
big grin of relief and decided to vent some stored-up anger of his own: He egged
on bystanders in their effort to rip up a damaged fire hydrant and he persuaded
a young kid named Timmy to throw the wire-mesh garbage can nearby. Timmy
was not much bigger than the can (and had just come out the week before), but
he gave it his all—the can went sailing into the plate-glass window (painted
black and reinforced from behind by plywood) that stretched across the front
of the Stonewall.

Stunned and frightened by the crowd's unexpected fury, the police, at the order
of Deputy Inspector Pine, retreated inside the bar. Pine had been accustomed to two

or three cops being able to handle with ease any number of cowering gays, but here the crowd wasn't cowering; it had routed eight cops and made them run for cover. As Pine later said, "I had been in combat situations, [but] there was never any time that I felt more scared than then." With the cops holed up inside Stonewall, the crowd was now in control of the street, and it bellowed in triumph and pent-up rage.

Craig dashed to a nearby phone booth. Ever conscious of the need for publicity—for visibility—and realizing that a critical moment had arrived, he called all three daily papers, the *Times*, the *Post*, and the *News*, and alerted them that "a major news story was breaking." Then he ran to his apartment a few blocks away to get his camera.

Jim Fouratt also dashed to the phones—to call his straight radical-left friends, to tell them "people were fighting the cops—it was just like Newark!" He urged them to rush down and lend their support (just as he had long done for their causes). Then he went into the nearby Ninth Circle and Julius' [bar], to try to get the patrons to come out into the street. But none of them would. Nor did any of his straight radical friends show up. It taught Jim a bitter lesson about how low on the scale of priorities his erstwhile comrades ranked "faggot" concerns.

Gary tried to persuade Sylvia to go home with him to get a change of clothes. "Are you nuts?" she yelled. "I'm not missing a minute of this—it's the revolution!" So Gary left to get clothes for both of them. Blond Frankie, meanwhile—perhaps taking his cue from Zucchi—uprooted a loose parking meter and offered it for use as a battering ram against the Stonewall's door. At nearly the same moment somebody started squirting lighter fluid through the shattered glass window on the bar's facade, tossing in matches after it. Inspector Pine later referred to this as "throwing Molotov cocktails into the place," but the only reality that described was the inflamed state of Pine's nerves.

Still, the danger was very real, and the police were badly frightened. The shock to self-esteem had been stunning enough; now came an actual threat to physical safety. Dodging flying glass and missiles, Patrolman Gil Weisman, the one cop in uniform, was hit near the eye with a shard, and blood spurted out. With that, the fear turned abruptly to fury. Three of the cops, led by Pine, ran out the front door, which had crashed in from the battering, and started screaming threats at the crowd, thinking to cow it. But instead a rain of coins and bottles came down, and a beer can glanced off Deputy Inspector Charles Smyth's head. Pine lunged into the crowd, grabbed somebody around the waist, pulled him back into the doorway, and then dragged him by the hair, inside.

Ironically, the prisoner was the well-known—and heterosexual—folk singer Dave Van Ronk. Earlier that night Van Ronk had been in and out of the Lion's Head, a bar a few doors down from Stonewall that catered to a noisy, macho journalist crowd scornful of the "faggots" down the block. Once the riot got going, the

Lion's Head locked its doors; the management didn't want faggots moaning and bleeding over the paying customers. As soon as Pine got Van Ronk back into the Stonewall, he angrily accused him of throwing dangerous objects—a cue to Patrolman Weisman to shout that Van Ronk was the one who had cut his eye, and then to start punching the singer hard while several other cops held him down. When Van Ronk looked as if he was going to pass out, the police handcuffed him, and Pine snapped, "All right, we book him for assault."

The cops then found a fire hose, wedged it into a crack in the door, and directed the spray out at the crowd, thinking that would certainly scatter it. But the stream was weak and the crowd howled derisively, while inside the cops started slipping on the wet floor. A reporter from *The Village Voice*, Howard Smith, had retreated inside the bar when the police did; he later wrote that by that point in the evening "the sound filtering in [didn't] suggest dancing faggots any more; it sound[ed] like a powerful rage bent on vendetta." By now the Stonewall's front door was hanging wide open, the plywood brace behind the windows was splintered, and it seemed only a matter of minutes before the howling mob would break in and wreak its vengeance. One cop armed himself with Tony the Sniff's baseball bat; the others drew their guns, and Pine stationed several officers on either side of the corridor leading to the front door. One of them growled, "We'll shoot the first motherfucker that comes through the door."

At that moment, an arm reached in through the shattered window, squirted more lighter fluid into the room, and then threw in another lit match. This time the match caught, and there was a whoosh of flame. Standing only ten feet away, Pine aimed his gun at the receding arm and (he later said) was preparing to shoot when he heard the sound of sirens coming down Christopher Street. At two-fifty-five a.m. Pine had sent out emergency signal 10-41—a call for help to the fearsome Tactical Patrol Force—and relief was now rounding the corner.

The TPF was a highly trained, crack riot-control unit that had been set up to respond to the proliferation of protests against the Vietnam War. Wearing helmets with visors, carrying assorted weapons, including billy clubs and tear gas, its two dozen members all seemed massively proportioned. They were a formidable sight as, linked arm in arm, they came up Christopher Street in a wedge formation that resembled (by design) a Roman legion. In their path, the rioters slowly retreated, but—contrary to police expectations—did not break and run. Craig, for one, knelt down in the middle of the street with the camera he'd retrieved from his apartment and, determined to capture the moment, snapped photo after photo of the oncoming TPF minions.

As the troopers bore down on him, he scampered up and joined the hundreds of others who scattered to avoid the billy clubs but then raced around the block, doubled back behind the troopers, and pelted them with debris. When the cops realized that a considerable crowd had simply re-formed to their rear, they flailed out angrily at anyone who came within striking distance. But the protesters would not be cowed. The pattern repeated itself several times: The TPF would disperse the jeering mob only to have it re-form behind them, yelling taunts, tossing bottles and bricks, setting fires in trash cans. When the police whirled around to reverse direction at one point, they found themselves face to face with their worst nightmare: a chorus line of mocking queens, their arms clasped around each other, kicking their heels in the air Rockettes-style and singing at the tops of their sardonic voices:

> We are the Stonewall girls
> We wear our hair in curls
> We wear no underwear
> We show our pubic hair . . .
> We wear our dungarees
> Above our nelly knees!

It was a deliciously witty, contemptuous counterpoint to the TPF's brute force, a tactic that transformed an otherwise traditionally macho eye-for-an-eye combat and that provided at least the glimpse of a different and revelatory kind of consciousness. Perhaps that was exactly the moment Sylvia had in mind when she later said, "Something lifted off my shoulders."

But the tactic incited the TPF to yet further violence. As they were badly beating up on one effeminate-looking boy, a portion of the angry crowd surged in, snatched the boy away, and prevented the cops from reclaiming him. Elsewhere, a cop grabbed "a wild Puerto Rican queen" and lifted his arm as if to club him. Instead of cowering, the queen yelled, "How'd you like a big Spanish dick up your little Irish ass?" The nonplussed cop hesitated just long enough to give the queen time to run off into the crowd.

The cops themselves hardly escaped scot-free. Somebody managed to drop a concrete block on one parked police car; nobody was injured, but the cops inside were shaken up. At another point, a gold-braided police officer being driven around to survey the action got a sack of wet garbage thrown at him through the open window of his car; a direct hit was scored, and soggy coffee grounds dripped down the officer's face as he tried to maintain a stoic expression. Still later, as some hundred people were being chased down Waverly Place by two cops, someone in the crowd suddenly realized the unequal odds and started yelling, "There are only two of 'em! Catch 'em! Rip their clothes off! Fuck 'em!" As the crowd took up the cry, the two officers fled.

Before the police finally succeeded in clearing the streets—for that evening only, it would turn out—a considerable amount of blood had been shed. Among the undetermined number of people injured was Sylvia's friend Ivan Valentin; hit in the knee by a policeman's billy club, he had ten stitches taken at St. Vincent's Hospital. A teenager named Lenny had his hand slammed in a car door and lost two fingers. Four big cops beat up a young queen so badly—there is evidence that the cops singled out "feminine boys"—that she bled simultaneously from her mouth, nose, and ears. Craig and Sylvia both escaped injury (as did Jim, who had hung back on the fringe of the crowd), but so much blood splattered over Sylvia's blouse that at one point she had to go down to the piers and change into the clean clothes Gary had brought back for her.

Four police officers were also hurt. Most of them sustained minor abrasions from kicks and bites, but Officer Scheu, after being hit with a rolled-up newspaper, had fallen to the cement sidewalk and broken his wrist. When Craig heard that news, he couldn't resist chuckling over what he called the "symbolic justice" of the injury. Thirteen people (including Dave Van Ronk) were booked at the Sixth Precinct, seven of them Stonewall employees, on charges ranging from harassment to resisting arrest to disorderly conduct. At three-thirty-five a.m., signal 10–41 was canceled and an uneasy calm settled over the area. It was not to last.

. . .

On the three hundred fiftieth anniversary of the Pilgrims' landing on Plymouth Rock, Massachusetts officials planned a celebration, and asked Wamsutta (Frank B.) James to deliver a speech. But James, an Aquinnah Wampanoag and a member of the United American Indians of New England, was never allowed to deliver the speech. Officials who checked the speech refused to let him speak the truth about the history of the colonization of Wampanoag lands. James and many other Native activists came to Plymouth Rock to declare a "National Day of Mourning for Native Americans," beginning a now-annual Thanksgiving Day protest against the genocide of the first peoples of the United States. Here is the speech James planned to deliver at Plymouth, Massachusetts, on September 10, 1970.

Wamsutta (Frank B.) James, Suppressed Speech on the 350th Anniversary of the Pilgrim's Landing at Plymouth Rock (September 10, 1970)[3]

I speak to you as a man—a Wampanoag Man. I am a proud man, proud of my ancestry, my accomplishments won by a strict parental direction ("You must succeed—your face is a different color in this small Cape Cod community!"). I am a product of poverty and discrimination from these two social and economic diseases. I, and my brothers and sisters, have painfully overcome, and to some extent we have earned the respect of our community. We are Indians first—but we are termed "good citizens." Sometimes we are arrogant but only because society has pressured us to be so.

It is with mixed emotion that I stand here to share my thoughts. This is a time of celebration for you—celebrating an anniversary of a beginning for the white man in America. A time of looking back, of reflection. It is with a heavy heart that I look back upon what happened to my People.

Even before the Pilgrims landed it was common practice for explorers to capture Indians, take them to Europe and sell them as slaves for 220 shillings apiece. The Pilgrims had hardly explored the shores of Cape Cod for four days before they had robbed the graves of my ancestors and stolen their corn and beans. Mourt's Relation describes a searching party of sixteen men. Mourt goes on to say that this party took as much of the Indians' winter provisions as they were able to carry.

Massasoit, the great Sachem of the Wampanoag, knew these facts, yet he and his People welcomed and befriended the settlers of the Plymouth Plantation. Perhaps he did this because his Tribe had been depleted by an epidemic. Or his knowledge of the harsh oncoming winter was the reason for his peaceful acceptance of these acts. This action by Massasoit was perhaps our biggest mistake. We, the Wampanoag, welcomed you, the white man, with open arms, little knowing that it was the beginning of the end; that before 50 years were to pass, the Wampanoag would no longer be a free people.

What happened in those short 50 years? What has happened in the last 300 years? History gives us facts and there were atrocities; there were broken promises—and most of these centered around land ownership. Among ourselves we understood that there were boundaries, but never before had we had to deal with fences and stone walls. But the white man had a need to prove his worth by the amount of land that he owned. Only ten years later, when the Puritans came, they treated the Wampanoag with even less kindness in converting the souls of the so-called "savages." Although the Puritans were harsh to members of their own society, the Indian was pressed between stone slabs and hanged as quickly as any other "witch."

And so down through the years there is record after record of Indian lands taken and, in token, reservations set up for him upon which to live. The Indian, having been stripped of his power, could only stand by and watch while the white man took his land and used it for his personal gain. This the Indian could not understand; for to him, land was survival, to farm, to hunt, to be enjoyed. It was not to be abused. We see incident after incident, where the white man sought to tame the "savage" and convert him to the Christian ways of life. The early Pilgrim settlers led the Indian to believe that if he did not behave, they would dig up the ground and unleash the great epidemic again.

The white man used the Indian's nautical skills and abilities. They let him be only a seaman—but never a captain. Time and time again, in the white man's society, we Indians have been termed "low man on the totem pole."

Has the Wampanoag really disappeared? There is still an aura of mystery. We know there was an epidemic that took many Indian lives—some Wampanoags moved west and joined the Cherokee and Cheyenne. They were forced to move. Some even went north to Canada! Many Wampanoag put aside their Indian heritage and accepted the white man's way for their own survival. There are some Wampanoag who do not wish it known they are Indian for social or economic reasons.

What happened to those Wampanoags who chose to remain and live among the early settlers? What kind of existence did they live as "civilized" people? True, living was not as complex as life today, but they dealt with the confusion and change. Honesty, trust, concern, pride, and politics wove themselves in and out of their daily living. Hence, he was termed crafty, cunning, rapacious, and dirty.

History wants us to believe that the Indian was a savage, illiterate, uncivilized animal. A history that was written by an organized, disciplined people, to expose us as an unorganized and undisciplined entity. Two distinctly different cultures met. One thought they must control life; the other believed life was to be enjoyed, because nature decreed it. Let us remember, the Indian is and was just as human as the white man. The Indian feels pain, gets hurt, and becomes defensive, has dreams, bears tragedy and failure, suffers from loneliness, needs to cry as well as laugh. He, too, is often misunderstood.

The white man in the presence of the Indian is still mystified by his uncanny ability to make him feel uncomfortable. This may be the image the white man has created of the Indian; his "savageness" has boomeranged and isn't a mystery; it is fear; fear of the Indian's temperament!

High on a hill, overlooking the famed Plymouth Rock, stands the statue of our great Sachem, Massasoit. Massasoit has stood there many years in silence. We the descendants of this great Sachem have been a silent people. The necessity of making a living in this materialistic society of the white man caused us to be silent. Today, I and many of my people are choosing to face the truth. We are Indians!

Although time has drained our culture, and our language is almost extinct, we the Wampanoags still walk the lands of Massachusetts. We may be fragmented, we may be confused. Many years have passed since we have been a people together. Our lands were invaded. We fought as hard to keep our land as you the whites did to take our land away from us. We were conquered, we became the American prisoners of war in many cases, and wards of the United States Government, until only recently.

Our spirit refuses to die. Yesterday we walked the woodland paths and sandy trails. Today we must walk the macadam highways and roads. We are uniting. We're standing not in our wigwams but in your concrete tent. We stand tall and proud, and before too many moons pass we'll right the wrongs we have allowed to happen to us.

We forfeited our country. Our lands have fallen into the hands of the aggressor. We have allowed the white man to keep us on our knees. What has happened cannot be changed, but today we must work towards a more humane America, a more Indian America, where men and nature once again are important; where the Indian values of honor, truth, and brotherhood prevail.

You the white man are celebrating an anniversary. We the Wampanoags will help you celebrate in the concept of a beginning. It was the beginning of a new life for the Pilgrims. Now, 350 years later it is a beginning of a new determination for the original American: the American Indian.

There are some factors concerning the Wampanoags and other Indians across this vast nation. We now have 350 years of experience living amongst the white man. We can now speak his language. We can now think as a white man thinks. We can now compete with him for the top jobs. We're being heard; we are now being listened to. The important point is that along with these necessities of everyday living, we still have the spirit, we still have the unique culture, we still have the will and, most important of all, the determination to remain as Indians. We are determined, and our presence here this evening is living testimony that this is only the beginning of the American Indian, particularly the Wampanoag, to regain the position in this country that is rightfully ours.

• • •

The pathbreaking poet Adrienne Rich, an outspoken feminist and lesbian, dedicated her book *Of Woman Born* to her grandmothers and "to the activists working to free women's bodies from archaic and unnecessary bonds." Through the book, Rich helped encourage a new discussion about the politics of motherhood, of sexuality, and of the body, topics that often were ignored or dismissed as apolitical. This selection appeared as the afterword to the first paperback edition of the book.

Adrienne Rich, *Of Woman Born* (1977)[4]

To seek visions, to dream dreams, is essential, and it is also essential to try new ways of living, to make room for serious experimentation, to respect the effort even where it fails. At the same time, in the light of most women's lives as they are now having to be lived, it can seem naive and self-indulgent to spin forth matriarchal utopias, to "demand" that technologies of contraception and genetics be "turned over" to women (by whom, and under what kinds of effective pressure?); to talk of impressing "unchilded" women into child-care as a political duty, of boycotting patriarchal institutions, of the commune as a solution for child-rearing. Child care as enforced servitude, or performed out of guilt, has been all too bitter a strain in our history. If women boycott the laboratories and libraries of scientific institutions (to which we have barely begun to gain access) we will not even know what research and technology is vital to the control of our bodies. Certainly the commune, in and of itself, has no special magic for women, any more than has the extended family or the public day-care center. Above all, such measures fail to recognize the full complexity and political significance of the woman's body, the full spectrum of power and powerlessness it represents, of which motherhood is simply one—though a crucial—part.

Furthermore, it can be dangerously simplistic to fix upon "nurturance" as a special strength of women, which need only be released into the larger society to create a new human order. Whatever our organic or developed gift for nurture, it has often been turned into a boomerang. . . .

When an individual woman first opposes the institution of motherhood she often has to oppose it in the person of a man, the father of her child, toward whom she may feel love, compassion, friendship, as well as resentment, anger, fear, or guilt. The "maternal" or "nurturant" spirit we want to oppose to rapism and the warrior mentality can prove a liability so long as it remains a lever by which women can be controlled through what is most generous and sensitive in us. Theories of female power and female ascendancy must reckon fully with the ambiguities of our being, and with the continuum of our consciousness, the potentialities for both creative and destructive energy in each of us.

I am convinced that "there are ways of thinking that we don't yet know about." I take those words to mean that many women are even now thinking in ways which traditional intellect denies, decries, or is unable to grasp. Thinking is an active, fluid, expanding process; intellection, "knowing" are recapitulations of past processes. In arguing that we have by no means yet explored or understood our biological grounding, the miracle and the paradox of the female body and its spiritual and political meanings, I am really asking whether women cannot begin, at last, to think through the body, to connect what has been so cruelly disorganized—our great mental capacities, hardly used; our highly developed tactile sense; our genius for close observation; our complicated, pain-enduring, multi-pleasured physicality.

I know of no woman—virgin, mother, lesbian, married, celibate—whether she earns her keep as a housewife, a cocktail waitress, or a scanner of brain waves—for whom the body is not a fundamental problem: its clouded meanings, its fertility, its desire, its so-called frigidity, its bloody speech, its silences, its changes and mutilations, its rapes and ripenings. There is for the first time today a possibility of converting our physicality into both knowledge and power. Physical motherhood is merely one dimension of our being. . . .

We need to imagine a world in which every woman is the presiding genius of her own body. In such a world, women will truly create life, bring forth not only children (if we choose) but the visions, and the thinking necessary to sustain, console, and alter human existence—a new relationship to the universe. Sexuality, politics, intelligence, power, motherhood, work, community, intimacy, will develop new meanings; thinking itself will be transformed.

This is where we have to begin.

• • •

In this essay, from *Negro Digest*, one of the nation's great jazz singers, Abbey Lincoln, speaks out forcefully against the abuse of black women, and raises issues that posed a challenge to feminists and others to address the specific struggles of African-American women.

Abbey Lincoln, "Who Will Revere the Black Woman?" (September 1966)[5]

Mark Twain said, in effect, that when a country enslaves a people, the first necessary job is to make the world feel that the people to be enslaved are sub-human. The next job is to make his fellow-countrymen believe that man is inferior and then, the unkindest cut of all is to make that man believe himself inferior.

A good job has been done in this country, as far as convincing them of their inferiority is concerned. The general white community has told us in a million different ways and in no uncertain terms that "God" and "nature" made a mistake when it came to fashioning us and ours. . . .

[S]trange as it is, I've heard it echoed by too many Black full-grown males that Black womanhood is the downfall of the Black man in that she (the Black woman) is "evil," "hard to get along with," "domineering," "suspicious," and "narrow-minded." In short, a black, ugly, evil you-know-what.

As time progresses, I've learned that this description of my mothers, sisters, and partners in crime is used as the basis and excuse for the further shoving, by the Black man, of his own head into the sand of oblivion. Hence, the black mother, housewife, and all-round girl Thursday is called upon to suffer both physically and emotionally every humiliation a woman can suffer and still function.

Her head is more regularly beaten than any other woman's, and by her own man; she's the scapegoat for Mr. Charlie; she is forced to stark realism and chided if caught dreaming; her aspirations for her and hers are, for sanity's sake, stunted; her physical image has been criminally maligned, assaulted, and negated; she's the first to be called ugly and never yet beautiful. . . .

Raped and denied the right to cry out in her pain, she has been named the culprit and called "loose," "hot-blooded," "wanton," "sultry," and "amoral." She has been used as the white man's sexual outhouse, and shamefully encouraged by her own ego-less man to persist in this function. Wanting, too, to be carried away by her "Prince Charming," she must, in all honesty, admit that he has been robbed of his crown by the very assaulter and assassin who has raped her. Still, she looks upon her man as God's gift to Black womanhood and is further diminished and humiliated and outraged when the feeling is not mutual. . . .

At best we are made to feel that we are poor imitations and excuses for white women.

Evil? Evil, you say. The black woman is hurt, confused, frustrated, angry, resentful, frightened and evil! Who in the hell dares suggest that she should be otherwise? These attitudes only point up her perception of the situation and her healthy rejection of same.

Maybe if our women get evil enough and angry enough, they'll be moved to some action that will bring our men to their senses. There is one unalterable fact that too many of our men cannot seem to face. And that is, we "black, evil, ugly" women are a perfect and accurate reflection of you "black, evil, ugly" men. Play hide and seek as long as you can and will, but your every rejection and abandonment of us is only sorry testament of how thoroughly and carefully you have been blinded and brainwashed. And let it further understood that when we refer to you we mean, ultimately, us. For you are us, and vice versa.

We are the women who were kidnapped and brought to his continent as slaves. We are the women who were raped, are still being raped, and our bastard children snatched from our breasts and scattered to the winds to be lynched, castrated, de-egoed, robbed, burned, and deceived.

We are the women whose strong and beautiful Black bodies were—and are—still being used as a cheap labor force for Miss Anne's kitchen and Mr. Charlie's bed, whose rich, black and warm milk nurtured—and still nurtures—the heir to the racist and evil slavemaster.

We are the women who dwell in the hell-hole ghettos all over the land. We are the women whose bodies are sacrificed, as living cadavers, to experimental surgery in the white man's hospitals for the sake of white medicine. We are the women who are invisible on the television and movie screens, on the Broadway stage. We are the women who are lusted after, sneered at, leered at, hissed at, yelled at, grabbed at, tracked down by white degenerates in our own pitiable, poverty-stricken and prideless neighborhoods.

We are the women whose hair is compulsively fried, whose skin is bleached, whose is "too big," whose mouth is "too big and loud," whose behind is "too big and broad," whose feet are "too big and flat," whose face is "too black and shiny," and whose suffering and patience is too long and enduring to be believed.

Who are just too damned much for everybody. . . .

We are the women whose husbands and fathers and brothers and sons have been plagiarized, imitated, denied, and robbed of the fruits of their genius, and who consequently we see as emasculated, jailed, lynched, driven mad, deprived, enraged and made suicidal. We are the women who nobody, seemingly, cares about, who are made to feel inadequate, stupid and backward, and who inevitably have the most colossal inferiority complexes to be found.

And who is spreading the propaganda that "the only free people in the country are the white man and the black woman"? If this be freedom, then Heaven is hell, right is wrong, and cold is hot.

Who will revere the black woman? Who will keep our neighborhoods safe for black innocent womanhood? Black womanhood is outraged and humiliated. Black womanhood cries for dignity and restitution and salvation. Black womanhood wants and needs protection, and keeping, and holding. Who will assuage her indignation? Who will keep her precious and pure? Who will glorify and proclaim her beautiful image? To whom will *she* cry rape?

• • •

In the era before the *Roe v. Wade* decision by the Supreme Court (January 22, 1973), abortions were illegal in the United States. Women were forced to carry unwanted pregnancies to term or to seek illegal abortions under dangerous and degrading circumstances, at great risk to themselves. In many cases, women died from back-alley abortions. The battle for abortion rights became a central part of the women's liberation movement. In the pre-*Roe* era, a number of women created their own networks to provide support and medical assistance to women who wanted to end their pregnancies. One of the most important of these efforts was the Chicago-based Abortion Counseling Service of Women's Liberation, or "Jane" as it came to be known. Here the feminist journalist and activist Susan Brownmiller, author of *Against Our Will: Men, Women and Rape*, recalls her own experience of having an abortion in the era before *Roe*, and describes how the women's movement successfully campaigned to overturn the federal ban on a woman's right to choose.

Susan Brownmiller, "Abortion Is a Woman's Right" (1999)[6]

Women's Liberation found its first unifying issue in abortion, and abortion became the first feminist cause to sweep the nation. From 1969 to 1972 an imaginative campaign—rash, impudent, decentralized, yet interconnected by ideas and passion—successfully altered public perception to such an extent that a "crime," as the law defined it, became a "woman's constitutional right." Its capstone was *Roe v. Wade*, the monumental Supreme Court decision of January 22, 1973.

Nineteen sixty-nine was a precisely defined moment, the year when women of childbearing age transformed a quiet back-burner issue promoted by a handful of stray radicals and moderate reformers into a popular struggle for reproductive freedom. The women had been dubbed the Pill Generation, and indeed, earlier in the decade many had heeded the persuasive call of the sexual revolution, only to be disenchanted. Exploring their sexual freedom with an uncertain knowledge of birth control and a haphazard employment of its techniques, they had discovered the hard way that unwanted pregnancy was still a woman's problem.

Unlike the isolated women of their parents' generation who sought individual solutions in furtive silence, they would bring a direct personal voice to the abortion debate. They would reveal their own stories, first to one another and then to the public. They would borrow the confrontational tactics of the radical-left movements from which they had come. They would break the law, and they would raise a ruckus to change the law, devising original strategies to fight for abortion through the courts.

Before the new militance erupted, abortion was a criminal act in every state unless a committee of hospital physicians concurred that the pregnancy endangered the woman's life. Three states had extended the largesse to women whose health was threatened—broadly interpreted, health could mean mental health, if two psychiatrists so attested—but no more than ten thousand "therapeutic" abortions were performed in a year. To the general public, abortion was the stuff of lurid tabloid headlines that underscored its peril: A young woman's body found in a motel room; she'd bled to death from a botched operation. A practitioner and a hapless patient entrapped in a midnight raid on what the police dubbed "an abortion mill." There were shining exceptions like the legendary Robert Spencer of Ashland, Pennsylvania, who ran a spotless clinic and charged no more than one hundred dollars, but venality ran high in an unlawful business in which practitioners were raided and jailed and patients were pressured to be informers. Money was not the only commodity exchanged on the underground circuit; some abortionists extorted sexual payment for their secret work.

One million women braved the unknown every year, relying on a grapevine of whispers and misinformation to terminate their pregnancies by illegal means. Those lucky enough to secure the address of a good practitioner, and to scrounge up the requisite cash, packed a small bag and headed for San Juan, Havana, London, or Tokyo, or perhaps across town. The less fortunate risked septic infection and a punctured uterus from back-alley amateurs willing to poke their insides with a catheter, a knitting needle, or the unfurled end of a wire hanger. Still others damaged their health with lye or Lysol, the last-ditch home treatments. *Life* magazine estimated in 1967 that "five thousand of the desperate" died every year.

The writer Jane O'Reilly's story gives the lie to the too simple myth that "rich" women could always find a connection. In the summer of 1957, she was a Catholic debutante from St. Louis who was looking forward to her senior year at Radcliffe when she discovered she was pregnant. Dr. Spencer was in one of his periodic shutdowns, Cuba sounded unreal and scary, and the trusted family doctor to whom she appealed insisted that she tell her parents. A classmate finally came up with an address in New York and lent her the six hundred dollars. O'Reilly recalls that a man with a mustache placed her on a kitchen table, prodded her with a knitting needle, and gave her some pills.

A month later she fainted in her college dormitory shower. Whatever had been done to her in New York, Jane O'Reilly was still pregnant. Moving out of the dorm, she joked about putting on weight and took her finals shrouded in a raincoat. The next day she gave birth at a Salvation Army hospital and signed away her baby daughter. For the next thirty-four years on every May 10, her daughter's birthday, O'Reilly plunged into a sobbing depression. In 1991 the pain partially lifted when her daughter found her through an adoption search.

Women of my generation still need to bear witness; we still carry the traumas. For my first abortion in 1960 I took the Cuba option that had scared O'Reilly. Here's what I remember: Banging on a door during the midday siesta in a strange neighborhood in Havana. Wriggling my toes a few hours later, astonished to be alive. Boarding a small plane to Key West and hitchhiking back to New York bleeding all the way. Bleeding? I must have been hemorrhaging. In which state did I leave the motel bed drenched with my blood?

• • •

Assata Shakur (Joanne Chesimard) was a member of Black Panther Party and the Black Liberation Army, and a target of repression under the FBI's counterintelligence program (COINTELPRO). On May 2, 1973, she was stopped by state police on the New Jersey Turnpike, along with two other people, and subsequently shot twice. In the confrontation, one of the state troopers and one of her two companions were killed. She was charged with the murder of both. Shakur was convicted in 1977 to a 33-year sentence, but escaped in 1979. She has been living since the 1980s in Cuba, where she wrote her autobiography, *Assata*. Here Shakur describes the conditions in Riker's Island Correctional Institution for Women, where many of the prisoners "come from places where dreams have been abandoned like the buildings." The use of the lower-case "i" for the first-person pronoun and other deliberate misspellings are from Shakur's original article, published by *The Black Scholar*.

Assata Shakur (Joanne Chesimard), "Women in Prison: How We Are" (April 1978)[7]

We sit in the bull pen. We are all black. All restless. And we are all freezing. When we ask, the matron tells us that the heating system cannot be adjusted. All of us, with the exception of a woman, tall and gaunt, who looks naked and ravished, have refused the bologna sandwiches. The rest of us sit drinking bitter, syrupy tea. The tall, fortyish woman, with sloping shoulders, moves her head back and forth to the beat of a private tune while she takes small, tentative bites out of a bologna sandwich. Someone asks her what she's in for. Matter of factly, she says, "They say I killed some nigga. But how could I have when I'm buried down in South Carolina?" Everybody's face gets busy exchanging looks. A short, stout young woman wearing men's pants and men's shoes says, "Buried in South Carolina?" "Yeah," says the tall woman. "South Carolina, that's where I'm buried. You don't know that? You don't know shit do you? This ain't me. This ain't me." She kept repeating, "This ain't me" until she had eaten all the bologna sandwiches. Then she brushed off the crumbs and withdrew, head moving again, back into that private world where only she could hear her private tune.

Lucille comes to my tier to ask me how much time a "C" felony conviction carries. I know, but i cannot say the words. I tell her i will look it up and bring the sentence charts for her to see. I know that she has just been convicted of manslaughter in the second degree. I also know that she can be sentenced up to fifteen years. I knew from what she had told me before that the District Attorney was willing to plea bargain: Five years probation in exchange for a guilty plea to a lesser charge.

Her lawyer felt that she had a case: specifically, medical records which would prove she had suffered repeated physical injuries as a result of beatings by the deceased and, as a result of those beatings, on the night of her arrest her arm was mutilated (she must still wear a brace on it) and one of her ears was partially severed in addition to other substantial injuries. Her lawyer felt that her testimony, when she took the stand in her own defense, would establish the fact that not only had she been repeatedly beaten by the deceased, but that on the night in question he told her he would kill her, viciously beat her and mauled her with a knife. But there is no self defense in the state of New York.

The District Attorney made a big deal of the fact that she drank. And the jury, affected by t.v. racism, "law and order," petrified by crime and unimpressed with Lucille as a "responsible citizen," convicted her. And i was the one who had to tell her that she was facing fifteen years in prison while we both silently wondered what would happen to the four teenage children that she had raised almost single handedly.

Spikey has short time, and it is evident, the day before she is to be released, that she does not want to go home. She comes to the Bing (Administrative Segregation) because she has received an infraction for fighting. Sitting in front of her cage and talking to her i realize that the fight was a desperate, last ditch effort in hope that the prison would take away her "good days." She is in her late thirties. Her hands are swollen. Enormous. There are huge, open sores on her legs. She has about ten teeth left. And her entire body is scarred and ashen. She has been on drugs about twenty years. Her veins have collapsed. She has fibrosis epilepsy and edema. She has not seen her three children in about eight years. She is ashamed to contact home because she robbed and abused her mother so many times.

When we talk it is around the Christmas holidays and she tells me about her bad luck. She tells me that she has spent the last four Christmases in jail and tells me how happy she is to be going home. But i know that she has no where to go and that the only "friends" she has in the world are here in jail. She tells me that the only regret she has about leaving is that she won't be singing in the choir at Christmas. As i talk to her i wonder if she will be back. I tell her good bye and wish her luck. Six days later, through the prison grapevine, i hear she is back. Just in time for the Christmas show.

We are at sick call. We are waiting on wooden benches in a beige and orange room to see the doctor. Two young women who look only mildly battered by life sit wearing pastel dresses and pointy-toed state shoes. (Wearing "state" is often a sign that the wearer probably cannot afford to buy sneakers in commissary.) The two are talking about how well they were doing on the street. Eavesdropping, i find out that the both have fine "old men" that love the mess out of them. I find out that their men dress fly and wear some baad clothes and so do they. One has 40 pairs of shoes while the other has 100 skirts. One has 2 suede and 5 leather coats. The other has 7 suedes and 3 leathers. One has 3 mink coats, a silver fox and a leopard. The other has 2 minks, a fox jacket, a floor length fox and a chinchilla. One has 4 diamond rings and the other has 5. One lives in a duplex with a sunken tub and a sunken living room with a water fall. The other describes a mansion with the revolving living room. I'm relieved when my name is called. I had been sitting there feeling very, very sad.

There are no criminals here at Riker's Island Correctional Institution for Women, (New York), only victims. Most of the women (95 percent) are black and Puerto Rican. Many were abused children. Most have been abused by men and all have been abused by "the system."

There are no big time gangsters here, no premeditated mass murderers, no godmothers. There are no big time dope dealers, no kidnappers, no Watergate women. There are virtually no women here charged with white collar crimes like embezzling or fraud. Most of the women have drug related cases. Many are charged as accessories to crimes committed by men. The major crimes that women here are charged with are prostitution, pick-pocketing, shop lifting, robbery, and drugs. Women who have prostitution cases, or who are doing "fine" time make up a substantial part of the short term population. The women see stealing or hustling as necessary for the survival of themselves or their children because jobs are scarce and welfare is impossible to live on. One thing is clear: amerikan capitalism is in no way threatened by the women in prison on Riker's Island.

One gets the impression, when first coming to Riker's Island that the architects conceived of it as a prison modeled after a juvenile center. In the areas where visitors usually pass there is plenty of glass and plenty of plants and flowers. The cell blocks consists of two long corridors with cells on each side connected by a watch room where the guards are stationed, called a bubble. Each corridor has a day room with a t.v., tables, multi-colored chairs, a stove that doesn't work and a refrigerator. There's a utility room with a sink and a washer and dryer that do not work.

Instead of bars the cells have doors which are painted bright, optimistic colors with slim glass observation panels. The doors are controlled electronically by the guards in the bubble. The cells are called rooms by everybody. They are furnished with a cot, a closet, a desk, a chair, a plastic upholstered headboard that opens for storage, a small book case, a mirror, a sink and a toilet. The prison distributes brightly colored bedspreads and throw rugs for a homey effect. There is a school area, a gym, a carpeted auditorium, two inmate cafeterias and outside recreation areas that are used during the summer months only.

The guards have successfully convinced most of the women that Riker's Island is a country club. They say that it is a playhouse compared to some other prisons (especially male): a statement whose partial veracity is not predicated upon the humanity of the correction facilities at Riker's Island, but, rather, by contrast to the unbelievably barbaric conditions of other prisons. Many women are convinced that they are, somehow, "getting over." Some go so far as to reason that because they are not doing hard time, they are not really in prison.

The image is further reinforced by the pseudo-motherly attitude of many of the guards; a deception which all too often successfully reverts women to children. The guards call the women inmates by their first names. The women address the guards either as Officer, Miss—or by nicknames (Teddy Bear, Spanky, Aunt Louise, Squeeze, Sarge, Black Beauty, Nutty Mahogany, etc.). Frequently, when a woman returns to Riker's she will make rounds, gleefully embracing her favorite guard: the prodigal daughter returns.

If two women are having a debate about any given topic the argument will often be resolved by "asking the officer." The guards are forever telling the women to "grow up," to "act like ladies," to "behave" and to be "good girls." If an inmate is breaking some minor rule like coming to say "hi" to her friend on another floor or locking in a few minutes late, a guard will say, jokingly, "don't let me have to come down there and beat your butt." It is not unusual to hear a guard tell a woman, "what you need is a good spanking." The tone is often motherly, "didn't I tell you, young lady, to. . . ."; or, "you know better than that"; or, "that's a good girl." And the women respond accordingly. Some guards and inmates "play" together. One officer's favorite "game" is taking off her belt and chasing her "girls" down the hall with it, smacking them on the butt.

But beneath the motherly veneer, the reality of guard life is ever present. Most of the guards are black, usually from working class, upward bound, civil service oriented backgrounds. They identify with the middle class, have middle class values and are extremely materialistic. They are not the most intelligent women in the world and many are extremely limited. Most are aware that there is no justice in the amerikan judicial system and that blacks and Puerto Ricans are discriminated against in every facet of amerikan life. But, at the same time, they are convinced that the system is somehow "lenient." To them, the women in prison are "losers" who don't have enough sense to stay out of jail. Most believe in the boot strap theory—anybody can "make it" if they try hard enough. They congratulate themselves on their great accomplishments. In contrast to themselves they see the inmate as ignorant, uncultured, self-destructive, weak-minded and stupid. They ignore the fact that their dubious accomplishments are not based on superior intelligence or effort, but only on chance and a civil service list.

Many guards hate and feel trapped by their jobs. The guard is exposed to a certain amount of abuse from co-workers, from the brass as well as from inmates, ass kissing, robotizing and mandatory overtime. (It is common practice for guards to work a double shift at least once a week.) But no matter how much they hate the military structure, the infighting, the ugliness of their tasks, they are very aware of how close they are to the welfare lines. If they were not working as guards most would be underpaid or unemployed. Many would miss the feeling of superiority and power as much as they would miss the money, especially the cruel, sadistic ones.

The guards are usually defensive about their jobs and indicate by their behavior that they are not at all free from guilt. They repeatedly, compulsively say, as if to convince themselves, "This is a job just like any other job." The more they say that the more preposterous it seems.

The major topic of conversation here is drugs. Eighty percent of inmates have used drugs when they were in the street. Getting high is usually the first thing a woman says she's going to do when she gets out. In prison, as on the streets, an escapist culture prevails. At least 50 percent of the prison population takes some form of psychotropic drug. Elaborate schemes to obtain contraband drugs are always in the works.

Days are spent in pleasant distractions: soap operas, prison love affairs, card playing and game playing. A tiny minority are seriously involved in academic pursuits or the learning of skills. An even smaller minority attempt to study law books. There are no jail house lawyers and most of the women lack knowledge of even the most rudimentary legal procedures. When asked what happened in court, or, what their lawyers said, they either don't know or don't remember. Feeling totally helpless and totally railroaded a woman will curse out her lawyer or the judge with little knowledge of what is being done or of what should be done. Most plead guilty, whether they are guilty or not. The few who do go to trial usually have lawyers appointed by the state and usually are convicted. . . .

For many, prison is not that much different from the street. It is, for some, a place to rest and recuperate. For the prostitute prison is a vacation from turning tricks in the rain and snow. A vacation from brutal pimps. Prison for the addict is a place to get clean, get medical work done and gain weight. Often, when the habit becomes too expensive, the addict gets herself busted, (usually subconsciously) so she can get back in shape, leave with a clean system ready to start it all over again. One woman claims that for a month or two every year she either goes to jail or to the crazy house to get away from her husband.

For many the cells are not much different from the tenements, the shooting galleries and the welfare hotels they live in on the street. Sick call is no different from the clinic of the hospital emergency room. The fights are the same except they are less dangerous. The police are the same. The poverty is the same. The alienation is the same. The racism is the same. The sexism is the same. The drugs are the same and the system is the same. Riker's Island is just another institution. In childhood school was their prison, or youth houses or reform schools or children shelters or foster homes or mental hospitals or drug programs and they see all institutions as indifferent to their needs, yet necessary to their survival.

The women at Riker's Island come there from places like Harlem, Brownsville, Bedford-Stuyvesant, South Bronx and South Jamaica. They come from places where dreams have been abandoned like the buildings. Where there is no more sense of community. Where neighborhoods are transient. Where isolated people run from one fire trap to another. The cities have removed us from our strengths, from our roots, from our traditions. They have taken away our gardens and our sweet potato pies and given us McDonald's. They have become prisons, locking us into the futility and decay of pissy hallways that lead nowhere. They have alienated us from each other and made us fear each other. They have given us dope and television as a culture.

There are no politicians to trust. No roads to follow. No popular progressive culture to relate to. There are no new deals, no more promises of golden streets and no place else to migrate. My sisters in the streets, like my sisters at Riker's Island, see no way out. "Where can I go?" said a woman on the day she was going home. "If there's nothing to believe in," she said, "I can't do nothing except try to find cloud nine."

• • •

In 1966, a group of black activists in Oakland, California—believing that the gains made in the civil rights struggle of the early 1960s were insufficient to deal with racism and poverty, and that violence was justified in self-defense against racists and the police—formed the Black Panther Party for Self-Defense. Huey P. Newton, Bobby Seale, and David Hilliard drafted the party's initial manifesto, which declared "We want land, bread, housing, education, clothing, justice and peace." Soon the party had members around the country. The party's ideas and its activities, like free breakfast programs, were attractive to young blacks in the ghettos around the country. But it also became a target of police and the FBI. The FBI, using various illegal tactics, set out to destroy the party. In one notorious raid in Chicago in December 1969, local police, supplied with FBI information, broke into an apartment and shot to death two Panther leaders, Fred Hampton and Mark Clark. Other leaders were arrested and harassed.

Kathleen Cleaver, an activist in SNCC, became a national spokesperson for the party and a member of its central committee soon after joining in the fall of 1967. Cleaver led a national campaign to free jailed Panther leader Huey Newton, and spoke and wrote regularly for the BPP. Cleaver here describes her experiences organizing in the BPP.

Kathleen Neal Cleaver, "Women, Power, and Revolution" (October 16, 1998)[8]

About two weeks before I joined SNCC, "Black Power" replaced "Freedom Now" as the battle cry. We, young women and young men who flocked to the front lines of the war against segregation, were contesting the remaining legacy of racial slavery. What we sought to eliminate were the legal, social, psychological, economic, and political limitations still being imposed on our human rights, and on our rights as citizens. That was the context in which we fought to remove limitations imposed by gender, clearly aware that it could not be fought as a stand-alone issue.

During that era, we hadn't developed much language to talk about the elimination of gender discrimination. Racism and poverty, imposed by bloody terrorists backed by state power, seemed so overwhelming then, and the ghastly backdrop of the war in Vietnam kept us alert as to what was at stake. It was not that gender discrimination wasn't apparent. It was evident in the most intimate matters—separate bathrooms marked "colored women" or "white ladies"; it was obvious in the facts that so many schools did not allow women to attend, and that so many jobs were not available if you were a woman. But from the early to mid-1960s, the first order of business was not how to advance our cause as women but how to empower the community of which we were a part, and how to protect our lives in the process.

Being in the Movement gave me and everyone who joined it a tremendous education. That experience taught us how to understand the world around us, how to think through the issues of what we could do on our own to advance our people's cause, how to organize our own people to change the world around us, and how to stand up to terrorism. Everything I learned in SNCC I took with me into the fledgling Black Panther Party. I started working there in November 1967, three or four weeks after Huey Newton was jailed on charges of killing an Oakland policeman in a predawn shoot-out. I organized demonstrations. I wrote leaflets. I held press conferences. I attended court hearings. I designed posters. I appeared on television programs, I spoke at rallies. I even ran for political office in order to organize the community around the program of the Black Panther Party and mobilize support to free Huey Newton.

At times, during the question-and-answer session following a speech I'd given, someone would ask, "What is the woman's role in the Black Panther Party?" I never liked that question. I'd give a short answer: "It's the same as men." We are revolutionaries, I'd explain. Back then, I didn't understand why they wanted to think of what men were doing and what women were doing as separate. It's taken me years, literally about twenty-five years, to understand that what I really didn't like was the underlying assumption motivating the question. The assumption held that being part of a revolutionary movement was in conflict with what the questioner had been socialized to believe was appropriate conduct for a woman. That convoluted concept never entered my head, although I am certain it was far more widely accepted than I ever realized.

Nowadays, the questions are more sophisticated: "What were the gender issues in the Black Panther Party?" "Wasn't the Black Panther Party a bastion of sexism?

Etc., etc., etc. But nobody seems to pose the question that I had: Where can I go to get involved in the revolutionary struggle? It seems to me that part of the genesis of the gender question, and this is only an opinion, lies in the way it deflects attention from confronting the revolutionary critique our organization made of the larger society, and turns it inward to look at what type of dynamics and social conflicts characterized the organization. To me, this discussion holds far less appeal than that which engages the means we devised to struggle against the oppressive dynamics and social conflicts the larger society imposed on us. Not many answers to the "gender questions" take into consideration what I've experienced. What I've read or heard as answers generally seem to respond to a particular model of academic inquiry that leaves out what I believe is central: How do you empower an oppressed and impoverished people who are struggling against racism, militarism, terrorism, and sexism too? I mean, how do you do that? That's the real question.

My generation became conscious during a period of profound world turmoil, when the Vietnam War and countless insurgencies in Africa, Asia, and in Latin America challenged the control of the resources of the world by the capitalist powers. They were facing a major assault. Those of us who were drawn to the early Black Panther Party were just one more insurgent band of young men and women who refused to tolerate the systematic violence and abuse being meted out to poor blacks, to middle-class blacks, and to any old ordinary blacks. When we looked at our situation, when we saw violence, bad housing, unemployment, rotten education, unfair treatment in the courts, as well as direct attacks from the police, our response was to defend ourselves. We became part of that assault against the capitalist powers.

In a world of racist polarization, we sought solidarity. We called for Black power for Black people, Red power for Red people, Brown power for Brown people, Yellow power for Yellow people, and, as Eldridge Cleaver used to say, White power for White people, because all they'd known was "Pig power." We organized the Rainbow Coalition, pulled together our allies, including not only the Puerto Rican Young Lords, the youth gang called Black P. Stone Rangers, the Chicano Brown Berets, and the Asian I Wor Keun (Red Guards), but also the predominantly white Peace and Freedom Party and the Appalachian Young Patriots Party. We posed not only a theoretical but a practical challenge to the way our world was organized. And we were men and women working together.

The women who filled the ranks of our organization did not have specifically designated sex roles. Some women worked with the newspaper, like Shelley Bursey, who became a grand jury resister when she was jailed because she refused to respond to one of the investigations into the Black Panther Party newspaper. Some of us, like Ericka Huggins, saw their husbands murdered, then were arrested themselves. In Ericka's case, she was jailed along with Bobby Seale and most of the New Haven chapter on charges of conspiracy to commit murder. She was later acquitted, but imagine what happens to an organization when fourteen people at once get arrested on capital charges. That doesn't leave much time to organize, or to have a family life. Maybe that was the kind of pressure that they hoped would force us to give up.

I created the position of Communications Secretary, based on what I had seen Julian Bond do in SNCC. I sent out press releases, I got photographers and journalists to publish about us, I wrote articles for our newspaper. I ran for political office on the Peace and Freedom Party ticket, against the incumbent Democratic state representative—who, by the way, was Willie Brown (now mayor of San Francisco). We ran a campaign poster in the *Black Panther* newspaper, which was a drawing of Willie Brown with his mouth sewed up, his body tied up in rope. The caption read: Willie Brown's position on the Vietnam War, political prisoners, and racism, you get the idea. We were imaginative in our approach to political organizing. Matilaba [J. Tarika Lewis], one of the earliest women members of the Black Panther Party, published drawings in the newspaper along with Emory Douglas. Connie Matthews, a young Jamaican who was working for the United Nations in Copenhagen, met Bobby Seale when he came over there on a tour, joined the Black Panther Party, and became our International Coordinator. Assata Shakur, who joined the New York chapter of the Black Panther Party, later became convicted of murdering a state trooper after a shoot-out on the New Jersey Turnpike in which she was wounded and another Panther, Zayd Shakur, was killed. Fearing that she would be killed, she escaped from prison, lived underground for a while, and eventually received asylum in Cuba.

In fact, according to a survey Bobby Seale did in 1969, two-thirds of the members of the Black Panther Party were women. I am sure you are wondering, why isn't this the image that you have of the Black Panther Party? Well, ask yourself, where did the image of the Black Panthers that you have in your head come from? Did you read those articles planted by the FBI in the newspaper? Did you listen to the newscasters who announced what they decided was significant, usually, how many Panthers got arrested or killed? How many photographs of women Panthers have you seen? Think about this: how many newspaper photographers were women? How many newspaper editors were women? How many newscasters were women? How many television producers were women? How many magazine, book, newspaper publishers? Who was making the decisions about what information gets circulated, and when that decision gets made, who do you think they decide to present? Is it possible, and this is just a question, is it possible that the reality of what was actually going on day to day in the Black Panther Party was far less newsworthy, and provided no justification for the campaign of destruction that the intelligence agencies and the police were waging against us? Could it be that the images and stories of the Black Panthers that you've seen and heard were geared to something other than conveying what was actually going on?

What I think is distinctive about gender relations within the Black Panther Party is not how those gender relations duplicated what was going on in the world around us. In fact, that world was extremely misogynist and authoritarian. That's part of what inspired us to fight against it. When women suffered hostility, abuse, neglect, and assault—this was not something arising from the policies or structure of the Black Panther Party, something absent from the world—that's what was going on in the world. The difference that being in the Black Panther Party made was that it put a woman in a position when such treatment occurred to contest it. I'll always remember a particular mini-trial that took place at one of our meetings. A member of the Party was accused of raping a young sister, who was visiting from the Los Angeles chapter of the Black Panther Party, and he got voted out of the Party on the spot. Right there in the meeting. In 1970 the Black Panther Party took a formal position on the liberation of women. Did the U.S. Congress make any statement on the liberation of women? Did the Congress enable the Equal Rights Amendment to become part of the Constitution? Did the Oakland police issue a position against gender discrimination? It is in this context that gender relations—a term that we didn't have back then—in the Black Panther Party should be examined.

I think it is important to place the women who fought oppression as Black Panthers within the longer tradition of freedom fighters like Sojourner Truth, Harriet Tubman, Ida Wells-Barnett, who took on an entirely oppressive world and insisted that their race, their gender, and their humanity be respected all at the same time. Not singled out, each one separate, but all at the same time. You cannot segregate out one aspect of our reality and expect to get a clear picture of what this struggle is about. In some cases, those who raise issues about gender are responding to what they think is the one-sided portrayal of the Black Panther Party as some all-male, macho revolutionary group. But look at where the picture is coming from before concluding that the appropriate response is to investigate gender dynamics within the Black Panther Party. I am not criticizing the project, but I am criticizing the angle.

The way Black women have sustained our community is phenomenal. Historically, we did not live within the isolation of a patriarchal world, we were thrust into that brutal equality slavery imposed. Our foremothers knew we would have to face the world on our own, and they tried to prepare us for that. What I think need to be examined and explained more fully are the powerful contributions women have made to our resistance against slavery, to our resistance against segregation, to our resistance against racism. Placing the participation of women in the Black Panther Party within that context illuminates a long tradition of fighting women.

CHAPTER TWENTY

Losing Control in the 1970s

Howard Zinn, "The Problem Is Civil Obedience" (November 1970)

George Jackson, *Soledad Brother* (1970)

Bob Dylan, "George Jackson" (1971)

Angela Davis, "Political Prisoners, Prisons, and Black Liberation" (1970)

Two Voices of the Attica Uprising (1971 and 2000)
Elliott James ("L. D.") Barkley (September 9, 1971)
Interview with Frank "Big Black" Smith (2000)

Leonard Peltier on the Trail of Broken Treaties Protest (1999)

Select Committee to Study Governmental Operations with Respect to Intelligence Activities, *Covert Action in Chile 1963–1973* (December 18, 1975)

Noam Chomsky, "COINTELPRO: What the (Deleted) Was It?" (March 12, 1978)

In the early 1970s, as a result of the movements of the 1960s, the system seemed out of control. It could not hold the loyalty of the public. As early as 1970, the University of Michigan's Survey Research Center found that "trust in government" was low in every section of the population. Interestingly, among blue-collar workers, 60 percent had "low" political trust in the government, compared to 40 percent among professional people.

There was also, by the 1970s, a reluctance by people in the United States to intervene with military force abroad. The result was that the government continued its attempt to expand power abroad, but covertly. For instance, a secret campaign was carried out to overthrow the government of Chile, which had elected a socialist president.

More voters than ever before refused to identify themselves as either Democrats or Republicans. In 1940, 20 percent of those polled called themselves "independents." By 1974, the number had risen to 34 percent.

Juries were acquitting radicals: the black radical Angela Davis, who was openly a Communist, was acquitted by an all-white jury on the West Coast. Pacifists who raided a draft board in Camden, New Jersey, were acquitted by a jury after the judge allowed testimony about the immorality of the Vietnam War.

The Nixon administration, widening the Vietnam War to Laos and Cambodia, aroused huge anti-war demonstrations all over the country, and then, facing enormous popular opposition to the war, moved slowly towards extricating the United States from Vietnam.

The 1970s was also the decade of the Watergate scandal. President Richard Nixon, fearful of being defeated in the election, authorized a secret break-in to Democratic National Headquarters. When discovered, the ensuing uproar led Congress to move to impeach Nixon, after which he resigned the presidency.

The war, the Watergate scandal, the decline in public confidence, led Congress to the unusual action of investigating both the CIA and the FBI. Reports were published that showed both those organizations were engaging in illegal activities, in this country and abroad.

The establishment was worried. Political leaders and certain intellectuals from the United States, Japan, and Western Europe organized the Trilateral Commission to develop a strategy for dealing with the upsurge of the 1960s and early 1970s. A report for the commission by Harvard political scientist Samuel Huntington concluded: "The essence of the democratic surge of the 1960s was a general challenge to existing systems of authority, public and private." According to Huntington, this "raised questions about the governability of democracy in the 1970s." Huntington cited an "excess of democracy," suggesting that there were "desirable limits to the indefinite extension of political democracy."

The establishment would now try to recoup its strength, while movements of the people continued their effort to create the democracy that the Trilateral Commission feared.

• • •

In November 1970, after my arrest along with others who had engaged in a Boston protest at an army base to block soldiers from being sent to Vietnam, I flew to Johns Hopkins University in Baltimore to take part in a debate with the philosopher Charles Frankel on civil disobedience. I was supposed to appear in court that day in connection with the charges resulting from the army base protest. I had a choice: show up in court and miss this opportunity to explain—and practice—my commitment to civil disobedience, or face the consequences of defying the court order by going to Baltimore. I chose to go. The next day, when I returned to Boston, I went to teach my morning class at Boston University. Two detectives were waiting outside the classroom and hauled me off to court, where I was sentenced to a few days in jail. Here is the text of my speech that night at Johns Hopkins.

Howard Zinn, "The Problem Is Civil Obedience" (November 1970)[1]

I start from the supposition that the world is topsy-turvy, that things are all wrong, that the wrong people are in jail and the wrong people are out of jail, that the wrong people are in power and the wrong people are out of power, that the wealth is distributed in this country and the world in such a way as not simply to require small reform but to require a drastic reallocation of wealth. I start from the supposition that we don't have to say too much about this because all we have to do is think about the state of the world today and realize that things are all upside down. Daniel Berrigan is in jail—a Catholic priest, a poet who opposes the war—and J. Edgar Hoover is free, you see. David Dellinger, who has opposed war ever since he was this high and who has used all of his energy and passion against it, is in danger of going to jail. The men who are responsible for the My Lai massacre are not on trial; they are in Washington serving various functions, primary and subordinate, that have to do with the unleashing of massacres, which surprise them when they occur. At Kent State University four students were killed by the National Guard and students were indicted. In every city in this country, when demonstrations take place, the protestors, whether they have demonstrated or not, whatever they have done, are assaulted and clubbed by police, and then they are arrested for assaulting a police officer.

Now, I have been studying very closely what happens every day in the courts in Boston, Massachusetts. You would be astounded—maybe you wouldn't, maybe you have been around, maybe you have lived, maybe you have thought, maybe you have been hit—at how the daily rounds of injustice make their way through this marvelous thing that we call due process. Well, that is my premise.

All you have to do is read the Soledad letters of George Jackson, who was sentenced to one year to life, of which he spent ten years, for a seventy-dollar robbery of a filling station. And then there is the U.S. Senator who is alleged to keep 185,000 dollars a year, or something like that, on the oil depletion allowance. One is theft; the other is legislation. Something is wrong, something is terribly wrong when we ship 10,000 bombs full of nerve gas across the country, and drop them in somebody else's swimming pool so as not to trouble our own. So you lose your perspective after a while. If you don't think, if you just listen to TV and read scholarly things, you actually begin to think that things are not so bad, or that just little things are wrong. But you have to get a little detached, and then come back and look at the world, and you are horrified. So we have to start from that supposition—that things are really topsy-turvy.

And our topic is topsy-turvy: civil disobedience. As soon as you say the topic is civil disobedience, you are saying our *problem* is civil disobedience. That is *not* our problem. . . .

Our problem is civil *obedience.* Our problem is the numbers of people all over the world who have obeyed the dictates of the leaders of their government and have gone to war, and millions have been killed because of this obedience. And our problem is that scene in *All Quiet on the Western Front* where the schoolboys march off dutifully in a line to war. Our problem is that people are obedient all over the world, in the face of poverty and starvation and stupidity, and war and cruelty. Our problem is that people are obedient while the jails are full of petty thieves, and all the while the grand thieves are running the country. That's our problem. We recognize this for Nazi Germany. We know that the problem there was obedience, that the people obeyed Hitler. People obeyed; that was wrong. They should have challenged, and they should have resisted; and if we were only there, we would have showed them. Even in Stalin's Russia we can understand that; people are obedient, all these herdlike people.

But America is different. That is what we've all been brought up on. From the time we are this high—and I still hear it resounding in Mr. Frankel's statement— you tick off, one, two, three, four, five lovely things about America that we don't want disturbed very much.

But if we have learned anything in the past ten years, it is that these lovely things about America were never lovely. We have been expansionist and aggressive and mean to other people from the beginning. And we've been aggressive and mean to people in this country, and we've allocated the wealth of this country in a very unjust way. We've never had justice in the courts for the poor people, for black people, for radicals. Now how can we boast that America is a very special place? It is not that special. It really isn't.

Well, that is our topic, that is our problem: civil obedience. Law is very important. We are talking about obedience to law—law, this marvelous invention of modern times, which we attribute to Western civilization, and which we talk about proudly. The rule of law, oh, how wonderful, all these courses in Western civilization all over the land. Remember those bad old days when people were exploited by feudalism? Everything was terrible in the Middle Ages—but now we have Western civilization, the rule of law. *The rule of law has regularized and maximized the injustice that existed before the rule of law, that is what the rule of law has done.* Let us start looking at the rule of law realistically, not with that metaphysical complacency with which we always examined it before.

When in all the nations of the world the rule of law is the darling of the leaders and the plague of the people, we ought to begin to recognize this. We have to transcend these national boundaries in our thinking. Nixon and [Leonid] Brezhnev have much more in common with one another than we have with

Nixon. J. Edgar Hoover has far more in common with the head of the Soviet secret police than he has with us. It's the international dedication to law and order that binds the leaders of all countries in a comradely bond. That's why we are always surprised when they get together—they smile, they shake hands, they smoke cigars, they really like one another no matter what they say. It's like the Republican and Democratic parties, who claim that it's going to make a terrible difference if one or the other wins, yet they are all the same. Basically, it is us against them.

Yossarian was right, remember, in *Catch-22*? He had been accused of giving aid and comfort to the enemy, which nobody should ever be accused of, and Yossarian said to his friend Clevinger: "The enemy is whoever is going to get you killed, whichever side they are on." But that didn't sink in, so he said to Clevinger: "Now you remember that, or one of these days you'll be dead." And remember? Clevinger, after a while, was dead. And we must remember that our enemies are not divided along national lines, that enemies are not just people who speak different languages and occupy different territories. Enemies are people who want to get us killed.

We are asked, "What if everyone disobeyed the law?" But a better question is, "What if everyone obeyed the law?" And the answer to that question is much easier to come by, because we have a lot of empirical evidence about what happens if everyone obeys the law, or if even most people obey the law. What happens is what has happened, what is happening. Why do people revere the law? And we all do; even I have to fight it, for it was put into my bones at an early age when I was a Cub Scout. One reason we revere the law is its ambivalence. In the modern world we deal with phrases and words that have multiple meanings, like "national security." Oh, yes, we must do this for national security! Well, what does that mean? Whose national security? Where? When? Why? We don't bother to answer those questions, or even to ask them.

The law conceals many things. The law is the Bill of Rights. In fact, that is what we think of when we develop our reverence for the law. The law is something that protects us; the law is our right—the law is the Constitution. Bill of Rights Day, essay contests sponsored by the American Legion on our Bill of Rights, that is the law. And that is good.

But there is another part of the law that doesn't get ballyhooed—the legislation that has gone through month after month, year after year, from the beginning of the Republic, which allocates the resources of the country in such a way as to leave some people very rich and other people very poor, and still others scrambling like mad for what little is left. That is the law. If you go to law school you will see this. You can quantify it by counting the big, heavy law books that people carry around with them and see how many law books you count that say

"Constitutional Rights" on them and how many that say "Property," "Contracts," "Torts," "Corporation Law." That is what the law is mostly about. The law is the oil depletion allowance—although we don't have Oil Depletion Allowance Day, we don't have essays written on behalf of the oil depletion allowance. So there are parts of the law that are publicized and played up to us—oh, this is the law, the Bill of Rights. And there are other parts of the law that just do their quiet work, and nobody says anything about them.

It started way back. When the Bill of Rights was first passed, remember, in the first administration of [George] Washington? Great thing. Bill of Rights passed! Big ballyhoo. At the same time [Alexander] Hamilton's economic program was passed. Nice, quiet, money to the rich—I'm simplifying it a little, but not too much. Hamilton's economic program started it off. You can draw a straight line from Hamilton's economic program to the oil depletion allowance to the tax write-offs for corporations. All the way through—that is the history. The Bill of Rights publicized; economic legislation unpublicized.

You know the enforcement of different parts of the law is as important as the publicity attached to the different parts of the law. The Bill of Rights, is it enforced? Not very well. You'll find that freedom of speech in constitutional law is a very difficult, ambiguous, troubled concept. Nobody really knows when you can get up and speak and when you can't. Just check all of the Supreme Court decisions. Talk about predictability in a system—you can't predict what will happen to you when you get up on the street corner and speak. See if you can tell the difference between the Terminiello [*Terminiello v. Chicago*] case and the Feiner [*Feiner v. New York*] case, and see if you can figure out what is going to happen. By the way, there is one part of the law that is not very vague, and that involves the right to distribute leaflets on the street. The Supreme Court has been very clear on that. In decision after decision we are affirmed an absolute right to distribute leaflets on the street. Try it. Just go out on the street and start distributing leaflets. And a policeman comes up to you and he says, "Get out of here." And you say, "Aha! Do you know *Marsh v. Alabama*, 1946?" That is the reality of the Bill of Rights. That's the reality of the Constitution, that part of the law which is portrayed to us as a beautiful and marvelous thing. And seven years after the Bill of Rights was passed, which said that "Congress shall make no law abridging the freedom of speech," Congress made a law abridging the freedom of speech. Remember? The Sedition Act of 1798.

So the Bill of Rights was not enforced. Hamilton's program was enforced, because when the whisky farmers went out and rebelled you remember, in 1794 in Pennsylvania, Hamilton himself got on his horse and went out there to suppress the rebellion to make sure that the revenue tax was enforced. And you can trace the story right down to the present day, what laws are enforced, what laws are not

enforced. So you have to be careful when you say, "I'm for the law, I revere the law."
What part of the law are you talking about? I'm not against all law. But I think
we ought to begin to make very important distinctions about what laws do what
things to what people.

And there are other problems with the law. It's a strange thing, we think that
law brings order. Law doesn't. How do we know that law does not bring order?
Look around us. We live under the rules of law. Notice how much order we have?
People say we have to worry about civil disobedience because it will lead to anarchy. Take a look at the present world in which the rule of law obtains. This is the
closest to what is called anarchy in the popular mind—confusion, chaos, international banditry. The only order that is really worth anything does not come
through the enforcement of law, it comes through the establishment of a society
which is just and in which harmonious relationships are established and in which
you need a minimum of regulation to create decent sets of arrangements among
people. But the order based on law and on the *force* of law is the order of the totalitarian state, and it inevitably leads either to total injustice or to rebellion—eventually, in other words, to very great disorder.

We all grow up with the notion that the law is holy. They asked Daniel
Berrigan's mother what she thought of her son's breaking the law. He burned draft
records—one of the most violent acts of this century—to protest the war, for
which he was sentenced to prison, as criminals should be. They asked his mother
who is in her eighties, what she thought of her son's breaking the law. And she
looked straight into the interviewer's face, and she said, "It's not God's law." Now
we forget that. There is nothing sacred about the law. Think of who makes laws.
The law is not made by God, it is made by Strom Thurmond. If you have any
notion about the sanctity and loveliness and reverence for the law, look at the legislators around the country who make the laws. Sit in on the sessions of the state
legislatures. Sit in on Congress, for these are the people who make the laws which
we are then supposed to revere.

All of this is done with such propriety as to fool us. This is the problem. In the
old days, things were confused; you didn't know. Now you know. It is all down
there in the books. Now we go through due process. Now the same things happen as happened before, except that we've gone through the right procedures. In
Boston a policeman walked into a hospital ward and fired five times at a black man
who had snapped a towel at his arm—and killed him. A hearing was held. The judge
decided that the policeman was justified because if he didn't do it, he would lose
the respect of his fellow officers. Well, that is what is known as due process—that
is, the guy didn't get away with it. We went through the proper procedures, and
everything was set up. The decorum, the propriety of the law fools us.

The nation then, was founded on disrespect for the law, and then came the

Constitution and the notion of stability which [James] Madison and Hamilton liked. But then we found in certain crucial times in our history that the legal framework did not suffice, and in order to end slavery we had to go outside the legal framework, as we had to do at the time of the American Revolution or the Civil War. The union had to go outside the legal framework in order to establish certain rights in the 1930s. And in this time, which may be more critical than the Revolution or the Civil War, the problems are so horrendous as to require us to go outside the legal framework in order to make a statement, to resist, to begin to establish the kind of institutions and relationships which a decent society should have. No, not just tearing things down; building things up. But even if you build things up that you are not supposed to build up—you try to build up a people's park, that's not tearing down a system; you are building something up, but you are doing it illegally—the militia comes in and drives you out. That is the form that civil disobedience is going to take more and more, people trying to build a new society in the midst of the old.

But what about voting and elections? Civil disobedience—we don't need that much of it, we are told, because we can go through the electoral system. And by now we should have learned, but maybe we haven't, for we grew up with the notion that the voting booth is a sacred place, almost like a confessional. You walk into the voting booth and you come out and they snap your picture and then put it in the papers with a beatific smile on your face. You've just voted; that is democracy. But if you even read what the political scientists say—although who can?— about the voting process, you find that the voting process is a sham. Totalitarian states love voting. You get people to the polls and they register their approval. I know there is a difference—they have one party and we have two parties. We have one more party than they have, you see.

What we are trying to do, I assume, is really to get back to the principles and aims and spirit of the Declaration of Independence. This spirit is resistance to illegitimate authority and to forces that deprive people of their life and liberty and right to pursue happiness, and therefore under these conditions, it urges the right to alter or abolish their current form of government—and the stress had been on abolish. But to establish the principles of the Declaration of Independence, we are going to need to go outside the law, to stop obeying the laws that demand killing or that allocate wealth the way it has been done, or that put people in jail for petty technical offenses and keep other people out of jail for enormous crimes. My hope is that this kind of spirit will take place not just in this country but in other countries because they all need it. People in all countries need the spirit of disobedience to the state, which is not a metaphysical thing but a thing of force and wealth. And we need a kind of declaration of interdependence among people in all countries of the world who are striving for the same thing.

• • •

At the age of sixteen, George Jackson was accused of stealing $71 from a gas station. At his trial, he was given a sentence of "one year to life." Every year, his case was reviewed but Jackson was never given parole. While in Soledad Prison in Salinas, California, Jackson was radicalized and became a leader in political struggles both inside and outside the prison's walls. His prison letters and other writings reached millions of people who were questioning racism, poverty, police brutality, and the injustices of the judicial system. In August 1970, Jackson's teenage brother, Jonathan, was killed in an attempt to rescue his brother from a courthouse in Marin County. George Jackson was then transferred to San Quentin Prison. On August 21, 1971, days before he was to go to trial, he was shot to death by prison guards. Two of his prison letters follow, the first to his father, Robert James Jackson, and the second to his attorney, Fay Stender.

George Jackson, *Soledad Brother* (1970)[2]

JULY 1965

Dear Father,

I am perplexed and hard pressed in finding a solution or reason that will adequately explain why we are so eager to follow Charlie. Why we are so impressed with his apparent know-how. A glance at his history shows that it has been one long continuous war. At no time in European history has there been a period of peace and harmony. Every moment of his past has been spent in the breakdown of civilization by causing war, disruption, disease, and artificial famine. You send me a date from the moment he emerged from his cave-dwelling days and I'll tell you which of his tribes were at war, either on us or on themselves. The whole of the Western European's existence here in the U.S. has been the same one long war with different peoples. This is the only thing they understand, the only thing they respect—the only thing they can do with any dexterity. Do you accept this miscreant as the architect of the patterns that must guide your future life! If so, we must part company, and it is best we do so now, before the trouble begins. But please stop and think so that you can turn yourself around in time, so that the developments to come won't shock you so badly. I have not wasted my time these last three or four years. I speak with some authority and people are listening. People like me are going to be shaping your tomorrows. So just sit back, open your mind, and watch, since you can't marshal the fundamentals to help me.

Yes, my friend, I remember everything, the reason that Delora [Jackson] and I had to spend that summer and winter in Harrisburg is known and remembered by me. I remember the garbage right under the side and back of our place on Racine. Mama [Georgia Jackson] having to wash and wring clothes by hand, carrying Penny [Jackson] and Jon[athan Jackson] while some fat redheaded mama sat on her behind. I remember how strange people looked to me when I finally had to be sent to Skinner School. You never knew why I was almost killed the first day I went, but I do. I remember how the rent and clothes for us children kept you broke and ragged. All of us hungry, if not for food—the other things that make life bearable. After you and Mama settled down you had no recreational outlets whatever. And everyone on Warren Blvd. knows how you would beat me all the way home from our baseball games in the alley. Robert, can you see how absurd you sound to me when you speak on "the good life," or something about being a free adult? I know you have never been free. I know that few blacks over here have ever been free. The forms of slavery merely *changed* at the signing of the Emancipation Proclamation from chattel slavery to economic slavery. If you could see and talk to some of the blacks I meet in here you would immediately understand what I mean, and see that I'm right. They are all average, all with the same backgrounds, and in for the same thing, some form of food getting. About 70 to 80 percent of all crime in the U.S. is perpetrated by blacks, "the sole reason for this is that 98 percent of our number live below the poverty level in bitter and abject misery"! You must take off your rose-colored glasses and stop pretending. We have suffered an unmitigated wrong! How do you think I felt when I saw you come home each day a little more depressed than the day before? How do you think I felt when I looked in your face and saw the clouds forming, when I saw you look around and see your best efforts go for nothing—nothing. I can count the times on my hands that you managed to work up a smile.

George

APRIL 4, 1970

Dear Fay,

... Down here we hear relaxed, matter-of-fact conversations centering around how best to kill all the nation's niggers and in what order. It's not the fact that they consider killing me that upsets. They've been "killing all the niggers" from nearly half a millennium now, but I am still alive. I might be the most resilient dead man in the universe. The upsetting thing is that they never take into consideration the fact that I am going to resist. No they honestly believe that shit. They do! That's what they think of us. That they have beaten and conditioned all the defense and attack reflexes from us. That the region of the mind that stores the principles upon which men base their rationale to resist is missing in us. Don't they talk of concentration camps?. Don't they state that it couldn't happen in the U.S. because the fascists here are nice fascists. Not because it's impossible to incarcerate 30 million resisters, but because they are humane imperialists, enlightened fascists.

Well, they've made a terrible mistake. I recall the day I was born, the first day of my generation. It was during the second (and most destructive) capitalist world war for colonial privilege, early on a rainy Wednesday morning, late September, Chicago. It happened to me in a little fold-into-the-wall bed, in a little half-flat on Racine and Lake. Dr. Rogers attended. The el train that rattled by within fifteen feet of our front windows (the only two windows) screamed in at me like the banshee, portentous of pain, death, threatening and imminent. The first motion that my eyes focused on was this pink hand swinging in a wide arc in the general direction of my black ass. I stopped that hand, the left downward block, and countered the right needle finger to the eye. I was born with my defense reflexes well developed.

It's going to be "Kill me if you can," fool, not "Kill me if you please."

But let them make their plans on the supposition, "like slave, like son." I'm not going for it, though, and they've made my defense easier. A cop gives the keys to a group of right-wing cons. They're going to open our cells—one at a time—all over the building. They don't want to escape, or deal with the men who hold them here. They can solve their problems only if they kill all of us—think about that— these guys live a few cells from me. None of them have ever lived, most are state-raised in institutions like this one. They have nothing coming, nothing at all, they have nothing at stake in this order of things. In defending right-wing ideals and the status quo they're saying in effect that ninety-nine years and a dark day in prison is their idea of fun. Most are in and out, and mostly in, all of their life. The periods that they pass on the outside are considered runs. Simply stated, they consider they periods spent in the joint more natural, more in keeping with their tastes. Well, I understand their condition, and I know how they got that way. I could honestly sympathize with them if they were not so wrong, so stupid as to let the pigs use them. Sounds like Germany of the thirties and forties to me. It's the same on the outside there. I'll venture to say that there's not one piece of stock, not one bond owned by anyone in any of the families of the pigs who murdered Fred Hampton. They organize marches around the country, marches and demonstrations in support of total immediate destruction of Vietnam, and afterward no one is able to pick up the tab. The fascists, it seems, have a standard M.O. [modus operandi] for dealing with the lower classes. Actually oppressive power throughout history has used it. They turn a man against himself—think of all the innocent things that make us feel good, but that make some of us also feel guilty. Think of how the people of the lower classes weigh themselves against the men who rule.

Consider the con going through the courts on a capital offense who supports capital punishment. I swear I heard something just like that today. Look how long [Lewis B.] Hershey ran Selective Service. Blacks embrace capitalism, the most unnatural and outstanding example of man against himself that history can offer. After the Civil War, the form of slavery changed from chattel to economic slavery, and we were thrown onto the labor market to compete at a disadvantage with poor whites. Ever since that time, our principal enemy must be isolated and identified as capitalism. The slaver was and is the factory owner, the businessman of capitalist Amerika, the man responsible for employment, wages, prices, control of the nation's institutions and culture. It was the capitalist infrastructure of Europe and the U.S. which was responsible for the rape of Africa and Asia.

• • •

Although he largely stopped writing what he once famously called "finger pointin' songs" in the mid-1960s, in 1971, moved by news of the murder of George Jackson, Bob Dylan went into a studio and recorded a new song mourning Jackson's death. He immediately released two versions of the song, one acoustic and one recorded with a band backing him, as a single.

Bob Dylan, "George Jackson" (1971)[3]

I woke up this mornin',
There were tears in my bed.
They killed a man I really loved
Shot him through the head.
Lord, Lord,
They cut George Jackson down.
Lord, Lord,
They laid him in the ground.

Sent him off to prison
For a seventy-dollar robbery.
Closed the door behind him
And they threw away the key.
Lord, Lord,
They cut George Jackson down.
Lord, Lord,
They laid him in the ground.

He wouldn't take shit from no one
He wouldn't bow down or kneel.
Authorities, they hated him
Because he was just too real.
Lord, Lord,
They cut George Jackson down.
Lord, Lord,
They laid him in the ground.

Prison guards, they cursed him
As they watched him from above
But they were frightened of his power
They were scared of his love.
Lord, Lord,
So they cut George Jackson down.
Lord, Lord,
They laid him in the ground.

Sometimes I think this whole world
Is one big prison yard.
Some of us are prisoners
The rest of us are guards.
Lord, Lord,
They cut George Jackson down.
Lord, Lord,
They laid him in the ground.

• • •

Angela Davis, who had been active in the solidarity campaign for George Jackson and two of his fellow inmates (known as the Soledad Brothers), was a leading Black activist, a professor at Berkeley, and a member of the Communist Party when she became the target of California authorities. They tried to implicate her in the deaths of three people involved in the August 1970 attempt to free George Jackson from the Marin County court house. She was not at the scene of the crime, but the police claimed that the guns used that day were registered in her name. Davis went underground. Soon she was named one of the Ten Most Wanted Criminals. Davis was captured soon after in New York City but an international campaign came to her support. She was acquitted by an all-white jury. Davis has continued to write pathbreaking work on women, racism, and prisons, and to take part in numerous movements for change. Here is part of an essay she wrote in 1970 on the prison system.

Angela Davis, "Political Prisoners, Prisons, and Black Liberation" (1970)[4]

In the heat of our pursuit of fundamental human rights, Black people have been continually cautioned to be patient. We are advised that as long as we remain faithful to the *existing* democratic order, the glorious moment will eventually arrive when we will come into our own as full-fledged human beings.

But having been taught by bitter experience, we know that there is a glaring incongruity between democracy and the capitalist economy which is the source of our ills. Regardless of all rhetoric to the contrary, the people are not the ultimate matrix of the laws and the system which govern them—certainly not Black people and other nationally oppressed people, but not even the mass of whites. The people do not exercise decisive control over the determining factors of their lives.

Officials' assertions that meaningful dissent is always welcome, provided it falls within the boundaries of legality, are frequently a smokescreen obscuring the invitation to acquiesce in oppression. Slavery may have been un-righteous, the constitutional precision for the enslavement of Blacks may have been unjust, but conditions were not to be considered so bearable (especially since they were profitable to a small circle) as to justify escape and other acts proscribed by law. This was the import of the fugitive slave laws.

Needless to say, the history of the Unites States has been marred from its inception by an enormous quantity of unjust laws, far too many expressly bolstering the oppression of Black people. Particularized reflections of existing social inequities, these laws have repeatedly born witness to the exploitative and racist core of the society itself. For Blacks, Chicanos, for all nationally oppressed people, the problem of opposing unjust laws and the social conditions which nourish their growth, has always had immediate practical implications. Our very survival has frequently been a direct function of our skill in forging effective channels of resistance. In resisting we have been compelled to openly violate those laws which directly or indirectly buttress our oppression. But even containing our resistance within the orbit of legality, we have been labeled criminals and have been methodically persecuted by a racist legal apparatus. . . .

The prison is a key component of state's coercive apparatus, the overriding function of which is to ensure social control. The etymology of the term "penitentiary" furnishes a clue to the controlling idea behind the "prison system" at its inception. The penitentiary was projected as the locale for doing penitence for an offense against society, the physical and spiritual purging of proclivities to challenge rules and regulations which command total obedience. While cloaking itself with the bourgeois aura of universality—imprisonment was supposed to cut across all class lines, as crimes were to be defined by the act, not the perpetrator—the prison has actually operated as an instrument of class domination, a means of prohibiting the have-nots from encroaching upon the haves.

The occurrence of crime is inevitable in a society in which wealth is unequally distributed, as one of the constant reminders that society's productive forces are being channeled in the wrong direction. The majority of criminal offenses bear a direct relationship to property. Contained in the very concept of property, crimes are profound but suppressed social needs which express themselves in anti-social modes of action. Spontaneously produced by a capitalist organization of society, this type of crime is at once a protest against society and a desire to partake of its exploitative content. It challenges the symptoms of capitalism, but not its essence. . . .

Especially today when so many Black, Chicano, and Puerto Rican men and women are jobless as a consequence of the internal dynamic of the capitalist system, the role of the unemployed, which includes the lumpen proletariat in revolutionary struggle, must be given serious thought. Increased unemployment, particularly for the nationally oppressed, will continue to be an inevitable by-product of technological development. At least 30 percent of Black youth are presently without jobs. In the context of class exploitation and national oppression it should be clear that numerous individuals are compelled to resort to criminal acts, not as a result of conscious choice—implying other alternatives—but because society has objectively reduced their possibilities of subsistence and survival to this level. This recognition should signal the urgent need to organize the unemployed and lumpen proletariat, as indeed the Black Panther Party as well as activists in prison have already begun to do.

In evaluating the susceptibility of the Black and Brown unemployed to organizing efforts, the peculiar historical features of the U.S., specifically racism and national oppression, must be taken into account. There already exists in the Black and Brown communities, the lumpen proletariat included, a long tradition of collective resistance to national oppression.

Moreover, in assessing the revolutionary potential of prisoners in America as a group, it should be borne in mind that not all prisoners have actually committed crimes. The built-in racism of the judicial system expresses itself, as [W. E. B.] Du Bois has suggested, in the railroading of countless innocent Blacks and other national minorities into the country's coercive institutions.

One must also appreciate the effects of disproportionately long prison terms on Black and Brown inmates. The typical criminal mentality sees imprisonment as a calculated risk for a particular criminal act. One's prison term is more or less rationally predictable. The function of racism in the judicial-penal complex is to shatter that predictability. The Black burglar, anticipating a two-to four-year term, may end up doing ten to fifteen years, while the white burglar leaves after two years.

Within the contained, coercive universe of the prison, the captive is confronted with the realities of racism, not simply as individual acts dictated by attitudinal bias; rather he is compelled to come to grips with racism as an institutional phenomenon collectively experienced by the victims. The disproportionate representation of the Black and Brown communities, the manifest racism of parole boards, the intense brutality inherent in the relationship between prison guards and Black and Brown inmates—all this and more causes the prisoner to be confronted daily, hourly, with the concentrated systematic existence of racism.

For the innocent prisoner, the process of radicalization should come easy; for the "guilty" victim, the insight into the nature of racism as it manifests itself in the judicial-penal complex can lead to a questioning of his own past criminal activity and a re-evaluation of the methods he has used to survive in a racist and exploitative society. Needless to say, this process is not automatic, it does not occur spontaneously. The persistent educational work carried out by the prison's political activists plays a key role in developing the political potential of captive men and women.

Prisoners—especially Blacks, Chicanos and Puerto Ricans—are increasingly advancing the proposition that they are *political* prisoners. They contend that they are political prisoners in the sense that they are largely the victims of an oppressive politico-economic order, swiftly becoming conscious of the causes underlying their victimization. . . .

Racist oppression invades the lives of Black people on an infinite variety of levels. Blacks are imprisoned in a world where our labor and toil hardly allow us to eke out a decent existence, if we are able to find jobs at all. When the economy begins to falter, we are forever the first victims, always the most deeply wounded. When the economy is on its feet, we continue to live in a depressed state. Unemployment is generally twice as high in the ghettos as it is in the country as a whole and even higher among Black women and youth. The unemployment rate among Black youth has presently skyrocketed to 30 percent. If one-third of America's white youths were without a means of livelihood, we would either be in the thick of revolution or else under the iron rule of fascism. Substandard schools, medical care hardly fit for animals, over-priced, dilapidated housing, a welfare system based on a policy of skimpy concessions, designed to degrade and divide (and even this may soon be canceled)—this is only the beginning of the list of props in the overall scenery of oppression which, for the mass of Blacks, is the universe.

In Black communities, wherever they are located, there exists an ever-present reminder that our universe must remain stable in its drabness, its poverty, its brutality. From Birmingham to Harlem to Watts, Black ghettos are occupied, patrolled and often attacked by massive deployments of police. The police, domestic caretakers of violence, are the oppressor's emissaries, charged with the task of containing us within the boundaries of our oppression.

The announced function of the police, "to protect and serve the people," becomes the grotesque caricature of protecting and preserving the interests of our oppressors and serving us nothing but injustice. They are there to intimidate Blacks, to persuade us with their violence that we are powerless to alter the conditions of our lives. Arrests are frequently based on whims. Bullets from their guns murder human beings with little or no pretext, aside from the universal intimidation they are charged with carrying out. Protection for drug-pushers, and Mafia-style exploiters, support for the most reactionary ideological elements of the Black community (especially those who cry out for more police), are among the many functions of forces of law and order. They encircle the community with a shield of violence, too often forcing the natural aggression of the Black community inwards. [Frantz] Fanon's analysis of the role of colonial police is an appropriate description of the function of the police in America's ghettos.

It goes without saying that the police would be unable to set into motion their racist machinery were they not sanctioned and supported by the judicial system. The courts not only consistently abstain from prosecuting criminal behavior on the part of the police, but they convict, on the basis of biased police testimony, countless Black men and women. Court-appointed attorneys, acting in the twisted interests of overcrowded courts, convince 85 percent of the defendants to plead guilty. Even the manifestly innocent are advised to cop a plea so that the lengthy and expensive process of jury trials is avoided. This is the structure of the apparatus which summarily railroads Black people into jails and prisons. (During my imprisonment in the New York Women's House of Detention, I encountered numerous cases involving innocent Black women who had been advised to plead guilty. One sister had entered her white landlord's apartment for the purpose of paying rent. He attempted to rape her and in the course of the ensuing struggle, a lit candle toppled over, burning a tablecloth. The landlord ordered her arrested for arson. Following the advice of her court-appointed attorney, she entered a guilty plea, having been deceived by the attorney's insistence that the court would be more lenient. The sister was sentenced to three years.)

The vicious circle linking poverty, police courts, and prison is an integral element of ghetto existence. Unlike the mass of whites, the path which leads to jails and prisons is deeply rooted in the imposed patterns of Black existence. For this very reason, an almost instinctive affinity binds the mass of Black people to the political prisoners. The vast majority of Blacks harbor a deep hatred of the police and are not deluded by official proclamations of justice through the courts.

• • •

On September 9, 1971, more than one thousand inmates in New York's Attica Correctional Facility rose up in protest against what they described as brutal conditions in the maximum security prison. They held more than forty guards hostage in an effort to draw public attention to their situation. In the prison yard they set up a remarkable community, with blacks and whites working together. Governor Nelson Rockefeller refused to meet their demands and on September 12, he ordered a military attack by state police and the National Guard, which resulted in the deaths of thirty-two prisoners and eleven guards. The troops fired more than two thousand rounds in the space of nine minutes, and brutalized prisoners as they retook the prison. Afterwards, no officials, police, or guardsmen were punished, but prison rebels were given life sentences. Here are two voices from the prisoners who took part in the Attica uprising. The first is L. D. Barkley, who read a statement written by the Attica prisoners. Barkley was only twenty-one years old when he was killed, only a few days after making this statement. The second voice is one of the survivors of Attica, Frank "Big Black" Smith, who spent years campaigning for recognition of the human rights abuses committed against the Attica prisoners before his death in 2004.

Two Voices of the Attica Uprising
(1971 and circa 1999)

ELLIOTT JAMES ("L. D.") BARKLEY (SEPTEMBER 9, 1971)[5]

The entire incident that has erupted here at Attica is not a result of the dastardly bushwhacking of the two prisoners [on] September 8th of 1971, but of the unmitigated oppression wrought by the racist administrative network of this prison throughout the year.

We are men! We are not beasts and we do not intend to be beaten or driven as such. The entire prison populace—that means each and every one of us here—has set forth to change forever the ruthless brutalization and disregard for the lives of the prisoners here and throughout the United States.

What has happened here is but the sound before the fury of those who are oppressed. We will not compromise on any terms except those terms that are agreeable to us. We call upon all the conscientious citizens of America to assist us in putting an end to this situation that threatens the lives of not only us, but of each and every one of you.

We have set forth demands that will bring us closer to reality of the demise of these prison institutions that serve no useful purpose to the people of America but to those who would enslave and exploit the people of America.

Our demands are certain. We want complete amnesty, meaning freedom from all and any physical and mental and legal reprisals. We want now speedy and safe transportation out of confinement to a non-imperialistic country. We demand that the federal government intervene so that we will be under direct federal jurisdiction. We want the governor and the judiciary to guarantee that there will be no reprisals. And we want all factions of the media to articulate this.

We guarantee the safe passage of all people to and from this institution. We invite all the people to come here and witness this degradation so that they can better know how they can bring this degradation to an end.

INTERVIEW WITH FRANK "BIG BLACK" SMITH (2000)[6]

PBS: What were the conditions people were looking to improve?

FRANK SMITH: First what we called . . . slave wages. Like myself, I was working for the warden, as the warden, they called me a laundry boy, and I was a fullgrown man, but that was the title. I was making 30 cent a day, you know, to hand iron, you know, shirts and sheets and tablecloths, and all that type of stuff.

It had a metal shop, you know, where you weren't making no money. You might make 25 cent a day, you know, to work in a sweatbox, 90- or 100-degree, all day, no shower, one shower a week, and when you wash up, you get two buckets of water, three gallons of water, one for the top and one for the bottom.

And the medical, you know, I lost just about all of my teeth in prison, because when you go to see a dentist you see the medical doctor, and we had two doctors that we call them refuge doctors, Steinberg and Williams. You had to go through them in order to get to the dentist, and if you go in to get an extraction they'll let you through, but if you're not going to go and get an extraction, then they give you two aspirins and you go back to your cell. You follow?

And the education department was really outdated, outdated books. We wanted to get books, the same as people got in the street.

And it was a lot of cell time and we wanted to get better upgraded food, because you had a lot of people there was on not eating meat, especially the pork and stuff. We wanted to change that type of stuff.

PBS: When the negotiations get going, what was the initial reaction?

FRANK SMITH: We were dealing with the commissioner, [Russell] Oswald, you know. "Yeah, that's right, yeah, we did that, that makes sense, we can change, and we going to do that, and we going to work on this and we going to work on that, and we going to deal with the really, really change," and all this. But then he went outside and he forgot that we on the national TV and we got a TV set up, and he go, "Oh, in there, they want everything, they want the whole world." He changes right up. So right then, you know, faith, you know, we said, "We don't want this reaction every person coming in here."

And then we start talking to the observers, you know, like Arthur Eve, Clarence Jones, [Tom] Wicker, and [John] Dunne, and all of them, that we needed the Governor, we needed somebody here that really, really want to take this on, because Oswald, ex-parole commissioner, and he didn't have no faith from Jump Street, you know, and he double-dealing, you know, he want to stroke somebody.

So that's when the issue, when it really came down to it, Rockefeller should be the person to come, you know, and talk to us as the chief executive of New York State, recognizing that his arm was reaching all the way to Washington, it wasn't just there, you know, because he had a little political thing in the wind, too, you know, he was scheming, you know. He could make a move in his career, too. But at that time, we didn't recognize that.

PBS: Why weren't Rockefeller's top aides good enough?

FRANK SMITH: I mean, it wasn't good enough, not only us, you know, it wasn't good enough for the observers. They felt that Rockefeller should be the person to come in and take charge and really deal with the situation. Because the faith of his commissioner wasn't any good, so what make his understudy going to be any better?

But now, we talk to the Governor, the highest executive, did not make the whole situation more real. You know, then we don't have to go through understudies. So you say something to them, and then they say something to Rockefeller. With his hidden agenda, he's scheming anyway, you know he's thinking about another position, or thinking about going on with his career, you know, and so he was reaching really all the way to Washington that we found out later. You know, so his concern really wasn't into it.

But then, you know, it's like I said earlier, you know, the apple don't fall too far from the tree. You got to go back to what happened with his daddy, you know, they know how to deal with violence. So that's what they do, they bring it in, they bring in their troopers and say, "You get rid of the problem," and that's what happened when he gave it to Oswald. He said, "You take care of it, you know, you know what to do." He didn't say, "Well, you go in there and kill them," but he knew something was going to happen. And they knew it, too, the observers. They knew something was up, because they was outside.

PBS: What did you see on Monday morning?

FRANK SMITH: The first thing I seen and hear was a helicopter circling over the yard, you know, and then gas, and then a loudspeaker, "Put your hand on your head and you won't be harmed," and all that type of stuff. But shooting at the same time, you follow, and everybody hit the ground, I hit the ground over by the observers' table.

And then they were coming over the wall, the assault forces, coming over the wall, shooting, and eventually I start hearing my name, you know, and then some friends of mine told me, you know, take my clothes off, because that gas that everybody burning and what we were doing we was putting milk on ourself, that supposedly, you know, prevented a lot of burns and stuff. So I finally got my clothes off.

But they were making people strip anywhere, as you come out of D Yard and go into A Block, and, and you fall on your stomach when you go through the door to A Block and you had to crawl, and I'm in A Block now and then I hear my name and the person that I worked for in the laundry said, "Here's Black, here he is," and they made me get up, beat me, and beat me into an area of the yard and laid me on the table and put a football under my neck, up under the catwalk, and told me that if it fall, they was going to kill me, and they spit on me and dropped . . . on me, and went through the torture word, you know, while I was laying there, "Nigger, why did you castrate the officers, why did you bury them alive? We going to castrate you," and I'm laying on the table spread-eagle, buck naked. But everybody in the yard was naked, the majority of the people, you know, and that went on for, like, three, four, five hours.

You know, and right behind me, I'm laying here, and here's the catwalk, and right here's the hallway, they had a gauntlet set up and it had glass broke on the floor, and they was running everybody through the gauntlet, beating them—they had 20, 30 people each side—with what they called their nigger sticks.

PBS: So even if Rockefeller did go, all it would have done is delay the inevitable, and what happened pretty much had to happen.

FRANK SMITH: He made a bad mistake. He made a very bad mistake, and you can't justify that by having one of your cronies, you know, like [Robert] Douglass, to come up and say all the things that they're saying, that we wanted every thing, and all we wanted was just a change in prison and understanding, recognizing that we were in prison, but the conditions in prison had to be changed, you know, because humans don't need to live that way.

So don't tell all the lies, you know. We need to get some factual stuff out of this, something has got to come out of this other than just people moving around, casting the blame, and moving the blame around. You know, Attica is more than that. Attica was a slaughter and it didn't have to be. And if the governor would have took it on, and would have really did the executive job that he's supposed to do, then it wouldn't have happened that way, instead of sending some cronies like the commissioner and people to come there, to give up some token, to give up some lineament. And now you got, you know, forty-three peoples in all, thirty-nine they say that got killed on the retaking, that's dead today.

• • •

The political prisoner and Native American activist Leonard Peltier was born on the Anishinabe/Chippewa Turtle Mountain Reservation in North Dakota. Moved by the treatment of indigenous peoples, Peltier joined the American Indian Movement (AIM) and in 1972 took part in the Trail of Broken Treaties. The protest, a response to the years of the United States breaking promise after promise in its treaties with Native peoples, culminated with the occupation of the Bureau of Indian Affairs building in Washington, D.C. Here is Peltier's account of the takeover.

Leonard Peltier on the Trail of Broken Treaties Protest (1999)[7]

In November 1972, we brought our grievances to Washington, D.C., in a mass demonstration for Indian rights. We called that cross-country march and demonstration the "Trail of Broken Treaties." It was our hope and intent to set up a series of wide-ranging meetings with government agencies to discuss a twenty-point spectrum of crucial issues, including an overhaul of the BIA, putting it under Indian control, and also the establishment of a commission to examine treaty violations by the U.S. government. What was to have been a peaceful meeting turned into an impromptu sit-in when government officials, reneging on their promises to see us, had BIA security guards try to oust us from the building. When the security guards started using strong-arm tactics on our women and Elders, the sit-in escalated into a tense confrontation.

We were not about to turn and run. The spirit of Crazy Horse was with us. We seized the BIA building right in the center of downtown Washington, allowed all employees to leave peaceably, and occupied it for five days—much to the outrage of the American public, who were, as usual, totally misinformed as to what had happened, or why. We were portrayed in the press as "thugs" and "hoodlums" and "violent militants." Yes, we "sacked" the BIA building, looking for—and finding in abundance—files that would reveal the government's duplicity in dealing with Indians. We piled up desks and anything else we could find to build barricades against the government's threatened assault. We broke sealed windows so that tear gas couldn't be used to suffocate us and force us out. The police themselves broke most of the lower-floor windows. Sure, some of the younger guys, infuriated by the government's lies and brutal mistreatment, started just breaking things up. We quickly put a stop to that. I remember Clyde Bellecourt announcing that, for every broken window in the BIA building, there were ten thousand hearts the BIA had broken in Indian country. He should have said a hundred thousand, even a million—that would have been nearer the mark.

One old Grandfather, a victim of the BIA throughout his life, took a fire ax, jumped up on the BIA commissioner's big mahogany desk, and split it in two! He laughed and wept ecstatically all the while, singing his death song as he chopped. "There . . . take *that* . . . and *that* . . . and *that!*" he cried between his gasps and his chants, righting an ancient wrong with every blow. It was beautiful. He was Crazy Horse incarnate at that moment.

Outside, the police and SWAT teams were gathered. If they wanted a bloodbath, we were prepared to give them one. We were ready to rain down desks and typewriters and filing cabinets and Molotov cocktails if they stormed the building. Some of the warriors put on their war paint. Every one of us was Crazy Horse. Seeing our resolve, the government itself had second thoughts. Murder four hundred Indians in a massacre a few blocks from the White House only days before the 1972 presidential election? No way. The FBI decided to end this thing for the moment, then hunt us down later one by one, which, indeed, is exactly what they did. That's when my name, as a security chief during the BIA takeover, appeared high on their list of secret targets as an "AIM agitator" and "key extremist." I'd already been arrested during the Fort Lawton take-over. I was permanently marked.

The government finally started negotiating with us, but only to end the occupation of the BIA building, not to resolve our original twenty-point list of grievances. We felt we'd made at least one point—that point being that *we exist!* We'd proven that. The government promised to look into our grievances (they never did) and they also promised not to prosecute us for the BIA takeover (a promise broken like all the others). We didn't believe them anyway. To defuse the situation and end their own embarrassment, they actually provided vehicles and an early-morning police escort out of town plus under-the-table money to pay our return travel expenses. Some of the Elders even received first-class tickets back home! The government thought they were sweeping us once more under the rug.

But this time we were not about to be swept.

• • •

The mid-1970s saw a general disillusionment in the nation with the president, the Congress, and government agencies like the FBI and the CIA. Part of this was a reaction to the Vietnam War, part a reaction to the "Watergate" scandal of President Nixon, whose men staged a break-in to the Democratic Party's National Committee offices in June 1972. Nixon was forced to resign on August 9, 1974. In 1974 and 1975, Congressional committees investigated the FBI and the CIA, revealing government crimes at home and abroad. One of their investigations was of the 1973 military coup that overthrew the democratically elected Salvador Allende government in Chile—a coup in which Nixon, Henry Kissinger, and U.S. corporations had conspired. Thousands were murdered, "disappeared," and tortured by the new regime, headed by President Augusto Pinochet. What follows is from the Senate report on covert action in Chile. This selection is from the section titled "Covert Action and Multinational Corporations."

Select Committee to Study Governmental Operations with Respect to Intelligence Activities, *Covert Action in Chile 1963–1973* (December 18, 1975)[8]

In addition to providing information and cover to the CIA, multinational corporations also participated in covert attempts to influence Chilean politics. The following is a brief description of the CIA's relationship with one such corporation in Chile in the period 1963–1973—International Telephone and Telegraph, Inc. (ITT). Not only is ITT the most prominent and public example, but a great deal of information has been developed on the CIA/ITT relationship. This summary is based on new information provided to this Committee and on material previously made public by the Subcommittee on Multinational Corporations of the Senate Foreign Relations Committee.

1. 1964 CHILEAN ELECTIONS

During the 1964 presidential campaign, representatives of multinational corporations approached the CIA with a proposal to provide campaign funds to the Christian Democratic Party. The CIA decision not to accept such funds, as well as other CIA contacts with multinational corporations during that campaign, are fully described in Part III.

2. 1970 CHILEAN ELECTIONS: PHASE I

In 1970, the U.S. government and several multinational corporations were linked in opposition to the candidacy and later the presidency of Salvador Allende. This CIA–multinational corporation connection can be divided into two phases. Phase I comprised actions taken by either the CIA or U.S.-based multinational companies at a time when it was official U.S. policy not to support, even covertly, any candidate or party in Chile. During this phase the Agency was, however, authorized to engage in a covert "spoiling" operation designed to defeat Salvador Allende. Phase II encompassed the relationship between intelligence agencies and multinational corporations after the September 1970 general election. During Phase II, the U.S. government opposed Allende and supported opposition elements. The government sought the cooperation of multinational corporations in this effort.

A number of multinational corporations were apprehensive about the possibility that Allende would be elected President of Chile. Allende's public announcements indicated his intention, if elected, to nationalize basic industries and to bring under Chilean ownership service industries such as the national telephone company, which was at that time a subsidiary of ITT.

In 1964 Allende had been defeated, and it was widely known both in Chile and among American multinational corporations with significant interests in Chile that his opponents had been supported by the United States government. John McCone, a former CIA Director and a member of ITT's Board of Directors in 1970, knew of the significant American government involvement in 1964 and of the offer of assistance made at that time by American companies. Agency documents indicate that McCone informed Harold Geneen, ITT's Board Chairman, of these facts.

In 1970 leaders of American multinational corporations with substantial interests in Chile, together with other American citizens concerned about what might happen to Chile in the event of an Allende victory, contacted U.S. government officials in order to make their views known.

In July 1970, a CIA representative in Santiago [Chile] met with representatives of ITT and, in a discussion of the upcoming election, indicated that [Jorge] Alessandri could use financial assistance. The Station suggested the name of an individual who could be used as a secure channel for getting these funds to the Alessandri campaign.

Shortly thereafter John McCone telephoned CIA Director Richard Helms. As a result of this call, a meeting was arranged between the Chairman of the Board of ITT and the Chief of the Western Hemisphere Division of the CIA. Geneen offered to make available to the CIA a substantial amount of money to be used in support of the Alessandri campaign. In subsequent meetings ITT offered to make $1 million available to the CIA. The CIA rejected the offer. The memorandum indicated further that CIA's advice was sought with respect to an individual who might serve as a conduit of ITT funds to the Alessandri campaign.

The CIA confirmed that the individual in question was a reliable channel which could be used for getting funds to Alessandri. A second channel of funds from ITT to a political party opposing Allende, the National Party, was developed following CIA advice as to a secure funding mechanism utilizing two CIA assets in Chile. These assets were also receiving Agency funds in connection with the "spoiling" operation.

During the period prior to the September election, ITT representatives met frequently with CIA representatives both in Chile and in the United States and CIA advised ITT as to ways in which it might safely channel funds both to the Alessandri campaign and to the National Party. CIA was kept informed of the extent and the mechanism of the funding. Eventually at least $350,000 was passed by ITT to this campaign. A roughly equal amount was passed by other U.S. companies; the CIA learned of this funding but did not assist in it.

3. FOLLOWING THE 1970 CHILEAN ELECTIONS: PHASE II

Following the September 4 elections, the United States government adopted a policy of economic pressure direct against Chile and in this connection sought to enlist the influence of Geneen on other American businessmen. Specifically, the State Department was directed by the 40 Committee to contact American businesses having interests in Chile to see if they could be induced to take actions in accord with the American government's policy of economic pressure on Chile. On September 29, the Chief of the Western Hemisphere Division of the CIA met with a representative of ITT. The CIA official sought to have ITT involved in a more active way in Chile. According to CIA documents, ITT took note of the CIA presentation on economic warfare but did not actively respond to it.

One institution in Chile which was used in a general anti-Allende effort was the newspaper chain EL MERCURIO. Both the United States government and ITT were funneling money into the hands of individuals associated with the paper. That funding continued after Allende was in office.

• • •

The MIT linguist Noam Chomsky was one of the most important voices against the war in Vietnam, writing scathing critiques of the justification for the war in *The New York Review of Books* and speaking on numerous anti-war platforms. In the 1970s, he also wrote a series of articles on U.S. imperialism around the world and the connections between U.S. domestic and foreign policies. Here Chomsky describes the FBI's Counterintelligence Program (dubbed internally COINTELPRO), begun in 1956 but escalated in the course of the 1960s. Using the cover of maintaining "internal security," the FBI investigated, harassed, and infiltrated groups like the Black Panthers, the American Indian Movement, the Committee in Solidarity with the People of El Salvador, Puerto Rican activists, the National Lawyers Guild, and Students for a Democratic Society.

Noam Chomsky, "COINTELPRO: What the (Deleted) Was It?" (March 12, 1978)[9]

It has often been observed that the United States is unusual, among the industrial democracies, in the narrowness of the spectrum of thought and political action, sharply skewed to the right as compared with other societies of comparable social and economic structure. Complex theories have been advanced to explain this intriguing phenomenon. No doubt subtle issues are involved, but it is important not to disregard some quite simple factors. For one thing, American business has been engaged for many years in massive organizing propaganda campaigns directed to what leading practitioners call "the engineering of consent." The scale is vast and the impact—on the media and school texts for example—quite substantial, far beyond anything to be found in the other industrial democracies. Another central element in the picture is the role of the national political police, the FBI, which for over half a century has been devoting major efforts to engineering of consent in a more direct way: by force. The character and scale of this enterprise is only now beginning to come to light, and the story that is being pieced together is quite a remarkable one.

J. Edgar Hoover rose to national prominence when he was appointed chief of the General Intelligence (anti-radical) division of the Justice Department in 1919, shortly before the notorious "Palmer raids," in which some 4,000 alleged radicals were rounded up in 33 cities in 23 states, while the *Washington Post* editorialized that "there is not time to waste on hairsplitting over infringement of liberty" in the face of the Bolshevik menace. Over 200 aliens were subsequently deported. The liberal Attorney General [A. Mitchell] Palmer proclaimed that "the government is now sweeping the nation clean of such alien filth," with the over-whelming support of the press, until they perceived their own interests were threatened. The "Red Scare" served to control labor militancy, dismantle radical parties, frighten liberals, and buttress an interventionist foreign policy. Hoover's FBI undertook the very same tasks, and has conducted them with considerable success.

The FBI casts a wide net. For example, the American Civil Liberties Union (ACLU) was infiltrated from 1920 to 1943 . . . and in the 1950s was secretly cooperating with the FBI in its programs of political and doctrinal control. Even the slightest departures from orthodoxy are not likely to escape the vigilant eye of the Bureau, as political activists have had many opportunities to discover. To cite one minor case of which I have personal knowledge, in 1969 I had two teaching assistants who were active in the civil rights and peace movements in an undergraduate humanities course at MIT. The Boston office of the FBI undertook to block their re-appointment, making sure to keep its activities confidential so that "the bureau's interest in this matter will be fully protected." An internal memorandum to the Director states that "an established source of the Boston office" at MIT (name blacked out) advised the Bureau that as a result of its efforts, "he was able to have their re-appointments to the staff of MIT canceled." In fact, the Bureau's efforts were irrelevant in this case, but the example illustrates very well the nature of its concerns, while raising interesting questions about our academic institutions.

In other cases the FBI went a few steps further. A former student of mine, also active in the peace movement, was teaching at San Diego State College in 1971. According to a report submitted to the Church Committee by the ACLU, the FBI provided defamatory information about him to the college administration (and also gained access to confidential college records). Three public hearings were held under college auspices. He was exonerated each time, then summarily dismissed by the chancellor of the California state college system, Glenn Dumke, one of the numerous examples of the treachery of the universities in those years. During this period the same student was the target of an assassination attempt by a secret terrorist army organized, funded, armed and directed by the FBI, which concealed evidence of the crime and prevented prosecution of the FBI agent in charge and the FBI infiltrator who led this organization in its rampage of fire-bombing, shooting, and general violence and terror aimed at the left, all with the full knowledge and cooperation of the Bureau.

In this case, the intended victim of the FBI assassination attempt escaped injury, though a young woman was seriously injured. Others were not so lucky. The most notorious case is that of Black Panther leader Fred Hampton, who, along with Mark Clark, was murdered in a pre-dawn Gestapo-style police raid— the phrase is accurate—in December 1969, with the complicity of the FBI, which had turned over to the police a floor plan of his apartment supplied by an FBI provocateur who was chief of Panther security. The floor plan no doubt explains the remarkable accuracy of police gunfire, noted by reporters. Hampton was killed in bed, possibly drugged; according to eyewitnesses, murdered in cold blood.

The FBI prank followed an earlier effort to have Hampton murdered by a criminal gang in the Chicago ghetto, the Blackstone Rangers. The Rangers were sent an anonymous letter by the local FBI office informing them that the Panthers were intending to murder their leader, but this effort to incite violence and murder failed. In other cases, the Bureau was more successful. Internal memoranda gloat over the success of the Bureau in fomenting gang warfare and violence in the ghetto, and disrupting such subversive activities as free breakfast programs for poor children in churches.

The record, which is by now extensive, demonstrates that the FBI was committed to attacking the civil rights movement, blocking legal electoral politics, undermining the universities and cultural groups (e.g., the largest black cultural center in the West, in the Watts ghetto), and disrupting political activities of which it disapproved by any means required, including the extensive use of provocateurs, arson, bombings, robbery and murder. Under COINTELPRO alone, its targets included the Communist Party, the Socialist Workers Party, the Puerto Rican Independence Movement, the various Black movements of the 1960's, and the entire "New Left." Though the left was not the sole target of the national political police, it was by a large measure the primary target. In scope of activities and level of violence, the criminal programs of the FBI far exceed anything known in other industrial democracies, and surely merit a prominent place in any investigation of "American exceptionalism" that deserves to be taken at all seriously.

There have been a few studies of these activities of the FBI. . . . But these studies have received little attention, and in fact the documentary record itself, despite its quite appalling nature, has barely created a ripple.

It is striking that the major revelations concerning FBI criminal activities appear precisely at the time of the exposure of the Watergate episodes, frivolous in comparison. It is interesting to contrast the concern accorded to Watergate and to the crimes of the national political police—which I stress again were incomparably more violent, far-ranging and significant in their effect on the cultural and political climate of American life. History has provided us with a controlled experiment to determine whether Nixon's critics were motivated by a concern for civil and human rights, or by the fact that Nixon, like Joseph McCarthy before him, was directing his weapons at the powerful, always an illegitimate target. The results of this experiment are quite clear-cut and leave little doubt that the furor over Watergate was largely an exercise in hypocrisy.

CHAPTER TWENTY-ONE

The Carter–Reagan–Bush Consensus

Marian Wright Edelman, Commencement Address at Milton Academy (June 10, 1983)

César Chávez, Address to the Commonwealth Club of California (November 9, 1984)

Testimony of Ismael Guadalupe Ortiz on Vieques, Puerto Rico (October 2, 1979)

Local P-9 Strikers and Supporters on the 1985–1986 Meatpacking Strike against the Hormel Company in Austin, Minnesota (1991)

Douglas A. Fraser, Resignation Letter to the Labor–Management Group (July 19, 1978)

Vito Russo, "Why We Fight" (1988)

Abbie Hoffman, "Closing Argument" (April 15, 1987)

Public Enemy, "Fight the Power" (1989)

In his book *The American Political Tradition*, the historian Richard Hofstadter examined U.S. political leaders from the time of Thomas Jefferson and Andrew Jackson to the modern era. He concluded that "the range of vision embraced by the primary contestants in the major parties has always been bounded by the horizons of property and enterprise. . . . [T]hey have accepted the economic virtues of capitalist culture as necessary qualities of man." Hofstadter noted, "That culture has been intensely nationalistic."

The Democratic administration of President Jimmy Carter and the Republican administrations of Ronald Reagan and George H. W. Bush clearly illustrated Hofstadter's thesis. Throughout those administrations, corporate power grew, enormous fortunes were created alongside desperate poverty, the militarization of the country continued, interventionism in foreign policy went on in support of corporate interests. Neither party would go beyond the limits of capitalism and nationalism.

• • •

In 1983, Marian Wright Edelman spoke at the elite Milton Academy in Massachusetts to the graduating class, urging them to take action against the injustices of a society that has money for B-2 bombers and tax breaks for rich corporations but not for health care, not for education, and not for programs to combat poverty. Edelman, a graduate of Spelman College and Yale Law School, became the first black woman admitted to the Mississippi Bar. She directed the National Association for the Advancement of Colored People (NAACP) Legal Defense and Educational Fund office in Jackson, Mississippi, and later worked as a counsel for the Poor People's March. In 1973, Edelman founded the Children's Defense Fund.

Marian Wright Edelman, Commencement Address at Milton Academy (June 10, 1983)[1]

Where is the human commitment and political will to find the relative pittance of money needed to protect children? What kind of world allows 40,000 children to die needlessly every day? UNICEF estimates that for $6 billion a year we could save 20,000 children a day by 1990 by applying new scientific and technological breakthroughs in oral rehydration therapy, universal child immunization, promotion of breastfeeding, and mass use of child growth charts. At home, where are the strong political voices speaking out for investing in children rather than bombs; mothers rather than missiles?

In 1953 Dwight David Eisenhower warned:

> Every gun that is made, every warship launched, every rocket fired signifies . . . a theft from those who hunger and are not fed, those who are cold and are not clothed.
>
> This world in arms is not spending money alone.
>
> It is spending the sweat of its laborers, the genius of its scientists, the hopes of its children.

And how blatant the world and national theft from needy children and the solution of pressing human needs is.

In its first year, the Reagan Administration proposed $11 billion in cuts in preventive children's and lifeline support programs for poor families with no attempt to distinguish between programs that work and don't work. The Congress enacted $9 billion in cuts.

In its second year, the Reagan Administration proposed $9 billion in cuts in these same programs; the Congress enacted $1 billion.

In its third year, the President is proposing $3.5 billion in new cuts in these same programs just as the effects of the previous cuts are being felt and millions of Americans are beset by joblessness, homelessness, and lost health insurance. Thousands of children face increasing child abuse, foster care placement, illness, and mortality because their families are unable to meet their needs while safety net family support, health and social services programs are being drastically cut back.

It is my strong view that the American people have been sold a set of false choices by our national leaders who tell us we must choose between jobs and peace; between filling potholes in our streets and cavities in our children's teeth; between day care for five million latchkey children and home care for millions of senior citizens living out their lives in the loneliness of a nursing home; between arms control and building the MX [missile]. There are other choices—fairer choices—that you and I must insist our political leaders make.

While slashing programs serving the neediest children, the President and Congress found $750 billion to give untargeted tax cuts mostly to non-needy corporations and individuals. And the Reagan Administration is trying to convince the American people to give the Pentagon $2 trillion over a seven year period in the largest arms buildup in peacetime history. Do you know how much money $2 trillion is? If you had spent $2 million a day every day since Christ was born, you would still have spent less than President Reagan wants the American people to believe the Pentagon can spend efficiently in seven years.

When President Reagan took office, we were spending $18 million an hour on defense.

This year, we are spending $24 million an hour.

Next year, President Reagan wants to spend $28 million an hour. The House Democratic leadership wants to spend "only" $27 million an hour and they are being labeled "soft" on defense.

By 1988, if the President had his way, we would be spending $44 million an hour on defense and every American would be spending 63 percent more on defense and 22 percent less on poor children and poor families. Just one hour's worth of President Reagan's proposed defense increase this year in military spending would pay for free school lunches for 19,000 children for a school year. A day's worth of his proposed defense increase would pay for a year's free school lunches for almost a half a million low income students. A week's worth of his proposed defense spending could buy a fully equipped micro computer for every classroom of low income children of school age in the U.S., assuming 25 children to a classroom.

How do you want to spend scarce national resources? What choices would you make in the following examples:

• Would you rather build one less of the planned 226 MX missiles that will cost us $110 million each, and that we still can't find a place to hide, or eliminate poverty in 101,000 female headed households a year? If we cancel the whole MX program we could eliminate poverty for all 12 million poor children and have enough left over to pay college costs for 300,000 potential engineers, mathematicians, and scientists who may not be able to afford college. Which investment do you think will foster longer term national security? President Reagan has cut safety net programs for poor families. He's building the MX missiles.

• Would you rather spend $100 million a year on 100 military bands or put that money into teaching 200,000 educationally deprived children to read and write as well as their more advantaged peers? American high school bands would be delighted to volunteer to provide music for patriotic events, I'll bet. President Reagan has cut compensatory education. He's not touched military bands.

• Would you rather keep or sell the luxury hotel the Department of Defense owns at Fort Dean Russey on Waikiki Beach which has a fair market value of $100 million, or provide Medicaid coverage for all poor pregnant women, some of whom are being turned away from hospital emergency rooms in labor? President Reagan has cut Medicaid. No one has seriously suggested curbing military luxuries like this hotel.

• We plan to build 100 B-1 bombers at a cost of $250 million each. If we build 91—nine fewer—we could finance Medicaid for all poor pregnant women and children living below the poverty level. Do you think this will threaten our national security?

• Whose hunger would you rather quench? Secretary Weinberger's or a poor child in child care? Every time Secretary [of Defense Caspar] Weinberger and his elite colleagues sit down in his private Pentagon dining room staffed by 19, they pay $2.87 a meal and we taxpayers pay $12.06. This $12.06 could provide 40 mid-morning milk and juice and cracker snacks President Reagan has forced poor children of working mothers in child care centers to give up. I think we should urge Secretary Weinberger to eat in one of the four other Pentagon executive dining rooms and give one million food supplements back to poor children instead.

Just as I believe we ought to weigh military nonessentials against civilian essentials—and apply the same standards of national purpose, efficiency and effectiveness to military programs as we do to domestic ones—I also believe that the non-needy should bear a fair portion of the burden of economic recovery. They have not. . . .

As you go out into the world, try to keep your eye on the human bottom line. I also hope you will understand and be tough about what is needed to solve problems, change attitudes, and bring about needed changes in our society. Democracy is not a spectator sport.

• • •

The farm worker leader César Chávez was born in Arizona, and grew up in migrant labor camps. In the early 1960s, he helped found the National Farm Workers Association, a precursor to the United Farm Workers Organizing Committee and, eventually, the United Farm Workers (UFW) union. Chávez came to international attention in March 1968, when he announced a boycott of California grapes. The popular boycott, in protest of the anti-union efforts of California growers, led to millions of dollars in losses for agribusiness and led to historic contracts with the UFW. But many of the growers broke the contracts or refused to negotiate new ones. In this speech, given in San Francisco in 1984, Chávez describes the unfinished struggle of farm workers for justice.

César Chávez, Address to the Commonwealth Club of California (November 9, 1984)[2]

Twenty-one years ago last September, on a lonely stretch of railroad track paralleling U.S. Highway 101 near Salinas, 32 Bracero farm workers lost their lives in a tragic accident.

The Braceros had been imported from Mexico to work on California farms. They died when their bus, which was converted from a flatbed truck, drove in front of a freight train. Conversion of the bus had not been approved by any government agency. The driver had "tunnel" vision. Most of the bodies lay unidentified for days. No one, including the grower who employed the workers, even knew their names.

Today, thousands of farm workers live under savage conditions—beneath trees and amid garbage and human excrement—near tomato fields in San Diego County, tomato fields which use the most modern farm technology. Vicious rats gnaw on them as they sleep. They walk miles to buy food at inflated prices. And they carry in water from irrigation pumps.

Child labor is still common in many farm areas. As much as 30 percent of Northern California's garlic harvesters are under-aged children. Kids as young as six years old have voted in state-conducted union elections since they qualified as workers.

Some 800,000 under-aged children work with their families harvesting crops across America.

Babies born to migrant workers suffer 25 percent higher infant mortality than the rest of the population.

Malnutrition among migrant worker children is 10 times higher than the national rate.

Farm workers' average life expectancy is still 49 years—compared to 73 years for the average American.

All my life, I have been driven by one dream, one goal, one vision: To overthrow a farm labor system in this nation which treats farm workers as if they were not important human beings. Farm workers are not agricultural implements. They are not beasts of burden—to be used and discarded. That dream was born in my youth. It was nurtured in my early days of organizing. It has flourished. It has been attacked.

I'm not very different from anyone else who has ever tried to accomplish something with his life. My motivation comes from my personal life—from watching what my mother and father went through when I was growing up; from what we experienced as migrant farm workers in California.

That dream, that vision, grew from my own experience with racism, with hope, with the desire to be treated fairly and to see my people treated as human beings and not as chattel. It grew from anger and rage—emotions I felt 40 years ago when people of my color were denied the right to see a movie or eat at a restaurant in many parts of California. It grew from the frustration and humiliation I felt as a boy who couldn't understand how the growers could abuse and exploit farm workers when there were so many of us and so few of them.

Later, in the '50s, I experienced a different kind of exploitation. In San Jose, in Los Angeles and in other urban communities, we—the Mexican American people—were dominated by a majority that was Anglo. I began to realize what other minority people had discovered: That the only answer—the only hope—was in organizing.

More of us had to become citizens. We had to register to vote. And people like me had to develop the skills it would take to organize, to educate, to help empower the Chicano people.

I spent many years—before we founded the union—learning how to work with people.

We experienced some successes in voter registration, in politics, in battling racial discrimination—successes in an era when Black Americans were just beginning to assert their civil rights and when political awareness among Hispanics was almost non-existent. But deep in my heart, I knew I could never be happy unless I tried organizing the farm workers. I didn't know if I would succeed. But I had to try.

All Hispanics—urban and rural, young and old—are connected to the farm workers' experience. We had all lived through the fields—or our parents had. We shared that common humiliation. How could we progress as a people, even if we lived in the cities, while the farm workers—men and women of our color—were condemned to a life without pride? How could we progress as a people while the farm workers—who symbolized our history in this land—were denied self-respect? How could our people believe that their children could become lawyers and doctors and judges and business people while this shame, this injustice was permitted to continue?

Those who attack our union often say, "It's not really a union. It's something else: A social movement. A civil rights movement. It's something dangerous."

They're half right.

The United Farm Workers is first and foremost a union. A union like any other. A union that either produces for its members on the bread and butter issues or doesn't survive. But the UFW has always been something more than a union—although it's never been dangerous if you believe in the Bill of Rights. The UFW was the beginning! We attacked that historical source of shame and infamy that our people in this country lived with. We attacked that injustice, not by complaining; not by seeking hand-outs; not by becoming soldiers in the War on Poverty.

We organized!

Farm workers acknowledged we had allowed ourselves to become victims in a democratic society—a society where majority rule and collective bargaining are supposed to be more than academic theories or political rhetoric. And by addressing this historical problem, we created confidence and pride and hope in an entire people's ability to create the future.

The UFW's survival—its existence—was not in doubt in my mind when the time began to come—after the union became visible—when Chicanos started entering college in greater numbers, when Hispanics began running for public office in greater numbers—when our people started asserting their rights on a broad range of issues and in many communities across the country.

The union's survival—its very existence—sent out a signal to all Hispanics:

That we were fighting for our dignity,

That we were challenging and overcoming injustice,

That we were empowering the least educated among us—the poorest among us.

The message was clear: If it could happen in the fields, it could happen anywhere—in the cities, in the courts, in the city councils, in the state legislatures.

I didn't really appreciate it at the time, but the coming of our union signaled the start of great changes among Hispanics that are only now beginning to be seen.

I've traveled to every part of this nation. I have met and spoken with thousands of Hispanics from every walk of life—from every social and economic class.

One thing I hear most often from Hispanics, regardless of age or position—and from many non-Hispanics as well—is that the farm workers gave them hope that they could succeed and the inspiration to work for change.

From time to time you will hear our opponents declare that the union is weak, that the union has no support, that the union has not grown fast enough. Our obituary has been written many times. How ironic it is that the same forces which argue so passionately that the union is not influential are the same forces that continue to fight us so hard.

The union's power in agriculture has nothing to do with the number of farm workers under union contract.

It has nothing to do with the farm workers' ability to contribute to Democratic politicians.

It doesn't even have much to do with our ability to conduct successful boycotts.

The very fact of our existence forces an entire industry—unionized and non-unionized—to spend millions of dollars year after year on improved wages, on improved working conditions, on benefits for workers. If we're so weak and unsuccessful, why do the growers continue to fight us with such passion? Because so long as we continue to exist, farm workers will benefit from our existence—even if they don't work under union contract.

It doesn't really matter whether we have 100,000 members or 500,000 members. In truth, hundreds of thousands of farm workers in California—and in other states—are better off today because of our work. And Hispanics across California and the nation who don't work in agriculture are better off today because of what the farm workers taught people about organization, about pride and strength, about seizing control over their own lives.

Tens of thousands of the children and grandchildren of farm workers—and the children and grandchildren of poor Hispanics—are moving out of the fields and out of the barrios and into the professions and into business and into politics. And that movement cannot be reversed!

Our union will forever exist as an empowering force among Chicanos in the Southwest. And that means our power and our influence will grow and not diminish.

Two major trends give us hope and encouragement:

First, our union has returned to a tried and tested weapon in the farm workers' non-violent arsenal—the boycott! After the Agricultural Labor Relations Act became law in California in 1975, we dismantled our boycott to work with the law.

During the early- and mid-'70s, millions of Americans supported our boycotts. After 1975, we redirected our efforts from the boycott to organizing and winning elections under the law. The law helped farm workers make progress in overcoming poverty and injustice.

At companies where farm workers are protected by union contracts, we have made progress in overcoming child labor, in overcoming miserable wages and working conditions, in overcoming sexual harassment of women workers, in overcoming dangerous pesticides which poison our people and poison the food we all eat. Where we have organized, these injustices soon pass into history.

But under Republican Governor George Deukmejian, the law that guarantees our right to organize no longer protects farm workers—it doesn't work anymore!

In 1982 corporate growers gave Deukmejian one million dollars to run for governor of California. Since he took office, Deukmejian has paid back his debt to the growers with the blood and sweat of California farm workers. Instead of enforcing the law as it was written against those who break it, Deukmejian invites growers who break the law to seek relief from the governor's appointees.

What does all this mean for farm workers?

It means that the right to vote in free elections is a sham!

It means that the right to talk freely about the union among your fellow workers on the job is a cruel hoax!

It means the right to be free from threats and intimidation by growers is an empty promise!

It means the right to sit down and negotiate with your employer as equals across the bargaining table—and not as peons in the field—is a fraud!

It means that thousands of farm workers—who are owed millions of dollars in back pay because their employers broke the law—are still waiting for their checks.

It means that 36,000 farm workers—who voted to be represented by the United Farm Workers in free elections—are still waiting for contracts from growers who refuse to bargain in good faith.

It means that, for farm workers, child labor will continue.

It means that infant mortality will continue.

It means malnutrition among our children will continue.

It means the short life expectancy and the inhuman living and working conditions will continue.

Are these make-believe threats? Are they exaggerations?

Ask the farm workers who are still waiting for growers to bargain in good faith and sign contracts!

Ask the farm workers who've been fired from their jobs because they spoke out for the union!

Ask the farm workers who've been threatened with physical violence because they support the UFW!

Ask the family of René Lopez, the young farm worker from Fresno who was shot to death last year because he supported the union. . . .

History and inevitability are on our side. The farm workers and their children—and the Hispanics and their children—are the future in California. And corporate growers are the past!

Those politicians who ally themselves with the corporate growers and against the farm workers and the Hispanics are in for a big surprise.

They want to make their careers in politics. They want to hold power 20 and 30 years from now.

But 20 and 30 years from now—in Modesto, in Salinas, in Fresno, in Bakersfield, in the Imperial Valley, and in many of the great cities of California—those communities will be dominated by farm workers and not by growers, by the children and grandchildren of farm workers and not by the children and grandchildren of growers.

These trends are part of the forces of history that cannot be stopped! No person and no organization can resist them for very long. They are inevitable! Once social change begins, it cannot be reversed.

You cannot uneducate the person who has learned to read. You cannot humiliate the person who feels pride. You cannot oppress the people who are not afraid anymore.

Our opponents must understand that it's not just a union we have built. Unions, like other institutions, can come and go. But we're more than an institution. For nearly 20 years, our union has been on the cutting edge of a people's cause—and you cannot do away with an entire people; you cannot stamp out a people's cause.

Regardless of what the future holds for the union, regardless of what the future holds for farm workers, our accomplishments cannot be undone! "La Causa"—our cause—doesn't have to be experienced twice. The consciousness and pride that were raised by our union are alive and thriving inside millions of young Hispanics who will never work on a farm!

Like the other immigrant groups, the day will come when we win the economic and political rewards which are in keeping with our numbers in society. The day will come when the politicians do the right thing by our people out of political necessity and not out of charity or idealism.

That day may not come this year.

That day may not come during this decade.

But it will come, someday!

And when that day comes, we shall see the fulfillment of that passage from the Book of Matthew in the New Testament, "That the last shall be first and the first shall be last."

And on that day, our nation shall fulfill its creed—and that fulfillment shall enrich us all.

• • •

Since its takeover of Puerto Rico in 1898, the U.S. government has treated it as a colony, using its land for military purposes whenever it wanted. The Puerto Rican islands of Culebra and Vieques were used for bombing practice, uprooting people from their homes, mutilating the countryside, causing a number of deaths. A long campaign of protest finally ended the bombing practice in Culebra in 1975, although residents complain that the toxic waste from the years of misuse still has not been cleaned up. Activists carried out a similar struggle on Vieques, as described in the following statement by a Vieques school teacher in 1979. The speaker, Ismael Guadalupe Ortiz, who had organized one of the first protests in Vieques against the U.S. military in 1964, was arrested after giving the address. In 1999, a Navy bomb killed a civilian guard on Vieques, David Sanes. Four years later, in 2003, the movement to free Vieques finally forced the U.S. military to end its use of the island for military practice.

Testimony of Ismael Guadalupe Ortiz on Vieques, Puerto Rico (October 2, 1979)[3]

My name is Ismael Guadalupe Ortiz. I am thirty-five years old. All my life I have lived in Vieques. For the past thirteen years I have been a high school teacher in the public school system of Vieques.

Many years ago, I began to fight for the right of my Viequense brothers to live in peace. Since 1978 I have been one of the directors of the Crusade to Rescue Vieques. This organization, that includes Viequenses of diverse political ideologies, religious philosophies, and various social positions, have carried on their shoulders the responsibility to unite in order to be most effective in our struggle against the U.S. Navy. When I speak of the struggle against the U.S. navy in Vieques, and what the presence of this armed force represents on our land, I am speaking of something concrete.

The violation of our land by the U.S. Navy began before I was even born. When I was born, La Isla Nena was already physically occupied and divided by this navy that today presumes to bring us here as the accused.

Today, I come here not as the accused, I come as the accuser. I accuse the U.S. Navy and the court of the U.S. in Puerto Rico, of conspiring to commit against all Viequenses, one of the greatest abuses ever brought against a people in our America.

I am not exaggerating. I accuse the U.S. Navy and its legal arm, the federal court, of expropriating and throwing into the street, thousands of human beings that live on these lands, and that now, this navy claims is theirs. Who are the witnesses that I will call to prove my accusation? To begin with, my own parents [Narciso Guadalupe Guadalupe and Mercedes Ortiz Maldonado] were victims of this expropriation. To continue, I call hundreds of Viequenses who are still alive to attest to how it was in the 1940s. Women who had to give birth in cane fields, because the birth coincided with the passage of the bulldozers that were knocking down their houses. Of men and women who woke up without a piece of land to cultivate for their or their family's sustenance.

I am not going to limit myself to generalities and damage to property. I am going to talk of lives, of precious Viequense lives that have been lost, and continue to be lost, as a consequence of the abuses and crimes of the U.S. Navy on our island of Vieques. I personally know and remember more than a dozen Viequenses who died or were assassinated at the hands of drunken marines or by bombs left on our land by this navy who today I accuse as a criminal. All Viequenses remember the death of Chulto Legrán, a twelve-year-old boy, victim of one of the many bombs that the navy left on our soil. This occurred in 1953. The elders tell us how the body of Alejandro Rosado was found on the lands occupied by the navy, buried with his head down and his feet up. This occurred in the early 1940s. The assassination of Felipe Francis Christian in April 1954 is still fresh in our memory. The elders tell us about the deaths of Anastasio and Domingo Acosta, father and son, victims of the navy's bombs. Juan Maysonet, Helena Holiday, and many more form links in the chain of victims, of flesh and blood, and of names and surnames.

We remember also the so-called riots of 1952, 1958, 1964, and 1968 that were no other than hordes of drunken marines who fell upon our civilian population like savages.

All these crimes have gone unpunished. The criminals roam free, and not this court or any other court has judged them. Nonetheless, today you judge me for getting together with my brother Viequenses in the Crusade to Rescue Vieques to fight against these injustices committed by the North American navy in my island of Vieques.

In addition to these crimes against individuals, there is the collective crime against the 8,000 Viequenses that live on this island. They have taken 26,000 of the 33,000 acres that we had for our economic development and have prohibited us from fishing in our waters, the source of sustenance for hundreds of Viequenses, and our free air and land transportation has been impeded by this North American navy that occupies our territory by force.

Viequenses are a people imprisoned between two bases, between the storage of explosives and bombing and shooting that little by little takes thousands of Viequenses away from their island in a forced exile.

We could continue speaking about the serious problems caused by unemployment, of an education system that offers nothing to children and young Viequenses, but I will not go on.

Suffice to say, that as a Viequense, as a Puerto Rican, and as the father of two children, I feel legitimately proud to be at the side of my people at this time. That my children will be able to say that I am a prisoner because I do not want Vieques to be for them what it was for me. That I do not want for them, or any other child of my small island, to be a land bombed and shot at wildly at the whim of foreigners. That I do not want for them to have a drunken marine corps, humiliating and abusing them on their own land. That for my children and for their little friends, the abuses of today will be a thing of the past, or perhaps a lesson in a schoolroom about what happened in Vieques, and never to let it happen again anywhere else. This is why I fight.

My crime is to walk on the land where I was born and have lived all my life. My crime is to fight along with my Puerto Rican and Viequense brothers against the abuses and injustices the United States navy represents. It is for these crimes that I am being tried in this court that represents the interests of the government of the United States in Puerto Rico and consequently the interests of the navy of that government. This is the same court that some days ago decided that the right of the navy to shoot and to bomb is more important than the right of 8,000 Viequenses to live in peace. This foreign court has no moral or legal authority to judge me. As a Puerto Rican, I will not find justice in the court of the invader that today attacks my people.

This court can today send me to prison, but outside remain thousands who will continue the struggle, which is the struggle of all the people.

• • •

In late 1984, members of Local P-9 of the United Food and Commercial Workers (UFCW) union began a coordinated campaign against major wage and benefit cuts by Hormel, a meatpacking company in Austin, Minnesota. In August 1985, more than 90 percent of the local voted to go out on strike, despite pressure from their international union officials to take concessions. The strike generated widespread solidarity from other trade unionists, some of whom were fired when they respected roving picket lines set up outside other Hormel plants. As labor historian Peter Rachleff writes in his book *Hard-Pressed in the Heartland*, "Both the UFCW and the AFL-CIO knew that Local P-9 represented a dangerous example for other labor activists and rank-and-file unionists. P-9 quickly came to symbolize democracy and membership participation, a willingness to oppose corporate demands for concessions, regardless of international union agendas or strategies, and a form of 'horizontal' solidarity that threatened the vertical, bureaucratic hold that international unions exercised over their locals." In 1986, the national union put Local P-9 into receivership and forced through the acceptance of a bad contract. The strike, which was ultimately defeated, was a classic example of how employer power is used to break unions and maintain their profits. Here several participants in the strike reflect on their struggle against Hormel and its lessons.

Local P-9 Strikers and Supporters on the 1985–1986 Meatpacking Strike against the Hormel Company in Austin, Minnesota (1991)[4]

JIM GUYETTE: I was born and raised here in Austin. This is my hometown. . . .
I started working at Hormel in July of 1968. In 1978, I got active in the union because they were negotiating a concessionary contract with the company. It was agreed that we would loan the company money to build a new plant, an interest-free loan, supposedly in return for never having our wages cut. I said, "The banks got more money than I do. Why are they coming to me for a loan?"

We were told we had to vote for the concessionary contract, but neither the company nor the union officials told us everything that was in it. It turned out to be open season for management to do whatever they wanted. It meant concessions in benefits. It meant concessions in every aspect of work. There was a no-strike clause for eight years and real speedup in production. At that speed, there were many injuries.

DENNY MEALY: I can recall as clear as day Chuck Nyberg, then Hormel's executive vice president, saying over TV that the workers will never receive any less in the new plant than what they earned in the old plant. But when I transferred to the new plant, I lost my incentive pay, which cost me a hundred dollars a week. The reduction in medical benefits was retroactive. I personally was paying back to the company forty-three dollars a week for medical expenses I had incurred. Between the transfer to the new plant and the concessions, I lost about one hundred sixty dollars a week. The working conditions had changed. The attitude of management to labor had changed. The injury rate was just phenomenal. It wasn't the same company.

JIM GUYETTE: The union meetings were held in the evenings. They would hold one the next day for those of us who worked nights. The president and one or two officers would sit up there and talk about what happened the night before. If one of us tried to make a motion, they would say that these meetings were simply a "courtesy," that all we could do was ask questions. But when we asked questions they didn't like, they'd get up and leave. Later, when I went to evening union meetings, they'd always rule me out of order. Finally, one of the older veterans said, "Look, I'm getting sick of all this 'out of order' stuff. He pays dues just like we do. Let's hear what the kid's got to say."

In 1981, I was on the executive board. We went to Chicago for a meeting before negotiations. What they did was booze you up, pound you on the back, and tell you what a great leader you were until your hat didn't fit. Then there was this big staged deal, that we had to take more concessions because everybody else was doing it.

Well, we had taken concession after concession. And I had pretty much stated where I was coming from in '78, '79, and '80. I mean, if the company wasn't making money, I could see the argument. But I couldn't see any rationale in offering new concessions to a profitable employer, one making more money than it ever had before. And I could see no rationale in beating the company to the punch. I just said, "Look, I'm going to tell you guys right up front, when we go home I ain't telling people to vote for this." They said, "We got to be united." I said, "Well, you be united all by yourselves—I want to give a minority report." I did, and we voted the contract down.

The international wasn't satisfied, so we had to vote again. Basically, it was "vote till you get it right." Well, the election was just a sham—I mean, there were ballots passed out wholesale. People were dropping in twenty-five at a time. I asked for a recount, but they destroyed all the ballots the next day. So it finally went through, and I was marked as a troublemaker.

Then I ran for president in '83. My opponent was John Ankor, who's now president of the scab union and was one of the first to cross the picket line. Before the election, I had made a motion that the rank and file choose an election committee from the membership itself. I asked the head of the committee if he would buy his own padlock to keep the ballot box from being stuffed. He did that. And, lo and behold, I won.

When I took over, we had friction within the union between the old leadership and the new folks coming up. The rumor through the plant was, "Guyette got elected, but nothing's going to get done because the executive board controls everything." But I went straight to the membership, and we started turning things around. What we said made sense to the rank and file. We were very upfront and honest with people and answered questions the best way we knew how. I think that's been the strength of what we've been able to do. I had confidence that if they were informed, if they knew the issues, they'd generally make the right decisions. And if they didn't, people had a right to be wrong.

Prior to my taking office, we'd be lucky to get a quorum of thirty-five people at the meetings. Our union hall held five hundred. Once we started communicating with everybody, we'd have to have four meetings a day to get them all in there. Issues got debated pro and con. Everybody got a chance to voice their opinions, whatever they were. That was just unheard-of.

CECIL CAIN: I came to Hormel about the time these rank and filers were taking over this local, Jim Guyette and Pete Winkels and a host of others. One of the first union meetings I recall was in July or August of 1984.

The union had already given a ton of concessions. Now the company was threatening to cut wages. Here I was, working for $10.69 an hour, and it still wasn't enough. So I went to that meeting. I remember Jim Guyette brought back a plan that the company wanted to offer us, paying $8.75 an hour. Good God, that's two dollars less! Here's a company, absolutely the most profitable meatpacker in the country, and they wanted more. And they didn't come after it nickel and dime.

I couldn't believe Jim was asking us what we thought. In my mind, he's the union president and he's supposed to take care of us. Why didn't he tell them to stick it? I walked right up to the podium and said, "I don't know why you even bother to come back and tell me this." But I found out that Jim Guyette doesn't make a move without coming to the rank and file. I got to appreciate it better. He would even present two or three aspects of a problem and say, "What do you want to do?" That's the way he always was: before the strike, during the strike, today.

JIM GUYETTE: Hormel had a tight control over everything. People in our community didn't see this complete domination so clearly before. Now they see how power corrupts, how power controls, how those who have so much money never seem to lose the desire for more and don't care how they get it or who they hurt. We could no longer stand by and watch people hurt to the tune of two hundred and two injuries per one hundred workers each year.

DENNY MEALY: My first five years with the company, I worked in the most dangerous area, the beef kill, doing the most dangerous job in the packinghouse industry. In that five-year span, I required a hundred and ninety-six sutures and ended up having two surgeries to realign my wrist. This injury rate was running rampant.

JIM GUYETTE: Young women, twenty-two years old, worked at the plant for less than two months and got carpal tunnel syndrome. They couldn't even pick up their kids anymore. People, thirty and thirty-two years old, big enough and mean enough to eat nails, couldn't lift a ten-pound box. Then the company retrains them to fry hamburgers at Hardee's and McDonald's and tells them to get on with their lives. After they've ruined people! We couldn't in good conscience stand by. We tried to approach the Hormel Company to create a safe place to work. They said to us: If you don't like it, there are plenty of others who will work under these conditions.

We saw the company's intent very early on. A year before the strike started, it became clear we were headed for confrontation. In order to avoid a war with

Hormel, we said, "We'll gamble with you. We'll tie our wages to your profits. We'll guarantee you more money than you made a year ago or take a cut in pay." It took the company a minute and thirty-five seconds to tell us that wasn't enough. When we asked how much was enough, they didn't have an answer. . . .

CECIL CAIN: When we first went on strike in August, Hormel's attitude was: They're going to get real tired and real hungry. The company "knew" that the strike would soon be ended. Only it didn't end in a couple or three months or four or five. We were real successful in staying out, and we were not going to buckle. But believe me, it's tough when you're getting forty bucks a week, now and then supplemented with twenty-five dollars. Then we started the Adopt-a-Family program that Corporate Campaign brought before us. We made an appeal to locals across the country at the end of November. By Christmas time, we started getting responses. Holy Christ, it was a way we were going to survive!

DENNY MEALY: By now, Hormel had been closed for five months, and their productivity had been cut because we were effective with the roving pickets. On January 13, 1986, Hormel reopened the Austin plant.

JIM GUYETTE: When they tried to fill the plant up with scabs, our people decided to show up for work the same time the scabs did. They drove around the plant about two miles an hour. There was a giant traffic jam in Austin, Minnesota! Nobody was really breaking the law, and the police were frustrated. . . .

DENNY MEALY: We decided on civil disobedience, a nonviolent protest. We would place ourselves strategically at the plant site, locked arm in arm. This was successful for several days until the company called the cops. The police would pull people out of the groups and immediately arrest them. Several times people were beaten to the ground. We went through a series of three arrests. On the day of the largest number, one hundred fifteen people were jailed. As our numbers increased, the police and the sheriff's department also increased their forces, calling in help from outlying communities. They used tear gas and riot dogs. For a situation we designed to be completely nonviolent, they employed force.

JIM GUYETTE: You see, they needed to use violence. So they had to try to make us into violent, crazy people. And that's something we've never become. The only violence in Austin was created by the company, the police, and by the National Guard. We preached nonviolence from the very beginning. We used ideas from Gandhi, from Martin Luther King, Jr. And we took a tremendous amount of time and conducted a lot of meetings to talk about what it was we wanted to do and how we wanted to do it without violence.

CAROL KOUGH: I was at the picket line most of the time. Basically, what everybody did was link arms. They stayed peaceful, linking arms. Terry Arens was the first one arrested. He was just talking to an officer. He said, "We're not doing anything wrong. We're not violent. I hope you guys remain the same." That made the officers mad. They said, "Let's get him." The officers pulled so hard, Terry said he thought his arms were going to come out of their sockets. When they couldn't get him loose, the police put their fingers in his eyes and pulled him down that way. Terry's a big guy, but they pulled him down to the ground. He had injury to his eyes.

Then they started macing people. They had police dogs there that could rip you apart. It got to the point where they didn't care what happened to a P-9er. That's an awful feeling, but that's the feeling people had. They didn't really care if they hurt you.

CECIL CAIN: We were winning at first. We'd turn out four or five or six hundred people there. We were effective in keeping it shut down. If you go down there and you're effective, here comes an injunction: You can only have three pickets per gate. In effect, they were outlawing pickets. The same difference to me. Then they started hauling up people, arresting them. Here they come on radio: "Violence!" "Mobs!" In comes the Guard. . . .

CAROL KOUGH: They had the nerve to claim that one of the reasons they needed the Guard was because there was a physical attack on the company photographer by one of the workers. I was out at the gate that morning. Traffic was circling both ways, plus people going into work. There was a mixture of strikers and scabs. The photographer from Hormel was purposely agitating. And if you read the police reports, they admit that this man was purposely agitating. Then he got out of his car and took a swing and a kick at one of the P-9 strikers. That's when the striker kicked him back. The photographer got in his car and drove over to the corporate office. All of a sudden, they take him away by ambulance, supposedly because he's been hurt. Yet he was able to drive over and walk into the office, no problem. I still feel it was a set-up—I really do—because of the way it happened. They said that was one of the reasons they called the Guard—a "physical altercation."

DENNY MEALY: The National Guard cut off every entrance except one, the very north gate. Then they formed a V, almost like a funnel, that led from Interstate 90 directly to the gate. Any way they could, they would get the replacement workers, scabs, into the plant. This "private security force" for Hormel cost the taxpayers of Minnesota over three million dollars.

We decided we would block that exit with cars and begin a bottleneck. Traffic started backing up. Now the Highway Patrol became involved. Hormel had the political power to get them to use their vehicles as tow trucks, pushing cars off the tops of bridges, down through the medians, through the intersections.

CECIL CAIN: I was in Fremont, Nebraska, with the roving pickets and freezing my tail off there. I came back here and heard that the National Guard had come. They were housed in St. Edward's Church; they just took it over. I drove in and went right to the interstate. I saw all those big National Guard trucks and the soldiers standing out there with shields on them. You see those things other places, you know, always on TV, but not where you live and not where your kids go to school and not against you. We didn't do anything. We didn't hurt anybody. We said, "They can't do that, can they?"

We used to say, "They can't do that, can they?" We don't say that anymore. When we hear somebody say it, we laugh, because they can do any damn thing they want to. Jesus Christ, I've worked all my life, paid all the goddamn taxes, did everything you're supposed to do, and these guys come in here. This was wrong, absolutely wrong.

PETE WINKELS: You can't imagine what it's like until you go through it. The actual military, the National Guard, comes in, exerts its authority, and blocks off half the town. And they have got absolute control. For the first time, people in this town saw them: What in the hell is going on? I mean, it really heightened everyone's consciousness. They could understand what it was like in Korea or Central America or Poland when someone voiced their dissent. . . .

CECIL CAIN: We wanted to get our jobs back, but it's changed a bunch. All those hundreds of years when people thought there was a difference between whites and Blacks, men and women, young and old—all that crap, it's changing. In a small town in the middle of no place in Minnesota—just a bunch of farmers, a bunch of white Caucasians, for cripe's sake, experience the same problems Black people have had trying to get a job and decent housing, the same problems Hispanics face getting jobs other than under-the-table dirt, or the same problems women have been facing, trying to get the same wage for the same job. Until you walk a mile in somebody else's moccasins, you really don't understand what they're talking about. The walls are coming down. These guys are looking at the country different, at the world different. We got a lot of people talking about their problems, talking about unionism, and a lot of people watching. We've got a lot of people holding hands together. And we've had quite an impact on the labor movement.

• • •

In 1978, a year after he became president of the United Autoworkers Union (UAW), Doug Fraser resigned from a committee of eight corporate executives and eight labor officials chaired by former Secretary of Labor John T. Dunlop. The Labor-Management Group represented an attempt to forge "cooperation" between workers and employers, but as Fraser noted in his resignation, U.S. corporations were proving with their actions that they had no genuine interest in working with labor, instead choosing "to wage a one-sided class war . . . against working people, the unemployed, the poor, the minorities, the very young and the very old, and even many in the middle class of our society." Here is the text of Fraser's open letter.

Douglas A. Fraser, Resignation Letter to the Labor–Management Group (July 19, 1978)[5]

I deeply regret that it was necessary to cancel the meeting of the Labor–Management Group scheduled for July 19. It was my intention to tell you personally at that meeting what I must now convey in this letter, because the Group is not planning to meet again until late September.

I have come to the reluctant conclusion that my participation in the Labor–Management Group cannot continue. I am therefore resigning from the Group as of July 19. You are entitled to know why I take this action and you should understand that I have the highest regard for John Dunlop, my colleagues on the labor side and, as individuals, those who represent the corporate elite in the Group.

Attractive as the personalities may be, we all sit in a representative capacity. I have concluded that participation in these meetings is no longer useful to me or to the 1.5 million workers I represent as president of the UAW.

I believe leaders of the business community, with few exceptions, have chosen to wage a one-sided class war today in this country—a war against working people, the unemployed, the poor, the minorities, the very young and the very old, and even many in the middle class of our society. The leaders of industry, commerce and finance in the United States have broken and discarded the fragile, unwritten compact previously existing during a past period of growth and progress.

For a considerable time, the leaders of business and labor have sat at the Labor–Management Group's table—recognizing differences, but seeking consensus where it existed. That worked because the business community in the U.S. succeeded in advocating a general loyalty to an allegedly benign capitalism that emphasized private property, independence and self-regulation along with an allegiance to free, democratic politics.

That system has worked best, of course, for the "haves" in our society rather than the "have-nots." Yet it survived in part because of an unspoken foundation: that when things got bad enough for a segment of society, the business elite "gave" a little bit—enabling government or interest groups to better conditions somewhat for that segment. That give usually came only after sustained struggle, such as that waged by the labor movement in the 1930's and the civil rights movement in the 1960's.

The acceptance of the labor movement, such as it has been, came because business feared the alternatives. Corporate America didn't join the fight to pass the Civil Rights Act of 1964 or the Voting Rights Act, but it eventually accepted the inevitability of that legislation. Other similar pieces of legislation aimed at the human needs of the disadvantaged have become national policy only after real struggle.

This system is not as it should be, yet progress has been made under it. But today, I am convinced there has been a shift on the part of the business community toward confrontation, rather than cooperation. Now, business groups are tightening their control over American society. As that grip tightens, it is the "have-nots" who are squeezed.

The latest breakdown in our relationship is also perhaps the most serious. The fight waged by the business community against the Labor Law Reform bill stands as the most vicious, unfair attack upon the labor movement in more than 30 years. Corporate leaders knew it was not the "power grab by Big Labor" that they portrayed it to be. Instead, it became an extremely moderate, fair piece of legislation that only corporate outlaws would have had need to fear. Labor law reform itself would not have organized a single worker. Rather, it would have begun to limit the ability of certain rogue employers to keep workers from choosing democratically to be represented by unions through employer delay and outright violation of existing labor law.

I know that some of the business representatives in the Group argued inside the Business Roundtable for neutrality. But having lost, they helped to bankroll (through the Roundtable and other organizations) the dishonest and ugly multi-million dollar campaign against labor law reform. In that effort, the business representatives in the Group were allied with groups such as the Committee to Defeat the Union Bosses, the Committee for a Union Free Environment, the Right-to-Work Committee, the Americans Against Union Control of Government and such individuals as R. Heath Larry, Richard Lesher and Orrin Hatch.

The new flexing of business muscle can be seen in many other areas. The rise of multinational corporations that know neither patriotism nor morality but only self-interest, has made accountability almost non-existent. At virtually every level, I discern a demand by business for docile government and unrestrained corporate individualism. Where industry once yearned for subservient unions, it now wants no unions at all.

General Motors Corp. is a specific case in point. GM, the largest manufacturing corporation in the world, has received responsibility, productivity and cooperation from the UAW and its members. In return, GM has given us a Southern strategy designed to set up a non-union network that threatens the hard-fought gains won by the UAW. We have given stability and have been rewarded with hostility. Overseas, it is the, same. General Motors not only invests heavily in South Africa, it refuses to recognize the black unions there.

My message should be very clear: if corporations like General Motors want confrontation, they cannot expect cooperation in return from labor.

There are many other examples of the new class war being waged by business. Everyone in the Group knows there is no chance the business elite will join the fight for national health insurance or even remain neutral, despite the fact that the U.S. is the only industrial country in the world, except for South Africa, without it. We are presently locked in battle with corporate interests on the [Hubert] Humphrey–[Augustus] Hawkins full employment bill. We were at odds on improvements in the minimum wage, on Social Security financing, and virtually every other piece of legislation presented to the Congress recently.

Business blames inflation on workers, the poor, the consumer and uses it as a club against them. Price hikes and profit increases are ignored while corporate representatives tell us we can't afford to stop killing and maiming workers in unsafe factories. They tell us we must postpone moderate increases in the minimum wage for those whose labor earns so little they can barely survive.

Our tax laws are a scandal, yet corporate America wants even wider inequities. If people truly understood, they would choose not Proposition 13's, but rather an overhaul of the tax system to make business and the rich pay their fair share. The wealthy seek not to close loopholes, but to widen them by advocating the capital gains tax rollback that will bring them a huge bonanza.

Even the very foundations of America's democratic process are threatened by the new approach of the business elite. No democratic country in the world has lower rates of voter participation than the U.S., except Botswana. Moreover, our voting participation is class-skewed—about 50 percent more of the affluent vote than workers and 90 percent to 300 percent more of the rich vote than the poor, the black, the young and the Hispanic. Yet business groups regularly finance politicians, referenda and legislative battles to continue barriers to citizen participation in elections. In Ohio, for example, many corporations in the Fortune 500 furnished the money to repeal fair and democratic voter registration.

Even if all the barriers to such participation were removed, there would be no rush to the polls by so many in our society who feel the sense of helplessness and inability to affect the system in any way. The Republican Party remains controlled by and the Democratic Party heavily influenced by business interests. The reality is that both are weak and ineffective as parties, with no visible, clear-cut ideological differences between them, because of business domination. Corporate America has more to lose by the turn-off of citizens from the system than organized labor. But it is always the latter that fights to encourage participation and the former that works to stifle it.

For all these reasons, I have concluded there is no point to continue sitting down at Labor–Management Group meetings and philosophizing about the future of the country and the world when we on the labor side have so little in common with those across the table. I cannot sit there seeking unity with the leaders of American industry, while they try to destroy us and ruin the lives of the people I represent.

I would rather sit with the rural poor, the desperate children of urban blight, the victims of racism, and working people seeking a better life than with those whose religion is the status quo, whose goal is profit and whose hearts are cold. We in the UAW intend to reforge the links with those who believe in struggle: the kind of people who sat down in the factories in the 1930's and who marched in Selma in the 1960's.

I cannot assure you that we will be successful in making new alliances and forming new coalitions to help our nation find its way. But I can assure you that we will try.

• • •

In 1979, doctors in Los Angeles and New York started to report unusual and hard to diagnose forms of pneumonia and cancer. In 1982, the Centers for Disease Control and Prevention (CDC) officially named the condition Acquired Immune Deficiency Syndrome (AIDS). Within two years, doctors had also identified the virus linked to AIDS, Human Immunodeficiency Virus (HIV). But the history of AIDS has been one of denial and suppression, because those most immediately affected by the disease in its early years were gays and lesbians, often people of color, and drug users. President Ronald Reagan did not make public mention of the epidemic until October 1987. People with HIV and AIDS and public health advocates have had to battle for recognition of the disease, affordable and effective treatment, and public education and health programs to prevent the spread of HIV. In March 1987, the political movement to confront the AIDS crisis found militant expression with the formation of ACT UP (the AIDS Coalition to Unleash Power) in New York. The group popularized the slogan "Silence = Death," and engaged in direct action and civil disobedience to confront complacent politicians, health officials, journalists, and other establishment figures. Here activist Vito Russo, the author of a groundbreaking book called *The Celluloid Closet* and a founding member of ACT UP and the Gay and Lesbian Anti-Defamation League, speaks of how people with AIDS were dying not of a disease, but of homophobia, of racism, and of indifference. Russo himself died as a result of AIDS in 1990, aged forty-four.

Vito Russo, "Why We Fight" (1988)[6]

A friend of mine in New York City has a half-fare transit card, which means that you get on buses and subways for half price. And the other day, when he showed his card to the token attendant, the attendant asked what his disability was and he said, I have AIDS. And the attendant said, no you don't, if you had AIDS, you'd be home dying. And so, I wanted to speak out today as a person with AIDS who is not dying.

You know, for the last three years, since I was diagnosed, my family thinks two things about my situation. One, they think I'm going to die, and two, they think that my government is doing absolutely everything in their power to stop that. And they're wrong, on both counts.

So, if I'm dying from anything, I'm dying from homophobia. If I'm dying from anything, I'm dying from racism. If I'm dying from anything, it's from indifference and red tape, because these are the things that are preventing an end to this crisis. If I'm dying from anything, I'm dying from Jesse Helms. If I'm dying from anything, I'm dying from the President of the United States. And, especially, if I'm dying from anything, I'm dying from the sensationalism of newspapers and magazines and television shows, which are interested in me, as a human interest story—only as long as I'm willing to be a helpless victim, but not if I'm fighting for my life.

If I'm dying from anything—I'm dying from the fact that not enough rich, white, heterosexual men have gotten AIDS for anybody to give a shit. You know, living with AIDS in this country is like living in the twilight zone. Living with AIDS is like living through a war which is happening only for those people who happen to be in the trenches. Every time a shell explodes, you look around and you discover that you've lost more of your friends, but nobody else notices. It isn't happening to them. They're walking the streets as though we weren't living through some sort of nightmare. And only you can hear the screams of the people who are dying and their cries for help. No one else seems to be noticing.

And it's worse than a war, because during a war people are united in a shared experience. This war has not united us, it's divided us. It's separated those of us with AIDS and those of us who fight for people with AIDS from the rest of the population.

Two and a half years ago, I picked up *Life* magazine, and I read an editorial which said, "it's time to pay attention, because this disease is now beginning to strike the rest of us." It was as if I wasn't the one holding the magazine in my hand. And since then, nothing has changed to alter the perception that AIDS is not happening to the real people in this country.

It's not happening to us in the United States, it's happening to them—to the disposable populations of fags and junkies who deserve what they get. The media tells them that they don't have to care, because the people who really matter are not in danger. Twice, three times, four times— *The New York Times* has published editorials saying, don't panic yet, over AIDS—it still hasn't entered the general population, and until it does, we don't have to give a shit.

And the days, and the months, and the years pass by, and they don't spend those days and nights and months and years trying to figure out how to get hold of the latest experimental drug, and which dose to take it at, and in what combination with other drugs, and from what source? And, how are you going to pay for it? And where are you going to get it? Because it isn't happening to them, so they don't give a shit.

And they don't sit in television studios, surrounded by technicians who are wearing rubber gloves, who won't put a microphone on you, because it isn't happening to them, so they don't give a shit. And they don't have their houses burned down by bigots and morons. They watch it on the news and they have dinner and they go to bed, because it isn't happening to them, and they don't give a shit.

And they don't spend their waking hours going from hospital room to hospital room, and watching the people that they love die slowly—of neglect and bigotry, because it isn't happening to them and they don't have to give a shit. They haven't been to two funerals a week for the last three or four or five years—so they don't give a shit, because it's not happening to them.

And we read on the front page of *The New York Times* last Saturday that Anthony Fauci now says that all sorts of promising drugs for treatment haven't even been tested in the last two years because he can't afford to hire the people to test them. We're supposed to be grateful that this story has appeared in the newspaper after two years. Nobody wonders why some reporter didn't dig up that story and print it 18 months ago, before Fauci got dragged before a Congressional hearing.

How many people are dead in the last two years, who might be alive today, if those drugs had been tested more quickly? Reporters all over the country are busy printing government press releases. They don't give a shit, it isn't happening to them—meaning that it isn't happening to people like them—the real people, the world-famous general public we all keep hearing about.

Legionnaire's Disease was happening to them because it hit people who looked like them, who sounded like them, who were the same color as them. And that fucking story about a couple of dozen people hit the front page of every newspaper and magazine in this country, and it stayed there until that mystery got solved.

All I read in the newspapers tells me that the mainstream, white heterosexual population is not at risk for this disease. All the newspapers I read tell me that IV [intravenous] drug users and homosexuals still account for the overwhelming majority of cases, and a majority of those people at risk.

And can somebody please tell me why every single penny allocated for education and prevention gets spent on ad campaigns that are directed almost exclusively to white, heterosexual teenagers—who they keep telling us are not at risk!

Can somebody tell me why the only television movie ever produced by a major network in this country, about the impact of this disease, is not about the impact of this disease on the man who has AIDS, but of the impact of AIDS on his white, straight, nuclear family? Why, for eight years, every newspaper and magazine in this country has done cover stories on AIDS only when the threat of heterosexual transmission is raised?

Why, for eight years, every single educational film designed for use in high schools has eliminated any gay-positive material, before being approved by the Board of Education? Why, for eight years, every single public information pamphlet and videotape distributed by establishment sources has ignored specific homosexual content?

Why is every bus and subway ad I read and every advertisement and every billboard I see in this country specifically not directed at gay men? Don't believe the lie that the gay community has done its job and done it well and educated its people. The gay community and IV drug users are not all politicized people living in New York and San Francisco. Members of minority populations, including so-called sophisticated gay men are abysmally ignorant about AIDS.

If it is true that gay men and IV drug users are the populations at risk for this disease, then we have a right to demand that education and prevention be targeted specifically to these people. And it is not happening. We are being allowed to die, while low-risk populations are being panicked—not educated, panicked—into believing that we deserve to die.

Why are we here together today? We're here because it is happening to us, and we do give a shit. And if there were more of us, AIDS wouldn't be what it is at this moment in history. It's more than just a disease, which ignorant people have turned into an excuse to exercise the bigotry they have always felt.

It is more than a horror story, exploited by the tabloids. AIDS is really a test of us, as a people. When future generations ask what we did in this crisis, we're going to have to tell them that we were out here today. And we have to leave the legacy to those generations of people who will come after us.

Someday, the AIDS crisis will be over. Remember that. And when that day comes—when that day has come and gone, there'll be people alive on this earth—gay people and straight people, men and women, black and white, who will hear the story that once there was a terrible disease in this country and all over the world, and that a brave group of people stood up and fought and, in some cases, gave their lives, so that other people might live and be free.

So, I'm proud to be with my friends today and the people I love, because I think you're all heroes, and I'm glad to be part of this fight. But, to borrow a phrase from Michael Callen's song ["Love Don't Need a Reason"]: all we have is love right now, what we don't have is time.

In a lot of ways, AIDS activists are like those doctors out there—they're so busy putting out fires and taking care of people on respirators, that they don't have the time to take care of all the sick people. We're so busy putting out fires right now, that we don't have the time to talk to each other and strategize and plan for the next wave, and the next day, and next month and the next week and the next year.

And, we're going to have to find the time to do that in the next few months. And, we have to commit ourselves to doing that. And then, after we kick the shit out of this disease, we're all going to be alive to kick the shit out of this system, so that this never happens again.

• • •

In November 1986, at a demonstration against recruitment by the CIA at the University of Massachusetts, police arrested twelve people, including Abbie Hoffman, one of the counter-culture heroes of the 1960s, and Amy Carter, the daughter of former president Jimmy Carter, and charged them with trespassing and disorderly conduct. The group had occupied a campus building to drive home their message. When the case came to trial in April 1987, the defense turned the court into a forum on abuses by the CIA, bringing in Daniel Ellsberg and others to give testimony. In a major victory, all of the defendants were acquitted of the charges against them. Here Abbie Hoffman—a cofounder of the Youth International Party (the Yippies) and one of the defendants in the famous Chicago Seven trial after the crackdown on protesters at the 1968 Democratic National Convention—presents his closing remarks to the jury. Hoffman acted as his own attorney in the case.

Abbie Hoffman, "Closing Argument" (April 15, 1987)[7]

Good morning, women and men of the jury:

At 50, I am the oldest of the student defendants. In a short time you will retire to deliberate your decision. In examining the exhibits before you, we would draw your attention to Exhibit No. 3, page 1, paragraph 1 of the letter from the administration to the University of Massachusetts community, dated November 21, 1986:

The university has consistently been committed to providing, promoting and protecting an environment which encourages the free exchange of ideas through formal classes, meetings, public addresses, private conversations, and demonstrations.

Also, we would like you to consider page 2, the first paragraph:

The university respects the rights of its students to express their views in whatever manner they see fit, including demonstrations, rallies and educational forums.

The defendants have not claimed that the CIA has no right to participate in that free exchange of ideas. To the contrary, the defendants encourage that right of free speech. But recruitment by a company, private or public, is not a right; it is a privilege which is regulated to insure that the laws of the University of Massachusetts, the commonwealth and the United States are being obeyed by the recruiter.

You heard Ralph McGehee's description of how he was recruited into the CIA. He was told that he would be gathering intelligence, and we don't object to that. The country needs intelligence. He wasn't told he would be part of an assassination team, that he would have to "arrange and doctor evidence" that would show the North Vietnamese were invading the South, that he would have to write a white paper to Congress that was a total lie so that Congress could authorize the first bombing of Hanoi. We would draw your attention to Mr. McGehee's remark that the big joke about Congress in the CIA was, "Treat them like mushrooms—keep them in the dark and feed them a lot of manure." Does anyone believe this is what recruiters say? Do they tell the recruitee (as witness Mort Halperin testified) that they might have to break the CIA's own charter and engage in domestic spying? That they might have to silence a Daniel Ellsberg? That they might have to engage in acts of war against a country we are formally at peace with? Mr. Halperin testified that during the Senate intelligence hearings chaired by Senator Frank Church in 1976 it was recognized that some covert or secret acts are necessary in the conduct of foreign policy. However, it was decided that a covert action or program could not be in direct conflict with publicly stated government policy. In other words, you can't tell your allies for six years not to do business with Iran and at the same time secretly sell Iran weapons yourself.

Free speech is not a license to misinform and lie without accepting challenge. The CIA has been invited to send representatives to debate with the defendants and our witnesses on campus and here in court. After all, in the "necessity defense," we have to prove that bigger laws are being broken. But where is the

CIA to refute the evidence we have brought before you? If you accept our necessity defense, the prosecutor must offer some proof that justification was absent beyond reasonable doubt, just as we must prove it was present.

When I was growing up in Worcester, Massachusetts, my father was very proud of democracy. He often took me to town hall meetings in Clinton, Athol and Hudson. He would say, See how the people participate, see how they participate in decisions that affect their lives—that's democracy. I grew up with the idea that democracy is not something you believe in, or a place you hang your hat, but it's something you do. You participate. If you stop doing it, democracy crumbles and falls apart. It was very sad to read last month that the New England town hall meetings are dying off, and, in a large sense, the spirit of this trial is that grass-roots participation in democracy must not die. If matters such as we have been discussing here are left only to be discussed behind closed-door hearings in Washington, then we would cease to have a government of the people.

You travel around this country, no matter where you go, people say, Don't waste your time, nothing changes, you can't fight the powers that be—no one can. You hear it a lot from young people. I hear it from my own kids: Daddy, you're so quaint to believe in hope. Kids today live with awful nightmares: AIDS will wipe us out; the polar ice cap will melt; the nuclear bomb will go off at any minute. Even the best tend to believe we are hopeless to affect matters. It's no wonder teen-age suicide is at a record level. Young people are detached from history, the planet and, most important, the future. I maintain to you that this detachment from the future, the lack of hope and the high suicide rate among youth are connected.

This trial is about many things, from trespassing to questioning acts by the most powerful agency in the government. And here we are in Hampshire District Court. You have seen the defendants act with dignity and decorum. You have seen our lawyers try hard to defend our position. Witnesses, many of whom occupied high positions of power, have come before you and have told you the CIA often breaks the law, often lies. The prosecutor has worked hard but has not challenged their sincerity. The judge is here, the public, the press. I ask you, Is it we, the defendants, who are operating outside the system? Or does what you have heard about CIA activities in Nicaragua and elsewhere mean it is they that have strayed outside the limits of democracy and law?

Thomas Paine, the most outspoken and farsighted of the leaders of the American Revolution, wrote long ago:

> Every age and generation must be as free to act for itself, in all cases, as the ages and generations which preceded it. . . . Man has no property in man, neither has any generation a property in the generations which are to follow.

Thomas Paine was talking about this spring day in this courtroom. A verdict of not guilty will say, When our country is right, keep it right; but when it is wrong, right those wrongs. A verdict of not guilty will say to the University of Massachusetts that these demonstrators are reaffirming their rights as citizens who acted with justification. A verdict of not guilty will say what Thomas Paine said: Young people, don't give up hope. If you participate, the future is yours. Thank you.

• • •

Rap music had since its inception featured songs about racism, alienation, and inequality in U.S. cities. But rap was also growing more commercialized by the late 1980s. When the group Public Enemy released its first album, *Yo! Bum Rush the Show* in 1987, its lyrics stood out starkly against the backdrop of Reagan-era conservatism and the still overwhelmingly white Music Television (MTV) programming. Here is a track from their third album, *Fear of a Black Planet*, that offered an uncompromising message of protest.

Public Enemy, "Fight The Power" (1990)[8]

1989 the number another summer (get down)
Sound of the funky drummer
Music hittin' your heart cause I know you got soul
(Brothers and sisters, hey)
Listen if you're missin' y'all
Swingin' while I'm singin'
Givin' whatcha gettin'
Knowin' what I know
While the Black bands sweatin'
And the rhythm rhymes rollin'
Got to give us what we want
Gotta give us what we need
Our freedom of speech is freedom or death
We got to fight the powers that be
Lemme hear you say
Fight the power

As the rhythm designed to bounce
What counts is that the rhymes

Designed to fill your mind
Now that you've realized the prides arrived
We got to pump the stuff to make us tough
From the heart
It's a start, a work of art
To revolutionize make a change nothin's strange
People, people we are the same
No we're not the same
Cause we don't know the game
What we need is awareness, we can't get careless
You say what is this?
My beloved lets get down to business
Mental self defensive fitness
(Yo) bum rush the show
You gotta go for what you know
Make everybody see, in order to fight the powers that be
Lemme hear you say. . .
Fight the power

Elvis was a hero to most
But he never meant shit to me you see
Straight up racist that sucker was
Simple and plain
Motherfuck him and John Wayne
Cause I'm Black and I'm proud
I'm ready and hyped plus I'm amped
Most of my heroes don't appear on no stamps
Sample a look back you look and find
Nothing but rednecks for 400 years if you check
Don't worry be happy
Was a number one jam
Damn if I say it you can slap me right here
(Get it) lets get this party started right
Right on, c'mon
What we got to say
Power to the people no delay
To make everybody see
In order to fight the powers that be

(Fight The Power)

Panama, the 1991 Gulf War, and the War at Home

Alex Molnar, "If My Marine Son Is Killed . . ." (August 23, 1990)

Eqbal Ahmad, "Roots of the Gulf Crisis" (November 17, 1990)

June Jordan Speaks Out Against the 1991 Gulf War
(February 21, 1991)

Yolanda Huet-Vaughn, Statement Refusing to Serve in the 1991 Gulf
War (January 9, 1991)

Interview with Civilian Worker at the Río Hato Military Base in Panama
City (February 23, 1990)

Mike Davis, "In L.A., Burning All Illusions" (June 1, 1992)

Mumia Abu-Jamal, *All Things Censored* (2001)

The administration of George H. W. Bush, coming into office in early 1989, seemed determined to eradicate the "Vietnam syndrome"—that is, the reluctance of Americans to go to war. Bush found an easy target in Panama, whose military dictator, Manuel Noriega, had once worked for the CIA, but was now becoming troublesome to the U.S. government. The excuse for the war was that Noriega was involved in drug trafficking—undoubtedly true, but not the real reason, which had more to do with U.S. control of the Panama Canal and proving its ability to openly intervene in another country's affairs.

It was a short war, totally one-sided. The bombardment of Panama City resulted in the destruction of neighborhoods and the deaths of at least a thousand ordinary citizens of Panama. Noriega was arrested and jailed. But the drug trade continued.

In 1990, Iraqi dictator Saddam Hussein, once befriended and given arms by the U.S. government, took over the neighboring oil sheikdom of Kuwait. Rejecting any possibility of negotiating with Iraq in order to end its occupation of Kuwait, the Bush administration, with the approval of Congress, went to war.

Once again, the invasion pitted against each other two very unequal military machines. There was a huge loss of life among Iraqis as a result of the heavy bombardment by the U.S. air force. A few hundred U.S. soldiers were killed, but tens of thousands, perhaps a hundred thousand Iraqis, civilians and soldiers died.

In the United States, there were protests all over the country against the war. In Washington, DC, 150,000 people marched against the war. There were huge demonstrations in New York and San Francisco.

Much of the public support for the war was based on the idea that "we must support our troops." A disabled Vietnam veteran named Philip Avilo, now a history professor at York College in Pennsylvania, wrote in a local newspaper: "Yes, we need to support our men and women under arms. But let's support them by bringing them home, not by condoning this barbarous, violent policy."

The black community was far less enthusiastic than the rest of the country about the war. An ABC News/*Washington Post* poll in early February 1991, in the midst of the war, found that support for the war was 84 percent among whites, but only 48 percent among African Americans. A meeting of black leaders in New York called the war "an immoral and unspiritual diversion . . . a blatant evasion of our domestic responsibilities."

As the United States entered the 1990s, the political system remained in the control of those who had great wealth, whether Democrats or Republicans were in power. The country was divided, although no mainstream political leader would speak of it, into classes of extreme wealth and extreme poverty, separated by an insecure and jeopardized middle class.

Yes there was, unquestionably, though largely unreported, what one worried mainstream journalist called "a permanent adversarial culture" that refused to surrender the possibility of a more equal, more humane society. If there was hope for the future of the United States, it lay in the promise of that refusal.

• • •

As Washington prepared for a war in Iraq in 1990, a father, and founder of the Military Families Support Network, sent an open letter to President Bush, which was published in the *New York Times*.

Alex Molnar, "If My Marine Son Is Killed . . ." (August 23, 1990)[1]

Dear President Bush:

I kissed my son goodbye today. He is a twenty-one-year-old marine. You have ordered him to Saudi Arabia.

The letter telling us he was going arrived at our vacation cottage in northern

Wisconsin by Express Mail on August 13. We left immediately for North Carolina to be with him. Our vacation was over.

Some commentators say you are continuing your own vacation to avoid appearing trapped in the White House, as President Carter was during the Iran hostage crisis. Perhaps that is your reason. However, as I sat in my motel room watching you on television, looking through my son's hastily written last will and testament and listening to military equipment rumble past, you seemed to me to be both callous and ridiculous chasing golf balls and zipping around in your boat in Kennebunkport.

While visiting my son I had a chance to see him pack his chemical weapons suit and try on his body armor. I don't know if you've ever had this experience, Mr. President. I hope you never will.

I also met many of my son's fellow soldiers. They are fine young men. A number told me that they were from poor families. They joined the Marines as a way of earning enough money to go to college.

None of the young men I met are likely to be invited to serve on the board of directors of a savings and loan association, as your son Neil was. And none of them have parents well enough connected to call or write a general to insure that their child stays out of harm's way, as Vice President [Dan] Quayle's parents did for him during the Vietnam War.

I read in today's Raleigh *News and Observer* that, like you, Vice President Quayle and Secretary of State [James] Baker are on vacation. Meanwhile, Defense Secretary [Dick] Cheney is in the Persian Gulf. I think this symbolizes a government that no longer has a non-military foreign policy vision, one that uses the military to conceal the fraud that American diplomacy has become.

Yes, you have proved a relatively adept tactician in the last three weeks. But if American diplomacy hadn't been on vacation for the better part of a decade, we wouldn't be in the spot we are today.

Where were you, Mr. President, when Iraq was killing its own people with poison gas? Why, until the recent crisis, was it business as usual with Saddam Hussein, the man you now call a Hitler?

You were elected Vice President in 1980 on the strength of the promise of a better life for Americans, in a world where the U.S. would once again "stand tall." The Reagan–Bush Administration rolled into Washington talking about the magic of a "free market" in oil. You diluted gas mileage requirements for cars and dismantled Federal energy policy. And now you have ordered my son to the Middle East. For what? Cheap gas?

Is the American "way of life" that you say my son is risking his life for the continued "right" of Americans to consume 25 to 30 percent of the world's oil? The "free market" to which you are so fervently devoted has a very high price tag, at least for parents like me and young men and women like my son.

Now that we face the prospect of war I intend to support my son and his fellow soldiers by doing everything I can to oppose any offensive American military action in the Persian Gulf. The troops I met deserve far better than the politicians and policies that hold them hostage.

As my wife and I sat in a little cafe outside our son's base last week, trying to eat, fighting back tears, a young marine struck up a conversation with us. As we parted he wished us well and said, "May God forgive us for what we are about to do."

President Bush, the policies you have advocated for the last decade have set the stage for military conflict in the Middle East. Your response to the Iraqi conquest of Kuwait has set in motion events that increasingly will pressure you to use our troops not to defend Saudi Arabia but to attack Iraq. And I'm afraid that, as that pressure mounts, you will wager my son's life in a gamble to save your political future.

In the past you have demonstrated no enduring commitment to any principle other than the advancement of your political career. This makes me doubt that you have either the courage or the character to meet the challenge of finding a diplomatic solution to this crisis. If, as I expect, you eventually order American soldiers to attack Iraq, then it is God who will have to forgive you. I will not.

$$\bullet \ \bullet \ \bullet$$

Eqbal Ahmad was born in India, before the partition of the country, and grew up in Pakistan. As Edward W. Said wrote in an obituary for Ahmad, who died in May 1999, "His life was an epic and poetic one, full of wanderings, border crossings, and an almost instinctive attraction to liberation movements, movements of the oppressed and the persecuted, causes of people who were unfairly punished—whether they lived in the great metropolitan centers of Europe and America, or in the refugee camps, besieged cities, and bombed or disadvantaged villages of Bosnia, Chechnya, south Lebanon, Vietnam, Iraq, Iran and, of course, the Indian subcontinent." In November 1990, two months before the U.S. launched its massive onslaught against Iraq, Ahmad gave a talk in Boston, Massachusetts, explaining the motives behind the drive to war. The speech was recorded by Ahmad's friend, crusading radio journalist David Barsamian, and broadcast on his program *Alternative Radio*.

Eqbal Ahmad, "Roots of the Gulf Crisis" (November 17, 1990)[2]

[W]e are coming to the end of—more or less to the end of—this century. It has been an extraordinary century, for many reasons. One of them is that this is the century during which the Western world started to count its wars. And so, we had World War I, and World War II, and the fears of World War III.

Before the twentieth century, for three and a half centuries, the West made wars upon the "other" without counting them. And a world system came into being (starting in the seventeenth century) marked by imperialism, marked by a global market, marked by capitalism, and marked above all by unrecorded and unremembered holocausts. Those were the centuries during which great civilizations—like those of the Mayas, the Incas, the Aztecs, the great civilized nations of this hemisphere—were destroyed. Those were also centuries during which other great civilizations—of Africa and China, and of India, and of the Middle East—were subjugated.

And those wars were not remembered, or I should say, were remembered only when a garden was besieged, or a Custer was killed. And the point of the twentieth century is that finally the colonial haves and the colonial have-nots began to fight with each other. And the West began to number its wars. It began also to realize fully the price of wars. And thus began a history not only of betrayals of humanity, but also of expressed hopes.

So I should begin by first reminding ourselves of the fact that World War I was probably the last "happy" war that the Western world has fought. Certainly the last war into which the West went joyously: there was dancing in the streets of London and Paris. And songsters sang about this wonderful war. After World War I, there was a genuine and massive recoiling from wars, and a yearning for peace. And such works as *When Peace Comes* became best-sellers. And such things as Woodrow Wilson's fourteen points came to be viewed as expressions of humanity's hopes. And the covenant of the League of Nations was widely welcomed.

It also witnessed betrayals of our hopes. Upon those betrayals were founded the premises of World War II. When World War II was over, the repugnance of war was so great that it had become inconceivable that we will accept another—or third—World War. It had also become conceivable that the colonized countries will witness decolonization, and freedom, and liberation. And the United Nations Charter was welcomed. And once again what we witnessed was disappointment—betrayals of those hopes which we nourished after World War II.

And now we have reached a third period of hopes and possible betrayal. For World War II, the post-war settlement essentially meant two things. . . .

The reality of the arms race (the strategic arms race) and massive defense spending and arms trades, on the one hand. And on the other hand, the continuation of warfare, with the Third World as its battlefield. So we had Greece, and we had Korea, and we had Vietnam, and we had the Cuban missile crisis. And we had those once-every-fifteen-month interventions of the United States in Third World countries, and once-every-six-year interventions by the Soviet Union in Eastern Europe (and finally in Afghanistan).

And now, something else has happened. And that is, one of the two major players in the Cold War game has walked out on the game, leaving the United States alone in front of the chess-board. That's what essentially has happened. And it is called an example of Russian weakness. It expresses the great Russian crisis and defeat that they walked out on the Cold War. So the question arises: what happens now? Is that one player which is left on the chess-board going to try to pick up all the counters, put them in the pocket, and bully everybody on the block? Or would it mean a New World Order? I think that is the question with which I have come to you. I don't (probably) have an answer.

I should perhaps remind us that in the past periods of hope and betrayal, there have been defining events. Not one, sometimes more than one event.

There was that invasion of Abyssinia. And those of you that have been reading history would remember that wispy, thin little man coming to the League of Nations, shaking his little wispy beard, and saying, "If you let it go this time, you will regret it." That was Haile Selassie after the invasion of his country.

After World War II, you would remember, it was, first Iran during the Azerbaijan crisis (in which for the first time after the bombing of Hiroshima and Nagasaki the United States used nuclear diplomacy). And soon after that there was the civil war in Greece, which led to the Truman Doctrine—whereby the United States promised to intervene anywhere where a government was threatened by external or internal forces (thus laying down the basis for continuous American interventions in the Third World). You would remember also that the next defining war was the Korean War, which followed soon after the National Security Council Memorandum No. 68. These were defining events.

I would submit to you that in this era of perestroika, the crisis in the Gulf may very well prove to be the defining event that would defeat our hopes, and start us out on a new period of betrayals. I would like to remind us also that both in 1936–37 and in 1945–55, the betrayals . . . occurred—and a new order of violence and domination began—with the complicity of the media, of the Congress, and (forgive me for thinking) of the public also.

For the media never asked what was behind the great crisis. It didn't even feel to ask why its own men—like George Polk—were being murdered in Greece (and by whom). It never asked who started—and how the Korean War started. What were the American objectives in the Korean War? You realize that the United States went into the Greek civil war, and it started—got into—the Korean War without public discussion. Without congressional authorization. Without declarations of war (as they did in Vietnam, too). And that there was one lone voice—that of I. F. Stone, [who] wrote *The Hidden History of the Korean War*. And it is only forty years later that we are now beginning to learn that the American government actually took the American people and Congress into the Korean War by lying.

And once again the media is doing exactly the same thing. And we must not be complicit this time. The media, the universities, the Congress, have all failed to ask fundamental questions about the crisis in the Gulf. No substantive discussion of this crisis has yet taken place—into the fourth month of this crisis, and nearly four hundred thousand troops to be dispatched (most already there, a few more to be dispatched).

First, there has been nothing (that I have seen) in the media about what compels Saddam Hussein's extraordinary ambitions. This fellow is being described as Hitler. As a dictator. As a tyrant. As a dangerous guy in that region. And nobody is asking why. Because this dictator has been around for fifteen years. What has suddenly in 1990 compelled his ambition, that requires three hundred and fifty thousand American troops to control? What did it?

No one has named the Camp David Accords. And Saddam Hussein's ambitions are directly attributable to the Camp David Accords. . . .

Remember the following. Since the decline of the Ottoman Empire (in other words, since the beginning of the nineteenth century), Egypt has played the role of the regional influential in the Arab world. Politically, culturally, even militarily, Egypt has led the Arab world (and ideologically). The Camp David Accords' supreme achievement was to isolate Egypt from its Arab milieu.

When Anwar Sadat signed that piece of paper, his hope had been that this would lead to the return of Egyptian territory to Egypt . . . which he did get. And two, a modicum of justice for the Palestinians. So that, over time, his isolation will be ameliorated. And that minimum that was promised to Sadat in the Camp David Accords was not honored. In fact, the maximum was dishonored.

To remind you of one reality alone, Carter, and [Harold] Saunders, and William B. Quandt—the three American negotiators from top to the bottom (with Carter at the top, Saunders in the middle, and Quandt at the bottom)—have testified and recorded in their books that in the last three days of the Camp David negotiations, the negotiations had broken down on one issue. And the issue was Sadat's insistence that there should be written in the Camp David Accords that Israel will put up no more settlements in the West Bank and Gaza. And [Menachem] Begin would say, "I am willing to agree on it informally, but won't do it in writing." And Carter weighs in and says, "You must understand Begin's difficult position. I give you guarantee that there will be no settlements."

And then that day they signed the piece of paper in front of the television camera, on prime time television. And Anwar Sadat and Begin and Carter kissed each other. (Sadat was particularly fond of kissing.) And then he went down and kissed his friend, Barbara Walters. And told Barbara Walters that there will be peace—and comprehensive peace—in the Middle East. This was confirmed by Carter and Begin. And the next day, around afternoon, Israel announced the setting up of new settlements. And Carter called poppycock.

But much more than that. It is after Camp David that the settlement process escalated. It is after Camp David that 60 percent of Palestinian lands were expropriated in the West Bank. It is after Camp David that nearly 80 percent of Palestinian water came under the Israeli occupying authority's control. And it was after Camp David that nearly eighteen thousand books were banned in the West Bank and Gaza. And it is after Camp David that Palestinian local leaders began to be deported (in violation of the Geneva Conventions).

Have you noticed what I have just said? It is after Camp David that the four elements of life, without which no community can survive, came under organized assault by the Israeli military occupation authorities. Those are: land, water, culture, and leaders. What underlies this extraordinary event called the Intifada is not merely Palestinian heroism, or its will to liberation. It is Palestinian desperation, and its will to survival. Literally, I mean, survival.

Now, obviously, Camp David meant moral, ideological, political isolation of Egypt from its Arab milieu. There would be a political vacuum in the Middle East after Camp David. And smaller players—like Syria and Iraq—would love, would aim at, would have the ambition, to fill that vacuum.

Saddam Hussein showed the first sign of wanting to fill that vacuum when he, in an unprovoked aggression, invaded Iran. And far from discouraging him, the United States encouraged him in that aggression. And Saudi Arabia and Kuwait paid his bills for warfare. To the tune of nearly $60 billion, they paid. He borrowed another $40 billion from them.

So now that he has invaded Kuwait, everybody is very upset about it. And the most extraordinary thing is, that they are still not talking about what underlay his extraordinary ambition.

Or take the second question: what is the politics of oil, that defines this conflict? How is it that through this inflationary cycle of the last ten years (1980 to 1990) oil has been the only product whose prices have been going down? You realize that oil prices have come down from about $42 a barrel to $14 a barrel. How? Why is it that from 1980–81 to 1990, the price of oil kept coming down? Who brought it down? How could they afford to bring it down? There should have been some discussion about it. . . .

Or, take the next question. There is an extraordinary international consensus behind America's interventionary initiative. Actually, this is the first time an American interventionary initiative has the support of all the great powers. Unusual. But it doesn't have the support of eleven—nearly half—of the Arab nations. . . .

Why are the Arab people so anti–American intervention? The answer is very simple: they don't believe that the Americans are doing it in Arab interests. They fear this is the beginning of recolonization. . . .

When Bush says, "Acquisition of territory by force is inadmissible," nobody believes it. When the American newspapers welcome the United Nations resolution of sanctions [on Iraq], it creates cynical feelings among the Arab masses, Arab people. The Israelis invaded Lebanon in 1982. No less than twenty thousand people were killed. And a very similar resolution before the Security Council was vetoed by the United States. The Israelis are occupying four Arab countries right now, and have annexed two of them. The United States has been sponsoring annexation and occupation. So there can be no trust, on this basis.

Or, has there been any discussion in the press as to why every day we hear, "This is the UN resolution. The UN has supported these things. American forces are behind the United Nations resolution"? But for three months the U.S. government has refused to form an allied UN command. They don't want their troops to be under UN command. The Russians have been pushing and shoving. (Quietly—they're not capable of doing much more anymore. Or not wanting to.) The Russians have been demanding over and over and over for the last two years that the UN Military Commission (which is under the control of the Security Council) should be activated. It's the United States which is refusing to activate the Military Commission. No discussion in the media. Why? Just discuss it. . . .

Finally . . . there has been no discussion in this country—at universities or in the media—of what are American objectives in the Persian Gulf? What are the goals of policy? What is it? Now, you will notice that President Bush (and [James] Baker) have done their best, surely, to produce debate. They cannot be blamed. They have tried their best to produce, to provoke, to encourage debate on this issue—because they have said too many things. They have said, "We are there to oppose aggression. Because that's a matter of principle." Number one. Number two, they say, "We are there because the United Nations asked us to be there," which it never did. The UN came after the Americans did (which has been forgotten). Then they are saying, "We are there because of oil." And most importantly, now they have said that "We are there to save American jobs." Now, with so many statements of objectives, and reports of total confusion in the American public, one would think that it would be the responsibility of the media, the universities, these scholars, these pundits, to at least start figuring out what the objectives are.

I would have really liked to talk about those objectives. Perhaps during some discussions, we will do that. For now, let me finish we two or three quick thoughts.

One, you will recall that since 1970, the United States has been desperate to insert . . . its military and political power in the Middle East. You would recall that it was through U.S. choices that the centrality for world struggle for power shifted in the 1970s. From the Atlantic and the Pacific in the 1950s and the '60s, it shifted in the 1970s to the areas bounded by the Mediterranean and Indian Oceans (i.e., the Middle East and southern Africa). You would recall that the Rapid Deployment Force and the new modernized navy were designed at the Middle East. At the beginning, a sixty thousand [person] Rapid Deployment Force, which by the Carter administration had reached two hundred thousand, and by Reagan had reached three hundred and fifty thousand. Much of the troops under the Rapid Deployment Force are now mobilized for this. You would recall that Saudi Arabia has been requested to provide bases since 1975, and had refused it. You would recall that Iran was built into a major force as part of America's southern strategy on the eastern flank of the oil belt (and Israel on the western flank).

I am merely suggesting that it is the great achievement of President Saddam Hussein that he opened the doors wide to American intervention. Those people who somehow think that Saddam Hussein has done something anti-imperialistic are thinking it wrong. Saddam Hussein is not only a tyrant and a dictator, he is also a fool. And that fool has created this situation.

Finally, I'll leave you with one simple suggestion: this is a war about staying number one. And this is a war about control of oil. And staying number one and controlling oil are not directed at the Arabs. It is directed at two large forces: Europe and the Third World. For the United States had exercised two leverages on its Western allies: the leverage of strategic weaponry (the strategic umbrella) and the leverage of economic dominance. It has lost both of them. Since 1970, American policy makers have been seeking new leverages over old allies—and control of oil will give that. And, over the Third World the United States would like to both have the leverage of oil and establish the principle that it remains—in the age of perestroika—the watchman on the walls of world freedom. Shall we let them have it? That's up to you.

• • •

The black feminist writer and activist June Jordan wrote of ordinary people's loves, desires, struggles, and passions—both personal and political. Jordan, who died of breast cancer in June 2002, was also an internationalist, committed to breaking down boundaries of nation and ethnicity. As her friend Alice Walker said, she was "an inhabitant of the entire universe." On February 21, 1991, the anniversary of the assassination of Malcolm X, she spoke at a rally in Hayward, California, against the war in the Gulf.

June Jordan Speaks Out Against the 1991 Gulf War (February 21, 1991)[3]

Correct me if I'm wrong, but this killer crusade, this conversion of a stranger's land into a killing field, this reduction of a people to a video display, this homicidal rhetoric that history does not support, that our common destiny is certain to condemn, this war has not saved one human being. This war has not saved a single American life. This war has not saved a single Israeli life. This a war has not saved a single Iraqi life. This war has not rescued the lives of Kuwait. This grand undertaking, this enormous, this infinitely casual overkill, this draining of our hearts, this annihilation of all tenderness, this erasure of every reason, every rational and civilized approach to dispute, this arched and leering assault upon all peaceable possibilities, this blasphemy unleashed against our shrunken trembling earth, that has become in the hellified lexicon of the killers ruling us, a target-rich environment, this war has not saved one human being from terror or from unspeakable agonies of extinction. Then, why do we permit this blasphemy to persist, expand, and explode our body politic as well as the entire Middle East? I grieve the sorrow roar, the sorrow sob. I grieve the monstrous consequences of this war. . . .

[But] I am reassured because not every American has lost her mind or his soul. Not every one of my compatriots who become a flag-wrapped lunatic, lusting after oil and power, the perversions of kicking ass, preferably via TV. A huge number of Americans has joined with enormous numbers of Arab peoples and European communities in Germany, England, France, Italy, Spain, and Muslim communities throughout India and Pakistan to cry out "Stop!" When I say huge, I mean it. If 1,000 Americans contacted by some pollster can be said to represent 250 million people, then how many multi-, multi-millions do we anti-war movement gatherings of more than 100,000 coast to coast and on every continent, how many do we represent? How come nobody ever does that kind of political math? Tonight, February 21, 1991, when yet again, the ruling white men of America despise peace and sneer at negotiations and intensify their arms-length arm-chair prosecution of this evil war, this display of racist value system that will never allow for any nationalism that is not their own and that will never allow third-world countries to control their own natural resources and that will never ever express—let alone feel—regret or remorse or shame or horror at the loss of any human life that is not white. Tonight, I am particularly proud to be an African American. By launching the heaviest air assault in history against Iraq on January 15, George Bush dared to desecrate the birthday of Martin Luther King, Jr.

Tonight, and 83,000 bombing missions later, is the twenty-sixth anniversary of the assassination of Malcolm X. On this sorry evening, the world has seen the pathological real deal behind the sanctimonious rhetoric of Bush and Company. The Persian Gulf War is not about Iraqi withdrawal from Kuwait. The war is not about Kuwait at all. Clearly, it's not about international law or respect or United Nations resolutions, since by comparison to Washington and Pretoria, the Butcher of Baghdad is a minor league Johnny-come-lately to the realm of outlaw conduct and contempt for world opinion. What has happened tonight is that the Soviet leader, Mikhail Gorbachev and the government of Iraq have reached an agreement whereby Iraq will withdraw from Kuwait, and that is a fact regardless of anything else included or omitted by the proposal. This agreement should provide for immediate ceasefire, a cessation to the slaughter of Iraqi men and women, and a halt to the demolition nationwide of their water supply, the access to food and security. What is the response of the number one white man in America? He's gone off to the theater. I guess that means that the nearest church was closed. Or that Colin Powell was busy dipping his spoon into the comfort of a pot of soup somebody else cooked for him. And that Dick Cheney was fit to be tied into any uniform so long has nobody would take away his Patriot missiles and Apache helicopters, and B-52 cluster bombers, and black and brown and poor white soldiers and sailors, and all of the rest of these toys for a truly big-time coward. Confronted with the nightmare prospect of peace, Bush goes off to the theater because he will be damned if he will acknowledge that Saddam Hussein is a man, is the head of a sovereign state, is an enemy to be reckoned with, an opponent with whom one must negotiate. Saddam is not a white man. He and his Arab peoples must be destroyed. No peace, no cease-fire, no negotiations.

And I am proud tonight to remember Dr. King and Malcolm X and to mourn their actions even as I pursue the difficult challenge of their legacy. Both of these men became the targets of white wrath when they in their different ways developed into global visionaries persisting against racism in Alabama, in Harlem, in South Africa, in Vietnam. Neither of these men could have failed to condemn this current attack against the Arab world. Neither of these men ever condoned anything less than equal justice and equal rights.

Hence, the undeniably racist double standards now levied against Saddam Hussein would have appalled and alienated both of them completely. I am proud to shake hands with the increasing number of African-American conscientious objectors. I am proud to remark the steadfast moral certainty of the United States Congressman Ronald Dellums's opposition to the war. I am proud to hear about the conscientious objections of Congressmen Gus Savage, and John Conyers, and Mervyn [Dymally] as I am proud to observe that even while African Americans remain disproportionately represented in the United States armed forces, we as a national community stand distinct, despite and apart from all vagaries of popular opinion. We maintain a proportionately higher level of opposition to this horrible war, this horrendous evasion of domestic degeneration and decay.

I want to say something else specific to you, Mr. President. It's true you can humiliate and you can hound and you can smash and burn and terrify and smirk and boast and defame and demonize and dismiss and incinerate and starve, and yes, you can force somebody—force a people to surrender . . . what happens to remain of their bloody bowels into your grasping, bony, dry hands. But all of us who are weak, we watch you. And we learn from your hatred, and we do not forget. And we are ready, Mr. President. We are most of the people on this god-forsaken planet.

• • •

At great risk to themselves, more than 220 soldiers declared themselves conscientious objectors to the 1991 Gulf War. Among the most eloquent was a Kansas doctor, Yolanda Huet-Vaughn. Huet-Vaughn, an immigrant from Mexico, had served five years in the military before receiving an honorable discharge in 1982. In 1989, she enlisted in the army reserves, and, after Iraq's invasion of Kuwait, was called up to go to Saudi Arabia. In the statement below, Huet-Vaughn explains her reasons for opposing the build-up to the eventual U.S. war against Iraq. As a result of her stance, she was identified as a "deserter," placed under house arrest for four months, court martialed, and sentenced to thirty months in prison. After Amnesty International labeled Huet-Vaughn a "prisoner of conscience" and organized a campaign around her case, she was released, having served eight months.

Yolanda Huet-Vaughn, Statement Refusing to Serve in the 1991 Gulf War (January 9, 1991)[4]

I, Yolanda Huet-Vaughn, M.D., am a board-certified family physician, a wife, a mother of three children ages two, five, and eight. I am also a member since 1980 of Physicians for Social Responsibility, the U.S. affiliate of the International Physicians for the Prevention of Nuclear War. In 1982 I cofounded the Greater Kansas City Chapter of Physicians for Social Responsibility. I am from Kansas City, Kansas. I am a captain in the U.S. Army Reserve Medical Corps. In connection with the Gulf crisis I was called to active duty service in December 1990.

I am refusing orders to be an accomplice in what I consider an immoral, inhumane, and unconstitutional act, namely an offensive military mobilization in the

Middle East. My oath as a citizen-soldier to defend the Constitution, my oath as a physician to preserve life and prevent disease, and my responsibility as a human being to the preservation of this planet, would be violated if I cooperate with Operation Desert Shield.

I had hoped that we as a people had learned the lessons of Vietnam—50,000 Americans dead—hundreds of thousands of civilian dead—and environmental disaster. What we face in the Middle East is death and destruction on a grander scale. Whereas in Vietnam we had 200 casualties per week, it has been projected that war with Iraq could result in 200 casualties per hour. . . .

The majority of casualties will be civilians, as 57 percent of the population of Iraq and Kuwait are concentrated in urban centers. Of this civilian population, 47 percent are children under the age of fifteen.

A bombing raid over Baghdad, a city of over four million, will not only target Saddam Hussein but also the civilian population, of whom two million are children. Are we as Americans, knowing this in advance, knowing that this is not fate but a choice, willing to live with the moral burden of these deaths? . . . .

From a medical point of view, the public has been misled concerning the catastrophic nature of wounds and injuries that will befall combatants and civilians. Are we as Americans willing to live through the evening news tallies of dead and wounded Americans knowing in advance that this war is avoidable?

As a mother I am keenly aware of the long-term medical and environmental consequences that may occur in the Middle East region and which may indeed have a global impact if war breaks out. A Jordan physicist estimates that burning of the oil fields could last six months with over one million barrels of oil burning per day. This burning would generate pyrotoxins that could accelerate global warming by two decades.

Perhaps the greatest medical catastrophe awaiting civilian and military personnel is the likely use of chemical, biological, or nuclear weapons. Never before have such vast arsenals of weapons of mass destruction been assembled. There is no guarantee that what may start as a conventional war won't quickly escalate to a war in which weapons designed to incinerate or irradiate massive population centers will be used.

Do we as Americans want the responsibility of going ahead with offensive maneuvers that could easily be the start of World War III? And I ask you, what is worth all of this death and destruction? What do we have after Vietnam except the tears and the pain and the loss?

As a doctor I know that where there can be no medical cure, prevention is the only remedy. I therefore commit my medical knowledge and training to this effort to avert war by refusing orders to participate in Operation Desert Shield. As Albert Einstein remarked with the advent of nuclear weapons, "If civilization is to survive, humankind will require a substantially new manner of thinking." I believe that we must all extend our thinking to a new level, and I urge our political and military leaders to acknowledge the severity of these medical and environmental consequences in committing themselves to diplomatic solutions.

I consider myself a patriot and have taken these actions in support of American troops who have been deployed in the Gulf region, in support of the American people, and in support of the children both here and in the Middle East who have no voice. I hope that in some small way my act of conscience will help promote a peaceful resolution of the Gulf crisis.

• • •

Although the United States would go to war in 1991, declaring that no large country (Iraq) should invade a smaller one (Kuwait), in December 1989 the U.S. military invaded tiny Panama, which it had long dominated, but which now was showing signs of independence. The United States had controlled Panama's strategic canal, a major shipping lane, from 1904, but the authority over the Canal Zone was scheduled to pass back to Panama, and the 1989 invasion was designed to install a government friendly to U.S. interests. President Bush said the war was needed to overthrow the Panamanian dictator, Manuel Noriega. Noriega had long been a friend of Washington, and had been funded by the CIA, but he had stopped doing Washington's bidding. The invasion of Panama destroyed whole neighborhoods and cost many lives. How many we do not know. As the human rights group Americas Watch commented at the time, "We have urged an examination of the military operations in Panama to determine individual and collective responsibilities for . . . serious violations of the laws of war. No such inquiry has taken place, and none is contemplated, as far as we can tell." Here is an interview describing what took place during the U.S. attack, from a report by the Independent Commission of Inquiry on the U.S. Invasion of Panama.

Interview with Civilian Worker at the Río Hato Military Base in Panama City (February 23, 1990)[5]

Q. You were at the military base at Río Hato?

A. Yes, I was at the base at Río Hato. I am a civilian—I was engaged in maintenance work at the base.

Located at that base at Río Hato were the Sixth Expeditionary Company, a tank unit of the Machos de Monte, and two schools. One is the officers' school, "Benjamín Ruiz." The other is a secondary school where they have the option of going on to pursue a military career or going to the university. These students are known as the Tomasitos.

That night of the 19th to the 20th of December we went to bed, but rumors were circulating that the 82nd [Airborne] Division had left the United States and that there was the possibility of an invasion.

Q. What time was this?

A. At about 7 p.m., maybe a little bit later. I think that none of us really believed that an invasion would actually happen, when you took into consideration the overwhelming difference in power between the two countries. I don't think that it would justify an invasion to remove Noriega, if that was its objective. Noriega had been near the base over the weekend taking in the fresh air with a small escort. If they had wanted to capture him they could have done it easily at that time or they could have done it the previous Sunday when he was there near the base in a public place with a friend of his. If there had to be bloodshed, they could have got him at that time with maybe 20 dead or, exaggerating the situation, 30 killed at the maximum—not the thousands of deaths which actually took place. An invasion was not justified to capture Noriega. We never believed this justification.

Then at about a quarter to one in the morning, we heard explosions and the helicopters buzzing the buildings. Then the machine guns started and we ran out of the barracks where we were staying. As there was a full moon, we could clearly see the paratroopers coming down. There was a plan for evacuation of the students, but the barracks were not close together, so the evacuation plan could only be carried out for a small group of students. Another group of students was captured by the U.S. soldiers. There were a number of these students killed.

This was because the U.S. troops didn't realize that they were practically children. They were all under 18 years old. They were machine-gunned before they could surrender. They were unarmed and before they told them to surrender they had opened fire.

Q. Did any of them have any weapons?

A. Among these kids? No, none of them. Some of them went to the armory to try to get weapons but they were not given to them. These were not streetwise kids. Well, anyway, they weren't given any weapons.

Q. How many were killed when they opened fire?

A. I didn't see it myself, but I heard the boys say that there were about 30 killed.

Q. Where were you at this time?

A. I ran towards the mountains, but I stayed close to the base. The helicopters fired at me. At that time I met up with two soldiers who were armed, and four boys, four Tomasitos who were unarmed. The boys were very frightened, they had no idea what the flares were. It was obvious that they had absolutely no military preparation. They have tried to say that this was a military training school but that isn't true.

They used lasers, they used these very large helicopters that fired missiles that caused multiple explosions, powerful explosions. They fired at us with machine guns. There were other bombs, which were very strange. They were strange in the sense that the explosion first produced a white light which then turned red. I have been told that this was the kind of bomb they used here in the neighborhood of El Chorrillo, to burn down the neighborhood. They were different, even the soldiers there had never seen that kind of explosion before.

When I was finally captured, they made me kneel against a wall, they put an M-16 against my neck and they threatened to kill me. The one who did this was very nervous. All of the U.S. soldiers that I saw at that moment seemed very nervous. They were also very young, about 20 years old, and it must have been their first experience in a genuine combat situation and maybe they expected more organized resistance. They seemed very frightened and very nervous.

One of them told the other not to kill me, that they would interrogate me. From there they transferred me to a place where they had the other prisoners. There they had a lot of the boys, the Tomasitos. They held them there tied up, with their hands tied behind their backs with a plastic band. They were treating them very badly there. They hit them, they beat them. There were some wounded and they kept them out in the sun. They were not given any medical attention. They poked them, took their personal belongings away from them like watches and money. They gave the impression that an army of mercenaries had arrived instead of a professional army. There was a scene where one U.S. soldier showed a watch to another and asked him if he liked it. The other one said, "If it works it's mine." And he kept it.

They were also gathering up a fair number of civilian prisoners. The civilians were not treated as badly as the military prisoners. They gathered up, for example, family members, small children, three-year-olds. This little girl was crying and saying that she wanted to go home but they couldn't, the whole family was being held prisoner.

We spent the whole day there, the 20th [of December]. They photographed us, took our names.

In the morning they began to look at some of the wounded. There was among them a youth who seemed pretty badly wounded—he had been wounded in the abdomen and in both arms. I don't know if they were bullet wounds or from shell fragments or shrapnel but he seemed to be in pretty bad shape. He was stretched out on the floor. Then a U.S. soldier came up, I think he was an officer, and he ordered that he be given medical care.

Q. What time was this?

A. I'm not sure, I think it must have been around 11 o'clock. He was wounded around 1:30 in the morning and he hadn't received any medical attention for about ten hours. But he was in very bad shape. He was left on the floor, and the floor was really filthy because it was the floor of the auto-mechanics' garage for the base. That's where we were being held.

I was also able to see the inside of one of the barracks, because I asked permission to go to the bathroom. The inside of the barracks was completely incinerated, but it was burned by a different kind of fire; when you touched something it turned to dust, things would seem to be whole, but when you touched them, they would completely disintegrate.

Officially they say there were twenty-three U.S. soldiers killed. Later I found out that at the Río Hato base two helicopters had been shot down. Already we can add up to perhaps nineteen dead, which would mean that in the rest of Panama, there would be only four killed. That's unbelievable, isn't it? The United States had many more deaths than have been officially acknowledged. . . .

They rounded up the entire civilian population. There are two towns very close to the base. They went to these towns and rounded up all of the males fourteen years old and older without any consideration—they arrested old men who, because of their advanced age and physical condition, it was impossible to imagine that they even had the strength to pick up a weapon. They took them prisoner, they took everyone prisoner. . . .

Since I was old enough to be aware of my environment, Panama has been a country that was relatively better off than the other Latin American countries that I know about. But during the last two years, with the economic pressure, the poverty level has risen terribly. Before, you never saw children begging on the streets, emotionally deranged people going around. The level of alcohol consumption has gone up.

We in Panama are not accustomed to those things and we say many applauding the fall of Noriega, believing in the promises that substantial economic aid would be forthcoming from the United States. And instead what we are seeing now is the application of the policies of the International Monetary Fund. One of these is the reduction of employment in the public sector, the payment of the foreign debt. This is going to wake up a lot of Panamanians from this illusion they had. I think they are waking up already.

• • •

Los Angeles, still remembering the Watts riot of 1965, exploded again in rebellion on April 29, 1992. The immediate cause was a jury verdict that found four white officers innocent of a brutal beating of a black motorist, Rodney King, on March 3, 1991. The incident was captured on videotape by an observer. The video showed police beating King repeatedly with their batons and kicking him, fracturing his skull. The trial had been moved from multiracial Los Angeles to the rich, white suburb of Simi Valley. When the verdict was announced, a multiracial rebellion erupted in Los Angeles, lasting for days. Like the urban rebellions of the 1960s, the uprising gave expression to long-held grievances about police brutality, racism, unemployment, and poverty. Here Mike Davis, the labor historian, writer, and author of *City of Quartz*, a fascinating study of Los Angeles, gives a first-hand account of the rebellion and the repression that followed.

Mike Davis, "In L.A., Burning All Illusions" (June 1, 1992)[6]

The armored personnel carrier squats on the corner like *un gran sapo feo*—"a big ugly toad"—according to 9-year-old Emerio. His parents talk anxiously, almost in a whisper, about the desaparecidos: Raul from Tepic, big Mario, the younger Flores girl and the cousin from Ahuachapan. Like all Salvadorans, they know about those who "disappear"; they remember the headless corpses and the man whose tongue had been pulled through the hole in his throat like a necktie. That is why they came here—to ZIP code 90057, Los Angeles, California.

Now they are counting their friends and neighbors, Salvadoran and Mexican, who are suddenly gone. Some are still in the County Jail on Bauchet Street, little more than Brown grains of sand lost among the 17,000 other alleged *saqueadores* (looters) and *incendarios* (arsonists) detained after the most violent American civil disturbance since the Irish poor burned Manhattan in 1863. Those without papers are probably already back in Tijuana, broke and disconsolate, cut off from their families and new lives. Violating city policy, the police fed hundreds of hapless undocumented saqueadores to the INS [Immigration and Naturalization Service] deportation before the ACLU or immigrant rights groups even realized they had been arrested.

For many days the television talked only of the "South Central riot," "black rage" and the "Crips and Bloods." But Emerio's parents know that thousands of their neighbors from the MacArthur Park district—home to nearly one-tenth of all the Salvadorans in the world—also looted, burned, stayed out past curfew and went to jail. (An analysis of the first 5,000 arrests from all over the city revealed that 52 percent were poor Latinos, 10 percent whites and only 38 percent blacks.) They also know that the nation's first multiracial riot was as much about empty bellies and broken hearts as it was about police batons and Rodney King.

The week before the riot was unseasonably hot. At night the people lingered outside on the stoops and sidewalks of their tenements (MacArthur Park is L.A.'s Spanish Harlem), talking about their new burden of trouble. In a neighborhood far more crowded than mid-Manhattan and more dangerous than downtown

Detroit, with more crack addicts and gangbangers than registered voters, *la gente* know how to laugh away every disaster except the final one. Yet there was a new melancholy in the air.

Too many people have been losing their jobs: their *pinche* $5.25-an-hour jobs as seamstresses, laborers, busboys and factory workers. In two years of recession, unemployment has tripled in L.A.'s immigrant neighborhoods. At Christmas more than 20,000 predominantly Latina women and children from throughout the central city waited all night in the cold to collect a free turkey and a blanket from charities. Other visible barometers of distress are the rapidly growing colonies of homeless compañeros on the desolate flanks of Crown Hill and in the concrete bed of the L.A. River, where people are forced to use sewage water for bathing and cooking.

As mothers and fathers lose their jobs, or as unemployed relatives move under the shelter of the extended family, there is increasing pressure on teenagers to supplement the family income. Belmont High School is the pride of "Little Central America," but with nearly 4,500 students it is severely overcrowded, and an additional 2,000 students must be bused to distant schools in the San Fernando Valley and elsewhere. Fully 7,000 school-age teenagers in the Belmont area, moreover, have dropped out of school. Some have entered the *vida loca* of gang culture (there are 100 different gangs in the school district that includes Belmont High), but most are struggling to find minimum-wage footholds in a declining economy.

The neighbors in MacArthur Park whom I interviewed, such as Emerio's parents, all speak of this gathering sense of unease, a perception of a future already looted. The riot arrived like a magic dispensation. People were initially shocked by the violence, then mesmerized by the televised images of biracial crowds in South Central L.A. helping themselves to mountains of desirable goods without interference from the police. The next day, Thursday, April 30, the authorities blundered twice: first by suspending school and releasing the kids into the streets; second by announcing that the National Guard was on the way to help enforce a dusk-to-dawn curfew.

Thousands immediately interpreted this as a last call to participate in the general redistribution of wealth in progress. Looting spread with explosive force throughout Hollywood and MacArthur Park, as well as parts of Echo Park, Van Nuys and Huntington Park. Although arsonists spread terrifying destruction, the looting crowds were governed by a visible moral economy. As one middle-aged lady explained to me, "Stealing is a sin, but this is like a television game show where everyone in the audience gets to win." Unlike the looters in Hollywood (some on skateboards) who stole Madonna's bustier and all the crotchless panties from Frederick's, the masses of MacArthur Park concentrated on the prosaic necessities of life like cockroach spray and Pampers.

Now, one week later, MacArthur Park is in a state of siege. A special "We Tip" hotline invites people to inform on neighbors or acquaintances suspected of looting. Elite L.A.P.D. Metro Squad units, supported by the National Guard, sweep through the tenements in search of stolen goods, while Border Patrolmen from as far away as Texas prowl the streets. Frantic parents search for missing kids, like mentally retarded fourteen-year-old Zuly Estrada, who is believed to have been deported to Mexico.

Meanwhile, thousands of *saqueadores*, many of them pathetic scavengers captured in the charred ruins the day after the looting, languish in County Jail, unable to meet absurdly high bails. One man, caught with a packet of sunflower seeds and two cartons of milk, is being held on $15,000; hundreds of others face felony indictments and possible two-year prison terms. Prosecutors demand thirty-day jail sentences for curfew violators, despite the fact that many of those are either homeless street people or Spanish-speakers who were unaware of the curfew. These are the "weeds" that George Bush says we must pull from the soil of our cities before it can be sown with the regenerating "seeds" of enterprise zones and tax breaks for private capital.

There is rising apprehension that the entire community will become a scapegoat. An ugly, seal-the-border nativism has been growing like crabgrass in Southern California since the start of the recession. A lynch mob of Orange County Republicans, led by Representative Dana Rohrabacher of Huntington Beach, demands the immediate deportation of all the undocumented immigrants arrested in the disturbance, while liberal Democrat Anthony Beilenson, sounding like the San Fernando Valley's Son-of-[Jean-Marie]-Le-Pen, proposes to strip citizenship from the U.S.-born children of illegals. According to Roberto Lovato of MacArthur Park's Central American Refugee Center, "We are becoming the guinea pigs, the Jews, in the militarized laboratory where George Bush is inventing his new urban order.". . . .

Unlike the 1965 rebellion, which broke out south of Watts and remained primarily focused on the poorer east side of the ghetto, the 1992 riot reached its maximum temperature along Crenshaw Boulevard—the very heart of black Los Angeles's more affluent west side. Despite the illusion of full-immersion "actuality" provided by the minicam and the helicopter, television's coverage of the riot's angry edge was even more twisted than the melted steel of Crenshaw's devastated shopping centers. Most reporters—"image looters" as they are now being called in South Central—merely lip-synched suburban clichés as they tramped through the ruins of lives they had no desire to understand. A violent kaleidoscope of bewildering complexity was flattened into a single, categorical scenario: legitimate black anger over the King decision hijacked by hard-core street criminals and transformed into a maddened assault on their own community.

Local television thus unwittingly mimed the [John] McCone Commission's summary judgment that the August 1965 Watts riot was primarily the act of a hoodlum fringe. In that case, a subsequent U.C.L.A. [University of California at Los Angeles] study revealed that the "riot of the riffraff" was in fact a popular uprising involving at least 50,000 working-class adults and their teenage children. When the arrest records of this latest uprising are finally analyzed, they will probably also vindicate the judgment of many residents that all segments of black youth, gang and non-gang, "buppie" as well as underclass, took part in the disorder. . . .

The balance of grievances in the community is complex. Rodney King is the symbol that links unleashed police racism in Los Angeles to the crisis of black life everywhere, from Las Vegas to Toronto. Indeed, it is becoming clear that the King case may be almost as much of a watershed in American history as Dred Scott, a test of the very meaning of the citizenship for which African-Americans have struggled for 400 years.

But on the grass-roots level, especially among gang youth, Rodney King may not have quite the same profound resonance. As one of the Inglewood Bloods told me: "Rodney King? Shit, my homies be beat like dogs by the police every day. This riot is about all the homeboys murdered by the police, about the little sister killed by the Koreans, about twenty-seven years of oppression. Rodney King just the trigger." . . .

For its part, the Bush administration has federalized the repression in L.A. with an eye to the spectacle of the President marching in triumph, like a Roman emperor, with captured Crips and Bloods in chains. Thus, the Justice Department has dispatched to L.A. the same elite task force of federal marshals who captured Manuel Noriega in Panama as reinforcements for L.A.P.D. and FBI efforts to track down the supposed gang instigators of the riot. But as a veteran of the 1965 riot said while watching SWAT teams arrest some of the hundreds of rival gang members trying to meet peacefully at Watts's Jordan Downs Housing Project: "That ole fool Bush think we as dumb as Saddam. Land Marines in Compton and get hisself re-elected. But this ain't Iraq. This is Vietnam, Jack."

• • •

The award-winning journalist Mumia Abu-Jamal has been on death row in Pennsylvania since a 1982 trial filled with procedural errors, in which he was convicted of shooting and killing police officer Daniel Faulkner. Abu-Jamal grew up in the projects of Philadelphia and became a member of the Black Panthers. He was well known as a crusading journalist and activist when his case went to trial. Despite appeals from numerous human rights groups for a new trial, international protests, and evidence of his wrongful conviction, Abu-Jamal remains behind bars. From prison, Abu-Jamal has recorded a series of radio commentaries and written a number of essays about the racism and injustice of the U.S. prison system and the war on the poor, inside and outside of prison. Here are two of these commentaries, from his book *Live from Death Row*.

Mumia Abu-Jamal, *All Things Censored* (2001)[7]

"LIVE FROM DEATH ROW"

Don't tell me about the valley of the shadow of death. I live there. In south-central Pennsylvania's Huntingdon County, a hundred-year-old prison stands, its gothic towers projecting an air of foreboding, evoking a gloomy mood of the dark ages. I, and some forty-five other men, spend about twenty-two hours a day in six-by-ten-foot cells. The additional two hours may be spent outdoors in a chain-link-fenced box, ringed by concertina razor wire, under the gaze of gun turrets.

Welcome to Pennsylvania's death row.

I'm a bit stunned. Several days ago, Pennsylvania's Supreme Court affirmed my conviction and sentence of death by a vote of four justices, three did not participate.

As a black journalist who was a Panther way back in my young teens, I've often studied America's long history of legal lynchings of Africans. I remember a front page of the Black Panther newspaper bearing the quote, "A black man has no rights that a white man is bound to respect," attributed to U.S. Supreme Court chief justice [Roger] Taney of the infamous Dred Scott case [*Dred Scott v. Sanford*], where America's highest court held that "neither Africans, nor their free descendants, are entitled to the rights of the Constitution."

Deep, huh?

Perhaps I'm naive, or maybe I'm just stupid, but I really thought the law would be followed in my case, and the conviction reversed. Really.

Even in the face of the brutal Philadelphia MOVE massacre on May 13 [1985], Ramona Africa's frame-up, Eleanor Bumpurs, Michael Stewart, Clement Lloyd, Allan Blanchard, in countless police slaughters of blacks from New York to Miami, with impunity, my faith remained. Even in the face of this relentless wave of antiblack state terror, I thought my appeals would be successful.

Even with all I knew, I still harbored a belief in U.S. law, and the realization that my appeal has been denied is a shocker.

Now, I could intellectually understand that American courts are reservoirs of racist sentiment and have been historically hostile to black defendants, but a lifetime of propaganda about American "justice" is hard to shrug off.

I need but look across the nation, where as of October 1986 blacks constituted some 40 percent of men on death row, or across Pennsylvania, where as of August 1988, 61 out of 113 men—some 50 percent—are black, to see the truth, a truth hidden under black robes and promises of equal rights.

Blacks are just 9 percent of Pennsylvania's population, just under 11 percent of America's. As I said, it's hard to shrug off, but maybe we can try this together. How? Try out this quote I saw in a 1982 law book by a prominent Philadelphia lawyer named David Kairys: "Law is simply politics by other means."

Such a line goes far to explain how courts really function, whether today, or 130 years ago in the Scott case. It ain't about law, it's about politics by other means.

Now ain't that the truth.

As time passes, I intend to share with you some truths. . . . I continue to fight against this unjust sentence and conviction. Perhaps we can shrug off and shred some of the dangerous myths laid on our minds like a second skin, such as the "right" to a fair and impartial jury of our peers, the "right" to represent oneself, the "right" to a fair trial even.

They're not rights.

They're privileges of the powerful and the rich. For the powerless and the poor, they are chimeras that vanish once one reaches out to claim them as something real or substantial. Don't expect the big networks or megachains of "Big Mac" media to tell you. Because of the incestuousness between the media and government, and big business—which they both serve—they can't.

I can.

Even if I must do so from the valley of the shadow of death, I will.

"WAR ON THE POOR"

In every phase and facet of national life, there is a war being waged on America's poor. In social policy poor mothers are targeted for criminal sanctions for acts that, if committed by mothers of higher economic class, would merit treatment at the Betty Ford Center. In youth policy, governments hasten to close schools while building boot camps and prisons as their "graduate schools." Xenophobic politicians hoist campaigns to the dark star of imprisonment for street beggars, further fattening the fortress economy. The only apparent solution to the scourge of homelessness is to build more and more prisons.

In America's 1990s, to be poor is not so a much socioeconomic status as it is a serious character flaw, a defect of the spirit. Federal statistics tell a tale of loss and want so dreadful that [Charles] Dickens, of *A Tale of Two Cities* fame, would cringe.

Consider: seven million people homeless, with less than two hundred dollars in monthly income. Thirty seven million people, 14.5 percent of the nation's population, living below poverty levels. Of that number 29 percent are African Americans, meaning that over 10.6 million blacks live in poverty.

Both wings of the ruling "Republicrat" Party try to outdo themselves in announcing new, ever more draconian measures to restrict, repress, restrain, and eliminate the poor. One is reminded of the wry observation of French writer Anatole France: "The Law, in its majestic equality, forbids the rich as well as the poor to sleep under bridges, to beg in the streets and to steal bread."

Already U.S. manufacturers have fled to NAFTA [North American Free Trade Agreement]–friendly Mexico, and only the Zapatista insurgency in Chiapas has slowed an emerging flood of Western capital. Outgunned in the industrial wars by Japan and Germany, the United States has embarked on a low-technology, low-skill, high-employment scheme that exploits the poor, the stupid, and the slow via a boom in prison construction, America's sole growth industry. Increasingly, more and more Americans are guarding more and more American prisoners for more and more years. And this amid the lowest crime rate in decades. No major political party has an answer to this social dilemma, short of cages and graves for the poor.

The time is ripe for a new, brighter, life-affirming vision that liberates, not represses, the poor, who after all are the vast majority of this Earth's people. Neither serpentine politics, nor sterile economic theory that treats them—people— as mere economic units offers much hope. For the very politicians they vote for spit in their faces, while economists write them off as "nonpersons."

It must come from the poor, a rebellion of the spirit that reaffirms their intrinsic human worth, based upon who they are rather than what they possess.

Challenging Bill Clinton

Bruce Springsteen, *The Ghost of Tom Joad* (1995)

Lorell Patterson on the "War Zone" Strikes in Decatur, Illinois (June 1995)

Winona LaDuke, Acceptance Speech for the Green Party's Nomination for Vice President of the United States of America (August 29, 1996)

Two Open Letters of Protest to the Clinton Administration
  Alice Walker, Letter to President Bill Clinton (March 13, 1996)
  Adrienne Rich, Letter to Jane Alexander Refusing the National Medal for the Arts (July 3, 1997)

Rania Masri, "How Many More Must Die?" (September 17, 2000)

Roni Krouzman, "WTO: The Battle in Seattle: An Eyewitness Account" (December 6, 1999)

Anita Cameron, "And the Steps Came Tumbling Down—ADAPT's Battle with the HBA" (2000)

Elizabeth ("Betita") Martínez, "'Be Down with the Brown!'" (1998)

Walter Mosley, *Workin' on the Chain Gang* (2000)

Julia Butterfly Hill, "Surviving the Storm: Lessons from Nature" (2001)

When President Clinton published his memoir, *My Life*, in 2004, reflecting on his eight years as president, the press concentrated on the scandal surrounding his sexual behavior. Clinton had been impeached by the House of Representatives and barely escaped removal from office because of the lies he told about his sex life.

Overlooked and underemphasized was the record of the Clinton years, the ending of the New Deal program guaranteeing aid to poor families with dependent children, the building of more prisons, the maintenance of a large military budget, and the fact that his legislation was largely supported by the Republican Party.

Overseas, Clinton's policy was marked by sporadic shows of military might. Barely six months in office, he sent the air force to drop bombs on Baghdad, on the basis of very weak evidence that Iraq was behind an alleged assassination plot against former President George Bush. Six people in a suburban neighborhood were killed, including a prominent Iraqi artist and her husband.

Clinton bombed Iraq on the grounds that they possessed "weapons of mass destruction," while maintaining comprehensive sanctions on that country that resulted in the deaths of hundreds of thousands of Iraqis. When U.S. embassies were attacked in Kenya and Tanzania, Clinton bombed Afghanistan and the Sudan, in the latter case mistaking a pharmaceutical factory for one producing chemical weapons.

Clinton sent troops into Somalia, intervening in a conflict between rival Somali leaders, but withdrew them after a clash in which nineteen U.S. troops were killed. Thousands of Somalis were killed by U.S. troops.

The following year, 1994, the United States was influential in withdrawing international peacekeepers from Rwanda. Thus, the international community, including the most powerful nation in the world, stood by while a large-scale massacre of perhaps a million people took place.

Throughout Clinton's administration, groups all over the country protested his foreign policy and carried on campaigns for economic justice. Toward the end of his administration, more than forty thousand people gathered to disrupt a meeting of the World Trade Organization in Seattle. The ensuing battle between demonstrators and police—broadcast around the world—was seen as a new chapter in the struggle against corporate globalization.

• • •

In 1995, in the middle of the Clinton era, the New Jersey–born rock musician and songwriter Bruce Springsteen released an album that consciously evoked John Steinbeck's *Grapes of Wrath* and the songs of Woody Guthrie. He wrote about the struggles of the working poor, undocumented immigrants, *braceros*. Returning to a folk idiom, which he had also explored in his album *Nebraska*, Springsteen gave voice to those who were left behind in the "boom" of the 1990s, those who made the rich even richer yet were nameless, those who died for corporate greed. Here are two songs from the album, the first, "Youngstown," inspired by the book *Journey to Nowhere* by Dale Maharidge and Michael Williamson.

Bruce Springsteen, *The Ghost of Tom Joad* (1995)[1]

"YOUNGSTOWN"

Here in northeast Ohio
Back in eighteen-o-three

James and Dan Heaton
Found the ore that was linin' Yellow Creek
They built a blast furnace
Here along the shore
And they made the cannonballs
That helped the Union win the war

Here in Youngstown
Here in Youngstown
My sweet Jenny I'm sinkin' down
Here darlin' in Youngstown

Well my daddy worked the furnaces
Kept 'em hotter than hell
I come home from 'Nam worked my way to scarfer
A job that'd suit the devil as well
Taconite coke and limestone
Fed my children and made my pay
Then smokestacks reachin' like the arms of God
Into a beautiful sky of soot and clay

Here in Youngstown
Here in Youngstown
My sweet Jenny I'm sinkin' down
Here darlin' in Youngstown

Well my daddy come on the Ohio works
When he come home from World War Two
Now the yards just scrap and rubble
He said, "Them big boys did what Hitler couldn't do"
These mills they built the tanks and bombs
That won this country's wars
We sent our sons to Korea and Vietnam
Now we're wondering what they were dyin' for

Here in Youngstown
Here in Youngstown
My sweet Jenny I'm sinkin' down
Here darlin' in Youngstown

From the Monongahela valley
To the Mesabi iron range
To the coal mines of Appalachia
The story's always the same
Seven-hundred tons of metal a day
Now sir you tell me the world's changed
Once I made you rich enough
Rich enough to forget my name

And Youngstown
And Youngstown
My sweet Jenny I'm sinkin' down
Here darlin' in Youngstown

When I die I don't want no part of heaven
I would not do heaven's work well
I pray the devil comes and takes me
To stand in the fiery furnaces of hell

"SINALOA COWBOYS"

Miguel came from a small town in northern Mexico
He came north with his brother Louis to California three years ago
They crossed at the river levee when Louis was just sixteen
And found work together in the fields of the San Joaquin

They left their homes and family
Their father said "My sons one thing you will learn,
For everything the north gives it exacts a price in return."
They worked side by side in the orchards
From morning till the day was through
Doing the work the hueros wouldn't do.

Word was out some men in from Sinaloa were looking for some hands
Well deep in Fresno county there was a deserted chicken ranch
There in a small tin shack on the edge of a ravine
Miguel and Louis stood cooking methamphetamine.

You could spend a year in the orchards
Or make half as much in one ten-hour shift

Working for the men from Sinaloa
But if you slipped the hydriodic acid
Could burn right through your skin
They'd leave you spittin' up blood in the desert
If you breathed those fumes in

It was early one winter evening as Miguel stood watch outside
When the shack exploded lighting up the valley night
Miguel carried Louis' body over his shoulder down a swale
To the creekside and there in the tall grass Louis Rosales died

Miguel lifted Louis' body into his truck and then he drove
To where the morning sunlight fell on a eucalyptus grove
There in the dirt he dug up ten thousand dollars, all that they'd saved
Kissed his brothers lips and placed him in his grave

• • •

At one point in the mid-1990s, one in ten workers in the small industrial town of Decatur, Illinois, were on strike or locked out. Labor activists around the world came to describe the central Illinois town as a "war zone," where the global attack on workers and unions was being dramatically played out. Members of the United Auto Workers were up against Caterpillar, the giant multinational known for its earth-moving equipment. Trade unionists in the United Rubber Workers faced tire manufacturer Bridgestone-Firestone. And, at same time, more than 750 chemical workers at A. E. Staley were locked out by the company after they challenged wage and benefit cuts and demanded action on workplace safety. Activists from all three struggles toured the country, raising money for the strikers and locked out workers. All the strikes were eventually defeated—in part because of the use of strikebreakers. (President Bill Clinton had promised to ban the use of replacement workers in strikes, but never fulfilled that promise.) Here Lorell Patterson, a Staley worker and a member of the Coalition of Black Trade Unionists, describes the "war zone" battles.

Lorell Patterson on the "War Zone" Strikes in Decatur, Illinois (June 1995)[2]

In Decatur, Illinois, we're fighting for justice and equal treatment. If we don't start counteracting what's going on today, we're all going to be going down the same cesspool. And that's what they're counting on—for us to sit and do nothing.

I think that the corporations are the worst conglomerate of idiots I've ever run across in my life. We like to bash Newt Gingrich and Bob Dole and Phil Gramm and all of them—but we've got to put a few Democrats in there, too. I've stood and watched these people—and some of them are African Americans—who are actually buying into crap like NAFTA (the North American Free Trade Agreement) and GATT (the General Agreement on Trade and Tariffs) as the best way to go to create jobs from everybody.

I wrote a letter to Senator Carol Moseley-Braun here in Chicago. And in her response, she proceeded to tell me that the reason that we're losing our jobs is because we're uneducated—that we only have twelfth-grade educations. But a few weeks later, these clowns turn around and start cutting programs for job training. We've got to let them know that we're not going to take this anymore.

We want education. We want livable wages. We want decent housing. And we want health care for the rest of our lives, not the life of the contract. It's very simple—it shouldn't be hard for the politicians to understand. Every human being has a right to those basic essentials.

The only way I can see that we're going to get that is to start organizing and educating. We've got to start standing up and telling them no. I have a right to be treated as a human being. And if we don't stand up and start forcing it out of their hands, we're never going to get it. You can send all the people to Washington that you want, you're not going to get it.

So when people try to tell me we can't change laws, I remind them that not so long ago, they made laws that excluded the poor, the minorities, the women—and everybody that wasn't rich. I tell people that if they believe that, then they're selling themselves short, and they're selling their children and their grandchildren short. It's time we start believing that we have the power, not the politicians.

Every once and a while, you meet people who want to blame everybody else for their problems. They want to blame Black people and other minorities. They want to blame welfare mothers. They want to blame immigrants. They want to blame poor people. You know, it's about time that we stop allowing ourselves to use each other as scapegoats.

I figured out a long time ago who my enemy was. The people who are my enemy are in some fancy house, wearing some fancy suit, and telling me that I don't deserve to have anything. These corporate goons have the politicians and the money. But there's one thing that they don't have, but we do—and that's each other. And there are more of us than there are of them. When we learn to stand up together as one, we can stop this mess, and there's no doubt about that in my mind.

The thing that we have in front of us is to organize the people out there that say that we can't win. I've been targeting these people in my community. I don't want to hear it anymore. After two years of being treated like less than dirt, I'm sick of it. I'm tired of people that say we can't do anything.

In Decatur, we're fighting not only the corporation, but also the judges. We're fighting the police department. We're fighting scabs. And every day that I live in this world and meet new people, I learn that this is a worldwide war on workers. It's gotten to the point where we need to stand up with one voice—people of all races.

I know what it's like to live in America and be a so-called American—and be treated like dirt. So I can imagine what immigrants are going through in this country—because I've been through most of it. And when Black people vote for Proposition 187, it makes me sick. One thing I've learned in this life is that you can't take away someone else's right and expect them not to come for you. . . .

So the next time that some of those people come up to you—none of them come up to me anymore, because of them know who I am—and they start squawking about how they can't win, I'd like you to say something to the effect of this: If you dare to struggle, you dare to win. If you dare not to struggle, you don't deserve to win. And if you are one of those people who's afraid of being arrested, going to jail and losing everything that you've worked so hard for—just go home. Because they'll come for you last, and they'll take every damn thing that you have and everything that your children and your grandchildren have.

So it saddens me that there are people in this world who don't believe that they have the power to be a human being. And I am fortunate that I was raised in a time and in a family where I was taught that there is always a reason to get up every morning—no matter how poor you are, no matter what you don't have. I was raised with what really counted—caring for other people and for myself and having the goddam gall to say, "I will not go back."

· · ·

The Native environmental activist and writer Winona LaDuke is an Anishinabe from the Mississippi Band of the White Earth reservation in northern Minnesota. LaDuke, who helped to begin the White Earth Land Recovery Project and the Indigenous Women's Network, has twice run as the vice presidential running mate of consumer advocate Ralph Nader, in 1996 and again in 2000, both times on the Green Party ticket. On the campaign trail, LaDuke raised issues ignored by the other candidates, and spoke to the record of the Clinton administration on the environment and on other vital issues. Here is the text of her acceptance speech for the 1996 election, delivered in Saint Paul, Minnesota.

Winona LaDuke, Acceptance Speech for the Green Party's Nomination for Vice President of the United States of America (August 29, 1996)[3]

I am not inclined toward electoral politics. Yet I am impacted by public policy. I am interested in reframing the debate on the issues of this society—the distribution of power and wealth, the abuse of power and the rights of the natural world, the environment and the need to consider an amendment to the U.S. Constitution in which all decisions made today will be considered in light of their impact on the seventh generation from now. That is, I believe, what sustainability is all about. These are vital subjects which are all too often neglected by the rhetoric of "major party" candidates and the media.

I believe that decision making should not be the exclusive right of the privileged. That those who are affected by policy—not those who by default often stand above it—should be heard in the debate. It is the absence of this voice which unfortunately has come to characterize American public policy and the American political system.

As most of you probably know I live and work on the White Earth reservation in Northern Minnesota, the largest reservation in the state in terms of population and land base. And as most of you know—in terms of recent political and legal struggles—the site of a great deal of citizen activism and change in recent months. That is how I view myself, as a citizen activist. Yet I find that as small and rural as is my area of the northwoods, as small as my pond is, the decisions made in Washington still affect me. And it is the fact that decisions made by others, people who have never seen my face, never seen our lakes, never tasted our wild rice, or heard the cry of a child in Ponsford, have come to impact me and my community. I am here to say that all people have the right and responsibility to determine their destiny and I do not relinquish this right to PACs [political action committees], to lobbyists, and to decision makers who are far away.

When you live in one of the poorest sections of the country and in the state of Minnesota, you are able to understand, perhaps better, the impact of public policy. It is indeed my contention that there is no real quality of life in America until there is quality of life in the poorest regions of this America.

For instance over half of the American Indians on my reservation live in poverty. This represents five times the state average. Of particular concern is that nearly two thirds of the children on my reservation live in poverty. Also 90 percent of the children in female-headed households live in impoverished conditions. Median family income on my reservation is just slightly above half the state average for median income. Per capita income is at the same level. Unemployment on the reservation is at 49 percent according to recent BIA statistics. And nearly one-third of all Indians on the reservation have not attained a high school diploma. Finally it is absolutely critical to note that approximately 50 percent of the population on the reservation is under 25 years of age, indicating that these problems will need to be addressed over the long term.

What does that mean in the larger picture? Let me give you some examples.

Welfare reform legislation: This is the nation leading the world in terms of number of people in poverty. There are some 9 million children in this country in poverty. Welfare reform eliminates the safety net for those children. Now let me tell you about some real people. Native Americans are the poorest people in the country. Four out of 10 of the poorest counties in the nation are on Indian reservations. This is the same as White Earth. My daughter's entire third grade class with few exceptions is below the poverty level. The only choice those parents have with any hope—with 45 percent unemployment—is to work at the casino at about six bucks an hour. With two parents working and paying child care expenses, this makes them ostensibly the working poor. Not much different than being in poverty. So my friends, a family of seven who live in a two-bedroom trailer down the road from me—a fifteen-year-old trailer—on AFDC [Aid to Families with Dependent Children] have few options under the new welfare reform plan. I will not stand by mute as the safety net is taken away from those children and that third grade class.

Environmental policy: WTI Incinerator is a hazardous incinerator in East Liverpool, Ohio, located less than 1,000 feet from a school. It was visited by Al Gore in 1992 where he pledged if elected, it would not open. It did.

Endangered species: Bill Clinton said in 1992 that he would not allow a weakening of the Endangered Species Act, yet he signed an appropriations bill in 1994 that prohibits any funds to be used to unlist or list any species under the Endangered Species Act. This put a freeze on any action on over one thousand species that are waiting to be listed under the act. . . .

How about Indian policy? Lots of promises and no action. Two free lunches, some Kodak moments, and immense budget cuts. Indian policy has come far in America, there's no question. Until almost the end of the nineteenth century Indians were dealt with by the Department of War. Since then Indian people have been in the Department of Interior. We are the only humans in the Department of Interior treated as a natural resource. . . .

[U]ntil American domestic and foreign policy addresses quality of life issues for the poorest people in the country, we cannot say that there is quality of life. Until all of us are treated as peoples—with full human rights—we cannot tout a human rights record. Until policy decisions are made that do not benefit solely the 1 percent of the population which has more wealth than the bottom 90 percent of the population, I do not think that we can collectively say that we are talking about real economic and social benefits. And finally, until we have an environmental, economic, and social policy that is based on consideration of the impact on the seventh generation from now, we will still be living in a society that is based on conquest, not one that is based on survival.

• • •

Here we include two letters of protest from the prominent writers and activists Alice Walker and Adrienne Rich.

Two Open Letters of Protest to the Clinton Administration

The Clinton administration, despite a few gestures toward easing travel restrictions for Americans traveling there, maintained the harsh embargo on Cuba, a Cold War policy that for decades has prevented vital goods from entering the island nation. When the embargo was further tightened by passage of the Helms-Burton Act, Clinton signed the legislation. Alice Walker, the novelist and poet, responded with an open letter, excerpted here.

ALICE WALKER, LETTER TO PRESIDENT BILL CLINTON (MARCH 13, 1996)[4]

Dear President Clinton:

Thank you very much for the invitation to visit the White House while I was in Washington in January. I am sorry circumstances made it impossible for us to meet. I was looking forward to experiencing the symbolic seat of North American government in a new way. In the past, I have only picketed the White House, and as a student walking up and down the street outside it, I used to wonder might be inside. It seemed to bee made of cardboard, and appeared empty and oppressive, remote from the concerns of a few black students—and their courageous white teacher—from the deep South. . . .

The bill you have signed to further tighten the blockade hurts me deeply. I travel to Cuba whenever I can, to take medicine and the small, perhaps insignificant, comfort of my presence, to those whose courage and tenderness have inspired me practically my entire life.

I have seen how the embargo hurts everyone in Cuba, but especially Cuban children, infants in particular. I spend some nights in utter sleeplessness worrying about them. . . . I have taken seriously the beliefs and values I learned from my Georgia parents, the most sincere and humble Christians I have ever known: Do unto others . . . Love thy neighbor. . . . All of it. I feel the suffering of each child in Cuba as if it were my own.

The bill you have signed is wrong. . . . The bill is wrong, the embargo is wrong, because it punishes people, some of them unborn, for being who they are. Given their long struggle for freedom, particularly from Spain and the United States, they cannot help taking understandable pride in who they are. They have chosen a way of life different from ours, and I must say that from my limited exposure to that different way of life, it has brought them, fundamentally, a deep inner certainty about the meaning of existence (to develop one's self and to help others) and an equally deep psychic peace. One endearing quality I've found in the Cubans I have met is that they can listen with as much heart as they speak.

I believe you and Fidel must speak to each other. Face to face. He is not the monster he has been portrayed; and in all the study you have done of Cuba surely it is apparent to you that he has reason for being the leader he is. Nor am I saying he is without flaw. We are all substantially flawed, wounded, angry, hurt, here on Earth. But this human condition, so painful to us, and in some ways shameful—because we feel we are weak when the reality of ourselves is exposed—is made much more bearable when it is shared, face to face, in words that have expressive human eyes behind them. . . .

Is Jesse Helms who speaks of Cuban Liberty, as he urges our country to harm Cuba's citizens, the same Jesse Helms who caused by grandparents, my parents and my own generation profound suffering as wee struggled against our enslavement under racist laws in the South? And can it be that you have joined your name to his, in signing this bill? Although this is fact, it strikes me as unbelievable. Inconceivable. I cannot think his is the name you will rejoice in later years to have associated with your own. I regret this action, sincerely, for your sake.

The country has lost its way, such as it was. Primarily because it is now understood by all that that resources and space itself are limited, and the days of infinite expansion and exploitation, sometimes referred to as "growth" are over. Greed has been a primary motivating factor from the beginning. And so the dream of the revengeful and the greedy to re-take Cuba, never mind the crises of children who can no longer have milk to drink, or of adults whose ration card permits them one egg a week? You are a large man, how would you yourself survive? . . . .

I often disagree with you—your treatment of black women, of Lani Guinier and the wonderful Joycelyn Elders in particular, has caused me to feel a regrettable distance—still, I care about you, Hillary and Chelsea [Clinton], and wish you only good. I certainly would not deprive you of food in protest of anything you had done!

Similarly, I will always love and respect the Cuban people, and help them whenever I can. Their way of caring for all humanity has made them my family. Whenever you hurt them, or help them, please think of me.

• • •

When the poet Adrienne Rich found out that she had been awarded the National Medal for the Arts in 1997, she refused to accept it. She was continuing a tradition of writers and activists who have rejected this and similar honors from a government they opposed. Rich was particularly incensed by the Clinton administration's destruction of the New Deal program to help poor families with dependent children.

ADRIENNE RICH, LETTER TO JANE ALEXANDER REFUSING THE NATIONAL MEDAL FOR THE ARTS (JULY 3, 1997)[5]

Dear Jane Alexander,

I just spoke with a young man from your office, who informed me that I had been chosen to be one of twelve recipients of the National Medal for the Arts at a ceremony at the White House in the fall. I told him at once that I could not accept such an award from President Clinton or this White House because the very meaning of art, as I understand it, is incompatible with the cynical politics of this administration. I want to clarify to you what I meant by my refusal.

Anyone familiar with my work from the early Sixties on knows that I believe in art's social presence—as breaker of official silences, as voice for those whose voices are disregarded, and as a human birthright. In my lifetime I have seen the space for the arts opened by movements for social justice, the power of art to break despair. Over the past two decades I have witnessed the increasingly brutal impact of racial and economic injustice in our country.

There is no simple formula for the relationship of art to justice. But I do know that art—in my own case the art of poetry—means nothing if it simply decorates the dinner table of power which holds it hostage. The radical disparities of wealth and power in America are widening at a devastating rate. A President cannot meaningfully honor certain token artists while the people at large are so dishonored. I know you have been engaged in a serious and disheartening struggle to save government funding for the arts, against those whose fear and suspicion of art is nakedly repressive. In the end, I don't think we can separate art from overall human dignity and hope. My concern for my country is inextricable from my concerns as an artist. I could not participate in a ritual which would feel so hypocritical to me.

• • •

At the end of the 1991 Gulf War, the U.S. government worked with the United Nations to maintain strict sanctions on Iraq, a country that had just had its infrastructure badly damaged in the war. The sanctions excluded not only weapons, but materials vital for civilian needs and Iraq's infrastructure. In March 1991, a United Nations mission to Iraq reported a situation of "near-apocalyptic" destruction in the wake of the Gulf War with "most means of modern life support . . . destroyed or rendered tenuous." Although humanitarian groups repeatedly documented the serious consequences sanctions had on ordinary people in Iraq, the Bush and Clinton administrations continued them. A number of activists began to work to end the embargo against Iraq, in some cases traveling to Iraq to bring food, medicine, and toys, in violation of government edicts. Some were fined and threatened with jail when they returned to the United States and spoke out about the truth of the sanctions. In addition to imposing a strict embargo, the Clinton administration oversaw routine bombing raids of Iraq, launched from Turkey and Saudi Arabia. Here Rania Masri, a leading voice against U.S. targeting of Iraq and a founder of the Iraq Action Coalition, calls for an end to the cruel embargo of Iraq.

Rania Masri, "How Many More Must Die?" (September 17, 2000)[6]

Imagine what it feels like to live for 10 years under sanctions and bombardment. You're in Basra, Iraq's southern-most city. It's morning and 120 degrees in the shade. The electricity is off three hours out of every six. You're thirsty, but the tap water is unsafe to drink. You're hungry, but the monthly food ration has almost run out, and all that is left is some rice and tea. Your 8-year-old son has started screaming in fright again, as he does every time a fighter jet flies overhead. He is scared of the bombs that have been dropped almost daily. Your 4-year-old daughter is suffering from diarrhea, as a result of the dirty drinking water, and the doctor has said the simple medicine needed to cure her is not available. Most likely, your little girl will die in your arms.

This story is replayed in homes throughout much of Iraq.

Sanctions supporters claim this siege on Iraq is required to ensure that Iraq is disarmed. Even if true, how can we permit this continued killing of children through disease and malnutrition? And how can we continue this policy—or remain silent about this tragedy—when former weapons inspectors have repeatedly documented that Iraq is already disarmed?

Former lead weapons inspector Scott Ritter wrote in the *Boston Globe* in March that ". . . from a qualitative standpoint, Iraq has in fact been disarmed. . . . The chemical, biological, nuclear and long-range ballistic missile programs that were a real threat in 1991 had, by 1998, been destroyed or rendered harmless."

These sanctions have cost the United States as much as $19 billion a year in lost exports, according to a study by the Institute for International Economics. The same study found that economic sanctions have rarely achieved policy goals.

Sanctions supporters in the United States and Britain complain that the sanctions have failed in achieving their unwritten goal—that of removing the Iraqi regime. They also state that the sanctions have hurt the Iraqi people, not the regime. So why maintain these sanctions when they cause so much suffering?

Denis Halliday, after resigning in protest from his post as U.N. humanitarian coordinator for Iraq and U.N. assistant secretary general, said: "We are in the process of destroying an entire country. It is as simple and as terrifying as that."

U.S. and British bombing attacks continue against Iraq. In the past two years, more than 20,000 sorties have flown over Iraq. These bombing raids, which are not sanctioned by the U.N. Security Council, have cost the taxpayer an average of $1 billion a year and have killed more than 300 civilians in Iraq since December 1998.

Despite the horror of the regular bombardment, the sanctions kill many more people. For the past 10 years, U.N. reports have regularly documented the fatal effects of these sanctions. A 1998 UNICEF report stated that approximately 250 people, including 150 toddlers and infants, die every day in Iraq because of the sanctions.

A 1999 U.N. report further documented that Iraq "has experienced a shift from relative affluence to massive poverty. In marked contrast to the prevailing situation prior to the events of 1990–91, the infant mortality rates in Iraq today are among the highest in the world. . . . Chronic malnutrition affects every fourth child under 5 years of age. . . . The Iraqi health-care system is today in a decrepit state."

It is particularly disheartening since Iraqis used to enjoy one of the world's best and most accessible health-care systems. Furthermore, nearly half of the people in Iraq today do not have access to safe drinking water, in contrast to more than 90 percent before the imposition of sanctions in 1990.

The U.N. oil-for-food program, presented as "humanitarian relief" by the mainstream media, provides less than 70 cents per person daily. It is no surprise that UNICEF found that "the oil-for-food plan has not resulted in adequate protection of Iraq's children from malnutrition/disease. Those children spared from death continue to remain deprived of essential rights addressed in the Convention of Rights of the Child."

The solution? Lift the economic sanctions on the people of Iraq.

Seventy-plus members of Congress, along with the National Gulf War

Resource Center, former weapons inspectors, the U.N. Human Rights Commission, numerous national and international human-rights organizations and religious leaders, more than a dozen U.S. universities, and tens of thousands of concerned Americans have called for the immediate lifting of these sanctions.

I repeat the question that Hans von Sponeck, the second U.N. humanitarian coordinator in Iraq, asked in February before resigning in protest, "How long [should] the civilian population, which is totally innocent on all this, be exposed to such punishment for something that they have never done?"

• • •

In late November and early December 1999, financial leaders from many nations came to a meeting of the World Trade Organization (WTO) in Seattle, Washington. The WTO, like the World Bank and International Monetary Fund (IMF), was set up to oversee the functioning and expansion of global capitalism. But activists from around the world had planned their own summit in Seattle, a global convergence of environmentalists, trade unionists, student activists, radicals, and others who rejected the vision of the IMF, World Bank, and WTO: a world where companies and profits can cross borders, but people cannot; where corporations have rights, but trade unionists and peasants who work in the factories and fields do not; where profit is valued above people. Despite the best-laid plans of the WTO organizers, and massive police repression, tens of thousands of people demonstrated on the streets of Seattle. In response to the enormous protests, city authorities declared a "civil emergency" and imposed a curfew. Police, backed by the National Guard and state troopers, fired round after round of CS gas, as well as rubber bullets, at demonstrators. But the demonstrations delayed the opening of the WTO meeting and then contributed to its early collapse. News of the protests spread quickly around the world as the Independent Media Center (Indy Media) allowed activists to get around corporate news filters to tell the story of Seattle. Here is a first-hand report from the "Battle of Seattle" by Roni Krouzman, a journalist and organizer of the Campus Action Network.

Roni Krouzman, "WTO: The Battle in Seattle: An Eyewitness Account" (December 6, 1999)[7]

As I looked upon the sea of people occupying Fourth Street in downtown Seattle last Tuesday, I could not help but feel energized and proud. We were occupying the city and dancing in its streets. We were nonviolently stopping the WTO and corporate globalization. We were making history.

But when I left the demonstrations and turned on the local news, I heard talk of rioters and chaos, not singing and dancing. I heard talk of police restraint in the face of "anarchist" violence, not police brutality against nonviolent direct action. I heard talk of a city driven to the brink of collapse by "angry protesters," and not an unjust system of exploitation creatively and beautifully stopped in its tracks.

They say that truth is the first casualty of war. Unfortunately, it is also the first casualty of popular rebellion. Now it's time to set the record straight about what happened and is still happening in Seattle.

I witnessed and took part in an incredible week of action and thought, one that united diverse interests to creatively challenge a global order that places profits over people. On Friday night and all day Saturday, 2,500 of us attended a series of lectures and were motivated and informed by intelligent, inspiring people from across the U.S. and around the world. But the media wasn't there.

Teach-ins and workshops continued on Sunday, when the first sign of protests emerged. Several hundred people, including French farmer and anti-globalization activist Jose Bové, demonstrated in front of a downtown McDonald's, creatively and energetically. Toward the end of the rally, someone broke a window, and that's what the media concentrated on.

That night I stumbled upon the Convergence Center, Seattle's grassroots direct action headquarters, and could not believe what I saw. Hundreds of young people filled this commercial space on Capitol Hill, milling about three massive rooms cluttered with flyers, banners and props. They all seemed so engaged, holding discussions in intimate circles, creating signs and teaching each other about civil disobedience and legal aid, and occasionally studying a giant 200 square foot map of the city that hung from a wall.

Suddenly, an activist barged in on a bustling meeting and announced that people had seized a vacant building downtown, and they needed our help to protect it from police. We walked those ten blocks briskly, and arrived just in time to see people in masks on top of the building unfurl a banner that read, "Housing is a right, not a privilege."

I returned to the Convergence Center the next day, and participated in the general spokescouncil meeting, a five hour affair during which delegates, representing one of thirteen clusters of three to four affinity groups each, each themselves composed of five to twenty members, finalized plans for Tuesday's actions. The meeting felt frustrating at times, but it was the essence of grassroots democracy, with each representative speaking his or her mind, and conferring with fellow affinity group representatives that sat beside them to plan a coherent, well-organized strategy.

After that meeting, I understood the giant map. Each cluster would occupy one of thirteen intersections surrounding the Washington Convention and Trade

Center, and nonviolently shut it down. Incredible that such a well-organized effort could be planned so creatively and democratically.

That evening, I attended the Peoples' Gala, an anti-corporate festival featuring music, comedy, and inspiring words. And seeing steelworkers sitting beside vegans, old lefties beside new, I was inspired indeed.

I could hardly relax enough to close my eyes that night, and awoke to my radio alarm at 5 a.m., one hour after I'd finally managed to fall asleep. I left my ID on the night table, donned a sweater, coat and poncho, packed my bag, and began my trek through the cold, wet, pre-dawn hours, confident that today, I would make history.

Our rain-soaked rally began shortly before 7 a.m., long after dozens of affinity groups had slipped in to the night to occupy the city. We sang and we huddled, and cheered when the head of the longshoreman union announced that there would be no business in West Coast ports that day. And over and over again, we hear the code of nonviolence repeated: no alcohol, no drugs, no physical or verbal assault, no property damage.

As the sun began to filter through the morning clouds, we began our march through a waking city, a contingent of steelworkers leading the way. We hit the first police barricade of many shortly thereafter, thousands of us facing down a few dozen cops, who stood guarding one of the many streets that led to the convention center. And so the march continued around the city, with groups of ten and twenty and fifty at a time leaving the procession to join the activists who had seized those 13 intersections. We cheered, and we chanted, and we felt in control everywhere I looked, I saw rivers of demonstrators milling excitedly through the streets.

And then the tear gas and the rubber bullets came. At midmorning, the police went on the offensive, demanding a mass of at least one thousand non-violent demonstrators positioned at the intersection of Sixth and Union disperse to make way for WTO delegates. We did not, and as dozens of demonstrators sat down in front of the police line, a squadron of ten officers carrying what appeared to be automatic or semi-automatic machine guns charged over them from behind, trampling several.

The crowd booed and jeered, refusing to disperse and chanting, "We're nonviolent, how about you?" Riot-gear clad police responded with a barrage of tear gas, overcoming dozens with noxious fumes and causing hundreds of us to flee the intersection. Some protesters quickly donned gas masks, refusing to give up their ground, and were met with a hail of rubber bullets. At least two were struck, one in the leg and one in the mouth. Legal observers reported that neither was seriously injured.

Demonstrators were shocked and confused, but did not panic, as direct action medics and other activists rushed to the aid of the injured. Thousands chanted,

"Shame!" and "The World is Watching!" amidst an eerie cloud of white gas and the steady hum of helicopters flying overhead.

By late morning, Seattle's coffee shops were buzzing with talk of the actions, which had now drawn over 5,000 demonstrators and hundreds of police, and diverted car and bus traffic from half the downtown area. As the day progressed and tensions mounted, some protesters adopted more aggressive tactics. Several young activists rolled van-sized garbage dumps into alleyways and intersections, including the intersection of Fourth and University. At noon, police ordered the raucous crowd there to disperse, and fired tear gas canisters when it refused. Hundreds of us fled yet again as some demonstrators threw the canisters back at the officers.

On the northern side of the Convention Center, along Pike Street, several small groups of youths dressed in black and donning ski masks or bandanas damaged property at stores including Nike Town, Old Navy, and Planet Hollywood. To the chagrin of activists who had attempted to enforce a code of nonviolence, they scrawled anti-corporate graffiti on walls and displays, and smashed corporate store windows with hammers, crowbars, and street signs, destroying a Starbucks storefront.

The overwhelming majority of activists did not engage in such activities, successfully blocking access to the Convention Center for 2,500 to 3,000 delegates through well-coordinated, nonviolent civil disobedience. In an effort to break the protesters' grip, police moved to take more intersections, shooting streams of pepper spray at nonviolent protesters who were sitting around the intersection of Sixth and Union, and attempting to break through their lines with an armored personal carrier. The police did not succeed, drawing chants of "Protect and Serve!" from an outraged crowd. Similar clashes erupted throughout downtown, with floods of protestors weaving in and out of key intersections—and securing them with barricades—visible in every direction. Police moved to take the intersections back one by one, and were often surrounded on both sides by thousands of demonstrators. I could not believe what I was seeing.

At 2 p.m., an estimated 25,000 activists, mainly union rank and file, marched into downtown from a rally at Memorial Stadium, joining the ten thousand or so direct action activists who had seized control of the city. The demonstrations displayed a level of diversity rare in American movements, as anarchists, environmentalists, and vegan hippies marched side by side with teamsters, steelworkers, and social justice activists. . . .

My week in Seattle was unlike anything I had ever seen, or ever thought I would see. Unlike many protests I had attended, the participants in Seattle were overwhelmingly young—people in their twenties, people in college, people in high school. The scope of the demonstrations was incredible as well; the Seattle protests were marked by a level of diversity, organization, and nonviolent direct action not witnessed in the United States in years, perhaps since Chicago, 1968, with activists of all stripes sharing thoughts and experiences with one another. Finally, we actually succeeded. We shut down the WTO, and prevented it from reaching a world trade agreement.

Our success had a lot to do with grassroots organizing processes and structures, made evident by a week of teach-ins, human chains, and grassroots mobilizations. It also had a lot to do with the issue. The WTO has managed to bring so many different and in the past, conflicting interests together because corporate globalization affects everyone and everything on the planet. This movement is not just about protecting labor rights or sea turtles. It's about demanding a say, and taking power back from the institutions, corporations, and governments that rule our lives and our communities.

The mainstream media have painted the story as one of police attempting to restore order, instead of police using police-state tactics to create chaos and trample on the constitutional rights of thousands of nonviolent demonstrators and bystanders. I know what really happened. I saw it with my own eyes. I took part in the meetings. I marched through the streets. I smelled the tear gas, and ducked to avoid the rubber bullets. Seattle marked a real watershed, with people of diverse beliefs coming together to demand a just, democratic world. Now we can only hope they return to their communities and begin the difficult work of making that world a reality. The Battle of Seattle may very well have been the first "shot across the bow" of a global peoples' movement grassroots organizers had hoped for.

• • •

The organization ADAPT (American Disabled for Attendant Programs Today) began as a part of the civil rights struggle to gain access to public transportation. It was also instrumental in forcing the government to pass the Americans with Disabilities Act of 1990. But the Act hardly resolved all of the problems facing the disabled, including forced institutionalization, inadequate health care, continued lack of access to buildings, and workplace discrimination. Here Denver-based activist Anita Cameron describes a protest against builders who refused to comply with federal regulations for constructing accessible homes.

Anita Cameron, "And the Steps Came Tumbling Down—ADAPT's Battle with the HBA" (2000)[8]

Thursday, March 2nd, as the Home Builders Association was having their Home Solutions 2000 Expo at Denver's Currigan Hall, ADAPT held its own Home Solutions Expo out front on its first of four days of protest against the Home

Builder's Association of Metropolitan Denver. ADAPT had tried to work with the HBA for about a year trying to get them to comply with the Fair Housing Law and build homes with access. Meetings, letters and committee work were to no avail. It is apparent that the HBA does not want their members building homes with access. The HBA actually wants the Fair Housing Law repealed! They feel that access should be provided on an as-needed basis, and feel that single-family detached homes, townhomes, and condos should continue to be exempted from accessibility requirements. Something had to be done.

That is why about 80 ADAPT members from Colorado and Kansas were at Currigan Hall on that cold Thursday evening, sending the HBA a strong message. We had great exhibits of our own to show. There was an accessible Barbie doll-house, complete with an elevator. We had two doorways—one accessible, and the other inaccessible, which we went through to demonstrate the usefulness of one, and uselessness of the other. There were pictures of the buildings that Atlantis had bought and remodeled for access, as well as educational materials on accessibility. We even had petitions and flyers with ADAPT's demands—30 percent of all new homes to be accessible, 30 percent of all new homes to be visitable, meaning a no-step entrance and an accessible bath on the first floor, and clear enforcement mechanisms in Colorado's Fair Housing Law. We marched, sang, and chanted and several ADAPT members spoke of the need for accessible homes and told stories of being forced to buy inaccessible homes, or even move out of state due to the lack of accessible housing. The cops came around trying to get us to leave, but there wasn't much they could do since we were on the sidewalk for the most part.

Friday, we were back with more awesome ADAPT stuff, including some gorgeous styrofoam steps that Pat [King], our wheelchair repair guy had made. After Dawn [Russell]'s rousing speech, everyone had a chance to tear down the steps with a wooden mallet. Afterwards, we formed a gauntlet in front of the steps to the front doors and passed out flyers. Later we made a human chain chanting "The People United Will Never Be Defeated."

On Saturday, back again, we saw that the cops had put up barricades which we quickly removed and got down to the business of letting the HBA know that they weren't going to "turn us around." Joe Ehman, an ADAPT member who is on the AIA [Architectural Inclusion and Access] committee, did a cool mock up of Roger Reinhardt, the HBA vice-president who had insulted ADAPT in a meeting a few weeks earlier by calling us simple-minded. Several of us gave interviews with the press, some of us paid to get inside the exhibit to speak with the various builders and contractors about access and pass out a couple of flyers, if we could. Only one small exhibit out of hundreds that had anything remotely to do with access. This time, the cops sent out a trained negotiator to tell us the police wanted ADAPT to stay in this "area" that they had designated by the barricades. We told him that if he brought Roger

Reinhardt out to speak to us, that we would leave. A few minutes later, he brought Roger out, but he had nothing to offer us but the same tired old discriminatory solutions that ADAPT would not accept. We kept our word, though, and left with a warning from the police that if we came back tomorrow, and did not stay within the barricades, that we would be arrested. Little did they know. . . .

On Sunday, we swept in, meaning nothing but business. We quickly sped up the ramps and began blocking and handcuffing ourselves to doors. The cops were there, but not quick enough to stop us. They began yelling out warnings, and soon, the arrests began. When the dust cleared, 17 ADAPT members were arrested and charged with blocking, and refusing to obey a lawful order.

The Home Builders Association tour of homes was another target of protests in July. After ignoring ADAPT's call for an accessible house in the Tour of Homes, for which the home builders build a series of new homes, this showcase even became an action packed showcase. Crawling into homes, picketing outside and eventually committing civil disobedience, Colorado ADAPT members sent the homebuilders a message that access can no longer be blown off. Challenging the Homebuilders to stop ignoring access to housing for people with disabilities, ADAPT continues their drive to end the excuses.

• • •

Elizabeth ("Betita") Martínez has spent years as a leading Chicana writer, educator, and organizer. A cofounder of the Institute for MultiRacial Justice in San Francisco, she was active in SNCC and then worked from 1968 to 1976 in New Mexico, where she edited the newspaper *El Grito del Norte* (Cry of the North) and co-founded the Chicano Communications Center. Martínez wrote and compiled the groundbreaking bilingual book *500 Years of Chicano History in Pictures*, a classic in people's history. Here Martínez reports from the front lines of youth protest against the criminalization of immigrants and young people in California.

Elizabeth ("Betita") Martínez, "'Be Down with the Brown!'" (1998)[9]

For ten days that shook Los Angeles, in March 1968, Chicano and Chicana high school students walked out of class to protest a racist educational system. The "blowouts," as they were called, began with several thousand students from six barrio schools, then increased every day for a week until more than 10,000 had struck. Shouting "Chicano Power!" and "¡Viva la revolución!" they brought the city's school system—the largest in the United States—to a total halt.

As scholar-activist Carlos Muñoz Jr. later wrote in his book *Youth, Identity, Power*, the strike was "the first time Chicano students had marched en masse in their own demonstration against racism and for educational change." Not only that; it was the first mass protest specifically focused on racism by any Chicanas or Chicanos in U.S. history. (This is not to deny the many huge strikes of Raza workers with labor demands that often had their roots in racist conditions on the job.) With the 1968 protests, students moved beyond the prevailing politics of accommodation to a new cry for "Chicano Power!"

The blowouts sparked other protests, including the first action ever by Chicano university students, at San Jose State College, and then Chicano participation in the long, militant Third World student strikes at San Francisco State and the University of California, Berkeley. New Raza college-student organizations emerged, while existing ones grew rapidly. All this took place at a time of youth rebellion nationwide and worldwide—from Mexico to France to Japan. Here, Raza students stood out because the great majority came from the working class. Their main goal was affirmation of their own culture's values and history rather than a counter-culture, such as many Anglo youth were celebrating.

Almost 30 years later, Raza high school students from California to Colorado repeated that history with new blowouts demanding more Latino teachers and counselors; Ethnic Studies (not only Latino but also African-American, Native American and Asian/Pacific Islander); bilingual education sensitive to students' cultural needs; and Latino student-retention programs. Other issues were often added; in California, these included combating repressive new anti-crime laws, preventing the re-election of right-wing Gov. Pete Wilson and fighting Proposition 187 with its inhumane call to deny educational and health services to anyone suspected of being undocumented.

California's blowouts focused on public schools in the northern part of the state at first, then spread south. The students, mostly of Mexican or Salvadoran background, came from high school, junior high and sometimes elementary school. Why a walkout during school hours rather than a march or rally on the weekend? Because, as they learned, California's public schools lose $17.20 or more for each unexcused absence per day. This pocketbook damage provided the economic centerpiece of the students' strategy. With it, they made history.

The first wave seemed to burst out of nowhere. On April 1, 1993, more than 1,000 mostly Latino junior high and high school students walked out of a dozen Oakland schools. On September 16, celebrated as Mexican Independence Day, more than 4,000 blew out in Oakland, Berkeley, San Jose, and the town of Gilroy. Arrests and violence were rare, although in Gilroy police did arrest teenager Rebecca Armendariz and harassed her for months with charges of contributing to the delinquency of a minor, apparently because she signed to rent a bus that students used. In right-wing-dominated Orange County, 300 students clashed with police while some were beaten and pepper-sprayed.

Another wave of student strikes unrolled in November and December in northern California. In Exeter, a small town in California's generally conservative Central Valley, 500 high school students boycotted classes when a teacher told an embarrassed youth who had declined to lead the Pledge of Allegiance in English: "If you don't want to do it, go back to Mexico." It was the kind of remark that had been heard too many times in this school where 40 percent of the 1,200 students—but only six of their teachers—are Latino.

At Mission High School in San Francisco, 200 Latino and other students demonstrated for the same anti-racist reasons as elsewhere, and also for being stereotyped as gangbangers if they wore certain kinds of clothing. The school board agreed to their main demand for Latino Studies, and then offered just one class—to be held before and after the regular school day. The basic message: this concession isn't for real.

On to February 2, 1994, which marked the anniversary of the signing of the 1848 Treaty of Guadalupe Hidalgo confirming the U.S. takeover of half of Mexico—today's Southwest. In Sacramento, the walkout movement spread like wildfire. Some 500 high school students and supporters from various districts shook up the state capital. "The governor wants more prisons, we want schools. He wants more cops, we want more teachers. We want an education that values and includes our culture. We want all cultures to know about themselves," they said, as reported by the local paper *Because People Matter*.

For César Chávez's birthday in March, nearly 150 Latino students from four city schools marched on district offices in Richmond. On April 18, half of the elementary school pupils in the town of Pittsburgh boycotted classes, with parental support, because a Spanish-speaking principal had been demoted. They had their tradition: 20 years before, Pittsburgh elementary school students had boycotted for lack of a Latino principal.

The spring wave climaxed on April 22 with a big, coordinated blowout involving more than 30 schools in northern California. It was unforgettable. Some 800 youth gathered in San Francisco under signs such as "Educate, Don't Incarcerate" and "Our Story Not His-story," and with beautiful banners of Zapata and armed women of the Mexican Revolution.

Calls for unity across racial and national lines and against gang warfare rang out all day. "Don't let the lies of the United Snakes divide us!" "Latin America doesn't stop with Mexico," said a Peruvian girl. Another shouted, "It's not just about Latinos or Blacks or Asians, this is about the whole world!" Some of the loudest cheers rang out from a 16-year-old woman who cried "We've got to forget these [gang] colors!"

In the town of Hayward that day, 1,500 high school and junior high students boycotted more than 20 schools. About 300 of them turned in their red or blue gang rags for brown bandannas—brown for Brown Power and unity. Later some of them set up a meeting to help stop the violence. "You wear the brown rag, be down. Be all the way down for every Raza," said Monica Manriquez, age 17.

Cinco de Mayo, May 5, brought more blowouts, followed by a June gathering in Los Angeles of 900 high school students. The youth themselves were startled by their own success. Sergio Arroyo, 16, of Daly City, spoke what others were thinking: "People didn't think it could happen, all that unity, but it did." Lucretia Móntez from Hayward High said "We're making history. Yeah, we're making history."

• • •

Author Walter Mosley is best known for his Easy Rawlins mystery series, which he started in 1990 with the novel *Devil in a Blue Dress*. Mosley, an Artist-in-Residence at the Africana Studies Institute, New York University, has also been active in encouraging independent publishing efforts by African Americans. In 2000, he published *Workin' on the Chain Gang*, raising important questions about a society that is ruled by the drive for profit.

Walter Mosley, *Workin' on the Chain Gang* (2000)[10]

The slaves in America and the serfs in Russia were freed at about the same time. The chains were laid out in front of them and the doors to the plantation were opened wide. Most slaves, most serfs, stayed on the plantation of their own accord, not because they liked it but because survival seemed reliant upon servitude.

Today the worker accepts more hours at a lower wage (or at an equal or higher wage that has lower value) or fewer hours, which mean the loss of health care and other benefits. All this for profit. When a slave is freed you can be sure that it is because she will make more profit for the plantation boss as a free agent. When a worker is lauded he's probably sweating gold.

Profit is made on a grand scale in America, but most of us don't share in it. Most of us work for dollars that fluctuate in value, at workplaces where the managers never really care about us or our hearts. We live within the margin of profit. We are the margin of profit. The money taken from our labor is used to buy political power that does not represent us. Our taxes pay for federally licensed air waves we do not control, for S&L [savings and loan] bailouts, for public inquiries into the president's privates, and for law enforcement agencies and judges who can't keep heroin out of our children's reach.

Broken roads and nonexistent stoplights, children who can't read, and prisons that are private businesses—this is also the margin, the margin of profit.

The verb, then, is marginalize. We are marginalized by the profit of capitalism. We are footnotes to Citibank and the Mobil Oil Corporation and Chiquita Brands International (once known as the United Fruit Company). We are the edges that form the outline of the behemoth that tells us he is the only way.

God, this monster would have it, is defined by the margin of profit. We pray to him and sacrifice to him, we give our children up to him, and he's never given a single sign that he cares. This is because he cannot care. Labor is a commodity that is useful only as long as it is disposable. Working hands can be replaced by cheaper or more efficient labor, but if those hands can't be cut away at a moment's notice, they become a liability.

The world of profit is a world of plunder. Advancement is defined by this margin but not by the quality of life or goodness. Fair, for profit, is what you can get away with. And everything is a commodity—love and hatred and the drugs you need to keep on breathing.

If profit is the only way, that is a sad state of affairs. It's a locked door, and somebody has thrown away the key. . . .

I'd like to say that the answer to the problem is the simple abandonment of the economic system that rules us. We should all work together, we should all live well. Give our all and share in the wealth; it's a beautiful notion, and maybe our children's children will have learned enough to make such a world work. But we, like the slaves of the nineteenth century, have been conditioned to imprisonment defined by the alienation of our labor: We give 100 percent and receive somewhat less in return. We take what we are given and make what we can of it between the demands placed upon us for the privilege of freedom.

Fine. For the moment, let's accept the system. Let's agree that the corporate, capitalist, alienated form of labor is what we have to work with. Still, can't we make a few demands? Can't we ask a few questions about ourselves on the coffee break and during commercials?

The margin of profit, among other things, defines our labor; more, it defines our humanity. The job you hold, the income you bring home, the recognition of your value to society, are all deeply informed by your labors. And if the system defines you, then it owes you something too. The question is, what are you owed?

This question must be articulated and answered by at least 10 percent of the population. Ten percent is an arbitrary number. I'm simply saying that the number of people that it takes to make political change is actually quite small. A fraction of the populace that is sure of what changes are necessary can change the minds of their neighbors. Truth . . . comes in small packages. During the twelve weeks of abstinence from arena sports and electronic media you could ask yourself what it is that you deserve for a lifetime of labor. Make a list. Share it with whoever will listen.

Maybe you think that a medical bill of rights makes sense. Maybe you think that every American child deserves an excellent education. Maybe you believe that the child-bearing job, not yet a property of capitalism, should be remunerated and revered by the state. Write it down and spread it around.

Maybe we need more doctors and scientists, and maybe the output from these laborers should be the communal property of the people. Maybe the margin of profit that works for cornflakes should be monitored more closely when it comes to medicine and war. Maybe profit and medicine don't mix.

Maybe you need a place to sleep and you won't sleep soundly until you know that everyone is safe and sound here in the bosom of the richest nation in the history of the world.

Make a list; put it in your wallet. Take it out now and then to tinker with it or expand it. Make decisions based on this list. Vote by it and argue for its claims. Compare the ideas of your bosses and political leaders with what you think is right. Then make another list, this time of those people and systems that support your notions. Notice who and what is missing from this list.

The goals of revolution are realized by personal enlightenment. Don't buy somebody else's list; don't clip one from the newspaper. It's not in Mao's "little red book" or in the Declaration of Independence either. Any life that you can attain must be, in part, the production of your own mind. What you need is missing from your life right now. Reach out for it. Define it. Then demand it from the world.

This simple exercise is nothing new, I know. I am not trying to innovate. Innovation, when it comes to a population in the billions, can easily lead to mass murder. I'm simply trying to lay a few notions next to each other: the margin of profit to the right, a list of my demands to the left. The TV is off, the election is next year, it's evening, and, like Sisyphus, I have a few moments before I have to continue the labors forced upon me by the gods.

Once you throw your chip into the game, the odds are changed, the revolution of enlightenment gains, and the margin of profit quavers toward a counter move.

• • •

Julia Butterfly Hill lived atop a 1,000-year-old redwood in Humboldt County, California, for 738 days to prevent the Pacific Lumber Company from chopping it down. From December 1997 to December 1999, Hill engaged in this act of civil disobedience to draw attention not only to the destruction of ancient redwoods, but to the global assault on the environment. Eventually, Pacific Lumber agreed never to cut down the tree, which she named Luna, and said it would also protect nearby trees. Here Hill reflects on her motivations for the protest.

Julia Butterfly Hill, "Surviving the Storm: Lessons from Nature" (2001)[11]

I didn't come from a background of activism, but when I first saw what was happening to the ancient redwoods in California, I fell to the ground and started crying and immediately got involved. It changed my life. Everyone thinks, when they hear I'm the poster child of tree huggers, that I must be a hard-core radical extremist, whacko, granola-munching, you name it—all in capital letters, with quotes. But, I was just dumped in the deep end of the entire movement—not just tree-sitting, not just forest issues, but the whole social, environmental, and consciousness movement—and said to myself: Better swim or you're going to drown! So I started learning how to swim.

Along the way I learned: by watching and talking, by asking questions, and by listening over and over during the 738 days that I sat in the ancient spreading branches of Luna. I saw how each different tactic is used and why it's being used. I realized that the best tools for dismantling the machine are the ones the mechanics are using to keep it running. I saw very early on that the mechanics in this situation are corporations, corporate media, and the government—all in a kind of collusion together. They say only a little bit, and usually a majority of what they say is skewed so that the participant on the other end (whether they're watching, listening, or reading) doesn't get the truth. And if you don't have the truth, then you cannot make an informed decision. And if you don't have an informed decision, then you cannot take a conscious act. And if you do not take a conscious act, then you're part of the annihilation of the gift of life, period.

I saw that some of the tactics activists were using were not working, because they weren't using the tools of the mechanic. They were going out there and sitting in trees. They were getting beaten up, killed, or thrown into jail with ridiculous charges by cops who pepper sprayed them. But nobody except the local community knew they were out there.

It was kind of like preaching to the choir. And we need to do that to inspire. I spend a lot of time preaching to the already converted because it hurts to care in today's world. It's easy to go numb and tune it out, whether you're 15, 25, or 50. But we still need to care, and to do that we need truth and inspiration, information and hope—that gives us the tools to take conscious actions toward positive change. At the same time, though, we must utilize the tools of the mechanics (who are trying to keep the machine running) in order to take it down. Otherwise, it's like trying to use a hammer to turn a screw.

I was in a situation with Luna where I had to learn to listen to nature and respect it, or die. My life was on such a precipice the entire time I was up there. It was just really fragile in so many ways. The first three months were so hard that I was praying to die. I didn't want to hurt that bad anymore. And yet at the same time I didn't want to give up. But, when death did start to come, I started praying for life. I was constantly on this emotional roller coaster—spiritually and physically. It was one assault after the other.

One day, they were cutting down trees all around me, and I started crying and hugging Luna. I was crying because I felt ashamed to be in white skin. I felt ashamed to be part of a race of people who perpetuated genocide thousands of years ago and have now made it our mission to perpetuate genocide on the rest of the planet and life in all its forms. It was eating me alive from the inside out. I was so angry and so hurt and ashamed, and I held onto Luna and was crying and apologizing over and over, saying: I'm so sorry. I'm so sorry.

When I finally sat up, I realized I was covered in sap. Climbing around in Luna before, I had gotten a little bit of sap on me, but I had never been covered like I was this day. I realized that sap was pouring out from all over her, actually pouring. I could see the sap flowing, which I had never really seen before, and it hit me: this was Luna communicating her grief. Sap is just like grief. It's not something you can wash away; it clings to you and becomes a part of who you are. And it was then that I realized nature was communicating to me. (Later on, people sent me scientific proof that sap is one of the ways trees communicate!)

I started paying attention. I started listening and getting answers from everything—from Luna, the birds, the bears, the shapes of the pine needles. Everything became my teacher when I opened up. My relationship with Luna grew. I realized that Luna has been communicating with humankind for 1,000 years, and we just forgot how to listen. But I learned how to listen, and from that moment on everything started coming to me. Sometimes, I'd have to get beaten over the head a little bit before I'd go: Oh yeah, thank you. What are you trying to tell me? My connection with Luna and my connection with nature is what kept me going, kept me alive, helped teach me the vital lessons I needed to learn when I was about to give up or make a very big mistake. I'm forever thankful for that.

One of the lessons I learned and something that I use a lot now is how to survive a storm. I nearly died up there, in the worst winter storms recorded in the history of California. The trees taught me that the way to make it through those storms (and the storms of life) is to stay rooted and centered but not rigid. The trees and branches that try too hard to stand strong and straight are the ones that break. The only ones that make it through are the ones that know to bend and flow and let go. So, I've been using that now in my life. I use it when I'm being bar-raged by the media, by grassroots activists, by mainstream community, by every-thing. I just bend and flow when I see the wind coming; I loosen up and get ready to get blown, and then I kind of flex back into place. And I'm ready to get up the next morning and do it all over again.

The legacy that I left behind was a vision of a better world. We protected a grove of old-growth forest. And we left a living embodiment of what that vision of a bet-ter world is all about: a world where the last of our ancient and old-growth forests and wild places are protected. A world where the watersheds we're all a part of are protected, even if we live in LA, Chicago, Detroit, or New York City. All those places that look nothing like nature anymore are actually a part of a watershed, and that watershed is the nature that beats its pulse underneath the asphalt and the concrete and steel. That watershed is our lifeblood, what keeps us alive.

To live a life of service for a better world is a legacy that doesn't disappear. It's an imprint, and that imprint can be negative or positive, depending upon the actions and choices we make every single moment of every single day. I have to tell you the coolest people I've ever met, young and old, are the ones who are out there giving their life for a good cause. They glow more; they're the most beauti-ful, magnificent, powerful people I've ever seen. They're much more powerful than the richest person and more beautiful than any model, because their beauty and power resonates from deep within the life force all the way through their body, and shines out. I've never wanted to kneel in front of a model or an actor or actress or a corporate billionaire, but I want to bow myself before people who are activists or who work for the common good. That's honor. Money is not honor. Doing something of real value with one's life is honor.

Bush II and the "War on Terror"

Michael Moore, "The Presidency—Just Another Perk" (November 14, 2000)

Orlando Rodriguez and Phyllis Rodriguez, "Not In Our Son's Name" (September 15, 2001)

Rita Lasar, "To Avoid Another September 11, U.S. Must Join the World" (September 5, 2002)

Monami Maulik, "Organizing in Our Communities Post–September 11th" (2001)

International Brotherhood of Teamsters Local 705, "Resolution Against the War" (October 18, 2002)

Rachel Corrie, Letter from Palestine (February 7, 2003)

Danny Glover, Speech During the World Day of Protest Against the War (February 15, 2003)

Amy Goodman, "Independent Media in a Time of War" (2003)

Tim Predmore, "How Many More Must Die?" (August 24, 2003)

Maritza Castillo et al., Open Letter to Colonel, U.S. Army (Ret.) Michael G. Jones (September 12, 2003)

Kurt Vonnegut, "Cold Turkey" (May 31, 2004)

Patti Smith, "People Have the Power" (1988)

The undemocratic nature of the American voting system, always dominated by the two major parties, became glaringly evident in the election of 2000. In that year, George W. Bush failed to get more votes than his opponent, Al Gore. But Bush was nonetheless installed as president by the Supreme Court. The Court refused a full recount of the votes in the state of Florida, where enormous voting problems had occurred, and gave Bush the election, declaring that he had won a majority of the electoral college.

On September 11, 2001, in one of the most horrific events in U.S. history, terrorists hijacked passenger planes and flew them into the Twin Towers of downtown

New York, and into the Pentagon, killing close to three thousand people. Bush immediately declared a "war on terror," and soon invaded and bombed Afghanistan, where Osama bin Laden, the presumed mastermind of the September 11 attacks, was hiding.

Thousands of Afghan people were killed in the ferocious bombing attacks, and hundreds of thousands displaced from their homes. The cruel Taliban regime was overthrown, but disorder continued in Afghanistan, Osama bin Laden was not found, and many of the same people were soon again in power.

The following year, 2002, the Bush administration began a propaganda campaign to convince the American people that Iraq had "weapons of mass destruction" and was a threat serious enough to warrant going to war. When the other countries in the United Nations were not entirely persuaded of this, the Bush administration, which had declared its right to wage a "pre-emptive" war unilaterally, attacked Iraq in March 2003.

The invasion began with a brief but intense bombing attack, and Baghdad was soon occupied. The U.S. government achieved its long-standing policy of "regime change" in Iraq. Saddam Hussein was removed from power. But several thousand Iraqi civilians were dead, and many more wounded after a deadly campaign called "Shock and Awe." The U.S. military occupation, with more than one hundred and forty thousand troops in the country, was resisted by the Iraqi population, with daily violent attacks and mounting casualties.

A majority of Americans at first supported the war, but disillusionment grew as it was revealed that the Bush administration had misled the public about Iraqi weapons and about Iraq's alleged links to the September 11 attacks. Families of people who had died on September 11 organized to protest the idea that war was the way to deal with terrorism. GIs in Iraq began to speak up against the war.

Amber Amundson, whose husband, an army pilot, was killed in the attack on the Pentagon, said: "I have heard angry rhetoric by some Americans, including many of our nation's leaders, who advise a heavy dose of revenge and punishment. To those leaders, I would like to make clear that my family and I take no comfort in your words of rage. If you choose to respond to this incomprehensible brutality by perpetuating violence against other innocent human beings, you may not do so in the name of justice for my husband. Your words and imminent acts of revenge only amplify our family's suffering."

That sentiment began to be felt by more and more people. By the summer of 2004, a national poll showed that a majority of the American public was opposed to the war.

· · ·

One of the most prominent voices against the Bush administration was that of Michael Moore, the documentary filmmaker and populist agitator. He sent out this column to the many readers of his Web site one week after the deeply flawed 2000 election.

Michael Moore, "The Presidency—Just Another Perk" (November 14, 2000)[1]

Dear Governor and President-in-Waiting Bush:

This has to be the first time in our history that a candidate who is losing *both* the popular vote *and* the electoral vote insists on being anointed President of the United States.

I can understand why you expect this title to be yours. You have spent your entire life having everything handed to you. You have never had to earn your place. Money and name alone have opened every door for you. Without effort or hard work or intelligence or ingenuity, you have been bequeathed a life of privilege.

You learned at an early age that, in America, all someone like you has to do is show up. You found yourself admitted to a wealthy New England boarding school simply because your name was Bush. You did not have to *earn* your place there. It was bought for you.

You then learned you could get into Yale with a "C" average. Other, more deserving, students who had worked hard for 12 years to earn their place at Yale were denied admittance. You got in because your name was Bush.

You got into Harvard the same way. After screwing off during your four years at Yale—and maintaining your "C" average—you took someone's else's seat at Harvard, a seat that they had *earned.*

You then pretended to serve a full stint in the Texas Air National Guard. But one day, according to the *Boston Globe*, you just skipped out and didn't report back for a year and a half to your unit. You didn't have to earn your military record because your name was Bush.

After a number of "lost years" that don't appear in your official biography, you were given job after job by your daddy and other family members—jobs you didn't have to earn. No matter how many of your business ventures failed, there was always another one waiting to be handed to you. Finally, you got to be a partner in a ball team—another gift—even though you put up only 1/100 of the money for the team. And then you convinced the taxpayers of Arlington, Texas, to give you another perk—a brand-new multi-million dollar stadium.

So it is no wonder to me why you think you deserve to be named President. You've haven't earned it or won it—therefore it must be yours!

And you see nothing wrong with this.

Why should you? It is the only life you have ever known.

I will never forget the footage of you sitting in your governor's mansion the night of the election when it was first declared that Gore had won Florida. Surrounded by Poppy and Mommy, and on the phone to your brother the governor of Florida, you were a picture of calm. You had not a worry in the world. You told the press that your brother had assured you Florida was yours. If a Bush said it was so, it was so.

But it ain't so. And when it dawned on you that the Presidency had to be earned and won by a vote of the people—yes, the people!—you went berserk. You sent in hatchet man James Baker ("F--- the Jews, they don't vote for us anyway" was his advice to Poppy in '92) to tell lies to the American people and stoke the nation's fears. When that didn't work, you went to federal court and sued to stop the votes from being counted because you knew how the vote would turn out.

What kills me is how you have turned to the big, bad, federal government for help! Was not your mantra, during every campaign stop, the following line:

"My opponent trusts the federal government. *I trust you, the people!*"

So now we learn the truth. You don't trust the people at all. You went running to the *federal* court to get your handout ("Trust the machines, not the people," you pleaded). But the judge didn't buy it, and for perhaps the first time in your life, someone said "no" to you.

What will you do now? According to the *New York Times*, 90 percent of your campaign funds came from just 775 American millionaires. Oh, that they could bail you out of this mess! I wouldn't count on them—it's not like they have suffered financially under Clinton/Gore. They know they will do just fine with the Kissin' Fool. I think, my friend, you are on your own.

Mr. Bush, your only hope is that Gore will wimp out and throw in the towel. There is ample evidence of how Democrats love to cave. You and your right-wing friends know the Democrats are weak-kneed and spineless. You remember how Al Gore and all the Democrats voted to put that anti-abortion zealot [Antonin] Scalia on the Supreme Court—and how 11 Democrats made the difference in placing Clarence Thomas there, too?

That's your ticket. Spook Gore and his party into believing a focus group is mad at them, take a phony poll that backs that up, get the gasbag pundits to yammer and hammer him and maybe, just maybe, you'll get the latest plum prize that is not yours to have.

• • •

On the morning of September 11, 2001, more than three thousand people perished when hijackers flew two planes into the World Trade Center in New York City, another into the Pentagon in Washington, and a fourth that crashed, after passenger resistance disrupted the hijackers, in Pennsylvania. In the wake of the attacks, President Bush and many other politicians voiced loud calls for retaliation, and it was soon clear that Afghanistan would be their target, even though a majority of the hijackers were from Saudi Arabia, and even though there was no clear evidence linking the government of Afghanistan to the attacks. There was widespread grief in the United States and some calls for revenge, but a number of family members who lost loved ones on September 11 spoke out against this course of action. A group of them gathered together to form an organization called September Eleventh Families for Peaceful Tomorrows. Two of the first people to speak out against the use of September 11 as a pretext for war were Orlando and Phyllis Rodriguez. Their son, Gregory, then only thirty-one years old, was killed that day while working on the 103rd floor of One World Trade Center. The Rodriguezes sent this open letter to the *New York Times* and other newspapers four days after the attack.

Orlando Rodriguez and Phyllis Rodriguez, "Not in Our Son's Name" (September 15, 2001)[2]

Our son Greg is among the many missing from the World Trade Center attack. Since we first heard the news, we have shared moments of grief, comfort, hope, despair, fond memories with his wife, the two families, our friends and neighbors, his loving colleagues at Cantor Fitzgerald/ESpeed, and all the grieving families that daily meet at the Pierre Hotel.

We see our hurt and anger reflected among everybody we meet. We cannot pay attention to the daily flow of news about this disaster. But we read enough of the news to sense that our government is heading in the direction of violent revenge, with the prospect of sons, daughters, parents, friends in distant lands dying, suffering, and nursing further grievances against us. It is not the way to go. It will not avenge our son's death. Not in our son's name.

Our son died a victim of an inhuman ideology. Our actions should not serve the same purpose. Let us grieve. Let us reflect and pray. Let us think about a rational response that brings real peace and justice to our world. But let us not as a nation add to the inhumanity of our times.

• • •

Rita Lasar, a founding member of September Eleventh Families for Peaceful Tomorrows, lost her brother Avrame ("Abe") Zelmanowitz, on September 11, 2001. He could have escaped, but stayed behind to help a quadriplegic coworker,

Ed Beyea. When President Bush mentioned Abe's heroic actions in a speech at the National Cathedral in Washington, DC, Lasar expressed outrage that her brother's sacrifice was being used to justify the invasion of Afghanistan. After the assault on Afghanistan began, Lasar joined a delegation to visit families who lost loved ones in the U.S. assault and to witness first-hand the impact of the bombings. Just before the one-year anniversary of her brother's death, Rita Lasar wrote this commentary.

Rita Lasar, "To Avoid Another September 11, U.S. Must Join the World" (September 5, 2002)[3]

When the planes hit the World Trade Center last September 11, my brother Avrame, who was in the North Tower, refused to join the evacuation because he was concerned for the safety of his close friend and fellow worker, a quadriplegic who could not easily leave. So Avrame stayed, hoping that help would arrive. When it didn't, he and his lifelong associate died together, along with thousands of others innocent New Yorkers.

That day changed my life. It changed the lives of all those who lost loved ones in the towers.

It changed the lives of the relatives of those on the flight that crashed in Pennsylvania. It changed the lives of hundreds of families who lost loved ones in the Pentagon. And, perhaps to a lesser extent, it changed the lives of most people living in the United States.

In the months after the disaster, I often heard how September 11 changed the world. But I don't think the attacks changed the world. And to the extent that Americans believe that September 11 changed the world, it is because they don't know much about the world in which they live.

I have never heard anyone say that the horrific massacres of 1994 in Rwanda—which took more than five hundred thousand lives—changed the world. Nor have I ever been told that Indonesia's massacre of two hundred thousand East Timorese during a twenty-year span changed the world. I have not even heard that the daily loss of eight thousand souls in sub-Saharan Africa due to AIDS changed the world.

Were these people less important than my dear brother?

Despite my own personal grief, I must conclude that, in light of these far greater calamities, September 11 did not change the world. What it did, in its own terrible way, was invite Americans to join the world, which is already a very troubled place. The question is whether we will accept that invitation.

Sadly, President Bush has no interest in doing so. He does not want the United States to join, or even cooperate with, the new International Criminal Court. He has also withdrawn the United States from the long-standing Anti-Ballistic Missile treaty with Russia, even as India and Pakistan shudder on the verge of nuclear war. He refuses to support international agreements that would alleviate global warming, and he will not seek to ratify the treaty banning land mines, leaving the United States in the company of Iraq, Iran and North Korea, Bush's "axis of evil."

And now the president is planning for a war against Iraq. Never mind that Iraq has committed no act of aggression against us that justifies war, that there has been no evidence linking Iraq to the September 11 attacks. Neither does the president seem to care that the world is opposed to an invasion of Iraq.

The international coalition that fought the first Gulf War was cemented by the principle that one country cannot invade another without provocation. Now the White House is poised to dismiss the coalition to launch an unprovoked invasion of Iraq.

An isolated United States is an unsafe country. As September 11 showed, there are no barricades high enough, no bombs big enough, no intelligence sophisticated enough to make America invulnerable.

We Americans have a choice.

We can conclude that we are alone, that we owe the world nothing and that the world owes us everything. This is the assumption implicit in Bush's "you're either with us or against us" stance, which is a shortsighted and self-centered philosophy.

Or we can open our eyes and see the abundance of opportunities for making the planet a safer and more just place, by actively participating in international organizations, multilateral treaties and protocols that advocate peace and social equality.

We can no longer afford a go-it-alone approach. If we want the world's help in getting at the roots of terrorism, we are going to have to start helping the rest of the world. We are going to have to comprehend that there are millions of people around the globe who understand all too well the horror of tragedies like September 11.

When that realization occurs, only then will we glimpse how September 11 changed the world.

• • •

In the aftermath of the September 11 attacks, the government passed a number of measures restricting civil liberties, most notoriously the USA PATRIOT Act (the Uniting and Strengthening America by Providing Appropriate Tools Required to Intercept and Obstruct Terrorism Act of 2001). Approved overwhelmingly by Democrats and Republicans in Congress, many of whom acknowledged not reading the bill, it gave the government broad powers to wiretap, arrest, and detain people "suspected" of having ties to terrorists. Although President Bush disclaimed anti-Muslim prejudice, it was clear that Muslims, South Asians, and other people of color were being targeted. These same groups were also subjected to verbal abuse and physical assaults, on the streets, in workplaces, and in their homes. As Monami Maulik, a community organizer of the Queens-based DRUM (Desis Rising Up and Moving), wrote soon after, "[D]uring this period of grief, we have had to endure perhaps the worst mass-scale anti-Arab, anti–South Asian, and anti-Muslim violence this country has seen." Maulik, born in Calcutta and raised in the Bronx, worked with the New York Taxi Workers' Alliance before helping to found DRUM in 1997. She wrote this essay on organizing after September 11 for *Manavi*, a South Asian newsletter based in New Brunswick, New Jersey.

Monami Maulik, "Organizing in Our Communities Post–September 11th" (2001)[4]

Since the tragic loss of lives on September 11th, I find the need for organizing in my community is even greater in the coming years. But this is not because September 11th was or will be the only mass-scale loss of human lives. Since the Gulf War, over 500,000 Iraqi children have died as a direct result of economic sanctions imposed by the U.S. against Iraq. Are the lives of these children any less valuable? In the midst of realizing the mass-scale inhumanity of war and imperialism, grassroots organizing can be the source of hope for a building a world centered on social justice. What distinguishes organizing from services, advocacy, and relief-work is that organizing seeks to change the root causes of social injustice as opposed to responding to its symptoms. But the question becomes whether we are organizing to challenge the institutions that create oppression or to maintain the status-quo?

The tragedies of September 11th continue to deeply hurt the South Asian community at large on multiple levels. First, we have lost members of our community in the World Trade Center. Moreover, a large number of those missing were low-wage, undocumented immigrant service workers whose families do not qualify for federal aid and benefits. Second, during this period of grief, we have had to endure perhaps the worst mass-scale anti-Arab, anti–South Asian, and anti-Muslim violence this country has seen. Hundreds of incidents ranging from threats to beatings to killings have been reported around the country. Our homes, communities, and places of worship have been under siege. And these are only the incidents that are reported. Moreover, this anti-immigrant backlash is currently being institutionalized via new anti-terrorist legislation, racial profiling, and the suspension of hard-won civil rights. Thousands of immigrants have been illegally detained and deported since September 11th, most of whom are Arab, South Asian, and Muslim. Third, U.S. bombing of Afghanistan and military presence in Pakistan to wage an endless war has many of us concerned with the possible impending devastation of our communities and families back home.

Given this hostile climate nationally for the South Asian immigrant community, particularly for undocumented immigrants in the years to come, there is an urgent need now more than ever to organize against the growing conservatism that can undo years of anti-racist, feminist, anti-homophobic, and pro-working class struggle. Our short-term objectives must be to re-build security in our communities against racial violence and provide emergency relief to undocumented families. Our long-term objectives need to challenge racism and xenophobia, organize to end state violence in the form of the Patriot Act and other racist, anti-immigrant legislation, and to build the emerging anti-war movement with the leadership of immigrant and people of color communities, particularly those whose voices are historically marginalized, such as women, queer people, undocumented immigrants, and low-wage workers.

But as socially conscious South Asians, perhaps our biggest challenge in organizing our communities in the coming years will be to counter the growing conservative backlash we are witnessing. In the past several weeks, mainstream South Asian organizations have followed the destructive path of blind patriotism that has fueled the horrific war against Afghanistan and the passage of the Patriot Act, one of the most anti-immigrant legislations passed by the U.S. in recent history. At the same time, conservative and communalist forces that have fueled anti-Muslim, anti-Dalit, and anti-Christian violence in India have been lobbying the U.S. government to inject its military might in South Asia to fuel the war over Kashmir.

This is the moment that we must ask ourselves what side of the fence do we stand on? The side that will only perpetuate more violence against Third World people around the world like that we have glimpsed so close to home on September 11th? Or the side that is for peace with justice both within the U.S., for immigrants, poor people, women, queer people, and people of color, and outside the U.S., for the people of Afghanistan and other nations targeted by U.S. militarism and imperialism? DRUM and the community organizing we practice stands for the latter.

• • •

When it became clear that President Bush would follow up the war on Afghanistan by attacking Iraq, a number of labor unions across the country passed resolutions against going to war. City councils in more than one hundred cities also passed anti-war resolutions. Here is one of the resolutions passed by Local 705 of the Teamsters, in Chicago, Illinois, one of the biggest Teamsters locals in the country.

International Brotherhood of Teamsters Local 705, "Resolution Against the War" (October 18, 2002)[5]

Whereas, we value the lives of our sons and daughters, of our brothers and sisters more than Bush's control of Middle East oil profits;

Whereas, we have no quarrel with the ordinary working-class men, women, and children of Iraq who will suffer the most in any war;

Whereas, the billions of dollars being spent to stage and execute this invasion, means billions taken away from our schools, hospitals, housing, and social security;

Whereas, Bush's drive for war serves as a cover and a distraction for the sinking economy, corporate corruption, lay-offs, Taft-Hartley (used against the locked out ILWU [International Longshore Workers' Union] longshoremen);

Whereas, Teamsters Local 705 is known far and wide as fighters for justice;

Be It Resolved that Teamsters Local 705 stands firmly against Bush's drive for war;

Further Resolved that the Teamsters Local 705 Executive Board publicize this statement, and seek out other unions, labor and community activists interested in promoting anti-war activity in the labor movement and community.

• • •

Rachel Corrie, a student at Evergreen College and member of the Olympia Movement for Justice and Peace, traveled to the Gaza Strip in Palestine in early 2003 as a volunteer with the International Solidarity Movement (ISM). On March 16, 2003, she was killed when she was run over by a Caterpillar bulldozer while trying to block the destruction of a Palestinian home. The bulldozer was driven by an Israeli, but built in the United States. The driver could not have failed to see Corrie, who was wearing a bright orange jacket and who announced her presence through a bullhorn. After her death, Corrie's family and friends released copies of her moving letters describing the struggle against the U.S.-backed occupation of Palestinian lands. Here is one of the letters she sent home.

Rachel Corrie, Letter from Palestine
(February 7, 2003)[6]

Hi friends and family, and others,

I have been in Palestine for two weeks and one hour now, and I still have very few words to describe what I see. It is most difficult for me to think about what's going on here when I sit down to write back to the United States. Something about the virtual portal into luxury. I don't know if many of the children here have ever existed without tank-shell holes in their walls and the towers of an occupying army surveying them constantly from the near horizons. I think, although I'm not entirely sure, that even the smallest of these children understand that life is not like this everywhere. An eight-year-old was shot and killed by an Israeli tank two days before I got here, and many of the children murmur his name to me—Ali—or point at the posters of him on the walls. The children also love to get me to practice my limited Arabic by asking me, "Kaif Sharon?" "Kaif Bush?" and they laugh when I say, "Bush majnoon," "Sharon majnoon" back in my limited Arabic. (How is Sharon? How is Bush? Bush is crazy. Sharon is crazy.) Of course this isn't quite what I believe, and some of the adults who have the English correct me: "Bush mish majnoon"—Bush is a businessman. Today I tried to learn to say, "Bush is a tool," but I don't think it translated quite right. But anyway, there are eight-year-olds here much more aware of the workings of the global power structure than I was just a few years ago.

Nevertheless, no amount of reading, attendance at conferences, documentary viewing and word of mouth could have prepared me for the reality of the situation here. You just can't imagine it unless you see it—and even then you are always well aware that your experience of it is not at all the reality: what with the difficulties the Israeli army would face if they shot an unarmed U.S. citizen, and with the fact that I have money to buy water when the army destroys wells, and the fact, of course, that I have the option of leaving. Nobody in my family has been shot, driving in their car, by a rocket launcher from a tower at the end of a major street in my hometown. I have a home. I am allowed to go see the ocean. When I leave for school or work I can be relatively certain that there will not be a heavily armed soldier waiting halfway between Mud Bay and downtown Olympia at a checkpoint with the power to decide whether I can go about my business, and whether I can get home again when I'm done. As an afterthought to all this rambling, I am in Rafah: a city of about 140,000 people, approximately 60 percent of whom are refugees—many of whom are twice or three times refugees. Today, as I walked on top of the rubble where homes once stood, Egyptian soldiers called to me from the other side of the border, "Go! Go!" because a tank was coming. And then waving and "What's your name?" Something disturbing about this friendly curiosity. It reminded me of how much, to some degree, we are all kids curious about other kids. Egyptian kids shouting at strange women wandering into the path of tanks. Palestinian kids shot from the tanks when they peek out from behind walls to see what's going on. International kids standing in front of tanks with banners. Israeli kids in the tanks anonymously—occasionally shouting and also occasionally waving—many forced to be here, many just aggressive—shooting into the houses as we wander away.

I've been having trouble accessing news about the outside world here, but I hear an escalation of war on Iraq is inevitable. There is a great deal of concern here about the "reoccupation of Gaza." Gaza is reoccupied every day to various extents but I think the fear is that the tanks will enter all the streets and remain here instead of entering some of the streets and then withdrawing after some hours or days to observe and shoot from the edges of the communities. If people aren't already thinking about the consequences of this war for the people of the entire region then I hope you will start.

· · ·

More than ten million people around the globe demonstrated against war on Iraq on February 15, 2003, in the largest coordinated international protest in human history. More than one million across the United States joined the demonstration, with some 500,000 coming out in New York, despite police edicts and barricades keeping people from marching. Two days after the demonstrations, a reporter wrote on the front page of the *New York Times*, "The fracturing of the Western alliance over Iraq and the huge antiwar demonstrations around the world this weekend are reminders that there may still be two superpowers on the planet: the United States and world public opinion. In his campaign to disarm Iraq, by war if necessary, President Bush appears to be eyeball to eyeball with a tenacious new adversary: millions of people who flooded the streets of New York and dozens of other world cities to say they are against war based on the evidence at hand." On February 15, dozens of activists addressed the demonstration in New York. Here is the speech of the actor and African-American activist Danny Glover.

Danny Glover, Speech During the World Day of Protest Against the War (February 15, 2003)[7]

We come here to reclaim our right as citizens of the world to peacefully protest! We must all stand as one voice to demand that the real users of weapons of mass destruction—our own country—dismantle them. That those who manufactured this climate of fear stop their lies, and heed the will of the people and the nation and the rest of the world to say no to war. That's why we come here!

We've overcome many obstacles in order to stand here this afternoon. For one, nature's unyielding and unforgiving reminder that this is February, and it's cold! But Mother Earth has smiled on us because she understands clearly that our voice must be heard. She knows that she is sick and only we, we the people, can heal her. She knows that.

We've overcome the obstacles that have been placed in our path on this journey by the city of New York and the state of New York and the federal institutions. Yet we've overcome our own fear to be here today because only with the acknowledgement of that fear do we demonstrate our real courage to stand up today. We stand here because our right to dissent and our right to be participants in a true democracy has been hijacked by an administration of liars and murderers who curse us because we stand in the way of their tyranny, who curse us because we stand in the way of their unholy and brutal agenda. An administration whose villainy and greed is insatiable. We stand at this threshold of history and say to them, "Not in our name! Not in our name!"

We stand here, and our stand is critical because inevitably in the future we'll have to challenge U.S. policy in the Gulf of Guinea. We'll have to challenge U.S. policy in other places and other oil producing countries in Africa. We'll have to do that. We have to challenge the potential recolonization of Africa.

But we stand here because we stand on the shoulders of others who have come before us and who have called for peace and justice. Men and women like Fannie Lou Hamer, Harriet Tubman, Martin and Malcolm, W. E. B. Du Bois, Toussaint L'Ouverture. Toussaint L'Ouverture, who at forty-seven years old led an assault against slavery on the island of Haiti two hundred years ago. And we stand here, yes we stand here, because Paul Robeson would be proud for us to stand here. And he would say to us that we are climbing Jacob's ladder! We are climbing Jacob's ladder! We are climbing Jacob's ladder!

. . .

In the Clinton and Bush years, the media became concentrated in fewer and fewer hands. In response, activists sought ways to build independent media outlets that would not sacrifice truth for profit. Among the most important of these efforts was the campaign to save the Pacifica Radio network and the program *Democracy Now!* The show, co-hosted by Juan Gonzalez and Amy Goodman, featured many stories largely excluded from the corporate media, particularly in the period after September 11, when establishment media outlets rallied around the flag to support the "war on terror." Here journalist Amy Goodman discusses the importance of independent media in the period of the 2003 invasion of Iraq.

Amy Goodman, "Independent Media in a Time of War" (April 21, 2003)[8]

A *Newsday* reporter asked me the other day, am I opposed to "embedded" reporters? You know they say it in the mainstream media: "Our reporter embedded with the Marines."

Even Walter Cronkite the other day raised some objections "What an unfortunate choice of words," he said. And he was critical. You rarely hear that criticism in the mainstream media, the working journalists today. What kind of critical reporting do we get?

It's this parade of retired generals that are on the network's payrolls. We now have people like Wesley Clark, General Wesley Clark, on the payroll of CNN, who is questioning their embedded reporter on the front line. He is questioning the reporter and the reporter is saying, "Yes, sir. No, sir."

This is journalism in America today. They have redefined "general news," and we have got to challenge that.

Why is it that if they have these retired generals on the payroll, they don't have peace activists and peace leaders also on the payroll? So let's have the same number of reporters embedded with Iraqi families, let's have reporters embedded in the peace movement all over the world, and maybe then we'll get some accurate picture of what's going on. Aaron Brown had some interesting comments. He said he admits CNN *Newsnight* came "a little late" to the peace movement. But once the war started, those voices are irrelevant because then the war is on.

We're seeing these romanticized pictures of soldiers against sunsets and the planes on those aircraft carriers that the embedded photographers are getting at the sunrise hour.

Think about Dan Rather the night that the bombs started falling on Iraq. He said, "Good Morning Baghdad." And Tom Brokaw said, "We don't want to destroy the infrastructure of Iraq because we're going to own it in a few days." And Peter Jennings was interviewing Chris Cuomo, who is a reporter for ABC, and he was out on the street, where we were, Times Square, with thousands of people in the freezing rain who had come out to protest the war. They had all sorts of signs that were sopping wet, and people were trying to keep the umbrellas up and the police charged a part of the crowd. Jennings said to Cuomo, "What are they doing out there? What are they saying?" And he said, "Well, they have these signs that say 'No Blood for Oil,' but when you ask them what that means, they seem very confused. I don't think they know why they're out here." I guess they got caught in a traffic jam. Why not have Peter Jennings, instead of asking someone who clearly doesn't understand why they're out there, invite one of them into the studio, and have a discussion like he does with the generals?

Why don't they also put doctors on the payroll? That way, you can have the general talking about the bomb that Lockheed Martin made, and the kind of plane that drops it, and whether it was precision guided or not. And then you can have the doctor talking about the effect of the bomb. Not for or against the war, just how a cluster bomb enters your skin and what it means when your foot is blown off, if you're lucky and you're not killed. So why not have doctors and generals at least? But this is just to show how low the media has gone.

You have not only Fox, but MSNBC and NBC—yes, owned by General Electric, one of the major nuclear weapons manufacturers in the world. MSNBC and NBC, as well as Fox, titling their coverage taking the name of what the Pentagon calls the invasion of Iraq: "Operation Iraqi Freedom." So that's what the Pentagon does, and you expect that. They research the most effective propagandistic name to call their operation. But for the media to name their coverage what the Pentagon calls it—everyday seeing "Operation Iraqi Freedom"—you have to ask: if this were state media, how would it be any different?

Even now, the media has had to start reporting a little bit on the protest. But it's not those events that we're talking about. It's the daily drumbeat coverage who is interviewed on the front pages of the *New York Times* and the *Washington Post* for the headline stories and the network newscasts that matters. They're the ones shaping foreign policy.

Fairness and Accuracy in Reporting did a study. In the week leading up to General Colin Powell going to the Security Council to make his case for the invasion and the week afterwards—this was the period where more than half of the people in this country were opposed to an invasion—they did a study of CBS *Evening News*, NBC *Nightly News*, ABC *World News Tonight*, and the *NewsHour with Jim Lehrer* on PBS. The four major newscasts. Two weeks. Three hundred and ninety-three interviews on war. Three were anti-war voices. Three of almost four hundred, and that included PBS. This has to be changed. It has to be challenged.

We are not the only ones—Pacifica Radio, National Public Radio stations— we are not the only ones that are using the public airwaves. They are, too. And they have to provide the diversity of opinion that fully expresses the debate and the anguish and the discussions that are going on all over this country. That is media serving a democratic society.

For awhile in talks before the invasion, I've been saying as we see the full-page pictures of the target on Saddam Hussein's forehead that it would be more accurate to show the target on the forehead of a little Iraqi girl, because that's who dies in war. The overwhelming majority of people who die are innocent civilians. And then what happens on the first night of the invasion? Missile strikes a residential area in Baghdad. They say they think they've taken out Saddam Hussein. Independent reporter May Ying Welsh, who stayed there as the bombs fell, who you heard on *Democracy Now!* on a regular basis, went to the hospital right after that first attack, and there was a four-year-old girl critically injured from that missile attack and her mother critically injured and her mother's sister. That's who dies, that's who gets injured in war. . . .

Our mission is to make dissent commonplace in America, so you're not surprised when you're at work, someone walks over to the water cooler and makes a comment, and someone isn't shocked and says, "What's that all about?" but that it comes out of the finest tradition that built this country. People engaged in dissent. We have parallel worlds in this country. For some, it's the greatest democracy on earth. There is no question about that. But for others, immigrants now in detention facilities, they have no rights, not even to a lawyer. And we have to be there and we have to watch and we have to listen. We have to tell their stories until they can tell their own. That's why I think *Democracy Now!* is a very good model for the rest of the media, as is the Indy Media Center all over the country and the world. Built on almost nothing except the goodwill and the curiosity and the interest and the passion of people who are tired of seeing their friends and neighbors through a corporate lens, and particularly tired and afraid of the fact that that image is being projected all over the world. That is very dangerous. Dissent is what makes this country healthy. And the media has to fight for that, and we have to fight for an independent media.

• • •

After the U.S. government, ignoring protests and world opinion, launched the attack on Iraq, on March 20, 2003, some of the most important voices of dissent were soldiers and their families. Where, they asked, was the threatening Iraq arsenal of the weapons of mass destruction that allegedly was the cause of the war? None could be found. In a stage-managed event, President Bush declared an end to "major combat operations" on May 1, but deaths of soldiers continued to mount, soon exceeding those who had died during the invasion. U.S. soldiers came to be seen not as liberators, but as an occupying army. In August 2003, while serving in Mosul, Iraq, Tim Predmore, a soldier with the 101st Airborne Division, wrote this statement, published in the Peoria *Journal Star* in Illinois and later in the *Los Angeles Times*.

Tim Predmore, "How Many More Must Die?" (August 24, 2003)[9]

"Shock and Awe" were the words used to describe the awesome display of power the world was to view upon the start of Operation Iraqi Freedom. It was to be an up-close, dramatic display of military strength and advanced technology within the arsenal of the United States and the United Kingdom's military.

But as a soldier preparing for the invasion of Iraq, the words "shock and awe" rang deeper within my psyche. These two great superpowers were about to break the very rules they demand of others. Without the consent of the United Nations, and ignoring the pleas of their own citizens, the United States and Britain invaded Iraq.

"Shock and Awe"? Yes, the words correctly described the emotional impact I felt as we prepared to participate in what I believed not to be an act of justice but of hypocrisy.

From the moment the first shot was fired in this so-called war of liberation and freedom, hypocrisy reigned. Following the broadcasting of recorded images of captured and dead U.S. soldiers over Arab television, American and British leaders vowed revenge while verbally assaulting the networks for displaying such vivid images. Yet within hours of the deaths of Saddam's two sons [Uday and Qusay Hussein], the American government released horrific photos of the two dead brothers for the entire world to view. Again, a "do as we say and not as we do" scenario.

As soldiers serving in Iraq, we have been told that our purpose here is to help the people of Iraq by providing them the necessary assistance militarily as well as in humanitarian efforts. Then tell me where the humanity was in the recent *Stars and Stripes* account of two young children brought to a U.S. military camp by their mother, in search of medical care? The two children had been, unbeknown to them, playing with explosive ordinance they had found and as a result were severely burned. The account tells how the two children, following an hour-long wait, were denied care by two U.S. military doctors. The soldier described the incident as one of many "atrocities" he has witnessed on the part of the U.S. military.

So then, what is our purpose here? Was this invasion due to weapons of mass destruction as we so often heard? If so, where are they? Did we invade to dispose of a leader and his regime on the account of close association with Osama bin Laden? If so, where is the proof? Or is it that our incursion is a result of our own economic advantage? Iraq's oil can be refined at the lowest cost of any in the world. Coincidence?

This looks like a modern-day crusade not to free an oppressed people or to rid the world of a demonic dictator relentless in his pursuit of conquest and domination but a crusade to control another nation's natural resource. At least for us here, oil seems to be the reason for our presence.

There is only one truth, and it is that Americans are dying. There are an estimated ten to fourteen attacks on our servicemen and women daily in Iraq. As the body count continues to grow, it would appear that there is no immediate end in sight.

I once believed that I served for a cause: "to uphold and defend the Constitution of the United States."

Now, I no longer believe; I have lost my conviction, my determination. I can no longer justify my service for what I believe to be half-truths and bold lies. My time is done as well as that of many others with whom I serve. We have all faced death here without reason or justification.

How many more must die? How many more tears must be shed before America awakens and demands the return of the men and women whose job it is to protect them rather than their leaders' interests?

• • •

Maritza Castillo and nineteen other relatives of national guard members sent to fight in Iraq signed this open letter to Colonel, U.S. Army (Ret.) Michael G. Jones of the Florida Department of Military Affairs.

Maritza Castillo et al., Open Letter to Colonel, U.S. Army (Ret.) Michael G. Jones (September 12, 2003)[10]

Dear Colonel Jones,

We, the relatives of the Florida National Guard soldiers want to express our position in relation to the last postponement of the return of our soldiers back home. We want to inform you that we are united in the fight for the return of our soldiers.

This letter shall serve to remind you that these soldiers have now been away from our homes for eight months, away from their children, wives and parents, away from their universities and jobs, involved in a guerilla war in an unknown country, not knowing the culture or the language of the place, menaced by mines, bombs and guns, risking their lives twenty-four hours a day, standing in their uniforms and carrying their equipment in temperatures of up to 130° F.

In less than three months, this small company has suffered countless attacks, leaving four soldiers crippled and another soldier in coma, not to mention the injured soldiers at the Ar Ramadi.

The National Guard soldiers are civilians, not active members of the Army. They have never received the training for combat in the desert or to face urban guerrillas. We know that, since their arrival at Ar Ramadi, our young soldiers have been patrolling and searching the houses of presumed guerrilla forces. We know that they lack adequate equipment, that in many cases they have patrolled without bullet-proof vests and without the necessary ammunition to face the guerrilla forces. Isn't this enough? How many months, how many abuses are we supposed to endure?

We will not mention each suffering and difficulty that our soldiers have endured. We just want to tell you that we know what they are going through and that we will not keep quiet in the face of this dishonor. We will not rest until our young soldiers come back to our homes.

We are determined to continue on this campaign to the end. If necessary, a group of mothers will go on an indefinite hunger strike. You will not only be responsible for the lives of our soldiers, but for that of their mothers. We shall not accept political apologies. Lack of governmental will by President Bush to work together with the United Nations and to restore the power to the Iraqis is the reason why the participation of an international force comprised by big nations is not possible. The coalition we are being told about does not really exist. It is our troops that carry the load of this war. It is our children who are being sacrificed due to an arrogant and unfair attitude.

For this and for other reasons, we demand the return of our soldiers now!! We shall not abandon our loved ones; we shall not abandon our troops. We shall continue demanding their return day-by-day, street-by-street, door-to-door. We will ask the world to join us. We will not abandon our fight until our soldiers are back in our homes.

• • •

Here the novelist and essayist Kurt Vonnegut, a frequent contributor to the independent magazine *In These Times*, issues a defiant call for honesty about the state of U.S. politics at the end of the first Bush II administration.

Kurt Vonnegut, "Cold Turkey" (May 31, 2004)[11]

Many years ago, I was so innocent I still considered it possible that we could become the humane and reasonable America so many members of my generation used to dream of. We dreamed of such an America during the Great Depression, when there were no jobs. And then we fought and often died for that dream during the Second World War, when there was no peace.

But I know now that there is not a chance in hell of America's becoming humane and reasonable. Because power corrupts us, and absolute power corrupts absolutely. Human beings are chimpanzees who get crazy drunk on power. By saying that our leaders are power-drunk chimpanzees, am I in danger of wrecking the morale of our soldiers fighting and dying in the Middle East? Their morale, like so many bodies, is already shot to pieces. They are being treated, as I never was, like toys a rich kid got for Christmas.

When you get to my age, if you get to my age, which is 81, and if you have reproduced, you will find yourself asking your own children, who are themselves middle-aged, what life is all about. I have seven kids, four of them adopted.

Many of you reading this are probably the same age as my grandchildren. They, like you, are being royally shafted and lied to by our Baby Boomer corporations and government.

I put my big question about life to my biological son Mark. Mark is a pediatrician, and author of a memoir, *The Eden Express*. It is about his crackup, straightjacket and padded cell stuff, from which he recovered sufficiently to graduate from Harvard Medical School.

Dr. Vonnegut said this to his doddering old dad: "Father, we are here to help each other get through this thing, whatever it is." So I pass that on to you. Write it down, and put it in your computer, so you can forget it.

I have to say that's a pretty good sound bite, almost as good as, "Do unto others as you would have them do unto you." A lot of people think Jesus said that, because it is so much the sort of thing Jesus liked to say. But it was actually said by Confucius, a Chinese philosopher, 500 years before there was that greatest and most humane of human beings, named Jesus Christ.

The Chinese also gave us, via Marco Polo, pasta and the formula for gunpowder. The Chinese were so dumb they only used gunpowder for fireworks. And everybody was so dumb back then that nobody in either hemisphere even knew that there was another one.

But back to people, like Confucius and Jesus and my son the doctor, Mark, who've said how we could behave more humanely, and maybe make the world a less painful place. One of my favorites is Eugene Debs, from Terre Haute in my native state of Indiana. Get a load of this:

Eugene Debs, who died back in 1926, when I was only 4, ran 5 times as the Socialist Party candidate for president, winning 900,000 votes, 6 percent of the popular vote, in 1912, if you can imagine such a ballot. He had this to say while campaigning:

As long as there is a lower class, I am in it.
As long as there is a criminal element, I'm of it.
As long as there is a soul in prison, I am not free.

Doesn't anything socialistic make you want to throw up? Like great public schools or health insurance for all?

How about Jesus' Sermon on the Mount, the Beatitudes?

Blessed are the meek, for they shall inherit the Earth.
Blessed are the merciful, for they shall obtain mercy.
Blessed are the peacemakers, for they shall be called the children of God....

And so on.

Not exactly planks in a Republican platform. Not exactly Donald Rumsfeld or Dick Cheney stuff.

For some reason, the most vocal Christians among us never mention the Beatitudes. But, often with tears in their eyes, they demand that the Ten Commandments be posted in public buildings. And of course that's Moses, not Jesus. I haven't heard one of them demand that the Sermon on the Mount, the Beatitudes, be posted anywhere.

"Blessed are the merciful" in a courtroom? "Blessed are the peacemakers" in the Pentagon? Give me a break!

There is a tragic flaw in our precious Constitution, and I don't know what can be done to fix it. This is it: Only nut cases want to be president.

But, when you stop to think about it, only a nut case would want to be a human being, if he or she had a choice. Such treacherous, untrustworthy, lying and greedy animals we are!

I was born a human being in 1922 A.D. What does "A.D." signify? That commemorates an inmate of this lunatic asylum we call Earth who was nailed to a wooden cross by a bunch of other inmates. With him still conscious, they hammered spikes through his wrists and insteps, and into the wood. Then they set the cross upright, so he dangled up there where even the shortest person in the crowd could see him writhing this way and that.

Can you imagine people doing such a thing to a person?

No problem. That's entertainment. Ask the devout Roman Catholic Mel Gibson, who, as an act of piety, has just made a fortune with a movie about how Jesus was tortured. Never mind what Jesus said.

During the reign of King Henry the Eighth, founder of the Church of England, he had a counterfeiter boiled alive in public. Show biz again.

Mel Gibson's next movie should be *The Counterfeiter*. Box office records will again be broken.

One of the few good things about modern times: If you die horribly on television, you will not have died in vain. You will have entertained us.

And what did the great British historian Edward Gibbon, 1737–1794 A.D., have to say about the human record so far? He said, "History is indeed little more than the register of the crimes, follies and misfortunes of mankind."

The same can be said about this morning's edition of the *New York Times*.

The French-Algerian writer Albert Camus, who won a Nobel Prize for Literature in 1957, wrote, "There is but one truly serious philosophical problem, and that is suicide."

So there's another barrel of laughs from literature. Camus died in an automobile accident. His dates? 1913–1960 A.D.

Listen. All great literature is about what a bummer it is to be a human being: *Moby Dick, Huckleberry Finn, The Red Badge of Courage,* the *Iliad* and the *Odyssey, Crime and Punishment,* the Bible and *The Charge of the Light Brigade.*

But I have to say this in defense of humankind: No matter in what era in history, including the Garden of Eden, everybody just got there. And, except for the Garden of Eden, there were already all these crazy games going on, which could make you act crazy, even if you weren't crazy to begin with. Some of the games that were already going on when you got here were love and hate, liberalism and conservatism, automobiles and credit cards, golf and girls' basketball.

Even crazier than golf, though, is modern American politics, where, thanks to TV and for the convenience of TV, you can only be one of two kinds of human beings, either a liberal or a conservative.

Actually, this same sort of thing happened to the people of England generations ago, and Sir William Gilbert, of the radical team of Gilbert and Sullivan, wrote these words for a song about it back then:

> I often think it's comical
> How nature always does contrive
> That every boy and every gal
> That's born into the world alive
> Is either a little Liberal
> Or else a little Conservative.

Which one are you in this country? It's practically a law of life that you have to be one or the other? If you aren't one or the other, you might as well be a doughnut.

If some of you still haven't decided, I'll make it easy for you.

If you want to take my guns away from me, and you're all for murdering fetuses, and love it when homosexuals marry each other, and want to give them kitchen appliances at their showers, and you're for the poor, you're a liberal.

If you are against those perversions and for the rich, you're a conservative.

What could be simpler?

My government's got a war on drugs. But get this: The two most widely abused and addictive and destructive of all substances are both perfectly legal.

One, of course, is ethyl alcohol. And President George W. Bush, no less, and by his own admission, was smashed or tiddley-poo or four sheets to the wind a good deal of the time from when he was 16 until he was 41. When he was 41, he says, Jesus appeared to him and made him knock off the sauce, stop gargling nose paint.

Other drunks have seen pink elephants.

And do you know why I think he is so pissed off at Arabs? They invented algebra. Arabs also invented the numbers we use, including a symbol for nothing, which nobody else had ever had before. You think Arabs are dumb? Try doing long division with Roman numerals.

We're spreading democracy, are we? Same way European explorers brought Christianity to the Indians, what we now call "Native Americans."

How ungrateful they were! How ungrateful are the people of Baghdad today.

So let's give another big tax cut to the super-rich. That'll teach bin Laden a lesson he won't soon forget. Hail to the Chief.

That chief and his cohorts have as little to do with Democracy as the Europeans had to do with Christianity. We the people have absolutely no say in whatever they choose to do next. In case you haven't noticed, they've already cleaned out the treasury, passing it out to pals in the war and national security rackets, leaving your generation and the next one with a perfectly enormous debt that you'll be asked to repay.

Nobody let out a peep when they did that to you, because they have disconnected every burglar alarm in the Constitution: The House, the Senate, the Supreme Court, the FBI, the free press (which, having been embedded, has forsaken the First Amendment) and We the People.

About my own history of foreign substance abuse. I've been a coward about heroin and cocaine and LSD and so on, afraid they might put me over the edge. I did smoke a joint of marijuana one time with Jerry Garcia and the Grateful Dead, just to be sociable. It didn't seem to do anything to me, one way or the other, so I never did it again. And by the grace of God, or whatever, I am not an alcoholic, largely a matter of genes. I take a couple of drinks now and then, and will do it again tonight. But two is my limit. No problem.

I am of course notoriously hooked on cigarettes. I keep hoping the things will kill me. A fire at one end and a fool at the other.

But I'll tell you one thing: I once had a high that not even crack cocaine could match. That was when I got my first driver's license! Look out, world, here comes Kurt Vonnegut.

And my car back then, a Studebaker, as I recall, was powered, as are almost all means of transportation and other machinery today, and electric power plants and furnaces, by the most abused and addictive and destructive drugs of all: fossil fuels.

When you got here, even when I got here, the industrialized world was already hopelessly hooked on fossil fuels, and very soon now there won't be any more of those. Cold turkey.

Can I tell you the truth? I mean this isn't like TV news, is it?

Here's what I think the truth is: We are all addicts of fossil fuels in a state of denial, about to face cold turkey.

And like so many addicts about to face cold turkey, our leaders are now committing violent crimes to get what little is left of what we're hooked on.

• • •

Here, to end, are lyrics to a song from poet, songwriter, musician Patti Smith, which she performed frequently in protest against the war on Iraq.

Patti Smith, "People Have the Power" (1988)[12]

I was dreaming in my dreaming
Of an aspect bright and fair
And my sleeping it was broken
But my dream it lingered near
In the form of shining valleys
Where the pure air recognized
And my senses newly opened
I awakened to the cry
That the people have the power
To redeem the work of fools
Upon the meek the graces shower
It's decreed the people rule

The people have the power
The people have the power
The people have the power
The people have the power

Vengeful aspects became suspect
And bending low as if to hear
And the armies ceased advancing
Because the people had their ear
And the shepherds and the soldiers
Lay beneath the stars
Exchanging visions
And laying arms
To waste in the dust
In the form of shining valleys
Where the pure air recognized
And my senses newly opened
I awakened to the cry

The people have the power
The people have the power
The people have the power
The people have the power

Where there were deserts
I saw fountains
Like cream the waters rise
And we strolled there together
With none to laugh or criticize
And the leopard
And the lamb
Lay together truly bound
I was hoping in my hoping
To recall what I had found
I was dreaming in my dreaming
God knows a purer view
As I surrender to my sleeping
I commit my dream to you

The people have the power
The people have the power
The people have the power
The people have the power

The power to dream to rule
To wrestle the world from fools
It's decreed the people rule
It's decreed the people rule
Listen. I believe everything we dream
Can come to pass through our union
We can turn the world around
We can turn the earth's revolution

We have the power
People have the power

Notes

EPIGRAPH

1   Frederick Douglass, "West India Emancipation" (August 3, 1857). Speech delivered in Canandaigua, New York, August 3, 1857. In Frederick Douglass, *Frederick Douglass: Selected Speeches and Writings*, ed. Philip S. Foner, abridged ed. by Yuval Taylor (Chicago: Lawrence Hill Books, 1999), p. 367.

INTRODUCTION

1   Howard Zinn, *A People's History of the United States: 1492–Present*, updated ed. (New York: HarperCollins/Perennial Classics, 2001).

CHAPTER ONE: COLUMBUS AND LAS CASAS

1   Christopher Columbus, *The Diario of Christopher Columbus's First Voyage to America, 1492–1493: Abstracted by Fray Bartolomé de las Casas*. Transcribed and translated from Spanish into English by Oliver Dunn and James E. Kelley, Jr. (Norman and London: University of Oklahoma Press, 1991), pp. 57–79. Based on the 1962 Carlos Sanz facsimile.

2   Bartolomé de Las Casas, *The Devastation of the Indies: A Brief Account* (1542). In Bartolomé de Las Casas, *The Devastation of the Indies: A Brief Account*, trans. Herma Briffault (New York: A Continuum Book from Seabury Press, 1974), pp. 37–44, 51–52.

3   Bartolomé de Las Casas, *In Defense of the Indians* (1550). In "Preface to the Defense of the Most Reverend Fray Bartolomé de Las Casas, of the Order of Saint Dominic, Late Bishop of Chiapa, to Philip, Great Prince of Spain," *In Defense of the Indians: The Defense of the Most Reverend Lord, Don Fray Bartolomé de Las Casas, of the Order of Preachers, Late Bishop of Chiapa, Against the Persecutors and Slanderers of the People of the New World Discovered Across the Seas*, trans. and ed. C. M. Stafford Poole (Dekalb, Illinois: Northern Illinois University Press, 1974), pp. 17–20. Translation of a circa 1552 Latin manuscript based on the 1550–51 debate. In the Bibliotheque nationale, Paris, France (Nouveux fonds latins, no. 12926).

4   Eduardo Galeano, *Memory of Fire* (1982). In Eduardo Galeano, *Memory of Fire*, vol. 1, *Genesis*, trans. Cedric Belfrage (New York: Pantheon Books/Random House, 1985; W. W. Norton and Company, 1998), pp. 45–51. Translated from the original Spanish edition, *Memoria del fuego, I. Los nacimientos* (Madrid: Siglo Veintiuno de España Editores, S.A., 1982).

CHAPTER TWO: THE FIRST SLAVES

1   Anonymous Letter to Mr. Boone in London (June 24, 1720). In Herbert Aptheker, *Negro Slave Revolts*, 50th anniversary ed. (New York: International Publishers, 1993), p. 175. From the Public Records of South Carolina, vol. 8, pp. 24–27.

2   Letter from Petersburg, Virginia (May 17, 1792). In Aptheker, *Negro Slave Revolts*, p. 211. First published in the *Boston Gazette and the Country Journal*, June 18, 1792.

3   Secret Keeper Richmond (Unknown) to Secret Keeper Norfolk (1793). In "A Letter to and From Slave Rebels," in Herbert Aptheker, *A Documentary History of the Negro People in the United States*, vol. 1 (New York: Citadel Press, 1951), p. 28. From the South Carolina Historical Commission, Columbia, SC.

4   "Felix" (Unknown) Slave Petition for Freedom (January 6, 1773). In Aptheker, ed., *A Documentary History of the Negro People in the United States*, vol. 1, pp. 6–7.

5   Peter Bestes and Other Slaves Petition for Freedom (April 20, 1773). In Aptheker, ed., *A Documentary History of the Negro People in the United States*, vol. 1, pp. 7–8. Leaflet in the collection of the New York Historical Society library.

6   "Petition of a Grate Number of Blackes" to Thomas Gage (May 25, 1774). In Aptheker, ed., *A Documentary History of the Negro People in the United States*, vol. 1, pp. 8–9. From the Massachusetts Historical Society, 5th series, vol. 3 (Boston, 1877), pp. 432ff.

7   "Petition of a Great Number of Negroes" to the Massachusetts House of Representatives (January 13, 1777). In Aptheker, ed., *A Documentary History of the Negro People in the United States*, vol. 1, pp. 9–10. From the Massachusetts Historical Society, 5th series, vol. 3 (Boston, 1877), pp. 432ff.

8   Benjamin Banneker, Letter to Thomas Jefferson (August 19, 1791). In Charles T. Cullen et al., ed., *The Papers of Thomas Jefferson, Volume 22: 6 August 1791 to 31 December 1791* (Princeton, NJ: Princeton University Press, 1986), pp. 49–52.

CHAPTER THREE: SERVITUDE AND REBELLION

1   Richard Frethorne on Indentured Servitude (March 20–April 3, 1623). In Susan Kingsbury, ed., *The Records of the Virginia Company of London* (Washington, DC: Government Printing Office, 1935), vol. 4, pp. 58–62.

2   *A True Narrative of the Rise, Progresse, and Cessation of the Late Rebellion in Virginia, Most Humbly and Impartially Reported by His Majestyes Commissioners Appointed to Enquire into the Affaires of the Said Colony* (1677). In Charles M. Andrews, ed., *Narratives of the Insurrections, 1675–1690* (New York: Charles Scribner's Sons, 1915), pp. 129–36.

3   Proclamation of the New Hampshire Legislature on Mast Tree Riot (1734). In Richard Hofstadter and Michael Wallace, eds., *American Violence: A Documentary History* (New York: Alfred A. Knopf, 1970), pp. 110–11. From *Documents and Records Relating to the Province of New Hampshire from 1722 to 1737*, vol. 4, p. 678.

4   Letter from William Shirley to the Lords of Trade (December 1, 1747). In Charles Henry Lincoln, ed., *Correspondence of William Shirley, Governor of Massachusetts and Military Commander in America, 1731–1760*, vol. 1 (New York: The Macmillan Company, 1912), pp. 412–17.

5   Gottlieb Mittelberger, *Gottlieb Mittelberger's Journey to Pennsylvania in the Year 1750 and Return to Germany in the Year 1754* (1754). In Gottlieb Mittelberger, *Gottlieb Mittelberger's Journey to Pennsylvania in the Year 1750 and Return to Germany in the Year 1754: Containing, Not Only a Description of the Country According to its Present Condition, But Also a Detailed Account of the Sad and Unfortunate Circumstances of Most of the Germans That Have Emigrated, Or Are Emigrating to That Country*, trans. from German by Carl Theo. Eben (1754) (Philadelphia: John Jos. McVey, 1898), pp. 19–29.

6   Account of the New York Tenant Riots (July 14, 1766). In Hofstadter and Wallace, eds., *American Violence: A Documentary History*, pp. 116–17. From the *Boston Gazetteer or Country Journal*, July 14, 1766.

CHAPTER FOUR: PREPARING THE REVOLUTION

1   Thomas Hutchinson Recounts the Reaction to the Stamp Act in Boston (1765). In Thomas Hutchinson, *The History of the Colony and Province of Massachusetts-Bay*, ed. Lawrence Shaw Mayo (Cambridge, Massachusetts: Harvard University Press, 1936), vol. 3, pp. 86–88, 89–90.

2   Samuel Drowne's Testimony on the Boston Massacre (March 16, 1770). In Anonymous, *A Short Narrative of the Horrid Massacre in Boston, Perpetrated in the Evening of the Fifth Day of March 1770: By Soldiers of the XXIXth Regiment, Which With The XIVth Regiment Were Then Quartered There: With Some Observations on the State of Things Prior to That Catastrophe: To Which Is Added, An Appendix, Containing The Several Depositions Referred to in the Preceding Narrative: And Also Other Depositions Relative to the Subject of It* (Boston: Printed by Order of the Town of Boston by Messrs. Eds and Gill, 1770), pp. 54–55.

3   George Hewes Recalls the Boston Tea Party (1834). In Henry Steele Commager and Richard B. Morris, eds., *The Spirit of 'Seventy-Six: The Story of the American Revolution as Told by Participants* (New York: Harper & Row, 1967), pp. 4–6.

4   New York Mechanics Declaration of Independence (May 29, 1776). In Peter Force, ed., *American Archives: Consisting of A Collection of Authentick Records, State Papers, Debates, and Letters and Other*

Notices of Publick Affairs, the Whole Forming a Documentary History of the Origin and Progress of the North American Colonies; of the Causes and Accomplishment of the American Revolution; and of the Constitution of Government for the United States, to the Final Ratification Thereof, 6 vols. (Washington, D.C.: M. St. Clair Clarke and Peter Force [Under Authority of Acts of Congress], 1846), 4th ser. (*A Documentary History of the English Colonies in North America from the King's Message to Parliament, of March 7, 1774, to the Declaration of Independence, by the United States*), vol. 6, pp. 614–15. Misspellings are in original.

5   Thomas Paine, *Common Sense* (1776). In Thomas Paine, *Collected Writings: Common Sense, The Crisis, and Other Pamphlets, Articles, and Letters, Rights of Man, The Age of Reason,* ed. Eric Foner (New York: The Library of America, 1995), pp. 20, 21–23, 24–28.

CHAPTER FIVE: HALF A REVOLUTION

1   Joseph Clarke's Letter about the Rebellion in Springfield (August 30, 1774). Letter to Major Joseph Hawley. In James Russell Trumbull, *History of Northampton, Massachusetts, From Its Settlement in 1654,* vol. 2 (Northampton, MA: Gazette Printing Company, 1902), pp. 346–48.

2   Joseph Plumb Martin, *A Narrative of Some of the Adventures, Dangers and Sufferings of a Revolutionary Soldier* (1830). First printed in Hallowell, Maine, by Glazier, Masters, and Co. in 1830. Reprinted as Joseph Plumb Martin, *A Narrative of Some of the Adventures, Dangers and Sufferings of a Revolutionary Soldier; Interspersed with Anecdotes of Incidents that Occurred within His Own Observation: Written by Himself,* ed. George F. Sheer (New York: The New York Times and Arno Press, 1968), pp. 283–89, 292–93.

3   Samuel Dewees Recounts the Suppression of Insubordination in the Continental Army after the Mutinies of 1781 (1844). First printed in Samuel Dewees, *A History of the Life and Services of Captain Samuel Dewees, A Native of Pennsylvania, and Soldier of the Revolutionary and Last Wars,* written and compiled by John Smith Hanna (Baltimore: Robert Neilson, 1844), pp. 228–32. Reprinted in Carl Van Doren, *Mutiny in January: The Story of a Crisis in the Continental Army Now for the First Time Fully Told from Many Hitherto Unknown or Neglected Sources Both American and British* (New York: Viking Press, 1943), pp. 253–56.

4   Henry Knox Letter to George Washington (October 23, 1786). In W. W. Abbott and Dorothy Twohig, eds., *The Papers of George Washington: Confederation Series, Volume 4: April 1786–January 1787,* vol. 4 (Charlottesville, VA: University Press of Virginia, 1995), pp. 299–302.

5   "Publius" (James Madison), *Federalist* No. 10 (November 23, 1787). Published on the Web site of the Library of Congress, American Memory: Historical Collections for the National Digital Library.

CHAPTER SIX: THE EARLY WOMEN'S MOVEMENT

1   Maria Stewart, "An Address Delivered at the African Masonic Hall, Boston" (February 27, 1833). In Maria Stewart, *Productions of Mrs. Maria W. Stewart, Presented to the First African Baptist Church & Society, of the City of Boston* (Boston: Friends of Freedom and Virtue, 1835), pp. 66–67.

2   Angelina E. Grimké Weld's Speech at Pennsylvania Hall (May 17, 1838). In *History of Pennsylvania Hall, Which Was Destroyed by a Mob, on the 17th of May, 1838* (Philadelphia: Merrihew and Gunn, 1838), pp. 123–26.

3   Harriet Hanson Robinson, "Characteristics of the Early Factory Girls" (1898). In Harriet Jane Hanson Robinson, *Loom and Spindle: Or, Life Among the Early Mill Girls* (New York, Boston, T. Y. Crowell & Company, 1898), pp. 37–40, 51–52.

4   S. Margaret Fuller Ossoli, *Woman in the Nineteenth Century* (1845). In S. Margaret Fuller Ossoli, *Woman in the Nineteenth Century: And, Kindred Papers Relating to the Sphere, Condition and Duties, of Woman,* Arthur B. Fuller ed. (New York: Greeley and McElrath, 1845), pp. 25–30.

5   Elizabeth Cady Stanton, "Declaration of Sentiments and Resolutions," Seneca Falls Convention (July 19, 1848). In Elizabeth Cady Stanton, Susan B. Anthony, and Matilda Joslyn Gage, eds., *History of Woman Suffrage, Volume I: 1848–1861* (New York: Fowler & Wells, Publishers, 1881), pp. 70–71.

6   Sojourner Truth, "Ain't I a Woman?" (1851). Quoted in Frances Gage, "Reminiscences by Frances D. Gage," in Stanton, Anthony, and Gage, eds., *History of Woman Suffrage,* vol. 1, p. 116. Text mod-

ernized for this edition by the editors. Compare with the account in "Women's Rights Convention: Sojourner Truth," *The Anti-Slavery Bugle* (Salem, Ohio), vol. 6, no, 41 (Whole no. 301) (June 21, 1851), p. 160.

7 Marriage Protest of Lucy Stone and Henry B. Blackwell (May 1, 1855). Quoted in T. W. Higginson, "Marriage of Lucy Stone Under Protest," *The Liberator* (Boston, Massachusetts), vol. 25, no. 18 (Whole no. 1085) (May 4, 1855), p. 71.

8 Susan B. Anthony Addresses Judge Ward Hunt, *The United States of America v. Susan B. Anthony* (June 19, 1873). In Ida Husted Harper, *The Life and Work Susan B. Anthony, Including Public Addresses, Her Own Letters and Many From Her Contemporaries During Fifty Years*, vol. 1 (Indianapolis: The Hollenbeck Press, 1898), pp. 438–41.

CHAPTER SEVEN: INDIAN REMOVAL

1 Tecumseh's Speech to the Osages (Winter 1811–12). In John D. Hunter, *Memoirs of a Captivity among the Indians of North America, From Childhood to the Age of Nineteen: With Anecdotes Descriptive of Their Manners and Customs: To Which Is Added, Some Account of The Soil, Climate, and Vegetable Productions of the Territory Westward of Mississippi* (London: Longman, Hurst, Rees, Orme, and Brown, 1823), pp. 45–48.

2 Cherokee Nation, "Memorial of the Cherokee Indians" (December 1829). First printed in from *The Cherokee Phoenix*, January 20, 1830. Reprinted as Cherokee Nation, "Memorial of the Cherokee Indians," *Niles' Weekly Register* (Baltimore, Maryland), vol. 38, no. 3 (Whole no. 965) (March 13, 1830), pp. 53–54.

3 Lewis Ross et al., Address of the Committee and Council of the Cherokee Nation, in General Council Convened, to the People of the United States (July 17, 1830). In *Niles' Weekly Register* (Baltimore, Maryland), vol. 38, no. 26 (Whole no. 988) (August 21, 1830), pp. 455–56.

4 Black Hawk's Surrender Speech (1832). In Samuel Gardner Drake, *Biography and History of the Indians of North America, from Its Discovery*, 11th ed. (Boston: B. B. Mussey,1851), pp. 656–57.

5 John G. Burnett, "The Cherokee Removal Through the Eyes of a Private Soldier" (December 11, 1890). In *Journal of Cherokee Studies*, vol. 3, no. 3 (1978), pp. 50–55. Special issue: *The Removal of the Cherokee*.

6 Chief Joseph's Surrender (October 5, 1877). Quoted in "The Surrender of Joseph" *Harper's Weekly*, vol. 21 (Whole no. 1090) (November 17, 1877), p. 906.

7 Chief Joseph Recounts His Trip to Washington, D.C. (1879). Quoted in Chester Anders Fee, *Chief Joseph: The Biography of a Great Indian* (New York: Wilson-Erickson, Inc., 1936), pp. 281–83.

8 Black Elk, "The End of the Dream" (1932). First printed in Black Elk, *Black Elk Speaks* (New York: William Morrow & Company, 1932). Reprinted as Black Elk, *Black Elk Speaks: Being the Life Story of a Holy Man of the Oglala Sioux: As Told Through John G. Neihardy (Flaming Rainbow)* (New York: Pocket Books/Bison Books, 1972), pp. 224–30.

CHAPTER EIGHT: THE WAR ON MEXICO

1 The Diary of Colonel Ethan Allen Hitchcock (June 30, 1845–March 26, 1846). In Ethan Allen Hitchcock, *Fifty Years in Camp and Field: Diary of Major-General Ethan Allen Hitchcock, U.S.A.*, ed. W. A. Croffut (New York: G. P. Putnam's Sons/The Knickerbocker Press, 1909), pp. 192, 198, 200, 203, 212–13.

2 Miguel Barragan, Dispatch on Texas Colonists (October 31, 1835). From a letter signed by José María Tornel, Miguel Barragan's secretary of war. Quoted in General Miguel A. Sanchez Lamego, *The Siege and Taking of the Alamo*, trans. Consuelo Velasco (Santa Fe: The Press of The Territorian, 1968), pp. 14–15. From the Historical Archives of the Secretary of National Defense, File XI/481.3/1145.

3 Juan Soto, Desertion Handbill (June 6, 1847). In Paul Foos, *A Short, Offhand, Killing Affair: Soldiers and Social Conflict During the Mexican-American War* (Chapel Hill and London: University of North Carolina Press, 2002), p. 106. Original handbill in the Beinecke Rare Book and Manuscript Library, Yale University, New Haven, Connecticut.

4   Frederick Douglass, Address to the New England Convention (May 31, 1849). Speech delivered at the New England Convention in Faneuil Hall Boston, Massachusetts. Printed in "Great Meeting at Faneuil Hall," *The Liberator* (Boston, Massachusetts), vol. 29, no. 23 (Whole no. 961), p. 90.

5   *North Star* Editorial, "The War with Mexico" (January 21, 1848). In the *North Star* (Rochester, New York), January 21, 1848.

6   Henry David Thoreau, *Civil Disobedience* (1849). In *Walden and Civil Disobedience*, ed. Paul Lauter (Boston and New York: Houghton Mifflin, 2000), pp. 17–23. This version is based on the 1866 text, "Civil Disobedience," as published in *A Yankee in Canada, with Anti-Slavery and Reform Papers*, rather than the 1849 version (titled "Resistance to Civil Government") from Elizabeth Peabody's *Aesthetic Papers* (1849), though there are only minor differences between the two.

CHAPTER NINE: SLAVERY AND DEFIANCE

1   David Walker's *Appeal* (1830). In David Walker, *David Walker's Appeal, In Four Articles; Together With a Preamble, to the Coloured Citizens of the World, but in Particular, and Very Expressly, to Those of the United States of America*, 3d ed. (Boston: David Walker, 1830; Baltimore: Black Classic Press, 1993), pp. 93–96.

2   Harriet A. Jacobs, *Incidents in the Life of a Slave Girl: Written by Herself* (1861). First printed in Boston, Massachusetts, in 1861. Reprinted as Harriet A. Jacobs, *Incidents in the Life of a Slave Girl: Written by Herself*, ed. L. Maria Child; enlarged ed., ed. Jean Fagan Yellin (Cambridge: Harvard University Press, 2000), pp. 68–71.

3   James Norcom's Runaway Slave Newspaper Advertisement for Harriet Jacobs (June 30, 1835). In *The American Beacon* (Norfolk, Virginia), July 4, 1835. Facsimile copy in Jacobs, *Incidents in the Life of a Slave Girl*, p. 237.

4   James R. Bradley, Letter to Lydia Maria Child (June 3, 1834). In C. Peter Ripley, ed., *The Black Abolitionist Papers, Volume III: The United States, 1830–1846* (Chapel Hill and London: University of North Carolina Press, 1991), pp. 136–37, 139–40. From the Anti-Slavery Collection, Boston Public Library, Boston, Massachusetts. All errors are in original.

5   Reverend Theodore Parker, "Speech of Theodore Parker at the Faneuil Hall Meeting" (May 26, 1854). In Charles Emery Stevens, *Anthony Burns: A History* (Boston: John P. Jewett and Company, 1856), pp. 289–95.

6   Henry Bibb, Letter to William Gatewood (March 23, 1844). In Henry Bibb, *Narrative of the Life and Adventures of Henry Bibb, An American Slave, Written by Himself* (New York: Published by the Author, 1850; New York: Greenwood Publishing Company/Negro Universities Press, 1969), pp. 176–78.

7   Jermain Wesley Loguen, Letter to Sarah Logue (March 28, 1860). First printed as "Mr. Loguen's reply," in *The Liberator* (Boston, Massachusetts), vol. 30, no. 17 (Whole no. 1531) (April 27, 1860), p. 1.

8   Frederick Douglass, "The Meaning of July Fourth for the Negro" (July 5, 1852). Speech delivered in Corinthian Hall, Rochester, New York. Printed in Frederick Douglass, *Frederick Douglass: Selected Speeches and Writings*, ed. Philip S. Foner, abridged ed. by Yuval Taylor (Chicago: Lawrence Hill Books, 1999), pp. 192, 194–95, 196–97.

9   John Brown, "John Brown's Last Speech" (November 2, 1859). In *Testimonies of Capt. John Brown, at Harper's Ferry, with his Address to the Court* (New York: American Anti-Slavery Society, 1860), pp. 15–16. No. 7, new series, of the Anti-Slavery Tracts.

10 Osborne P. Anderson, *A Voice from Harper's Ferry* (1861). First printed in Osborne P. Anderson, *A Voice from Harper's Ferry: A Narrative of Events at Harper's Ferry; With, Incidents Prior and Subsequent to its Capture by Captain Brown and His Men* (Boston: Printed for the author, 1861). Reprinted in Jean Libby, *Black Voices from Harper's Ferry: Osborne Anderson and the John Brown Raid* (Palo Alto, California: Jean Libby, 1979), pp. 59–62.

11 Martin Delany's Advice to Former Slaves (July 23, 1865). The speech was reported in the letter of Lieutenant Edward M. Stoeber to Major S. M. Taylor of the Bureau Refugees, Freedmen, and Abandoned Lands South Carolina, Georgia, and Florida, sent from Beaufort, S.C., July 24, 1865. Printed in part in Ira Berlin, Steven Hahn, Steven F. Miller, Joseph P. Reidy, and Leslie S. Rowland,

"The Terrain of Freedom: The Struggle over the Meaning of Free Labor in the U.S. South," *History Workshop*, no. 22 (Autumn 1986), pp. 123–27. From the U.S. National Archives and Records Administration, Freedman's Bureau Records, Washington, D.C., S-5 1865, Registered Letters Received (series 2922), South Carolina Assistant Commissioner, BRFAL, NA.

12 Henry McNeal Turner, "On the Eligibility of Colored Members to Seats in the Georgia Legislature" (September 3, 1868). In Edwin S. Redkey, ed., *Respect Black: The Writings and Speeches of Henry McNeal Turner* (New York: Arno Press/The New York Times, 1971), pp. 14–15, 16, 25.

CHAPTER TEN: CIVIL WAR AND CLASS CONFLICT

1 An Eyewitness Account of the Flour Riot in New York (February 1837). First printed in the *Commercial Register* (New York, New York), February 14, 1837, and then in *Niles' Weekly Register* (Baltimore, Maryland), 5th series, vol. 1, no. 26 (February 25, 1837), pp. 433–44.

2 Hinton Rowan Helper, *The Impending Crisis of the South* (1857). First printed in New York by Burdick Brothers in 1857. Reprinted in Hinton Rowan Helper, *The Impending Crisis of the South: How to Meet It*, ed. George M. Frederickson (Cambridge, Massachusetts: The Belknap Press of Harvard University Press, 1968), pp. 42–46.

3 "Mechanic" (Unknown), "Voting by Classes" (October 13, 1863) . In *Columbus* [Georgia] *Daily Sun*, October 13, 1863, p. 1.

4 Joel Tyler Headley, *The Great Riots of New York* (1873). First printed as *The Great Riots of New York, 1712 to 1873: Including a Full and Complete Account of the Four Days' Draft Riot of 1863* (New York: E. B. Treat, 1873). Reprinted as Joel Tyler Headley, *The Great Riots of New York: 1712–1873* (New York: Thunder's Mouth Press, 2004), pp. 109–13.

5 Report on a Bread Riot in Savannah, Georgia (April 1864). In the *Augusta Chronicle and Sentinel* (August, Georgia), April 22, 1864, n.p.

6 "Exempt" (Unknown), "To Go, Or Not to Go" (June 28, 1864). In the *Milledgeville Confederate Union* (Midgeville, Georgia), June 28, 1864, n.p.

7 O.G.G. (Unknown), Letter to the Editor (February 17, 1865). In the *Macon Daily Telegraph and Confederate* (Macon, Georgia), February 24, 1865, n.p.

8 *Columbus Sun*, "The Class That Suffer" (February 1865). In the *Augusta Chronicle and Sentinel* (Augusta, Georgia), February 17, 1865, n.p.

9 J. A. Dacus, *Annals of the Great Strikes in the United States* (1877). In J.A. Dacus, *Annals of the Great Strikes in the United States: A Reliable History and Graphic Description of the Causes and Thrilling Events of the Labor Strikes and Riots of 1877* (St Louis: Scammell and Company, 1877), pp. 21–23, 42–43, 98–99.

CHAPTER ELEVEN: STRIKERS AND POPULISTS IN THE GILDED AGE

1 Henry George, "The Crime of Poverty" (April 1, 1885). In Henry George, *The Crime of Poverty: An Address*. Delivered in the Opera House, Burlington, Iowa, April 1, 1885, Under the Auspices of the Burlington Assembly, No. 3135, Knights of Labor (Glasgow: "Land Values" Publication Department, n.d.), pp. 5–6, 7, 9–10, 11, 12, 13–15, 18, 19, 25–26.

2 August Spies, "Address of August Spies" (October 7, 1886). In *The Accused [and] the Accusers: The Famous Speeches of the Eight Chicago Anarchists in Court: When Asked If They Had Anything to Say Why Sentence Should Not Be Passed Upon Them: On October 7th, 8th, and 9th, 1886: Chicago, Illinois* (Chicago: Socialistic Publishing Society, n.d.), pp. 1, 9–10.

3 Anonymous, "Red-Handed Murder: Negroes Wantonly Killed at Thibodaux, La." (November 26, 1887). In *The Weekly Pelican* (New Orleans, Louisiana), vol. 1, no. 52 (November 26, 1887), p. 2.

4 Reverend Ernest Lyon et al., Open Letter from the New Orleans Mass Meeting (August 22, 1888). First printed by the *Louisiana Standard* (New Orleans), August 25, 1888. Reprinted in *Congressional Record*, 50th Cong., 1st Sess., vol. 19, part 9, appendix, pp. 8993–94.

5 Mary Elizabeth Lease, "Wall Street Owns the Country" (circa 1890). Quoted in William E. Connelley, ed., *History of Kansas, State and People: Kansas as the First Quarter Post of the Twentieth Century*, vol. 2 (Chicago: The American Historical Society, Inc., 1928), p. 1167.

6   Mary Elizabeth Lease, Speech to the Woman's Christian Temperance Union (1890). In Joan M. Jensen, ed., *With These Hands: Women Working on the Land* (Old Westbury, NY: The Feminist Press; New York: McGraw-Hill Book Company, 1981), pp. 154–55, 158–60.

7   The Omaha Platform of the People's Party of America (July 4, 1892). First printed in "Omaha," *The National Economist,* vol. 7, no. 17 (July 9, 1892), p. 257.

8   Reverend J. L. Moore on the Colored Farmers' Alliance (March 7, 1891). First printed as J. L. Moore. "The Florida Colored Farmers' Alliance, 1891," in *National Economist* (Washington, DC), March 7, 1891. Reprinted as Reverend J. L. Moore, "We Join Hands . . . ," in Milton Meltzer, ed., *In Their Own Words: The History of the American Negro 1865–1916,* vol. 2 (New York: Thomas Y. Crowell Company, 1965), pp. 109–11.

9   Ida B. Wells-Barnett, "Lynch Law" (1893). In Ida B. Wells-Barnett, *Selected Works of Ida B. Wells-Barnett,* ed. Henry Louis Gates, Jr. (New York: Oxford University Press, 1991), pp. 74–77.

10   Statement from the Pullman Strikers (June 15, 1894). In U.S. Strike Commission, *Report on the Chicago Strike of June–July, 1894, by the United States Strike Commission* (Washington, DC: Government Printing Office, 1895), pp. 87–88.

11   Edward Bellamy, *Looking Backward: 2000–1887* (1888). First printed in New York by Ticknor and Company in 1888. Reprinted as Edward Bellamy, *Looking Backward: 2000–1887* (New York: Penguin Books, 1982), pp. 67–70.

CHAPTER TWELVE: THE EXPANSION OF THE EMPIRE

1   Calixto Garcia's Letter to General William R. Shafter (July 17, 1898). In Philip Foner, ed., *The Spanish–Cuban–American War and the Birth of American Imperialism, vol. II: 1898–1902* (New York: Monthly Review Press, 1972), pp. 369–70.

2   Lewis H. Douglass on Black Opposition to McKinley (November 17, 1899). First printed in *American Citizen* (Kansas City), November 17, 1899. Reprinted in Foner, ed., *The Spanish–Cuban–American War and the Birth of American Imperialism,* vol. 2, pp. 824–25.

3   Missionary Department of the Atlanta, Georgia, A.M.E. Church, "The Negro Should Not Enter the Army" (May 1, 1899). In *Voice of Missions* (Atlanta, Georgia), May 1, 1899, p. 2.

4   I. D. Barnett et al., *Open Letter to President McKinley by Colored People Of Massachusetts* (October 3, 1899). Statement read by Archibald M. Grimké at Charles Street Church, Boston, Massachusetts. First printed in I. D. Barnett et al., *Open Letter to President McKinley by Colored People Of Massachusetts* (n.p.: n.p, n.d.), pp. 2–4, 10–12.

5   Samuel Clemens, "Comments on the Moro Massacre" (March 12, 1906). First published in *Mark Twain's Autobiography,* ed. Albert Bigelow Paine (New York: Harper and Brothers, 1924). Reprinted in *Mark Twain's Weapons of Satire: Anti-imperialist Writings on the Philippine-American War,* ed. Jim Zwick (New York: Syracuse University Press, 1992), pp. 170–73. From the Mark Twain Papers, The Bancroft Library, University of California at Berkeley.

6   Smedley D. Butler, *War Is a Racket* (1935). First printed in New York by Round Table Press in 1935. Reprinted in Smedley D. Butler, *War Is a Racket: The Antiwar Classic by America's Most Decorated General, Two Other Anti-Interventionist Tracts, and Photographs from the Horror of It* (Los Angeles: Feral House, 2003), pp. 23–26.

CHAPTER THIRTEEN: SOCIALISTS AND WOBBLIES

1   Mother Jones, "Agitation—The Greatest Factor for Progress" (March 24, 1903). Speech delivered in the Memorial Hall, Toledo, Ohio. First printed in *The Toledo Bee,* March 25, 1903. Reprinted in *Mother Jones Speaks: Collected Writings and Speeches,* ed. Philip S. Foner (New York: Monad Press, 1983), pp. 95, 96–98.

2   Upton Sinclair, *The Jungle* (1906). In Upton Sinclair, *The Jungle* (New York: Doubleday, Page & Company, 1906), pp. 401–05, 409–10.

3   W. E. B. Du Bois, *The Souls of Black Folk* (1903). First printed in Chicago by A.C. McClurg & Co. in 1903. Reprinted as W. E. B. Du Bois, *The Souls of Black Folk* (New York: Penguin Classics, 1989), pp. 3–12.

4   Emma Goldman, "Patriotism: A Menace to Liberty" (1908). First printed in New York by Mother
      Earth Publishing Association in 1908. Reprinted in Emma Goldman, *Anarchism and Other Essays* (New
      York: Dover Publications, Inc., 1969), pp. 127–28, 128–29, 135–36, 144.

5   "Proclamation of the Striking Textile Workers of Lawrence" (1912). In Charles P. Neill, ed., *Report
      on the Strike of Textile Workers in Lawrence, Massachusetts in 1912*, 62nd Congress, 2nd Session, Senate
      Document 870 (Washington, D.C.: Government Printing Office, 1912), pp. 503–04.

6   Arturo Giovannitti's Address to the Jury (November 23, 1912). First printed in *Ettor and Giovannitti
      Before the Jury at Salem, Massachusetts, November 23, 1912* (Chicago: IWW, n.d. [circa 1913]).
      Reprinted in Joyce Kornbluh, ed., *Rebel Voices: An IWW Anthology* (Ann Arbor: The University of
      Michigan Press, 1964), pp. 193, 194, 195.

7   Woody Guthrie, "Ludlow Massacre" (1946). First recorded for Moe Asch in 1946. First printed in
      Sing Out!, vol. 8, no. 3 (1959).

8   Julia May Courtney, "Remember Ludlow!" (May 1914). First printed in *Mother Earth*, vol. 9, no. 3
      (May 1914), pp. 77–78, 79. Reprinted in Peter Glassgold, ed., *Anarchy! An Anthology of Emma
      Goldman's Mother Earth* (Washington, D.C.: Counterpoint, 2001), pp. 345–46, 347.

9   Joe Hill, "My Last Will" (November 18, 1915). First printed in the *Herald-Republican* (Salt Lake
      City, Utah), November 18, 1915. Reprinted in Franklin Rosemont, *Joe Hill: The IWW and the
      Making of a Revolutionary Workingclass Counterculture: Profusely Illustrated* (Chicago: Charles H. Kerr,
      2002), p. 132.

CHAPTER FOURTEEN: PROTESTING THE FIRST WORLD WAR

1   Helen Keller, "Strike Against War" (January 5, 1916). Speech delivered at Carnegie Hall, in New
      York City, sponsored by the Women's Peace Party and the Labor Forum. First printed in *The Call* (New
      York, New York), January 6, 1916. Reprinted in Helen Keller, *Helen Keller: Her Socialist Years*, ed. Philip
      S. Foner (New York: International Publishers, 1967). pp. 75–81.

2   John Reed, "Whose War?" (April 1917). First printed in *The Masses*, vol. 9, no. 6 (whole no. 70)
      (April 1917), pp. 11–12. Reprinted in James C. Wilson, ed., *John Reed for The Masses* (Jefferson,
      North Carolina: McFarland & Company, Inc., 1987), pp. 164–66.

3   "Why the IWW Is Not Patriotic to the United States" (1918). Quoted in National Civil Liberties
      Bureau, *The Truth About the IWW: Facts in Relation to the Trial at Chicago by Competent Industrial
      Investigators and Noted Economists* (New York: National Civil Liberties Bureau, April 1918), p. 38.
      See also Carleton H. Parker, *The Casual Laborer and Other Essays* (New York: Harcourt, Brace and
      Howe, 1920), p. 102.

4   Emma Goldman, Address to the Jury in *U.S. v. Emma Goldman and Alexander Berkman* (July 9,
      1917). Delivered in New York, New York. In *Anarchy on Trial: Speeches of Alexander Berkman and Emma
      Goldman Before the Federal Jury in the City of New York, July, 1917* (New York: Mother Earth
      Publishing Association, 1917), pp. 58–60, 61, 64–65.

5   Eugene Debs, "The Canton, Ohio, Speech" (June 16, 1918). In Jean Y. Tussey ed., *Eugene V. Debs
      Speaks* (New York: Pathfinder Press, 1970), pp. 251–52, 253, 256–57, 260–61.

6   Eugene Debs, Statement to the Court (September 18, 1918). In William A. Pelz, *The Eugene V. Debs
      Reader: Socialism and the Class Struggle* (Chicago: Institute of Working Class History, 2000), pp.
      170–72.

7   Randolph Bourne, "The State" (1918). First printed in Randolph Bourne, *Untimely Papers*, ed. James
      Oppenheim (New York: B. W. Huebsch, 1919). Reprinted in Lillian Schlissel, ed., *The World of
      Randolph Bourne* (New York: E. P. Dutton, 1965), pp. 245–46, 247–49, 250–51, 254–55, 257, 260,
      264–65.

8   e. e. cummings, "i sing of Olaf glad and big" (1931). In e. e. cummings, *The Complete Poems:
      1904–1962*, ed. George J. Firmage (New York: Liveright, 1994), p. 340.

9   John Dos Passos, "The Body of an American" (1932). In John Dos Passos, *U.S.A.* (New York: The
      Modern Library/Random House, 1939), pp. 470–73.

10   Dalton Trumbo, *Johnny Got His Gun* (1939). In Dalton Trumbo, *Johnny Got His Gun* (New York: J.
      B. Lippincott Company, 1939), pp. 289–96.

CHAPTER FIFTEEN: FROM THE JAZZ AGE TO THE UPRISINGS OF THE 1930S

1 F. Scott Fitzgerald, "Echoes of the Jazz Age" (1931). First printed in *Scribner's Magazine*, vol. 40, no. 5 (November 1931), pp. 459, 460–61, 464–65. Reprinted in Arthur Mizener, ed., *The Fitzgerald Reader* (New York: Charles Scribner's Sons, 1962), pp. 323, 324–25, 330–31.

2 Yip Harburg, "Brother, Can You Spare a Dime" (1932). Printed in Yip Harburg, *The Yip Harburg Songbook*, ed. Tom Roed (Miami: CPP/Belwin, Inc., 1994), pp. 13–16.

3 Paul Y. Anderson, "Tear-Gas, Bayonets, and Votes" (August 17, 1932). In Paul Y. Anderson, "Tear-Gas, Bayonets, and Votes: The President Opens His Reelection Campaign," *The Nation*, vol. 135, no. 3502 (August 17, 1932), pp. 138–40.

4 Mary Licht, "I Remember the Scottsboro Defense" (February 15, 1997). In the *People's Weekly World* (New York), February 15, 1997.

5 Ned Cobb ("Nate Shaw"), *All God's Dangers* (1969). In Theodore Rosengarten, *All God's Dangers: The Life of Nate Shaw* (Chicago: University of Chicago Press, 2000), pp. 295, 296–98, 544–45, 546.

6 Billie Holiday, "Strange Fruit" (1937). Lyrics by Abel Meeropol ("Lewis Allan"). First printed as Abel Meeropol, "Bitter Fruit" in *New York Teacher*, vol. 1, no. 12 (January 1937), p. 17.

7 Langston Hughes, "Ballad of Roosevelt" (1934). First printed in *The New Republic*, vol. 81, no. 1041 (November 14, 1934), p. 9. Reprinted in Langston Hughes, *The Collected Poems of Langston Hughes*, ed. Arnold Rampersad and David Roessel (New York: Alfred A. Knopf, 1994), pp. 178–79.

8 Langston Hughes, "Ballad of the Landlord" (1940). First printed in *Opportunity*, vol. 18, no. 12 (December 1940), p. 364, and then incorporated in 1951, with slight alterations, reflected here, in "Montage of a Dream Deferred." Reprinted in Hughes, *The Collected Poems of Langston Hughes*, pp. 402–03.

9 Speech to the Court of Bartolomeo Vanzetti (April 9, 1927). In Marion D. Frankfurter and Gardner Jackson, eds., *The Letters of Sacco and Vanzetti* (London: Constable and Company, 1929), Appendix II, pp. 362–63, 370–72, 376–77.

10 Vicky Starr ("Stella Nowicki"), "Back of the Yards" (1973). In Alice Lynd and Staughton Lynd, eds., *Rank and File: Personal Histories by Working-Class Organizers* (Boston: Beacon Press, 1973), p. 69, 70–73, 75, 76, 83, 84, 85–86.

11 Sylvia Woods, "You Have to Fight for Freedom" (1973). In Lynd and Lynd, eds., *Rank and File*, pp. 113, 115, 116, 119, 123–24, 128–29.

12 Rose Chernin on Organizing the Unemployed in the Bronx in the 1930s (1949). As recounted by her daughter, Kim Chernin, in Kim Chernin, *In My Mother's House* (New Haven, CT: Ticknor and Fields, 1983), pp. 92–98.

13 Genora (Johnson) Dollinger, *Striking Flint: Genora (Johnson) Dollinger Remembers the 1936–37 GM Sit-Down Strike* (February 1995). Interview by Susan Rosenthal conducted February 1995. In Genora (Johnson Dollinger), with Susan Rosenthal, *Striking Flint: Genora (Johnson) Dollinger Remembers the 1936–37 GM Sit-Down Strike* (Chicago: L. J. Page Publications, 1996), pp. 5, 7, 8, 11–12, 14–16, 25. Available from Haymarket Books (Chicago, IL).

14 John Steinbeck, *The Grapes of Wrath* (1939). First printed in New York by Viking Press in 1993. Reprinted as John Steinbeck, *The Grapes of Wrath* (New York: Penguin Books, 1992), pp. 568–73.

15 Woody Guthrie, "This Land Is Your Land" (February 1940). Woody Guthrie wrote "This Land Is Your Land" in February 1940, but first recorded the song for Moe Asch and released it on Folkways Album #FP27 (*This Land Is My Land*) in 1951.

CHAPTER SIXTEEN: WORLD WAR II AND MCCARTHYISM

1 Paul Fussell, "'Precision Bombing Will Win the War'" (1989). In Paul Fussell, *Wartime: Understanding and Behavior in the Second World War* (New York: Oxford University Press, 1989), pp. 13–16.

2 Yuri Kochiyama, "Then Came the War" (1991). In Joann Faung Jean Lee, *Asian American Experiences in the United States: Oral Histories of First to Fourth Generation Americans from China, the Philippines, Japan, India, the Pacific Islands, Vietnam, and Cambodia* (Jefferson, North Carolina: McFarland and Company, Inc., 1991), pp. 10, 11–15, 16–17, 18.

3   Yamaoka Michiko, "Eight Hundred Meters from the Hypocenter" (1992). In Haruko Taya Cook and
    Theodore F. Cook, *Japan at War: An Oral History* (New York: New Press, 1992), pp. 384–87.
4   United States Strategic Bombing Survey, *Summary Report (Pacific War)* (July 1, 1946). In United
    States Strategic Bombing Survey, *United States Strategic Bombing Survey: Summary Report (Pacific
    War)* (Washington, DC: Government Printing Office, 1946), pp. 22–26.
5   Admiral Gene Larocque Speaks to Studs Terkel About "The Good War" (1985). In Studs Terkel,
    "*The Good War": An Oral History of World War Two* (New York: Pantheon, 1984; New York: New Press,
    1997), pp. 189–93.
6   Kurt Vonnegut, *Slaughterhouse-Five* (1969). First printed as Kurt Vonnegut, Jr., *Slaughterhouse-Five:
    Or, The Children's Crusade, A Duty-Dance with Death* (New York: Delta Book/Dell, 1969), pp.
    129–32. Reprinted as Kurt Vonnegut, *Slaughterhouse-Five* (New York: Laurel Book/Dell Publishing,
    1991), pp. 149–52.
7   Paul Robeson's Unread Statement before the House Committee on Un-American Activities (June
    12, 1956). In Paul Robeson, "A Statement by Paul Robeson" (June 12, 1956), Appendix 3, in Eric
    Bentley ed., *Thirty Years of Treason: Excerpts from Hearings Before the House Committee on Un-American
    Activities, 1938–1968* (New York: Thunder's Mouth Press/Nation Books, 2002), pp. 977–80. See also
    Robeson's testimony before HUAC, pp. 770–89.
8   Peter Seeger, "Thou Shall Not Sing" (1989). In Bud Schultz and Ruth Schultz, eds., *It Did Happen
    Here: Recollections of Political Repression in America* (Berkeley: University of California Press, 1989),
    pp. 15–17.
9   I. F. Stone, "But It's Not Just Joe McCarthy" (March 15, 1954). First printed in *I. F. Stone's Weekly*,
    vol. 2, no. 8 (March 15, 1954). Reprinted in I. F. Stone, *The I. F. Stone's Weekly Reader*, ed. Neil
    Middleton (New York: Random House, 1973), pp. 39–44.
10 The Final Letter from Ethel and Julius Rosenberg to Their Children (June 19, 1953). In Michael
    Meeropol, ed., *The Rosenberg Letters: A Complete Edition of the Prison Correspondence of Julius and Ethel
    Rosenberg* (New York: Garland, 1994), p. 702–03.

CHAPTER SEVENTEEN: THE BLACK UPSURGE AGAINST RACIAL SEGREGATION

1   Richard Wright, *12 Million Black Voices* (1941). First printed in New York by Viking Press in 1941.
    Reprinted as Richard Wright *12 Million Black Voices: A Folk History of the Negro in the United States*
    (New York: Thunder's Mouth Press, 2002), pp. 98–102.
2   Langston Hughes, "Dream Boogie" (1951). In Hughes, *The Collected Poems of Langston Hughes*, p.
    368. This poem and "Harlem" are both part of *Montage of a Dream Deferred*.
3   Langston Hughes, "Harlem" (1951). In Hughes, *The Collected Poems of Langston Hughes*, p. 426.
4   Anne Moody, *Coming of Age in Mississippi* (1968). In Anne Moody, *Coming of Age in Mississippi*
    (New York: Dial Press, 1968), pp. 235–39.
5   John Lewis, Original Text of Speech to Be Delivered at the Lincoln Memorial (August 28, 1963). In
    Clayborne Carson et al., eds., *The Eyes on the Prize Civil Rights Reader: Documents, Speeches, and
    Firsthand Accounts from the Black Freedom Struggle, 1954–1990* (New York: Penguin, 1991), p.
    163–65.
6   Malcolm X, "Message to the Grass Roots" (November 10, 1963). Speech delivered in Detroit,
    Michigan, at the Northern Grass Roots Leadership Conference. In Malcolm X, *Malcolm X Speaks:
    Selected Speeches and Statements*, ed. George Breitman (New York: Grove Weidenfeld, 1990), pp 4–5,
    6–8.
7   Martha Honey, Letter from Mississippi Freedom Summer (August 9, 1964). In Elizabeth Sutherland
    Martínez, ed., *Letters from Mississippi* (Brookline, Massachusetts: Zephyr Press, 2002), pp. 222–24.
8   Testimony of Fannie Lou Hamer (August 22, 1964). Joseph L. Rauh, Jr., papers, Library of Congress,
    Manuscript Division, Washington, DC. In the original, Hamer's name is misspelled "Fanny."
9   Testimony of Rita L. Schwerner (1964). In *Mississippi Black Paper: Fifty-Seven Negro and White
    Citizens' Testimony of Police Brutality, the Breakdown of Law and Order and the Corruption of Justice in
    Mississippi* (New York: Random House, 1965), pp. 59–60, 61, 62–63.

10   Alice Walker, "Once" (1968). In Alice Walker, *Once: Poems by Alice Walker* (New York: Harcourt, Brace & World, 1968), pp. 23–36.

11   Sandra A. West, "Riot!—A Negro Resident's Story" (July 24, 1967). First printed in *The Detroit News*, July 24, 1967, p. 7A. Reprinted in *Reporting Civil Rights: Part Two: American Journalism 1963–1973* (New York: The Library of America, 2003), pp. 596–97.

12   Martin Luther King, Jr., "Where Do We Go from Here?" (August 16, 1967). Annual Report Delivered at the 11th Convention of the Southern Christian Leadership Conference. The Martin Luther King, Jr. Papers Project, Stanford University, Stanford, California.

CHAPTER EIGHTEEN: VIETNAM AND BEYOND: THE HISTORIC RESISTANCE

1   Mississippi Freedom Democratic Party, McComb, Mississippi, Petition Against the War in Vietnam (July 28, 1965). First circulated as a leaflet and then published in the McComb, Mississippi, Mississippi Freedom Democratic Party newsletter, July 28, 1965. Reprinted in Joanne Grant, ed., *Black Protest: History, Documents, and Analyses: 1619 to the Present*, 2nd ed (Greenwich, CT: Fawcett, 1968), pp. 415–16.

2   Martin Luther King, Jr., "Beyond Vietnam" (April 1, 1967). Speech delivered in Riverside Church, New York, New York, sponsored by Clergy and Laity Concerned. Martin Luther King, Jr., Martin Luther King Papers Project at Stanford University, Stanford, California.

3   Student Nonviolent Coordinating Committee, Position Paper on Vietnam (January 6, 1966). In Grant, ed., *Black Protest*, pp. 416–18.

4   Bob Dylan, "Masters of War" (1963). In Bob Dylan, *Lyrics, 1962–1985: Includes All of Writings and Drawings Plus 120 New Writings,* 2nd ed. (New York: Alfred A. Knopf, 1985), p. 56.

5   Muhammad Ali Speaks Out Against the Vietnam War (1966). Quoted in Mike Marqusee, *Redemption Song: Muhammad Ali and the Sprit of the Sixties* (New York: Verso, 1999), p. 214–15.

6   Jonathan Schell, *The Village of Ben Suc* (1967). In Jonathan Schell, *The Village of Ben Suc* (New York: Borzoi/Alfred A. Knopf, 1967), pp. 122–30, 131–32.

7   Larry Colburn, "They Were Butchering People" (2003). In Christian G. Appy, *Patriots: The Vietnam War Remembered From All Sides* (New York: Viking, 2003), pp. 346–49.

8   Haywood T. "The Kid" Kirkland, from *Bloods: An Oral History of the Vietnam War by Black Veterans* (1984). In Wallace Terry, *Bloods: An Oral History of the Vietnam War by Black Veterans* (New York: Random House, 1984), pp. 94–95, 103–05.

9   Loung Ung, "People Just Disappeared and You Didn't Say Anything" (2003). In Appy, *Patriots,* pp. 526–28.

10   Tim O'Brien, "The Man I Killed" (1990). In Tim O'Brien, *The Things They Carried* (New York: Broadway Books, 1998), pp. 124–30.

11   Maria Herrera-Sobek, Two Poems on Vietnam (1999). In Maria Herrera-Sobek, "Cinco Poemas," in George Mariscal, ed., *Aztlán and Viet Nam: Chicano and Chicana Experiences of the War* (Berkeley: University of California Press, 1999), pp. 234–35.

12   Daniel Ellsberg, *Secrets: A Memoir of Vietnam and the Pentagon Papers* (2003). In Daniel Ellsberg, *Secrets: A Memoir of Vietnam and the Pentagon Papers* (New York: Penguin, 2003), pp. vii–ix.

CHAPTER NINETEEN: WOMEN, GAYS, AND OTHER VOICES OF RESISTANCE

1   Allen Ginsberg, "America" (January 17, 1956). First composed in Berkeley, California. In Allen Ginsberg, *Collected Poems 1947–1980* (New York: Harper and Row, 1984), pp. 146–48.

2   Martin Duberman, *Stonewall* (1993). In Martin Duberman, *Stonewall* (New York: Dutton, 1993), pp. 197–202.

3   Wamsutta (Frank B.) James, Suppressed Speech on the 350th Anniversary of the Pilgrim's Landing at Plymouth Rock (September 10, 1970). United American Indians of New England, East Weymouth, Massachusetts.

4   Adrienne Rich, *Of Woman Born* (1977). In Adrienne Rich, *Of Woman Born: Motherhood as Experience and Institution,* 10th anniversary ed. (New York: W. W. Norton, 1986), pp. 281–86. The afterword,

excerpted here, does not appear in the original 1976 edition, but in the 1977 Bantam paperback edition and in the tenth anniversary Norton edition, reissued in 1995.

5   Abbey Lincoln, "Who Will Revere the Black Woman?" (September 1966). In *Negro Digest*, vol. 15, no. 11 (September 1966), pp. 16–17, 18, 19–20.

6   Susan Brownmiller, "Abortion Is a Woman's Right" (1999). In Susan Brownmiller, *In Our Time: Memoir of a Revolution* (New York: Dial Press/Random House, 1999), pp. 102–04.

7   Assata Shakur (Joanne Chesimard), "Women in Prison: How We Are" (April 1978). In *The Black Scholar: Journal of Black Studies and Research*, vol. 9, no. 7 (April 1978), pp. 8–11, 13. The original text uses the lower-case first-person pronoun "i" except when it is the first word of a sentence.

8   Kathleen Neal Cleaver, "Women, Power, and Revolution" (October 16, 1998). Based on a talk given October 16, 1998, at Howard University, Washington, DC. In Kathleen Cleaver and George Katsiaficas, eds., *Liberation, Imagination, and the Black Panther Party: A New Look at the Panthers and their Legacy* (New York: Routledge, 2001), pp. 123–26.

CHAPTER TWENTY: LOSING CONTROL IN THE 1970S

1   Howard Zinn, "The Problem Is Civil Obedience" (November 1970). First printed in Hugh Davis Graham, ed., *Violence: The Crisis of American Confidence* (Baltimore: Johns Hopkins Press, 1971), pp. 154–62. Reprinted in Howard Zinn, *The Zinn Reader: Writings on Disobedience and Democracy* (New York: Seven Stories Press, 1997), pp. 403–11.

2   George Jackson, *Soledad Brother* (1970). First printed in New York by Coward-McCann in 1970. Reprinted as George Jackson, *Soledad Brother: The Prison Letters of George Jackson* (Chicago: Lawrence Hill Books, 1994), pp. 67–68, 233, 234–236.

3   Bob Dylan "George Jackson" (1971). In Dylan, *Lyrics, 1962–1985*, p. 302.

4   Angela Davis, "Political Prisoners, Prisons, and Black Liberation" (May 1971). Written in the Marin County Jail. First printed in Angela Y. Davis, ed., *If They Come in the Morning: Voices of Resistance* (New York: Third Press/Joseph Okpaku Books, 1971; San Francisco: National United Committee to Free Angela Davis, 1971), pp. 19–20, 27, 28–29, 31–33. Reprinted in Angela Y. Davis, *The Angela Y. Davis Reader*, ed. Joy James (Malden, Massachusetts: Blackwell Publishers, 1998), pp. 39–52.

5   L. D. Barkley (September 9, 1971). Transcribed from the Freedom Archives compact disc *Prisons on Fire: George Jackson, Attica and Black Liberation* (Oakland: AK Press/Alternative Tentacles, 2002). 60 mins. Produced by Anita Johnson and Claude Marks in cooperation with the Prison Radio Project.

6   Interview with Frank "Big Black" Smith (2000). In *The Rockefellers*, PBS, "The American Experience" Series (2000), two parts. Written, produced, and directed by Elizabeth Deane and Adriana Bosch.

7   Leonard Peltier on the Trail of Broken Treaties Protest (1999). In Leonard Peltier, *Prison Writings: My Life Is My Sundance*, ed. Harvey Arden (New York: St. Martin's Press, 1999), pp. 99–102.

8   Select Committee to Study Governmental Operations with Respect to Intelligence Activities, *Covert Action in Chile 1963–1973* (December 18, 1975). 94th Congress 1st Session, Staff Report of the Select Committee To Study Governmental Operations With Respect to Intelligence Activities, United States Senate, December 18, 1975 (Washington, DC: U.S. Government Printing Office, 1975).

9   Noam Chomsky, "COINTELPRO: What the (Deleted) Was It?" (March 12, 1978). In Noam Chomsky, "COINTELPRO: What the (Deleted) Was It?: Engineering of Consent," *The Public Eye* (The Repression Information Project, Washington, DC), vol. 1, no. 2 (April 1978), pp. 14–16.

CHAPTER TWENTY-ONE: THE CARTER–REAGAN–BUSH CONSENSUS

1   Marian Wright Edelman, Commencement Address at Milton Academy (June 10, 1983). Speech delivered in Milton, Massachusetts. Personal manuscript of Marian Wright Edelman. Selection from pp. 2–5, 6.

2   César Chávez, Address to the Commonwealth Club of California (November 9, 1984). In César Chávez, *The Words of César Chávez*, ed. Richard J. Jensen and John C. Hammerback (College Station: Texas A&M University Press, 2002), pp. 122–26, 128–29. From the United Farm Workers Papers, Wayne State University, Detroit, Michigan.

3   Testimony of Ismael Guadalupe Ortiz on Vieques, Puerto Rico (October 2, 1979). Text first printed in Spanish in Arturo Meléndez López, *La Batalla de Vieques* (Bayamón, Puerto Rico: COPEC, 1982). Translation courtesy of Ismael Guadalupe Ortiz.

4   Local P-9 Strikers and Supporters on the 1985–1986 Meatpacking Strike against the Hormel Company in Austin, Minnesota (1991). In Bud Schultz and Ruth Schultz, *The Price of Dissent: Testimonies of Political Repression in America* (Berkeley: University of California Press, 2001), pp. 96–102, 104–08, 118.

5   Douglas A. Fraser, Resignation Letter to the Labor–Management Group (July 19, 1978). In Box 1, UAW President's Office: Douglas Fraser Collection, Archives of Labor and Urban Affairs, Wayne State University, Detroit, Michigan.

6   Vito Russo, "Why We Fight" (1988). Based on a transcript of two speeches delivered at ACT UP demonstrations: the first in Albany, New York, May 9, 1988, and the second in Washington, DC, at the Department of Health and Human Services, October 10, 1988. Published on the web site of the AIDS Coalition to Unleash Power (ACT UP), New York.

7   Abbie Hoffman, "Closing Argument" (April 15, 1987). In *The Nation*, vol. 244, no. 17 (May 2, 1987), pp. 562–63.

8   Public Enemy, "Fight the Power" (1990). From Public Enemy, *Fear of A Black Planet* (New York: Def Jam, 1990). Lyrics by Keith (Boxley) Shocklee, Eric Sadler, and Carlton Ridenhour, reprinted from the album liner notes, p. 6.

CHAPTER TWENTY-TWO: PANAMA, THE 1991 GULF WAR, AND THE WAR AT HOME

1   Alex Molnar, "If My Marine Son Is Killed . . ." (August 23, 1990). In the *New York Times*, August 23, 1990, p. A23.

2   Eqbal Ahmad, "Roots of the Gulf Crisis" (November 17, 1990). Speech delivered in Boston, Massachusetts. Recorded by David Barsamian, Alternative Radio, Boulder, Colorado (program no. AHME001).

3   June Jordan Speaks Out Against the 1991 Gulf War (February 21, 1991). Speech delivered in Hayward, California. Transcription by *Democracy Now!*

4   Yolanda Huet-Vaughn, Statement Refusing to Serve in the 1991 Gulf War (January 9, 1991). Press release supplied by the author.

5   Interview with Civilian Worker at the Río Hato Military Base in Panama City (February 23, 1990). In the Independent Commission of Inquiry on the U.S. Invasion of Panama, *The U.S. Invasion of Panama: The Truth Behind Operation "Just Cause"* (Boston: South End Press, 1991), pp. 115–18, 119.

6   Mike Davis, "In L.A., Burning All Illusions" (June 1, 1992). In *The Nation*, vol. 254, no. 21 (June 1, 1992), pp. 743–45.

7   Mumia Abu-Jamal, *All Things Censored* (2001). In Mumia Abu-Jamal, *All Things Censored*, 2nd ed., ed. Noelle Hanrahan (New York: Seven Stories Press, 2001), pp. 202–06.

CHAPTER TWENTY-THREE: CHALLENGING BILL CLINTON

1   Bruce Springsteen, *The Ghost of Tom Joad* (1995). From Bruce Springsteen, *The Ghost of Tom Joad* (New York: Columbia Records/Sony, 1995). Lyrics from album liner notes pp. 4–5.

2   Lorell Patterson on the "War Zone" Strikes in Decatur, Illinois (June 1995). Speech delivered in Chicago, Illinois, at =the 1995 Socialist Summer School sponsored by the International Socialist Organization. In Lorell Patterson, "'If You Don't Dare to Fight, You Don't Deserve to Win,'" *Socialist Worker* (Chicago), no. 227 (July 7, 1995), p. 6.

3   Winona LaDuke, Acceptance Speech for the Green Party's Nomination for Vice President of the United States of America (August 29, 1996). Speech delivered in Saint Paul, Minnesota. Transcript by the 1996 Ralph Nader Campaign.

4   Alice Walker, Letter to President Bill Clinton (March 13, 1996). Copy in the collection of the editors.

5   Adrienne Rich, Letter to Jane Alexander Refusing the National Medal for the Arts (July 3, 1997). Published on the Web site of the Barclay Agency, agents for Adrienne Rich.

6   Rania Masri, "How Many More Must Die?" (September 17, 2000). In *The News and Observer* (Raleigh, NC), September 17, 2000, p. A25.

7   Roni Krouzman, "WTO: The Battle in Seattle: An Eyewitness Account" (December 6, 1999). Published on the Web site TomPaine.com, December 6, 1999.

8   Anita Cameron, "And the Steps Came Tumbling Down—ADAPT's Battle with the HBA" (2000). In *Incitement* (Austin, TX), vol. 16, no. 2 (summer 2000).

9   Elizabeth ("Betita") Martínez, "'Be Down with the Brown!'" (1998). In *De Colores Means All of Us: Latina Views for a Multi-Colored Century* (Boston: South End Press, 1998), pp. 210–13.

10   Walter Mosley, *Workin' on the Chain Gang* (2000). In Walter Mosley, *Workin' on the Chain Gang: Shaking Off the Dead Hand of History* (New York: The Library of Contemporary Thought/Ballantine, 2000), pp. 82–84, 89–93

11   Julia Butterfly Hill, "Surviving the Storm: Lessons from Nature" (2001). In Neva Walton and Linda Wolf, *Global Uprising: Confronting the Tyrannies of the 21st Century: Stories from a New Generation of Activists* (Gabriola Island, BC: New Society Publishers, 2001), pp. 224–28.

CHAPTER TWENTY-FOUR: BUSH II AND THE "WAR ON TERROR"

1   Michael Moore, "The Presidency—Just Another Perk" (November 14, 2000). Published on the web site Michael Moore.com on November 14, 2000.

2   Orlando Rodriguez and Phyllis Rodriguez, "Not in Our Son's Name" (September 15, 2001). Press release, September 15, 2001.

3   Rita Lasar, "To Avoid Another September 11, U.S. Must Join the World" (September 5, 2002). Syndicated by Knight Ridder Tribune news service for the Progressive Media Project. Printed as Rita Lasar, "9-11 Shattered U.S. Isolation," *Milwaukee Journal Sentinel*, September 9, 2002, p. 13A.

4   Monami Maulik, "Organizing in Our Communities Post–September 11th" (2001). In *Manavi Newsletter* (New Brunswick, New Jersey), vol. 12, no. 3 (Winter 2001). Revised by the author in February 2004 for this volume.

5   International Brotherhood of Teamsters Local 705, "Resolution Against the War" (October 18, 2002). Press Release, Teamsters Local 705, Chicago, Illinois.

6   Rachel Corrie, Letter from Palestine (February 7, 2003). In "Rachel's War," *The Guardian* (London), March 18, 2003, p. 2.

7   Danny Glover, Speech During the World Day of Protest Against the War (February 15, 2003). Speech delivered in New York, New York.

8   Amy Goodman, "Independent Media in a Time of War" (April 21, 2003). Speech delivered in Troy, New York. In *Independent Media in a Time of War* (Troy, New York: Hudson Mohawk Independent Media Center, 2003), 29 minutes.

9   Tim Predmore, "How Many More Must Die?" (August 24, 2003). First printed as "A U.S. Soldier in Iraq Wonders: 'How Many More Must Die?'" *Peoria Journal Star*, August 24, 2003, p. A5. Predmore's essay was also syndicated by the Copley News Service, September 17, 2003, and published as "A U.S. Soldier in Iraq Questions His Mission," *Los Angeles Times*, September 21, 2003, p. 4.

10   Maritza Castillo et al., Open Letter to Colonel, U.S. Army (Ret.) Michael G. Jones (September 12, 2003). Published on the Web site of Military Families Speak Out.

11   Kurt Vonnegut, "Cold Turkey" (May 31, 2004). In *In These Times*, vol. 28, no. 14 (May 31, 2004), pp. 32–34.

12   Patti Smith, "People Have the Power" (1988). First recorded on Patti Smith, *Dream of Life* (Arista, 1988). Lyrics in Patti Smith, *Patti Smith Complete: Lyrics, Reflections and Notes for the Future* (New York: Doubleday, 1998), p. 135–36.

Credits and Permissions

CHAPTER 1: COLUMBUS AND LAS CASAS

The *Diario* of Christopher Columbus.
From *Diario of Christopher Columbus's First Voyage to America, 1492–1493*, translated and edited by Oliver C. Dunn and James E. Kelly, Jr. Published by the University of Oklahoma Press, 1989. Reprinted by permission.

Bartolomé de Las Casas, *In Defense of the Indians*.
From *In Defense of the Indians: The Defense of the Most Reverend Lord, Don Fray Bartolomé de Las Casas, of the Order of Preachers, Late Bishop of Chiapa, Against the Persecutors and Slanderers of the People of the New World Discovered Across the Seas*, translated and edited by C. M. Stafford Poole. Copyright © 1974. Used with permission of Northern Illinois University Press.

Eduardo Galeano, *Memory of Fire*.
From *Memory of Fire: Genesis*, by Eduardo Galeano, translated by Cedric Belfrage. Copyright © 1985 by Cedric Belfrage. Used by permission of Pantheon Books, a division of Random House, Inc.

CHAPTER 2: THE FIRST SLAVES

Anonymous Letter to Mr. Boone in London.
Copyright © 1993 by International Publishers. Reprinted by permission.

Benjamin Banneker, Letter to Thomas Jefferson.
From Thomas Jefferson, *The Papers of Thomas Jefferson, Vol. 22: Aug. 1791 to Dec. 1791*. Copyright © 1986 Princeton University Press. Reprinted by permission of the Princeton University Press.

CHAPTER 3: SERVITUDE AND REBELLION

Proclamation of the New Hampshire Legislature on the Mast Tree Riot.
From *American Violence: A Documentary History* by Richard Hofstadter and Michael Wallace. Copyright © 1970 by Alfred A. Knopf, a division of Random House, Inc. Used by permission of Alfred A. Knopf, a division of Random House, Inc.

Account of the New York Tenant Riots.
From *American Violence: A Documentary History* by Richard Hofstadter and Michael Wallace. Copyright © 1970 by Alfred A. Knopf, a division of Random House, Inc. Used by permission of Alfred A. Knopf, a division of Random House, Inc.

CHAPTER 4: PREPARING THE REVOLUTION

Thomas Hutchinson Recounts the Reaction to the Stamp Act in Boston.
Reprinted by permission of the publisher from *The History of the Colony and Province of Massachusetts Bay: Volume III*, by Thomas Hutchinson, edited by Lawrence Haw Mayo, pp. 86–90, Cambridge, Mass.: Harvard University Press. Copyright © 1986 by the President and Fellows of Harvard College.

CHAPTER 8: THE WAR ON MEXICO

Henry David Thoreau, *Civil Disobedience.*
> From Paul Lauter, editor, *Walden and Civil Disobedience.* Copyright © 2000 by Houghton Mifflin Company. Used with permission.

CHAPTER 9: SLAVERY AND DEFIANCE

David Walker's *Appeal.*
> Copyright © 1993. Reprinted by permission of Black Classic Press.

Harriet A. Jacobs, *Incidents in the Life of a Slave Girl: Written by Herself.*
> Reprinted by permission of the publisher from *Incidents in the Life of a Slave Girl: Written by Herself* by Harriet A. Jacobs, editied and with an introduction by Jean Fagen Yellin, pp. 68–71, Cambridge, Mass.: Harvard University Press. Copyright © 1987, 2000 by the President and Fellows of Harvard College.

James R. Bradley, Letter to Lydia Maria Child.
> From *The Black Abolitionist Papers: Volume III: The United States, 1830–1846,* edited by C. Peter Ripley. Copyright © 1991 by the University of North Carolina Press. Used by permission of the publisher.

CHAPTER 12: THE EXPANSION OF THE EMPIRE

Calixto's Letter to General William R. Shafter.
> Copyright © 1972 by MR Press. Reprinted by permission of the Monthly Review Foundation.

Lewis H. Douglass on Black Opposition to McKinley.
> Copyright © 1972 by MR Press. Reprinted by permission of the Monthly Review Foundation.

Smedley D. Butler, *War Is a Racket.*
> From Smedley D. Butler, *War Is a Racket: The Antiwar Classic by America's Most Decorated General, Two Other Anti-Interventionist Tracts, and Photographs from the Horror of It* (Los Angeles: Feral House, 2003). Copyright © 1935 (Renewed). Reprinted by permission.

CHAPTER 13: SOCIALISTS AND WOBBLIES

Mother Jones, "Agitation: The Greatest Factor for Progress."
> Copyright © 1983 by Philip S. Foner. Reprinted by permission.

Arturo Giovannitti's Address to the Jury.
> Copyright © 1998. Reprinted by permission of Charles H. Kerr, Chicago, IL.

Woody Guthrie, "Ludlow Massacre."
> Copyright © 1959 (Renewed) by SANGA MUSIC, INC. All rights reserved. Used by permission.

CHAPTER 14: PROTESTING THE FIRST WORLD WAR

Helen Keller, "Strike Against War."
> Copyright © 1967 by International Publishers. Reprinted by permission.

Eugene Debs, "The Canton, Ohio, Speech."
> Copyright © 1970 by Pathfinder Press. Reprinted by permission.

Eugene Debs, "Statement to the Court."

From *The Eugene V. Debs Reader* edited by William A. Pelz. Copyright © 200 by William A. Pelz. Used by permission of the Institute of Working Class History.

e. e. cummings, "I sing a song of Olaf glad and big."

Copyright © 1931. Copyright © 1959, 1991 by the Trustees for E. E. Cummings Trust. Copyright © 1979 by George James Firmage, from *Complete Poems: 1904–1962 by E. E. Cummings*, edited by George J. Firmage. Used by permission of Liveright Publishing Corporation.

John Dos Passos, "The Body of an American."

From *U.S.A.* by John Dos Passos. Published by The Modern Library. Copyright © 1932 by John Dos Passos. Used by permission of the Modern Library, an imprint of Random House, Inc.

Dalton Trumbo, *Johnny Got His Gun.*

Copyright © 1939 by Dalton Trumbo. Renewed 1983. Reprinted by permission of Lyle Stuart, Inc.

CHAPTER 15: FROM THE JAZZ AGE TO THE UPRISINGS OF THE 1930S

F. Scott Fitzgerald, "Echoes of the Jazz Age."

From *The Crack-Up*. Copyright © 1945 by New Directions Publishing Corp. Reprinted by permission of New Directions Publishing Corp. Reprinted in the UK by permission of David Higham.

Yip Harburg, "Brother, Can You Spare a Dime?"

E. Y. "Yip" Harburg. Published by Glocca Morra Music (ASCAP) and Gorney Music (ASCAP). Administered by Next Decade Entertainment, Inc. All Rights Reserved. Used by permission.

Paul Anderson, "Tear Gas, Bayonets, and Votes."

Reprinted with permission from the August 17, 1932, issue of *The Nation*. For subscription information, call 1-800-333-8536. Portions of each week's *Nation* magazine can be accessed at http://www.thenation.com.

Mary Licht, "I Remember the Scottsboro Defense."

From *People's Weekly World* (New York, NY), February 15, 1997. Copyright © 1997 by Mary Licht. Reprinted by Permission.

Ned Cobb ("Nate Shaw"), *All God's Dangers.*

From *All God's Dangers* by Theodore Rosengarten. Copyright © 1974 by Theodore Rosengarten. Used by permission of Alfred A. Knopf, a division of Random House, Inc.

Billie Holliday, "Strange Fruit."

Words and Music by Lewis Allan. Copyright © 1939 (Renewed) by Music Sales Corporation (ASCAP). International Copyright Secured. All Rights Reserved. Reprinted by permission.

Langston Hughes, "Ballad of Roosevelt" and "Ballad of the Landlord."

From *The Collected Poems of Langston Hughes* by Langston Hughes. Copyright © 1994 by The Estate of Langston Hughes. Used by permission of Alfred A. Knopf, a division of Random House, Inc.

Bartolomeo Vanzetti, Speech to the Court.

From *The Letters of Sacco and Vanzetti*, edited by Marion D. Frankfurter and Gardner Jackson. Copyright © 1928, renewed © 1955 by The Viking Press, Inc. Used by permission of Viking Penguin, a division of Penguin Group (USA), Inc.

Vicky Starr ("Stella Nowicki"), "Back of the Yards."
Copyright © 1973 by MR Press. Reprinted by permission of the Monthly Review Foundation.
Sylvia Woods, "You Have to Fight for Freedom."
Copyright © 1973 by MR Press. Reprinted by permission of the Monthly Review Foundation.
Rose Chernin on Organizing the Unemployed in the Bronx in the 1930s.
From *In My Mother's House* by Kim Chernin. Copyright © 1983 by Kim Chernin. Reprinted by permission of Houghton Mifflin Company. All rights reserved.
Genora (Johnson) Dollinger, *Striking Flint: Genora (Johnson) Dollinger Remembers the 1936–37 GM Sit-Down Strike.*
Copyright © 1995 by Susan Rosenthal. Reprinted by permission.
John Steinbeck, *The Grapes of Wrath.*
From chapter 28. Copyright 1939. Renewed © 1967 by John Steinbeck. Used by permission of Viking Penguin, a division of Penguin Group (USA) Inc. Reprinted in the UK by permission of William Heinemann, Ltd.
Woody Guthrie, "This Land Is Your Land."
Words and Music by Woody Guthrie. TRO-© Copyright 1956 (Renewed) 1958 (Renewed) 1970 (Renewed) by Ludlow Music, Inc., New York, NY. Used by permission.

CHAPTER 16: WORLD WAR II AND MCCARTHYISM

Paul Fussell, "'Precision Bombing Will Win the War.'"
From *Wartime: Understanding and Behavior in the Second World War* by Paul Fussell. Published by Oxford University Press. Copyright © 1989 by Paul Fussell. Reprinted by permission of Oxford University Press.
Yuri Kochiyama, "Then Came the War."
From *Asian American Experiences in the United States: Oral Histories of First to Fourth Generation Americans from China, the Philippines, Japan, India, the Pacific Islands, Vietnam, and Cambodia.* Copyright © Joann Faung Jean Lee. Reprinted by permission of McFarland & Company, Inc., Box 611, Jefferson, NC, 28640.
Yamaoka Michiko, "Eight Hundred Meters from the Hypocenter."
Copyright © 1993. From *Japan at War: An Oral History* by Haruko Taya Cook and Theodore F. Cook. Reprinted by permission of The New Press: (800) 233-4830.
Admiral Gene Larocque Speaks to Studs Terkel About "The Good War."
Copyright © 1984, 1997. From *"The Good War:" An Oral History of World War II* by Studs Terkel. Reprinted by permission of The New Press: (800) 233-4830.
Kurt Vonnegut, *Slaughterhouse-Five.*
Published by Laurel Book/Dell Publishing. Copyright © 1965 by Kurt Vonnegut. Reprinted by permission of Dell, an imprint of Random House, Inc.
Paul Robeson's Unread Statement before the House Committee on Un-American Activities.
Copyright © 1956 by Paul Robeson. Reprinted by permission of Paul Robeson, Jr.
Peter Seeger, "Thou Shall Not Sing."
From *It Did Happen Here: Recollections of Political Repression in America*, edited by Bud Schultz and Ruth Shultz. Published by University of California Press. Copyright © 1989. Used by permission.

I. F. Stone, "But It's Not Just Joe McCarthy."
> From *The I. F. Stone's Weekly Reader,* edited by Neil Middleton. Copyright © 1954 by I. F. Stone. Reprinted by permission of Random House, Inc.

The Final Letter from Ethel and Julius Rosenberg to Their Children.
> Copyright © 1994. From *The Rosenberg Letters: A Complete Edition of the Prison Correspondence of Julius and Ethel Rosenberg,* edited by Michael Meeropol. Reproduced by permission of Routledge/Taylor & Francis Books, Inc.

CHAPTER 17: THE BLACK UPSURGE AGAINST RACIAL SEGREGATION

Richard Wright, *12 Million Black Voices.*
> From *12 Million Black Voices: A Folk History of the Negro in the United States* by Richard Wright. Published by Thunder's Mouth Press. Copyright © 1941 by Richard Wright. Reprinted by permission of Thunder's Mouth Press.

Langston Hughes, *Montage of a Dream Deferred.*
> From *The Collected Poems of Langston Hughes* by Langston Hughes. Copyright © 1994 by The Estate of Langston Hughes. Used by permission of Alfred A. Knopf, a division of Random House, Inc.

Anne Moody, *Coming of Age in Mississippi.*
> Copyright © 1968 by Anne Moody. Reprinted by permission of Delta, a division of Random House, Inc.

John Lewis, Original Text of Speech to Be Delivered at the Lincoln Memorial.
> Copyright © 1963 by John Lewis. Reprinted by permission.

Malcolm X, "Message to the Grass Roots."
> From *Malcolm X Speaks: Selected Speeches and Statements,* edited by George Breitman. Copyright © 1963 by Malcolm X. Reprinted by permission of Pathfinder Press.

Martha Honey, Letter from Mississippi Freedom Summer.
> Copyright © 1964 by Martha Honey. Reprinted by permission of the author.

Testimony of Fannie Lou Hamer.
> Copyright © 1964 by Fannie Lou Hamer. Reprinted by permission.

Testimony of Rita L. Schwerner.
> Copyright © 1964 by Rita L. Schwerner. Reprinted by permission.

Alice Walker, "Once."
> Copyright © 1968 by Alice Walker. Reprinted by permission.

Sandra A. West, "Riot!—A Negro Resident's Story."
> Copyright © 1967 by Sandra A. West. Reprinted by permission of the *Detroit News.*

Martin Luther King, Jr., "Where Do We Go from Here?"
> Reprinted by arrangement with the Estate of Martin Luther King, Jr., c/o Writers House as agent for the proprietor, New York, NY. Copyright © 1967 Martin Luther King, Jr. Copyright renewed 1991 by Coretta Scott King.

CHAPTER 18: VIETNAM AND BEYOND: THE HISTORIC RESISTANCE

Mississippi Freedom Democratic Party, McComb, Mississippi, Petition Against the War in Vietnam.
> From *Black Protest,* edited by Joanne Grant. Copyright © 1968 by Joanne Grant. Used by permission of Fawcett Books, a division of Random House, Inc.

Adrienne Rich, *Of Woman Born.*
From *Of Woman Born: Motherhood as Experience and Institution* by Adrienne Rich.
Published by W. W. Norton. Copyright © 1977 by Adrienne Rich. Reprinted by permission of W. W. Norton, Inc.
Abbey Lincoln, "Who Will Revere the Black Woman?"
Copyright © 1966 by Abbey Lincoln. Reprinted by permission.
Susan Brownmiller, "Abortion Is a Woman's Right."
From *In Our Time: Memoir of a Revolution* by Susan Brownmiller. Published by The Dial Press. Copyright © 1998 by Susan Brownmiller. Reprinted by permission of the Dial Press, an imprint of Random House, Inc.
Assata Shakur (Joanne Chesimard), "Women in Prison: How We Are."
Copyright © 1978 by Assata Shakur. Used by permission.
Kathleen Neal Cleaver, "Women, Power, and Revolution."
Copyright © 1998. From *Liberation, Imagination, and the Black Panther Party: A New Look at the Panthers and Their Legacy,* edited by Kathleen Neal Cleaver and George Katsiaficas. Reproduced by permission of Routledge/Taylor & Francis Books, Inc.

CHAPTER 20: LOSING CONTROL IN THE 1970S

Howard Zinn, "The Problem Is Civil Obedience."
Copyright © 1970 by Howard Zinn. Used by permission of the author.
George Jackson, *Soledad Brother.*
Copyright © 1970 by George Jackson. Used by permission of IMG Literary.
Bob Dylan, "George Jackson."
Copyright © 1971 by Ram's Horn Music. Copyright renewed by Special Rider Music. All rights reserved. International copyright secured. Reprinted by permission.
Angela Davis, "Political Prisoners, Prisons, and Black Liberation."
Copyright © 1971 by Angela Y. Davis. Reprinted by permission of the author.
Elliott James ("L. D.") Barkely.
From the compact disc *Prisons on Fire: George Jackson, Attica and Black Liberation* (Oakland: AK Press/Alternative Tentacles, 2002). Copyright © Freedom Archives. Used by permission of AK Press (http://www.akpress.org).
Leonard Peltier on the Trail of Broken Treaties Protest.
From Leonard Peltier, *Prison Writings: My Life Is My Sundance,* edited by Harvey Arden. Copyright © 1998 by Crazy Horse Spirit, Inc. & Arden Editorial Services, L.L.C. Reprinted by permission of St. Martin's Press.
Noam Chomsky, "COINTELPRO: What the (Deleted) Was It?"
Copyright © 1978 by Noam Chomsky. Reprinted by permission of the author.

CHAPTER 21: THE CARTER–REAGAN–BUSH CONSENSUS

Marian Wright Edelman, Commencement Address at Milton Academy.
Copyright © 1983 by Marian Wright Edelman. Reprinted by permission of the author.
César Chávez, Address to the Commonwealth Club of California.
TM/Copyright © 2004 the Cesar E. Chavez Foundation (http://www.chavezfoundation.org).
Testimony of Ismael Guadalupe Ortiz on Vieques, Puerto Rico.
Copyright © 1979 by Ismael Guadalupe Ortiz. Reprinted by permission of the author.

CHAPTER 22: PANAMA, THE 1991 GULF WAR, AND THE WAR AT HOME

CHAPTER 23: CHALLENGING BILL CLINTON

CHAPTER 24: BUSH II AND THE "WAR ON TERROR"

Index

About the Authors

HOWARD ZINN is professor emeritus at Boston University. He is the author of the classic *A People's History of the United States*, "a brilliant and moving history of the American people from the point of view of those ... whose plight has been largely omitted from most histories" (*Library Journal*). The book has now sold more than one million copies.

Zinn has received the Lannan Foundation Literary Award for Nonfiction and the Eugene V. Debs award for his writing and political activism, and in 2003 was awarded the *Prix des amis du Monde Diplomatique*.

Zinn is the author of numerous books, including *The Zinn Reader*, the autobiographical *You Can't Be Neutral on a Moving Train*, and the play *Marx in Soho*.

Zinn grew up in Brooklyn and worked in the shipyards before serving as an air force bombardier in World War II. Zinn was chair of the History Department at Spelman College, where he actively participated in the civil rights movement, before taking a position at Boston University. While there he became a leader in the movement to end the war in Vietnam.

He now lives with his wife, Roslyn, in Massachusetts and lectures widely on history, contemporary politics, and against war.

ANTHONY ARNOVE is an editor, author, and activist based in Brooklyn, New York. He is the editor of *Terrorism and War*, an interview collection with Howard Zinn, published by Seven Stories Press, and *Iraq Under Siege: The Deadly Impact of Sanctions and War* (Cambridge: South End Press; London: Pluto Press, 2000; updated ed., 2003).

Arnove is a regular commentator for ZNet. His writing has also appeared in the *Financial Times*, *Le Nouvel Observateur*, *L'Humanité*, *International Socialist Review*, *Socialist Worker*, *Left Business Observer*, *Red Pepper*, *Mother Jones*, *Diaspora*, *Race and Class*, *Monthly Review*, *In These Times*, *The Nation*, and other publications.

He is a member of the International Socialist Organization and the National Writers Union.

About Seven Stories Press

SEVEN STORIES PRESS is an independent book publisher based in New York City, with distribution throughout the United States, Canada, England, Australia, and New Zealand. We publish works of the imagination by such writers as Nelson Algren, Octavia E. Butler, Assia Djebar, Ariel Dorfman, Barry Gifford, Peter Plate, Lee Stringer, and Kurt Vonnegut, to name a few, together with political titles by voices of conscience, including the Boston Women's Health Book Collective, Project Censored, Noam Chomsky, Nat Hentoff, Gary Null, Greg Palast, Robert Scheer, Barbara Seaman and Howard Zinn among many others. Our books appear in hardcover, paperback, pamphlet, and e-book formats, in English and in Spanish. We believe publishers have a special responsibility to defend free speech and human rights wherever we can.

For more information, visit www.sevenstories.com; for a free catalogue, write to Seven Stories Press, 140 Watts Street, New York, NY 10013.

Books By Howard Zinn

Artists in Times of War. New York: Seven Stories Press, 2003.

Passionate Declarations: Essays on War and Justice. New York: Harper Perennial, 2003.

You Can't Be Neutral on a Moving Train: A Personal History of Our Times, 2d ed. Boston: Beacon Press, 2002.

Terrorism and War, with Anthony Arnove. New York: Seven Stories Press, 2002.

Emma. Cambridge: South End Press, 2002.

A People's History of the United States: 1492–Present, updated ed. New York: HarperCollins/Perennial Classics, 2001.

Three Strikes: Miners, Musicians, Salesgirls, and the Fighting Spirit of Labor's Last Century, with Dana Frank and Robin D. G. Kelley. Boston: Beacon Press, 2001.

Howard Zinn on War. New York: Seven Stories Press, 2001.

Howard Zinn on History. New York: Seven Stories Press, 2001.

La otra historia de los Estados Unidos. New York: Seven Stories Press, 2001.

Marx in Soho: A Play on History. Cambridge: South End Press, 1999.

The Future of History: Interviews with David Barsamian. Monroe, Maine: Common Courage Press, 1999.

The Zinn Reader: Writings on Disobedience and Democracy. New York: Seven Stories Press, 1997.

Failure to Quit: Reflections of an Optimistic Historian. Monroe, Maine: Common Courage Press, 1993. Reprint ed., Cambridge: South End Press, 2002.

The Politics of History, 2d ed. Urbana: University of Illinois Press, 1990.

Justice: Eyewitness Accounts. Boston: Beacon Press, 1977. Reprint ed., Cambridge: South End Press, 2002.

Postwar America: 1945–1971. Indianapolis: Bobbs-Merrill, 1973. Reprint ed., Cambridge: South End Press, 2002.

Disobedience and Democracy: Nine Fallacies of Law and Order. New York: Vintage Books, 1968. Reprint ed., Cambridge: South End Press, 2002.

Vietnam: The Logic of Withdrawal. Boston: Beacon Press, 1967. Reprint ed., Cambridge: South End Press, 2002.

SNCC: The New Abolitionists. Boston: Beacon Press, 1964. Reprint ed., Cambridge: South End Press, 2002.

The Southern Mystique. New York: Knopf, 1964. Reprint ed. Cambridge: South End Press, 2002.

LaGuardia in Congress. Ithaca, NY: Cornell University Press, 1959.